The Infamous Mrs. Gallagher

The Infamous Mrs. Gallagher

Prolific Victorian Brothel Keeper

Susan Bennett

First printed 2020
Reprinted 2021

ISBN –9798568832478

To Doreen and Gerald, without whom this would never have been written....
and Jane Gallagher, of course!

Contents

Preface...9

Prologue..13

Part One - Early Years..15

Chapter 1 - Jane's Story..15

Chapter 2 - Building the Brothel Empire 26

Chapter 3 - Social Evil 32

Chapter 4 – Prostitutes, Poverty and Punishment..............42

Chapter 5 - Coverture..50

Chapter 6 - William Seabrook Chalkley 55

Chapter 7 - Married – or not? 66

Part Two - Shocks and Surprises.................................77

Chapter 8 - London Connections 77

Chapter 9 - The Missing Will 92

Chapter 10 - Charles Pollard..............................100

Chapter 11 - Pretty Pickles and a Dish of Salmon.............115

Chapter 12 - Furnishers and Furniture 124

Chapter 13 – Death, Love and Marriage 130

Chapter 14 - Controlling Social Evil................................144

Part Three - Triumphs, Trials and Tribulations....................162

Chapter 15 - The Talking Fish 162

Chapter 16 - Beshemel v Gallagher 174

Chapter 17 - Johnson v Gallagher..........................182

Chapter 18 - Chalkley's Downfall 192

Chapter 19 - Life in the Brothel Streets 201

Chapter 20 - Preying on the Vulnerable 211

Chapter 21 - Hidden Houses of Ill Fame 226

Part Four - Judgement Day..236

Chapter 22 - Jane is appealing 236

Chapter 23 - Combative Cooper..........................243

Chapter 24 - Chalkley the Fugitive..........................257

Chapter 25 - Chalkley Faces Judgement 278

Chapter 26 - Transported to Australia 284

Chapter 27 - Fallout..291

Chapter 28 - Sins of the Father..............................300

Part Five - What happened next?....................................307

Chapter 29 - Prosecuted as a Procuress 307

Chapter 30 - Tussles over Tyrer Street 319

Chapter 31 - Revolving Doors 327

Chapter 32 - The Final Curtain..............................334

Chapter 33 - Lust and Money 347

Chapter 34 - 'Anything, in fact, with walls and a ceiling' ... 367

Part Six - Missing, presumed dead 374

Chapter 35 - Where is Jane?... 374

Chapter 36 - Ireland?.. 379

Chapter 37 - Social Evil in Dublin..................................... 389

Chapter 38 - Misnomer... 397

Chapter 39 - Madams and Mayhem 403

Chapter 40 - Eight Days, Two Deaths............................... 411

Chapter 41 - The Gold Rush 421

Chapter 42 - Denouement 429

Chapter 43 - Twists and Entanglements........................... 437

Mrs. Gallagher.. 441

Epilogue 442

Acknowledgements 444

Table of Figures 446

References... 450

Preface

It was a miserable February day in 2018 when I received an email from the Museum of Liverpool. 'We've got a new project for you, interested?' I had just finished the latest on Fabric and Garment Trades in Victorian Liverpool and only a few months before I had completed the first: research into people who had lived in the last remaining court houses in the city. It was all part of a Heritage Lottery Funded Project: 'Galkoff's Jewish Butchers and the Secret Life of Pembroke Place,' which resulted in an exhibition launched at the Museum in November 2018. I read on eagerly, for the last two projects had been fun.

'We want you to find out as much as possible about brothels and prostitution in Victorian Liverpool.'

Well, as a volunteer researcher, how could I refuse this one? No matter what came of it I would be able to dine out on the stories for months, if not years. Off I went, finding very quickly that the only available sources of information were newspaper reports, as court records were either non-existent or very short on detail and work already done on prostitution in the Victorian period was mainly about London, so there was a huge amount to discover. It was a rip-roaring ride, totally exhilarating, completely unpredictable and tremendously exciting. I surged through information about prostitutes where they lived, who they were and the offences they committed.

Once I had dispatched a blog and reported on what the museum needed, I thought it might be interesting to delve deeper into the detail and see if I could trace the lives of some of the prostitutes and brothel keepers whose names recurred with great regularity and then tell their real stories in the context of Victorian life. This seemed like a plan, as it would do justice to what I had uncovered in Liverpool and relate it to the city's position in the world at that time as a leading port and a centre of innovation.

I hit the jackpot almost immediately purely by picking on a name I had seen more than a few times in my research: Jane Gallagher. Using family history research techniques, I tackled her life like I would do anyone's and was staggered by the amount she threw up. Trails led to other trails and I was soon researching French history, the law, the rights of married women, bigamy, the law again and again, wills and probate, land registers, street directories, maps and tracking court cases across the country, as well as following her children's lives and those of her grandchildren, as far as I could.

It was almost too much input so I had to discipline myself to be very methodical, which worked for a while, collecting tables of data and recording links under emerging themes. However, resisting the compulsion to follow interesting snippets was soon overwhelming. I mean, who could have put to one side a report about a vicar being found dead in a brothel, being moved to the workhouse to avoid clerical embarrassment, then finding that the coroner refused to allow public access to his pocket book as it was too salacious? I immediately devoured the lot, created a sub - topic for vicars and priests, added to my search terms and very quickly had a bulging folder.

As I continued to discover more and more interesting seams of inquiry, it became a huge project, tricky too, like trying to trace a virus and as the work multiplied, I came across very unlikely people. Far from becoming disillusioned about ever reaching a point where I could start amalgamating, synthesising and making sense of it all, it only spurred me on. I was amazed at how urgent it became every morning to ignore all other calls on my time and get going again. My online storage had to be trebled as information and archive material increased and I became known, affectionately, I might add, as the 'Brothel Woman' as I bothered and pressed everyone I could in my search for more and more.

Eventually, I started to realise that I was finding reports and websites, research and archive material coming up with the same names and topics many times, a sure sign I had reached some sort of watershed, so I gave myself permission to jump off the treadmill, get an eye test as things were becoming fuzzy round the edges with all that scrolling, and sit back, relax and read it all properly. Only then was I able to indulge and enjoy, which in its turn gave rise to yet another list of interesting topics to pursue.

It was sensational who Jane Gallagher was linked to, and how she blazed a life for herself that could either be described as a ruthless pursuit of self-interest, or one driven by an overwhelming need to provide for her children and protect their futures. I became not just absorbed in her life but wholly immersed, as Jane was notorious throughout the kingdom. From curious researcher, I morphed into a detective as Jane became the centre of multiple investigations and so complex were the links and the task of evidencing the truth, I dare not let any of it out of my head.

I visited the scenes of various 'crimes' in Liverpool, haunted their Archives and ransacked their microfiche records, battled to stay on track when faced with huge, creaky volumes of leather bound A3 tomes complete with original dust and even ventured to the National Archives to brave their systems, filthy ancient pages and 38 degrees of heatwave in the summer of 2019. Field trips followed to graveyards galore, endless tramps taking photos of the brothel streets, venturing far into Cheshire, Lancashire, the Isle of Man and down to Leicestershire, London, Southampton and beyond to find original sources.

I never knew what I would find next as the best information always popped up when I was looking for something else. I did not so much suffer from writer's block, as over stimulation as I encountered revelations and incredible situations you could never invent or get away with in a novel. If truth is stranger than fiction, then Jane Gallagher's life must be a supreme example.

The biggest challenge was to get at the truth, and Jane was certainly not to be trusted with it, as I found to my cost. The Court of Appeal in Chancery Lord Justice Knight Bruce in exasperation in 1861 summed her up exactly:

'No reliance can be placed on what this woman has stated...'

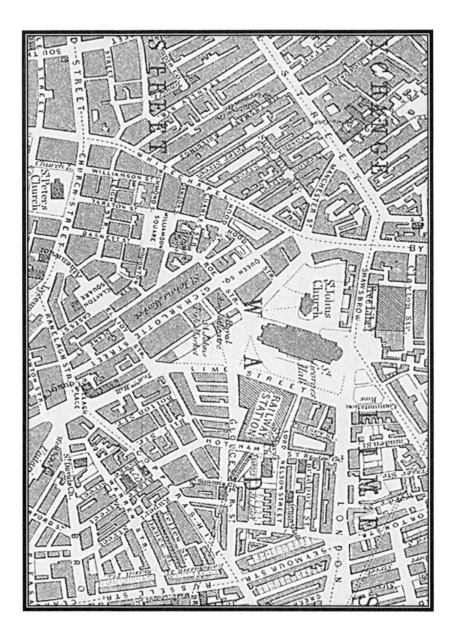

Figure 1 Weekly Dispatch Atlas of Liverpool 1860

Prologue

It is Saturday 12.5.1860 at the recently opened Vice Chancellor's Court, St George's Hall, Liverpool and the *Johnson v Gallagher and Another* trial was about to begin. Resplendent as always and in the height of fashion, Jane Gallagher presented a confident and regal figure on that chilly, still wintry day in mid-May. She was then aged forty-four, respectable looking, a middle-class widow and known mother of seven children, the eldest being twenty-seven, the youngest just twelve. She was also about to become a grandmother for the first time.

There would have been quite a crowd both inside and out as the newspapers described this event in their biggest headlines: 'Scandalous Revelations in the Chancery Court'[1] claimed one. Another, only slightly less restrained, disclosed: 'Some of the most revolting and disgraceful aspects of Social Evil.'[2]

These then, were the very first major newspaper reports I found about Jane and the reason why I chose her, for who could fail to be curious with such coverage? What struck me immediately was that in spite of these dramatic headlines, the case was not about Jane Gallagher's ownership and management of her many brothels in Liverpool town but about her failure to pay the money she owed to a fashionable furnishing company called Burton and Watson.

In its heyday, up to 1858, it was a very successful business providing quality furnishings to those who could afford it and they also fitted out the luxury cabins of ships. Their furnishings were highly regarded in Liverpool and one of their adverts reads:

'Amongst (our) drawing-room articles, which are formed of choice walnut wood and rosewood, may be enumerated beautifully designed chiffoniers, with Italian marble tops and plate-glass backs and panels, chairs in Utrecht velvet, couches and lounging chairs to match, centre and occasional tables, whatnots and music stands, papier-mache and other fancy chairs and tables. This stock being formed of the very best of materials, and manufactured from perfectly seasoned and dry woods, is well worthy of the attention of gentlemen furnishing or families replenishing their furniture.'[3]

Between the years 1849 and 1856, Burton and Watson supplied Jane Gallagher with furniture and other goods for the classy houses she set up as brothels in Liverpool. They were aware she was at that time a married woman living separate from her husband who was said to be in Manchester.[4] These furnishings consisted of the finest Italian and French designs, she even had Old Master paintings by Van Dyck and Poussin. The houses were carpeted, she provided expensive food and drink, had wine cellars, cooks and housekeepers and her girls wore silken gowns, each worth at least £550 in today's money. Her brothels were either rented or bought and sumptuously furnished to the greatest quality, so that 'the gentleman could be comfortable...'

These were definitely not common street brothels, back street cellars or miserable hovels as Jane's clientele were educated, higher middle-class gentlemen and their sons who were making vast sums of money in the growing international port of Liverpool. It was the very furnishing and maintenance of these, as there had been great wear and tear as you might expect, and for not paying her bills that she was in court. She had other creditors too: the suppliers of the gorgeous gowns the young women wore, plus she paid fees for sending her children to live with hired nurses in the Isle of Man, later to expensive boarding schools away from her business and when they were adults, she bought houses for them in other parts of the country so they never needed to be associated with what she actually did for a living.

Burton and Watson were represented in court by a man called Johnson, who was the official receiver nominated to recover debts owed to the company which became bankrupt and all their stock had to be sold in April 1858 – two years before the court case of *Johnson v Gallagher and Another*.[5] The reference to 'Another' also intrigued me until I found an account which named this person as 'William Seabrook Chalkley,' who was at that time secretary of the Liverpool Tradesman's Loan Company, and his back story is truly remarkable.

But how much did Jane owe them? No official court records of this particular case have survived but according to the newspaper reports and bearing in mind this was only her debt to Burton and Watson, not what she owed all her creditors in total, it was about £372 2 shillings and 6 1/2d [worth £22,003.45 at 2017 values].

We therefore begin our journey in the middle, to work our way backwards, forwards, sideways and sometimes around in dizzying circles and spirals, as Jane weaves fantasy and fiction with facts that suit her, truth and tragedy intermingle with hilarious adventures, she being the pivot around which all other lives turn.

Part One - Early Years

Chapter 1 - Jane's Story

Jane, by now no stranger to the courts, has the presence of a much-loved actress and the confidence of one who is unassailable. She exudes a powerful presence, knowing she has the skills to amuse, shock, entertain and run rings round the Victorian legal system just as she has for the previous ten years. Very sure of her audience, I can just picture the scene as she gazes around, a small smile twitching her lips, recognising many of her brothel clients among the professionals before her, their sons and nephews too, along with members of the public who managed to find a space.

Figure 2 Jane Gallagher, St George's Hall 1860 by George Jones 2019

Her defence lawyer invites Jane to describe her early life and she responds telling them her parents were Jane Rowlinson and Samuel Oakes, who were married in Backford, Cheshire on 22.10.1797 when Samuel was 27 and his bride just 20. They had five children who survived and lived initially in Backford where the eldest, Margaret, was born in 1808.

Samuel was a labourer over the next ten years and he brought his wife and family to Liverpool, probably in search of work, somewhere between 1809 and 1810 when Mary, their second daughter was born. He then became a cart owner, plying his trade between the docks and warehouses of Liverpool. Ann was born next in 1813, then Ellen, the youngest in 1821. Jane was the fourth child, born on 13.6.1816 and baptised on 7.9.1816 at St Martins in the Field church in Liverpool.[6]

I wondered where Jane had picked up her literacy skills and sharpness as when I examined all their marriage certificates, I found she was the only one who could sign her name, the others put an 'x' in its place. School attendance was not mandatory until 1880 and even then, children only went until they were ten years old. She could have gone voluntarily to a protestant school from about 1820 onwards, unless her parents taught her to read and write, which is rather unlikely, but where and which schools accepted girls to be educated in that period?

In 1823, Liverpool had 32 day-schools 'for the education of the poor,' catering for 7,441 children. 14 of these were church schools (2,914 pupils), two Roman Catholic (440 pupils), and 18 Nonconformist (4,087 pupils). By 1826, when Jane would have been ten, two elementary public schools were founded by Liverpool Corporation.[7] For working class girls and boys there were also places in what was known as 'Dame' schools for children between ages of four and eight. They have been described by a former pupil as:

'A very antique specimen of humanity,' under whose tuition she 'learnt nothing, or next to nothing.'[8]

These dames were generally:

'Elderly and impoverished widows [who] stirred the soup with one hand and held a penny cane in the other.'

That is, they could be equally if not more concerned with ordinary domestic duties than with actual instruction. It seems they provided only the most basic of education: children generally learned reading, scripture and spelling from an unqualified teacher, and in 1835, James Kay-Shuttleworth, the secretary of the Supervisory Committee of the Privy Council on Education, commented on their deficiencies, saying:

'The [teachers'] only qualification for employment seems to be their unfitness for every other... regular instruction among their scholars is absolutely impossible.'[9][10]

For girls, this instruction was mostly in needlework as not only did it function as vocational training for a possible future in low-paid textile work, but it also equipped them for domestic work in their own homes.[11] Regardless, Jane did emerge with the ability at least to write her own name and the potential to hold more than her own, and she needed to as the world she grew up in changed exponentially in her childhood.

By the beginning of the 1800s, Liverpool had replaced London as the principal port in the country. Cotton was imported and eight new docks were built between 1815 and 1835, her childhood years. As the population grew in proportion to its wealth, there was a need in Liverpool from the early 1800s for more and more housing and speculators were not slow to see the opportunities. However, there was nothing humanitarian about their projects as the homes were designed to accommodate as many people as they could in order to maximise their gains and a simple design did just that. It was known as court housing, which was nothing like the court houses where magistrates and judges sat. Jane's family lived in Renshaw Street and Leece Street between 1810 - 1820 when her father graduated from being a labourer to being a cart owner when she was about five years of age. In 1821, they lived in court houses in Skelthorne Street and Hanley Street until 1832, then by 1833, they had moved to Lime Street.

A reconstruction of a court house can be seen in the Museum of Liverpool where it is a part of the People's Republic exhibition, along with the frontage of the last standing court house in the city, which was the site of the former Galkoff's Butchers. The design of a typical block was of two rows of terraced houses, back-to-back, each sharing a common wall which ran like a spine down the centre of the building. Each side of the dividing wall consisted of a cellar dwelling and three stories above ground level. Sanitation was almost non-existent and the communal latrine was emptied on a 'need-to-do' basis, when it was overflowing. Only then did men or 'scavengers' drain the whole putrid mess and remove it, until next time.

These cellar dwellings, literally the lowest of the low, were reliably described by Dr William Henry Duncan, a GP in Liverpool who became the country's first Medical Officer of Health in 1846, as:

'Being 10 to 12 feet square, sometimes flagged but more often than not with an earthen floor, windowless and with no source of light or air but a door standing lower than street level.

'Washing facilities were also lacking and if they existed at all were situated in the communal courtyard along with a single source of cold water. In the more luxurious yards, there was a communal washing area consisting of a stone-bench.[12] A court of between 2 to 12 hovels would be lucky to have one tap, each of which operated for a little over an hour three times a week, and this would cost up to £10 (£678.01) a year, [a massive amount even by today's standards.] Poorer people were known to queue for two or three hours for water, perhaps at four o'clock in the morning to make sure of getting some.[13]

'In the streets inhabited by the working classes, I believe that the great majority are without sewers, and that where they do exist, they are of a very imperfect kind unless where the ground has a natural inclination, therefore the surface water and fluid refuse of every kind stagnate in the street, and add, especially in hot weather, their pestilential influence to that of the more solid filth. With regard to the courts, I doubt whether there is a single court in Liverpool which communicates with the street by an underground drain, the only means afforded for carrying off the fluid dirt being a narrow, open, shallow gutter, which sometimes exists, but even this is very generally choked up with stagnant filth.'[14]

Probably as consequence of the poor living conditions of those families like Jane's, the average age of death for the people of Liverpool in 1842 as compared to other areas of the country was 35 for those in professional trades, 22 for ordinary tradesmen and for a labourer 15. But, as the rate of infant mortality was also very high, these averages are somewhat skewed.[15] This is the environment in which Jane grew up: one of five girls, living in Liverpool's centre in the worst sort of housing, her father subject to the unpredictability of work on the docks and they were all probably very hungry for most of her young life. Her prospects were bleak: early marriage, children and probably more poverty.

But the railway line opened between Liverpool and Manchester in 1830 and, age 14, Jane must have taken part in the celebrations in the September. Work had begun in the 1820s to connect the major industrial city of Manchester with the nearest deep water port in Liverpool, 35 miles away. Although horse-drawn railways already existed elsewhere, and a few industrial sites used primitive steam locomotives for bulk haulage, L&M was the first locomotive-hauled railway to connect two major cities and the first to provide a scheduled passenger service.

The opening day was a major public event attended by Arthur Wellesley, the Duke of Wellington, who rode on one of the eight inaugural trains, as did many other dignitaries and notable figures of the day. Huge crowds lined the track to watch the trains depart for Manchester[16] which left Liverpool on time and without any technical problems. The Duke of Wellington's special train ran on one track and the other seven trains on an adjacent and parallel track, sometimes ahead and sometimes behind the Duke's train. Around 13 miles out of Liverpool the first of many problems occurred when one of the trains derailed and the following train collided with it. With no reported injuries or damage, the derailed locomotive was lifted back onto the track and the journey continued.

At Parkside railway station, near the midpoint of the line, the locomotives made a scheduled stop to take on water. Although the railway staff advised passengers to remain on the trains while this took place, around 50 of the dignitaries got off when the Duke of Wellington's special train stopped. One of those was William Huskisson, former cabinet minister and Member of Parliament for Liverpool. He had been a highly influential figure in the creation of the British Empire and an architect of the doctrine of free trade, but had fallen out with Wellington in 1828 over the issue of parliamentary reform and had resigned from the cabinet. Hoping to be reconciled with Wellington, he went to the Duke's railway carriage and shook his hand. Distracted by the Duke, Huskisson did not notice a locomotive on the adjacent track, the *Rocket*. On realising it was approaching, he panicked and tried to get into the Duke's carriage, but the door of the carriage swung open leaving him hanging directly in its path. He fell onto the tracks in front of the train, suffering serious leg injuries, dying later that night.

The Duke of Wellington felt that the remainder of the day's events should be cancelled following the accident and proposed to return to Liverpool. However, a large crowd had gathered in Manchester to see the trains arrive and was beginning to become unruly so Wellington was persuaded to continue. By the time they reached the outskirts of Manchester the crowd was hostile and spilling onto the tracks. With the local authorities unable to clear the tracks, the trains had to drive at low speed into the crowd, using their own momentum to push people out of the way.

Eventually, they arrived at Liverpool Road railway station in Manchester to be met by an angry crowd, who waved banners and flags against the Duke and pelted him with vegetables. Wellington refused to get off and ordered the trains to return to Liverpool. Mechanical failures and an inability to turn the locomotives meant that most of the trains were unable to leave. While the Duke of Wellington's train left successfully, only three of the remaining seven locomotives were usable and they were used to slowly haul a single long train of 24 carriages back to Liverpool, eventually arriving six and a half hours late after being pelted with objects thrown from bridges by the drunken crowds lining the track.[17] All this Jane would have known and it must have been very exciting for a young girl.

The next record to be found for Jane after her baptism is of her marriage to Thomas Gallagher, a tailor in 1833, living at Whitechapel, Liverpool. How Jane met him when she was only two months off seventeen and why she married him is a matter for speculation. She wasn't pregnant as she did not have their first child, Ann Elizabeth, until nearly ten months later. Little is known of Jane's early married life, apart from what she said in subsequent court cases, as she and her family were not newsworthy during her early years, but they lived in a small world, as Liverpool at that time was still a town and nothing like the sprawling city of today. People walked everywhere as only the rich could afford horse-drawn carriages and all shops, such services as there were, pubs and limited amusements were very close together. Jane probably knew Thomas by sight to begin with as they only lived around the corner from each other and she might have bought some clothes from his father's shop.[18]

There are few facts about Thomas' parents or possible Irish connections. Given the commonality of his name, tracing his ancestry is virtually impossible without more information, but what I do know about him is he was born between 1809 - 810 in Lancashire, which could be anywhere in the county including Liverpool, and in 1821 a Thomas Gallagher, a spirit dealer lives at 83 Whitechapel. He is likely to be Thomas' father as he himself would have only been about ten at the time.[19] By 1824, Thomas senior is a tailor and still living at 83 Whitechapel and Jane's future husband Thomas would have been 14. When he was 18 in 1828, Thomas is a clothes dealer at 83 Whitechapel until 1832.

Jane recalls:

'I remember my father's death, which was 27 years ago... He kept a cart and two horses. I was married in the year 1833, the year my father died, being then about sixteen years of age. He resided in Lime Street at the time of his death, the rent of the house being £13 a year [£881.32 at 2017 values]. He left no will and no property but the cart and horses and furniture. His widow [Jane's mother] continued the carting business for about twelve months afterwards. The business was lucrative but the parties managing it did not give her satisfaction and she was compelled to sell it and also some part of her furniture, altogether not realising more than £20 [£1,356.03].

'After disposing of the cart and horses, my mother took a smaller house at a rent of £10 [£678.01] a year, and commenced business as a greengrocer. No portion of the house was sub-let at first, but after about four months my mother had only the cellar, where she carried on the greengrocery business, and continued there for six or seven months. That business did not prove lucrative and she went to live in Manchester with a daughter whose husband was a clock and watch maker and who maintained her there for about four years. My mother was not there in the character of a servant.'[20]

In 1839, her mother, Mrs. Oakes, came to live with Jane in a small house in Silver Street, Copperas Hill, Liverpool because her husband Thomas, reputedly a drunkard, had sold off what there was in the place and left her with four children. When Mrs. Oakes came to the rescue, no doubt on the train, about £12 [£813.62] or £14 [£949.22] was spent in refurnishing the house and 'lady lodgers' were taken in to help with the cost of maintenance - these ladies being prostitutes. It seems Mrs. Oakes also had several of these houses in Manchester, all doing very well too.

This was startling. How had Mrs. Jane Oakes, who would have been trained for a life of motherhood, wifely and domestic duties, developed the skills and found the money and energy to cultivate several brothels when she was a 62-year-old widow? Enterprising, indeed.

Jane continued her testimony, saying:

> 'They lived in the house for two or three years, her mother paying the rent. Had the furniture been hers, her husband would have taken it, as he had done before. It became a gay house; her mother was the landlady and she managed the business. There was no servant, Jane did the housework and as regards profits, they sometimes did very well.'

Mrs. Oakes took all the money, supporting Jane and her children using the proceeds from her lucrative houses in Manchester to furnish the house in Liverpool.

This much told me all I need to know to get cracking, using online genealogical databases, Liverpool Archives records, newspaper reports, anything I could get my hands on. I was eager to track Jane, her family and the facts, to make sure they added up. And I am so glad I did as it was not long before I realised that, for Jane, the truth was malleable.

Some differences were neither here nor there. For example: '*I remember my father's death, which was 27 years ago....*' This would make it 1833, when in fact her father was buried on 2.2.1834, at St John's Church in Liverpool, age 64, according to his death certificate, though he did die in his home in Lime Street. She gets it sort of right in another statement: '*I was married in the year 1833, the year my father died, being then about sixteen years of age.*' In fact, she was seventeen in 1833.[21] A more serious discrepancy was the fact that Jane said Thomas deserted her in 1839 leaving her with four children, when she only had three at that time. As Thomas' desertion and the reasons for it were to become a key issue in not only the 1860 court case but others before it, I knew I needed to check this out.

Civil Birth, Death and Marriage registration only started in 1837 therefore parish baptism records are the only sources available to show the birth of some of Jane and Thomas's children. Ann Elizabeth, their eldest was their only child when Samuel, Jane's father, died in 1834. She was baptised on the 18.2.1834 at St Peter's Church in Liverpool and Jane and Thomas lived on Lime Street where Thomas worked as a tailor.[22] Selina is the next child to be born[23] and was baptised on 6.6.1836 also at St Peter's Church in Liverpool and by this time the family are living on Jones Street. Thomas is still a tailor. Caroline follows, born between January and March 1839 [24] but there is no baptism certificate, just the civil registration of her birth.

They are the only children born by 1839 and the 1841 census which took place on 6th June, over two years after Jane said Thomas deserted her, showed Jane and Thomas living with their children at Skelthorne Street, Liverpool with her sisters Ellen and Ann almost next door. Her other sister Mary lived in Skelthorne Street too in 1839, so there would have been plenty of family witnesses around to see Thomas still living with Jane at least until 1841.

William Thomas, Jane's eldest son and fourth child, was actually born on 15.3.1841[25] at Skelthorne Street, Liverpool and in 1843 at Silver Street, the youngest Alfred Hugh[26] was born. On both their baptism certificates their father is named as Thomas Gallagher, a tailor. So now we have a total of five children fathered by Thomas Gallagher by 1843, four years after Jane claims Thomas deserted her.

And if this was not enough murky water, on the 11.1.1848, the *Liverpool Mercury* reports on a case brought by Thomas Gallagher, a tailor, who formerly lived in Gill Street, Liverpool against Mr. Christopher Macrae, a broker of Great John Street, who lived in the West Derby area of the town. This Thomas Gallagher argued that in May the previous year, which would have been in 1847, he and his wife [not named] called on him at his property in Gill Street where there were lodgings to be let. Thomas Gallagher agreed with Christopher Macrae a rent of 15 shillings a week [worth £45.31] and he and his wife moved in until August, about three months. By that time, he had only repaid £2 [£120.83] of the 15 shillings a week owing and Christopher Macrae had also lent Thomas money over that period when he had asked for it. An accountant called Joseph Brace was produced who proved that Thomas Gallagher had frequently promised to pay the money back.

In Thomas' defence, Mr. James his counsel, urged the court to disbelieve the whole of the evidence and called upon several witnesses to prove that Thomas Gallagher did not owe this money. The jury, after some deliberation, found in Thomas' favour, subject to him paying the outstanding rent money.

Is this tailor Thomas Gallagher our Jane Gallagher's husband? I am not sure at all but I do know that a lawyer called Mr. James also represented Jane in the 1860 court case so if she is the wife mentioned in this news report then she was still living with Thomas as man and wife as late as 1847, eight years later than Jane claimed in her testimony, and a date we need to remember.

Something is definitely awry. Maybe Jane is mistaken in saying that Thomas deserted her in 1839 and her mother Jane Oakes did not come to her rescue that year but Jane sticks to it in every court case over the years. Maybe Jane continued to cohabit with Thomas after 1839, in which case he could not legally have been said to desert her until after 1843 and the birth of Alfred Hugh their youngest son. Or, the only other scenario that springs to mind is that the sons are not Thomas' children at all but someone else's and Jane gave Thomas' name as their father to keep the boys' legitimacy. If this is true, then Jane knowingly lied to the church when they were baptised and the registration authorities, which was a criminal offence.

The boys were brought up and carried the Gallagher name until the 1851 census which shows them under another name. On William Thomas' marriage certificate, he named Thomas Gallagher as his father, however, Alfred Hugh, the youngest son, didn't. This issue of the boys' parentage niggled me throughout for I knew legitimacy would determine their inheritance rights to Jane's fortune, but I parked this for the moment due to lack of information and moved on to consider Jane's sisters. How did they figure in their mother's brothel business empire?

Jane had this to say about them:

> 'I have three sisters at present: they are in indigent circumstances - some of them very... they were continually asking my mother for money and were a great nuisance to her...'

With comments like these, I appreciated that all might not have been cosy in her family, but which one had offered Jane Oakes a place to live after her green-grocer's business failed until she came to rescue Jane Gallagher when Thomas (allegedly) deserted her? The only clues I had were:

- It could have been anytime from 1839 to 1843 after Jane's fifth child was born

- The sister's husband was a clockmaker

- They lived in Manchester

Seeing as two of Jane's sisters married two brothers and both were clockmakers this was not as easy as it looks! Mary married Edward Bellion and Ellen married William Bellion which means they were all brothers or sisters-in-law to their siblings. This inter - marrying occurs more than once in our story as many peoples' worlds in Victorian times were so narrow, they bordered on the incestuous. To find out which sister their mother lived with I started with Margaret, the eldest and worked down the list, at least that was the plan.

Margaret Oakes married John Rutherford, a fruit seller, on 6.10.1828 at Manchester Collegiate Church.[27] Neither she nor her husband appear in the 1841 census and John Rutherford at some point dies. I can find no trace of Margaret after this, but she does appear as the widow of John Rutherford in her mother's will which was drawn up in 1851.[28] There is no conclusive evidence of where they lived, or anything more about her life or death but she had died by 1860.

Mary Oakes married Edward Bellion, a clockmaker on 22.9.1827 in Liverpool and by the 1841 census was living with her husband and family on Cookson Street. All their children were born and baptised in Liverpool apart from Edward who was baptised on 27.5.1838 in St Helens.[29] Maybe that was by chance for in both the 1851 and 1861 censuses the family were living in Greenland Street, Liverpool, not in Manchester.

Ann Oakes is the third sister and married William Gill on 31.8.1828 in Liverpool at St John's Church.[30] Their first two children were born in Manchester and by the 1841 census they all lived in Upper Medlock Street, Hulme, Manchester, but her husband is described as a maker up of twist, not a clockmaker. William Gill died after 1841 and Ann married again to a man called Glen, a whitesmith in 1854, a month before her mother died in May Street, Liverpool. The couple married from Devon Street, where Jane had a brothel, but no house number is given on their marriage certificate.

In Jane's 1860 court case,[31] Ann Glen was called as a witness against her. She confirmed that Mrs. Oakes, their mother, returned to Liverpool after a long stay with another sister in Manchester, note not her, where this sister assisted Jane in the sub-letting, 'the delicate term for fitting up houses as receptacles for girls of loose character,' and that she, Ann Glen, had also assisted in the same way at another house, one of those on Tyrer Street and possibly the one at Devon Street as well. You can judge the validity of her evidence against a response in court when asked if she and Jane were on good terms. Her lawyer replied: 'She is on terms of utter enmity with her.'

Ellen Oakes, the youngest sister, married William Bellion, a clockmaker, at St Paul's Church, Liverpool on 29.1.1838 nearly ten years after her sister Mary married his brother Edward. Both bride and groom show as their address 6 Mount Pleasant, Liverpool on the marriage certificate. Their first two children were born in Liverpool and their youngest in Manchester in October 1840. By April 1841, the census listed them all as living at Jodrell Street, Manchester and Jane Oakes, her mother, is there too.[32] Whilst she appears in their household that night, she could have just been staying over, not actually living there. However, Ellen's husband is a clockmaker and if we take Jane's other reckoning of 1843 as being the date of Thomas' desertion then it does seem reasonable that Ellen was the daughter their mother lived with for two years from 1841 to 1843.

In 1851 Ellen and William were living in Hulme, Manchester and also took in Jane's husband Thomas when he left Liverpool. He is recorded in the census as being a tailor, the brother-in-law of William Bellion and born in Liverpool around 1810. Ellen's husband is described in the 1841 census as an optician and also in her mother's will of 1851.[33] Perhaps Ellen was the one sister in the family who felt she had a responsibility to look after those in vulnerable circumstances.

It is also very telling that Ellen and William thought enough of Thomas to name one of their sons William Thomas in 1849, well after whatever date Thomas is said to have deserted Jane. It certainly looks like Ellen at least did not think he was a drunken brute.

Chapter 2 - Building the Brothel Empire

Being left alone with young children between 1839 - 1843 was a horrifying prospect for any young woman in her twenties with no benefits, rights or any place to go except the streets or the workhouse so Jane must have been very glad her mother left her brothels in Manchester and rushed back to Liverpool to help. They came to an arrangement with Thomas whereby they paid him regular sums of money to 'keep him quiet, for he had led a very dissipated life' and drank to excess. They also took great measures to ensure he never knew how she made her money.

By 1841, Jane Gallagher is busy going around the brothel houses every day collecting the money due and looking out for their girls. She managed the empire on a day-to-day basis ordering goods and services, maintaining the furnishings, making sure the girls were well dressed and that there was good quality food and drink. She and her mother also lived in the houses in rotation so they could make sure all was well. It was on such a daily visit that Jane was an unwitting witness to an attack.

'At the police court, Mary Ann Duffy, a well-dressed female of disreputable character, appeared to complain against a fashionably attired man named John Hooton, said to be a son of the master tailor of that name, for having thrown upon her a bottle of vitriol which destroyed a velvet shawl and a satin dress worth £9 [£543.75 at 2017 values].

'Mary Ann Duffy stated that she had apartments at a beer house in Blake Street. On the evening of the previous Friday, she went into the parlour preparatory to going out. The defendant was then lying on the sofa. When she entered, he rose, followed her round the room and threw upon her the contents of a small phial. A female named Jane Gallagher, who was waiting for her at the parlour door said, "That young gentleman has thrown something upon you." Mary Ann put her hand behind her and felt her clothes were wet, but she observed "Oh, it is nothing but lavender water."'

But it was vitriol, it destroyed her silken gown and she was lucky not to be seriously injured. The magistrate, Mr. Rushton said:

'It is very fortunate for you, young man, that the statute which makes this offence a felony [a crime of high seriousness] has been repealed. All I can do at present is make you pay a penalty of £5 [£302.09.']³⁴

Vitriol, the most commonly available type of which today is sulphuric acid, is a highly corrosive liquid first made on a large scale in the 18th century, where it was known as oil of vitriol and used in many manufacturing processes. The first vitriol factory was set up on the Thames at Twickenham in 1736. Others followed in Birmingham and Prestonpans near Edinburgh, which by 1776 had become the largest in Britain. A Glasgow newspaper, the *Reformers Gazette* in 1834,³⁵ reported that a Hugh Kennedy had been hung for throwing vitriol, 'wilfully and maliciously' on the face of a fellow servant while he slept. Kennedy's victim had woken in agony, 'One of his eyes being literally burned out!' The writer grieved to say that the crime of throwing vitriol had become so common in the Glasgow area that it was:

'Almost a stain on the national character. No punishment could be too severe for the culprits. We would have their arms cut off by the shoulders, and, in that state, send them to roam as outcasts from society, without the power of throwing vitriol again.'

As the 19th century wore on, the crime developed a name: vitriolage.

'Despoliation prompted by jealousy and rejection was often the motive and women threw it at other women, men at men, men at women and women at men.'

The necessity of protecting their girls must have been an occupational hazard for Jane and her mother but it did not stop them expanding their brothel empire. Continuing her testimony in court Jane describes how her mother Jane Oakes took another house and business at 12 Tyrer Street, which later was renumbered to become No 8, about two years after they lived in Silver Street, then another at 6 Tyrer Street, which is later renumbered to No 10 at the same time. As Caroline, Jane's third daughter was born at Silver Street in 1839 we can assume that these two houses on Tyrer Street were taken around 1841. Both houses were furnished by her mother. The rent of one house was £13 [£785.42] a year and the other £15 [£906.26]. Jane estimated that £40 [£2,416.68] was spent on No 6 and about £30 [£1,812.51] on No 8. Besides these they had another house in Gill Street at the same time, her mother furnishing that at a cost of about £40 [£2,416.68]. This could have been the same house as mentioned in the last chapter.¹

The money is piling up already as this amounts to £8,337.55 at current values for only one year's rent and the initial furnishing of two houses out of the 22 to 25 Jane spoke

---

¹ See page 16

of as being in use at various times. They then bought or leased other 'gay' houses which had all previously been brothels and carried on the tradition. In all, as far as I can ascertain, Jane and her mother between them acquired – rented or then bought - the following properties in Liverpool. Where I know the exact address, it is given.

6 Blandford St	60 Devon St	6 Finch St
4,5 Hotham St	4,5,8 + 9 Houghton St	42 Lord Nelson St
6,7 May St	Pellew St	13 Pembroke Gardens
41 Russell St	10,12 Silver St	1 Springfield St
St Vincent St	8 Trafalgar St	2,6, 8 Tyrer St
10,12 Upper Dawson St		

The map below shows the town centre where Jane had nine houses in just three streets, her others being just a little further way.

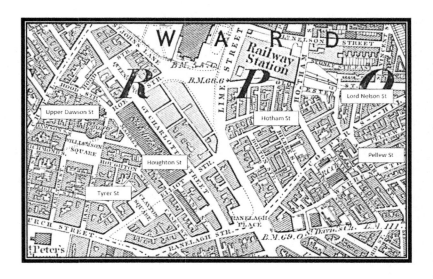

Figure 3 Jane's city centre brothels: OS 6" map of Liverpool 1845-1864

To fund this massive expansion, Jane borrowed from the Liverpool Tradesman's Loan Company via its secretary William Seabrook Chalkley.

'All the furniture was obtained from Mr. Watson, who had previously sold the furniture to other ladies who could to pay for it and she and her mother had to take the houses furnished - all the houses they took had been houses of that sort previously – Mr. Watson furnished those sorts of houses. We had a house in Manchester; my mother went there and disposed of it. She took it about eleven years ago [1849]. The furniture in the house stood on precisely the same footing as those in Liverpool. I think it was better furnished than the house in Tyrer Street where the furniture cost £30 [£1,812.51].'

The carpets, furnishings, wines and spirits, everything that the houses needed to act as comfortable brothels, was paid by instalments from the income from their houses, sometimes by Jane and her mother and at other times by their servant.

'Mr. Watson too used to call for the instalments, and when he called at the houses and found the "ladies" in bed, he would wait until they made their appearance downstairs, in order to secure the cash.'[36]

The vice chancellor hearing the case, reeling from Jane's descriptions, said:

'That seems pretty clear now, I think.' At which point there was much laughter in the court.

Jane was at pains to emphasise that she had no financial interest in the houses, but her children had, for they were sent to the Isle of Man to be nursed and afterwards to expensive boarding schools on the proceeds of the brothel empire. Their bills were paid by her mother, Jane insisting she only helped out with the houses where she could, though many 'presents' were made to her by gentlemen frequenting the houses. When asked for more detail, Jane said that furnishings were sent out from Burton and Watson in her name.

'They would let her have anything she wanted and would have furnished half of Liverpool for her if she wished.'

The cross examination went as follows:

Lawyer: Did you pay for them on your own account or your mother's?

Jane: Why, Mr. Watson knew how the money was got.

Lawyer: Was there a single particle of that furniture bought for your mother?

Jane: Oh, yes.

Lawyer: In her name?

Jane: I don't know, Mr. Watson will tell you. This money is part of the £3,000 [£177,387.60] I have stated I had spent with Messrs Burton and Watson.

'The house at No 6 Tyrer Street was the next to be purchased and Messrs Holden were the solicitors and I went with my mother to Messrs Holden about it. I think the purchase money was about £60 [£3,625.02] or £70 [£4,229.19] which was paid by instalments and I remember taking the money down. No part of the money either for No 6 or No 8 was raised by mortgage.

'I had no money at this time: if I had, my husband would have taken it from me. At this time, I was not living on hostile terms with my husband; we were partly supporting him; we were obliged to do so to keep him quiet, I never spoke to him; I did not see him. He would have taken the clothes off his children's backs if I had not sent them away; he had done so before. He was a very drunken man; he drank his senses away.

'My husband lived in Manchester. It is seventeen years since I separated from my husband [1843]. He never lived with me after my mother came to live with me. We never paid any rent for the house. I went to keep an establishment there and I keep it now. It was my mother's house, and in her occupation previous to 1851. That had been a 'gay house' about 35 years,' [since 1808 but not necessarily owned by Jane's mother.]

'I do not know when my mother purchased that house: Mr. Lowndes [solicitor] will tell you. I went with her and saw the money paid for it and two shops behind it were bought together. It was not furnished when we bought it. Messrs Burton and Watson furnished it; it is the same furniture that there is now and it was paid by instalments in the same manner as the other houses.

'No 4 Houghton Street belongs to Mr. Sheffer. I have had it and No 2 Tyrer Street about eleven years [since 1849] but I had nothing to do with the business of those houses until after my mother's death [in 1854]. Mr. Watson furnished it and I paid him. Nos 10 and 12 Upper Dawson Street were included in the same purchase. Part of the purchase money for those houses was raised by mortgage; what was paid, was paid by instalments for as my mother made it, she sent it. Mr. Morris paid the interest upon the mortgage; rents behind paid the mortgage; Mr. Morris was a clerk in Messrs Holden. They were not the solicitors of my mother in the purchase.

'The house belonged to Mr. Lowndes and he sold it to my mother. I used to take the instalments down to Messrs Holden for the purchase of No 6 and so I became acquainted with Mr. Morris. There was nobody with me and my mother at Messrs Lowndes, Bates and Robinson's office when the purchase was made that I can remember, we did not think there was any occasion for it. Since the death of my mother [in 1854] I could not interfere as to the disposal of that property [No 6 Houghton Street].'[37]

At this point I stopped trying to add up just what Jane's houses costs to buy, rent or furnish as her evidence was dotted all over the place and differed significantly from what she admitted in subsequent cases. At no time does she give any indication of what the profits were.

This is a lot to take in as there are many unanswered questions and one wonders if she deliberately employed the smoke and mirrors approach. However, it is very clear that in the years 1839 to 1850 Jane and her mother were on a roll, renting then buying properties all over Liverpool, developing their brothel empire. It wasn't hard to see a strategy emerging:

- Jane was the real force behind the empire, her mother the public front

- Jane contracted with suppliers via her mother to provide for their brothels

- She was kept by her mother in comfort and luxury

- They borrowed money, paid by instalments, ran up debts to fund expansion

- They employed people to run their houses, to take the fall if the police were involved and they kept behind the scenes

- The children were sent away in blissful ignorance to the Isle of Man to be nursed and later to a succession of private schools and tutors

- Thomas was paid off monthly to 'keep him quiet' and Jane's sisters, by and large, kept out of it

Chapter 3 - Social Evil

Quietly tolerated, prostitution has existed throughout history
An accepted, if unspeakable, part of society
Always lurking just out of sight
Based on centuries of understanding prostitution as a 'safety
valve' for women
And an outlet for men's insatiable sexual urges
It came to be considered an inevitable part of any civilisation
A necessary evil - A Social Evil
'Evil Becomes Her' by Jacqueline Shelton 2013[38]

Was Jane Gallagher's brothel empire a ruthless exploitation of vulnerable people or a business opportunity? Immoral, illegal or just pure social evil?[39] The Victorians themselves were ambivalent, revealing a fascinating duality of public morality and private debauchery, for they were caught between two stools:

'If society was to allow men comparative sexual freedom and at the same time keep single women virgin and married women chaste then a solution had to be found which would gratify the former without sacrificing the latter and the answer lay in prostitution... a class of fallen women was needed to keep the rest of the world pure.'[40]

For the Victorians there were at least three sub-classes of these women, the first being:

'Genteel, lady-like, educated, exotically delightful and acceptable companions like the high-class courtesans who were furred and attractive professional ladies who take midday and afternoon walks in the better parts of town.'[41][42]

Their boudoirs offered the best surroundings to make Victorian gentlemen feel like they were merely cultivating intelligent conversation instead of indulging in 'criminal conversation,' which was a Victorian euphemism for prostitution. It was this sort of 'silken' prostitute' that Jane Gallagher offered the wealthy middle and upper classes of Liverpool. Those of this type include women who:

- Are kept by men of independent means

- Live in apartments and maintain themselves by entertaining men

- Live in or work from high class brothels
- Are well-dressed but also frequent the better streets and attend society events

The second sub-class were common street prostitutes, seen by respectable Victorians as infesting low neighbourhoods: debauched, evil seducers of the innocent, absolutely beyond redemption.[43] Certainly, the invective hurled at them by some worthy gentlemen is very strong and their passions are mighty to behold, in both the brothel and the pulpit for the '*Great Social Evil*' was very much feared by the middle classes in the nineteenth century who worried that:

> 'Prostitution would pollute respectable society, wrecking marriages, breaking up the family home, destroying the very fabric of the nation.'[44]

But what was life like for street prostitutes? The unpublished diaries of three Liverpool girls tell their stories.[45] Ellen Reece, Jane Shaw and Jane Doyle ran away from home to live in a cellar with other girls, under the care of 'old granny' and an elderly man. From shoplifting and robbing drunks, they graduated to prostitution, fighting a constant battle of wits with constables they could sometimes buy off with a glass of gin. If arrested, even a girl with no money was sure of a lawyer, since there was an understanding with them that they should defend the girl without charge and in return she should afterwards spend the night in their bed.

It was usual for common Victorian prostitutes to work in pairs and for a man to hire them both simultaneously and Jane Doyle explained how she had worked with Jane Shaw. On the first occasion, a prosperous-looking man of about fifty had wanted them both. They had gone to a room with him where Jane Doyle had watched Jane Shaw lose her virginity, for which the man paid 10 shillings [£30.21].

This trade was loosely organised, the Liverpool girls simply renting rooms in such notorious houses as the *Cheshire Cheese* in Newton Lane, sometimes at a shilling [£3.02] for 10 or 15 minutes. The girls and their customers were guaranteed very little privacy in such places and Ellen Reece reported that there were as many as six or seven beds in a room with men and women in them. Robbing clients was an essential part of the trade of the freelance prostitute but it was important that the stolen money was not to be found on her if she was arrested.

Ellen Reece described the way in which girls learnt to hide gold sovereigns in their vaginas, as from experience, she knew that she could carry thirty sovereigns in this manner. The police matrons who searched the girls were usually fooled but a girl who tried to conceal money from her pimps was made to stand on a bed and jump off, again and again, until the coins were shaken out. Some girls hid sovereigns by swallowing them before they were searched, and then relieved themselves on the floor of the bridewell [police lock up]. If the coins had not reappeared after a day or two, the girls would complain of being constipated and ask for 'opening medicine.' According to Ellen Reece, she had never known any girl come to harm through swallowing sovereigns, even though a few girls well known to the police were obliged to swallow their takings almost every night.

One girl got away with it when she found herself in front of a gullible judge. A respectably attired foreigner had followed the woman into a disorderly house on Tyrer Street where he says she robbed him of a sovereign, which she immediately swallowed. He threatened to have her charged, but in only three minutes after swallowing the coin, by an extraordinary effect of nature, she again produced the sovereign and returned it to the man. The woman was then arrested and taken to court. And the verdict?

> The magistrate said: 'It was contrary to the law of nature for the prisoner to part with the sovereign in so short a time,' and ordered her discharge. Obviously, the magistrate had never seen a sword swallower!

Nevertheless, common prostitution was viewed by prominent Victorians as a terrible threat.

> 'Too long, from a morbid sense of delicacy, have we suffered ourselves to remain in a happy but culpable innocence respecting this horrid and most colossal vice [of prostitution] ... which, more than any other, fed like some infernal and insatiable canker worm on the vitals of society, sapped the foundations of our entire social fabric and destroyed unheeded and disturbed, the flower and hope of mankind...'

So said Mr. J.H Marshall, superintendent of Bradford town mission who came to lecture in Liverpool to the worthy gentlemen of the town in 1859 on Yorkshire's good work to manage their levels of prostitution.[46] They were strong words indeed and Bradford only had 60 brothels and 177 prostitutes in 1859, who he referred to as 'kept mattresses,' as compared to Liverpool which had 700 known brothels and 2,256 prostitutes in that year alone. This figure was to peak in 1861 to 1,000 known brothels and over 3,000 prostitutes. Police figures are the tip of the iceberg however, the actual numbers being inevitably much higher as many women, like those employed by Jane, never came to the attention of the police.

The last category of prostitutes contains women and young girls for whom there was no choice, who had, according to Victorian researchers such as the worthy Mr. Logan from Glasgow,[47] experienced:

- Ill-considered and ill-assorted marriages
- Inadequate renumeration for female work

- Want of proper surveillance of servants on the part of masters and mistresses
- Harsh and unkind treatment by parents and other relatives
- Attendance at evening dancing schools and dancing parties
- Theatre-going
- Improper works and obscene prints
- A lack of encouragement for virtue
- Temptation by the rewards given to vice, leading to dishonesty and a desire for property

And pressure from those who profited from social evil such as:

- Procuresses, or females who visit country towns, markets and places of worship for the purpose of decoying good-looking girls
- Children who have been urged by their mothers to become prostitutes for a livelihood

But were these women victims of, or the sole perpetrators of social evil? The personal observations conducted by another worthy, Mr. Tait in 1848 in an 'Inquiry into the extent, causes of prostitution in Edinburgh', and the same Mr. Logan cited above,[48] revealed some 'natural causes' or character failings of women who became prostitutes:

Licentiousness of inclination	Irritability of temper
Pride and love of dress	Indolence

More vociferous was an article in the Liverpool *Porcupine* magazine in 1861 entitled, 'Slatternly Wives,' which proclaimed that:

'Thousands of working men are driven from their homes to the brothel, grog shop or beer house by reason of the inconsideration, ignorance, slovenly conduct or slatternly habits of their wives.'

But less sensational studies concluded that most common prostitution stemmed from desperation, deprivation or the threat of starvation, because of:

- Ignorance or defective education or religious instruction
- Desecration of the Sabbath

- Tales of love, murder, superstition strongly interwoven with a hollow profession of morality which is evidently intended as a cloak for many sins[49]

- The corrupting influence and intermixing in factories where chastity is almost unknown

- Intemperance

- Being servants in taverns and public houses where women have been seduced by men frequenting those places of dissipation and temptation

- Insufficient space in homes with no room for decency

- Lack of parental discipline and bad examples

Most managed to agree that poverty was the biggest single cause of prostitution and the Reverend Abraham Hume, a Scottish-Irish Anglian priest working in Liverpool published a book in 1858 called 'Conditions in Liverpool, Religious and Social' which shone 'a piercing light' on the actual differences in the qualities of life experienced by people living in different wards of the town. Not surprisingly the most deprived wards were those with the poorest housing and the highest social evil, drunkenness and crime rates and Hume produced a map showing where these wards were.

His research of coroner's reports of these areas revealed that in 1847 the average life expectancy in Liverpool was twenty years and five months as compared to that of those who lived in Ulverston on the Cumbrian coast, which was 41 years and eight months. Another startling statistic he gave was that the average age of death in people who attended St Anne's Dispensary on Rose Hill in Liverpool was 14 years and 11 months. Both averages are again well skewed by the high mortality rates of children in Liverpool but nevertheless, they do indicate the extent of atrocious living conditions in the town. He also quotes police figures for that period showing there were 7,862 inhabited cellars in Liverpool where they estimated 32,584 people lived, 15% of the total population of Liverpool, making an average of 4.14 people per cellar.

Dr Duncan, Liverpool's Public Health Officer, and who we have already heard of in respect of court housing,[50] claimed in the *Times* newspaper:

'Liverpool is notoriously the unhealthiest, the worst drained and the most miasmatic city of the empire,' and according to Sir Arnold Knight MD, feeble Liverpudlians 'were unfit to be shot at,' since approximately 70% of recruits for the army in the 1840s were rejected.[51]

Women were also more vulnerable to poverty as work for them was scarce and unreliable. Apart from domestic service and bar work, they had little choice but to sell their wares on the streets, not only their bodies but flowers, fish, pig's feet, watercress, cockles and firewood and they were continually harassed by the police for violating by-laws. Women also worked in the 'sweating' shops as shirt makers, dressmakers and tailoresses but wages, conditions and job security were very poor. Cotton picking was another option but this was thirsty work and the women in this trade were known for their drinking and rough habits. Father James Nugent, Roman Catholic chaplain of Walton Gaol and a social reformer, described cotton pickers, who kept late hours and went to the most disreputable public houses in Marybone, as 'very little removed from the girls of the streets.'[52]

Work for men was more available but unpredictable as Liverpool, being dependent on the sea for most of its economy, used predominantly casual labour, like Jane's father Samuel, the carter, who worked at the docks on an 'as and when' basis. Subject to the vagaries of the weather, the sea, gales and fog meant that employment was feast or famine for the majority of the population and in times of slump there was a great tendency to resort to public houses.

In 1863, a pamphlet was produced by the Rev R. Jones[53] which showed that 115 people had died prematurely through drink that year and featured extracts from coroner's reports and comments made at inquests. Some of those who died met with an accident whilst drunk:

- In charge of a cart, called at three public houses and became drunk. Falling off shafts, the wheel passed over him and he was picked up dead

- Drinking with some friends, became intoxicated. He was seen walking along the edge of the quay at George's Dock. He fell in and was drowned

- Name unknown. She was found lying on her face in a ditch with a bottle beside her, which had contained rum. The surgeon attributed death to suffocation while drunk

7,550 people in Liverpool in 1863 were patients of the hospitals and dispensaries through drink and 17,010 had been in the hands of the police. The Rev R. Jones also told the stories of the families of drunken men, families like Jane's:

- Being drunk on Saturday, the couple quarrelled. She was struck on the head and died from the injuries received

- She said her husband drank and that he was spending his wages and leaving her and the children without bread. She died in a room without furniture, barely covered with a few filthy rags and having bruises on her person

In 1864, 143 children in Liverpool were suffocated, three quarters of them between Saturday night and Sunday morning, when drinking was at its height.

'In one case an infant was suffocated in the midst of a fight which took place in a public house.'

This pamphlet goes on to quote a medical writer who noted:

'The blood of the professed drunkard .... differs from that of a sober man; it is darker and approaching the character of the venus [vein]. Drunkards are exceedingly subject to all kinds of inflammation, both from the direct excitement of the liquor and from their often remaining in a state of intoxication exposed to cold and damp. Hence inflammatory affectations of the lungs, intestines, bladder, kidneys, brain etc.' [54]

Whilst the connection between factory work and social evil might not be immediately obvious, there is plenty of evidence to support it. The *Liverpool Mail* in 1842 ran a long article about the impact on families. One woman said, with tears in her eyes:

'The factories had been their ruin, their eldest daughter being only sixteen years of age, had had one child; the other although fourteen years old, was pregnant!'

The reporter was informed by a person well acquainted with the factory system, that within the last few years, since wages have been reduced, the prostitution of female factory workers had increased at least 50%.

'It is neither more nor less than manufacturing goods with the proceeds of prostitution... These poor girls wish to keep up appearances, which they cannot do, as they have parents to keep, which would not be the case if there was an efficient poor law. There are a great number of instances where the children leave their parents at 13 or 14 years of age and go into boarding houses, where they learn all kinds of bad practices as well as in the factories.

'He saw a young man with two little girls, nine and twelve years old. He asked him: "Where are you going?" The man replied: "To seek work for these children," adding, "It is hard work to be thrown out of work and be forced to turn these poor things into the factories." The man had been a spinner but his spinning frame was double decked, which means joined to another, so one man works them both. The man could not get any other work anywhere "so these children must earn my bread."'[55]

This is not an isolated report and eight years later in 1850 little seems to have changed. The *Liverpool Mercury* published the revelations of a female pickpocket.

She speaks of leaving the factory when she was 12, where she worked as a piecer in a room with seven other piecers under a spinner and a cypher.

'The spinner would let off two girls for the purposes of spending the afternoon in thieving. The girls principally stole handkerchiefs, boots etc and let the spinners have their share of the plunder either for nothing, or for a very small price. One shilling [£4.01] for a handkerchief worth five [£20.05] or six shillings [£24.06].'

She said she knew many factory girls in Manchester who, when they leave work, go on the streets.

'I had personal knowledge of seven girls of this kind. Any man might see it any night in Oldham Street. These girls were from different families and their families must have known by their fine clothes, that they were not living properly. There are many girls who work the streets. They only go to the factory as a blind. I do not think there is a mill in Manchester where this is not done. In one way the overlookers are worse than the spinners, because having the power of "bagging" the piecers, the girls dare not deny them; but they would visit the spinners. Ever since women ceased to be spinners and the men took their places, there has been many more girls thrown on the town.

'I know a young woman named Agnes Rowley about eighteen or nineteen years of age, who has lost her place four times through resisting the spinners she pieced for. The spinner in No 5 tried to seduce her and bothered her so that she could not stand it and left that room to go to No 4. She had previously worked in No 6 and got bagged because she would not submit to the spinner. Afterwards she lost her place at the mill... I know many cases in which the piecers have children to the overlookers or spinners. Ann Modruff has a child to an overlooker, a married man, and Jane Bostock has a child to an overlooker, again a married man. Ann Rogers has a child to the spinner and Ann Hickey, also to a spinner.'

When the newspaper quite rightly seeks corroboration of these revelations, the Reverend Mr. Clay said:

'He has learned so much as to satisfy him that there is some foundation for her account.'[56]

The awful fact is, with the limited life expectancy for a common prostitute once engaged in sex work, life was a hell hole in the back streets of Liverpool. Many died terrible deaths:

- Grace Mc Connell, a prostitute in 1849, attempted suicide by throwing herself in the river, saying she preferred it to cutting her throat to end her existence[57]

- Ann Swift a prostitute in 1846 is accused of murdering another prostitute in Mason Street[58]

Was it worth it? James Nugent, chaplain at Liverpool borough prison, estimated that the maximum wage earned by a woman doing sewing in 1850 was ten shillings a week [£40.09], with younger sewers averaging between two [£8.02] and four shillings [£16.04]. But a woman who picked up a sailor or an officer from a ship in one of the many dancing saloons in the city, could easily earn £2 [£160.37] or £3 [£240.56] a week.[59]

There was always the risk of venereal disease, but for the most desperate women it was a case of eat today or starve tomorrow or possibly die of disease very soon. For others it was a chance to be free from poverty by entering into a life of glamour and excitement, to wear fashionable clothes and be taken out to the theatres, music halls and be seen on the arm of wealthy, influential men.

So, who was exploiting who? Were these women wrong to use men to make easy money and gain a better life for themselves? Or were they slaves to the bullies and madams, mistreated, abused, exploited until they became riddled with disease, alcoholics or wrinkled crones with no beauty left and no alternative but an early death by their own hands or from unforgiving street living?

The Victorian view that social evil was down to women when it takes two to tango, would not be acceptable today.

This *Punch* cartoon illustrates graphically how such convictions were ingrained in young males by the time they were in long trousers. The young boy by the mantelpiece is parroting views he has often heard his male elders express:

'Women are a decidedly inferior animal.'

What is worse, these assumptions were not only accepted without question; they were enshrined in law.

Figure 4 'Women are a decidedly inferior animal.' Punch 1859

Chapter 4 – Prostitutes, Poverty and Punishment

Was prostitution legal? Well, not since the *Vagrancy Act 1824* introduced the term 'common prostitute' into English Law with a punishment of up to one month's hard labour.[60] The *Town Police Clauses Act 1847* [61] made it an offence for common prostitutes to assemble at any 'place of public resort,' such as a coffee shop and there were many controversial cases prosecuted on these grounds against establishments in Liverpool town between 1850 - 1889.[62]

It was not until 1885 before the age of consent went up from 13 to 16 with legislation which also said any person who kept, managed or assisted in the management of premises used as a brothel, or was the tenant or landlord of such premises was liable to a hefty fine or a maximum of three months' imprisonment. But we had to wait until 1895 before the case *Singleton v Ellison*[63] defined a brothel as premises used by more than one woman for the purposes of prostitution. Therefore, while many brothel keepers were arrested for keeping a disorderly house or one of ill fame and many women for soliciting on the streets, Jane avoided being prosecuted for over twenty years until 1862, partly thanks to her strategy of owning nothing on paper and paying others to operate brothels on her behalf.

Having laws against prostitution in place is one matter and the ability of the police to enforce it quite another. They had an unenviable job because the law as it stood throughout the 19th century did not give them any real means for closing down brothels until 1885 and the force itself was only created in the 1830s. Police powers simply failed to grow in line with the resulting disorder and they struggled desperately even in normal circumstances to keep the levels of prostitution down.

Exceptional weather conditions, such as occurred when an adverse east wind arrived in Liverpool, did not help either. This happened in 1855 when it blew for so long that many sailors were trapped in the port and it was largely responsible for food shortages and bread riots. Why? Because an east wind meant that a ship could not get in or out of Liverpool therefore seamen stuck on land spent their time in the brothels and drinking establishments.

Policing as we know it only became possible with the *Reform Act* of 1832[64] which had been enacted to curb what was known as the 'rotten boroughs' and said those over a certain population should establish a police or constabulary force, Liverpool being one of them. In 1836, the Liverpool Watch Committee offered the post of head constable to Michael Whitty at a time when there were three police groups: the Night Watch, the Day Police and the Dock Police. Whitty was regarded as the first full-time senior permanent official of Liverpool Corporation and the police force itself was the first large body of municipal employees. He had previously been the superintendent in charge of the Night Watch[65] but as Liverpool's first head constable he also had responsibility for establishing a Fire Brigade as well. Up to this point fire-fighting was provided by fire brigades owned by various insurance companies.

The new force was created on 29.2.1836 and consisted of 290 men, 24 inspectors and four superintendents, plus 40 policemen, bridewell [local lock up] keepers and indoor officers. It was suggested that the Town Police and Night Watch were amalgamated and adverts were placed throughout the town to attract new volunteers to the force. About twelve months later, the dock police, which had been the most efficient of the three groups, was subsumed when Liverpool town's first unified police force was set up and it reported on the state of the town, as it then was, to the Improvement Committee of the council in February of that year drawing attention to these facts:[66]

- There were between 3 - 400 public houses in the town

- A quarter of the entire number were licensed victuallers, whose houses were kept open until after midnight

- Even on Sundays many were open between 4 - 6.00 am when they were filled with 'the most depraved characters,' until church time

- There were between 60 - 70 tap rooms and several hundreds of beer shops which were supported by the most infamous individuals

- Before public houses had been ordered by the mayor to be closed at stated hours, between 100 and 120 people were brought before the courts for drunkenness every day

With the new rules about opening hours in operation this reduced to about 50 a day.

In Williamson Square in the town centre and its immediate vicinity [where Jane later had several houses] there were around 20 saloons where thieves and prostitutes nightly entertained and crime abounded, for they 'possessed allurements of the dance, the song and the comic recitation.' Further facts were:

- There were around 300 brothels, some containing females as young as ten

- Known robberies in brothels came to £1,000 [£67,801.30] a week and by 1843 this had almost doubled

- That in all brothels, spirits could be obtained and 100 of these establishments were within a fifteen-minute walk of the city centre

- Each prostitute was said to live with a man who benefitted from this plunder

- There were upwards of 1,000 male thieves, 500 of whom worked at intervals and stole when they could and 600 congregated at the docks on a regular basis to entrap disembarking sailors newly paid off

- 1,200 thieves were under the age of fifteen and worked with the older men

- The combined amount reckoned to be stolen in this way was £700,000 a year [£47,460,910.00]

This was the starting position of the police and the scale of what an untrained and inexperienced force had to contend with, their men being ordinary males recruited off the streets who would probably find themselves having to choose between their drinking mates and the law in any street confrontation. Sometimes they were victims themselves:

> 'After a policeman came home from duty early and went to bed, he got up to get his wife a brandy as she felt ill. Dressed in trousers, he felt in his pocket for some money to pay for the brandy and found he had several sovereigns. They were not his trousers!' Another man had been in his bed while he was at work and the *Liverpool Mercury* said his wife, 'left the house...'

From 1836, the police were fighting a losing battle and their Watch Committee reported two years later in 1838 that there were:[67] 431 brothels and 154 houses in which prostitutes lodged. By 1840[68] the numbers had risen to 568 brothels and 209 houses in which prostitutes lodged, bringing the total number of prostitutes known to the police to 2,489.

So, what were the police doing about it? In 1840, 72 brothels were closed and 133 opened. 28 houses where prostitutes lived were closed and 43 new ones opened, showing that while the police could close a house, they had no power to get rid of the nuisance. In 1841, there were only these statistics available: 561 brothels and 2,899 prostitutes known to the police. The census showed that year the population of Liverpool was 271,824 of which 131,292 were male,[69] therefore there was one brothel for every 234 men including boys, and 45 men and boys in Liverpool for every prostitute.

The police also reported the following, which says a lot about the professionalism of the police force at that time. For the period 1840-1842:

'The conduct of the police force exhibits considerable improvement. There has been during the year fewer constables suspended, or otherwise punished for disobedience of orders, or neglect of duty than in any preceding year since the establishment of the force.'

There then followed, at the height of Liverpool's notoriety, between the late 1840s to 1852, a succession of head constables, whose service was less than satisfactory. This coincided with the rise in immorality and probably compounded the problems the police had trying to contain it. In April 1844, Henry Miller was appointed the head constable and sworn in before Liverpool's mayor, Thomas Sands, and the town's chief magistrate Edward Rushton. Within six months the *Liverpool Albion* on 25.10.1844 was expressing concern about the leadership of the police force. Its readers were told that the Watch Committee had convened a sub-committee to look into the state of the force generally and to seek assurance as to whether the printed rules and regulations were fully carried out. Then came a Minute of the Watch Committee of Liverpool council, which oversaw the police force:

'The Daily Board of yesterday think it their duty to report to the committee, on the earliest opportunity, that the head constable has been guilty of a flagrant disobedience of orders, given to him by the chairman in the presence of three members.'

Miller resigned in December 1844 after only nine months in the service of Liverpool town and Matthew Dowling was appointed the next head constable in 1845 where once more, he blotted his copybook - he had previously been dismissed by Sir Robert Peel, the Home Secretary in 1829 for leaking some documents. Dowling was described as 'a curious individual who could not be said to lack intelligence,' and who on 10.1.1838 became a barrister in Liverpool and was called to the bar on 30.1.1841 prior to being appointed head constable. However, it was reported that in 1852, in an effort to preserve an unblemished record, he removed a portion of a critical report from the north division police book and on Thursday 4.3.1852 both he and superintendent John Towerson were dismissed from Liverpool police.

It was not until the appointment of Major John James Grieg as head constable of Liverpool police on 27.3.1852 that this rotten run of chief constables ended. Major Grieg had the unenviable task of restoring the general public's confidence in the police and also the magistracy as well, for in 1859 Mr. Mansfield, while being careful not to criticise Major Grieg himself said:

'As a stipendiary magistrate for Liverpool I very much doubt [the official returns of the numbers of brothels and prostitutes] ... I have seen so much dishonesty in these matters that I cannot believe them... The police lied through thick and thin... There was something extremely wrong, so far as the police were concerned... There were underhand dealings with the police... There was something roguish, foul and corrupt in the administration of justice...'

The Watch Committee were: 'Greatly surprised at the above statement....' and ordered an investigation.[70]

Vulnerable women in Liverpool also needed the head constable's protection from the very police who were supposed to be looking out for them. In 1853, Sarah Gill of Glover Street was assaulted in her home by two constables who were then found guilty and fined.[71] Annie Williams, a respectable girl, claimed she was picked up by police and assaulted by them for being a prostitute, another was dragged into a cellar by a policeman who intended to rape her. In all, 40% of all victims of alleged police assaults reported by the Liverpool press of the time were female.

The plight of prostitutes in Liverpool was also the subject of Dr Bevan's lecture on 3.6.1843 on 'Female Prostitution'.[72] He was the minister of Newington Chapel.

'They are exposed to every inclemency of the weather, ill-clad to resist rude assault; their wretched dwellings, as in the majority of cases they are cellars, hovels, to which they herd from the ornate and fashionable rooms in which they receive their visitors; the inconceivable brutalities to which they are compelled to submit at the hands of their licentious customers, and their own associates or bullies; their ejection from the higher to the lower grade, as their beauty is deflowered, and their health undermined. "We have been knocked about long enough," they told me.'

As a minister, he had gathered information about the variety of diseases common amongst prostitutes, the inevitable sexual infections and conditions but also rheumatism, fevers, skin and pulmonary disorders. The women in their turn infected their children and their husbands as well as their customers. He reiterated that the average life span of a prostitute from when they took up the work, was six years and that:

'The greater portion of this period is occupied in the endurance of suffering, which at last makes a miserable exit welcome.'

The Mr. Logan, the Glasgow researcher, depicts the closing scene of a young person, who, having been turned out of the house where she had ministered to the lust of the visitors, and the cupidity of the mistress, could find no shelter but in an empty house. Her pangs became so intolerable that she cried out to a few of her old associates:

'Oh! Women! Smother me! I cannot bear this! Do smother me!' He added: 'They did smother her!'

Mr. Lowndes, a Liverpool surgeon who worked at the Lock(e) hospital, also sheds light on their situations, saying even in the last days of prostitutes:

'The agony of their dissolution is often unseen and unheard. No friendly arm supports the pillow, no tender voice whispers consolation into the ear, no kindred hand closes the glazed and sightless eye.'

You will have noticed the many different estimates so far of the life expectancy of prostitutes, which reflects the state of knowledge at that time and the differing definitions of who was counted and which sources of information they had access to.

It was against this background of poverty, desperation and depravity that back street brothel keepers plied their trade and prostitutes tried to survive and look after their children. Many took to drink to cope. It was reported on 20.10.1852 that a prostitute Isabella Shepherd died the previous Tuesday at a brothel in Hotham Street kept by Samuel Wood. She was of very drunken habits and had complained of being ill the past two weeks. An inquest was ordered. The coroner was more outraged at the death taking place in a brothel than the fact the unfortunate woman died and he railed against a witness called Ellen Rooney who had lived in this 'den of infamy' as housekeeper for four years. He asked:

'What thoughts she had of another world and whether the example and the miserable death of her co-partner in sin was likely to produce any effect on her?'

She said she hoped it would. He strongly advised her to leave off her dissolute life and turn her attention to some honest mode of getting a livelihood.[73]

The body of Mary McNeil, a prostitute, who lived at a brothel kept by Mary Leary in 2 Court, Bickerstaffe Street, was found dead in bed, after a fit of drunkenness. The medical evidence showed that death had resulted from disease of the heart, lungs and liver, induced by excessive drinking and the jury found a verdict accordingly. [74]

In 1864 Bridget Kelly, a prostitute who lived in a brothel kept by Annie Maxwell in No 4 Court, Scotland Road, killed Mary Ann her sixth child, all of whom were then dead. Witnesses were called who said that Bridget was a drunken woman who had been intoxicated the previous night. Early on the Sunday morning the son of the brothel keeper found Bridget lying in the kitchen with the child by her side. He tried to take the child away from her but she sat up and gave him a slap in the face. The son again asked Bridget for the child and she threw the child out of her arms down the steps of the door, its head coming in contact with the flags. The child did not cry but instantly went into convulsions. Bridget said 'Now you can have it.' She was in a great passion but the son did not know the cause of it. The brothel keeper told him to take the child up from where it was lying on the outside of the door and carry it upstairs to bed. The verdict was manslaughter.[75]

Not only were prostitutes and their children dying horribly, they were brutally misused, beaten, stabbed. In June 1843, Margaret Anderson, a prostitute living on Albion Street in a brothel stabbed another prostitute called Hannah Power. She received a wound three inches long in the back of her head, another on the throat near the jugular vein and one on the angle of her eye.[76] In October 1849, Morris Whaling was committed for trial on a charge of brutally ill-using a prostitute at a public house in Canning Place. He broke three jugs and two glasses on her head. She was taken to hospital.[77] Michael Riley in 1876, a cabman, was charged with raping a prostitute called Margaret Foyle.[78]

These individual stories give life, and death, to the statistics and show how conditions in parts of Liverpool were dreadful, not only for prostitutes but young innocent widows with many children suddenly left to fend for themselves and unable to work, as well as pregnant respectable girls like Catherine Comerford in 1846, a servant who was inseminated by one of the family and thrown out and ended up giving birth in squalor in a brothel, or those simply abandoned or alone. Alternatives were as bad: the workhouse, the last resort short of prostitution for many, where conditions described by a gentleman, Mr. Nightingale, were 'worse than Scutan in the Crimea...' was not appealing.

In 1846, the Female Penitentiary in Liverpool published figures showing that 'over 500 miserable creatures in this town alone, fall into a premature grave, victims of the horrible consequences of a life of prostitution.'[79] Most were continually arrested and overcrowding in prisons was rife. A spot audit on one day in 1867 showed 306 females had been in prison 15 times, of these 41 had been in prison 30 times and 175 had been in prison in the last three months. The sad truth is, no woman chose to be a prostitute, the majority bewailed their wretched fate, wished their lives over and Liverpool was said to be in 1867 a 'hotbed of syphilis.'[80] Common prostitution did not:

'Free women from a life of poverty and insecurity but further subjected them to physical dangers, alcoholism, venereal disease and police harassment.'[81]

And if that was not enough, then came the *Contagious Diseases Acts* of 1864, 1866 and 1869 which were meant to lower the rates of venereal disease amongst the armed forces of the day. By 1864, any woman identified as a common prostitute by a plain clothes policeman was subject to two weekly internal examinations. The men who frequented brothels and used prostitutes were not similarly required to have an internal examination. These Acts were based on the idea that women, not men were responsible for the spread of venereal disease and that while men would be degraded if subjected to physical examination, the women who satisfied male sexual urges were already so degraded that further indignities scarcely mattered.[82]

If a woman was found to be diseased, she was interned in a special Lock(e) hospital of which there was a very busy one in Liverpool where Mr. Lowndes, the surgeon, worked.[83] And within these Acts, there was deliberate and sanctioned discrimination as the police were told:

'Do not concern themselves with the higher class of prostitutes: indeed, it would be impossible and impertinent as well, were they to make the attempt.'[84]

Those prostitutes, such as the ladies employed by Jane, would have found themselves truly above these laws, though they were just as likely to be diseased and infect others in their turn.

This muddled state of the law is the result of the ambivalence of Victorian social attitudes towards social evil. It was 1886, 22 years later before the *Contagious Diseases Acts* were repealed and the barbaric targeting of vulnerable women was ended, thanks to the efforts of activist Josephine Butler[85] from Liverpool and others. Liverpool, therefore, at this time, 1830 to 1850, provided Jane and others, with a wonderful business opportunity to make money.

- The newly created police force was struggling

- There were no laws against owning or even running a brothel, as long as they were not 'disorderly houses'

- Liverpool financers were overflowing with money and almost queuing to supply the madams with loans and mortgages

- There was an unlimited market of wealthy educated men to enjoy her silken brothels

- Jane's women were not subject to the *Contagious Diseases Acts*

They certainly made the most of it.

Chapter 5 - Coverture

'If a wife tries to eke out a scanty subsistence for herself and her children by working the husband could seize the proceeds of her work and if he wishes bestow them on his mistress.'
'Continuity and Change' by Joanne Bailey 2002

This was lived reality for married but separated women in the middle of the 19th century and in order to understand Jane's rights, or lack of them, from either 1839 or after 1843, whichever date she actually separated from her husband Thomas, and her right to own property and to keep the proceeds of the brothels, we have to have some knowledge of the law in Victorian times. The fact she made her living from immoral earnings is beside the point, it would have been the same if she had been employed in a more respectable capacity.

Under common law, Jane was governed by the system of coverture. Sir William Blackstone, in his 1765 authoritative legal text 'Commentaries on the Laws of England,'[86] said this about it:

'The very being and legal existence of the woman is by the common law suspended during marriage, or at least is incorporated and consolidated into that of her husband, under whose wing, protection and cover she performs everlasting.'

Jane, therefore, had no legal separate entity from Thomas and in law he owned everything she had. Blackstone went on to say that:

'Under the influence and protection of her husband she was in a relationship similar to that of a subject to a baron or lord. A husband could not grant to his wife anything such as property, and could not make legal agreements with her after marriage, because it would be like gifting something to one's self or making a contract with one's self. Existing contracts made between a future husband and wife were void upon marriage.'[87]

Yes, you did read that right. The Select Committee actually said:[88] 'The wife is incapable of contracting, of suing and of being sued.'

Furthermore, a husband's consent to his wife pledging his credit was assumed from the couple's cohabitation. If there was cohabitation, retailers and traders could deal with a wife without checking whether she had her husband's permission to spend.[89]

We now see this as nothing but appalling but how did it work? Did grocers hide in cupboards to spy on couples?

'The condition of English wives under coverture was both defended as one of privilege and attacked as worse than slavery.'[90]

However, this truly was the law. You can now see why Jane was so anxious to appear to have nothing, earn nothing and be wholly dependent on her mother, who was a widow and therefore an independent woman, to provide directly for her and her children. It was the only way she could protect the brothel monies being taken by Thomas, who if she is right about his tendencies, would have drunk them all away.

The issue of whether Jane had any separate estate at any point until Thomas' death in 1858 was the key to all the major court cases she was involved in during that period. Whilst married women enjoyed the evasion or mitigation of punishment in certain types of offences, for example, a woman could not be punished for committing a theft in the company of her husband because the law assumed that she acted under his coercion, they were unable to make financial transactions in their own name. However, a distinct advantage, as far as Jane was concerned, was the fact that this also prevented her from being sued and therefore imprisoned for debts.[91]

This might explain why Jane was still living, if she was, with Thomas up until 1843 when she claimed to have been deserted by him in 1839 and why she later took such desperate measures to keep her independence and her fortune, for there were few choices for women in unhappy, brutal or equally impossible marriage circumstances, apart from carrying on the best she could. You might wonder at this point why didn't she get a divorce?

Easier said than done as before 1857 to obtain a divorce meant submitting a private bill to parliament, a process which cost around £1,000 (£80,186.10) and, not surprisingly as few people then had 1,000 pennies let alone pounds, only around ten were granted a year. On top of this there were different rules about which grounds men and women could sue for divorce and only four such divorces were granted to women between 1800 – 1857. Rich as she was, Jane could not afford it or to let it be known she had that sort of money.

One woman who could, Caroline Norton, had a very difficult time of it, and she was an aristocrat. The collapse of her marriage culminated in June 1836 when Tory MP

George Norton sued the then prime minister, Lord Melbourne - a Whig - claiming he had had an affair with Caroline. He not only wanted to prove his wife had committed adultery, which would be the first step towards obtaining a divorce, but the rumour was that his action was part of a plot by the Tories to try to bring down the Whig government.[92]

Whilst Lord Melbourne was successful in defending the action, Caroline's reputation was ruined and she was labelled a 'scandalous woman.'[93] She and George then separated but Caroline, under coverture, remained George's property. She was unable to divorce him and had no legal rights, which George knew and would not let Caroline have access to their children. Caroline, in desperation, tried to get a change in the law. She was already an established writer so she used her skills to produce a series of political pamphlets to educate the public about this and other injustices and persuaded MPs to support her cause.

Published in 1837 under the title: 'Observations on the Natural Claims of a Mother to the custody of her Children as Affected by the Common Law Rights of the Father,' the first pamphlet argued that all children under the age of seven should remain in the custody of their mother and that the decision as to where older children would live should be decided by the court – not the father. She made five hundred copies and circulated them privately.

Caroline, with the help of upper-class friends also tried to introduce a bill into parliament to give judges the power to allow either parent to have access to children under the age of 12. She published another pamphlet called: 'The Separation of Mother and Child by the Law of Custody of Infants Considered '[94] in which she wrote:

> 'The fact of the wife being innocent and the husband guilty, or of the separation being an unwilling one on her part, does not alter his claim: the law has no power to order that a woman shall have even occasional access to her children, though she could prove that she was driven by violence from her husband's house and that he had deserted her for a mistress. The father's right is absolute and paramount, and can be no more be affected by the mother's claim than if she had no existence.'

It was a struggle but the bill eventually became law in August 1839, so that if a wife was legally separated or divorced from her husband and had not been found guilty of adultery, she was allowed custody of her children up to the age of seven and access thereafter. While Caroline Norton's campaign had brought the issue into the public domain and worn away opposition to the bill, it did not mean Caroline got her children back. The law only applied in England, Wales and Ireland so George took the children to Scotland where she could not claim access and only when one of her sons died, was she allowed to see them.

Caroline didn't give up and continued her campaign, publishing 'English Law for Women in the Nineteenth Century' in 1854 and in June 1855 wrote 'A Letter to Queen Victoria on Lord Chancellor Cranworth's Marriage and Divorce Bill.' The letter was very powerful as she used own experiences to show that what was a matter of law, was a travesty of justice for women. In it she showed how a wife, like Jane, deserted by or separated from her husband for years, was still tied to him forever, because they were still legally married. She was not entitled to keep any of her possessions:

'Even her own clothes or ornaments; her husband may take them or sell them if he pleases even if they be gifts of relatives or friends before the marriage. An English wife could not make a will. Any money she earned belonged to her husband. If she was paid for work and he had not agreed to the payment, he could insist that a second payment was made to him.'

As his wife, she was his possession.

'A married woman was not allowed to move out of her husband's house. If she did, he could sue her for the restitution of conjugal rights, could enter the place where she was and carry her away by force, with or without the aid of the police. If a wife tried to separate from her husband for reasons of cruelty, it had to be cruelty that endangers life or limbs. If she had forgiven him in the past for such treatment, the law considered she had condoned his offences and could not complain of subsequent cruelty. Separated wives were not entitled to financial support as a matter of right and when a husband deserted his wife and was living off her money [as Thomas was with Jane], if he could prove that friends or relations had the means to help her, he could legally avoid making any payment to her.

'When a marriage failed it was the wife who suffered most; even having a spotless character gave her no advantage in the eyes of the law. She may have left if her husband lived and slept with the "faithful housekeeper," or having suffered personal violence at his hands, or he may have shut the doors on her, none of this mattered. The law took no notice of who is to blame. As her husband, he had a right to all that is hers; as his wife she had no right to anything that is his. As her husband he may divorce her. The most she can obtain is permission to live alone, still married to his name. The marriage ceremony was a civil bond to him and an indissoluble sacrament for her, and the rights of mutual property that marriage was supposed to confer, are made absolute for him and null for her.'[95]

It was a very powerful piece of lobbying from Caroline Norton in 1854, and shows us just what Jane was up against legally. But she did have privileged free access to legal advice from her grateful professional clients who must have pointed out that there was one clause she could use to her advantage.

'English wives could not sue for libel, sign leases or do any business which involved signing a contract.'

On the face of it, this does not appear to be a very useful edict, but Jane found a way to bend coverture to her own purposes, 'sometimes in ways that constituted active collusion,'[96] but it won for her many cases where she was sued for not paying her debts.

In 1857, the *Matrimonial Causes Act* became law but there were still inequalities. Men were able to 'petition the court' for a divorce on the basis of their wife's adultery, which would have to be proved, as would the absence of any collusion or an indication that the adultery was condoned. Women who wanted to divorce their husbands in addition had to prove an aggravating factor of the adultery, such as rape or incest. The High Court in London was the only place to get a divorce and proceedings were held in open court, enabling society to be scandalised by the personal details revealed during the process.[97]

That Jane survived financially is a miracle. It was not until 1858 that she became a widow and reverted to being a single woman, free to marry and conduct her own business, so the issues around her rights and whether she could be sued or contract services was to prove very important to her, embroiled as she was from the mid-1850s in various court cases which threatened her independence and the profits of the brothel business.

Looking back from the relatively secure position of today, we women have to consider ourselves fortunate that from the moment of separation we do not face living as Jane was:

'In a state of outlawry. She [the wife] many not enter into a contract, or, if she does, she has no means of enforcing it. The law, so far from protecting, oppresses her. She is homeless, helpless, hopeless and almost wholly destitute of civil rights.'[98]

As well as contending with coverture, Jane also had to wriggle round the law regarding brothels, prostitution and the efforts of almost vigilante organisations such as the *Society Against Vicious Practices* and the *Society for the Suppression of Vice*, as well as prosecution by the police.

But Jane broke the back of coverture more than once. In fact, the judgement in her 1861 appeal was often quoted in legal precedents and appears in law books available to this day.

Chapter 6 - William Seabrook Chalkley

Figure 5 Impression of W.S. Chalkley by George Jones 2019

Who? This is the person referred to as 'Another' in Jane's 1860 case: *Johnson v Gallagher*, her co-defendant and financer. But where did he spring from? One of the first clues appeared in the *Liverpool Daily Post* at the time of the 1860 trial which said Chalkley was born in Dover, Kent. I checked, and from there it was fairly plain sailing to track his early life. [99]

His parents were Thomas Chalkley and Mary Ann Cook[100] who were married in Dover in 1810 at St Mary the Virgin, a Roman Catholic Church.[101] They had many children of which nine survived. William Seabrook Chalkley, hereafter referred to as 'Chalkley,' was the eldest, born in 1812 in Dover, [102] along with two sisters, Sophia

Seabrook and Matilda Sophia. Other siblings, William and Mary Ann (Jane) were baptised in Chingford, Essex, Eliza Mercy and Sarah Jane in Southwold, Suffolk and Betsy Ann and Thomas Richard in Corton, Suffolk.

What all these places had in common was water, the sea or major rivers, so it did not surprise me when one of the baptism records showed their father Thomas to be a boatman. The next place I found the family was in the Isle of Man, also surrounded by water, where he is listed in a street directory in 1837 as a tide waiter, a customs official who boarded and inspected boats and ships to check for smuggled goods and to collect the duty. Thomas' wife Mary Ann is also listed in 1837 as being a baker of College Street, Ramsey and a milliner and dressmaker. Chalkley, age 25 by then, was living in Liverpool, working in his own bakery, as he had been an apprentice in his mother's establishment.

College Street still exists in Ramsey, though it has deteriorated and been built around in recent times. It is only a few yards away from the quayside, the Customs Toll House where Thomas would have worked and the Market Square, both very busy places in 1837. *Mona's Herald* of the 14.5.1839 featured an advert for the sale of Thomas Chalkley's house and gives us a good description of the place.[103]

HOUSE, SHOP, AND BAKERY.

TO be LET, and entered upon at May,—That convenient DWELLING HOUSE, SHOP, and BAKERY, situate in College Street, in the Town of Ramsey, with an excellent Garden attached, in which is a plentiful Supply of good Spring Water, at present in the occupation of Mr. THOMAS CHALKLEY, and well suited for the purposes of a Baker or general Dealer.

For Particulars, apply to Mr. EDWARD CHRISTIAN, Baldroma, in the Parish of Maughold, or on the Premises.

Figure 6 'For Sale' the house of Thomas Chalkley: 1839

By the 1841 census, only some of the family are still living in the area, but now on Cardle Street, Maughold, near Ramsey: Thomas and Mary Ann, Thomas Richard who was 14 and Elizabeth, who must be their daughter Eliza Mercy, wife of William Lewis. She was pregnant at the time of the census as she had a daughter Mary Ann in September of the same year. The other children, when adults, had relocated to Liverpool, while their parents moved again to Waterloo Road in Ramsey sometime before 1847. The Methodist Centre opened in 1846 when they lived across the road, which was interesting because when Chalkley's parents were married it was at a Roman Catholic Church in Dover. At some point therefore between 1827 and 1848 the Chalkley family became Methodists themselves and records show Chalkley was passionately involved in what was then, the radical preacher movement.

Methodism first came to the Isle of Man in 1758 when one John Murlin was diverted by a storm in the Irish Sea. However, Murlin made very little impact on the island and Methodism was not really established until the arrival of John Crook in 1775. Crook based himself in Peel, where for part of each summer the main fishing port on the west coast welcomed the herring fisheries fleet. [104] The first Methodist meeting place on the Isle of Man was a summer house at Mount Morrison, overlooking Peel Bay and St Patrick's Isle. By the time of John Wesley's first visit in 1777, a chapel had been built in the town near the sea front in Shore Road. This building, now a youth centre, was used by Wesley both during this and a further visit in 1781, at the end of which, he wrote in his journal:

> 'Having now visited the Island round, east, south, north and west, I was thoroughly convinced that we have no such circuit as this, either in England, Scotland or Ireland.'

There is no actual date for when the Chalkley family converted but it was in the early days of January 1823 when the Rev. John Butcher landed at Derbyhaven as the first pioneer of Methodism on the island, having been sent by the Bolton circuit on the strength of having sixpence balance in hand at the December quarterly meeting. The resolution in their minute book says:

> 'That Brother J. Butcher go to the island for three months... to discipline the circuit.'

In a few months the greater part of the island had been visited by Butcher and his fellow-workers. He preached in the market-place and occasionally on the beach somewhere near the site of the Methodist Loch Parade Church, on Douglas Bay. Butcher was joined by his son and later by Thomas Sharman. In 1824, a chapel was built in Wellington Street costing £935 [£53,697.42]. [105] Therefore, when the Chalkley family arrived on the Isle of Man, Methodism was a relatively new.

Thomas Chalkley was also committed to the Ramsey Temperance Society where he was one of the key people to address a meeting in May 1842. [106] I dare say he would have seen more than enough alcohol in his official duties as a tide-waiter and confiscated many gallons in the course of his duties to be at all tempted by drink. He is obviously very much on the side of law enforcement and as such he was regarded as a respectable and professional person.

Smuggling had been a real problem in the late 1700s as the Isle of Man up to 1765 operated a free-trade policy, but the Manx were not fond of the English customs duties and found ways round them. Merchants importing goods from mainland

Britain claimed a refund of the import duty paid and the now uncustomed goods were then shipped back to England. This system was very popular, ships began to sell direct to the Manx and the simple drawback fraud soon became wholesale smuggling. [107] At the same time, brewing became a major industry on the Isle of Man. Malt was bought from England and strong beer brewed to sell to ships sailing to the New World. Much of it found its way back to England and Scotland and resulted in a loss of revenue to the government. Because the Manx brewers bought raw barley, they didn't pay malting duty, neither did they pay duty on the beer they brewed. At one stage it was estimated that 40% of all British beer was brewed in the Isle of Man, though this estimate should probably be taken with a pinch of salt.

A letter in the *Gentleman's Magazine* in 1751 rained abuse on the island, calling it *'The great STOREHOUSE or MAGAZINE for the French.'* It sets out the main contraband as wine, brandy, coffee, tea and 'other Indian goods' from Denmark, Holland and France. The local parliament, the Tynwald, did take steps to stop illegal trading, but at the same time claimed it was those from the mainland, including Liverpool merchants and 'Irish bankrupts and fugitives' who were the bad apples.

What they were referring to was the English customs vessels which harassed legitimate merchants going about their honest business. In one example the customs men swarmed aboard a wherry that had brushed against her side and, finding no cargo, stripped the crew of their clothes and robbed a passenger of 25 guineas. This incident caused a near riot and could not have engendered much sympathy for the English.

Smugglers were a close - knit bunch and seemed to have much unofficial support on the Isle of Man, so much so the Scottish customs authorities complained that:

'Their correspondence with the common people of these coasts... on the south and north sides of the Solway Firth is so well established, that the least appearance of danger from thence is conveyed to them by signals which, at the same time, inform them to what parts they may with safety steer.'

But not all Manx smugglers made a fortune.

'Myles Crowe was once a schoolteacher, but was persuaded to invest his savings in a smuggling enterprise. He was successful for a while in his trade with the Solway, but an informer revealed his 'cog-hole' to the customs authorities, and Myles was a ruined man.

'He spent some time living in Kirkcudbright, working as an assistant to more fortunate free-traders but returned annually to the Isle of Man, to collect the rent from some small property he owned there, investing the income in contraband. These enterprises were hardly more successful: on one occasion his breeches, stuffed with tea, burst as he was boarding a ship in Douglas Harbour; and on another trip, he was overcome by the narcotic effect of tobacco wrapped round his body next to the skin! In old age, the smuggler manqué became an assistant ferryman, plying from Kirkcudbright to Castelsod, and died a miserable end at the hands of a poisoner who sold his corpse for dissection.'

Nevertheless, Thomas Chalkley was still kept busy in the 1840s as a tide waiter and earned many commendations:[108] On 2.3.1846 the master and crew of the *Sea Horse* were apprehended in Ramsey on a charge of conveying and concealing one and half gallons of British spirits on the vessel. Thomas Chalkley was the officer who found the spirits 'in places of concealment' on the vessel when it arrived from Port William. Everyone involved was fined 20 shillings each [£60.42] or faced imprisonment for one month. [109]

A case of attempted smuggling took place at Port Lewague near Ramsey in July 1846. A man called Mc Kinnon, a spirit dealer living in Glasgow, brought a large chest by coach from Douglas, the capital of the Isle of Man and left it at the *Heelis's Hotel* in Ramsey. He then hired a horse and cart to take it back to Port Lewague, about a mile away, but here his troubles began. Instead of carrying the chest to a man who kept a boat who was going to take it to the Glasgow steamer, it went to the house of Mr. Christian, a retired preventative officer and the chest was seized by the authorities but Mc Kinnon got away. The trunk was found to contain 18 gallons of rum, gin and brandy in three tin cases constructed exactly to fit and were apparently made expressly for smuggling. Mc Kinnon was captured and brought to court and sentenced to six months imprisonment in Castle Rushden on the island if he did not pay the fine of £25 [£1,510.43]. The news report ended:

> 'We understand Mr. Chalkley, the active officer, is entitled to much praise, for his zeal and vigilance in this case.' [110]

For Thomas Chalkley it must have been very exciting work: the stealth, secrecy, the chase, the moonlit stake-outs and triumphant arrests, as a single report following a very hectic weekend shows:

On a Friday, four pounds of tea, four bottles of wine, soap, brandy and gin were found on the schooner *Sarah* moored in Ramsey but based in Runcorn. The crew were fined £5 each [£302.09 at 2017 values] and their boat seized. On the Saturday, five pounds of tea were seized from two seamen who were about to board the *Mary Helena*, a cutter bound for the *Firefly*, a steam surveying vessel moored in Ramsey bay. They were fined £2 14 shillings [worth £163.13] which was three times what the tea was worth and their boat was seized. It was noted in the news report that had the maximum penalty been imposed on these two sets of smugglers and if the full value of the property seized was taken into account it would have amounted to nearly £300 [£18,125.10].

In May 1847, two months later, there were another two high profile successful seizures for the tide waiters in Ramsey.[111] In the first John Atkinson, master of the schooner *Isabella* and David Mc Donald, master of the smack *Rose* both from Berwick were charged with having in total: 20 gallons of spirits, 48 pounds of soap, four and half pounds of tea and quantities of sugar, coffee and tobacco. They were fined the full penalty of £100 each [£6,041.70] and their vessels were detained.

'Great praise is due to the officers Messrs Chalkley and Corlett, for their vigilance.'

In the second, the schooner *Mary and Frances* was preparing to sail from Ramsey to Maryport, on the Cumberland coast when she was boarded by the tide waiters who found in the ballast: two boxes of tea, two boxes of cigars and two rolls of tobacco. The master and the mate were taken into custody when it was found that these items belonged to Mr. Clarke, a grocer, whose shop had recently been broken into and cash taken along with these goods.

'A great sensation was produced throughout the town and gratification prevailed that the real robber was taken. Much praise is due to the vigilant officers for their activity on the occasion.'

I was surprised to find that tea and soap were more often featured on the lists of contraband than alcohol and tobacco. When I did a bit of digging, I found that there were very high customs duties on not only these items but ashes, bay-salt, cotton, copper, coals, drugs, flax, fruit, furs, hemp, iron, leather, linens, oil, paper, rice, tobacco, tallow, threads, tapes, silks and sugar.[112] Why anyone would want to smuggle ashes though I cannot imagine.

In 1848, Thomas Chalkley retired with a good character and a superannuated pension after 48 years in the customs service, more than 20 of which he spent on the Isle of Man.[113] What happened to Thomas and Mary Ann, Chalkley's parents after 1848 is not clear until they appear in Liverpool in the 1851 census. Thomas Chalkley is said to be retired and they lived in Sandon Street, Liverpool, next door but one to their daughter Mary Ann who is by then married to James Sayle. Future street directories show Thomas Chalkley to be a gentleman with other various business connections, such as being a land agent.

Chalkley himself, back in 1835, was a baker working in his mother's establishment on the Isle of Man, where he met and married Jane Key. She was born in 1818 in Marown,[114] her parents being Anne Craine and her father Robert Key. The wedding took place in 1835 at Bride, Ayr. Chalkley was 23 and Jane only 17. They had seven children, five of whom did not survive infancy. The first, born in Douglas on Isle of Man in 1836 was Christian Mary Chalkley who died there in 1837.[115] Chalkley and his wife then moved to 19 Duckenfield Street, Liverpool where he set up as a baker. All their other children are born in Liverpool.

We can trace the family's location in the next ten years via the addresses the children were baptised from and Chalkley's occupation is set out on most of their baptism certificates.

- Sarah Ann Chalkley was born on 24.3.1837, died on 26.7.1837 of convulsions and was buried at the Wesleyan Chapel crematorium only four months old and the whole family lived at Duckinfield Street, Liverpool[116]

- Matilda Sophia Chalkley, was born on 22.9.1839.[117] Chalkley was recorded as a baker. However, she died of inflammation of the lungs on 15.3.1840 and was buried at the Wesleyan Chapel crematorium only six months old. She and her family lived at Pembroke Gardens, Liverpool

By this time, some of Chalkley's siblings have moved to Liverpool too, as we can see from their marriage records. Two of them were married on the same day 12.2.1839 and in the same place as each other, the parish church in Liverpool.[118] Chalkley and his sister, Sarah Jane were witnesses at Mary Ann's wedding to James Sayle, a sailmaker from the Isle of Man and Eliza Mercy married William Lewis, a plasterer from Liverpool.

- Chalkley's first son, Thomas Chalkley was born on 14.4.1841 and died in July 1854 age thirteen in Liverpool. His father was a baker[119]

- Chalkley's sister Sarah Jane, married from Dansey Street, Liverpool on 19.9.1842 at St Martin's in the Field church in Liverpool. Chalkley by then was a book keeper living on Great Orford Street

- William Chalkley, another son, was born on 22.6.1843 and died on 11.12.1843 of bronchitis and was buried at the Wesleyan Chapel Crematorium, age five months. Chalkley, was listed as a baker, and his family lived at Vine Street[120]

- Sarah Jane Chalkley's, born on 5.12.1844, the youngest daughter, is the only child who survived to adulthood. Chalkley's occupation has switched again to bookkeeper and they lived at 31 Spring Place, Springfield Street, Islington, Liverpool [121]

- In 1847, William Seabrook Kitchenman Chalkley was born and he died on 22.5.1848 at 28 Warren Street, Liverpool age seven months having had diarrhoea for seven days and convulsions for 28 hours. His father's occupation is still that of a bookkeeper [122]

Therefore, by 1847 when Chalkley was 35 and Jane was 29 they had experienced the deaths of all but two of their children and Thomas their only eldest son died when he was thirteen, just when they must have thought he was safe. Sarah Jane is the only child who had a full life. We can only imagine the impact on Chalkley and his wife of losses on such a scale, and wonder how well Chalkley's faith as a Wesleyan Methodist sustained him in those awful years. I wondered, had there been an epidemic?

Typhus, the spotted fever, mixed for the first time with enteric fever, was something new, resulting in not only fever, but an ulcerated intestine and was rampant in the town in the years between 1838 - 1842. It spread through the air and in Liverpool alone the epidemic in 1839 caused 358 deaths, hitting mostly the poor, as the pathetic scenes in Manchester portrayed in Mrs. Gaskell's novel *Mary Barton* showed. As the first four of Chalkley's children died between 1837 and 1843 and all of them had infections of the lungs or convulsions they could have been victims of this epidemic. The Chalkley's were far from poor compared to street children,[123] but there were many other childhood diseases about and in 1839 alone as many nationally as 9,131 died from smallpox, 10,937 from measles, 8,165 from whooping cough, 19,816 from scarlatina [scarlet fever], 4,192 from croup and 2,482 from diarrhoea.[124]

In between Matilda's birth and death in 1840 and Thomas' birth in 1841 when Chalkley and Jane must have been grieving for the loss of their third child yet looking forward to the birth of the fourth, *Perry's Bankruptcy Gazette* contained a notice dissolving a partnership between Chalkley and Shadrach Roberts in a bakery and biscuit making business on Wednesday 19.8.1840.[125] A news report[126] also dated the same day, spoke of the disappearance of Shadrach.

'On Monday last, Mr. Roberts, of the firm of Chalkley and Roberts, Vine Street, left his pace of business with a cart load of bread, which he expected to dispose of in Wavertree and the neighbourhood. Having finished his business, he was seen to pass through the gate at the railway, on the Wavertree Road, on his return home, about half past nine the same evening, but has not since been heard of. The cart and horse were discovered in the road and the remainder of the bread was undisturbed and about ten shillings was found in the cart box. No reason can be assigned for his absence. The police have been informed of these facts and we hope some satisfactory information may soon be obtained.'

The same article was widely reported around the country and the *Staffordshire Gazette* had some additional information about Shadrack:

'No reason can be assigned for his absence – he was prospering in business, has never been known to remain from home longer than might be reasonably expected... As may be supposed the family of Mr. Roberts are in the greatest distress – and we need scarcely add, that any intelligence that might be conveyed to them respecting their relative will be most gratefully received.'[127]

This cannot be a coincidence! Shadrack went missing on Monday 11.8.1840 and Chalkley did not waste any time in declaring their business partnership 'dissolved' and making it public. One wonders what really happened to their working relationship? I tried to find out.

There is a Shadrach Roberts in the 1841 census, age 20, living at Mann Street, Upper Westside, Toxteth Park, West Derby, Liverpool and he is described as a bread baker,[128] but there is no other evidence that leads to him, despite there being several Shadrach Roberts listed on national databases. For example, the 1851 census shows one with his wife Ann and children working as a storekeeper in Walton on the Hill in Liverpool at 15 Manchester Street but is this him? Maybe he did find a happy ending after all or, more likely, he simply vanished.

The 1841 census confirms Chalkley kept a bakery at 35 Vine Street, Liverpool, and he must have taken on yet another partner straight away for the *Globe* on 16.4.1841 reported that a partnership in the bakery and grocery business between William S. Chalkley and David Stuart Whitelaw had also been dissolved, the second one in less than a year - eight months in fact.

When I looked closer at the 1841 census, I found James Heyes a baker and David Whitelaw, a baker, living in Chalkley's house on Vine Street, so Chalkley must have promoted David from within his ranks. He is only 20 and the partnership has barely got going. Again, what happened there? I don't know but Chalkley had left baking to become a bookkeeper in 1844, though why anyone employed him as such with two bankruptcies behind him, is remarkable, and by the time the Liverpool Tradesmen's Loan Company set up in 1846, he was their secretary. Jane Gallagher says she and her mother took loans from the company from 1849, via Chalkley and by 1850 the company was so successful they were offering wider services without security or collateral.[129]

Meanwhile, Thomas Richard, Chalkley's younger brother by fifteen years had moved from the Isle of Man and was living at Benson Street, Liverpool in Chalkley's house from where he married Mary Craig at Mount Pleasant Chapel on 24.9.1849, giving his profession as customs officer, like his father. How true this is I am not sure as he appears in all other public records as a joiner and builder. 1850 brought two family celebrations as Thomas Richard and Mary had a son in May who they named after Chalkley, so he became the second William Seabrook Chalkley, and their sister Betsy

Ann married Francis Denison, a fish merchant living in Manchester, on 23.12.1850 at St Jude's Church in West Derby, Liverpool and Chalkley was a witness. Chalkley claimed to own a timber yard on Chatham Street from 1852 but the truth is the joinery and building business was in joint ownership with Thomas Richard, his brother,[130] yet another ill-fated partnership for Chalkley, number three at that time and this one went bankrupt too in 1854.[131]

Chalkley was not just a multiple bankrupt, but also by now a Wesleyan Methodist Minister. He became conspicuous for his piety and ardour in good work, was an eminent preacher, a class leader and was looked up to as a pillar of his church.

'From his first appearance in town, he made a glaring profession of religion and united himself to the Wesleyan body of Methodists.'[132]

A split between the Methodists and the Wesleyans occurred in 1849, the year when Chalkley first becomes associated with Jane Gallagher. Simultaneously, he rises to religious prominence as a key speaker aligned with the leaders of the Liverpool Wesleyan Reformers who maintained their witness as a separate body among the Free churches.

After reformers were expelled from the mainstream Wesleyans,[133] the *Liverpool Mail* [134] listed Chalkley as one of the preachers present at their key meeting in Liverpool.[135] It was held at the *Amphitheatre* and admittance was by ticket only, for those who supported the notables expelled from the Methodist movement. The preachers invited to the stage included Chalkley. The rebels' message was:

'It was a movement of thought, a movement of inquiry, of freedom. They were bursting at their fetters; they were looking round about them. The world was always in motion; everything was in progress; it was the age of railways and of steam; it was the age of the electric telegraph; it was the age of improvement. Everything was improving, and should not Methodism?'

Chalkley was so passionately involved, he proposed the first resolution:

'That this meeting having heard the statements of the Revds. Messrs. J Everett, S Dunn and W Griffith jun., in reference to their recent expulsion by the Wesleyan conference, deeply sympathises with them in the painful circumstances in which they find themselves.'

Unfortunately, the remainder of his eloquence is lost due to the poor quality of the copy in the archives, but be sure it was important as the account of the meeting takes up five whole columns of the six available in the large broadsheet of the *Liverpool Mail* – with no adverts at all.

We leave Chalkley here for the moment, coming into his own, from his lowly beginnings as a baker in his mother's shop on the Isle of Man to being a successful accountant, despite several bankruptcies, secretary of the Liverpool Tradesman's Loan Company, a well-respected Wesleyan Methodist Minister and, from 1849, negotiator of loans for Jane Gallagher, notorious brothel keeper of Liverpool town.

Chapter 7 - Married – or not?

It was New Year's Eve 2018 and I was at my desk when the celebrations to welcome 2019 began. Fireworks were soaring, shooting, shattering and slashing the sky as far as I could see, but I was distracted by this, in the *Liverpool Daily Post* in 1862 which popped up when I was looking for something else completely.[136]

'William Mercer – This bankrupt, described as a licensed victualler and saddler in Liverpool... stated that he formerly kept a public house in Houghton Street... that he is the husband of notorious Mrs. Gallagher but the house in Houghton Street was kept in his name and not in hers. He did not know when he married her whether her former husband was living or not; in fact, never inquired. Found out, about eighteen months after his marriage that Gallagher was still living. His marriage to her took place about eighteen years ago. Had been separated from her about ten years. Does not know how many houses of ill fame she keeps.'

Seconds later I was quivering with excitement, elated, exhilarated, fascinated. Abandoning the New Year, I set to work knowing that I could not let myself get carried away with this dramatic news, or even afford to speculate yet on the new avenues this might lead me into as Jane had shunted me miles off track a few times already with her web of half-truths. First and fast, I needed to establish beyond doubt that the newspaper report was accurate, after all Jane was still married to Thomas Gallagher who did not die until 1858, and I had his death certificate to prove it, so it couldn't be true, could it?

'The bankrupt [William Mercer], on examination, stated that he formerly kept a public house in Houghton Street'

This is confirmed by the 1851 census for 8 Houghton Street, Liverpool, a place Jane in various court cases admits was one of her many brothels. In the census, Jane Mercer, not Gallagher, appears as the victualler William Mercer's wife and her age is correct and her birthplace. [A victualler is a formal name for the landlord of a public house or similar licensed establishment.]

'The house in Houghton Street was kept in his name not hers......'

This we have come to expect from Jane. Whilst William Mercer was listed by street directories as head of the household for the years 1851 – 1853, this does not tell us whose house it really was. Jane did inherit in trust for her children a house in Houghton Street from her mother when she died in 1854 but this was after 1853 when William Mercer is no longer living in the street. However, Jane had at some point, according to her sworn testimony in 1860, owned numbers 4,5,8 and 9 Houghton Street.

'He is the husband of the notorious Mrs. Gallagher...'

Was this official or was she 'living over the brush' as they say in Lancashire? We already know ordinary people could not afford a divorce as before 1858 it could only be granted by a private act of parliament and living together, bigamy or, more dubiously, selling your wife, were the only options, none of which was legally a marriage nor do they make any sense for Jane in her situation.

Yes, wife selling. According to Rebecca Probert's book: 'Divorced, Bigamist, Bereaved,' [137] there are lots of examples of money or goods being given by another man to a husband in exchange for his wife, either in private or sometimes in the market place. Some thought it would legitimise a separation in the eyes of the married couple and of the wider community and a wife sale even appeared in Thomas Hardy's novel: *The Mayor of Casterbridge.*

A newspaper report: 'Public Sale of a Wife' describes such a sale. It took place in front of a beer house at Shear Bridge, Little Horton, near Bradford. Hartley Thompson offered his wife, Martha, for sale. She was said to be: 'of prepossessing appearance.' They had not been married long but had been very unhappy together and believed, in ignorance, this sale was as good as a divorce, and much cheaper. A large crowd gathered after the sale was announced by the bellman of the pub. The wife, it was said,

'Appeared before the crowd with a halter, adorned with ribbons round her neck.'

The sale, however, was not completed because of a disturbance created by a crowd from a neighbouring factory and Ike Duncan, the prospective buyer, was detained at his work beyond the time.[138]

In 1870, a man from Bury sold his wife by public auction to her lover, then she was led away to his home with a rope around her neck. This caused such a scandal that effigies of the husband and wife were burned. Thankfully, by the end of the nineteenth century, the custom seems to have disappeared. Many people really did come together in this way, ignorant of either the fact that their marriage would be declared void or in defiance of law but until 1907 it was NOT a criminal offence. They might have faced proceedings in the ecclesiastical courts, but in the 19th century this rarely happened.

According to William Mercer in 1862: 'His marriage took place about eighteen years ago....' which would make it 1844. But the actual marriage of Jane to William Mercer took place in 1850, according to the certificate I found quite easily, now knowing which names to look for.

On it, Jane declared herself to be a widow and thus free to marry when Thomas was still alive, spelt her name slightly wrong as 'Gallaher' and said her father was a farmer not a carter, three erroneous statements. As we have noted before, to do this knowingly is perjury. It is also telling that no family members were witnesses. William Boyd, was the sexton of the church and the other witness, Fanny, could not sign her name and probably worked for Jane. She also took a big risk she would be denounced at the altar when she married in St Mark's church which was on Upper Duke Street in Liverpool, less than a mile away from where she lived in Houghton Street and not much further from St Martin's in the Fields Church where she married Thomas in the first place in 1833. Other bigamists were more discrete and travelled away from the area where they were known, but not Jane. I think she was truly an advocate of the old adage: 'If you can't hide it, flaunt it!'

I kicked myself for not picking this up sooner, but you cannot search for what you do not know. Whilst I suppose I should have been more cynical and checked out the possibility of a second marriage much earlier, all I can only say is that I was blind-sided by the fact that Jane continued to use 'Gallagher' officially, according to Liverpool street directories and censuses, even after she married William Mercer so I had no idea that any Jane Mercer I came across was probably Jane Gallagher until I saw the news report. The fact remains she married him and in doing so committed bigamy and was liable to be prosecuted as the only legal grounds for a second marriage at that time were that the first spouse had died or if there was a valid assumption the first spouse had been absent for seven years without contact, as the courts then assumed the absent spouse was dead. However, there is ample proof that Jane bigamously married William Mercer in the full knowledge that Thomas was still alive:

Thomas was living in Leece Street, in Liverpool from 1847 - 1849, quite near to her. In 1850 he may have already moved to Manchester for in the 1851 census he was living with Jane's sister, Ellen Bellion in Hulme. Surely family would have known about the second wedding? Her mother must have as when writing her will in 1851 she did not refer to Jane as her widowed daughter but as the wife of Thomas Gallagher. It is therefore hard to believe Jane did not know Thomas was still alive when she tricked William Mercer into a bigamous marriage in 1850. Life must have been very complicated for her at this time, managing a supposedly dead or missing husband who she was still paying every month to keep quiet and at the same time keeping the second one a secret whilst living openly with him in Houghton Street, Liverpool, even putting his name over the door as the licensee.

'He found out about eighteen months after the marriage that Thomas Gallagher was still living. He had separated from her about ten years before,' [which would be 1852, only two years after the marriage.]

I therefore I think it is safe to say William Mercer was probably not amused by being deceived. However, he was still listed in a street directory as living at 8 Houghton Street, Jane's brothel, in 1853. This could be because the directory was compiled in 1852 but not published until a year later. By 1854, Jane is living in her May Street brothel and sometime before 1856 she moves back to Houghton Street to live there with her next lover. William Mercer is by then living in Hotham Street, maybe in yet another of Jane's brothels. So why on earth did she marry William Mercer, a man eighteen years older than her? Jane could have made a far better choice from amongst her connections with the wealthy middle - class folk of Liverpool.

Figure 7 Impression of William Mercer by George Jones 2019

There are well researched reasons why people committed bigamy, none of which were legitimate in the eyes of the law in this period. Rebecca Probert lists them:[139] They :

- Were unaware that they were committing bigamy

- Thought having their first spouse's permission is enough – this still does not make the second marriage legal

- Alleged the first spouse had behaved very badly

- Were acting on the spur of the moment

- Were drunk at the time

- Or using repeat marriage as a career, marrying for financial gain

- Wanted to debauch the innocent, then leave them, but this was rape

- Wished to gain respectability for children born out of the second marriage

Given that Jane was so well advised legally, had independent means and no need of a husband to keep her, in fact she had more to lose financially by marrying again, it is hard to see why she did it. William Mercer was hardly a young man, not rich, exciting or glamourous. Perhaps it was because she thought she could legitimise two further children.

Yes, that was a surprise too. I found when searching birth records using Gallagher as Jane's maiden name and Mercer as the surname of the child, that Jane had had two girls by William Mercer, years before she married him. Rosanna was born in 1845, only two years after the birth of Alfred Hugh, and Maria Jane in 1848, which again begs the question why did she do it? These children were illegitimate and marrying after their births did not change their status, not even when Jane became a widow in 1858.

According to official public records, the couple seemed to live in different houses as well. William Mercer in 1845 was listed in a Liverpool street directory as having a business at 173 London Road, Liverpool, but a *Liverpool Mercury* report of the 22.6.1845 showed that he was a publican of Leeds Street who had been robbed of £1 17s 6d [£113.28] by someone called William Walsh. A month later Rosanna Mercer was born at one of Jane's three houses on Tyrer Street in Liverpool on 22.3.1845 and baptised on 13.7.1845 at St Nicholas' Church, Chapel Street which is on the river front and in centre of Liverpool. But William, a saddler, does not live at Tyrer Street and neither of his two addresses above are associated with Jane. [140]

Then I found two baptism entries for the other child born in 1848, the first being for Mary Jane Mercer, daughter of William and Jane Mercer, baptised on 11.6.1848 at St Nicholas' Church, Liverpool. William and Jane say they lived at Devon Street, one of Jane's houses. William's occupation is that of a saddler. [141] Then there is another record for Maria Jane Mercer, who was baptised on 16.11.1848 five months later at St Peter's Church, Church Street, Liverpool but is recorded as being born at Greek

Street. All the other details are correct. Maria Jane is the name she is known by in the future 1851 census and later on her marriage certificate, so Maria Jane she will remain from this point. All sorts of explanations could be suggested for her having two baptism certificates:

- Maybe Jane organised one baptism and didn't invite William Mercer so he organised a separate event and didn't invite Jane

- Perhaps they argued about the name and the parent who chose Maria instead of Mary won at the end of the day

- Or as St Peter's is a Roman Catholic Church and she was baptised as Maria and St Nicholas' church is Church of England, where the child was christened Mary, the couple were covering both their options

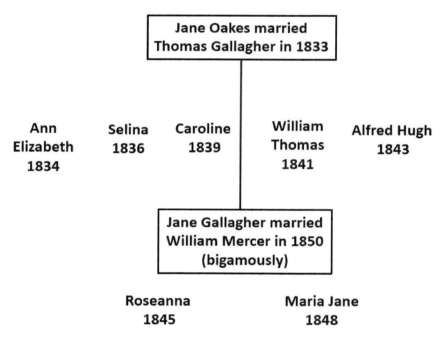

Figure 8 Jane's marriages and children

I doubt we will ever be sure. But what we do now know is that by 1850 Jane has two living husbands, a child baptised twice out of seven living children between two fathers. When I looked at the dates of these events, I found Jane was either pregnant or had just had a child every year from 1833 to 1848 apart from 1837 and 1846. How, then did Jane have time to run a brothel empire? Well, having the money to send the children out to private nurses, tutors and boarding schools certainly must have helped.

But I still find it hard to believe she took the risk.[142] Quite apart from the emotional damage inflicted by the act of bigamy, there were also significant legal consequences. And I am still questioning whether the father of Jane's sons was Thomas Gallagher as William Mercer could well have been on the scene by that time. Is the simplest explanation that she was drunk when she married a second time?

The *Bigamy Act* of 1603 aimed:

'To restrain all persons from marriage until their former wives and former husbands be dead.' It also said that persons who entered into a second marriage while their first spouse was alive would 'suffer death, as in cases of felony.'[143]

The last sentence for such a crime was 1693 so Jane was spared that.

- From then to the middle of the 1700s the usual sentence was branding on the hand
- By 1779 a fine could be substituted, usually just one shilling, but with imprisonment as well
- In 1795 legislation was passed that allowed for bigamists to be transported, though only for cases judged to be serious
- In the 1820s the use of this option declined, so Jane was safe from transportation too by 1850

It was at this time people began to see bigamy in a lighter manner. The *Public Advertiser* joked that the punishment for bigamy in Norway was:

'That the guilty person should be obliged to live with both wives at once.'[144]

Another popular joke quipped:

Boy: Pa, what's a bigamist?

Father: Oh, a man who makes the same mistake twice.[145]

The police could arrest the bigamist but they did not usually prosecute. It was down to the individuals involved as anyone could bring a prosecution for bigamy.[146] In the majority of cases it was the second spouse who did, people like William Mercer, who believed he was entering into a lawful marriage. Why he didn't we can only speculate. Maybe Jane paid to keep him quiet as well, but if he had prosecuted her then the chances of a conviction were high, for there were two marriage certificates and witnesses to both weddings who could be called to testify they took place and others who could testify that Thomas was very much alive in 1850. If the prosecution had taken place after 1861 and he won, the *Offences against a Person Act* allowed punishment of up to seven years penal servitude, which meant imprisonment with hard labour was the maximum sentence. But the reality was much less harsh, as a few examples in Liverpool newspapers show:

- John Conlin, 46, pleaded guilty to marrying Alice Ward at Belford, his first wife being then alive. The prisoner said he was led to commit the offence in consequence of the profligate habits of his wife, and under the supposition that she was dead. He was sentenced to six months hard labour[147]

- George Critchley who pleaded guilty of bigamy said his second wife was cognizant of his previous marriage before his marriage with her. This was seen as mitigating the offence and his sentence was a more lenient two months' hard labour[148]

In 1850, the following sentences were handed down for female bigamists in the same sitting: Margaret Leek, Bridget Jackson and Ann Carroll, one month in prison in December 1850.[149] Jane was therefore very lucky neither William Mercer or Thomas Gallagher chose to prosecute, such is the power of money.

I had tried for a long time at this point to find Jane's children by Thomas Gallagher in the 1851 census but as I was using the Gallagher surname for queries, nothing came up. Now knowing she had married William Mercer I searched again and a hidden door swung wide bringing an avalanche of new information.

Jane's two eldest daughters Ann Elizabeth (17) and Selina (16), using the Mercer surname are at a boarding school, at 59 Poulton Street in Kirkham, Lancashire in 1851. It was run by Mary Whalley, the head teacher, age 50 and widow who also came from Kirkham. One of her daughters, Sarah Whalley, 25, taught there and her three brothers and servant were also in residence, so it must have been a large establishment for there were thirteen pupils on census night with ages from 9 -17, Ann Elizabeth being the eldest. No doubt she was next in line to leave.

The three youngest Gallagher children were also found under the surname Mercer and were being looked after by William Mercer's widowed mother Rosanna at Moor Hall, near Aughton, Ormskirk where she was the housekeeper. They are described as her grandchildren, which they were, sort of. The two Mercer girls are also there, Rosanna and Maria Jane. This meant the youngest five children were all brought up together at Moor Hall and the legitimate and illegitimate and must have known each other well. It says a lot about the heart of William Mercer's mother, who took them all in regardless of legal parentage and looked after them away from the brothels. All the children are described as scholars of the household in the 1851 census:

- Rosanna Mercer, widow, age 70, born 1781 living at Moor Hall, Prescot Rd, Aughton, a housekeeper from Sunderland

- Caroline Mercer granddaughter age 13

- William Thomas Mercer grandson age 11

- Alfred Hugh Mercer grandson age 9

- Rosanna Mercer granddaughter age 6

- Maria Jane Mercer granddaughter age 3

Aughton, near Ormskirk, 12 miles north of Houghton Street in Liverpool, must have been a wonderful place to grow up: clean air, open spaces, with no immoral influences, diseases, noise, drunkenness, open sewers, drunks, or the hassle of a big city. Ormskirk was also quite well connected, despite it being a rural area and by 1820 stage coach services had developed bringing regular one penny post between Ormskirk and Southport for letters and newspapers twenty years ahead of Rowland Hill's national penny post. It was also growing fast and in 1800 Ormskirk had a population of 2,554 which by 1821 rose to 3,838. There was weekly cartage to and from Liverpool and the railway between Liverpool, Ormskirk and Preston opened in 1849, giving Jane easy access to her children. Gas street lighting even arrived on Easter Monday 1835.

Moor Hall itself is in Aughton, two miles south of Ormskirk, set in five acres of gardens with views to the south over a beautiful lake, said to be the remains of a medieval moat. A grade II listed gentry house of mid-sixteenth century origin, it is one of the most important listed buildings in the UK. It was first recorded in 1282 and in 1533 it was acquired by Peter Stanley of Bickerstaffe, who built the present manor house.[150] In 1824, Baines street directory shows Richard Alison, a gentleman lived in Moor Hall.[151] The estate then passed to the head of the family, Sir William Stanley of Hooton. On the sale of the Hooton estates in 1840 it was purchased by the Rev John Rosson, who would have owned it in 1851 when the children lived there. He is registered in the 1854 street directory as a landowner of Moor Hall and was a county magistrate. Age 50, he lived with his unmarried sister, Frances age 44 also from Liverpool. They had a house maid, a dairy maid and a kitchen maid living with them. I wonder if he knew he was harbouring the children of the notorious Jane Gallagher?

The other adults living at Moor Hall in 1851 were directly related to William Mercer's mother Rosanna and to William Mercer's daughters. They are described in relation to Roseanna Mercer, William's mother:

- Elizabeth M Turner married daughter and a gentlewoman age 40 born in Lancaster born 1811

- Ann Turner granddaughter age 20 governess, born 1831

- Ann Raynor married daughter age 30 gentlewoman born in Lancaster, born 1821

The young Rosanna and Maria Jane would have been nieces of Elizabeth Turner and Ann Raynor and cousins of Ann Turner. To Jane's children by Thomas, the same women and child were step relations. No doubt Ann Turner taught the children, being a governess, but it would not all be work for there was the splendid house to explore and outside all the fields, woods and farmland.

I used this opportunity to find out more about where William Mercer and his mother came from and found William Mercer, 54, was born around 1797 in Lancashire. His father was Thomas Mercer, a farmer, and his mother Rose Gildart (1773).[152] William had several siblings and the family moved from Lancaster to Liverpool between 1803 and 1805.

William's parents didn't actually marry until 20.1.1798 in Lancaster, Rose being from Glasson Dock and Thomas from Hornby, near Lancaster in the Lune Valley. This was nearly a month after William was born and his mother was only seventeen. In order to marry, William's father had to either publish the banns or get a licence, which, since an act in 1753, meant you could shorten the waiting time involved in publishing banns and the marriage could take place sooner. Obtaining a licence required a bond to guarantee that the information given as to age and parental consent was true. The bond was for £200 [£15,352.22] and was the penalty threatened for false swearing, not the cost of the licence. John Townley of Lancaster was the guarantor and neither he nor Thomas could sign their names, each marked the document with an 'x.'[153] With it, Thomas and Rosanna were able to be married quickly in January 1798.

The only information about him, after William separated from Jane, is in a newspaper report in the *Liverpool Mercury* dated 10.9.1852 which showed that William Mercer applied to renew his drink licence for the premises at 8 Houghton Street and Jane's name appears there as well. Whilst he said he kept a saddler's shop in Church Street, Liverpool, he maintained he still lived at Houghton Street and that a Mrs. Callaghan, a misspelling of Gallagher, 'conducted' the house but the magistrates, having a great deal of information about it, knew it was Jane. They stipulated as a condition of granting William Mercer's drink licence, that in future he must conduct this house himself, and by implication keep Jane out of it.

The *Liverpool Mercury* on 28.6.1856, shows Jane using the Gallagher name again, clearly living with her next lover in Houghton Street, while William Mercer, then a provision dealer, was prosecuted at Hotham Street, Liverpool for 'lead underselling scale' and fined plus costs. Whilst Jane did have brothels in Hotham Street, it was not at this time and William appears to have moved on and is well clear of Jane, apart from the fact she was mother to his two daughters. He kept in close contact with them both and later in life lived in their houses after they married.

In conclusion, it is very hard to justify that Jane did not know Thomas her husband was still alive in 1850 when she bigamously married William Mercer. It is equally difficult to appreciate why she married him anyway as there seemingly was no advantage in doing so. And what is more surprising is that none of her future court cases or any of the resulting newspapers reports, apart from the one which revealed her second marriage in the first place, ever referred to her bigamy - it was as if it had never happened.

Part Two - Shocks and Surprises

Chapter 8 - London Connections

Meanwhile, as the brothel empire expanded, Jane's children were becoming adults and at some point, they must have found out what their mother did to keep them in the style they were accustomed to. By the late 1850s, the two eldest girls left boarding school so, because Jane also needed to find somewhere away from the brothels for them to live, she bought Bird Cottage in Rossett, Denbigshire, just across the water from Liverpool, from where Ann Elizabeth is married in 1859. Her sister, Selina was a witness so she too must have been at Rossett that summer, and maybe Caroline as well but neither are to be found in the 1861 census anywhere, either as Gallagher or Mercer, though once again by accident, I did find a marriage record, in London.

Wherever they had been, they were back in time for Selina, age 26, to marry Frederick Fox Cooper, age 56, an author and widower, on 12.7.1862 at St Mary's Church in Lambeth, Brixton, Surrey. The certificate tells us both bride and groom were living at Chester Place, London, Frederick's father was said to be a gentleman, and Selina's a merchant tailor, which is rather a grand title for Thomas. I suppose Selina had to reinvent her family's back story to keep up appearances when she came to London, though given the sort of man I now know Frederick Fox Cooper was, I think he would have dined out forever on the back of his mother-in-law being a notorious brothel keeper! Caroline, her sister and Alfred Edgar Cooper, Frederick Fox Cooper's youngest son, were witnesses at the wedding.

But why would Selina, only 26, marry a man 30 years older than her? Or maybe that is the wrong question. What did Fox Cooper gain from marrying Selina? Apart from a young and I assume good-looking wife, Selina would have come into her share of the brothel empire at 21, so was he in need of money?

The marriage certificate said he was an author so I searched for titles and found a very long list of plays, mostly adaptations of famous others, with very little original material of his own, so I did not pay him much attention at the time. However, in another chance search, a year later, merely tying up loose ends, or so I thought, I found there was picture of Frederick Fox Cooper in the *Theatrical Times* dated 1847 held in the *Victoria and Albert Museum* in London. This was enough to rekindle my interest so I set about finding out more about him. He is certainly a fine figure of a man, and what a life I discovered![154]

If you rolled Jane's legal manipulations, fearlessness in court and love of the limelight with a readiness to take great financial gambles, along with Frederick Fox Cooper's own involvement with fighting, drinking, rioting, brawling and bankruptcy, ebullience, bravado and refusal to conform, then you have some measure of the man. And whilst I can appreciate how Selina would have been very attracted to one so fearless, dashing, bold and confident, Jane had at least the sense to realise that you do not marry them.

Figure 9 Frederick Fox Cooper:Theatrical Times: 1847: © V&A Museum

I will start at the end for Fox Cooper, as I will call him from now on, died on his birthday 4.1.1879, and who else in the world could manage that? Age 73, he had by that time been married to Selina for seventeen years and they had no children. The obituaries are very telling as their writers were more able to be honest once he was dead, knowing that Fox Cooper could not sue them in court from beyond the grave.[155]

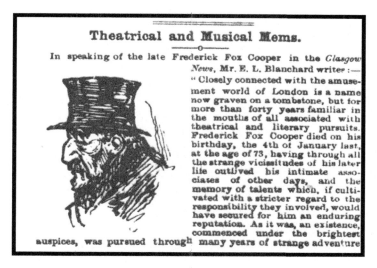

Theatrical and Musical Mems.

In speaking of the late Frederick Fox Cooper in the *Glasgow News*, Mr. E. L. Blanchard writes :—
" Closely connected with the amusement world of London is a name now graven on a tombstone, but for more than forty years familiar in the mouths of all associated with theatrical and literary pursuits. Frederick Fox Cooper died on his birthday, the 4th of January last, at the age of 73, having through all the strange vicissitudes of his later life outlived his intimate associates of other days, and the memory of talents which, if cultivated with a stricter regard to the responsibility they involved, would have secured for him an enduring reputation. As it was, an existence, commenced under the brightest auspices, was pursued through many years of strange adventure

Figure 10 Fox Cooper's Obituary: London, Provincial Entr'acte: 25.1.1879

It continued:

'As it was, an existence commenced under the brightest auspices, was pursued through many years of strange adventure amidst continual struggles with adversity, and his history, truly told, would serve us another example of the utter uselessness of intellectual gifts without the ballast of strong moral principles.'

Follow that!

Fox Cooper got his second name from his godfather, the famous Charles James Fox, who led the Whig political party and was close friend of George, Prince of Wales. He held office briefly as a Tory under Lord North but soon switched sides leading the opposition through a long political life. His uncle, Sir Edward Fox Cooper, the antiquarian, was an intimate friend of the famous Richard Brinsley Sheridan, the famous Irish satirist, a playwright, poet and long-term owner of the *London Theatre Royal*, Drury Lane. Sheridan is known for his plays such as *The Rivals, The School for Scandal, The Duenna* and *A Trip to Scarborough*. He was also a Whig MP for 32 years in the House of Commons for Stafford (1780-1806) and Ilchester (1807-1812).

These two friends of Fox Cooper's father featured in a satirical cartoon produced by James Gillray (1756-1815), a well-known caricaturist. Gillray's plates were exposed in shop windows where eager crowds examined them and this one was about the imposition of Dog Tax.[156]

It was first proposed in 1758, along with, interestingly, a tax on bachelors aged over 25 and widowers under 50 having no children and took nearly 40 years to pass as nobody could agree on how to implement it.[157] To begin with, the plan was simple but then, as is the tendency for all legal documents, it became so precise as to be unclear:

'From and after the 5th day of July 1796, every person who shall keep any Greyhound, Hound, Pointer, Setter dog, Spaniel, Lurcher or Terrier or who shall keep two or more dogs, of whatever description or denomination shall be charged and assessed annually with the sum of five shillings [£19.19] for each Greyhound, Pointer, Setter dog, Spaniel, Lurcher or Terrier; and also, for each dog, where two or more dogs shall be kept, and every person who shall inhabit any dwelling house, assessed to any of the duties on inhabited houses, or on windows or lights, and shall keep one dog and no more, such dog not being a Greyhound, Pointer, Setter dog, Spaniel, Lurcher or Terrier, shall be charged and assessed annually, with the sum of three shillings [£11.51] for such dog.

Upset Victorians did, of course, find ways round this as the act remained in place until 1882.

'A gentleman near Warwick, who keeps only one dog merely for the purpose of a house-dog, returned it as such to the Surveyor of Taxes. That return was objected to because, it was insisted, the dog, of a spaniel kind, was liable to the higher rate of duty, the same as a sporting dog. The gentleman remonstrated; stating that the dog not being, in his opinion, a true sporting spaniel, but a common mongrel, did not, therefore, come within the letter of the Act of Parliament; and, at all events, not being trained nor even used for the purpose of sporting, most certainly did not fall within the spirit and meaning of the act. The remonstrance was, however, unavailing: and notice of an appeal was given. The case was heard before the Commissioners at Wellesbourne, when, without a moment's hesitation, it was decided against the Surveyor of Taxes.'

James Gillray first learnt letter-engraving, then wandered for a time with a company of strolling players. After a colourful life, he returned to London and became a student in the Royal Academy, supporting himself by engraving and producing many caricatures under fictitious names. His publisher and print seller, Hannah Humphrey, whose shop was first at 227 Strand, then in New Bond Street, then in Old Bond Street, and finally in St James's Street, London, lived with Gillray and he thought of marrying her. On one occasion they were on their way to church, when Gillray said:

'This is a foolish affair, methinks, Miss Humphrey. We live very comfortably together; we had better let well alone.'

Gillray's eyesight began to fail in 1806 and he started to wear spectacles but they were unsatisfactory. Unable to work to his previous high standards, he became depressed and started drinking heavily and he produced his last print in September 1809. Drink caused his gout and in July 1811, Gillray attempted to kill himself by throwing himself out of an attic window above Humphrey's shop in St James's Street. He became insane and she looked after him until his death on 1.6.1815 in London when he was buried in St James's churchyard, Piccadilly.

Fox Cooper's parents were Henry Fox Cooper (1771-1838) and Elizabeth Ann Nicholls (1777-1822) and he was the youngest of two children, the eldest being Henry Octavius William Fox Cooper (1804–1874) and they were both born in Westminster, London. His father, Henry Fox, first appeared in the newspapers in 1805[158] when it is announced he has already:

> 'Given many specimens of his elegant poetic taste, and is about to publish a volume of poems, of the merits of which report speaks in the highest terms of praise. We are happy to find he is patronised on this occasion by several persons of the first rank and consequence, among whom are the Prince of Wales, the Duchess of Bedford, the Dukes of Manchester and Gordon etc.'

We even have an example; a sonnet called *The Anxious Lover* which was published less than a month later in February 1805[159] and begins:

> *The sun has risen, and I must haste away*
> *To meet My LOVE, or else in accents sweet,*
> *She'll chide my lingering footsteps when we meet,*
> *And question 'Why I could so long delay?'*

By May he has published his poems, price five shillings [£11.02] and, canny man as he was, dedicated them to the Duchess of Manchester. They were connected in that Henry Fox Cooper and his family lived at 2 Little George Street in the parish of St Marylebone in London between 1769-1770 and children of the fourth Duke and Duchess were baptised in the same parish, Manchester Square being in the same area.[160] This connection was not as illustrious as it sounds though for the 5th Duchess was Lady Susan Gordon who bore the Duke two sons and five daughters before they separated. The Duke became governor of Jamaica and the Duchess ran off with a footman in 1812.[161]

Things could not have gone well for Fox Cooper's poet father for within ten years, on 4.8.1815 Henry Fox Cooper was arrested for debt and detained in Fleet debtor's prison in London until the middle of December.[162] He is described as a translator of languages and he owed someone called John Henderson £100 [£4,652.52].

In January 1817, Henry Fox Cooper had recovered sufficiently from this setback and started a Sunday paper called *The Legislator* but it only lasted until 1818. It was a radical publication and stood for the rights of the working classes. In it, Henry Fox Cooper claims: 'He will unceasingly persevere... to advocate and elicit Truth...' Nevertheless, it did not survive as Truth, it seems, is unprofitable. This put Henry Fox Cooper in prison again for debt as he owed Thomas Hague just over £100 [£4,652.52]. He was not released for five months, until October 1818.[163]

Undeterred, Henry Fox Cooper began work as the editor of *John Bull*, a publication founded in 1820. Its purpose seemed to be to defame the characters of all those connected to Queen Caroline, who lived at Brandenburgh House, and her supporters. It even listed the clergy who prayed for the Queen. There is some doubt about who the real owner of *John Bull* was but most suspected someone called Theodore Hook, a notorious man who had been charged with money that went missing when he was treasurer of Mauritius and he was arrested there in 1825.

It appears that Henry Fox Cooper was therefore only a nominal editor, a front, to cover for Hook, being paid three guineas a week which must have come in handy as he and his wife had by then six children. Even so, Henry Fox Cooper had to take the rap when the paper was accused of libel in 1821 and was put in Newgate prison, from where he produced the next two issues of *John Bull*. He was editor until 1825 during which time there were three more legal events for which Henry seems to have somehow avoided being blamed for. But regardless, the efforts of *John Bull*, whilst being pursued through the courts, received the appreciation of King George IV who said:

'Neither he or his ministers nor his parliament nor his courts of justice all together had done so much good as John Bull.'

After leaving *John Bull* in 1825, Henry Fox Cooper brought out his own version of the paper, called *Fox Cooper's John Bull*. First published in 1826, it only survived for twenty-three issues and there is a suggestion that something not quite right was going on which Henry Fox Cooper refused to talk about. He died of dropsy on 21.8.1838 at Shaftesbury Place in London, leaving a second wife Harriet, his first having died in 1822, and the following children: our own Frederick Fox Cooper, Foster, Henry Octavius William and three daughters. Fox Cooper's father therefore, in the words of one of his descendants, was:

'A journalist of average distinction... wrote a book of verse of fair merit and enjoyed some patronage from the Manchester family, if not that of Charles James Fox as well.'[164]

Little is known of Fox Cooper's childhood apart from his birth as the second son in Westminster in 1806 and what we can infer from his father's newsworthy career. He must have felt pretty insecure growing up with his father in prison for debt more than once and again for libel in respect of the *John Bull* publication, and acutely aware of their financial situation. It was intended that he be articled to a relation, Isaac Fox Cooper, a stockbroker, who died worth a million pounds, but there is no evidence this happened.

Well-connected and rebellious, Fox Cooper was destined for a life similar to his father's, one of constant debt, not rising wealth and or fame, as he was never able to build up sufficient capital to tide over the financial troubles which came with his brightest ideas and worse, he failed to realise, in spite of several downfalls, that it made the slightest difference. He earned not fame and respect but notoriety and mockery.

He married Ann Foxhall, born on 2.12 1805 in Brecon, Wales, at St Giles in Camberwell, London in 1823 when they were both under eighteen. Ann was the daughter of a vet who had married a sister of Alderman Garratt, tea merchant and one-time Lord Mayor of London. There may have been tensions between Fox Cooper and his family even then as there was a story about him having to borrow his brother's breeches for the wedding. They had three sons:

- Frederick Harwood was born on 24.11.1826

- Henry Fox who died in 1832, probably as a result of the cholera epidemic that year

- Alfred Edgar, who did not follow until 1.2.1840, after a gap of nearly eight years

Not only a writer and playwright, Fox Cooper was also a competent actor, a skill he put to good use in his later court appearances, always playing to the gallery. Even as young as fifteen, he was treading the boards and in the 1820s he actually appeared occasionally at the *Adelphi*, as we know from the programmes.[165] Fox Cooper did claim that he had been trained as a parliamentary reporter and shorthand writer like Charles Dickens and others have speculated he learnt his writing skills assisting his father at the *John Bull* publication before rejecting the family's efforts to determine his future. What is certain is that he quarrelled with his parents and began writing articles for *Drama*, or the *Theatrical Pocket Magazine* in May 1821 though he did have his share of rejections. In March 1822 he expressed his feelings on the raw deal given to dramatic authors:

'Of all the miseries of human life, authorship is the worst. If a man should wish to spend a life void of perplexity, he should apprentice himself to a knife-grinder or a bellows-mender.'[166]

His first stage play appeared in 1827 and was called *The Sons of Thespis*. It was followed by the drama *The Deserted Villa* which was produced at the *Adelphi* in 1835, then by pieces such as *The Spare Bed* and *Hercules, King of Clubs* and other dramatic sketches.

Then, on Friday 2.12.1831, Fox Cooper is arrested for felony by James Thompson,[167] which resulted in the first of his many appearances in London's courts of justice.

'BOW STREET: During the business yesterday morning a constable named Smith entered the office, accompanied by a gentleman called Frederick Fox Cooper, whom he said he had been instructed to take into custody upon a charge of felony alleged to have been committed by him whilst in the employ of a person named James Thompson, the sworn printer, publisher and editor of a Sunday newspaper.'[168]

Constable Smith handed a placard over to the magistrate at Bow Street court in which:

'The person of Mr. Cooper is described and a reward of £20 [£1,356.03] offered for his apprehension, it being stated that he had absconded with various sums of money which he had embezzled whilst in the employ of Mr. Thompson.'

Constable Smith further explained that he had seen the placards around town and had 'accidentally' met with Mr. Cooper and taken him into custody in the hope of collecting the reward.

Fox Cooper told the magistrate he was willing to wait a reasonable time as the charge was unfounded and atrocious. He had already, before he was apprehended, gone to the Lord Mayor to get his advice and was told to leave the case in his solicitor's hands. The magistrate said:

'There was not the slightest need to detain Mr. Cooper. If he would leave his name and address, he would doubtless be forthcoming to meet any charge.'

The next day, Saturday 3.12.1831, a letter from Fox Cooper appeared in the *Morning Post*, dated the previous day, which shows he had wasted no time making his grievances known to London's newspaper readers:[169]

'Sir- Presuming that your Bow Street reporter has furnished you with an account of the proceedings at that office this day, in which my name is painfully conspicuous, I trust to your candour for the insertion of certain contradictions to the infamous and abominable placard which was handed in to the Magistrates Court for perusal.'

He objects in the strongest terms saying he was never employed by Thompson nor has he absconded with various sums of money with which he was supposed to be on his way to France. Fox Cooper claims that the real proprietors of the *Satirist* are Mr. Barnard Gregory and Mr. Rose who opened an account for him for advertisements in May 1831 not long after the *Satirist* set up.

Whilst it was true that he was engaged at the *Satirist*, Fox Cooper says it was only for one month. He was to receive a salary from them for his services and was held responsible for the payment of the advertisements he inserted in their paper, for which he signed for Mr. Gregory before he sent them to the printers. At the end of one month, Fox Cooper said he thought it fit to have nothing more to do with the *Satirist* and he went to be the editor of a North Wales newspaper where he remained all the previous summer.

'With regard to the motives which led me to withdraw my services from the Satirist, out of respect to the feelings of a Noble Marquis and his amiable consort, I am precluded at present from saying anything further than that they must ultimately redound to my credit.'

A true dramatist, Fox Cooper has told us just enough to spike our interest and left us with tantalising questions. What had the scandalous Marquis done? Why was Fox Cooper accused of stealing money and fleeing to France? Did he really leave for North Wales instead?

Gregory was not slow to respond and got this into the late editions the same day.

'Sir – Having in your Paper of this day used my name in connexion with some proceedings in which a person of the name of Frederick Fox Cooper appears, I trust to your fairness and impartiality to give insertion to the following:

'In the month of May last, Mr. Thompson having been applied to by this Cooper for a situation in his establishment, and being unwell and out of town, he requested me as a favour to communicate with him and abide by certain instructions conveyed to me in a note. I did so. Cooper was in a state of distress and solicited some apparel in order to enable him to enter upon the duties for which he was engaged. With this Mr Thompson liberally furnished him, and in the arrangement, it was expressly stipulated he should receive no monies.

'Ingratitude such as he has exhibited, happily for the world, is of rare occurrence. My evidence, as well as that of a respectable person who was present at that time, I communicated to him on behalf of Mr. Thompson, will go to support the preliminary engagement.' B. Gregory.

And there was a P.S. 'I beg it may be contradicted that I am, as stated in your journal, the proprietor of the Satirist. I am no way connected with that objectionable Print than as being security for Mr. Thompson at the Stamp Office;

and if I choose to become or continue such security, it is a matter which can concern no person but myself!'

Methinks he doth protest too much. Regardless, what was the truth of the matter?

Well, the *Satirist* was first published weekly on 10.4.1831 and released on Sundays, costing 7d [£1.98].[170] At its height the paper had a weekly circulation of over 9,000 and it shut in 1849. The paper became notorious for the allegations it published and the legal battles they provoked; no doubt inspired by its motto which was displayed on the front page:

> 'Satire's my weapon. I was born a critic and a satirist; and my nurse remarked that I hissed as soon as I saw light.'[171]

The *Stamps Act* of 1694 imposed Stamp Duty and during the early part of the 18th century, it was extended to cover a number of items. Somerset House in London hosted the Stamp Office and staff had the task of applying an impressed duty stamp to items to show that the required duty had been paid.[172] Up until 1855, every newspaper produced in the country had to be brought to Somerset House to be stamped.[173]

Later, on Sunday the 4th, following the quick volleys of Fox Cooper and Mr. Gregory, the *Morning Post* gave their version of events:

> 'About two o'clock yesterday, Mr. Frederick Fox Cooper presented himself before the bench of magistrates at Bow Street, and said he attended the office in consequence of a paragraph daring him to do so, which appeared in the Satirist newspaper of last Sunday.'

Fox Cooper handed over the paper to the magistrate and pointed out some editorial comments which used 'the most scurrilous language' about the proceedings at Bow Street the preceding week.

The *Satirist* objected to the *Morning Post* publishing Fox Cooper's letter saying:

> 'Will the sapient personage of the Post who has been imposed upon by the false statement of this vagabond answer for his appearance at Bow Street on Tuesday? We doubt this.'[174]

Upon which, Fox Cooper marched, well, perhaps not quite so quickly, as it was two days later, to Bow Street court on 6.12.1831 demanding to be heard as a much-maligned innocent. No stage directions, use your imagination, it even has a strapline which would look well on a bill board and a wonderful teaser to whet your appetite.[175] After making his entrance, he proclaimed:

'A duty which he owed to his family to demand an instantaneous investigation of the atrocious hand-bills which the Satirist people had been circulating against him.'

In what could have easily been an aside to the audience, he confidentially reminds the magistrate that he had been taken into custody on the previous Friday on a charge of felony, and that, after waiting a considerable time upon that occasion, no charge whatever was brought against him. The police officer went from Bow Street to the *Satirist's* office, only saw a lad, who could not tell him where Mr. Thomson resided but hinted that there was a claim at the Stamp Office unsatisfied by him, and that the *Satirist's* people only wanted to get him arrested for it.

The magistrate then read a copy of the *Satirist*, which was helpfully provided by Fox Cooper and enquired 'What was his object in surrendering himself?'

'To clear my character, sir; and you will presently see that I have sacrificed my liberty, nay my very means of providing for my family, in order to accomplish this. The object of the Satirist people is to get me thrown into prison for a civil debt. I was never employed by James Thompson, the sworn printer and publisher of the paper, nor should I know him if I see him. I court the fullest inquiry, and will thank you to despatch one of your officers to say that I am in attendance to meet my accusers.'

The magistrate asked Fox Cooper to take a seat and obediently sent the gaoler to request the attendance of Mr. Thompson, or someone on his behalf. About an hour later, during which Fox Cooper no doubt made the most of his aggrieved dignity, a Mr. Cannon on behalf of Mr. James Thompson appeared to prefer a charge of felony on Fox Cooper and said he had brought witnesses with him to support the charge. He then called a man called Eve who was a collecting clerk employed by Mr. Thompson at the *Satirist* office.

Mr. Eve: He had heard that Mr. Cooper was in the employ of the *Satirist*, but did not know that fact of his own knowledge. He had never seen Mr. Fox Cooper in his life and could not swear the gentleman present was the Mr. Cooper meant.

Fox. Cooper: Mr. Eve, I will save you that trouble, I admit...

Magistrate: There is no need for you to make the slightest admission, Mr. Cooper.

Eve continued: He had seen a receipt for £1 2 shillings [£74.58] in the handwriting of Mr. Cooper for payment of an advertisement.

Magistrate: That is, you believe it to be the handwriting of Mr. Cooper. Can you swear it?

Eve: I cannot.

The magistrate then said it was extraordinary that nobody attended to identify Mr. Cooper, and asked if there was any other witness. Where was Thompson? Mr. Cannon said Mr. Thompson had gone a little way into the country. He knew, however, that Mr. Fox Cooper had been in the employ of that person.

Magistrate: Will you swear it, sir?

Mr. Cannon: He objected to being sworn. He only attended as professional adviser to Mr. Thompson, but if the magistrates would only postpone the case, he would come provided with plenty of witnesses.

Attention was then called to the paragraph in the *Satirist* of the previous Sunday and the magistrate commented:

> 'It was a curious circumstance that, after such a notice, Thompson should absent himself... Mr. Cooper had attended voluntarily to meet so serious an accusation.'

Cannon: He had another witness, Mr. Morris Salmon, the printer, who would be forthcoming, as well as many others, if the case was postponed a short time.

Magistrate: Well then, as this young gentleman is desirous of the fullest investigation, I shall remand him until seven o'clock.

But, dramatically, and right on cue, a gentleman from the Stamp Office stepped forward and said he had instructions to arrest Mr. Cooper for dues upon a paper called *Paul Pry*, of which he was the proprietor. It was then ascertained that private instructions had been given to the Stamp Office and its officers had no alternative but to take Mr. Cooper into custody.

I was loving this and eager to find out what on earth this *Paul Pry* publication had to do with anything. I found the title comes from the play written by John Poole, first presented in London at the *Haymarket* on 13.9.1825. The character is described as a comical, idle, meddlesome and mischievous fellow consumed with curiosity who conveniently leaves behind his umbrella in order to have an excuse to return and eavesdrop, often using the catchphrase 'I hope I don't intrude.' In the end, however, Pry becomes a hero for rescuing papers from a well.[176]

The first performance of the play was on the 13.7.1826 at the *Theatre Royal* in Angel Street. Only six weeks after the first night the *Morning Chronicle* recorded that:

> '*Paul Pry* has attracted more graphic notoriety than most of his characters, as there is hardly a print-shop in the metropolis that does not present that whimsical actor in one or other scene of this ludicrous performance.'[177] [178]

Paul Pry was also a Sunday newspaper published by Fox Cooper from 28.2.1830, from 13 Wellington Street, Strand in London. It claimed to possess political spirit, a radical outlook, humour, wit, fun and eccentricity and was of all-round interest. Tending to be flippant with a high moral tone, it also featured divorce court proceedings.[179] In September 1830, *Paul Pry* was bought by another publisher, after the printing of thirty issues but it does not appear to have been very profitable and perhaps, as one commentator said, '*Paul Pry* had seen enough.[180]

But before Fox Cooper was removed from court, the magistrate directed that he should be taken into a private room and not placed amongst the disorderlies. At eight o'clock the *Satirist* case was reheard but Mr. Cannon said he had no further witnesses to offer as the notice was so short, he had not been able to procure any, they were all out. The magistrate then discharged Fox Cooper and announced to Mr. Cannon:

'I feel bound to say that, as he has been here twice upon this charge, and came of his own accord to meet it, I shall not listen to a third application. If you have any more evidence, then you can take it to the sessions.' [Quarter Sessions.]

Mr. Cannon said he was instructed by the proprietors of the *Satirist* to do so. Fox Cooper was then discharged, from this charge, but was marched out of court in the custody of the King's officers on behalf of the other charge from the Stamp Office for not paying the tax due and spent time in prison while he raised the money.[181]

What a farce! It is also ironic, in that Fox Cooper had written a *Burlesque* in 1829 about low-level society and insolvency set in the King's Bench prison, where he himself was to be incarcerated for debt only two years later. He probably based it on what he had seen when visiting his father who was also imprisoned for debt in 1815 and 1818 for:

'It showed what places of jollity our prisons were, and what cruel privations poor debtors received from their hard-hearted creditors.'[182]

But Fox Cooper was not finished with the *Satirist* yet. In a later court case in which the paper was sued by a man called Dicas, Fox Cooper was a witness for the prosecution. On oath he confirmed that Gregory was the proprietor, but that he did not like people to know this, which is why Gregory had engaged him at his private address rather than at the newspaper's office. When Fox Cooper was cross examined it was put to him that the magistrate had discharged him from this case we have just been hearing about in December 1831 because he had received money from certain gentlemen for suppressing scurrilous articles about them which the *Satirist* was going to publish.[183] The Noble Marquis?

But Fox Cooper protested:

'He never wrote to noblemen and gentlemen that he would suppress letters.'

One such letter was handed to him as evidence and he denied it was his handwriting. The *Satirist* then dredged up another charge of him pawning things in a furnished lodging. Fox Cooper said his wife had done so, not him, because she would not let her children starve!

Just what are we to believe? If this had been on the stage I doubt Fox Cooper would have received anything except rotten vegetables, but he still got off the charges.

Within three months of selling *Paul Pry* in December 1830, Fox Cooper was indeed living at Rue des Marches in Paris, so there was some truth in that allegation, and the rest of his family followed early in 1831. This would not have been a comfortable journey for them as they would have had to take a coach and horses to Dover, wait for the weather, the tide and other passengers before a rowing boat took them out to a cutter or maybe a steam mailboat, then have to get on another coach, with horses, to Paris.

He might have gone to get new material for a play, or to get wider experience but given what he goes on to do in the future, a better suggestion was that Fox Cooper was laying-in a stock of French plays which he could take home and plagiarise at his leisure, probably the enforced sort of leisure he enjoyed seven times at least in the debtors' prisons.[184]

The Fox Cooper family did not stay in Paris very long for later in 1831 they lived at Segontium Terrace, Caernarvon, North Wales where there was a small but neat theatre, thus fulfilling another part of the testimony given in the *Satirist* case. But Fox Cooper was back in London by November and had been arrested for another debt of £256 4 shillings [£17,370.69] by 8.12.1831. Fox Cooper must have known it was coming but took the risk anyway even though he knew it was a crime to have used unstamped paper in the publication of *Paul Pry*. He served six months in the Fleet prison in London for that one and was released on 8.6.1832.

To be fair, there were many such prosecutions before the reduction of stamp duty and its eventual abolition in 1855 and in the Victorian period, many popular novels featured men who had fallen foul of their creditors and ended up in debtors' prisons, such as Charles Dicken's *Mr. Pickwick* [published in 1836], who spent some time in Fleet prison. The plot of Anthony Trollope's *Mr. Scarborough's Family* published in 1883 revolves around the gambling debts of the eldest son, Mountjoy Scarborough, and shows how rife was the curse of the sons of the rich who ran up debts, placing great burdens on their parents or guardians to settle with creditors on their behalf. Sometimes, the sons went too far for even parental patience and ended up in the Fleet Prison in London.

However, this cannot have been a good time for any of his family but it is not thought that they were incarcerated with him, as was often the case at that time. From 1824, prisoners had been allowed to lodge within a certain radius of the prison and a note left in the Fox Cooper family's papers suggests[185] that he may have stayed in Surrey Street, Strand while the family spent Christmas 1831 and Easter 1832 at Union Row, Kent Road in London.

After his release, Fox Cooper bounced back and became a theatrical manager and devoted more energy to writing for the stage producing four plays in 1833. Between times, he is involved in another case regarding non-payment of money, but this time on the other side of the fence, for he is the creditor of a young man called Joseph Sladen Smith. In July 1835, described as a 'fashionably dressed young man,' Smith's story is told in court:

'In the year 1831, he graduated from Oxford age nineteen and by the time he had finished his three years he had about £800 [£54,241.04] worth of debts. £86 [£5,830.91] of this he owed to a wine merchant and £74 [£5,017.30] for jewellery, some of which he admitted he had given to young ladies.'

Smith was arrested on 11.7.1834, the very day he became part proprietor of the *City Theatre*, Milton Street, London with a Mr. Carter. A few days previously he had sold his reversionary interest under the will of his grandfather to the *Globe Company* and received £785 [£53,224.02], with which he opened an account at Barclays on 27.7.1834 and by the end of that day he only had £321 [£21,764.22] left as he had made various payments. A few days later he went to prison and he now had no money to pay his creditors. Whilst in there, a fellow from his college mentioned a scheme to him to make money. He had a friend called Comber in Horsemonger Lane gaol who could purchase horses and dispose of them to great advantage. Smith, somehow, advanced him £80 [£5,424.10], Comber was set free and Smith then advanced him another £30 [£2,034.04], all of which Comber never returned.[186]

Smith had been in court as an insolvent debtor several times already, owing in total £1,505 [£102,040.96] of which he had been able to pay back £985 [£66,784.28] and he had about £344 [£23,323.65] in assets. His lawyer argued:

'Opposing creditors had pandered to the extravagance of the insolvent [Smith], and had, in his opinion, created it: they, therefore, had no right to complain of the disposition of the money in question.'

The case was adjourned and nothing further was reported in the press about Joseph Sladen Smith and his debts.

Thus, was the heady life and free and easy times of young gentlemen like Fox Cooper, Selina's future husband, between 1830-1835, before she was even born.

Chapter 9 - The Missing Will

On the 18.7.1854,[187] Mrs. Jane Oakes, Jane's mother, a very healthy, active woman and probably the oldest brothel madam in Liverpool, died age 77 at one of her houses at 6 May Street. According to the *Liverpool Daily Post*,[188] she had been in the business since 1839.

Jane, as one of the executors of the will, organised the funeral but said:

'Her mother did not have much ready money when she died, scarcely as much as paid the expenses of her funeral. It was all tied up in the business and property, but I buried my mother respectably.'[189]

As this was late spring, with few facilities for keeping bodies, the funeral was probably held very quickly. The Victorians had strict rituals to follow when someone died and:

- They would use crepe to cover mirrors in the house to avoid trapping the spirit of Mrs. Oakes in the looking glasses

- The family would draw the curtains and stop the clocks at the time of death to mark the exact moment she passed away

- Family photos would be turned face down throughout the house to prevent her spirit from possessing relatives and friends

- The family would hang a wreath of laurel and yew or boxwood, tied with black crepe or ribbons, on the front door as a signal to neighbours and visitors that a death had occurred[190]

- The bell knob or door handle would also be draped with black crepe and tied with a ribbon – black because Mrs. Oakes had been married[191]

- When her body was removed from the house, it was taken head-first, so that she would be unable to call others to follow her[192]

- Funeral invitations, which were engraved on a small square of paper with a wide black border and delivered by private messenger, would be sent out

The viewing was likely held at the Mrs. Oakes' house. The family was expected to view the remains before guests, which made it important they arrived at the right time and not earlier. The family would be seated in the order of relation to the deceased, closest relative at the head of the line, and whenever possible, family were seated in a separate room thus protecting any show of grief from the eyes of their guests. [193] The coffin would remain open so that guests could view the body before the start of the funeral; however, it would not be opened in the church unless a lot of guests were expected to view.

After the service ended, the guests would remain in the church until the family and those attending the interment were escorted from the building in preparation for the procession.[194] The first carriage would contain the clergyman and the pall bearers, with six (maybe eight) intimate friends of Mrs. Oakes to carry the coffin. The next carriage would be the hearse, followed by the carriage of the nearest relatives, which would be followed by more distant relatives and friends.[195]

A basic Victorian hearse was an elaborate carriage, black or white (in the case of children), with glass sides, silver and gold decorations, dressed - up according to budget. Other extras included multiple black horses drawing the carriage, velvet coverings for the coffin and the horses, ostrich plumes decorating every corner, or even an entire canopy of ostrich feathers covering the hearse. Flowers would have surrounded the coffin so they could be seen through the glass windows.

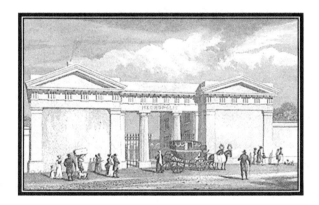

Figure 11 Low Hill Cemetery and Necropolis, 1825-1898 Everton, Liverpool

She was buried at Liverpool's Necropolis on Low Hill which was built because it was urgently needed to cope with the expansion of Liverpool in the early 19th century.[196] Covering five acres, it was opened at the corner of the Everton and West Derby Roads and designed by John Foster junior. The grounds were laid out by the curator of the Botanic Gardens and cost £8,000 [£542,410.40]. It filled up quickly in the following 70 years with 80,000 burials, the first taking place on 1.2.1825.[197]

By 1896, the Necropolis had caused such serious unsanitary conditions in the surrounding area that it was closed on 31.8.1898. The council took over responsibility and in 1913 the lodges, gates and walls were demolished, monuments, large gravestones were removed and the area was landscaped with ornamental gardens. On 22.4.1914, the area was renamed and opened as Grant's Gardens, after Alderman J.R. Grant who was the chairman of the Corporation Parks and Gardens Committee.

Mrs. Oakes' will, dated 12.3.1851[198] said she lived in Manchester and represented less than £450 [£36,083.75.] The normal procedure after the funeral would then have been for Jane and her co - executor John Heales James to apply for probate, which Jane did, but not until ten years later in 1864. This she admitted in 1860 saying 'she had thus rendered herself liable for a penalty of £100.' [£8,018.61]

Normally in Victorian times wills were not prepared until the last few weeks of life to avoid having to change names and circumstances at the last minute. The fact Mrs. Oakes' was prepared over three years before shows her concern about how the brothel empire would be managed after her death. But the will was very elusive. It could not be located for the 1860 court case, few people knew it existed, the sisters did not challenge it and probate was only finally achieved ten years later, long after Jane had done what she liked with the brothel empire. Once more Jane puzzled me as I could not see what she gained by delaying probate. It was only after substantial research that I realised what a very long game she was playing.

It was just as difficult for me to find the will as well. I searched all the obvious official records but could not even locate a newspaper death notice and I only made progress when I tried the national databases for probate looking at dates over a decade after she had died. However, whilst this gave me the precise date of death and probate it did not help me find an actual copy. I became mired in many maze-like dead ends until eventually, on the Family Search website of the Church of the Latter-Day Saints [Mormons], I found they had an actual copy of the will. But, as it was not available online, I had to go personally to one of their few research centres in England to download a copy.

Well, it was at least a chance to get away from my computer and out into the field as quite by chance one of these Mormon places happened to be about thirty miles away, so off we went, my cousin and I. The staff were wonderful and about four of them furiously chased the website reference, there was much coming and going as logic was useless for this search as the will was written in 1851, Jane Oakes did not die until 1854 and the staff found it inexplicable probate was dated 1864. After half the day it was finally located on their worldwide system but it was not, as expected, downloadable or printable from the Mormon research centre. All was not entirely lost though, as I had an address to apply to and enough detailed references to send away for it.

In the course of us saying 'thank you' we were treated to some additional information by one of the on-site researchers who explained why the Mormons had invested so much time and energy in developing family history records and an extensive world-wide database. The Mormons were committed to saving souls so they could enjoy the afterlife as true believers and they had extended their attention not just to people alive now but to their ancestors. They allocated huge resources to make it possible for their fellow Mormons to research their family trees and compile family histories like genealogists do, so Mormons can now bind their ancestors to them, by something described as 'celestial glue.' According to them, whole generations can, as a result, be saved by the current descendant, which is why the Family Search website is free to all.

This was rather unexpected so I looked it up when I got home and found:[199]

'One of the core tenets of Mormon faith is that the dead can be baptised into the faith after their passing. Baptism of the dead evolved from the beliefs that baptism is necessary for salvation and that the family unit can continue to exist together beyond mortal life if all members are baptised.

'Mormons trace their family trees to find the names of ancestors who died without learning about the restored Mormon Gospel so that these relatives from past generations can be baptised by proxy in the temple. For Latter-Day Saints, genealogy is a way to save more souls and strengthen the eternal family unit.'

Well, that's one way of looking at it, but I could not help picturing Jane's face if ever she learnt one of her descendants had presumed to save her soul in this way, and as a strategy for saving souls, it has not been without controversy in our time either.

'In the mid-1990s, there was a backlash when it was uncovered that the names of about 380,000 Jewish Holocaust victims had been submitted for posthumous baptism by what church historian Marlin Jensen calls "well-intentioned, sometimes slightly overzealous members."

'In 1995, the church agreed to remove the names of all Holocaust victims and survivors from its archives and to stop baptising Jews unless they were direct ancestors of a Mormon or unless they had the permission of all the person's living relatives. However, Jewish names have periodically been discovered since the 1995 agreement, including that of Holocaust survivor and Jewish human rights activist Simon Wiesenthal, which was found and removed in 2006. Catholics and members of other faiths have also been upset at the practice.'

But I could not disagree with their following statement.

'Despite the controversies, the Mormon archives are a boon to professional and amateur genealogists.'

As I found the will and had an interesting day out, I filed this information away for future reference.

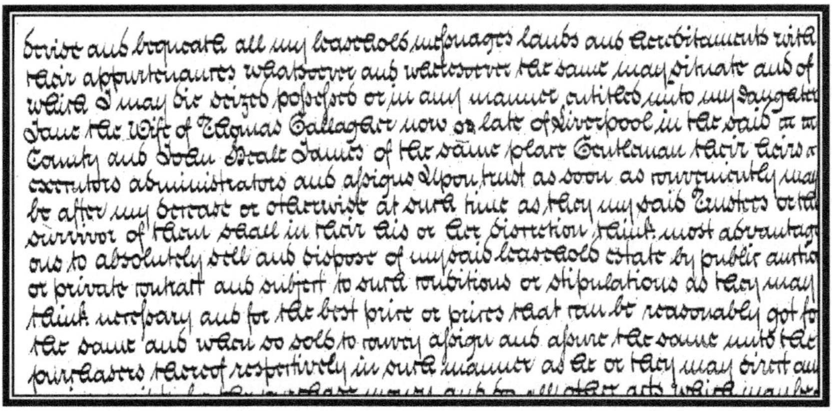
devise and bequeath all my leaseholds messuages lands and hereditaments with
their appurtenances whatsoever and wheresoever the same may situate and of
which I may die seized possessed or in any manner entitled unto my daughter
Jane the Wife of Thomas Gallagher now or late of Liverpool in the said
County and John Heale James of the same place Gentleman their heirs
executors administrators and assigns Upon trust as soon as conveniently may
be after my decease or otherwise at such time as they my said Trustees or the
survivor of them shall in their his or her discretion think most advantag
ous to absolutely sell and dispose of my said leasehold estate by public auctio
or private contract and subject to such conditions or stipulations as they may
think necessary and for the best price or prices that can be reasonably got fo
the same and when so sold to convey assign and assure the same unto the
purchasers thereof respectively in such manner as he or they may direct an

Figure 12 First section of Jane Oakes will 1851

Above is an extract of Jane Oakes' will. Granted, it is not easy to read, and not just because of the handwriting. The wording is torturous and there is not one full stop or paragraph break in two very large sheets of paper. But over a week, with a guide to Victorian script on my knee, I managed almost a complete transcript, most of which is repetition, so it is not as long as it felt while I struggled to make it out.

Jane, of course, knew what it said but did not give anyone a chance to challenge it. She went ahead in 1854 and:

'Paid all the debts that she [her mother] left as far as I could, these were loan debts... She had a sum of money in the savings bank at Manchester, I don't know how much. She gave that money to my younger sister [Ellen] and she drew it out before she died."[200]

But Mrs. Oakes' will is actually more complicated than Jane said. It set up a Trust for Jane's five legitimate children which included everything in the brothel empire. Jane and a lawyer were named as trustees, but once again on paper, she could not be sued or forced to liquidate the assets to pay her debts as they were her children's property.

Between them Jane Oakes and Jane Gallagher had prevented control of the empire and its profits being passed to Thomas as Jane's husband or to her creditors and it was all perfectly legal, thanks no doubt to her very able lawyer clients. Here is the relevant section, to which I have added much needed punctuation to make it comprehensible:

'Trust dividends, rents and annual profits arising from the said trust monies, stocks, funds and sureties upon trust to pay the same rents, dividends and annual profits of the said trust monies as and when the same shall be received unto the proper hands of my daughter, the said Jane Gallagher, during the term of her natural life to and for her sole use and for the maintenance, education and support of all and every one of the children of my said daughter by the said Thomas Gallagher.'

Only after Jane Gallagher died was the money to pass to the children over 21, the legitimate children that is, and only Jane's eldest Ann Elizabeth was already 21 in 1854. There was also a single item left specifically to one of Jane's daughters, Caroline, her best bib, which might have looked like this, and was a very fashionable item.[201]

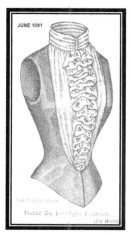

Figure 13 Victorian bib or plastron: 1891

My immediate concern was for the two illegitimate girls. Were they to miss out completely? Not exactly. They are mentioned by name and described as the daughters of William Mercer, not as Jane's, which shows that by 1851 when she drew up her will, Jane Oakes must have been well aware of their status and that Jane had entered into a bigamous marriage.

> 'If more than one provided also that in case all of them, the said children of my daughter Jane Gallagher, shall die before attaining the said age of twenty-one years unmarried and without leaving lawful issue then and in such case, I direct my said trustees or their survivors of them to pay and divide the same between Rosanna Mercer and Maria Jane Mercer, daughters of William Mercer of Liverpool, aforesaid Saddler.'

Nice thought, but as every one of Jane's legal children did survive beyond 21, married and as far as I had been able to trace them at this time, two had children, the two illegitimate daughters would receive nothing. Meanwhile Jane could do as she liked with impunity, and did, 'treating the property in every respect as if it were exclusively her own.'[202] She continued to expand the business, giving even more bills of sale on the furniture and mortgaging the houses in order to raise extra finance via the Liverpool Tradesman's Loan Society and her good friend Chalkley.

She was called to account in the 1860 case though. Then, only Jane, Chalkley and Jane Oakes' solicitor knew what was in the will. Chalkley said it was:

> 'Rather general ... not particularly specifying the property... but I knew that the word property was mentioned in the will and that that was left to the children.'

But Johnson, the official receiver on behalf of Burton and Watson, had more specific questions for Jane:

Lawyer: When your mother died, to whom did you consider this furniture belonged?

Jane: To me. I have got it still. My mother left a will, which I believe is here. I only saw one will, which my mother gave me in some papers, telling me it was for my children. I don't know that the will has ever been proved. I have read that will. There is a distinction made in it between furniture and houses.

But when the will was called for, 'it could not be found...' Mr. Roby, the solicitor for Jane, had 'mislaid it,' but promised that he would produce it the next day. The judge remarked:

> 'If it was not forthcoming, he should of course place great importance upon the absence of such a document.'

Indeed.

There does not seem to have been any protest from her sisters at that time, who Jane said:

'Were continually asking her mother for money. There never was another will of my mother's that I know of. My sisters are married and have families. None of them ever asked to see my mother's will: I have assisted them all. They have never expressed any annoyance at not being mentioned in the will; my mother told them they need not expect anything at her death. I told my mother that if she meant to give to my sisters, she had better give it to them before her death, for they would only come to annoy me afterwards.

'We had a house in Manchester: my mother went there and disposed of it. She told me she would put in her will that at her death it was to be sold at once and divided equally among the girls, and I said there is no point keeping it on if I am to sell it when anything happens to you; you had better do it yourself; and she went up to Manchester and sold it by auction – I mean the furniture in the house. I don't know what it realised: she never told me.'

Jane's impatience with the sisters and irritated dismissal of her elderly mother's wish to have everything signed off neat and tidy does not sit well. Certainly, by that time she was very confident in her role as head of the business and as a result of her most recent successful skirmishes in the law court, possibly becoming arrogant.

But it would be a while yet before this pride would lead to her fall. Her first priority was to consolidate the brothels and make the most of the Liverpool's lucrative prostitution market.

Chapter 10 - Charles Pollard

'Charles Pollard, a sporting character, was brought up upon a warrant, charged with entering the house of Richard Chilcott in Houghton Street early in the morning last Friday week and putting him in bodily fear. The defendant was bound over in his own recognisances of £50 [£4,009.51] to keep the peace for twelve months.'[203]

Figure 14 Impression of Charles Pollard by George Jones 2019

This was the first I knew of Charles Pollard, who, the article went on to describe, was living at No 5 Houghton Street in 1856, one of Jane's brothels. It was a mere snippet I stumbled on, tucked away at the bottom of a page in the *Liverpool Mercury*.

Well, he wasn't just a lodger or a visitor for Charles and Jane presented as man and wife, though they both heavily denied it in every court case they appeared in. How, when Jane was dealing with her mother's death, estate and the new Trust, on top of everything else, had she found time for another live-in relationship? I blame the train.

The lines from Liverpool to the capital had opened in 1838, I knew Jane had started to go to London quite often by the 1850s[204] and Charles Pollard had been living there since 1840s, so it is highly likely they met there. But who was this man?

He was born in 1814 in Stamford, Lincolnshire. His parents were William and Mary Pollard[205] and his baptism record shows his father was a fishmonger.[206] His local newspaper, the *Stamford Mercury* on 16.7.1847,[207] which reported on one of Charles' more notable court cases, casually mentioned that he married a woman from King's Cliffe, six miles south of Stamford. There is a possible marriage in 1836 on record between Charles Pollard and an Ann S. Pearson at Newington St Mary, which was then in Surrey, but now Southwark, when Charles would have been 18,[208] but none in King's Cliffe. As there were so many other Charles Pollards around at that time it is difficult to find out which he really was, even the 1841 census is little help.

Charles Pollard though is no Irish tailor nor a Lancashire saddler/publican or a Manx Methodist Minister. This man is powerfully built, flashy, fearless, a risk taker, good looking, makes and loses money as fast as others change their shirts and is not frightened of using his fists in an argument or to defend his friends. More like Fox Cooper, life is boom or bust for him, no wonder Jane was captivated.

There was a lot to investigate and I found almost immediately so many articles about him and Louis-Napoleon Bonaparte in 1847 this chapter might more aptly be entitled 'The Fish Monger and the Prince-President of France,' if it hadn't been for other equally extraordinary accounts of his misdoings. As we will find out, Charles Pollard was quite a character.

Louis-Napoléon Bonaparte, as we probably know, was the last monarch of France, reigning from 1852 until 1870. Born in Paris on 20.4.1808 and named Charles-Louis Napoléon Bonaparte, he is usually known as Louis-Napoléon. His parents were Louis Bonaparte, King of Holland, the younger brother of Emperor Napoleon I and Hortense de Beauharnais, the daughter of Emperor Napoleon I's first wife, Joséphine de Beauharnais. He had two elder brothers: Napoléon Louis Charles Bonaparte (1802) who died in childhood and Napoléon Louis Bonaparte, King Louis III of Holland (1804) who married Charlotte Bonaparte, but they had no children.

Louis - Napoleon was christened at the Palace of Fontainebleau on the 4.11.1810, which was more than two years after he was born and his godparents were the first Emperor Napoleon and his Empress, Marie Louise. Following Emperor Napoleon I's defeat at Waterloo and the subsequent Bourbon Restoration, all members of the Bonaparte family were forced to leave France. Louis-Napoleon and his mother settled in Switzerland, where she bought Schloss Arenberg. He studied for some time in Augsburg in Bavaria and developed a slight German accent which he kept all his life.

In 1823, the family moved to Rome and Louis-Napoleon became involved with the Carbonari, fighting against Austria's presence in northern Italy. Forced to flee in 1831, he soon made his way back to France, traveling incognito with his mother, using the name Hamilton, and arrived in Paris on 31.4.1831. In a secret meeting, the then French King Louis-Philippe permitted them to remain in Paris, provided they remain incognito and that their stay was brief. However, their identities were soon discovered and they were forced to leave the city just a week later, making their way back to Switzerland.

Louis - Napoleon then joined the Swiss Army and began writing about his political views. After an unsuccessful coup attempt in October 1836, King Louis Philippe demanded that he be turned over to France, but the Swiss government refused as he was a Swiss citizen. He later travelled to London, Brazil, New York and returned to Switzerland in 1837 to be at his mother's deathbed.

After her death on the 5.10.1837, Louis-Napoleon spent some time at Schloss Arenberg before returning to London the following year. He soon made plans for another attempt to take the French throne but sailing to Boulogne in 1840, he was arrested. A quick trial took place and he was sentenced to life in prison in the fortress of Ham. Whilst there, he spent much time writing, publishing essays and articles in numerous newspapers and magazines throughout France.

Still hoping to fulfil his ambition to claim the French throne, Louis-Napoleon managed to escape from Ham in May 1846. While renovations were being made to his cell, he disguised himself as one of the workers and walked right out through the main gates and made his way back to England. Once there, he lived for a brief time in lodgings off Lord Street in Southport, just sixteen miles north of Liverpool. It is claimed Lord Street is the inspiration behind the tree-lined boulevards of Paris, which he went on to have constructed in 1854.[209] But first, his cousin died, leaving Louis-Napoleon as the sole heir to the Bonaparte dynasty.[210]

The French Revolution of 1848 led to the abdication of King Louis-Philippe and the declaration of the Second Republic. Louis-Napoleon quickly left for France, while the deposed King went into exile in England, an ironic reversal in situations. Ignoring his advisers who urged him to cease his claims on power, Louis-Napoleon instead declared his loyalty to the Republic and returned to London where he closely watched events unfold in his homeland.

In September of that year, he was elected to the French National Assembly and returned to Paris as the country prepared to elect the first President of the French Republic. He immediately entered the contest and on 20.12.1848, was declared the winner. Taking the title Prince-President, Louis-Napoleon went to live at the Élysée Palace.[211]

Slotted between his valiant fighting, political manoeuvring, dramatic escape, and his sojourn in Southport, Prince Charles Louis - Napoleon Bonaparte lived in 1847, the year before his return to France and becoming the Prince-President, at No 3 King Street, near St James Park in London. [212] The Army and Navy Club was nearby at the junction of St James Street and King Street and became very prosperous having established itself on equal terms with the older Service Clubs. Its many distinguished members included Prince Louis-Napoleon, who after his return to France presented the club with the Gobelin tapestry which still adorns the staircase of the inner hall. [213]

Figure 15 Louis - Napoleon at the time of his failed coup in 1836

It was at King Street that Napoleon first met Charles Pollard. [214] Napoleon explains how:

'In the month of June last [1847], in consequence of the non-arrival of a remittance from Florence, I was desirous of obtaining £2,000 [£120,834.00] for a temporary purpose...'

Then on 10.6.1847, out of the blue, he received a letter from Charles Pollard:

'Mr. Pollard presents his respects to Prince Napoleon and Mr. P will do himself the honour of calling upon the Prince tomorrow morning at twelve o'clock on private business.'

Napoleon says he only communicated his need for funds to Mr. Orsi, who was acting as his secretary and lived at 18 Stockbridge Terrace, Pimlico, and nobody seems to know how Pollard heard about it. Mr. Orsi claims he had only spoken to a Mr. Arnold, bill discounter, of 37 Sackville Street.[215] According to a street directory of London in 1848, Arnold was a solicitor[216] and whilst he knew Charles, he said did not instruct him to call upon Napoleon on his behalf. However, when later cross examined in court at the Old Bailey, Mr. Arnold admitted he had told three other people about the request from Napoleon.

Whatever, Napoleon goes on to say Pollard came as arranged and introduced himself as the writer of the letter. Pollard was a perfect stranger to him at that time but he told Napoleon that he had heard he needed some funds and that he had between £2-4,000 [£120,834.00 - £241,668.00] to offer if he wished.

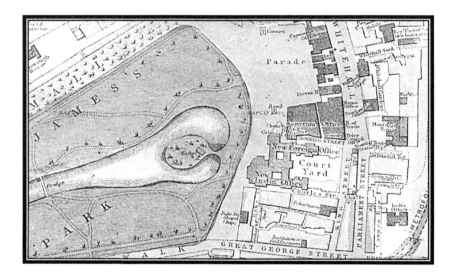

Figure 16 King St on map of London 1868, by Edward Weller, F.R.G.S.

Napoleon's response was, understandably, to ask how he knew he wanted money. Pollard said he was a man of business and it was his business to provide money to noblemen and that he was currently trying to find a loan of £40,000 [£2,416,680.00] for a friend of Napoleon's too. Napoleon was not sure about still wanting money as he was currently selling some investments in the French railways but Pollard nevertheless stated his terms were 5% and that he lived at 10 Essex Street, the Strand, London. When I checked I found that Pollard had only lodged there for three months at the time of this meeting, so was this just a convenient address?

Napoleon told him to come back on Monday 14.6.1847 and Pollard produced some stamps and asked Napoleon to sign on them, but he declined. Once Pollard had gone, Napoleon instructed 'a certain person, Mr. Sams, a book seller,' to make enquiries about him.

Mr. W.H. Sams had a shop on the corner of St James Street, opposite the palace, which was well known in the fashionable and aristocratic circles as 'Sam's Library.' He carried on his father's business as a librarian-publisher and his shop windows were covered in caricatures of well-known politicians and other celebrities such as Lord Lytton. '*Lodge's Peerage*' in its first edition printed in 1827 was published at Sam's Library and called '*Sam's Peerage.*'

His name rang a bell with me, so I went back through my databases to find out why.[217] It led me to re-read an 1861 *Stamford Mercury* report on another court case where Pollard was questioned about his past alleged criminal activities. In it he admitted his involvement with Louis-Napoleon but denied another accusation saying: 'He was never charged with causing the death of Dutch Sam's widow. '[218]

Well, there are no flames without fire, and this set me off on another track, as if Napoleon wasn't exciting enough. Had he killed Dutch Sam's widow, whoever she was? Now I do know who Dutch Sam was I wondered how I never knew at all, but there you go. First though, I had to check and initially found nothing as I did not go back far enough or query the right words: trying 'Coroner Courts, London, murders' brought me nothing but a headache and asking for 'Dutch Sam' was equally frustrating.

Eventually I struck gold with 'Dutch Sam's Widow,' after dialling the dates significantly backwards to the 1830s and drew a good handful of newspaper reports, all about boxing, for Young Dutch Sam was a world class boxer or pugilist. He was also agreed to be a rather handsome fellow, standing about five feet nine inches and in fighting trim, weighing ten stones twelve pounds. He first appeared in public on the stage of the *Old Fives Court*, St Martin's Lane, London. This performance and those that followed earned him a reputation as 'the everlasting and sure leveller of all.'

Born plain Samuel Evans on 30.1.1808, his parents were Blanche and Samuel, who was sometimes known as Elias, a Jew of Dutch extraction and a hawker, [a street seller] in East Stepney in London. Sam was taught to read and write 'and placed early in the world to get a living,' first as a shop boy in a potato house, though another newspaper reported he was employed by a baker, subsequently as a press boy and folder of sheets in a printing office. However, the 'jog trot progress of a typo did not suit his active genius...' and he was obviously destined to cause more headlines than compose them in a newspaper office. Sam then became a marker at the King's Bench where:

> 'He learnt to play that manly and scientific game with consummate skill and bid fair with greater practice to rival the characters of the day.'[219]

But his greatest ambition was to distinguish himself and Young Dutch Sam won his first fight at age 15 and fell in with the renowned Richard Curtis, who not only taught all the 'essential acquirements of the art pugilistic', but as King Dick, was his advisor.[220] Young Dutch Sam's extraordinary severity of hitting and constant victories earned him the nickname the *Phenomenon*. Sam, like his father who was also a pugilist, dared to list opponents in weight above his standing, 'all of whom fell beneath his conquering arm.' He was never beaten and became the world welterweight champion in the 1820s.

Figure 17 Young Dutch Sam – Wikipedia

Bell's Life in London and Sporting Chronicle's obituary of Sam said:

> 'He spoke well, and when he chose could "do the agreeable" with a suavity highly creditable to his class, securing to himself throughout his career the patronage of many noblemen and gentlemen of highest distinction. His temper was cheerful and he possessed a flow of natural humour which rendered him an agreeable companion in social circles.

'His practical jokes were, however, often characterised by an utter disregard to the feelings of his victims ......What was pleasure to him was destruction to them. This, with a reckless disregard to his own interests and an unhappy disposition to mix in those scenes which constitute what is known as "Life in London" and in which he was often the companion of sprigs of nobility, to whose wild vagaries he was but too much inclined to pander, led him to scrapes from which he had some difficulty in escaping.

'From all that we have seen of his career we cannot compliment him as having been either steady or persevering in his efforts to realise independence or secure respect. His opportunities for wooing Dame Fortune were numerous, but the wildness of his disposition prevented his taking advantage of them. He was twice installed in public houses, the first in Castle Street, Leicester Fields, London and the next the *Coach and Horses*, St Martins Lane, but could not be prevailed upon to attend to his duties as landlord, hence those speculations were abandoned.

'It was not until he married a woman who was his faithful and attached companion till the moment of his death, that the foundation of prosperity was laid. She, luckily, was a woman of good sense, and considerable experience in the public line, and possessed an influence over his erratic disposition which enabled her to "carry on the war" with success, commencing at the *Black Lion*, Vinegar Yard and finally casting anchor in 1842 at the *Old Drury Tavern*, Brydges Street, Covent Garden where despite of Sam's still volatile disposition, she continued to "Increase his store." '[221]

To put it more plainly than *Bells' Life* wanted to do, young Dutch Sam drank too much, was always up until the early hours of the morning carousing with his wealthy friends and dissipate gentry, ignoring medical advice until such a time as, only 35, he relapsed, was seized with inflammation of the lungs, and gave up the ghost in November 1843. [222] [223]

But *Bell's* was quite enamoured with young Dutch Sam's wife:

'Throughout his last illness he was attended with kindness by his exemplary wife, who spared neither pains nor expense to alleviate his disease. He died calm and collected, surrounded by several of his friends, who, while they pitied him, could not but condemn the headlong folly which had distinguished his passage through his short but eventful existence.'[224]

We have now reached the point where Dutch Sam's widow exists in her own right, but I still need to bring her and Pollard together to find out whether he did in fact murder her.

Dutch Sam's widow continued to run the *Old Drury Lane Tavern* on Brydges St but it became very rowdy without her husband to keep order. Headlines certainly confirm this. The *Lloyds Weekly* newspaper sported:[225] 'A row at Young Dutch Sam's' and was dated New Year's Eve 1843, barely a month after he died. At 3am some men came into the pub after drinking elsewhere and one of them struck Sambo Sutton, the black prize fighter, 'who waded in with his feet and fists.'[226] What more than one newspaper describes as a 'Glorious Row' was the result and the police were called. A court case followed, brought by Dutch Sam's widow, against the man who started the fight and he was bound over to the next session. The account ended with these words:

> 'The dark gentleman alluded to was in court during the whole of the investigation and seemed to enjoy the situation in which the defendant was placed, for he showed his teeth continually.'

In June 1844, young Dutch Sam's widow is in court again this time for harbouring prostitutes. She had allowed four young women of dubious character to drink in her establishment, which was technically illegal even though they only stayed for three minutes before she got the pot boy to evict them.[227] It therefore came about, only seven months later on 30.6.1844, that she married Thomas William Burford. Quite why she did and to such a loser, no one knows but she must have felt the lack of her husband's fists in the bar, his reputation and maybe thought a male presence on the premises would help. Little did she know....[228]

Now she is Mrs. Sophia Burford, though the press continues to label her Young Dutch Sam's widow, Thomas William Burford became the landlord and responsible person for the management of the *Old Drury Lane Tavern*. The next we hear is in a newspaper report about a bankruptcy in January a year later in 1845. It has a strange title: *Bankruptcy Court Re: Burford*.[229] There is no '*Somebody versus Somebody else.*' Intriguing. I soon found out why, for the new Mrs. Burford appears to have engineered the bankruptcy of her second husband, though she quite charmingly denied it. When you the read the full story, you can't really blame her... The *Morning Advertiser* sets the scene:

> 'A great many persons connected with the trade were present during the proceedings, which were continued until a late hour and which seemed to be particularly attractive in consequence of the bankrupt having married the widow of Dutch Sam the prize fighter and within a few months afterwards he [the bankrupt] having been arrested at the alleged instigation or requisition of his wife through the distillers who served the house.'[230]

The debts were estimated at about £1,000 [£80,186.10]. Mr. Burford himself couldn't remember, when asked in court, when he had married Dutch Sam's widow, as 'he had been now in prison for about a month awaiting trial.' He was questioned at length about the alleged abstraction of certain books containing an account of his business, without which nobody could verify his accounts of what had happened to the money. It appeared that at the time of his arrest he had only £27 [£2,165.02] in his possession. When he married Dutch Sam's widow, he had about £50 [£4,009.31] of his own and he believed the business his wife brought with her was worth about £2,000 [£160,372.20], which obviously made it good idea to marry her. When pressed, Burford claimed the business was managed purely by his wife and the barmaid, that he had received no money from the estate and effects since he had been sent to prison and the books were with the person overseeing the bankruptcy.

I expect the spectators were really there to hear his wife, Sophia, and she did not disappoint. She told them that since her marriage to Burford she had kept a day book of accounts which she had not seen since he went into prison. He had taken her purse with around £85 [£6.815.82] in it from a table in her bedroom which she usually kept 'in her bosom,' which meant she could not use it to pay the distiller.

'My husband never restored to me a farthing of that money, as he said he was cash keeper; and always helped himself from the till when he wanted money... He had taken money very often and from within three days of their marriage he had pocketed £10 [£801.86].'

It came out that shortly after the marriage there had also been a 'family difference' between them with the result that her barmaid was brought before the magistrate on an assault warrant, remanded and ultimately discharged. This, unfortunately, I could not find anything else about. Under cross examination Mrs. Burford was asked:

Lawyer: Upon your oath, didn't you yourself state your anxiety to get rid of him, and that he was about to leave the country!

Sophia: He told me himself shortly after our marriage, that he would be very glad to leave the country.

Lawyer: Upon your oath, did not you, upon your representations, induce the petitioning creditor to issue the fiat?

Sophia: I do not know what you mean. My barwoman knows all about our accounts as well as I do and I swear that I never lent myself to his imprisonment or arrest. He used the till whenever he thought proper and all I can add is, that he has ruined "My house!"

The result was that Mr. John Nicholson, for the distillers was chosen as assignee, in other words, both Burfords lost control of the money and on 8.3.1844, Burford came up again at the bankruptcy court for examination of his books but they were 'not exactly ready' and the hearing was adjourned. But all is not lost for this lady who is the darling of the press for Sophia springs back to our attention on 1.11.1846 under her old married name.[231] The *Era* says:

> 'Mrs. Evans, widow of the late Dutch Sam, has taken the Old Bell, Wellington Street, Strand where a harmonic meeting [an amateur choir], supported by known talent, is held every Monday and Friday evening. We trust that this "Belle" may never have to sound the alarm of distress.'

They continue to report her 'harmonious evenings' over the next six months saying they are well attended; the music is first rate, and:

> 'The strenuous efforts of Mrs. Evans to please is deserving of every success. May the undertaking be prosperous, and we sincerely hope that this "Belle" and the Bell may never have to ring changes.'[232]

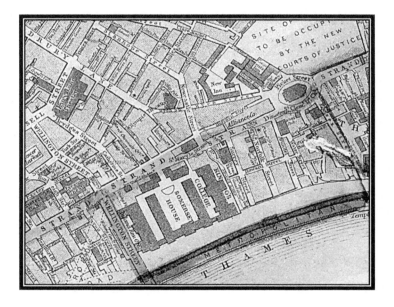

Figure 18 Map of London 1868, by Edward Weller, F.R.G.S.

I cannot tell if Thomas William Burford was in residence with her at the *Old Bell* from 1846 to 1847 or where he was as he does not appear in the London street directories, but he died a short time later and was buried on 17.4.1847 in Godstone, Surrey age 34, leaving young Dutch Sam's widow, a widow a second time after only three years of marriage.[233] A month later, the licence for the *Old Bell* is transferred from William Burford to Sophia Burford.[234] The *Era* again reports:

'The Bell Tavern, Wellington Street, under the able management of Mrs. Evans, widow of the late Dutch Sam, continues to prosper. A new billiard table has been added to the numerous attractions of this rendezvous for the Fancy [the boxing fraternity].'[235]

Meanwhile, Charles Pollard, a month later in June 1847, was well embarked on his efforts to ensnare Louis-Napoleon. On the 14th he visited him again and spoke of the commercial crisis and how hard to come by cash was at the time. Louis-Napoleon said Pollard did not need to proceed if he did not want to, at which point Pollard produced two pieces of paper he had with him and asked Napoleon to take a copy.[236] The bills [cheques] were not directed at anyone at this time so Pollard asked Napoleon to accept this and to add at the bottom that he was to be the drawer of these bills. In doing so he explained that he would be responsible if Napoleon did not pay the bills in two months as agreed. Pollard then asked how he wanted the money and left promising to come back the next day with it.

It is very strange that the well-educated Louis-Napoleon, noble warrior, astute politician and future Prince-President of France, was so gullible. Why had he signed bills to someone he never met before or would have sought out? Well:

'He was a nobleman of distinction and considerable property, residing at present in this country, who had unguardedly entrusted, for the first time in his life, into the hands of the prisoner a valuable security for the purpose of getting discounted. (He) had never before had recourse to such a proceeding, and he would not have done so on this occasion had his revenue been at this moment available, and had he not a considerable sum of money just now locked up in French railways. He had never accepted a bill before, and was not acquainted with the distinction between a cheque and a bill. He had never before had occasion to raise money.' [237]

So, he was desperate for ready money, but that does not account for this foolishness or innocence in financial matters. His secretary should have advised him better.

Charles did go back to see Napoleon but only spoke again about the state of the money market and advised that he would lose a lot of money by selling his stock at that time. He wanted to wait a few days until the market recovered, but he would have the money in the next few days.[238]

Mr. Orsi, the secretary, subsequently visited Pollard more than once in Essex Street on 19th and 20th June, to find he was not in. However, he did meet Mrs. Lee, the landlady, with a servant, Ann McLelland, and a woman who represented herself as Mrs. Pollard. On the first occasion Napoleon went as well and Pollard was actually in, but Mrs. Pollard told the girl to inform him that he was out. Still Napoleon did not get his money, so he wrote to Pollard the day after. Back came a letter from him, supposedly in Birmingham, but nothing else. Napoleon only then sprang into action, instigating enquiries into the bills and placing adverts asking for information.

Meanwhile, on 25th June, Pollard and a friend called Watson called on Alexander Symons, a wine merchant, who lived at 16 London Street. Watson had known him when he had been a commercial traveller for some years but as Pollard was until then unknown to Symons, Watson, acted as the go-between. Once introduced, Pollard asked Symons to discount a bill for £1,000 [£60,417.00] which he said was 'as good as a bank note and would be paid when it was due.' Pollard's terms were: he would take two hogs-heads of wine, give £75 [£5,312.75] for discount and would take the remainder in cash. Symonds refused and offered £750 [£45,312.75] and two hogs-heads of wine, taking the balance for his discount. [239]

The following day Pollard and Watson returned with a man who said he was Mr. Smith and that he came to prove the handwriting of Napoleon. Pollard added that he had pawned the bill for £300 [£18,125.10] with a silversmith on the Strand and he wanted Symonds to go with him to pay to get the bill out of pawn. He refused and saying: 'that was not the way he did business.'

During this conversation, by curious coincidence or not, Mr. Orsi, Louis - Napoleon's personal secretary, happened to call upon Symonds and was told to wait upstairs. Pollard, Watson and Smith immediately left saying they would go and get the bill and return in 30 minutes. Neither Pollard or Smith came back but Watson did within half an hour. However, after seeing Mr. Orsi, Symonds said he no longer intended to discount any bills Pollard gave him and had committed to help to get the bills back. The cat was out of the bag.

Cross examined in court Symonds said that if Louis - Napoleon had applied to him for the money, he would have advanced it without question as he had previously occasionally discounted bills for a friend, but he wanted to make it clear, he was not in the habit of doing so. The difference between what Pollard offered for discounting the bill and what he would have given was about £25 [£1,510.43].

However, after the second visit of Pollard and Watson with Mr. Smith, Symonds claimed he had had information of the peculiar circumstances of the bill from a French gentleman, with whom he was acquainted and had the bills been brought to him on that visit he would have tried to gain possession of them, with the view of assisting Napoleon. He stated quite clearly that he had seen Mr. Orsi several days prior to the first interview with Pollard – and what? Set this up?

Eager to further distance himself, Symonds confirmed he did not know Pollard previously but that someone had pointed him out the previous week in *Crockford's Club* in St James' Street, London.

Pollard, described as a gentleman when he appeared in court, was arrested in Bow Street by the police and taken into custody at Vine Street station where he was charged by Napoleon in person with:

> 'Stealing, on the 15.6.1847, bills of exchange for the repayment and value of £2,000 (£120,834.00), the property of Charles Louis - Napoleon, Bonaparte, Prince of the Kingdom of France.'

Another police officer went to Essex Street later that same night to search the house. There he met Mrs. Pollard and found adverts for money lending services and letters addressed to Charles Pollard at 6 Salisbury Street as well as 10 Essex Street. After the day's proceedings at Marlborough Street Court, Pollard, described as 'a stout, middle aged man, dressed in the first style of fashion,'[240] was then fully committed without bail.

The notorious case was heard on 7.7.1847 at the Old Bailey. The *Morning Post* reports that:

> 'The court was crowded, and among the crowd might be seen several persons known at this court as being connected with a peculiar class of bill discounters.'[241]

These were commission agents, such as Charles described himself on many occasions, men who derived their income solely from commission on sales.

Now it is obvious to us all that Charles Pollard's intentions were to defraud Napoleon, but he was acquitted.

What?[242]

Pollard's counsel argued:

> 'The prisoner was clearly not guilty of stealing the bills of exchange, for the paper and stamps were his, he having bought them with his own money for the lawful purpose of using them, as soon as they acquired a money value by the signature of the Prince. Aye, what is more, the right to make that use of them was actually intended to be conferred upon him, by the Prince, who intended to part with them, and never wishes to see them again.

> 'Nor the £2,000 of course – for if the Prince had received their value, he must have wished to see them again, when at maturity, in order to discharge his debt. The moment the bills acquired any value beyond that of mere paper and stamp, the Prince, by his own voluntary act, made it over to the prisoner.'[243]

The fact that Charles never intended to give the £2,000 to the Prince is irrelevant as he was charged with larceny [theft or stealing] and this he did not do. Had it been fraud, then there would probably have been quite a different outcome. [244] Why

Napoleon didn't later arrange unofficial punishment for Pollard, given his new powers as Prince-President of France, I will also never understand.[245] It is bizarre.

After the trial, I reluctantly had to admire Charles' utter cheek whilst at the same time could not help thinking of the Charles Dickens quote: 'The Law is an Ass.' It is a wonder Dickens never included a parody of this case in one of his very popular novels.

But what of the little matter of the death of Dutch Sam's widow? I still needed closure on that.

Chapter 11 - Pretty Pickles and a Dish of Salmon

Charles Pollard is just as much phenomenon as young Dutch Sam, moving up the social scales from his fishmonger heritage to become a self-made gentleman accepted in exclusive London clubs, at ease in aristocratic circles, with a viable commission agent business. He also moved around a lot that's for sure as by the age of 34 he had gone way beyond the fish markets of Stamford to make a living as:[246]

- A general dealer in Birmingham

- A commission merchant in Bridges Street and Salisbury Street, on the Strand in London

- A sporting gentleman

In a bankruptcy hearing in 1848, Charles said he lived principally by betting on horse races, estimating his profits to be about £200 [£12,083.40] a year for the four years between 1844 and 1848. He further admitted to working with someone else in negotiating a loan for £36,0000 [£2,175,012.0] for a gentleman during which they divided a bonus of 0.5% [£108,750.06]. Knowing how economical he was with the truth and prone to boasting, I am yet to be convinced.

What connected Charles Pollard and Sophia Burford, was the *Old Bell* public house or tavern on Wellington Street, the Strand. She had the license between 1845 and 1849[247] and in March 1848[248] Charles, at his bankruptcy hearing, said he had had it from 1840. However, the list of licensees for the *Old Bell* from 1841 to 1854 shows that Sophia was right:

- 1841-42   J. Lomas

- 1843 -47   Richard Pyne

- 1845-49   Sophia Burford – until her death in 1851

- 1851–53   No entries in the street directories

- 1854   Charles Pollard

The next entry for the *Old Bell Tavern* is in 1857 when J.O.G. Hunter is listed, therefore Charles could only have been the leaseholder and not the tenant or licensee. Maybe he acquired the *Old Bell* leasehold as a result of gambling, or took it in exchange for granting someone a loan who then defaulted? But, back in his own bankruptcy court, the judge decided that, given Charles' past financial dealings, he was not entitled to the protection of the court for his bankruptcy, living as he did by his profligate habits. The case was adjourned to enable a broker to inspect the property in Wellington Street he claimed for his own.

The first point I can find Charles and Sophia together is the 1851 census, which shows he is living with his wife Sophia Pollard, though I cannot find any record of their marriage. Her entry appears [249] with three untruths. First, she is listed as married to Charles, then being 32 years of age when she was 37 and finally as being born in Lincolnshire, not Kent.[250] Like Jane, she was not above lying on official documents. But is she the same woman who was living at Essex Street with Charles and a house keeper called Mrs. Lee in June of 1847? I don't know. I have looked but can find no marriages for Charles that fit other known facts.

If Charles was the leaseholder of the *Old Bell* and Sophia became the tenant then maybe that is how they met, as the *Drury Lane Tavern* was only round the corner from Wellington Street and the Strand. Charles was a sporting, betting and drinking man's man and maybe he knew Young Dutch Sam the boxer? Charles did apply for a drink license that year, but for a house at 16-17 Fish Street Hill, next door to the *Monument Hotel* in London, which was refused with no reason given. His name is however, on London's rates books between 1852-1853 for the *Old Bell Tavern* and for a house on Warwick Street in Westminster for 1853.

Life goes on very quietly for a while at the *Old Bell*, as far as Charles and Sophia are concerned, living in bliss perhaps? Certainly nothing happened to cause any headlines until Sophia dies on 10.7.1851 under suspicious circumstances. The inquest was held on 14.7.1851 and Sophia was buried at St Paul's church, Covent Garden on 17.7.1851. We now come to the central issue. Did Charles murder her or not?

Newspaper reports on the inquest held on 15.7.1851 [251] shed a new light on the saintly, long suffering, hard-working, harmonic society hostess Sophia. Let's see what the *Era* had to say.[252]

> 'An inquiry which excited a most extraordinary degree of interest in the neighbourhood, took place this morning before Mr. Bedford, the Coroner and a respectable jury, on Monday at the York Hotel, Tavistock Street, Covent Garden, on the body of Mrs. Sophia Burford, aged thirty-seven, the landlady of the Old

Bell, Wellington Street, Strand whose death was alleged to have been caused by violence. A solicitor was retained on behalf of her relatives.'

They first called Sambo Sutton, the boxer involved in the fracas at the *Old Drury Inn* in 1843, whose real name is Thomas. He stated that he was in the *Old Bell* three weeks previously and Mrs. Burford had told him:

'She had been very ill and had cut her head open, for she fell, the blood trickling down her neck.'

He'd told her to seek advice and had not seen her alive since. The next witness was Mr. Joshua Anderson, who described himself as an artist and an eminent singer, living at the *White Bear*, Piccadilly.

'On the night of the 18.7.1851 he was sitting in the bar parlour at the Old Bell with Mr. Crotty and Mr. Charles Pollard, (with whom Mrs. Sophia Burford lived), who sent for some pickled salmon for supper. When it was on the table Mrs. Burford came in, and having closed the door, attempted to take hold of the dish, but Mr. Pollard prevented her.

'She then took up a handful of salmon and threw it in Mr. Pollard's face, which he returned, and so they went on until all the salmon was finished. [Laughter.] She then insisted that he and Mr. Crotty should quit the room, but this Mr. Pollard would not allow, as they were friends of his, and he would send for some more salmon. As the waiter was coming in with it, she took it from his hand, threw it into the street, and then placed the empty dish on the table. Mr. Pollard observed he would have some more. When she rose from her seat Sophia said: "Then you shall swallow the dish," and tried to reach it.

'Mr. Pollard put up his own hand to prevent her from getting it and the other he placed open on her face to keep her back and she fell backwards in her chair and the hinder part of her head struck against a piece of wood. She sat for several minutes and the two abused each other very much. She put her handkerchief up to her neck and a little blood trickled down.

'Upon this she went to the bar and said Pollard had struck her. She ordered a cab and said she would go to her brother but Pollard persuaded her to stay. Pollard did not strike her and that was the only injury she received.'

Mr. Crotty was also examined but his evidence was the same. A Mr. Roberts and Mr. Brooks, surgeons, were then questioned at great length. Mr. Roberts had attended Mrs. Burford for four years during which he said she had suffered from great mental excitement which produced inflammation of the brain. After she died on the 10.7.1851, a post mortem was undertaken and her body was found to be a mass of disease, which fully accounted for her death. There was no trace of any blow. Mrs.

Bellamy, her nurse, swore that Mrs. Burford had never stated to her that Pollard had struck her. The coroner said he did not think any other evidence necessary and the jury returned a verdict of 'Died from Natural Causes.'

So, there you have it. All I can say is that Charles Pollard was fast losing his nine lives... But wait, would you like to know what Sophia Burford put in her will? And maybe it would help to say that the will was written and dated 1.7.1851 after the pickled salmon incident on 18.6.1851, and she attached her mark instead of her signature. We know she could read and write for the news reports spoke of her keeping account books so she must have been too ill to sign properly. Maybe the will was dictated by her and written up after the fact, which was quite common in Victorian days. Whether she actually put her mark on it is debatable. However, it was proved in court on 26.7. 1851 as being her last Will and Testament.

Below is the second page of Sophia Burford's will.[253] George White is Sophia's solicitor and his statement is at the top of the page saying Sophia died on 10.7.1851, that her will was written on 1.7.1851 and that the estate does not exceed £2,000 [£160,372.20]. It is counter signed by the Judge, J.G Middleton. Thus, the will was proved to be legal and actionable on 26.7.1851.

Figure 19 Sophia Burford's proven will dated 1851

The rest of this will, as written down by another, is fairly easy to read and you can see who the beneficiaries are. Sophia must not have borne any ill feelings towards Pollard in her last few weeks as the residue, after bequests, is equally divided between the solicitor and Pollard, who is said in the will to live at the *Monument Hotel* on Fish Hill Street, and Pollard is given permission to carry on running the *Old Bell* after her death until such time as her estate is settled.

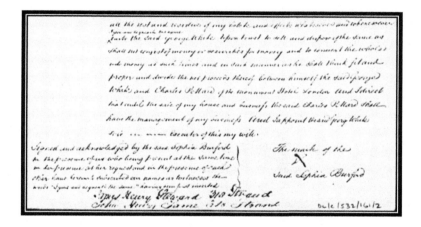

Figure 20 Signatures on Sophia Burford's will 1851

Guilty or not, Charles obviously relishes risk, lives quite happily at the sharp end of life and is unbothered by the legal challenges of Sophia's relations. He gets on with managing the *Old Bell* and the *Monument Hotel*, where he is the proprietor, or so he says.

Just 14 months later, Charles back is in court, this time in the case *Curzon v Pollard*. The woman, Curzon, was formerly his housekeeper and she sought to recover from Charles three months' wages. It appeared that she gave notice on 21.1.1852 to leave in a month's time but to suit Charles she agreed to stay a month longer. If fact she stayed until 25th March and her argument was that she was therefore entitled to a quarter's wages. However, the judge ruled that she was only entitled to two months and four days.[254]

Bankrupt or insolvent, Charles continues to flit from one court case to another, between London and Liverpool, and later all over the country. In 1853, creditors were still pursuing Charles for money and he was formally listed after a long process of examinations in the court in Basinghall Street in London, between 8th and 17th October 1853.[255]

Two years after Sophia died on 25.10.1853, a notice appeared in the *London Morning Advertiser*, placed by the assignees of Charles Pollard, a bankrupt, regarding the *Old Bell* wine vaults on Wellington Street saying they are up for auction to be held in the next month. The advert confirms it is only the lease and goodwill that were for sale, though there were some issues about the tenant's [Sophia's] property and belongings which no doubt Charles would have had to sort out with the executor, Mr. White, but it was still Charles who owed his distiller creditors £2,612 [£209,446.09]. On 16.11.1853[256] his last examination as a bankrupt was held at the Court of Bankruptcy in London chaired by Mr. Commissioner Evans. He was questioned about removing goods from the premises and the case was adjourned for seven weeks.[257]

Meanwhile, Alexander Ford, a wine and spirit merchant of Hemmings Row, London also sued Charles privately in court in 1853 for an unpaid bill of £80 [£6,414.89] for wine to supplied to him and on 3.5.1854, the court in London announced they would finally be declaring dividends on Charles' bankruptcy on 25.5.1854.[258]

At this stage Charles disappears to avoid his creditors[259] and nobody could locate him, though sometime in the next couple of years he does find another strong, independent, wealthy woman, Jane Gallagher, and bursts far more dramatically into Liverpool life than we previously thought. The brief news report about Charles being accused of inciting *Bodily Fear* in Richard Chilcott quoted at the beginning of Chapter 10 is technically correct but it does not give us the glorious detail of the *Northern Times*.[260]

'Some interest was manifest at the Police Court yesterday by certain parties who attended to hear details of a case ...'

Briefly, Mr. Richard Chilcott of Basnett Street, Liverpool complained about Mr. Charles Pollard, described as a powerfully sized gentleman residing some distance from Chester [at Houghton Street as it turns out], though this newspaper did not say so.

On the Friday night in question about 1am, Charles Pollard called at Richard Chilcott's house, created a disturbance, struck him and threatened to take his life. And we have almost a transcript of the case, courtesy of the reporter from the *Northern Times*:

Magistrate:	What sort of house is it?
Prosecutor:	A private house.
Magistrate:	Were the parties acquainted before?

Prosecutor: Yes, and although Mr. Richard Chilcott has been very badly used, he only wishes to call on Charles Pollard to enter into sureties to keep the peace.

Richard Chilcott was then called to give his evidence.

'At 1am Charles Pollard knocked at my door, which I opened myself; there were two men as big as himself along with him; he rushed in and struck me violently, and then ran up to my private apartment, where some friends were assembled, and created a disturbance.'

Prosecutor   Did he threaten to take your life on that occasion?

Richard Chilcott: He did, not only on this but on fifty other occasions.

Prosecutor: Are you afraid of your life of him?

Richard Chilcott: I   am, because I am a cripple in one of my hands and cannot use it.

Prosecutor: And therefore, you cannot protect yourself?

Richard Chilcott: I cannot.

Magistrate: Was he sober at that time?

Richard Chilcott: He was not drunk.

Magistrate: What have you [Charles Pollard] to say to this charge?

Charles Pollard: I admit I went into the house. It is a common gambling house, and a friend of mine lost a great deal of money there.

Prosecutor: I object to this. If it is, let it come before the court in a proper way and not by this scandalously false assertion.

At this point, a Mr. Goodier, an attorney who had previously sent a note from where he sat to Charles Pollard in the dock, jumped up and said in an excited manner. 'I appear for the prisoner.' The prosecuting lawyer objected saying that it was not professional to offer to defend Charles Pollard after he had started his own defence.

Mr. Goodier: Lord Campbell has decided –

Prosecutor: I don't care about Lord Campbell! Sit down sir. [Laughter in court.]

Mr. Goodier: No, I won't, sir. [Renewed laughter.]

The magistrate then intervened to ask Charles Pollard if he had retained this man Goodier to which Charles replied: 'Just now I have, but not before.' And this seemed to settle the legal question of a retainer, and introduced an element of chaotic consternation into the proceedings. Whether this was orchestrated between Charles Pollard and Mr. Goodier or not, they were now firmly in control. Fox Cooper would have been very proud.

Mr. Goodier drew himself up under the witness box where Richard Chilcott stood and the contrast between the two men's appearance caused an involuntary shout of laughter. Richard Chilcott was a powerful and well-made man, Mr. Goodier very small, so small the contrast resembled a tomtit and an eagle, and caused even more laughter but Mr. Goodier definitely had the advantage.

Mr. Goodier: How many glasses did you drink before 1am that night?

Richard Chilcott: None, at all. I never drank a drop the whole week.

Mr. Goodier: What did Charles Pollard say when he came into your house?

Richard Chilcott: He said, you b-------y thief. I will have your life.

Mr. Goodier: He didn't kill you, did he?

Richard Chilcott: No, for you may see I am here. [Laughter.]

Mr. Goodier: Do you allow gambling in your house?

Prosecutor: I object to this – if the learned advocate has anything to say about gambling in the house, let him bring it forward in a proper manner and we will repel it.

Mr. Goodier: Ha!

Prosecutor: Hah! Hah! Go on young gentleman. [Laughter.]

Richard Chilcott said he was not aware that there was anyone in his house that Charles Pollard wanted to see. He had known him for a long time but did not know the two men who were with him, did not even speak to them except when he was introduced to one of them in Wales, who dined where he dined, and Charles introduced them.

Mr. Goodier: How many stone do you weigh?

Richard Chilcott: I should like to know how many stone you weigh [loud laughter] or your client?

Mr. Goodier: You weigh fourteen stone?

Richard Chilcott: That's more than you will ever weigh, I know. [Renewed laughter.] How much does your client weigh?

Mr. Goodier:	One of your hands is crippled?
Richard Chilcott:	Yes, for the last twelve months.
Charles Pollard:	Oh! That's from fighting.

Richard Chilcott: Yes, that's right enough, it's from fighting; but if I had the use of it such blackguards as you would not insult me.

It was only after this piece of theatre that it was agreed between them that Charles Pollard would be bound over for twelve months in his own recognisance to keep the peace by a bond of £50 [£4,009.51].

Who was in the right? We know about Charles' dubious track record but was Richard Chilcott the innocent victim he appeared to be? I found he was the proprietor of a cigar and billiard divan [many of which in Liverpool were fronts for brothels] at various addresses on Houghton Street from 1845, and also at times owned Nos 23, 27, 29, and 12, therefore he was a neighbour of Jane's and would know her well.

In 1848, he was in court on a charge of taking a cherry and imprisoned for eight hours while it was sorted out. I kid you not, this really happened. He had been in St John's market and started to eat cherries from a stall belonging to George Taylor, who told him to desist. Richard refused saying he could 'Go to hell,' and that he would eat what he liked.

The superintendent of the market then intervened but Richard was belligerent, maybe drunk, who knows, and said: 'If I eat another cherry shall I be imprisoned?' The answer was: 'Yes.' Richard defiantly took another cherry and was taken into custody. In court Richard was really indignant:

'I have been an inhabitant of this town for twenty years and I shall proceed against the man for false imprisonment. I have been eight hours in gaol for taking one cherry.'

If he did, it was not reported in the newspapers.[261]

So, by 1856 Charles is firmly established in Liverpool town and has brought his London ways with him. Jane must have been dazzled as for the next few years she and Pollard are not just living as man and wife, they become partners in more than one court case and introduce a fabulous creature to Victorian society.

Chapter 12 - Furnishers and Furniture

Times are a-changing, even though Jane is still legally married to Thomas, she must have felt somewhat exposed in spite of the Trust her mother set up to provide for her children and future grandchildren. So, in 1855, what did she do? Spent lots of money and acquired more and more houses, for her eldest child Ann Elizabeth was now 21 and a single, independent female not yet married or subject to her husband's rule and coverture.

Jane began negotiations to buy the leasehold of a house they rented on Tyrer Street, Liverpool.[262] It was paid for by Jane but actually the title was assigned to Ann Elizabeth, who became the new business front for Jane's money laundering. Thus, she continued the successful strategy of owning nothing on paper, but managing everything. The other children at this time were teenagers and not old enough to be involved, but it was only a matter of time.

It was a large house having eight bedrooms, two parlours and one kitchen and Jane furnished it courtesy of the ever-obliging Messrs Burton and Watson.[263] According to the legal documents, the property was on the west side of Tyrer Street and on the 24.2.1855, only one year after Jane's mother died, Ann Elizabeth entered into an agreement to buy the house and abide by the usual covenants, one of which was that the house would not be used for offensive purposes, not that Jane took any notice of course.[264] An indenture was drawn up assigning the property to her, from its owners on the payment by her of £150 (£8,869.38).

So that there could be no actual doubt about who pulled the strings, a document dated 12.12.1855 stated that while Ann Elizabeth Gallagher was of age to sign in her own right as a single woman, her name was used in the indenture purely as a trustee, the money having been paid by her mother, and that she had no interest in the property. More importantly it added that Anne Elizabeth would assign it back to her mother whenever she asked.

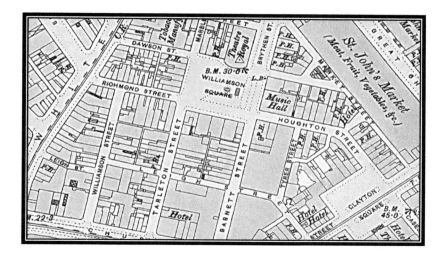

Figure 21 Tyrer St in Liverpool City Centre. OS 25" map 1890

At the same time, and in the same way, around 1856, Jane bought Bird Cottage in Rossett, where Ann Elizabeth later got married, for her children with their Trust money. Here she was free to present as a respectable, well-educated middle-class woman, who dressed lavishly and owned a horse and carriage. It was a very desirable property in the lovely countryside, now a conservation area, as the advert for Rossett Hall in 1856 shows.[265] Note, it was the cottage, not the hall that Jane acquired.

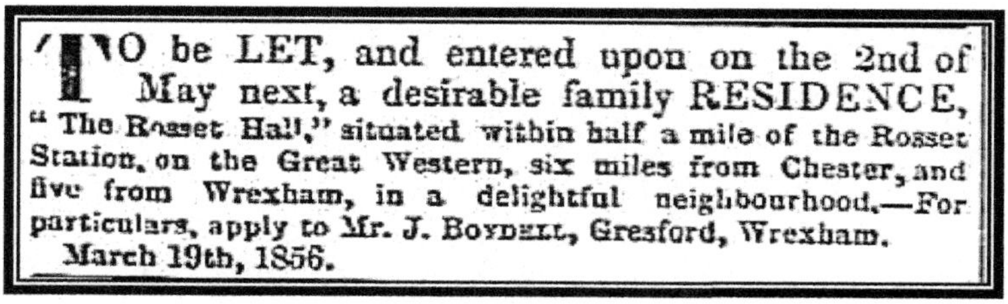

'TO be LET, and entered upon on the 2nd of May next, a desirable family RESIDENCE, " The Rosset Hall," situated within half a mile of the Rosset Station, on the Great Western, six miles from Chester, and five from Wrexham, in a delightful neighbourhood.—For particulars, apply to Mr. J. Boydell, Gresford, Wrexham. March 19th, 1856.

Figure 22 Advert for Rossett Hall, Chester Chronicle, 1856

A station was built in Rossett by Great Western Railways in 1846 and acted as the catalyst for the development and growth of the village. It was then easy to get to from Liverpool, across the River Mersey. The next 20 years or so saw new large detached and semi-detached Victorian villas and mansions being built along Station Road, where the *Golden Lion* pub and Bird Cottage are, and out towards Burton and

Croeshowell where the new wealthy business class lived who employed staff for their properties and gardens from the village.

Jane claims it was her daughter's idea to buy the cottage for herself and her siblings, who had equal shares and proportions in the Trust, Jane adding she was more than pleased to help with it as 'I did not wish my children to know about me...' and her life as a brothel madam in Liverpool. Previous to this the children had been kept well away from the empire, in private education, boarding and finishing schools.

She paid £900 [£72,167.49] for it, but the completion date however, is not clear, and was one of the key bones of contention in the 1860 court case. Jane alleged it was before 1856 and Burton and Watson said in a sworn affidavit it was after. According to Jane:

> 'Mr. Watson had called upon her at No 4 Hotham Street to solicit from her an order to furnish the house at Rossett and that he suggested that he should accompany her to the Rossett, and he did in fact accompany her there; that he had obtained an order from her to furnish the house; of an expensive character even though the house was only a small one, for £615 [£49,314.45].'[266]

Mr. Watson said he met Jane at Chester station in February 1856 and was informed by her she had purchased Bird Cottage for which she was yet to pay. She picked him up in her Brougham carriage and told him:

> 'They should have no fear, she would be able to pay any day before moving into the house.'

At this point, as Jane was recounting the tale to the court hearing in 1860, the Vice Chancellor said: 'Well, but Mr. Watson got a ride in the carriage included.'

Mr. Watson is also clear she distinctly ordered the furniture, which was of excellent quality, upon her own responsibility, not on behalf of her husband.[267] He admitted the furniture Jane ordered was of an expensive character but he maintained his prices were fair and reasonable.

A few days later he actually saw in the possession of Mr. James of 70 Gloucester Street, Liverpool, who had been lawyer for Thomas Gallagher in 1847, a contract for the purchase of Bird Cottage and a receipt from the seller for 10% deposit.

We have already heard how Burton and Watson:

> 'Had been in the habit of furnishing for Mrs. Gallagher a great number of "gay" houses and had given her credit to a very large amount, £372 2s 6½d [£22,003.45].'

And to be fair, Jane had paid back quite a bit,[268] but the outstanding amount was enough to threaten Burton and Watson's financial viability. Later, Jane 'absolutely refused to pay the balance due for the furniture at Bird Cottage.' Why, only she knows and it never really came out, but I suspect it might have had something to do with the fact that Jane had won a case in 1857 which made her think she could get away it.

It happened in January of that year when a carpet manufacturer called George Woods took Jane Gallagher to court to recover the balance of a debt due to him. Jane pleaded coverture saying she did not possess a separate estate apart from her husband. In other words, she used one of the few benefits of coverture which meant that as a married woman she could not legally contract services, nor could she be sued.

There was no case to answer as George Woods should have checked if she had a separate estate from her husband before he supplied her with goods.[269] The fact Jane had another husband, William Mercer, by that time was irrelevant as that marriage, being bigamous, was null and void. Burton and Watson, caught in the same trap of assuming she had a separate estate, were in much deeper.

Another case at that time, which was headlined in local newspapers as: 'Supplying furniture to a house of ill fame,'[270] may also have affected Jane's decision to stop paying. It had nothing to do with Jane, but everything to do with Burton and Watson. John Burton himself was suing a brothel keeper called Ellen Ellis on behalf of the company, to recover £14 14 shillings [£1,138.64]. They had been supplying her goods for the previous 18 months from 1852 to 1854 to the value of £130 [£10,424.19] and she had only paid £116 [£9,301.59] back by instalments up to 1855.

Ellen Ellis' defence was that Burton and Watson knew that the goods were being used to support a brothel, which was illegal, as the law as it stood then said: 'No man should trade on the immorality of another and that other a woman.'[271] Ellen's defence lawyer exclaimed:

'He could not perceive how ignorance of the purpose could be at all supposed to exist. Here was a person furnishing a house, in all respects apparently intended for the purpose stated. Mr. Burton went there week by week and received his 20 shillings [£80.90], 30 shillings [£120.28] or £2 [£160.37] a week and must have been cognisant at least to some extent of the character of the house.'

The judge found for Ellen Ellis.

Burton and Watson had been in business since at least 1848 when John Burton lived at 25 Montague Street and had another address on Low Hill in Liverpool. The 1851 census shows him to be 55, a cabinet maker from Lincolnshire with a wife called Mary who is 51. They have two sons, Howard age 25 who is also a cabinet maker and a young boy, George, age eight. His wife's mother is living with them at 1 Moor Place in Liverpool and a servant.

William Watson, upholsterer, the other half of the company, lived at 2 York Terrace in Everton in 1848. By 1851, William had moved to 44 Paddington in Liverpool, then in 1856 to 40 Radcliffe Street in Everton, and 3 Russell Street by 1859. [Incidentally, Jane lived at 4 Russell Street in 1864.] He was responsible for sales and for collecting the payments from those customers paying by instalments and would have been the one who should have checked Jane's financial status.

With their prime business site at 79 London Road, Liverpool,[272] by 1856 Burton and Watson had a lucrative Furniture, Bedding and Upholstery Warehouse and were quite prosperous, as providers of:

'First class goods of every description of drawing room, dining room, library, hall and bedroom furniture at moderate prices.'[273]

They confidently announced their expansion in the *Liverpool Mercury* in 1857, moving to better premises at 26 London Road, which was formerly the Blind Asylum, the first to be opened in England in 1791.[274] It was designed by John Foster junior (later architect and surveyor to Liverpool Corporation) on the site later occupied by the *Odeon* cinema on London Road in 1942. This is where the Beatles famously played on 8.12.1963 and where in the following year the premier of the Beatles' first film 'A Hard Day's Night' was shown.[275]

But Burton and Watson, the 'Celebrated Cabinet Manufacturers' ambitious plans were halted by a bankruptcy notice of the sale of their stock on 19.8.1858 announced in the *Liverpool Mercury*,[276] ordered by the trustees under a Deed of Assignment and without reserve. They also had to dispose of a house they rented on Finch Street for £24 [£1,924.47] a year.'[277]

What had gone wrong? Scouring the newspapers, I found that Burton and Watson had been extending credit to a number of people, like Ellen Ellis and Jane Gallagher, who had not kept up with their payments. They had taken some to court in an effort to avoid bankruptcy but without much success. Put simply, they had let their desire to make money exceed not only their Victorian scruples but their legal obligation to check the financial status of those they extended credit to and they did not pay attention to the law which forbade them profiting from immoral earnings. The latter led to more than Burton and Watson regretting their liberality towards brothel keepers, who gleefully used it as a defence when taken to court for non-payment of instalments.

Burton and Watson sailed the same boat' as Woods, the carpet manufacturer and after they lost the Ellis case they knew 'they had no remedy,' but via Johnson, the official receiver.

Chapter 13 – Death, Love and Marriage

Figure 23 A Victorian Tailor

By this time, after paying Thomas, her husband, off for at least sixteen years, Jane, must have realised that while being married to Thomas had come in handy when avoiding coverture, he was a big liability. With the bill Caroline Norton had helped draft making its way through parliament as the *Matrimonial Causes Act*, which included a woman's right to form a contract, to keep possession of her own earnings, she began in 1856 to rid herself of the risk that Thomas might still be able to claim her ill-gotten gains.

I often wonder what life for Thomas was like, being on the receiving end of a woman such as Jane. A tailor by trade, poorly paid, working long hours, knowing every shirt he made for the fancy rich folk Jane associated with meant 20,619 stitches. Working an average of 30 stitches per minute at a gauge of 10 stitches per inch, it would take approximately eleven and a half hours to stitch just one shirt. That doesn't take into account time for cutting threads, finishing a thread, or threading needles, nor for cutting out the pieces to be sewn, or make allowances for an individual tailor's speed.[278] All that for little money and awful conditions. The tailors and shoemakers, in the big cities at least, were militant and organised strikes and campaigned vigorously for better wages and conditions, but there were usually too many men desperate to fill the strikers' places for agitation to have much effect.[279]

Little is known about Thomas Gallagher beyond his approximate birth date, his actual marriage and eventual death apart from statements made by Jane, her family and Chalkley in their court cases. If he hadn't married Jane he would have sunk into the past without a trace, just another tailor trying to earn a living in Victorian Liverpool. But he was Jane's husband, legally entitled to command her and any money she earned, and named father of five of her children.

Whilst Jane and her mother paid him off regularly, Jane's mother made doubly sure he and William Mercer could not benefit from her estate by stating in her will that all the property and assets that she left Jane should be:

'Free from the control, debts and engagements of the said Thomas Gallagher or any future husband with whom my said daughter may intermarry...'

Other lawyers in Jane's cases dismissed him too:

'Her husband was a drunk, dissipated man and was maintained by his wife out of the proceeds of the houses.'[280]

But we do know he signed something very important and rather inexplicably, in 1856. In an almost prescient move a trust deed arrangement between Jane and her husband Thomas, described by one present day legal commentator as a 'smart move,[281] catapults Thomas from being side-lined by all into prime position in the 1860 court case, as it is this deed upon which the whole business of Jane's separate estate is debated and ends up becoming a legal precedent.

'There was a deed drawn up in 1856 with respect to my property, and I asked him to sign it and he did so. He read that deed. I don't remember I ever communicated to him anything about myself.' [282]

Jane considered this deed: 'To have effect over everything that I had; all that I had in trust for my children.... I never had any property in my life but I owed Mr. Chalkley a good deal of money and I was obliged to give him that: I was obliged to do what I was told. I came to an arrangement with Mr. Chalkley that all my property should be assigned for any advances that he or the Tradesman's Loan Society afterwards made to me. I did not tell Mr. Chalkley at that time that my property consisted of anything.'[283]

The deed was both Chalkley's idea and negotiated by him. When later questioned in court in 1860, he confirmed:

'He proposed that he should have an assignment of the household property in order to secure the loans granted and these which might be granted.[284] The assignment was made, with the consent of Thomas: to whom when the deed was read over, signed it, well knowing that he was signing away his interest and not only in that which he was then possessed [by right of being her husband], but which he might in the future possess by right of his wife.'

The deed actually said: that Jane and Thomas lived separately and that Thomas would execute the assignment below and enter into the covenants it contained:

'To William S. Chalkley all the money, securities, household chattels, stock in trade, and personal estate which she then possessed or had in trust for her and all sums of money which were then due in respect of the said trade or business, and all interest due or thenceforth to grow due upon any of the same premises should be available to Jane for her sole and separate use or that she could appoint a trustee to manage it for her.'

The 1856 deed then allowed Jane via Chalkley the power to invest the money or goods or sell them without her husband's permission and a covenant set out that it should be lawful for Jane to in future live separate from him:

'Without any interference from him and to carry on any trade or business she might think fit and that all real and personal estate to which she might become entitled should be held and disposed of by her solely as she might think fit.'

Chalkley was to indemnify and protect Thomas from all debts then incurred or thereafter by Jane while she was living apart from Thomas.

- To be clear, Jane was a married woman and legally everything she had belonged to Thomas who signed to say he passed all his rights as her husband to possess and benefit from her assets and the Trust to Chalkley

- In return Chalkley protected Thomas against any future claims made against Jane, who, in law, was still his wife and his responsibility

- And Chalkley held all Jane's assets as security against her existing loans, debts and instalments due to creditors and any future loans she might apply for

But why did Chalkley stand as surety to protect Thomas from being prosecuted for his wife's debts when he did not know Thomas Gallagher at all?

Chalkley: I saw her solicitude to keep her children right and I endeavoured to assist her.

Lawyer: Then it was from purely moral principles?

Chalkey: Yes, on moral principles. I did not know that the money was to pay for furniture for "Gay" houses.

Which is exactly what you would expect from a righteous, pious and well-respected Wesleyan Methodist Minister, but his words would very soon come back and bite the ruthless money man he truly was in the mouth.

What is unusual is the fact that the business Jane ran and referred to in this deed was that of a 'wine and spirit merchant.' It is the one and only use of this euphemism for brothels, which when read out in court in 1860 produced gales of laughter and smirks.

When cross examined as to whether Thomas really knew what he was doing and had been informed exactly what difference it would make to his expectations, Chalkley replied:

'Mr. Stevenson, my solicitor, communicated my suggestions about the assignment to the husband, and Mr. Stevenson told me he told Gallagher that his wife was largely indebted to the Tradesman's Loan Society; he said he had explained all. At that time Gallagher must have known he was signing away every penny that he had or had any right to. I don't know whether Mr. Stevenson has made an affidavit in this case...'[285]

Not everyone believed this. In a notable statement to the court the lawyer for Burton and Watson in 1860 disputed that:

'Mrs. Gallagher's husband would have assented to such an agreement if he had known at the time that the property was all to be swept away for loans and that there were then debts more than the value of the furniture. Was it to be believed that a man who was said to be so greedy and so grasping as to strip the clothes off his children's backs would so readily give away all that property and pay the debts incurred with Mr. Chalkley on account of the Liverpool Tradesman's Loan Society? It was not worth commenting further upon such an improbable case.'

The judge intervened saying, 'It has only been alleged that the husband was grasping for drink,' to which the prosecuting lawyer snapped back:

'Well, this would have supplied him with the most excellent drink; he might have swum in what he could have purchased with this money. It was contrary to all common sense!'

And he proceeded to urge that the deed of assignment could be held to include the property at the Rossett, which was subsequently acquired; and it was meant only to apply to property in existence at the time the assignment was made.

Now we know why Jane was so keen to muddy the waters about when exactly Bird Cottage at the Rossetts was purchased. Whether it was before or after this deed of assignment is crucial to her hanging on to it and her considerably expensive furniture.

But you cannot help but wonder why Thomas signed this deed in 1856. He could have continued to live easily without working and drink as much as he liked with regular payments from Jane and before that her mother. Maybe Thomas was scared about his wife's debts and saw this as a way of getting rid of his responsibility in law for them, a chance to officially separate from her, thus avoiding the damage to his 'reputation' from being openly cuckolded by her with Mercer and Pollard.

Or he might not have been in a state to understand just what he was giving up.

A year later in 1857, Thomas is living in 3 Court, Bakehouse Lane, Liverpool, from where, age 48, he was admitted as number 3998 to the West Derby workhouse in Liverpool by G. Whyte, his location described as 'Lunatic,' [probably the name of the ward] on 11.8.1857 and discharged from the Asylum Ward on 16.9.1857 just over six weeks later.[286]

Being in the workhouse in Victorian times was the last resort of the poor, those having no work or no home, in other words being a vagrant, situations which have never been looked on sympathetically in any of the previous ages:

- By an act of Edward III (1312-1377) a labourer leaving his service was to be branded with a letter 'F' (in token of falsity)

- Henry VI (1421-1471) decreed: Every loitering and idle wanderer was to be branded with the letter V and be judged as a slave for two years... to be fed on bread and water and refused meat and caused to work at such labour how vile so ever it be, as he shall be put to beating, chaining or otherwise. If he ran away within the two years, he was to be branded in the cheek with the letter S and be adjudged a slave for life, and if he absconded a second time, he was to suffer death as a felon

- By another act in the same reign, it was decreed that the loitering and idle wanderer should have a V marked on his breast with a hot iron then sent to the place where he was born there to be compelled to labour in chains or otherwise on the highways or at common work

- In the reign of Henry VII, an act was passed in which sheriffs, mayors and constables should make due search and cause to be taken, all such vagabonds, idle and suspected persons living suspiciously and them to set into the stocks, there to remain three days and three nights with no other sustenance but bread and water and after that to be set at large and commanded to leave the town

- The end of Henry VIII's reign (1587) shows that every vagabond was to be whipped through the town where he was arrested: at a cart's tail, naked til his body be bloody of such whipping [287]

- Fortune tellers and mendicant monks, proctors and pardoners were to be put into the pillory and have an ear cut off and ruffelers or sturdy vagabonds were to have the upper part of the gristle of the right ear cut off and be set to labour. If they reoffended, they were liable to be arrested and suffer death as felons

- Queen Anne (1665-1714) defined who these rogues, vagabonds and sturdy beggars were and the terms included: all persons able in body who run away and leave their wives and children to the parish and not having means otherwise to maintain themselves

This last category would certainly have included Thomas, if Jane's testimony is to be believed. Therefore, measures to deal with 'the idle poor' were not new in Victorian times and workhouses began around 1620, but what had changed by the time Thomas was an inmate in 1857 was the introduction of the *Poor Law Amendment Act* in 1834. Based on the recommendation of a royal commission, relief for the poor was still to be funded by rate payers, but for the first time it was to be administered by unions, groupings of parishes, presided over by a locally elected Board of Guardians. Each union was responsible for providing a central workhouse for its member parishes. For the able-bodied poor, like Thomas, it was the workhouse or nothing and sometimes, nothing was preferable.

The Brownlow Hill workhouse in Liverpool was enlarged in 1842-1843. It grew to become one of the largest workhouses in the country, housing 3-5,000 people,[288] and it set on fire in 1862, long after Thomas had been moved. The church was destroyed and one of the children and two nurses were burnt to death. Life was cruel in the workhouse, particularly for those who did not have their full wits about them.

This workhouse was claimed to be the largest brothel in England, due to lax supervision. The *Satirist* published statements made at a meeting by Mr. Rushton, the Liverpool stipendiary magistrate who alleged that:

'In the classification ward, known profligates were associating freely with ordinary decent people and there was indiscriminate prostitution going on. An access route had been created over the wall between the male and female wards by knocking the glass bottles off from the top and women wearing only shifts were going over the top to the men's ward at night.'

As a result, the governor was afraid to go to some parts of the workhouse after dark.

In December 1857, some months after Thomas left the workhouse, an article appeared in *Liverpool Mercury* called 'Our Pauper Population.'[289] It describes Liverpool workhouse, which it says has over 1,000 sick beds on its site making it one of the largest hospitals in the whole kingdom. Sickness, it claimed, is one of the biggest causes of poverty, but it claims that nine tenths of those who enter do simply for the medical treatment and leave very soon after as they are not without means. There were also around 440 births a year and very few of the women were married:

> 'Perhaps one in ten of the children born are illegitimate; the workhouse affords a secret retreat; and there is no doubt that this department of the workhouse, as respects admissions, is open to considerable abuse.'

One of the staff said:

> 'We have some very superior women indeed who come. He recognised a patient, a young girl, who would have soon come into £2,000 a year [£118,258.40].

> 'In another instance there was discharged the daughter of a highly respectable gentleman from Manchester. Her afflicted father, we believe, was prepared to pay £100 [£8,020.61] a year for her maintenance in any establishment where she would have the opportunity to reform, but the girl refused and returned to her vicious course of life.

> 'Another very respectable lady, the sister of a professional gentleman of this town, and gifted with every accomplishment and grace to make her the delight of the social circle in which she moved, in an unfortunate hour, began to indulge privately in drink; the vice increasing soon resulted in public shame. Intoxication paved the way for the other vice and the result was her ultimate admittance into this department of the workhouse.'

These people could well afford to pay for their hospitalisation and should not have received free and discrete services from the workhouse hospital, but it was a scandal nobody was prepared to do anything about.

It was reported in the same article that about twenty deaths a week occurred in the workhouse. In October 1857, one month after Thomas left the lunatic ward of the workhouse, another man, John O'Hare, who was similarly very much addicted to drink, was also confined there suffering from delirium tremens. In November he committed suicide and the coroner's verdict was: temporary insanity.[290]

As Thomas was designated 'a lunatic,' the workhouse wanted nothing to do with him and he was admitted to Rainhill Hospital, St Helens, Lancashire on the same day as he was discharged from the workhouse, 16.9.1857, his feet hardly touching the ground. [291] The hospital was designed by Harvey Lonsdale Elmes (1814-1847), who was one of England's most talented architects. He is best known as the architect for St George's Hall in Liverpool, which has been described as the finest neoclassical building in Europe. It was built when the quality of the environment was considered to be important and access to spacious grounds and a rural setting, with fresh air and natural light was thought to be therapeutic.

The Rainhill and Prestwich asylums were set up in Liverpool and Manchester in 1851. Both institutions were originally built to accommodate between 400 and 500 patients but the pressure of admissions was both immediate and immense. By 1856, the year before Thomas admitted, and five years after Rainhill opened, its superintendent Dr John Cleaton reported overcrowding and commented that recovery rates were lower and death rates higher amongst patients 'shattered in bodily health and condition.'[292]

Thomas' file [293] shows he is a Protestant, married but said to have deserted his wife. He is declared to have been insane for three months, which would have been from when he was admitted into the workhouse, and that he has impaired senses. Today, questions would have been asked about his mental state when he signed the 1856 deed, less than a year before.

Then we are given a physical description, the first real picture of Thomas. He has a light complexion with grey hair and eyes, and a bilious temperament. Technically, this can mean three things: of or relating to bile or suffering from liver dysfunction (and especially excessive secretion of bile), or indicative of a peevish ill-natured disposition. [294]

But then the report says Thomas is happy and contented. He has an ordinary physique, with no bruises and moderate nutrition. We even have his heart rate, a pulse of 80. According to today's NHS, most adults have a resting heart rate of 60 to 100 beats per minute so Thomas was within the normal range. They diagnosed him as having dementia and general paralysis on his admittance form.

Here is a transcription of the doctor's notes:

'He states he has come to the wards as a visitor, sees all things done well, has plenty of tobacco, fruits and is remaining for some time as he likes it very much, seems merry, laughs a good deal.'

Later he adds: 'This man is incoherent and passes sleepless nights,' and on November 23rd [1857] another condition is added to his record: 'Dementia with epilepsy, has had no fit since admission. Labours under the belief that he only came here for a few days but says he feels very comfortable and does not care about leaving. Has deluded notions on other matters. Eats, sleeps and works well.'

It was commonly thought at the time:

'That the causes of epilepsy are very numerous...a fact no doubt to be accounted for by the difficulty which poor people have in their own wretched homes, of giving sufficient attendance to keep out of danger those suffering from this distressing malady, liable as they are at any moment to fall down in a fit.'[295]

Current research has also shown that excessive alcohol consumption is a potential problem for any patient with epilepsy, and particularly teenagers. Seizures can occur within 48 hours of excessive and, often, binge drinking.[296] Alcohol may also increase seizure frequency through disturbed sleep. Thomas' lunacy therefore could have been a combination of alcohol and other side effects of the treatments available at that time for epilepsy.

Before 1912, the only effective agent was potassium bromide, and a major problem was keeping a balance between suppressing fits and the frequent side effects. A German report showed that 10 grains (0.66 g) of potassium bromide taken three times a day caused reversible impotence. Sir Samuel Wilks (1824–1911) also observed that: [297]

'It is a great question whether this remedy which has so powerful an influence in checking the fits is really curative; and whether indeed it has a permanent effect on the brain to render it less unstable.'

Gowers, in Chapter XIII of his book called 'Epilepsy and Other Chronic Convulsive Diseases' says that:

'Potassium bromide has almost superseded other drugs in the treatment for the disease ... the influence of bromide is in the majority of cases, transient not permanent...and has a direct effect on the nerve elements, diminishing for instance, reflex action in the spinal cord, and... on the nerve cells of the brain.'

Regardless, bromides, although initially slow to gain acceptance, were used from the 1870s until well into the 20th century[298] when Hauptmann (1881–1948) in 1912 discovered the anti-epileptic properties of phenobarbitone by accident when studying the anxiolytic effects of various drugs. [299]

By January 16th [1858] Thomas' record shows he still has had no fits since admission and is mentally unchanged, which makes you wonder if he was an epileptic or an alcoholic at all. By 29.3.1858 the record shows:

'This case has turned out to be one of general paralysis and he is becoming gradually feebler since admission with increasing amounts of mental torpor. Has been brought to the infirmary, is incapable of employment.'

The same year, Jane is forty-two and has been living with her exciting and flamboyant lover, Charles Pollard for some time in Houghton Street, who whilst she might have admired him for wading into Richard Chilcott's house fists flying on behalf of a friend, cannot have been much amused to find his court case and her address syndicated across the country. It was seen by one of his creditors, Alexander Ford in London who quickly travelled by train to Liverpool, armed with an execution order against Charles which entitled him to recover the money he was owed, £80 [£4,730.34] by seizing the goods in what he thought was Charles' house.

And that was a big, big mistake! You can imagine Jane's outrage as bailiffs arrived to seize her precious furniture, exotic, very expensive and, above all, nothing to do with Charles Pollard's debts. The neighbours must have enjoyed the eruption that day and I am sure those who tried to remove it were given very short shrift and probably a lot more than fleas in their ears.

Once this little 'misunderstanding' was sorted out the fact remained that Charles Pollard had absconded three years before to avoid his debts. He was seized and taken to Lancaster Castle prison.[300] Jane must have been very much in love for she set her lawyers to work, arranged a meeting with Alexander Ford and agreed a settlement with him.

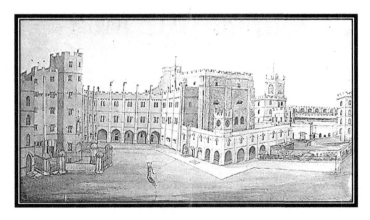

Figure 24 An interior view of Lancaster Castle in 1824, J. Weetman.

Meanwhile Charles was enjoying the hospitality of Lancaster Castle which was, in the mid-1800s, the largest debtor's prison outside London. Unlike the Marshalsea, Fleet and Horsemonger gaols in London and many others, archives show that conditions in Lancaster Castle were rather good, so much so it was nicknamed *Hansbrow's Hotel*, after the governor which is an indication that incarceration, at least for Charles, was tolerable, maybe even truly enjoyable. There are tales of events being held like fairs, mock elections and concerts. Etchings produced by a man who was himself imprisoned for debt, show well-appointed rooms, complete with servants, fires and what seems to be a plentiful supply of food and drink. There were rewards for good behaviour, as well as social clubs with well-thought-out constitutions, and even a savings club at one time.

That is not to say there were no rules, or that debtors were not expected to behave while in prison: the dungeons of the castle were used from time to time to punish those who transgressed, and the debtors had to exist alongside crown prisoners and criminal lunatics. There are stories of the whole prison falling silent when the great brass execution bell was tolled for some unfortunate soul being despatched at *Hanging Corner*, and the arrival of the Assize Court each spring and autumn must have had an effect on the atmosphere in the castle as well. But this was tempered by the freedom most debtors enjoyed: the chance to spend time with their families, and in some cases even work to pay off debts, though I doubt that would have attracted Charles.[301]

Having neatly avoided all previous attempts to incarcerate him, despite his daring and audacious financial dealings, Charles must have felt it really bad luck to be imprisoned in a fortress for such a small amount having got away scot free with cheating the current Prince-President of France. No doubt he regaled his fellow prisoners with his exploits and became a popular gentleman inmate, but it would not have done his street cred any good when it became known that a mere woman was negotiating with Alexander Ford to pay his debts.

Jane met with Ford and offered him £15 in cash [£886.94] and bills accepted by her for the remainder of the debt £65 [£3,843.40] and he agreed, probably thinking this was better than the nothing he had had from Charles so far. The fact Jane could put her hands so easily on ready money when she was keeping her younger children in expensive finishing schools, buying houses and paying lawyers to defend her in court, shows just how much she must have been making from the brothels.

Charles was duly set free after Jane produced the cash and the bills and I assume they resumed their exciting life together at Houghton Street. But when Alexander Ford tried to cash one of the bills, he found it was worthless, as Jane was still a married but separated woman and under the laws of coverture, she could not make a contract to pay any money and could not be sued, which Jane knew full well. Alexander Ford was rightly furious and took her to court in March 1858 while Thomas was sinking further into torpor in Rainhill Hospital in St. Helens, only ten miles away.

Jane produced witnesses to show she was married to Thomas Gallagher, despite the fact that the 1856 deed granted her the right to live separately from him. Witnesses like Mr. James, the lawyer, who vouched for Jane's intention to pay for the furniture at Bird Cottage, represented her in 1860 court case as well and lived at 70 Gloucester Street, Liverpool, who said he had known Jane for some time, that she was a married woman and she lived with Charles in a coffee house 'or something of that sort...' in Houghton Street, Liverpool. He obviously hadn't been a witness when Jane bigamously married William Mercer in 1850.

Then Mary Bellion, Jane's sister, was called to prove that she had lived with her husband for many years and had nine children with him. Actually, as far as we know, there were only five children ever baptised or entered under the Civil Registration of Births as his and two more which weren't. However, Jane could have miscarried or had children who died very quickly and were never registered.

The judge, having heard the facts, was not a happy man, and said so, bluntly.

> 'The defendant was a married woman. Nobody could pretend to say for a moment that it was not very wrong that being a married woman the defendant should give a bill for the purpose of getting a man out of gaol and then turn round upon the person to whom she had given the bill and say "It is true I gave you the bill as if I were a single woman but I am a married woman and my husband is still alive." Nobody could defend such conduct; but if it was true that she was a married woman, it was a defence according to law and the jury were bound to give a verdict for the defendant.'[302]

As Alexander Ford could not contend the evidence, he had to submit. Jane won her case and he lost £65 [£3,843.40]. This was coverture Jane Gallagher style, twisted beyond bent to be sure, used in action by a woman in love who knew the law.

Thomas's record meanwhile, by August 1858, shows:

> 'His mind is almost completely and irrecoverably gone, frequently passes his evacuations involuntarily, is destructive to his clothing.'

On the 19th October 1858 Thomas died of general paralysis. His death is officially registered on the 20th at St Helens, the nearest registered office to Rainhill Hospital. Today we know that general paralysis is the outcome of untreated syphilis that finally attacks the brain and renders its victims utterly helpless and is referred to as tertiary or neurosyphilis.[303]

Thomas' condition was mirrored in asylums across Britain in the 1800s, with hundreds of people receiving the diagnosis of general paralysis of the insane. The majority of these were men in their 30s and 40s, all exhibiting one or more of the disease's tell-tale signs: grandiose delusions, a staggering gait, disturbed reflexes, asymmetrical pupils, tremulous voice and muscular weakness. Their prognosis was bleak, most dying within months, weeks, or sometimes days of admission.

Among the causes listed were excessive mental labour, heavy physical work, emotional strain, alcohol and sexual excess. Others suggested it could be brought about by a blow to the head, or as a consequence of railway accidents that injured the spine. It would be 'wine and women' however, that came to be seen as the most relevant factors, based on the demographic characteristics of the disease.[304]

The predominance of men among the sufferers was notable, with the military particularly susceptible, yet many experts noticed that the clergy tended to escape its ravages. On those occasions when the disease appeared in women, they were said to be prostitutes or innocent victims infected by their philandering husbands. It was also frequently characterised as 'a disease of civilisation' in the sense that with progress came a risk of 'de-evolution,' a regression back to man's primal nature.

Present at death was Joseph Bellhouse, who could not write as it is his mark, not his signature which appears on Thomas' death certificate. The official date of burial is 23.10.1858 and took place at Toxteth Park Cemetery, Liverpool, register number 4442. His details were given as: tailor, the address as Rainford Asylum in St Helens, he had a single grave reference number 907 and his burial was overseen by the Reverend Mr. Clementson. [305]

Figure 25 Thomas' Death Certificate 20.10.1858

His actual grave is in section L, which has two parts. One is in the consecrated area of public graves and plot 907 is a single public grave with no headstone. In the other general section L, plot 907 is a private grave with a headstone with names, Hughes, Morris and Green. It is therefore likely that Thomas is buried in the public grave without a headstone and there is no record of any of the family arranging or attending the funeral, even though Jane was a mere ten miles away.

Who was Thomas, really? Hospital observations portray a decent simple man, who liked a drink, but who maybe had epilepsy at a time when there was no definitive treatment and had caught a venereal disease, maybe from one of his wife's employees. They also say he was a man who:

'Sees all things done well...... seems merry, laughs a good deal.'

Jane's sister took him into her house where she had young children and named a son after him but according to Jane, he was 'a very grasping, sordid man.'

Six months later, his eldest daughter Ann Elizabeth married William Brindley on 26.4.1859, at Christ Church, Rossett in Denbigshire where Bird Cottage was. It is not known who gave her away, maybe William Mercer her stepfather? Thomas, her real father is down as a draper and not noted as deceased and Selina, her sister, is a witness. [306]

As a newly married woman, control of Ann Elizabeth's property would have automatically passed over to her husband, but Jane had dealt with that. Nine months previously another indenture dated 1.7.1858, had been drawn up whereby Ann Elizabeth passed trusteeship, on Jane's instructions, of the Tyrer Street property to William Seabrook Chalkley himself, not the Liverpool Tradesman's Loan Society, as this was Chalkley conducting business privately, off the books. He, on paper, paid £150 for the house, the exact amount Jane had in 1856.

By 1858 therefore, Chalkley was sole trustee of the Trust left by Jane Oakes for the benefit of her legitimate grandchildren. Jane must have had some sort of hold over him to allow him such control for I refuse to believe she, of all people, just did as she was told. Jane was nobody's victim and now she was a widow, she was free to contract, sue and be sued.

Chapter 14 - Controlling Social Evil

There were many desperate attempts by Victorians throughout the period to find solutions to this sticky problem as social evil by the late 1850s had spiralled into an epidemic. A whole variety of measures were applied, as different as prosecution was to reform, as inevitable as demonisation and marginalisation, as ignorant as shaming and as predictable as cashing in. But whatever was done had little impact and respectable gentlemen were not slow to find scapegoats, as this letter to the editor in the *Liverpool Mercury* in 1858[307] shows:

'The shameful, disgraceful and bold effrontery of harlotry in our streets lies at the door of the magistrates themselves. For do not they licence houses in Lime Street that are noted for being vile dens of prostitutes? Has not the stipendiary magistrate issued an order that protects, under certain stipulations, from the annoyance of police information, some of the filthiest sinks of iniquity of that street which are not licensed?

'And when informations are laid against these resorts of prostitutes, did not one of the officials appear more like an advocate of the proprietors of these infamous establishments than an assistant to those who had in view the protection of public morals?'

Another contributor, similarly enraged, fairly spittled the page with invective:

'Who have allowed this evil to grow to its present fearful dimensions by their encouragement of that apathy to public morals and public decency which seldom fails to interpret the law's technicalities favourably to the fattening of those wretches who feed on the debasement of woman.

'The chief obstacle of the removal of obtrusive harlotry lies in the Magistracy of the GOOD OLD TOWN.'[308]

Well, that's pretty clear. But how true was it that the magistracy was responsible for failing to control the rapid expansion in social evil?

From 1837, as Britain's second city, only behind London in size and commerce, social upheaval in Liverpool was marked. Between 1845 and 1849 it bore the impact of the potato famine in Ireland and received the vast numbers of Irish people who migrated to England, some on the way to America, though the majority stayed in Liverpool. This led to tensions in the local community and violence between Catholics and Protestants. By 1841, there were almost 50,000 Irish people in Liverpool and in the next ten years this figure had risen to 80,000. All the organisations which existed to improve social welfare felt the strain which resulted in slum housing, over-crowding, high mortality rates and epidemics of smallpox, cholera and typhus. [309]

Figure 26 Lime Street, Liverpool 1890

The population of Liverpool continued to grow rapidly to 649,613 in 1881,[310] and it was a most notorious blackspot in country. Between 1834, when Jane Gallagher had her first child and her last one in 1848, 49 out of every hundred children died before the age of nine. In the Vauxhall wards this went up to 64.[311] By 1867, 48,782 children aged between five and thirteen were not attending school and 25,000 of them lived on the streets with no natural protectors. In 1868, Liverpool had more than double the prostitutes and more than twice the number of brothels than Manchester.

In the first fifty years of the 1800s the town was known as a hotbed of squalor, crime and violence. As Liverpool grew in size as England's largest port, so did the numbers and prosperity of cotton brokers, shipping companies and insurance agencies, railway, police and fire services, lawyers, merchants, wine and spirit providers, clothing and furnishing businesses. These entrepreneurial, wealthy, middle-class men were the prime customers for all luxury goods and silken services, including those offered by Jane Gallagher's empire. The market for common prostitution was even larger.

In this fast - paced environment, women like Jane Gallagher, mere daughter of a carter, achieved what would have been impossible for most in her situation. As a mother of seven children, left to raise them by herself, with no welfare benefits, she, by exploiting the male demand for social evil, ensured every one of them survived into adulthood, had a private education and the means to live a better life. Between 1839 - 1860 little stopped her as the prevention or control of social evil by social reformers, magistrates and the police force, was, at best, a muddle and at worst chaotic. The authorities blamed each other as they fought to contain the highly visible seamier side of the business, common prostitution, in the streets of Liverpool every day. The results, judging by even more outraged letters to the editor, were not impressive.

'Gentlemen, Lime Street is a high change for prostitutes and that public mart for prostitution, virtually under the protection of the bench of magistrates, abound in and about it.

'Carloads of girls of a tender age, in the company of painted, diabolical brothel keepers and procuresses, arriving at those marts, which are now adding to their other conveniences one which can scarcely be alluded to, and which renders them liable to be proceeded against as common brothels.

'I humbly entreat those who have the power to put the existing laws in force, and brand with public infamy those loathsome wretches who cause the evil.'[312]

The head constable himself admitted, writing in his defence in 1889, that back then they did not make much difference until at least 1870 because of the police rule book which said brothels are [only] proceeded against under the following circumstances where:

- Very young girls are kept

- The police are satisfied that a robbery has taken place, whether there has been a conviction or not

- The houses are of notoriously bad character, such as to become a public nuisance

- Brothels are opened in a respectable street or leading thoroughfare

- They are complained of by two or more of the inhabitants of the street, who will substantiate the complaint in court

Even when this last method was utilised, procedures were complicated. The neighbours had to raise a memorial or a petition of respectable gentlemen, submit it to a constable then to the magistrate, 'praying for the removal of the brothel' and with the support of an inspector of police appear and present the case to the magistrates for judgement, the neighbours bearing all costs. Poorer areas were unable to afford a petition and had no remedy at all.

This did not stop the *Social Purity* branch in Liverpool, which survived thanks to rich benefactors, seeking to abolish prostitution and other sexual activities that were considered immoral, according to their Christian morality. They were very active from the late 1860s to about 1910, along with other aggressively named organisations such as: [313]

- Society for the Suppression of Vice and Immorality
- Association for the Prevention of Immorality and Vice
- Society for the Suppression of Vicious Practices and Resorts
- Society for Reclaiming Unfortunate Females

This last organisation proclaimed:

'An aggression into the region of Satan [is] in order to rescue perishing souls from his dominion.'

The law courts were their battle ground and passionate speakers exhorted respectable Victorian gentlemen and their good ladies to support them. In the quest for suppression and repression, with prostitutes their satanic enemy, they took on high profile cases and blamed the magistracy when they were unsuccessful. But the police and magistrates could only enforce existing laws, none of which made it illegal to run a brothel until 1885 when greater powers were given. The police until then had to rely on the *Town Police Clause Act of 1847*[314] which made it an offence for common prostitutes to assemble at any 'place of public resort' such as a coffee shop, cause a nuisance or solicit in the streets.

Over the 19th century, Liverpool civic leaders recognised that drunkenness along with poverty were social problems which exacerbated crime, immorality and other forms of social evil and turned to the licensing system of public and other houses in an effort to reduce it. They initially focused on what went on in pubs, especially around the Sailors' Home near the docks and the city centre streets near Williamson Square where Jane Gallagher had, over 25 years, nine of her many Liverpool houses.

The head constable of the time instructed his police to enforce the offence of 'harbouring prostitutes' by watching pubs, charging their owners and arresting prostitutes who remained longer than a few minutes, which was deemed to be sufficient time for them to have refreshment but not long enough for them to assemble or solicit on the premises.[315] This led to a display of notices saying: 'Ladies are requested not to stay longer than ten minutes for refreshments,' and there was much confusion between the police, magistrates and licensees about just how long a lady could remain for refreshment purposes. Some said twenty minutes, others ten minutes, some an hour and others protested that there was no law at all which prevented prostitutes having a drink. Owners also challenged magistrates over how they were to know if a well-dressed lady was a prostitute or not?

Looking at published cases in Liverpool newspapers the inconsistencies around prosecutions are there for all to see. Regardless, the proprietors of places of amusement, pubs, dancing salons, coffee houses and other amenities found themselves up in court, many on multiple charges of 'harbouring prostitutes.'

Figure 27 The Hop on Lime Street, mid-1800s

The Hop, which was a large dancing salon underneath the Teutonic Hall on Lime Street was one of the *Society for the Suppression of Vicious Resorts'* targets in 1860. This building was originally designed by Edward Tuton and opened in the late 1840s as the Teutonic Hall. However, after only ten years the building was converted and split into two. On the ground floor was *Allsopp's New Crystal Palace Waxworks* whilst upstairs was a new version of the Teutonic Hall which showed dioramas. The building was again converted in 1859 and the top hall renamed the *Theatre Variete*.[316] But why were they targeted?

'There you will find between 80 to 100 abandoned women a night, their expensive, gaudy and tasteless array of finery serves but to display their wanton depravity and wretched mode of life. The male portion of the audience consisted of young men, clerks, merchant's sons, shop keeper's assistants, a few smartly dressed, rakish-looking sailors and several well-seasoned, vicious-looking middle aged women and old men. When not engaged in dancing, they spent time in walking about smoking cigars, professional harlots leaning on their arms, or, seated on the crimson cushions, they dallied with vice.'[317]

The Hop was charged with harbouring prostitutes in 1858, and again in 1860 with mixed success. *Bendino's Cigar Divan* was prosecuted six times for the same offence: four times the owner was fined the maximum amount £5 [£295.65] and twice the case was dismissed.

Another place of amusement was the *Zoological Gardens*.

'Its glory is brightest after nightfall, when surrounding walks and gardens are shaded... it bursts into splendour... the noisy band in the orchestra strikes up a lively dance-tune, scores of couples enter the charmed and mystic circle, and hundreds of nimble feet keep time to the merry music... If any disappear beneath the surface, they are not missed...'

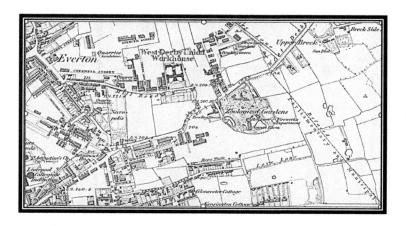

Figure 28 Ordnance Survey 6" map of the Zoological Gardens 1851

'Beauty abounds in shadow like the ghosts of lovely faces that have died; in a wreck, mingled with all that is loathful; in transit, pairing off with care, or with misery, or with shamelessness; and in bloom, just entering into the deceptive shadow of the maze which this place represents.

'Young lads, apprentices, mechanics, some not old enough to be either, poverty stricken, pay the cost of the silks and satins and Tuscan shawls of their partners; they pay for the expensive liquor served in the refreshment rooms and snug little cabins beneath the orchestra; they pay, at least they find the money and somebody pays. If wan faces and lack lustre eyes and hollow laughter and stooping shoulders be credible witnesses, they do pay, too, whoever else may bleed for the cash.'[318]

The *Zoological Gardens* are near to Pembroke Place and Boundary Place, slightly out of town, the proprietor was Thomas Atkins and they opened in 1833.[319] The owners cooperated with the police in 1857 and cleared it of obvious prostitutes by paying for a man to stand and vet women at the gate and a policeman was provided to point out those who were known to police. The societies for the 'repression or suppression of social evil' however, were not convinced the problem had been solved:

'Still, it is a respectable institution. It is sanctioned by the magistrates and guarded by the police. Places of healthful amusement are denounced from the pulpits; but this passes un-condemned. If two women of doubtful character attend the Amphitheatre, there is a stir amongst the justices and noises in the journals; but if a hundred light women dance upon this [platform], the magistrates grant licences and stamp the place respectable.'

Figure 29 Liverpool Zoological Gardens

The *Porcupine* in 1863 reported:

'Hundreds of decent girls go... but in no one instance can they possibly escape a degree of pollution... There is hardly anything in the amusing, certainly nothing of the proper sense, there is much that is positively dangerous. The "Zoological Pleasure Gardens" is perhaps not a name for them, for what pleasure there is in them is certainly part animal in its tendency.' [320]

The gardens closed in 1863. Nevertheless, the owners of other places of amusement fought back, saying there was no disorder on their premises and prostitutes had the right to seek refreshment and at the same time highlighted again and again the inconsistent judgements between judges for the same type of cases.

In three cases brought by one society, evidence was strong and police expelled the prostitutes and gave warnings. However, the owners continued to admit prostitutes and magistrates renewed their drink licences while awarding fines which owners could well afford given the amount of business they did. Procuresses of the higher class of women continued to display their latest acquisitions with impunity, as they knew the more well-dressed, the less likely they were to be turned away. Therefore, not much of a dint was made in social evil and the police, magistrates and the law were easy targets for indignant, respectable Victorians frustrated with the lack of progress in tackling the nuisance.

The police then tried other tactics, focusing on the brothel keepers but the madams simply paid the fine, closed the house and moved somewhere else. Letters to the editor continued.[321]

'Gentlemen, having shown in my last letter that contrary to the report put forth by the Watch Committee, there had been an increase in the number of brothels in Liverpool, it is now my intention to show that they are also more barefaced and impudent.

'Hitherto the keepers of these places have generally located themselves in back or retired streets, avoiding public situations. Now we have one of these houses, or, as I should say, shops, in one of the most public streets and greatest thoroughfares in the town, and within a short walk of your own office: it is also one of the worst and most dangerous nature, professing to be a respectable fruit shop, but, in reality, a most infamous brothel, in which are kept six young prostitutes and when young boys go in to purchase fruit or cigars (for the keeper deals in both), they are invited into a back room and are frequently tempted to toss for bottles of wine with the keeper of this den of infamy. I know of more than one young man that has been nearly ruined for life for visiting this abode of vice.'

When loud voices in the press maintained that the police were not doing enough, Nott Bower, the head constable, in a report of December 1889 pointed out that notable cities such as Manchester and Glasgow had special local powers for dealing with brothels and for granting search warrants, which the Liverpool police did not have:

> 'Brothels and prostitution have existed in all ages of the world and the evils in connection therewith may be checked and tolerated, but cannot be suppressed by human effort and the attempt to effect suppression by men of the highest character and with the best possible intentions, has frequently served only to aggravate the evils they desired to subdue.'

He ended with expressing the opinion, using the words of Major Greig [a previous head constable in 1875] that:

> 'We must look to moral means as the only efficient one by which any considerable improvement can be effected.'

Coincidentally, this comment is almost word for word what Josephine Butler said well before him.

Jane and other madams who met the demands of the middle and higher-class men were relatively free to continue with their trade, as instructions issued to those responsible for enforcing the *Contagious Diseases Acts* of the 1860s allowed their employees to continue their trade unchallenged. There were also privileges such as Mrs. Davies enjoyed when she was arrested for keeping an improper house in 1871 and was allowed to be tried by a jury out of town as hers was a 'genteel establishment.' However, this did not stop her absconding. You will be pleased to hear the privilege of her class was withdrawn on her arrest and she was still prosecuted.[322]

The majority of charges brought against brothel keepers were therefore for the more visible 'lower order' establishments. Any madams arrested were usually brought in for other offences, such as being drunk and disorderly, fighting, failing to pay their bills or using young children. Note the age of consent was 13 until 1885. As the head constable pointed out to the public:

> 'In order to deal with prostitution in the streets, the police had, by law to be satisfied that soliciting gives annoyance to any inhabitant or passer-by or that while the prostitute is on the streets, she was behaving in a riotous or indecent manner.
>
> 'The mere fact of a prostitute walking in the public streets, though there may be no moral doubts as to her purpose in doing so, is not an offence against the law and any constable interfering with her would be liable to be convicted of assault,

should he apprehend her and would be outside the protection of the law should he himself be assaulted in endeavouring to do so.'

Increases in arrests of common prostitutes also put tremendous strain on the prisons which had to contain those in their care. By 1869, the annual report for Liverpool's Borough Prison[323] shows that for the first time there were more females than men in the cells. The greatest number of females locked up at one time was 586 and there were only 407 cells, so women had to share. This jeopardised the 'Silent System' which was in operation, the policy that kept people confined in single cells alone. Of these women, of those who were Catholics, mostly Irish, 45% were prostitutes, half of whom could not read or write. [324]

The prison chaplain, James Nugent, pointed out in 1877 that the 5,000 committals of women that year represented only 700 women, for most of the women were prolific offenders who almost served life sentences – very short lives too – in instalments. Such as:

- Mary Cook, first arrested in April 1840, age 18-19 for vagrancy. By 1842, age 20, she had been arrested once for stealing money and three times for common prostitution. In 1843, she had two convictions for common prostitution, in 1844 three more with another for being drunk. Four times in all that year she was in prison and she was only 22 by that time

- Margaret Vernon had her first conviction for common prostitution in 1839 when she was 17. During the next fifteen months, she added another four and one for stealing

- Ann Shield's first conviction at age 19 in 1839 for common prostitution became 10 in total by 1845. In-between times she was convicted of being drunk three times and stealing twice

As Nugent reported:

'Without bread, without shelter and above all, destitute of friends, it requires a strong resolution and a high standard of moral principle to resist the temptations that surround them.' [325]

By 1893, nothing has changed, as the *Liverpool Review*[326] showed. Their reporter spoke to an officer who by repute was known to be smart, intellectual and conscientious. He said:

'That more attention was being given to the lower class of immoral women while the swell women are gradually getting back to their old haunts... [they] can always square the police and they leave many loop holes for the better class while they dragoon the lower classes. It is rare that a better class woman is arraigned in the dock, yet hundreds of such women can be found on the streets. They solicit openly, frequent the same haunts night after night and are unmolested by the police. At the same time poorer women are hounded to suicide, the gaol, the workhouse or one of the many refuge homes – only to emerge again and carry on the old life at the first opportunity.'[327]

They asked other policemen 'If there was any diminution in the number of common prostitutes in the streets as result? The answer was an emphatic 'No.'

'But,' said one of the officers, 'they are more difficult to catch.'

'Indeed, how's that?'

'Oh, sir, they have so many more runs and go to ever so many different places.'

'But can't you follow them?'

'Yes, but while we are following one, or a couple, for maybe an hour or so, half a dozen others take their place. They watch us as sharply as we watch them.'

'And what is your honest opinion of the crusade against this class of women?'

'That it has given us a lot of work to little or no purpose, sir.'

What about the efforts of the church? Ministers of various religions were excellent at setting down their views on social evil and its attendant, the evils of drink, and proposing solutions. Cardinal Manning condemned parents who sent their children to pubs to fetch beer and spirits, Thomas Burke[328] set out in detail the social and drink problems of Liverpool in 1910 and Father James Nugent founded the *League of the Cross*, a temperance organisation.[329]

The Reverend John Jones called attention to the dire consequences of excessive alcohol in his book 'Slain in Liverpool in 1866 by Drink,'[330] the Reverend R.C. Armstrong in 1890 produced the 'Deadly Shame of Liverpool, an appeal to Municipal Voters, which highlighted the 'gay equipages rolling down Bold Street with the brilliant shop fronts and the gaunt faces of the poor and abandoned.'[331] The Reverend Abraham Hume,[332] saw very clearly the distinction between the rich and poor and condemned immorality which he divided into two: intemperance and the social evil. His resulting report and 1858 map showed: 'The Condition of Liverpool: Religious and Social.'

Using his experience as the incumbent of the parish of Vauxhall, Hume divided the town into to 36 districts and shaded each area according to its police statistics for crime, health data and the clergy's knowledge about life in those areas. It resulted in useful hard evidence that social evil springs from a wide range of roots causes. But what was more interesting was that after urging all societies, charities, benevolent gentleman and public agencies to work closer together to tackle the many causes to, 'maximise the good and minimise the evil, he observed:

- Social evil is a subject of still greater solemnity yet it is one which from its very character the clergy seldom notice...'

- Crime is beyond clerical influence...'

- We [the clergy] are links between the various ranks and are fitted to be the almoners of the rich and benevolent...' [where it is far less uncomfortable]

- 'It is self-evident that what is given for the poor should actually reach the poor...'.

In 1857, another gentleman was quite outspoken about what he considered were the Christian duties of clergymen and how far he felt they fell short.

'It is the duty of the clergy to endeavour to reclaim those poor miserable fallen ones – outcasts, adjudged unworthy of the eternal world, as some people look upon them.... Some clergymen, I apprehend, look upon it not altogether a healthy kind of mental occupation to devote themselves too exclusively, or even at all, to the study of individual fallen man or woman, and to help them, where needs be, out of their downward course of life.

'I can well understand and account for this. The fact is, the work is rather too disagreeable – not altogether fitting their prominent situation in life – something too low and dreadfully commonplace to exercise their talents in. Yes, this is the clerical world all over. Alas, methinks we have fallen on an evil age. If these phenomena be not humbug at the bottom, so much the worse for us. Talk about Christian charity, indeed! Where do we find it nowadays? Not very often, I fear.'[333]

The rather aptly named Rev J.J. Skewes from the Holy Trinity Church, Liverpool is a case in point and he began this particular controversy by writing a letter to Detective Hale on 4.12.1883 entitled 'The Plague Spots of Liverpool,' about which he claimed a series of articles were to appear in the *Liverpool Albion*. Skewes wrote to:

'The best detective that I can think of, for detailed information about the numbers of brothels, the types of people who frequent them, details of the more respectable class of men who have been seen going to those places and whether they were sober or otherwise.'

He assured the detective that he was empowered by the proprietors of the *Albion* to ask for this information and would provide him with fair renumeration for his services. He ended the letter by saying:

'I may add that nothing is asked that need in any way affect your position, and all that you may communicate will be so arranged that there will be no need for anyone to know your name in the matter but yourself and myself.'

He then asked the detective to call upon him to discuss his offer, but he, quite rightly, passed the letter on to his head constable whose response was sent to a newspaper, not the Rev Skewes. It said:

'Sir, - Detective Hale has handed to me the (as I must designate it) most improper letter you have thought fit to address to him. I am surprised you should consider it becoming to try and induce a subordinate officer, by the offer of "renumeration" and "utmost confidence" to do that which is contrary to the regulations of the police force. I am at the same time pleased to find that Detective Hale has a better idea of what his only proper course is when such an offer is made to him.

'I forward this letter, together with the one you sent to Detective Hale, to the press, that the public may know the sort of attempt which has been made to obtain information in violation of those regulations which a police officer is bound, in common honesty, to comply with. – I am your obedient servant.' J.W. Nott Bower, Head Constable.

But that was nowhere near the end of the matter. What began on 4.12.1883 continued in sometimes twice daily correspondence between the clergyman and the head constable, all appearing in the *Liverpool Mercury*.

The Rev Skewes maintained in his next letter he had done nothing wrong as Detective Hale had three years previously freely given him information and nothing was said about it being against the police code of conduct at that time. Nott Bower claimed that Skewes' account and that of Detectives Hale's differed substantially and that his detective said he had refused to give the Rev Skewes the information he wanted three years previously.

These two determined opponents went at it hammer and tongue, which while selling many newspapers, did nothing for the reputations of either the police or the clergy. Nor did it make any impression on the spread of prostitution. I expect the madams were laughing their socks off as these increasingly hostile letters were printed in the *Liverpool Mercury*.

Skewes retaliated with an attack on all those influential people in the city who took rents from brothels and made money from supplying them, offering to name and shame them. He claimed personal credit for getting 61 houses closed three years before as a result of the information the police had given him.

Nott Bower, from his command post, produced letters from Major Grieg, the previous head constable showing that the Rev Skewes had been refused his information requests and was only given data that had been made public. No police officer had supplied him with any information at all.

After this exchange, the Rev Skewes said in what became the last letter published by the *Liverpool Mercury*, that he would give out the names and details of every man on the police force who had given him information in the past. That stopped the correspondence dead in its tracks on 15.12.1883 after a full ten days of washing dirty linen in public.

Other worthies too had meanwhile added their views, most of them urging the Rev Skewes to keep out of police business and tend to the needy in his congregation. Some made very personal attacks on him and congratulated the police on exposing his attempt at bribery. Others were more far more cutting.

'Gentlemen, the publication of the letter appropriately headed "The Plague Spots of Liverpool" must have affected the Rev Henry Skewes somewhat after the manner of a severe cold douche....[334]

'If the Reverend gentleman is the person of the same name who gave up a considerable portion of his apparently not very valuable time to certain of Mr. Irving Bishop's [a spiritualist performer[335]] pin finding, banknote telling experiments (of course in the cause of science) and also figured on the platform of that persecuted saint "The Escaped Nun" [a series of reports in mid 1800s about women escaping Roman Catholic convents,[336]] it seems to me that he might perhaps find other means of filling up his spare time, which appears to hang heavily on his hands.

'If the Reverend gentleman is so anxious to obtain information on matters which to most people's minds hardly come within a clergyman's province, why not have interviewed another reverend gentleman lately before the public – who apparently takes great interest in researches of the same kind?'

Now that, whilst true, was rather beneath the belt. He was referring to a case which had come up only the month before and had scandalised Liverpool. Ernest James Augustus Fitzroy, vicar of St Jude's in Liverpool in 1883[337] was charged with drunkenness and of immorality with Emma Smith alias Mary Dynock, who is referred to as a mere strumpet. He had been ordained late in life after previously being a newspaper owner who lost all his money. He was found guilty by a clerical court of being drunk and suspended from office for three years, but not found guilty of immorality based on the evidence of a woman of the town.[338]

As if that was not enough to shake confidence in the clergy, these following cases of deliberate clerical action clinched it as some clergymen were simply unable to resist pursuing immorality instead of immortality:

- A Church of England vicar, M.A Gathercote in 1838, claimed nunneries in Scorton and Darlington were being used by Roman Catholic vicars for fornication and child murder[339]

- The Reverend Anthony Cosslett was found unconscious in a brothel in Liverpool's notorious Albion Street in 1854, and so salacious was his pocket book that the coroner refused to allow extracts to be published. He was removed quickly so officially he died in the workhouse[340]

- John Fenton, whose father was the incumbent of St Mary's church in Wavertree denied being the father of Sarah Davies' child in 1856, despite overwhelming evidence. The good reverend when called upon to give evidence to support his son said, 'I refuse to open my mouth until my expenses are paid. I demand £8 16 shillings [£705.64]'[341]

- The Reverend Canon Wilberforce said he heard the Bishop of Manchester remark in 1880 that he felt convinced that: 'He would sooner keep a brothel than a spirit vault.' What is more, Canon Wilberforce endorsed the sentiment, for he 'believed that of the two evils, the public house was the worse'

Meanwhile social evil businesses boomed, social reformers continued to expostulate in the newspapers as they had since the 1830s and the *Liverpool Society for Reclaiming Unfortunate Females* were doing their sums:

'According to the latest calculation, a sum not less than £3,000 weekly (£181,251.00) is expended in the support of prostitution in this town alone... whilst probably not more than £20 [£1,208.34] a week is contributed for the rescue of its wretched victims!

'Should this be so? What! £3,000 weekly to spread crime, disease and even death; and only £20 to arrest their fearful programs! For the destruction of bodies and souls of a numerous class of wretched beings, £3,000; and for their present and eternal welfare, only one hundred and fiftieth part of that amount!

'Men of Israel, help! And wipe away this terrible reproach, by liberally supporting a society whose objective is, by the blessing of God, to make a determined stand against prostitution so awfully prevalent, and to seek and save its perishing victims.'

Other more moral alternatives for women were available but sadly restricted by the extent of charitable donations. Some lucky prostitutes were offered the chance to volunteer to enter such places, however, efforts to rehabilitate the penitents were doomed not just by a lack of funding, but basic conditions, stringent rules and much compulsory religious instruction. Some of the women eventually gained domestic work in the homes of respectable Liverpool ladies, others fell afoul of the rules and were expelled, and many returned to prostitution through lack of choice and imminent starvation, as the *Liverpool Society for Reclaiming Unfortunate Females* reported:

> 'During the year of 1839, the society has had under its care 200 females, 67 of them left or were dismissed for improper conduct before they had been with the society for a month, 45 before they had been with the society for three months, and 16 before they had been with the society for six months; making a total 128 who have voluntarily left the society or forfeited its protection by inattention to its rules.

> 'Of the remaining number, two have died in possession of Christian consolation, 18 have been returned to their friends, and 32 have been placed in situations to provide honestly for themselves, making a total of 52 who have been saved from crime and wretchedness by means of the society's exertions, during its first years. The remaining 20 are still in the society's lodgings.

> 'The committee are happy to report that several even of those who have left the society or been dismissed from its lodgings, have not returned to their wicked course but are employing honest means to obtain a livelihood.'

Not impressive statistics at all but maybe understandable as some prostitutes played the system. By the end of the 19th century, when reformatories were more widely available as an alternative to prison, prostitutes would express penitence and plead with a magistrate to be sent to a refuge instead, as it was a softer option. After a good wash, clean clothes and a hearty meal, they would sign themselves out and go back to prostitution.[342]

But still the figures for social evil rose and more letters were written to the editors, some offering novel solutions.

Cut off their hair!

> 'It may not be out of place to notice that one of the regulations of the Female Penitentiary which, in the opinion of many, is an excellent institution. It is, we believe, one of the rules that a female on entering must submit to have her hair cropped short. Now, if there be anything more than another upon which a

woman prides herself, it is her hair. To deprive her of that, stamps, as it were, a brand upon her.'

Bring back the pillory!

'If ancient acts are to be resorted to in order to suppress prostitution, could not ancient punishments be equally as well adapted? I mean the pillory. If the keepers of all disreputable houses, when convicted at the sessions, were sentenced, in addition to their imprisonment, to stand at the end of London Road, in Lime Street, in a pillory, for two hours each Saturday, it would greatly diminish the evil complained of.'

And the national call from the Society for the Protection of Young Women:

'Seduction ought to be made a penal offence. All over 15 who voluntarily choose this life to be registered...'

Yet other less punitive and more sustainable means of reducing social evil had been eloquently advocated since the beginning of the 19th century.[343]

'We forget that the object is not to produce outward compliance with the law, but to raise up the inward feeling, which secures the outward compliance. You may drag men into church by main force and prosecute them for buying a pot of beer – and cut them off from the enjoyment of a leg of mutton – and you may do all this, till you make the common people hate Sunday, and the clergy and religion and everything which relates to such subjects.

'There are many crimes, indeed, where persuasion cannot be waited for and where the untaught feelings of all men go along with the violence of the law. A robber and a murderer must be knocked on the head on the head; but we have no great opinion on the possibility of indicting honest men into piety or calling in the Quarter Sessions to the aid of religion. You may produce outward conformity by these means but you are so far from producing the inward feeling that you incur a great risk of giving birth to a totally the opposite sentiment.'

But by 1861, in Liverpool, there were still 1,829 brothels and 3,190 prostitutes, known to police, with many more unknown and in spite of the law and the societies against this, that and the other, some churches and reformers working together, current tactics were ineffective. Vested interests were far too powerful.

What was next then? The following letter had a suggestion: Zoning, the herding of brothels into 'Designated 'Areas' away from the respectable streets, raises its head.

now witnessed in our highways. Instead of driving these unfortunate women into the streets, the authorities should try and keep them out of them. In consequence of the late crusade against places of resort for these creatures, our suburbs are infested with them, and they are constantly to be seen in parts of the town where heretofore we were free from such society.—Yours, &c., January 29, 1869.   A LOVER OF DECENCY.

Figure 30 'A Lover of Decency.' Letter to the Liverpool Mercury 1869

Part Three - Triumphs, Trials and Tribulations

Chapter 15 - The Talking Fish

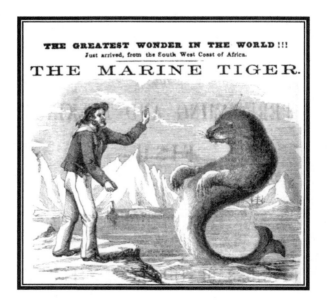

Figure 31 The Marine Tiger – Congleton Mercury 5.3.1859

What is this creature? Described in 1858 as being the only one of its species ever publicly exhibited, 12 feet in length, weighing six hundred weight, it had been caught by Senor Cavana and his intrepid crew, 'who encountered much personal danger in the River Senegal off the coast of Africa,' on 5.5.1854. According to the *Congleton Mercury*:

'It had two fore flappers, shoulder blades, bones, arms and wrist bones, which were of great strength, and it could extend either the right or the left one, elevating both in an appealing attitude. Its brain cavity was large and the brain highly convoluted.'[344]

We recognise this creature as a seal but the Victorians first called it a monster specimen and then very soon it became the *Talking Fish*, as according to the popular press, it did.[345]

'We do not know the method by which it has been trained, but it is very docile, and to some extent intelligent, and appears readily to comprehend what is said to it by its keeper, obeying commands like a dog.

'If it be told to skip and dance, or turn over, it at once obeys the command, and repeats the evolution as often as directed. Although possessing a mouth full of formidable teeth, it will kiss its keeper with an appearance of affection, and when desired, pronounce the words "Mama" and "Papa" with considerable clearness of articulation.

'The animal subsists upon fish and consumes about 30lb weight of whiting per day. One peculiar habit it displays is that after it has swallowed its first food in the morning, which it does not appear to masticate, it disgorges once, and often twice or thrice, and then despatches again with an evident relish. It is about seven feet long, is amphibious and possesses the power of standing erect at pleasure.'

That's just a seal just being a seal, but the Victorians loved curiosities, like those promoted in shows organised by Phineas Taylor Barnum who founded the *Barnum and Bailey Circus*. He had a variety troupe called *Barnum's Grand Scientific and Musical Theatre*, and soon after, by purchasing *Scudder's American Museum* which he renamed after himself, he promoted such wonders as the *Fiji Mermaid and General Tom Thumb*.[346]

Barnum profited from the masses who were hungry for spectacle. Human curiosities, or *lusus naturae*, freaks of nature, were among the most popular travelling entertainments of the late eighteenth and early nineteenth centuries and by the 1830s:

'The display of grotesquely embodied human forms was for some populists, carnivalesque entertainment and for others an offence to genteel sensibilities.'[347]

The time was indeed ripe for the appearance of a *Talking Fish* during the nineteenth century for the exotic animal trade was gaining support as the British Empire extended. Capturing unusual creatures represented, for those wealthy enough to pay and see them, the conquest of distant and exciting lands and showing these across the country was a demonstration of imperial might. As a result, Victorians developed an appetite for these creatures and many were drawn to the dockside when they heard that interesting cargo was to be unloaded.[348]

But the papers were wrong when they said in 1859 that the *Talking Fish* was the first to be seen in England for one had come ashore off the Sussex coast in December 1749, nearly a hundred years earlier.[349] Jane Gallagher had also seen one in Liverpool in 1856, paying tuppence for the privilege, so when another such specimen was unloaded at the port in December 1858, she used Charles Pollard as her agent and bought it. Charles paid Senor Cavana, a man who obviously appreciated how lucrative the previous one had been, £300 [£17,738.76] for which Jane also received the services of the *Talking Fish's* keeper, John Beshemel as part of the bargain.

The brothel business was obviously doing well and after winning her recent court cases, Jane must have been very happy to have a more legitimate distraction and offer England a chance to queue and pay to see her curious creature. It also gave Charles something to do and kept him out of trouble as he became the road manager for the *Talking Fish*. She lost no time making the fish pay and had exhibited it in Liverpool by the beginning of February 1859 where it became not only the talk of the town but the entire kingdom as news reports about this wonder of the world appeared in all major cities as well as London.

Many journalists went along to see it ready to be scathing about the claims made of the *Talking Fish* as they suspected it was Barnum type bunkum. One cynic said the seal was starved:

> 'The highest manifestation of the seal's intelligence could be observed whenever the keeper's movements take the direction of the cupboard where the fish which it feeds upon is kept.'

The *Liverpool Herald* said quite plainly:

> They were intent on 'exposing what we considered to be a wretched imposition... One of the highest functions of the British Journalist could not, we are persuaded, be placed in abler or more uncompromising hands [than theirs].'

However, the Earl of Sefton was an early visitor in Liverpool along with numerous members of parliament and came out on the side of credulity and so the *Talking Fish* triumphed over the doubters. From week to week the gentility of the visitors increased and the enthusiasm of previously cynical newspapers like the *Liverpool Herald* was evident:

'The sea lion really speaks and it all but reasons,' they proclaimed and 'Quite a sensation had been created in the town of Liverpool.'

So great was popular demand that Jane and Charles had to extend its stay for a further week.[350]

In due course, the show moved on to Manchester where the *Talking Fish* was interviewed by the satirical Mr. Punch who had taken the express train from London as soon as he heard about it. The result was an amusing conversation printed in the magazine and a telling cartoon:

Figure 32 Punch cartoon of the Talking Fish June 1859

By the 5th May, having triumphed in the provinces, the *Talking Fish* arrived in London for its first public levee at 191 Piccadilly, London, which was referred to as the home of Jane and Charles.[351] The *Morning Post* was invited to the preview and concluded that:[352]

'The exhibition is not what many of our readers have no doubt been led to believe, a pure Barnum invention, but it is really and truly a highly educated seal. It is of a dark slate colour on the back, the under parts being a dirty white. It inspires a large quantity of air, and closes its nostrils for a time.

165

'We have spoken of the performance of the fish, but not of its powers in that department of education. We do not mean to tell our readers that it is yet so far advanced in the knowledge of the English language as to hold a conversation on the state of the weather or the prospects of the present European crisis; but it has two deep sounds which it repeats as directed and which bear a striking resemblance to "Mama" and "Papa" – its desire to meet with "Mama" appearing to predominate over every other feeling.'

THE PERFORMING AND TALKING FISH.— Daily at 191, Piccadilly, opposite the Albany. Admission One Shilling. A FASHIONABLE MORNING EXHIBITION every Saturday, from 11 a.m. to 6 p.m., 2s. 6d. ; Children, 1s. After Six the usual prices.

Figure 33 'The Talking and Performing Fish' The Field 7.5.1859

'The *Talking Fish* is shown in a large tank of water during the day, we are assured the water is always drawn off at night and the fish, being supplied with blankets, rolls herself into them to take her night's rest with evident satisfaction.

The *London Morning Herald*[353] also attended the preview:

'Although we were somewhat prepared to witness something wonderful, from reading in the Liverpool and Manchester papers, we deemed those accounts to be huge exaggerations of the fact... [due to their] taste for Munchausen-like-marvels. That has not been the case so we have no hesitation in declaring: everything that has been said upon the subject, we believe to be strictly true... We were not five minutes in the room when we were impressed with the conviction that this is one of the greatest natural curiosities that has ever come under the notice of the public.

'In offering this curious animal to public view, the proprietor wishes to inform visitors that they are not to confound it with the marine wolf as it is quite a different species... The creature has with difficulty been tamed and, in a sense, domesticated. Such is its present docility and obedience that it has left its locality at night in search of its keeper and has laid down to sleep by his side.'

Maybe its docility has also something to do with its increased weight, up from 6 cwt to 9 cwt since Jane bought it six months before.

The *Daily Telegraph* really worked themselves up to be disappointed with the *Talking Fish*, speculating that it was a relation of Barnum favourites: *the Rumtifoozle, the Poasokus, the Oozly Bird and the Pig-faced Lady*, but even they had to reluctantly admit that:[354]

'This strange animal really does all that his proprietors advertise it of being capable of doing. From the general ferocity of the fish's appearance, we should on no account like to pass a night alone with her in a double-bedded room with the door locked!'

The *Standard* reports the proprietor of the *Talking Fish*, who would have officially been Charles: [355]

'Invited a number of gentlemen who were present at this exhibition to a dinner at the *Gordon Hotel*, for the purpose, as it were, of inaugurating the public opening of his most interesting exhibition. Many expected that the great seal itself would be one of the guests but the presence of the creature was excused on the grounds of the fatigue it had suffered on account of its extraordinary labours of the day.

'The obliging and urbane attention of the proprietor deserves also to be especially mentioned; and we can assure our readers that should they pay a visit to this most wonderful of Nature's freaks, they will come away both astonished and highly gratified.' [356]

Praise indeed from cynical journalists. Jane must have been preening herself as she became more socially acceptable to those of highest rank in London. It was definitely a lucrative investment for over 150 people attended the private preview alone and many more at the first public viewing in London. When you add the countless multitudes, who would have seen the *Talking Fish* in the provinces on its tours, then possibly this fish in its limited life made Jane more money in personal performances than did her prostitutes.

At the same time, in June 1859, Charles was in the insolvent debtor's court before Mr. Commissioner Murphy on the instigation of two more debtors, Harrop and Watling. The principal inquiry was whether Charles had any interest in the *Talking Fish*. Charles said it belonged to Jane Gallagher who he lived with at 191 Piccadilly in London and in Liverpool and proof was submitted.

Someone in the court suggested that the '*Talking Fish*' should be produced and the learned Commissioner said 'It had better be brought under the "seal" of the court.' [Laughter.] It appeared that Charles had been called 'Charles Stuart' by some of his friends, but he denied it. Commissioner Murphy said 'Perhaps it was on account of his resemblance to "the Pretender."' Inspite of the laughter, the court refused to allow an adjournment to produce evidence as to the name Stuart, and Charles would have been discharged if not for an informality. [357]

However, managing the *Talking Fish* entourage on the road, or the train, proved to be another challenge Charles struggled with. In July 1859, the support team reached the Midlands where it was presenting the fish at Warwick Agricultural Show, and the *Morning Chronicle* [358] reports the showground was:

'Full to overflowing, the weather brilliant. Concerts, balls, comic songs, Howes and Cushing, Wombwell and the *Talking Fish*, drama, balloons and pyrotechnic, all make demands on the votaries of pleasure.'

The paper assures everyone that all week these amusements would be largely patronised. It should have been a wonderful occasion for the *Talking Fish*. But...

Charles said he had arranged and paid for adverts to be placed in the local newspapers and arrived on the Saturday night, 9th July with the fish in the care of two men, but the booth for its reception was not ready. He was obliged to hire a stable to house it until the afternoon of the Tuesday, when it would be finished and it could be exhibited as intended at nine in the morning, but a day later than planned. Mr. Wilson, who was paying Charles for a week's exhibition time for the *Talking Fish*, refused to give him the balance owing as they had lost income. They parted on bad terms, with Charles, no stranger to the courts, vowing to sue.

The *Talking Fish* did not fare much better at a Summer Fair a week later on the 16th July. The *Leeds Times* described what happened: [359]

'Hundreds of people attracted by an elaborate puff, rushed to see the *Talking Fish*, which was said to be the mama uttering phoca [a genus of the earless seal] so immensely popular in London, Manchester and Liverpool, but they were deceived.

'The fish was a seal, a common seal, and not like its popular namesake, an uncommon fish. All that it did in the shape of performance was to roll over and over in its tank at the word of command, and kiss or shake fins with its keeper. These little tricks it did to perfection but it had no talk in it. The showman attempted to make out that the unfortunate fish did speak occasionally, to a select circle, but his audience heard him with disbelief, and were rather severe in their remarks.

'If this fish, however, was not an extraordinary one, the fry around were, for our reporter lost his handkerchief within a couple of minutes of entering the show.'

Perhaps the final word on the *Talking Fish*'s performance in 1859 should be from *Saunders Newsletter* published in Dublin in August 1859. [360]

'I have been to see the *Talking Fish*, but in this, as in many instances, many of our own animals speak a single word each more distinctly than the *Talking Fish*, which is only a seal, speaks its one word. Our duck says "quack," our sheep "mah", and our calf "bah" much more plainly that the seal says "pah-pah."'

The tour laboured on: Brighton, Ramsgate and Dover in September, until on 24th October a headline announced a court case Charles had found time to take out against Mr. Wilson of the Warwick Agricultural Show to get his money back:[361]

THE *TALKING FISH* AGAINST THE JUMPING BABIES - *Pollard v Wilson*

What?

Charles was suing Mr. Wilson, who turns out to be the patentee of the 'Elastic Baby Jumpers' of No 144, High Holborn, London to recover £41 [£2,424.30], the balance of £100 [£5,912.92] for one week's hire of the said fish. Charles presented his version in court with confidence and humour then sat back, no doubt pleased with his performance. However, Mr. Wilson, himself a showman and his solicitor, were no pushover and responded to Charles' theatrics with:

'If the fish could speak it would tell a different story.' [Laughter in court.]

'Have you brought the fish here today?' [Laughter.]

'Or perhaps if you had it might have told a different tale? [More laughter.]

They went on to claim that as a result of Charles' failure to fulfil his part of the agreement, the speculation made a loss. The booth was ready at the proper time but the fish was not, being without water and fish to eat and Charles had not got the adverts out in time nor had he adapted them to the Warwick country - style event, for they read like a London advert.

The judge of Westminster County Court ruled for Mr. Wilson saying that Charles had not performed his contract and could not, therefore, recover his costs.[362] The *Elastic Baby Jumpers* had the last laugh, winning easily over the *Talking Fish*.

But who were the *Elastic Baby Jumpers?* I could not let this go unexplored and I discovered an illustrated article in the May - June 1848 edition of the *Punch* magazine, Isn't it wonderful? What these items really did is explained here in the *Aberdeen Press and Journal* in 1848.[363]

'Baby Jumpers – an amazing article for the nursery by which infants from the age of three months are enabled to exercise and amuse themselves when alone without the possibility of being injured.'

In other words, they made the Baby Bouncers we dangle from doorways. What I find truly amazing is that these articles were in use in 1848 and imported from America.

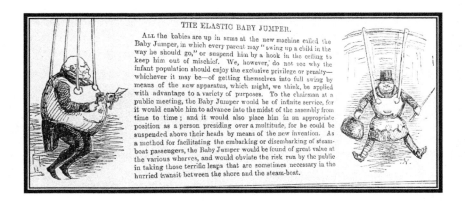

Figure 34 'The Elastic Baby Jumpers' Punch 1848

In November 1859, there was more bad publicity for Charles and Jane must have been furious that her risk taking, powerful and exciting lover was turning out to be practically useless. The *Leeds Times* referring to their Winter Fair said that

'If the *Talking Fish* had been good enough to turn up the whole countryside would have flocked to see it...' [364]

By the 18th November the *Belfast Morning News* is poking fun...[365]

'We hear the *Talking Fish* is under engagement to teach a large party of ladies to swim. He offers to teach them swimming, if they in return will give him lessons in talking...'

Unfortunately, in December, one year after Jane had bought the *Talking Fish*, everything came to a slow halt. The newspapers reported that: [366]

'The fish's constitution had been gradually breaking up for some time past, owing to the artificial habits which its position as a public fish compelled it to adopt, and for a period had been forced to withdraw into private life. The recent hard frost had affected it severely and the interesting sufferer was wrapped in blankets and eminent medical men were called in. Their efforts, however, proved unavailing.'

After three days of painful illness, the fish died on 21.12.1859. The *Stamford Mercury* reported:[367]

'It is gravely asserted that the wife of the proprietor, Mr. Charles Pollard, formerly of Stamford, went to see it on the day of its death, when, although at the point of death, it recognised her, and tried to raise itself up to come near to her, but the effort was too great for its strength, and it fell over on its side and expired.'

The *Morning Post*: remarked the fish was: [368]

'Said to have "the gift of the gab," and three causes seemed to have helped it on its way: bad water, bad air, and bad diet. There is many a man who has died from less.'

And *Punch*? Well, punched:[369]

'The loss of the *Talking Fish* will be largely felt in the circle in which it moved - by which we mean, the large tub in which it was in the habit of taking his daily rounds. According to the information we have received... it is to be buried not in Westminster Abbey but in Billingsgate Market. Its epitaph is to be simply "In Sealo Quis."'

The *Banffshire Journal and General Advertiser* did not hold back either[370]:

'We need not state that the *Talking Fish* died deeply regretted by its keepers, who will feel its loss most deeply in that part where losses are generally felt by persons the most deeply - viz. the breeches pocket. What complaint the *Talking Fish* had, beyond receiving every now and then a scant supply of flounders, we cannot state, but we understand that it took its final leap from this world into the next in its rash efforts to combine in his own person the Seal and Die Department.'

The *Talking Fish's* legacy quickly became a matter of humour, rumour, speculation and imagination.

'Its owner, it is also said, will be a heavy loser by its death, as he was getting a good income from its exhibition, and was not long since offered a large sum for it by a speculator.'

This is confirmed by the *Westmorland Gazette*:

'Unlike human creatures, the fish has contrived, in one sense at least, to take some £1,500 [£88,693.80] with it out of this world, that sum having been very recently offered to its bereaved proprietor for the possession of its person.'

The *Talking Fish* died the week before Christmas but by January 1860 it is in a pantomime called: *Barber, barber shave the cat*. It is a tale that references a strike in the building trade in 1859. The fictional *Talking Fish* plays the part of a rifle volunteer and is the lover of young Alice, the daughter of a poor barber.[371]

Jane and Charles were not slow to ride on the back of the deceased fish either as this exhibition advertised in the *Morning Post* on 13th February shows:

'On Monday Feb 27th and until further notice the largest collection of walking, talking and performing mechanical figures ever will be exhibited in the Exhibition Room of the *Talking Fish* at 191 Piccadilly, in addition to the preserved remains of that extraordinary phenomenon.'

There was also a rumour that the proprietor of the *Talking Fish* had already commissioned another seal to be trained, and satirists used comparisons of the fish's verbal dexterity with the dumb silence of members of parliament on vital issues of the day. Meanwhile, in 1861 the Great Maccomo produced another *Talking Fish* in Liverpool as part of his wonderful exciting performances and display of the *Largest Zoological Collection left in England*![372] And in Newcastle on Market Street in 1862, another *Talking Fish*:

'May be heard daily in its large bath where it rears its vasty head and dripping mane high above the splashing billows lashed into motion by its own fins and tail, where it says much better than any ordinary fish could say: "Papa and Mama."'[373]

Even Charles resurrected it in 1864 in a letter to the editor.

'Sir, In your Impression of this date I observe a notice of the "Performing and Musical Fish." Your paragraph is not very clear. In one line you call it "no fish" and in the third below speak of it as "the fish" but upon one point I must comment which is your remark upon "the *Talking Fish*" which, at this period of its exhibition, was pronounced by all the press to be one the most wonderful exhibitions ever witnessed.

'Why then should you, in order to advance the interest of the present exhibition of a fish of the same species, but, as a specimen, far inferior to the *Talking Fish*, publish a paragraph not only inaccurate but utterly false!

'If you choose to promote the present exhibition it does not require that others should be stigmatised. Well knowing your desire to do justice, I doubt not that you will insert this in the columns of your valuable journal. Charles Pollard. Late proprietor of the *Talking Fish*.' Dec 5.'[374]

It was a very long time before the *Talking Fish*, which became more famous the longer it was dead, stopped appearing in newspapers.

It all makes for a good read, but throughout this adventure I could not help wondering who actually was the proprietor of the *Talking Fish*. Jane said she paid for it, or gave Charles the money to pay for it, but Charles ran the road show, hosted the gentlemen's dinners and took people to court in its name. With coverture as it was and Jane a new widow, she probably had little choice but to use Charles as the official front so none of her creditors could force her to pay them out of the proceeds of the

Talking Fish. It also touched William Mercer's financial affairs in 1862 when he was asked at his bankruptcy hearing if he had any financial interest in the *Talking Fish*.[375]

One person who is clear about the true proprietor was John Beshemel, the *Talking Fish*'s keeper. He was so convinced Jane was the person who employed him, he took her to court for his unpaid wages in 1860 and again in 1861 to prove it.

Chapter 16 - Beshemel v Gallagher

This court case was heard twice as Jane refused to accept the first verdict. Most of the evidence was the same so what follows is a composite of both trials and the final judgement.

John Beshemel was claiming £1 [£60.61] a week for the 61 weeks he had looked after the *Talking Fish*, a claim Jane vehemently denied. He began the proceedings at the Bail Court at Nisi Prius at Westminster before Mr. Justice Crompton and a jury, by describing how he came to be employed by Jane to look after the *Talking Fish*:[376]

Figure 35 Illustration of the Talking Fish by George Jones, Formby 2019

'I am a native of Gibraltar and I was at Liverpool in December 1858 in the employ of Mr. Cavana who intrusted to my care the *Talking Fish*. A Mr. Pollard, a friend of Mrs. Gallagher, came and asked me if Mr. Cavana would sell the fish and she bought it for £300 [£17,7738.76]. I asked her to let me go into the service of the fish as I was very anxious to be in the society of the fish. [Laughter in court].

'We entered into an agreement for my services. I was to have my board and lodging, two suits of clothes, £1 [£59.13] a week and anything I got from the visitors. I continued with the fish in all its exhibitions until it died and for some time afterwards, I remained with Mrs. Gallagher, doing what I was told.

'She let me have pocket money when I wanted it, to pay for my washing and such matters and sometimes used to give me a shilling [£2.96] to go out with on a Sunday. The visitors used to give me money. One lady gave me 5 shillings [£14.78] and another 2 shillings and 6d [£7.39].'[377]

Questioned further, Beshemel said he was sleeping with the *Talking Fish*, eating by it and never leaving it, to the extent that he was obliged to sleep at its side even when they were exhibiting in a tent.[378]

'He acted as its companion and the fish was useless without the person who used to exhibit it, feed it, and had in fact taught it to perform. He was therefore engaged to attend to the fish and show it and "go the circuit" with the fish.' [Laughter in court.]

Jane's lawyer:	Then your perquisites depended on the number of visitors?
Justice Crompton:	No, on their liberality. [Laughter in court].
Justice Crompton:	I thought you dined with her every day?
Jane's lawyer:	No, my lord; Mrs. Gallagher's residence and the exhibition were at different places.
Justice Crompton:	Oh! Then you dined with the fish?
Beshemel:	Yes, my lord.
Justice Crompton:	Had you your meals with it?
Beshemel:	In the same room.
Jane's lawyer:	Did not Mrs. Gallagher give you a watch?
Beshemel:	Yes, and here it is; it is worth 35 shillings [£223.21].
Jane's lawyer:	Did she not say it cost her £5 [£297.12]?

Beshemel: I believe she did. I don't recollect. I did not say that while I was in her employ, I saved £10 [£606.10], which I had sent to a relative. I could not save £1 [£60.61]. She said to me after the fish died that she would give me some money when she sold her wax figures.

Mrs. Francis, who then kept a confectioner's shop at Edge Hill, Liverpool, but who was previously Jane's housekeeper at her private hotel [brothel], gave, amidst much laughter, the following account of a conversation she had with Beshemel shortly after he had entered Jane's service.

Mrs. Francis: John, how smart you look.

Beshemel: I was a poor man the other day, I am a gentleman now.

Mrs. Francis: John, do you get any wages?

Beshemel: No, I've got good clothes, plenty of meat and a good bed to lie on, and I get what the company give me. When that is not sufficient, my mistress supplies my wants.

Mrs. Francis: John, you are better off than I am, for I have to find my own clothes.

She said she behaved towards Beshemel as if he had been her own child, giving him money to spend when he asked for it.

'When the seal died, he cried and I told him he might continue where he was until he obtained another situation and I maintained him for four months. He could scarcely speak English when he first came to England. He sometimes wore five shirts at a time, because they could not make him understand that he must change his linen.'[379]

Beshemel, cross-examined, struggles on:

'I did not say to Mrs. Francis I got money from the visitors or when I did not get enough my mistress was to give me something. I did not say to her that I had my board and lodging and two suits of clothes a year and that therefore I had a good place. I dined with the defendant two or three times.'

Mrs. Francis, cross-examined:

'I got money from persons who used the hotel. I had no wages. Of course, many gentlemen brought their wives there. I did not ask for marriage certificates, but many showed them to me unasked.' [Loud laughter].

Jane's lawyer addressed the jury briskly: 'Although this was an action about a *Talking Fish*, there would be no occasion for much talk on either side.' He was at pains to show how Beshemel had 'filled a very menial office' in Jane's employment. 'It was his duty to give the *Talking Fish* his bath and to wrap him in flannels afterwards,' and he maintained there had been no agreement to pay Beshemel £1 a week.[380]

Jane Gallagher was then called, which is what the crowded court had been waiting for, and it was clear Jane was to all appearances the proprietress of the *Talking Fish*, and directed Beshemel in his work. He was kept on after the death of the fish in the hope of getting another fish, but this failed and Beshemel was discharged. She denied her liability, throwing it onto Charles Pollard, who was not to be found, even though she was said to be 'on intimate terms with him.'[381]

I assume Charles was absent as he had been to Worcester's Races at the beginning of the month where he was arrested for assaulting a police officer and in court the very next morning, the 1.11.1860.[382] It was packed as Charles was billed as the proprietor of the great *Talking Fish* and he appeared with all his gentlemen sporting friends. It seems that in the early hours of that morning, about 1.30am, PC Clements:

'Heard a noise of people talking near the Duke of York Inn, Worcester. On proceeding in that direction, two or three girls who had been conversing with some gentlemen ran away. He spoke civilly to the gentlemen telling them they must not make any disturbance at that late hour and he must request them to leave the street.'

The gentlemen, Charles included, said: 'They would not leave, called him a scamp and said he was drunk.'

PC Clements threatened to take them to the station if they persisted in this sort of conduct and laid hold of one of them. At this stage Charles came up to him and said they were his friends and he, [the officer] 'should not interfere with them.' He then struck PC Clements a blow on the forehead, knocked him to the ground and also struck him with his knee.

PC Clements then had to struggle and Charles ran into the *Duke of York Inn*, shut the door and several gentlemen threw water on the poor policeman from a window. Detective Richardson however, came up while this was going on, demanded admission to the house and arrested Charles, who offered not the least resistance and he was taken to the police station.

This certainly sounds very much like him! But in court Charles, 'who had the demeanour of a gentleman,' had a different story to tell. He said the officer laid hold of him by the collar, which he could not allow him to do. He denied striking him and said he never touched him at all.

A man named Kayle, of Farringdon, Hertfordshire who witnessed the affray, voluntarily gave evidence.

'He saw the policeman go to the gentlemen, heard him tell them to disperse and not make a noise, then they became very abusive and Charles taxed him with exceeding his duty, called him a know-nothing b...... and told him he better be off. The officer remained, upon which Charles began pushing him with his hand and his knee across the street and they struggled together. They were up and down like fighting dogs. During the struggle the PC lost his man. He was certain Charles struck the policeman many times.'

Mr. Castle, of the *Great Western Hotel* in London, who was one of the gentlemen with Charles, was the next witness. He said he was standing opposite the group with two friends when the policeman came up and said they must leave the street. Mr. Castle told him they were not interfering with any person and that by his manner he was exceeding his duty. Some further remarks were made then Charles came up, told the officer not to interfere, as he would not allow him to take any of his friends to the station. Mr. Castle did not believe that Charles touched PC Clements at all.

Charles' friends then waded in saying the PC was uncivil and another friend said he, not Charles, had been 'tumbling' about with the policeman. The magistrate judged the assault was proved and he fined Charles £1 [£60.61] and costs of 6 shillings and 6d [£19.22].

It says something about Charles' arrogance and self-assurance that he interrupted saying he considered he had been wrongly convicted.

'Upon which some murmuring took place amongst the spectators and a gentleman giving his name as Christopher William Bolton, living in Chanceley Court, offered further evidence in mitigation of the fine.'

The magistrate said: 'It was useless as there could be no denial of the assault but that Charles could have the witness sworn if he chose to do so, but it would only be putting him to the expense of another shilling. [£2.96]'

A voice called out: 'Have another shilling's worth!' [Laughter in court].

Mr. Bolton was duly sworn and claimed the PC took hold of Charles by the collar who said 'If he was to go, he would go quietly.' Bolton saw the PC was down, but it was not by Charles. Charles then pledged his honour that he never gave the officer a blow and after some further remarks, the magistrate reduced the fine to 10 shillings [£29.56] and costs.

Charles left saying: 'I am much obliged to you, sir; I think I have had a good shilling's worth this last time.'

I feel sorry for the PC.

Meanwhile, the *Talking Fish* case went on without Charles Pollard and Jane played to the gallery denying in the most positive terms that she had engaged Beshemel at £1 a week, the agreement being that he should be boarded and lodged, have two suits of clothes in the year and the monies given by visitors.

Questioned by her own solicitor, Jane said:

'Beshemel had made more money than she had by the exhibition of the *Talking Fish*, by which she had lost £1,000 [£59,129.20].'[383]

Lawyer: How came you first to see the fish?

Jane: Paid tuppence. [Laughter]

Lawyer: It was the first *Talking Fish* that ever came to this country?

Jane: Oh no. There was one on Elliot Street, Liverpool, four years before this one. Beshemel never asked me for money before he was leaving.

Lawyer: There was no great art in feeding this fish?

Jane: Oh no, sir.

Lawyer: He did not take food out of a baby's bottle, I suppose, though he did say 'Ma!' What did he eat?

Jane: Fish.

Lawyer: Fish that did not talk. [Great laughter in court.]

When asked where Pollard was:

Jane   :   I do not know where Pollard is now. I decline to say whether Pollard and I cohabited as man and wife.

Lawyer: You decline to answer that?

Jane: I do; and it is very impertinent of you to ask the question. [Laughter]

Lawyer: Where do you live in Liverpool?

Jane: I keep a private hotel called Detmore's Coffee House.

Lawyer: Is it an improper house, frequented by loose characters?'

Jane: I don't know. You may have been there for all I know. [Laughter in court.]

This then, was the grand finale of the first *Talking Fish* Court case in 1860. Jane lost, had to pay John Beshemel £61 [£3,606.88] back wages and £45 [£2,660.81] costs in all. She refused to accept the verdict and a completely new trial was ordered which took place in the same bail court in London on almost the same dates in November the following year, 1861. By now the case was notorious, and many rushed to attend, but this time the focus is slightly different, as Charles Pollard has been found, hasn't been fighting in recent days, and makes an appearance. He confirms he bought the fish, but does not say he was acting on behalf of Jane in doing so.

Charles also admitted he agreed the terms of Beshemel's employment which he says did not include the £1 a week and he disagreed that very few people gave Beshemel tips, saying he frequently had 10 shillings [£29.56] and 15 shillings [£44.35] a day. Under cross examination Charles continued to contradict much of Jane's evidence and admitted:

- He and Jane were living together as man and wife

- He had not been found guilty of stealing £2,000 worth of bills from Louis - Napoleon fourteen years previously and that he was honourably acquitted, not by a flaw in the indictment but on the merits of the case

- No one had charged him with the death of Dutch Sam's widow. The verdict was 'Death from natural causes'

- He did not keep a brothel in Liverpool but barristers sometimes stayed at the house

- He had another house but did not know if it was a brothel

- He did not know much of Jane's private history, nor how long he had lived with her

- He was a commission agent but did not sell goods

- He was a racing broker and did the best he could, like any other gentleman

That must have been quite a session but how much of it is true? Well, at last one of them admits they were living together as man and a wife but, a year later, we still are not clear who owned the *Talking Fish*, even though Jane is the one being prosecuted for not paying John Beshemel's wages.

I find it hard to believe Charles denied knowing anything about Jane's past for he had lived her life in Liverpool since 1856 at least and at 191 Piccadilly in London too, both of them splitting their time between the two cities. From 1857-1859, street directories show Pollard was living at 7 May Street in Liverpool, one of Jane's houses which did have an illustrious London barrister staying there on the night of the 1851 census, though Charles was not listed and the house does not appear in the 1861 census.

In this trial Fanny Francis, who gave evidence at the last one, was said to be a Charles' housekeeper but was equally recorded by court reporters as being Jane's in the previous trial. She actually was a long-time employee and had managed many houses for Jane in the past, though I have no record of her working at 7 May Street as Pollard claims. But the 1861 census shows her living with Jane Gallagher and others at 9 Houghton Street, another brothel, and in 1862 she was charged with keeping a brothel at Detmer's Coffee House at 5 Houghton Street which had been a notorious establishment of Jane's since 1847.

All the evidence was now in, for the second time, and as his lordship was about to rise, the jury said there was no chance of their agreeing. An attempt was then made to settle. Beshemel offered to take the money which had been paid into court from the first trial and said he would pay his own costs if Jane would. The learned judge expressed a strong opinion that the previous verdict had been very good terms, but Jane again insisted on taking the chance of overturning it.

The jury after being locked up for some time, found for Beshemel and Jane had to pay the £61 and damages of £45, exactly the same as before. She gained nothing.[384]

The last word has to go to the *Morning Herald* quoted in *Lloyds Weekly Newspaper*[385] written straight after the second trial in 1861. It went far beyond the frivolous and to the very core of the dispute.

> 'Mrs. Gallagher, who rejoices in the unquestionably Celtic name, has had to pay the price of the bad repute of her own character and that of her witnesses, through a verdict given against her on the single testimony of an interested party, and for which the weight of evidence was probably less than for the losing version.

> 'And in this way the chief moral lesson that is taught by the incident we have been reviewing may perhaps turn out to be, that if people will follow immoral callings and give themselves up to what is an irregular system of gain, the wages of their sin will not only follow in the daily incommodities of the life they have chosen, but also in those accidents of judicial procedure, which, like a judgement, offer up their private history to public ridicule.'

And I am quite sure Jane did not like that one bit, nor would she have been very pleased with Charles Pollard.

Chapter 17 - Johnson v Gallagher

Sandwiched between the two *Talking Fish* trials was the now infamous 1860 case, *Johnson v Gallagher*, which began on Saturday 12th May. We are back where we started, but knowing much more about Jane. The glamour of Charles Pollard might have been fading by then with his failure to turn up for the first *Talking Fish* case and subsequent poor showing and there is no indication he stayed around to support Jane in her biggest trial so far.

Maybe William Mercer was there? Strangely enough, even though he had been approached to contribute towards her defence in the *Talking Fish* trial and refused:

'He did join with Mr. Roby, the attorney who had defended her acceptance of a note for £30 [worth £1,773.88] to the Imperial Loan Company. Mercer said he did not know then what the money was wanted for... he gave the note simply because Mr. Roby asked for it.'[386]

Incidentally, this Loan Company by 1868, in just eight more years, would be managed by Chalkley's future son in law, Edwin Carver, husband of his only surviving daughter, Sarah Jane Chalkley.

No court records exist for the 1860 hearing, but there are many accounts in the press, most of which differ greatly in what they chose to print, but we do also have a later court transcript which neatly summarises the key issues and the judgements made when the matter went to the Court of Appeal in London in 1861. Between the shocking revelations and financial complications, important points of law had to be debated and judged against the changes to women's rights embedded in the 1857 Act Caroline Norton had championed.[387] The opening statement sets the tone for the rest of this trial.

'The action was brought to recover the balance of an account due to the insolvents [Burton and Watson] and the defence was that at the time the debts were contracted Mrs. Gallagher was a married woman. From the peculiar nature of the proceedings in this court, the precise cause of action against Mr. Chalkley was not stated.'

It turned out that Chalkley was being sued as the trustee of Jane Oakes' will and custodian of the brothel empire Jane assigned to him in the form of the Trust created by her mother, to benefit her five legitimate children.

Whilst still pleading penury, Jane appeared to be anything but poverty stricken that day as she faced a packed to bursting court to describe her early life, marriage and the development of the brothel empire. Somewhere in the second day the salacious details were put aside and the lawyers concentrated on the really sticky issue of what, if anything, Jane owed Burton and Watson for the furniture. The court took no account of the fact that what they were dealing with was immoral earnings, much as the public wanted to hear more lurid details, as it was not illegal to keep a brothel until 1885. Instead, the bulk of the case is about the complexities of the law of coverture as it applied at the time to separated but married women. Quite tedious stuff, and I expect most people didn't bother queuing for that.

Figure 36 Jane in court illustrated by George Jones 2019

We already know that Burton and Watson had for many years been supplying Jane with furniture for her brothels in the knowledge that she was a married woman living apart from her husband Thomas, to whom she paid a regular allowance. Their big mistake was to assume she had a separate estate and that she was legally able to order, contract and pay for the furniture. On this basis they extended credit to her and between 1856 and 1858, Jane paid £284.10 shillings towards her account and then refused to pay the rest, which amounted to £372 2 shillings and 6 1/2d [£22,003.45].[388] Then Burton and Watson became bankrupt and assigned all their assets, including Jane's debt, to Johnson who acted on behalf of their creditors.

Jane and Thomas had executed a deed of separation in June 1856 which involved placing all her property, especially the assets of her business as a 'wine and spirit merchant' in Liverpool, in trust for her sole use 'not withstanding her coverture.' When Thomas died in October 1858, Jane became a widow, *a sole femme*, a woman with the power to contract who could live at last as an independent person, which was an entirely new status for Jane after over 20 years of marriage.

This made 1859 a very busy year for Jane, who continued to take significant action to protect her assets. By September 1859, Jane's daughter Ann Elizabeth had married a bank clerk in Rossett, Denbighshire and Jane had taken back ownership of the Tyrer Street property and Bird Cottage in Rossett, along with the excessively expensive furniture. On the 10th October, whilst Charles was preparing to sue the *Elastic Baby Jumpers* over the *Talking Fish*, Jane executed a bill of sale in favour of Chalkley selling him the furniture for £1,390 [£82,189.59], which just happened to be how much she then owed him, but moved to London without telling him, where she had rented a house at 1 Vassall Rd, Brixton for her unmarried children, 'so that they were not contaminated' by the court case.

When Burton and Watson heard about the disappearance of the furniture, they were quick to act. On the 2nd December, Jane was back in the Chancery Court at St George's Hall, Liverpool [389] to defend an action Johnson, on behalf of Burton and Watson, had taken. They wanted the court to put a charge on her furniture in order for them to recover the amount owing, arguing that Jane did have the financial means to pay them as she owned two houses in her own right at the bottom of London Road. They also claimed she had tried to mortgage them not long ago but had since dropped the application as she had found the money another way. They added 'there was also a *Talking Fish* in her possession, for which a considerable sum had been paid.'[390]

The lawyers for Burton and Watson stated that the bill of sale Jane had given to Chalkley was 'defective' and that there was a high risk that Jane could consequently pursue a course which would leave them without 'remedy.' In other words, there would be nothing left in her separate estate to pay them. They wanted an immediate court order to rescind the bill of sale.

Actually, there were two of these. A second bill of sale was executed on 29th November to correct the first one, so someone with a legal background was making sure it was cast iron. This new bill included a clause which said that Chalkley could also hold the furniture as security for any future loans Jane might incur.

Not surprisingly, Johnson thought this was fraudulent preference of one creditor over others, as many more people were owed money by Jane. The judge refused to act, saying Burton and Watson had to wait for this main case, which was due to be heard in the Chancery Court two months' later. The wrangling therefore was all about Jane's separate estate, how much it was worth, what was included, or not, and the correct interpretation and validity of the deed of separation Thomas signed in 1856. Lawyers argued:

> 'It was contrary to all common sense that the deed should include the property of Bird Cottage at the Rossett as it was bought after the deed was signed and the deed was only meant to apply to property in existence at the time it was signed. The only effect of that deed upon the property at Rossett was to create a separate estate and the legal estate in it never passed to Chalkley until the bill of sale [October 1859] for the furniture which was subsequently given to him by Mrs. Gallagher.'[391]

The prosecution then set out the legal reasons why they were:

> 'Disputing both the legality and the equity of a preference being given to Chalkley to the disadvantage of the other creditors.'

It was also suggested that property which had been acquired in the name of Jane Oakes during her lifetime was put in her name merely to exclude Thomas from the right of possession. In other words, Jane had callously used her mother as a front. What was new was an affidavit from Ann Glenn, Jane's sister, made voluntarily before the registrar on the 6th May 1860. In it, Mrs. Glenn stated that:

> 'She was married and living in Liverpool, that she was always on intimate and affectionate terms with Mrs. Oakes her mother, and was with her the day before she died and was well acquainted with her affairs. She had never heard that her mother ever owned or was entitled to, and did not believe that she ever owned or was entitled to, or had any beneficial interest in the houses at No 5 Houghton Street, Nos 6 and 7 Tyrer Street, May Street or the house known as the Cottage in St Vincent Street, all of which houses Mrs. Glenn had on several occasions, both before and after the death of her mother, been told by Mrs. Gallagher to be, and believed to be up to the present time, the absolute property of Mrs. Gallagher.

> 'The only property her mother was possessed of at the time of her death was a sum of about £17 [£1,005.20] in a savings bank in Manchester, whence she came to Liverpool to be the servant and manage the "sub-letting" of a house in Tyrer

Street for Mrs. Gallagher, which house the latter had just bought. Mrs. Glenn admitted she had also managed for Mrs. Gallagher the "sub-letting" of the adjoining house.'

Mrs. Glenn obviously had never seen her mother's will which set out all the property she owned. Jane's response was rapid and rapier sharp:

'She had been credibly informed and believed that Mrs. Glenn had been dragged through the streets by Maguire, the detective, to the offices of Messrs Evans, Son and Sandys, [Johnson's solicitors], where the statement which had been read had been forced from her...'

And nothing more is reported on the matter apart from a remark that a 'too zealous detective has been employed, that is all.'

Next in the stand was Chalkley. He had been secretary of the Liverpool Tradesman's' Loan Society for many years and said he became acquainted with Jane eight or nine years previously when she first made an application for a loan. This would make it 1851 by his reckoning, when Jane was bigamously married to William Mercer and maybe even separated from him by that time, but Jane said she had known Chalkley since 1849. In either case he might not have known Jane as Gallagher but Mercer, yet no mention is made of her bigamous marriage or other surname.

Chalkley said on the occasion of Jane's first loan he did not make enquiries 'respecting the persons applying' as Jane was known to the directors of the company and 'they did not tell me of her position.' When he laid Jane's applications before the directors, 'they were immediately passed and they never did that unless they knew the party.' It was previous to 1852 when he learned she was the proprietress of a number of gay houses in different parts of the town, but 'I did not satisfy myself on the subject.'

At this time, legally, Jane as a married woman, could not make any contracts or be sued, but once again the loan company, just like Burton and Watson, assumed she had a separate estate, so eager were they for her business.

Chalkley claimed: 'He had never heard it hinted that the property belonged to her children, that he did not know until after the first loan that she was a married woman and it was only then that he suggested that everything be assigned to him, in order to receive the loans and she immediately acceded, saying she "had no other desire than to pay the loans off."'

But he was one of the very few who had seen Jane Oakes' will which assigned everything to her grandchildren and at that point he said he advised Jane to have the will proved, which she did not do until 1864. The loans Jane had, he said were always properly paid and it was only latterly, that they were not properly paid and renewed.

'I have not my books here, I had no notice to produce them, I have my personal books here, but I have no books belonging to the society. I have no power to produce those.'

Johnson's lawyer pounced:

'We have now brought it down to the loans from the society and I submit we are entitled to have the books.'

The judge refused saying: 'The society are not the defendants.'

Chalkley reveals Jane told him that the furniture in her houses was the only property she had, adding:

'My opinion of Mrs. Gallagher's moral character was not very high in 1856, but as far as truthfulness is concerned, she has always been very correct as far as I know.'

As the furniture at Bird Cottage is the key issue in this trial, Chalkley is then questioned about where the funds came from to buy it:

'No one came to me to negotiate loans in that respect, there was no loan made through the Liverpool Tradesman's Loan Company or our building society but I know they got the money from another building society. I did not know until after the purchase that it was intended to be a residence for Mrs. Gallagher and her children, I know nothing about the furniture, I had nothing to do with it at the time.

'My making continual loans to her was no reason why I should know all her affairs. Mrs. Gallagher told me that her girls were coming home from school, that she must have a separate place for them. It was sometime after the cottage was completely furnished that I learned it had been furnished by Burton and Watson and that the furniture had not been fully paid for.'

His examination went on and on.

Lawyer: Don't you know it is the custom of these women to clothe their lodgers?

Chalkley: No, I do not. I never had any idea that the children were at extravagant schools; I don't swear that I thought all the loans were for the purpose of paying for their education. All I knew about her solicitude for her children was from what she told me, but I did not believe all she said.

But he admitted he received the rents of many of Jane's houses for which he held the deeds as surety.

'I neither consented nor objected to the houses being used as gay houses, except so far as advice went. I did not know that I had power as a trustee to put a stop to them being used in that way.

'I was not aware of Mrs. Gallagher removing her furniture from Rossett to London; she had promised me she would not remove it. She has not given me a fresh bill of sale for it.'

The prosecuting lawyer at this point injected saying:

'I am now in possession of the property which has been removed from the Rossett, I have put a man in possession, Mr. George Best in London.'

This effectively prevented Jane from selling the furniture and squirreling the money away where the court could not take it to pay her debts. That concluded the second day of the hearing.

It struck me when I first read this that an awful lot of Chalkley's evidence was contradictory. It is astonishing a pious preacher would present in this way, his moral compass whirling and wavering, prevaricating every time he was called to account, repeating the same mantra over and over: 'I did not know.' It was his business, as secretary of the Liverpool Trademan's Loan Company, to know.

On 17th May, the final day of the hearing, the judge said:

'He did not wish to hear any observations in support of the proposition that the "business" carried on in the houses mentioned in the evidence was Mrs. Gallagher's business.'

Later he enlarged again saying: 'He regarded Mrs. Gallagher's description in the deed of assignment as a wine merchant a mere colourable description....'[392]

He then ruled that Jane was not to be charged with fraud with regard to the original transaction for the furniture purchased from Burton and Watson as she had paid off a portion of what she owed. This meant that Jane's lawyer was able to argue that she was at perfect liberty to deal with Chalkley for the purpose of giving him security for a bona fide existing debt and that Burton and Watson had no existing lien on the furniture which could claim priority over the demand of Chalkley, a bona fide creditor, who had taken a specific security, the bill of sale, on it.

Eventually, all the scandalous headlines boiled down to was a feud about furniture which used as its weapons the law regarding married women and coverture. Now desperate, an injunction was demanded by the prosecution to prevent the furniture being sold as:

'It might be at any moment removed and the evidence which had been given showed that nothing short of the appointment of a receiver could protect the interest of Burton and Watson.'

The value of the furniture was estimated by Mr. George Best, the auctioneer in London, as £153 6 shillings six pence [£9,065.98] and the original value of the furniture to be £284 13 shillings [£16,831.13], for which sum he would undertake to execute work of the same value and finish. In other words, sell it off at auction and pay the proceeds after his costs into court so that Burton and Watson could be paid the outstanding balance Jane owed.

Jane's lawyer made the point that it was only Burton and Watson's claim that could be adjudicated that day, not the claims of the many other creditors, there was no fraud in Jane giving the security to Chalkley and she had nothing which should render her liable for costs. The order had to be made out for the separate estate only, the furniture, and if there was not enough in the proceeds of the sale then Burton and Watson had to look to another remedy for the outstanding debt.

Chalkley's lawyer continued to defend him by saying that he was not liable to pay anything to Burton and Watson as the amount they charged Jane for the furniture £615 [£49,314.45] was vastly in excess of its value and that what Mrs. Gallagher had already paid back was ample. He stated strongly that Chalkley did not connive in the removal of the furniture from Bird Cottage.

The judge summed up declaring that what was in question was simple, Burton and Watson's claim on the furniture.

'It was one of the most startling propositions he had ever heard, one which could not be carried out and one which had no authority, that a married woman having a separate estate and becoming discovert [a widow]:

- Paid out of the general assets a separate debt

- Then stood as against separate creditors in the position of the separate creditors whom she had satisfied

He maintained that all creditors who were separate creditors during coverture and who were separate creditors now, ought to come in pro rata. This was because nobody knew just how much Jane owed everyone else and in order to find out, he instigated an inquiry into the value of the estate Jane had at the time of Thomas' death, the value at the time of Chalkley's bill of sale and the present value. The furniture in London was to be sold and any property of Jane's in the houses in London she had taken.

Officially, the Vice Chancellor decreed:

'The separate estate of Jane Gallagher at the time of her husband's death, and Jane Gallagher personally to the value of that estate at that time, were liable to the plaintiffs [Johnson representing Burton and Watson]; and that William Seabrook Chalkley took no higher interest in the separate estate than Jane Gallagher had therein at the date of the bill of sale.'[393]

Jane had to pay the costs but was imprisoned for not doing so. [394] It is not clear whether this was because she had no money or that she refused. They are both declared insolvent debtors within the month and adverts were placed asking for creditors to come forward.[395] That was it.

The new Borough Gaol at Liverpool opened in 1855 and was explicitly designed and built to offer separate confinement or single cells with enforced rules of silence. Talking was forbidden.[396] Confined to their cells, prisoners started work at 6am and went to bed at 8pm and were under constant supervision. However, even that early in the prison's existence, the issue of separate confinement was a problem for their female population for no matter how many extra beds they brought, in the system collapsed.

'In the door of the cell.... there is a pierced eye-hole by which the turnkeys can look in upon the prisoner at any time, without being observed by them... The officers are to be seen quietly walking about and although there is a population of above 1,200 persons within a narrow compass everything is as silent as the tomb, the light sombre, the whole effect saddening and impressive.'[397]

Penologists, alienists and social reformers, like Dr Thomas Laycock of Edinburgh University argued that the habitual or incorrigible criminal was essentially unreformable.

'They were a class of people numbering tens of thousands who possess no self-control beyond that of an ordinary brute animal, nay, less than a well-bred horse or dog. They are for the most part immoral imbeciles.'[398]

Luckily for Jane, treadmills were not in full operation until 1868, after she had been freed, as prisoners were spending six to seven hours a day on it. Some chaplains opposed its use, 'due to its physical effects, which can result in irreparable injury and causes much anxiety.'[399] The prison surgeon, Francis Archer, however, who was responsible for certifying prisoners as 'fit' to be placed on it:

'Did not think it had prejudicially affected the gelato of the prisoners; persons of a weak frame of body, and those encumbered with an unnecessary amount of fat, of course feel it the most.'

But officials agreed the harsher regime had not 'proved a deterrent to the old thieves' and the number of committals continued to grow, from 884 in the second quarter of

1866 to 1,011 for the same period in 1867. Picking oakum, was another common form of punishment Jane may have endured but Liverpool justices were advised in 1864 this practice endangered prisoner's health. Instead, it was suggested they should be given access to books, always assuming they could read, and greater opportunities to attend the chapel. Only some recommendations were accepted.[400]

Suicide attempts in the gaol were common but, following investigation, were often dismissed as shamming and the prisoners punished. In 1864 when two male prisoners attempted to hang themselves, the governor claimed that 'neither had any intention of injuring himself.' Prisoners, rather than prison discipline and the system, were blamed for their mental disorders.

This then was where Jane spent the next months of her life while she waited for her appeal to be heard.

But what of the hapless Chalkley?

Chapter 18 - Chalkley's Downfall

After his disastrous appearance in court, Chalkley must have panicked. The Liverpool Tradesman's Loan Society immediately instigated a searching enquiry into the state of their business and Chalkley's management of both the Liverpool and Manchester offices as its secretary. It was some time, however, before certain facts became known but meanwhile rumours were rampant and Chalkley disappeared. He was last seen on 25.5.1860[401] and headlines like this blazed across Liverpool and the entire country, accusing him of embezzlement on a massive scale.

Figure 37 'Embezzlement by the Secretary of a Loan Company' 16.6.1860

'Chalkley, a few weeks ago underwent a long examination in the Chancery Court of Lancaster touching the transactions of himself individually and as an officer of the loan society, with Mrs. Gallagher, one of the most notorious brothel keepers in Liverpool. The charges against Chalkley are embezzlement and forgery. The exact amount of his deficiencies has not been ascertained but rumour places them as not less than £5,000 [£295,646.00]. What renders the proceedings more disgraceful is the fact that Chalkley was a preacher in the reformed body of the Wesleyan Society and was well known as such all over Lancashire and particularly in the railway stations.'

The very nature of Chalkley's duties for the loan society [sometimes referred to as the loan company] had given him many opportunities for embezzlement as he was often away from home for up to a week at a time visiting a number of other northern towns such as St Helens, Manchester, Preston, Rochdale in Lancashire and parts of

Yorkshire, Cheshire and Wales, hence him being well known in all the region's railway stations.[402] A police notice, offering a considerable reward of £200 [£11,825.84] for Chalkley's arrest, was issued in which he was described as being:

'From 47-50 years of age, about five feet three inches high, proportionate make, between dark and fair complexion, a little colour in his cheeks, rather long face, grey hair, curls up behind, bald on top of the head, the backs of his hands are mottled in patches with brown marks. General dress, frock coat, trousers and vest.'

The Loan Society's investigations revealed that whenever Chalkley desired a day or two's absence, his other work for the society was delegated to his Manchester agent, a man called Goodall. He had also been speculating in coal mines and other mining operations near Nantwich, Cheshire. Below is a notice published in 1862 about a Birmingham Bankruptcy case which stated Chalkley had been in co-partnership with William Bott in the company of Presgwyn, Quinton and Berthlandeg Collieries.[403]

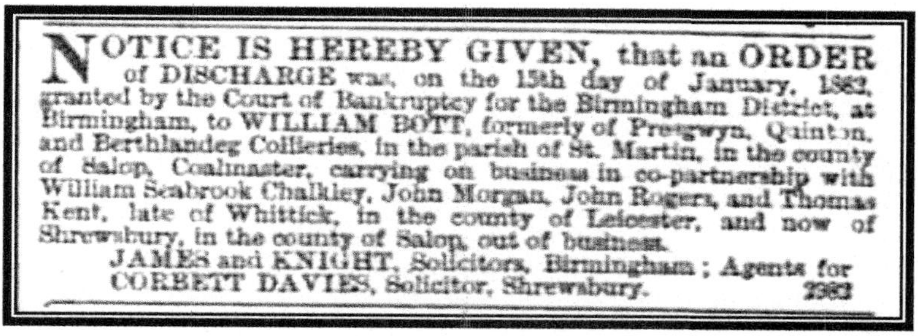

NOTICE IS HEREBY GIVEN, that an ORDER of DISCHARGE was, on the 15th day of January, 1862, granted by the Court of Bankruptcy for the Birmingham District, at Birmingham, to WILLIAM BOTT, formerly of Presgwyn, Quinton, and Berthlandeg Collieries, in the parish of St. Martin, in the county of Salop, Coalmaster, carrying on business in co-partnership with William Seabrook Chalkley, John Morgan, John Rogers, and Thomas Kent, late of Whittick, in the county of Leicester, and now of Shrewsbury, in the county of Salop, out of business.
JAMES and KNIGHT, Solicitors, Birmingham ; Agents for CORBETT DAVIES, Solicitor, Shrewsbury.   2963

Figure 38 'Bankruptcy Notices' Birmingham Journal 18.1.1862

People also said he had 'irons in the fire' in various other directions as well and that his affairs were considerably involved. Next came the rumour that Chalkley had swindled the Tradesman's Loan Society out of between £20 and £30,000, [£1,182.58 - £1,773,876.00], which eventually was shown to be true. No wonder he fled![404]

The *Northern Whig* agreed the offences were more to do with the Manchester Office of the Trademan's Loan Society than Liverpool,[405] the *Liverpool Daily Post* reported Chalkley had been declared bankrupt as well as an insolvent debtor and that his poor wife was examined privately,[406] and the *Glasgow Herald* made much of the great scandal Chalkley's business dealings had caused amongst the Wesleyan Methodists.[407]

The actual bankruptcy notice for Chalkley as published in *Perry's Bankruptcy and Insolvency Gazette* on 27.6.1860[408] was also a surprise, as it shows that Chalkley was a ship owner in Liverpool. There was more detail in this next notice. [409] I got a little excited when I found there was a ship called the *William Seabrook Chalkley* ploughing the waters around America, but it turned out to belong to a completely different family, so I am still looking for Chalkley's ship.

William Seabrook Chalkley, Liverpool, ship owner, coal owner, and coal merchant, agent, and money scrivener, June 27, July 9, at one, at the Court of Bankruptcy, Liverpool. Off. assignee, Mr. Cazenove, Liverpool ; sol., Mr. Rymer, Liverpool.

Figure 39 'Bankruptcies,' the Globe 20.6.1860

Now, all this amounts to far more money than one would expect someone in his position to have at his disposal. It makes you want to cry out 'Will the real Chalkley please stand up?' Devout minister, conniving embezzler, distraught middle-aged man who lost six out of seven children, baker, shop owner, coal owner, merchant and multiple bankrupt and now a ship owner. It makes you wonder what else might be lurking under this pious cloak of respectability?

The investigation into Chalkley's handling of the company's finances revealed more shocks and surprises. It came out that a Mr. Charles Harber, who said he had acted as the deputy chair of the Liverpool Tradesman's Loan Society five years previously, around 1853, commissioned an audit and found the bad debt account was very considerable. It was Chalkley's responsibility as secretary to keep it under control, so the board instructed him to reduce it, which he did, but not as you might have thought proper, as an account of a court case reported in the *Lancaster Gazette* on Saturday 14.8.1858 reveals.

It described how a Mr. Dale in 1853 had approached the society to request a loan, offering as security a guarantor in the person of Mr. Gribbon. In due course the loan of £30 [£2,405.58] supported and backed by the signatures of both Mr. Dale and Mr. Gribbon was granted by the committee of the Loan Society on the recommendation of Chalkley, their secretary.

Mr. Dale paid one instalment back on this loan, but no more. He had in fact, done a moonlight flit [disappeared] and his guarantor Mr. Gribbon was therefore called in to pay the balance due, £28 4 shillings, a lot of money (£2,261.25). But it came out in evidence that Mr. Dale had, five years before in 1853:

- Obtained a loan from the society for £20 [£1,603.72] and he actually received £18 [£1,443.35], the rest being the costs of the loan
- He was not very regular in his repayments
- He then obtained a second loan from the society
- Then he got a third loan for £30 [£2,405.58] from the society
- And was still not very regular in his repayments, in fact he was fined £3 [£240.56] or £4 [£320.74] for irregularity
- But he got a fourth loan of £30 [£2,405.58], the current one, as a renewal of the previous £30 loan on the advice of the society

It was this amount that was still owing. By this point, you would quite right to question why on earth the Loan Society and Chalkley as its secretary with responsibility for checking the ability of applicants to service their loans and for keeping the company accounts, allowed Mr. Dale to carry on borrowing when he had previously been fined for irregularities? Well, you only have to look at the practices of present Payday Loan Companies for your answer. However, Chalkley was a Methodist preacher and I certainly expected him to be more scrupulous with other people's money than that.

Mr. Gribbon, it turned out, had only agreed to be a guarantor for the fourth loan of £30 because Chalkley had assured him that Mr. Dale had made his previous repayments very well and that he, Chalkley, believed Mr. Dale to be a respectable man. Mr. Monk, the lawyer speaking for Mr. Gribbon, pointed out that:

'His client, Mr. Gribbon, was misled in consequence of information being kept back from him but which if he had known, would have prevented him from giving the guarantee.'

Mr. Brett, solicitor for the Trademan's Loan Society and Chalkley its employee, argued:

'There was no fraud to say that Mr. Dale had paid up very well for in point of fact he had paid up very well. Of course, it was only now that Mr. Dale was off [gone, as in disappeared] that Mr. Gribbon alleged that he had been deceived in order to avoid being responsible for the debt... '

So, who was right? His Lordship, Baron Pollock, who presided over this case held at Lancaster Crown Court, summed up for the jury and after explaining the law as to the avoidance of a contract, said that if the jury thought Mr. Chalkley made his statement to Mr. Gribbon, the proposed guarantor of the latest loan to Mr. Dale, knowing that Dale had not paid up regularly, and for the purpose of inducing the defendant to become a guarantor, then the contract was voided and the jury should find for the defendants.

They did. Gribbon won his case and Chalkley and the Liverpool Tradesman's Loan Society had egg on their face. You would have thought that Chalkley would have learnt his lesson at this point, but then another case came along.

Two ladies, both named Dickinson had been granted loans in the past from the Liverpool Tradesman's Loan Society's Manchester Office, which Chalkley supervised, and deposited security in the form of some title deeds for the amount borrowed. One of the loans was paid off in 1857 and the other in 1858 and since then they had applied for no other loans at all. The original loan had been repaid and the title deeds returned to them.

In June 1859, an application from Ann Dickinson was filled in for £200 [£11,825.84] and presented to the directors citing their deposited deeds as surety as before. The loan was granted by the directors, who did not ask to see the deeds again, and, as was the custom of the loan society, the cheque was handed to Chalkley who had the responsibility of handing it over to the borrower, Ann Dickinson. It was also Chalkley's duty to enter this cheque in the books as being handed over. All well and good, except for the fact that Ann Dickinson had not applied for a second loan.

The investigation set in process by the Loan Society in May 1860 after Chalkley fled, led to the opening of a safe in which they found promissory notes for Ann Dickinson's money, the second loan she never had, and details of her title deeds held as security, which had been back in her possession since 1858. Questions were then asked in Chalkley's absence, and a youth called George Richardson, who had been a clerk in the company, said he had filled up the application at Chalkley's direction, and that it was his handwriting.[410] Richard Barlow Pots, who in June 1859 was a director and treasurer of the Loan Company, had signed the cheque for Ann Dickinson even though all the details were in Chalkley's handwriting. The cheque directed Messrs. Moss and Co to pay to 'self' £185 5 shillings [£11,825.84], the difference being the costs of the loan, the words 'or bearer' being struck out and it was signed William Chalkley, secretary.

When this was investigated, William Cotterill, a clerk to the Loan Society, produced Chalkley's cashbook where there was another entry for the 1859 loan application by Ann Dickinson for a further £200 [£11,825.84] and on 29.6.1859 Chalkley credited himself with having paid £289 8 shillings and 5d into the bank. The promissory note for this loan was found in the cash book, it bore Chalkley's mark and he was the only person who had charge of the cash book.

William Pitt Hornby, clerk to Messrs Moss and Co Bankers, said the money was paid into the Loan Company bank account along with two other cheques, not into

Chalkley's bank account, something he thought was to Chalkley's advantage as it meant he did not personally benefit from this fraud as the money went straight back in the company account to reduce the bad debt account, but this ignores the fact that Chalkley had to balance his books having previously withdrawn heavily from the company bank account on false loan applications in his own interest.

The company's auditor, James Underhill, had audited the company accounts in January 1860. At that time Chalkley produced the notes for the loans and referred to an entry in his cash book: 'By loan to Ann Dickinson, £200.' The promissory note was produced and the auditor passed the transaction. When pressed, the auditor said that not all the necessary promissory notes were there when he audited the cash book but he was told by Chalkley that they were in the hands of the solicitor. Underhill believed him.

Finally, the two Dickinson sisters made a statement. Alice Isabella who lived at 48 St Stephen Street in Salford and Ann Dickinson confirmed they had taken loans in 1856 and 1857 and had deposited title deeds as security and that they did not take out a loan in 1859 nor was that promissory note signed in their handwriting. They confirmed they had undertaken all their transactions in 1856 and 1857 with Mr. Goodall and had never even seen Chalkley.

Goodall managed the Manchester branch of the society and, it turns out, was not employed by the society but was a servant of Chalkley's, whom he supervised in weekly visits. Goodall too had absconded by 1860 and had taken with him funds from the loan society. None of this bode well for the Loan Society.

The Dickinson case and subsequent investigations in 1860 revealed that this was not an isolated case, but the thin end of a very large wedge and Chalkley's modus operandi for accumulating a personal fortune was revealed: when it came to signing these documents, which was supposed to be done by the applicant and their guarantors or sureties, most of the people concerned were fictitious.

Chalkley's clerks under his instruction completed the details in the application forms. At the committee where applications for loans were presented by Chalkley for approval, he was given a cheque for the borrower and the fiction was never discovered for Chalkley kept the cheque for himself or he would take it to the bank and credit the company to hide the many defaulters and the then missing instalment payments from fictitious borrowers. This situation continued to such a considerable extent that in 1860 Chalkley, after appearing in Jane's case and fearing exposure, felt obliged to disappear.

The society's initial investigation found that there was a deficiency in his cash-book and on the promissory notes to the extent of £15,000 [£886,938.00] - £16,000 [£946,067.20], the majority of which was down to paperwork completed from persons whose signatures were attached to the notes, but who themselves could not be found.

This estimate changed as investigators continued to unravel new frauds and schemes which Chalkley had woven into the very structure of the loan society. More and more cases came to light and became part of the evidence against Chalkley. Another such example involved a man called William Henry Astin, who was a clothes dresser living in Huddersfield. He had stood surety for two loans from the Tradesman's Loan Society for £450 [£26,608.14] borrowed by Joshua Hanson who had since paid them off in full. Astin had provided and signed the promissory notes.

Another application with William Astin as one of the sureties was made, but the signature was not in his handwriting. He did not know the people named in the form, neither had he authorised any person to make use of his name. He had lived in Huddersfield for 27 years and knew the neighbourhood well and there was no other clothes dresser there of the same name as himself.

How did Chalkley get away with it? The directors and board members of the Loan Company who signed the cheques must have been either negligent or complicit. When they were questioned as part of the investigation, they admitted they signed the cheques but did not ask to see all the paperwork for loans, but claimed the chairman of the board did. They also denied noticing that on the applications they were presented with, that the handwriting on each was the same.

The consequences for the Liverpool Trademan's Loan Society were significant. It was established in 1846 and was a large business. The *Liverpool Mercury* understood that Chalkley had officially given security to the extent of £1,000 [£62,609.00] and that Messrs. Potts and Tuton were his guarantees. The loans guaranteed in 1846 amounted to £58,000 [£3,631,322.00] and the amounts repaid reached £54,000 [£3,380,886.00] and the company had 1,200 shares held by 13 shareholders with a paid-up capital of £30,000 [£1,773,890.78]. The previous half yearly dividend in 1859 was 8% per year free of income tax.[411]

The company in addition to their paid-up shares, traded with a very large amount of borrowed capital and many industrious and frugal people, misled by Chalkley's specious and plausible representations of the success and the safety of the society, having been induced to invest the whole of their savings in it, were now suffering for Chalkley's fraudulent behaviour.

Six months after Chalkley disappeared the statement below appeared in a letter to the editor of the *Liverpool Mercury* using the facts from the principal statement made to shareholders in November 1860[412] and shows just how bitter these investors were and how little was left in the society's coffers after Chalkley's disappearance.

'Chalkley has been permitted to rob the unfortunate shareholders of about £25,000 [£1,478,230.00]. And in addition to this, through the mismanagement and carelessness of somebody, loans have been contracted for £11,550 [£682,942.26] which are estimated to realise only £2,200 [£130,084.24] thus all the capital of the company has been lost and something more.

'What those individuals may think who have been sitting on the board of directors and have been in the receipt of pay for watching over the affairs of the company, I cannot say; I will leave them to their own thought. An inspector's report speaks of "Great laxity in the supervision of the company's affairs by the directors and a discrepancy so palpable that an ordinary degree of attention only was necessary to discover it."

'Whether any legal proceedings will eventually be taken against the directors or not rests with the shareholders. It is hoped they will sift the matter to the bottom; such gross carelessness and bad management should not be allowed to go unpunished. The misery, inconvenience and probable ruin that will fall upon many poor widows and orphan children loudly demand that justice should be done for them.'

'Yours - A VICTIM'

The society soon found itself in the bankruptcy court and eventually in voluntary liquidation.[413] By 1861, the Liverpool Trademan's Loan Society's investors were 'well-nigh ruined' and the estimated losses were rumoured to be as high as £40,000 [£2,365,168.00].[414] The absent Chalkley was comprehensively derided in a booklet entitled 'The Doings of W.S Chalkley' published in 1861.[415]

'Whilst for six days a week he was the associate of women, notorious even in Liverpool as keepers of innumerable "gay houses," he was on the seventh day assembling with a religious body, having the revolting profanity and the hypocrisy to ascend the pulpit, and the effrontery to pollute with his presence the homes of true worshippers who respected him, nay revered him, and welcomed him into their family circle, because they believed him to be sincere and devout in his professions of piety.

'We know as a fact that not only in this town, but in various other parts of the country, he was regarded as a model Christian man - as a most zealous advocate of Christian truth - as a man to be looked up to as an example of all that was holy and good - as one who not only preached, but himself obeyed the precepts of the gospel and, as a fitting illustration of the success which even in this life is sometimes the reward of a career of strict honour and integrity.

'And yet, at this very time, there can be no question that he was leading a life grossly immoral - that he was associating continually with women of the most abandoned character, and receiving, in one form or other, a share of the proceeds of infamy.

'Amongst skeletons of sermons found in his possession we see hazarded the assertion that "Man does not love sin for itself any more than men love the devil." Chalkley however, must himself either have possessed a strong attachment for the arch enemy of mankind, or he was himself living a most forcible contradiction of his public sermonising, though it is true his career might be cited in support of the truth of another portion of the same address, in which he maintains, we need not say how theoretically, that "Sin prostrates all the energies of the soul... sin is ruinous, it leads to hell!"

'In the gratification of his lust he sacrificed all; and for the society of the most degraded and depraved he left a home where he was fondly and dearly loved by a wife and daughter, against whom, we believe, there has never been even a breath of suspicion - who appear throughout to have had not the least idea of the true character of the serpent whom they nested in their bosoms, and who even yet still cling to him with the fondness of a woman's love.

'But indeed, such an adept does he appear to have become in the art of hypocrisy, that not only does he seem to have averted suspicion from the minds of all with whom he came into contact, but even to have deceived himself as to the true character of the course he was pursuing.'

Amen.

Chapter 19 - Life in the Brothel Streets

While Jane is languishing in prison as an insolvent debtor for not paying the costs of the *Johnson v Gallagher* court case and investigations begin into what exactly she does owe, I thought I would try to establish just how extensive her holdings were, the houses she owned, rented and ran as brothels. In the process I discovered much more about what everyday life was like in Liverpool, not only for Jane and her women, but her neighbours as well.

As the houses Jane lists in her testimony appear in clusters on various street maps, I started with those in the very centre of the town.

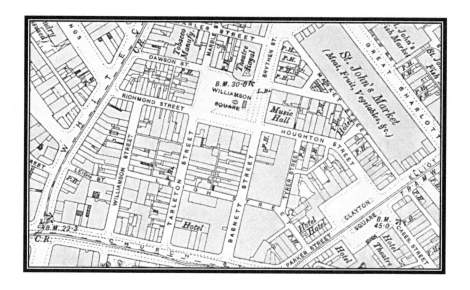

Figure 40 Houghton, Tyrer, Upper Dawson Street. OS Liverpool 1890

They are Nos 4,6,8 and 9 Houghton Street; Tyrer Street Nos 2,6 and 8 which are adjacent to Houghton Street and Upper Dawson Street Nos 10 and 12 which are parallel to Houghton Street, quite a cosy clutch of brothels, right in the centre of the town and near to several theatres. Houghton Street links Williamson Square with Clayton Square and beyond via Roe Street, Queen's Square, all very important focal points in the city. It was also the heart of Jane's brothel empire.

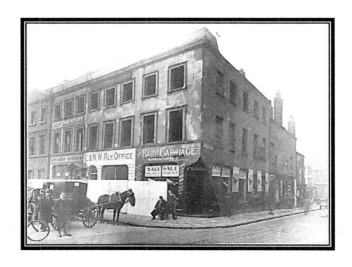

Figure 41 Clayton Square, corner of Houghton Street, Richard Brown 1923

Williamson's Square in 1807 housed the *Theatre Royal*, rich merchants, gentlemen, ladies of independent means, and hotels or boarding houses. In Clayton Square there were ten merchants, two physicians, a counting house, a gentleman and lady of independent means and a draper's shop. Both squares and Houghton Street hosted vibrant street markets at various times during the week and the whole area was very busy.

The *Playhouse Theatre*, referred to as a music hall, appears on the map at the end of Houghton Street facing Williamson Square where today it is the only surviving Victorian theatre still in active theatrical use. It must have extended down Houghton Street as far as No 26 where there was a theatre entrance. In 1866, it was the site of the former *Star Music Hall*, the name coming from the fact that the music hall was itself built on the site of an even earlier concert hall, run by Jem Ward, called the *Star Concert Hall*, which was active in the mid-19th century. Jane and her customers would probably have visited all three of these theatres over the years, calling into her high-class brothels either before or after the shows.[416]

The 1851 census that shows Houghton Street had: two cabinet makers, three plumbers and glaziers, a sailmaker, an auctioneer and a hairdresser, two shoe makers, two poulterers, a grocer and a tobacconist. To cater for less respectable tastes, it was also the home of Jane's brothels disguised variously as eating houses, lodging houses, coffee houses, oyster rooms or billiard halls, hidden alongside two other billiard halls, two victuallers and beer houses, two lodging houses and a Temperance Hotel.

Figure 42 Corner of Williamson Sq with Houghton St. 1858 W.G. Herdman

Five of the Jane's immediate neighbour's premises on Houghton Street sold alcohol and the impact of drunkenness, seen nightly in the town, was no respecter of class.

'A person of respectable appearance, whose eyes shot forth a rather insane expression, booked in the lockup record as Charles Simeon, was charged with drunk and disorderly conduct in the streets on the previous evening, 3.9.1835.'

Watchman: Last night, about two o'clock this morning, I found the prisoner....

Prisoner: Mr. Magistrate, let him speak deliberately and slowly, as I intend to take down his words and make an example of him.

Watchman: I found him drunk and disorderly in Houghton Street and as he would not go about his business, I walked him to the bridewell.

Prisoner: Me drunk! Me the devil. What, I drunk? No such thing. I am a captain in his Majesty's navy and have seen very glorious service. Me drunk! Ag, ah! Me drunk! Very good! I'll tell you, sir, all about it. I am a magistrate of two counties and have committed many for that crime, consequently it cannot be supposed that I would commit myself. [Laughter in court.] I have not the honour of your acquaintance, sir, but the last time I had the felicity of appearing in this place, I had two public dinners given to me.

Magistrate: That may be, sir, most persons in your situation as prisoners, receive a dinner at the public expense. Your statements, however have nothing to do with the charge.

Prisoner: I think they have, if law and justice go hand in hand. The fact is, that constable has been telling lies of a most extraordinary calibre. I went to the lockup for the purpose of charging the man with a most gross assault upon my person, and when I arrived there with one of the constables, the station house keeper and the constable seized upon me and kept me on this charge.

Watchman: The prisoner was in company with ladies of questionable character, who, in chorus with him, created a great disturbance by knocking at the doors of public and other houses, at two o'clock in the morning. He, the watchman, had desired them to desist.

Prisoner: I am a member of the Common's House of Parliament, and can do as I like.

Watchman: Not as I knows in this mere town of Liverpool.

Upon which, 'issue was joined,' and the prisoner booked for the night. The magistrate said it was evident the prisoner was both drunk and disorderly, and therefore, he must pay a fine of five shillings [£16.95].

> 'The prisoner did not like the decision in the least and had evidently still a wish to carry the matter before the House of Commons; but the police court in this instance being the "Imperial Parliament," £4 15 shillings [£322.06] was given to him in change out of a £5 note [£339.01], which was in his possession when he was taken. The prisoner received the change with much chagrin and left the court threatening the powers that be in the lower courts with the vengeance of the courts above. From his appearance, we should judge the prisoner to be a mad man.'

So said the *Liverpool Standard and General Advertiser*.[417]

Whilst drink was without doubt the greatest contributor to social evil in Liverpool, gambling was a big problem too.

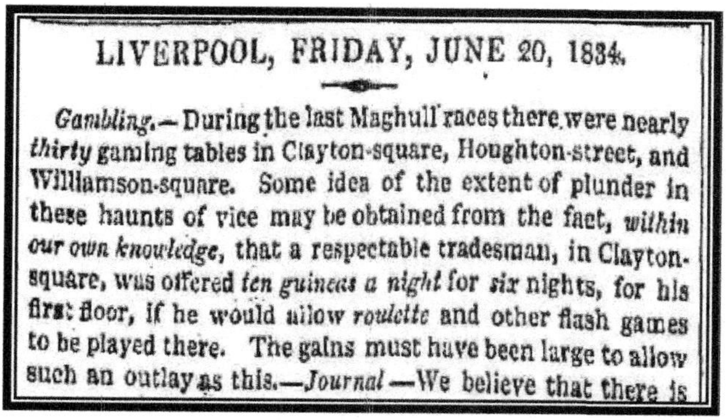

LIVERPOOL, FRIDAY, JUNE 20, 1834,

Gambling. — During the last Maghull races there were nearly thirty gaming tables in Clayton-square, Houghton-street, and Williamson-square. Some idea of the extent of plunder in these haunts of vice may be obtained from the fact, *within our own knowledge*, that a respectable tradesman, in Clayton-square, was offered *ten guineas a night* for *six* nights, for his first floor, if he would allow *roulette* and other flash games to be played there. The gains must have been large to allow such an outlay as this.—*Journal*—We believe that there is

Figure 43 Gambling - Liverpool Mercury 20.6.1834

The money that changed hands was significant, when ten guineas a night in 1834 was worth £711.91 at current values. For six nights anyone offering their premises would have received the equivalent of £4,271.46. Later in the 1860s, the area was the scene of organised fist fighting contests, illegal cock and dog fighting with the best money to be made when the horse races were on at Chester or Aintree.

Four houses on Houghton Street were occupied by brothels owned by Jane or her mother at various times, who sub-let to ladies who would pay for their rooms. There would be a person in charge, a cook, someone to serve food and alcohol, maids to clean up and probably a man on the door to keep the riff - raff out. All four establishments appear on the Liverpool council's lease registers so in one sense the council made money from immorality too, against the terms of their own leases.

The best madams made sure that their women were free of disease, clean, smelt nice, wore beautiful clothes, could read and talk intelligently. We know from lists of contents how valuable Jane's furniture was, enough for it to be keenly fought over in court cases, and in these luxurious surroundings, Jane could bill gentlemen additionally for food, wine and spirits. She would have made as much money, if not more, from extras than from the acts of social evil, for her brothels added the illusion there was no vice involved and men could go home well satisfied with their consciences intact.

Jane is reported to have said in one of her court cases that No 4 Houghton Street was run by her mother as a brothel. No 4a was a respectable business until 1856 and the premises of both were big enough for multiple occupancy. Jane's mother was the tenant of a Mr. Sheffer who owned the house for 11 years from 1849.

Year and Source	Occupants of No 4 Houghton Street
9.6.1796 lease register	Executors of Mary Park in the name of Richard Sanday
1827 -1829 Street Directories	David Morris, Livery Stables
1841 Census	Mary Winstanley 30, children: Edward 8, Maisie 6, Thomas 5 months. John Clay 30, Painter, Elizabeth Clay 30, Mary Tunstall 60, Francis Tunstall 30 and Catherine Conley 20
1841- 1843 Street Directories	John Winstanley
1845-1851 Street Directories and 1851 Census	James Dawber, a vet. The 1851 Census shows Fanny Hughes, age 24, is a House Keeper, plus Harriet Hughes, a house servant.
1851-1855 Street Directories, Liverpool Mail 5.4.1851	James Dawber is still head of the household, but he gives up the Vet practice due to ill health and a Mr. John Turner takes over in March 1851 until 1855
1855-1856 Street Directories	1855 No 4 was split and 4 was occupied by John Platt and 4a by John Turner, who was a Car Proprietor between 1855/6

Neither Mr. Sheffer's, Jane's or her mother's name appears anywhere on the table, so we have only her word for this. The first real indication that No 4 was anything but a legitimate domestic household is in the census of 1851 where Fanny Hughes, age 24, from Boston in Lincolnshire, with a servant Harriet Hughes, age 43, from Ireland appears. As the girls lived elsewhere and only rented rooms for the night, when Jane claims to keep a hotel there, she is 'sort of' right.

Gore's 1862 street directory shows Jane is the head of the household at No 4 and the place is described as a 'Coffee House,' and on 8.1.1862, Emma Studdart of No 4 Houghton Street is in court for keeping a disorderly house there while Jane is living in London. [418]

5 Houghton Street, prior to Jane and her mother taking it over, had been a Timber Merchants and a Spirit Vault and therefore was in effect commercial premises and probably quite large, possibly in multiple occupancy. Jane claimed it had been a 'gay house' for the previous 35 years, since 1816.

I can find no information about when Jane's mother acquired it with a mortgage of £1,000 [£59,129.20] via Mr. Lowndes of Messrs Lowndes, Bateson and Robinson solicitors, but it was also known as a 'Coffee House' from around 1845 and when Jane's mother died this became part of her estate and Jane took over the tenancy but paid no rent. The furniture was by paid for by instalments.

Jane says she became the tenant of No 8 in 1851, but did not pay rent, claiming it had been her mother's house prior to her moving in and it had been a 'gay house' before that, like No 5, where Margaret Davies, a spirit dealer ran it as the *Grapes Hotel* and a brothel.

No 8 Houghton Street had a wide variety of occupants too, mostly respectable traders until around 1839:

- A merchant
- A Pen, Quill and Feather dealer
- A carver and gilder

Before more dubious occupations then started to appear:

- Spirit Dealers
- Billiard Halls
- Lodging Houses
- Jane's establishments

Then came James Clark's court appearances from 1857, as his beer licence for No 8 is refused more times than it is granted and he is fined for serving out of hours, organising both dog and cock fights as well as allowing betting on his premises. He is also reputed to be a teacher of martial arts. On this occasion only, against all the odds, James Clark's licence was granted. The magistrates might have been influenced by the fact that the clerk to court pointed out that the Duke of Wellington was also a fighting man...

By 1869, 8 Houghton Street was frequented by:

'Betting men, sparring men and fighting men. There was a very large sparring room upstairs. Thieves, also of the lowest order, went there.'

The census of 1861, when Jane was living at No 9, shows that Janet Johnson, age 40 born in Ireland, is the head of the household and a cook, also from Ireland. But who are they keeping house and cooking for? In this instance the girls do live on the premises, or were just caught there on census night for there are several young women, age 18-23, none of whom are related. Four of the girls come from Ireland, two from different parts of Lancashire and one from Plymouth.

Year and Source	Occupants of No 8 Houghton Street
1807 Street Directory	Thomas Wattleworth, a merchant
1829 Street Directory	Thomas Reilly, a Pen, Quill and Feather dealer
1839 -1849 Census and Street Directories	Margaret Davies, spirit dealer of the Grapes Hotel, who could have managed this as a brothel for Jane and her mother
And at the same time in 1841	John Ayres, secretary of the Rotunda (a theatre) and also Edward Simkin Morris, a billiard table maker, live here. Property must have been divided into two shops as well as a house
1847 Street Directory	John Whiteman, a carver and guilder moves in and John Ayres now has a billiard room on the premises
1850 Marriage certificate	Jane Gallagher marries from here.
1851 Census	Jane and William Mercer, living with Fanny Magee, age 60 and her family
Liverpool Mail 3.4.1852	Advert for a furniture sale of items at 8 Houghton Street which is the property of Jane Gallagher
Liverpool Mercury 10.9.1852	Run by William Mercer, Jane's second husband. He was bound over by the magistrate to 'Get his house in order…'
1853 Street Directory	William Mercer
1855 Street Directory	William and Thomas Bailiff, cabinet makers

Such a gathering of unrelated girls in the same house is characteristic of other known brothels I have looked into, especially when you add to the mix the fact that they are either milliners or dressmakers. That is not to assume their professions mean they were automatically prostitutes but, many were.

Year and Source	Occupants of No 9 Houghton Street
1825	George Beaden, a Stay Maker (corset maker),
1839 to 1848	John Ayres, billiard table maker, lived at No 9 and also at No 8 from 1841 – as they were next to each other
Advert 1844	Edwin Simkin Morris who has Billiard Rooms here which he says are 'spacious and commodious' and to which he has 'fitted up with every comfort and convenience.'
1851 Census	William Bailiff, a cabinet maker at No 9 until 1859 and at No 8

An entry in the Council's Lease Register dated 26th May 1825 shows that Charles Lowndes, a gentleman, owned 9 Houghton Street, the same Mr. Lowndes from the solicitors who sold No 5 to Jane's mother.

The lease register describes the property:

'All that piece or parcel of land, with the two several messuages or dwelling houses or shops... containing in front to Houghton Street 18 ft 6 inches and running in depth on the South East side 60 ft and to the North West side 40 ft 10 inches and from thence in a circular form to the front of Market Street 20 ft 4 inches.'[419]

Conditions of the lease are:

- Not to put warehouse doors to Houghton Street
- Not to carry out offensive trades

Nevertheless, Jane ran it as a brothel until 1862 when she was forced to close it by the police.

Edwin Simkin Morris not only confirms the use of 9 Houghton Street in the 1840s but also provides us with an idea of how big the house was, and more interestingly, that it had a private side entrance on Upper Dawson Street, which no doubt came in useful as Jane's clientele could come and go discretely.

In 1859, the place was a 'Coffee House' run by Mary Detmer who gave it the name while she also seemed to be running No 5. She managed this house for Jane and the 1861 census lists Jane living there with Fanny Francis, the housekeeper, who appeared for Jane in the *Talking Fish* cases in 1860 – 1861, along with a seaman boarder, chief mate and three other staff.

As we have seen, social evil and drink sustain each other on Houghton Street, spiced up with entertainment in the form of the theatres, and as a result:

'There were 2,912 publicans and tavern keepers and around 3,000 manufactories of human degradation and wretchedness. If all the churches and preaching rooms were counted, there would be only around 300.

'This meant, there were twenty taverns to one church, twenty chaplains of darkness to one minister of light.'[420]

Social reformers had an unenviable task.

Chapter 20 - Preying on the Vulnerable

'There are about 200 prostitutes on the streets of Liverpool under 12 years of age.'
The chaplain of Liverpool workhouse in a public meeting, July 1854.

There are many reasons why young children ended up mired in a life of social evil in Liverpool in the Victorian period. For some, it was due to the failings or vicious practices of their parents, for others it was procuresses who lured them into their brothels where they were compelled to provide personal services. Most often it began for children as young as three years of age when they were stripped, robbed of everything they stood up in and abandoned. If they were lucky, they were found and taken to a policeman. What is not known is how many weren't and were never heard of again. [421]

'In February 1842 an eleven-year-old girl called Jane Whalley was sent by her parents from Ormskirk [12.5 miles from Liverpool] to act as a servant and milk girl for a cow-keeper. After she had lived in her place a week or so, she was found, from her size and strength, not to suit, so her master determined on sending her back to her father and mother.

'Accordingly, on Saturday last, she was despatched, with her bundle under her arm, to find a cart by which she could be conveyed home. It seems she missed her way and after rambling about the town till twelve o'clock at night, fell in with some prostitutes who took her to one of Mrs. Donnell's five brothels in Albion Street, Liverpool. Here she was reduced to nearly a state of nudity and the whole of her clothes pawned.

'On Tuesday she was found in the brothel by a police officer and taken to a bridewell for safety. When the case came up on the Wednesday, it was found her clothes had been pledged by a young woman at the shop of Mr. Holland, pawnbroker on London Road, who said in her defence that another girl named Eliza Higgie had given them her to pledge. Eliza was ordered to pay a penalty of forty shillings [£132.92], the costs for illegally pledging, and two shillings [£6.04], the sum the articles were pledged for, or be imprisoned and the clothes were ordered to be returned by the pawnbroker to the girl.'

This was not an isolated case. [422]

'In September 1847, an elderly man named John Smith was committed for trial charged with robbing Ann Walker, a little girl. She was going up Prescot Street in Liverpool with a basket when the man gave her something wrapped in paper, which he said was a shilling, telling her to go and purchase pears with it. He then took charge of her basket and ran off but was apprehended in Moss Street. It was found out afterwards that the shilling was a farthing he had folded in the paper.'

And in 1857:

'A well-dressed scoundrel, named Joseph Clare, described as a porter but who was actually the keeper of two houses of ill fame, one at 1 Springfield Street and the other at 38 Hotham Street, was brought up by a detective officer on a charge of having committed a felonious assault on his own daughter, a girl named Mary Ann, twelve years of age. The case excited horror and disgust in all who heard it.[423]

'The girl who is a handsome, intelligent person, very well dressed and who appeared large for her age, said she was twelve years old on the 13.12.1856. She went to bed in Hotham Street about nine on that night, when her father proceeded to commit the offence. She screamed and her half-brother heard her, a boy of about fourteen years of age, then her father ran out of the room.'

The girl said her father had attempted the assault three times before. The doctors who examined Mary Ann said there had been violence but they could not say from what cause. They did not think she had been penetrated. Joseph, her half-brother, who said his role was 'to collect the bed money from the girls who go to the house,' confirmed he had rushed to his sister's aid when she screamed and found his stepfather lying on the bed where Mary Ann and he usually slept.

Joseph Clare was Irish and a street directory in 1848 listed him as the publican of the *Eagle Tavern* in Liverpool so he must have brought his family over from Ireland before then, as Mary Ann Clare and her brother Joseph were both born there. He was about 30, but said to be 40 in a different newspaper, and admitted he had taken some liberties with his daughter but nothing of a criminal description. The jury found him guilty and the judge summing up said his conduct:

'Was the most horrible and disgusting he had ever heard of, and that he was sorry that the law only allowed him to pass a very lenient sentence for this offence, but the highest that the law did allow him, he should inflict.'

Two year's imprisonment with hard labour was the result.[424] Joseph Clare must have been known to Jane Gallagher for one of her brothels was at No 1 Springfield Street and she had others on Hotham Street. There was a similar case in the Liverpool press ten years later. Charles Jack, a labourer age 42 was arrested on 13.2.1867 and sentenced to twelve months' imprisonment for having carnal knowledge of a little girl age 10 called Emma Allcock. He had no previous convictions.[425]

Until 1885, the age of consent was thirteen and amongst wealthy Victorian men there was much demand for young girls as one prevailing belief was that intercourse with a child cured syphilis, and they paid a great deal for a virgin. It was a lucrative business, had an unlimited male market and there was a lot of money to be made by those with few scruples.

The Liverpool *Porcupine* magazine in 1857 reported there were 680 children wandering the streets of the town in 1856 alone. Procuresses:

> 'Lurked at the corner of streets watching for (their) prey... Younger and younger girls, either through desperation or more often, by being enticed, decoyed or abducted by other females, were persuaded or forced into prostitution. Many were invited into brothels for refreshment by 'kind' ladies who then initiated them into the trade.'

This led to the prominence of procuresses like Harriet Brunell. Under the headline: 'A House of Assignation,'[426] the *Liverpool Mercury* describes how, in August 1862, a young attractive girl under sixteen, who was not named, but had been living respectably in Chester with her mother, was one day walking in Clements Walk in the city. A woman known as Polly Stanley asked her into a house to help with some cleaning, but then kept her there overnight, locking her into a bedroom with a strange man.

The next morning Polly Stanley took the girl to Harriet Brunell's brothel at 53 Warren Street, Liverpool and handed her over. The girl was then renamed 'Minnie St Clare', to prevent her mother from finding her and forced to give herself to numerous visitors who left her various sums of money, from 10 shillings and sixpence [£31.04] to £5 [£295.65], which was taken off her by Harriet Brunell the moment the men had gone.

Another girl called Martha Freeman age 18 said she had been taken on as a domestic servant in Harriet Brunell's house and at that time, she did not know what sort of house it was. Before that she had been living in respectable situation in Tuebrook, Liverpool. After a few days she realised it was a brothel but Harriet Brunell told her she would forfeit a month's wages if she left. She was then compelled to become a prostitute. Harriet Brunell was sentenced to six months hard labour. Such procuresses were well known, lived raucous lives and appeared often in the newspapers. Hotham Street, near to Lime Street, was one of the most popular places for trade in young girls.

Johanna Rosenberg, of German descent, commonly known as Madam Anna, supplied young girls for many years. Described as a 'portly-looking lady, elegantly attired,' she is in court almost as many times as Jane Gallagher, both as accused and accuser, but for very different reasons. Very handy in a cat fight, she managed lower class brothels and was involved in more than one assault case, unlike Jane who was mostly in court for owing money.[427]

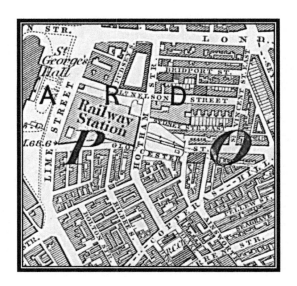

Figure 44 Hotham St adjacent to Lime Street Station. OS map. 1846-1864

The first we hear of her is in 1850 when she is characterised as a 'Liverpool lady in the habit of visiting the races.' Madam Anna was in a booth on the 9th October at Chester Races when she saw a friend playing roulette. As she knew he was likely to lose his money she went up to him to draw him away but Job Walker, aged 42, who had the management of the roulette table along with a Mr. Williams, resented her interference and a scuffle took place. During this it was alleged that a gold watch on a chain round Madam Anna's neck was snatched and went missing. When the watch could not be found, Job Walker was arrested.[428]

At the subsequent court case, Madam Anna admitted she had been drinking champagne before the watch went missing but said she had not had much. When asked how much she considered this to be for one person she replied, 'About a couple of bottles.'

A private in the 2nd Dragoon Guards was called as a witness. He said he had been with the party before the scuffle and Madam Anna and her group of six or seven people had drunk between six and eight bottles of champagne and that she had definitely been tipsy. Two other females who had a booth nearby were called as witnesses and said when Madam Anna had been in the tent before the scuffle, she did not have the gold watch round her neck, only a vinaigrette [an ornamental bottle for holding smelling salts] and that she had been so drunk she had set herself on fire. Job Walker was acquitted.

In July 1851, Madam Anna is in court again this time accused of assaulting Ann Jones. They both lived on Hotham Street, where each kept an establishment. Ann Jones claimed that Madam Anna threw water at her from an upstairs window, then came down and thrashed her with a whip. Madam Anna was fined 20 shillings [£80.90].[429]

Evidently a spirited woman, Madam Anna in March 1852 was arrested for an assault on Catherine Smith and again fined 20 shillings. Catherine was also fined 16 shillings [£64.15] for breaking Madam Anna's windows.[430]

Later in May 1852, Madam Anna was in court for the assault of Emma Goldsmith and Ann Parsons. It took place in a cellar in Hotham Street on 6th May. Madam Anna had hair torn from her head, lost a bracelet valued at £35 [£2,806.51] and a pin shaped like a snake set with diamonds worth £55 [£4,410,24]. She claimed the two women had tried to throw her on the fire. When she extricated herself, she threw a tumbler at the head of Ann Parsons, which left a severe wound. Witnesses said that Madam Anna was the aggressor throughout but the verdict was a 20 shilling fine for Ann Parsons and costs or 14 days imprisonment and Emma Goldsmith had to pay a 40 shilling fine [£160.37] or suffer one month's imprisonment.[431]

In September 1854, another court case involving Madam Anna actually disappointed the people of Liverpool waiting eagerly to hear some scandal. She was summoned by prostitute Margaret Anna Esser.

'As the court began to fill and a few minutes before the time appointed, there was a regular rush of persons into the lobbies. Human hopes are made for disappointment and in this case the consternation was great when the expectants were informed it was "No Go."'

Madam Anna had settled with the young girl and paid money into court to avoid further exposure:

'As it was likely that, had the case gone ahead, the names of certain persons who visited her house would be revealed and it would not be pleasant or convenient that such names should appear in newspapers.'

The case was discharged.[432]

In 1855, Madam Anna 'the celebrated keeper of a disorderly house on Hotham Street,' was summoned for selling foreign sherry wine without a license. An excise officer proved that on the 5th March they were supplied in her house with three bottles of sherry. In her defence, Madam Anna said she had bought the wine from Taylor's public house in the neighbourhood, but at five shillings [£20.05] less for each bottle than she charged the excise officers, an enormous profit. She was fined £50 [£4,009.31.][433]

In September 1856, Madam Anna, 'A lady so well known in the annals of Hotham Street,' was summoned by the police for using obscene language in the streets, but she did not condescend to appear in court and was fined £1 [£80.19] in her absence.[434]

Finally, in December 1857,[435] another court heard how Madam Anna kept five or six young girls in each brothel, each aged between fifteen and twenty, many of whom had been imported from abroad to meet the demand. She was also said to export English girls to Hamburg for the same purpose. Evidence was produced which had been gathered by the Home Office about this illegal trade which included:

'Harrowing disclosures as to the manner of treatment received by these unfortunate foreign girls.'

They described of how Madam Anna called on them in their homes, induced them to enter her establishments and brought them to Liverpool herself. English girls from other parts of the country were also found in her houses by anxious parents and the police.

The exact charge was:

'Having kept and maintained a certain common, ill maintained house for her lucre and gain, caused to come together certain persons, as well as men and women, of evil name and fame, for the purpose of drinking, tippling and otherwise misbehaving themselves.'

As Madam Anna held her handkerchief to her eyes, appearing to be weeping, the Recorder delivered judgement on 16.12.1857, there being no need to hear evidence as she had pleaded guilty.[436]

'It appears that you, not being an Englishwoman but a foreigner, have for five years or more resided in this town and kept a brothel. It appears that the inmates of this house for the most part were girls, young girls, English and foreign, and under your auspices, under your eye, and in your house, many immoralities have been practised and much harm, no doubt, has been done.

'If, as it is alleged, young girls have been induced by you to enter into this course of life attended by misery and ending in destruction, you have indeed much to answer for. There must be a heavy burden on your conscience if you rightly consider these things. A just sense of such conduct ought to fill you with apprehension more serious than can attend the sentence of any earthly judge.

'However, I don't exactly know how these things are, and I can only deal, by your plea, to justice, with what is certain against you. If and considering how long you have carried on with this brothel in this town and how much mischief must have been done there, the sentence of the court is that you must be imprisoned and kept to hard labour for four calendar months and in addition to that, pay to the Queen a fine of £25 [£1,478.23] and be further imprisoned till that fine is paid.

'One thing I will add, that I hope the landlord of this house, Mr. John Shallcross, whoever he may be, will be more careful of the next tenant that he gets into it.'

After the sentencing, the *Liverpool Daily Post* observed:

'In the neighbourhood of Madam Anna's late residence, the auctioneer is busy in houses of similar character. Three out of the seven or eight houses forming one cluster of infamy in Hotham Street are thus closed up and the fear of fine, imprisonment and hard labour will, we have no doubt, have its influence on many others.'

This included Jane Gallagher who also closed up her establishment(s) in Hotham Street around this time.

But Madam Anna had not finished yet. She still had powerful and influential friends in Liverpool two years later. In 1859, she was the subject of searching questions after gaining bail with two gentlemen providing sureties for her. The *Liverpool Daily Post* tried to identify them but their names were not to be found on the official register or their addressees nor a description of the monies deposited as bail. The newspaper demanded to know:

'Why an exception was made for this woman and why there should even be the appearance of sympathy in official quarters with a lady of Madam Anna's class and character.'

I wonder, was this pay-back from the 1854 case where she did a deal with the complainant to avoid embarrassment to unknown gentlemen?[437]

Madame La Farcie, another keeper of many brothels on Hotham Street, was a similar larger than life procuress, 'Well dressed, portly, of rather dissipated appearance,' she had a long list of aliases: [438]

- Mathilde Schwendler, late of 48 Lime Street (Café de L'Empire), housekeeper to a hotel and Coffee House keeper
- Mathilde Schwendler Colbert
- Mathilde Colbert
- Mathilde de la Farcie
- Madame de la Farcie

On the 13.8.1862, a case came to the notice of the press because Mary Ann Jones, age 14, was charged with theft and found in a brothel at 52 Hotham Street, owned by Madam la Farcie. She was the daughter of a joiner living in Smithdown Lane in Liverpool, had run away from home and stolen a cloak and skirt belonging to her mother and sister. Finding Mary Ann led to the arrest and charging of Madam la Farcie:

'A second edition of Madam Anna, for keeping an abominable house for the purposes of prostitution.'

It was reserved for the reception of young girls and this was not the first time a complaint had been 'urged' against her house.

Mary Ann's mother, a decent, respectable looking woman, said her daughter had been a very naughty and cruel girl for some length of time. On the Saturday night she had told her she was going to the *Zoological Gardens* with a companion who she [the mother] knew to be a decent girl. Mary Ann did not return home until after eleven o'clock and her mother scolded her for being out so late. The next day Mary Ann left home taking with her the clothing she stole and information was given to the police.[439]

Mary Ann was remanded for seven days. Matilda la Farcie was formerly charged with keeping a brothel for about six years [from 1856] and procuring young girls at No 52 Hotham Street, where she acted as the manager. The landlady of the house was a Mrs. Mandeville.

A good-looking girl, age seventeen, but of meretricious appearance and bearing, called Margaret Tobin, was called as a witness and she told how, about six weeks previously in June as she was walking along Ranelagh Street in Liverpool one afternoon with another girl, she met two young women. They asked her 'Have you any money, miss?' She went with them to a public house where they said she could live at 52 Hotham Street. She went there but not with the girls. If she had not met the girls, she said she 'had always intended going to some other house on that street.'

Once there, Margaret asked Madam la Farcie if she could stay. She agreed and stated her terms: she would supply Margaret with board, lodgings and the clothes she was to wear 'when going out' These were only lent to her by Madam la Farcie. This was a common practice designed to prevent girls from leaving as their own clothes were sold by the brothel madam. Many who tried were arrested for 'stealing' the fine clothes. Margaret was to give Madam la Farcie all the money she earned

In the evening, Madam la Farcie gave her some clothes and asked her if she had parents in Liverpool but she did not remember what answer she gave but told her she was about eighteen. Madam la Farcie took the girl to some public places, to the supper rooms and the *Turkish Divan*, the *German Coffee House* and other places, showing off her new acquisition. She stayed at the house in Hotham Street for about two weeks and there were other girls living there. People who visited the house sometimes gave her money and sometimes gave it to Madam la Farcie.

The jury returned a verdict of 'Guilty.' The Recorder judged her case to be of an aggravated character as :

'She had allowed children of about fourteen years of age to go into her house for the purposes of turning them into prostitutes with the intention of profiting from their wages.'

The Recorder, said: 'He could not conceive of anything more abominable in a Christian country than such a mode of proceeding.'

She was sentenced to 18 months imprisonment with hard labour and was not seen in Liverpool again. [440]

The police did not collect and publish figures for the number of child prostitutes known to police under the age of 16 in 1854, and by 1858 the numbers are much less than the 200 alleged by the chaplain of Liverpool workhouse, but it is inevitable there were far more. What was known about them was that most girls began their lives with stealing, simply because they were starving, around 13 years of age and cases recorded in the Liverpool's Quarterly Sessions books show a clear progression from lesser crimes to common prostitution and worse. [441] Given the lack of credible alternatives, it was inevitable that some children grew into hardened professional prostitutes and criminals very quickly.

However, many of the young women had no choice but to remain on the streets of Liverpool or trapped in back street brothels. Ann Williams's career is set out overleaf and shows her convictions began with drinking at twenty, moving onto vagrancy by age twenty-two with many following sentences for prostitution, ending at age thirty-two as a reputed thief.[442]

Ann W	Offence	Sentences
1839 – age 20	Drunk x 3	2 days
1840-41 - age 21 -22	Prostitution x 6 Vagrancy x2	7 – 14 days 3 months
1842-43 – age 23-24	Prostitution x 10	7 days – 1 month
1844-46 – age 25-27	Drunk x 3 Stealing and Prostitution	3 days 1 month
1847-48 – age 28 -29	Prostitution x 8 Drunk	1 month 3 days

The authorities did try, but often to no avail.

In December 1841, a child not yet fourteen and a prostitute was found drunk and disorderly in Dale Street, Liverpool molesting every gentleman who came near her. She was sent to the House of Correction.[443] In 1869, Mary Ann Rawthorne, another child of only 14 years of age, was brought in and charged by Mr. Graham, reformatory agent, under the following circumstances:

'In March 1886, she was sent to a reformatory from whence she absconded twice, the last time being two months since. A letter sent by Mr. Cropper stated that the authorities were totally unable to manage her. She was found on Saturday last in one of the vilest brothels in Ben Johnson Street and had been walking the streets of the town as a prostitute. She was sentenced to three months hard labour after which an endeavour would be made to get her into a penitentiary.'

Why was nothing more done by the authorities to protect these young people? Well, there was some perception in Victorian society that the exploitation of young girls only happened in 'foreign parts,' where the people were barbarians anyway. The newspapers certainly showcased the more extreme cases for polite society to read and be scandalised about, whilst at the same time encouraging them to think it was a distant problem. For example, in 1845 the *Liverpool Mercury* reported:

'The Russian government is about to authorise the sale of Circassian children, principally for the purpose of prostitution to the Turks.'

Later, in 1858, they told of how Mr. Toogood, the magistrate of Monghyr in Bengal, India, discovered that the clerks were in the habit of registering the sale of girls to brothel keepers on legal documents. Three girls in particular had been sold to one American woman via deeds of lease, which assigned them to her for 90 years, and all their children. She, as their new owner was entitled to 'extract any kind of service whatever' and bound only to furnish food and clothing.

At the resulting trial the nameless American woman admitted that the girls were intended for prostitution: one admitted she followed that trade, another said she was young, but that 'she was being brought up to it.' What is even more startling is the fact that a higher court, whilst admitting all the facts were true, censured the original magistrate for interfering with matters with which he had nothing to do with. The clerk who signed the deeds was acquitted. The American brothel-keeper was given two years imprisonment by two judges as the hiring of a girl for immoral purposes was illegal but a third judge, a Mr. Colvin, disagreed. He said that the proceedings were null and void. A Mr. Sconce went even further and claimed the American woman was rather an injured individual than otherwise. Hiring a child, he said, does not 'constitute a crime.'[444]

Women could also find they were exploited and trafficked by men they had previously lived with as man and wife. In October 1867, a young Frenchwoman named Margaret Gandi was charged with assaulting Louis der Gest, an agent for a Brussels lace house.[445] The charge was dismissed as trivial but it came out in evidence that der Gest, having tired of Margaret Gandi, took her over to Brussels saying he had got her a job in a hotel. Once there she was introduced to a Madame Julie and after being in her house for a day or two found that instead of the place being an hotel, it was a brothel and that der Gest had actually sold her for 250 francs for the purposes of prostitution. Horrified at the situation, she persuaded a friend to pay the money and release her and got a receipt from Madame Julie. No more is known but one can only imagine what happened next as she ended up in court on a charge of assault.

Victorian society was slow to waken up to the problems on their own doorsteps but in 1854, the *Liverpool Mail* ran a long article on the front page of its Saturday

Supplement on 19th August showing how trafficking in young girls for prostitution was fast becoming an urgent concern in England as well as in foreign parts. [446]

'At almost all of the principal railways stations are to be found wretches whose sole occupation it is to be on the watch for suitable victims. Hundreds of men and women are constantly employed in the diabolic trade of seduction, enticing young girls between ten and seventeen years of age to leave their homes to devote themselves to the shameful service of prostitution. Young people are traded as if they were so many bales of Manchester cotton, decoyed and entrapped under the pretence of teaching them some trade or bettering their prospects in life.'

They analysed recent court cases and found that there was an ongoing price for such services. £8 [£641.49] secured a young person, who had to pay the brothel keeper for their board and lodging but they then shared the profits from monies they generated for the business.

'Such a trade is worse than that of a Virginian slave trader. Five years is the working life expectancy for a prostitute, as against 30 years for a slave.'

The newspaper points to opening comments in court made by the official Recorder showing that female profligacy and crime existed in Liverpool in a far greater proportion to the population than in other large towns, the cause being drunkenness, and again the magistrates are scapegoated.

'We cannot help thinking that our local magistracy has not been sufficiently active in availing themselves of existing legal means for abating and repressing those dreadful evils. The evil is a most fearful one, morally, socially, physically, its baneful effects are spreading far and wide. Our legislators will incur a tremendous responsibility if now that the disease has become so patent, they do not at once apply to it every remedy in their power.'

Once enticed and used to the life and attention, not every attempt to rescue girls thus abducted succeeded. Two girls in 1867 were lured from their homes in Belgium and inquiries were made in all directions to find them, all in vain. The father, heartbroken, returned to his ordinary life, but was then told his daughters were in London. He went immediately, with the help of an inspector from Scotland Yard, to the house where they were kept as ordinary prostitutes. [447] The girls said on their way to church they had been accosted by a female called Ems who promised them good situations so they went with her to Anvers, then Le Havre and afterwards to London where they were placed in a brothel. They positively refused to return home and their father cast them off and left them to their fate.

Hamburg appears many times in these abduction situations: Susannah Evans age 16 was from taken there from Liverpool in 1856, a case which came to the attention of the government,[448] and Liverpool had its own child procuresses with links to the city, like Madam Anna.

The government finally does act but not until as late as 1885 when the *Criminal Law Bill* attempted to protect the innocence of children and raised the age of consent to 16. In a public meeting at the town hall in Liverpool in October 1885, those attending heard from local MP Mr. Samuel Smith who wrote of his outrage and proposed amendments to the bill:

'There is no doubt now than an organised trade in young girls exists on a large scale and in certain parts of the metropolis the daughters of the poor are hardly safer than in the wilds of Africa. [Loud applause.] We now see the cause of the terrible increase in juvenile prostitution of late years. It is largely the result of the trade in little girls mostly between the ages of 13 and 16 who are sold to wealthy debauchers by the vile women who are their accomplices. [Cries of "Shame!"] Those children are often kidnapped in the streets, put under the influences of drugs and ruined and the law seems utterly unable to reach the offenders.

'Men make open boast of the number of their victims and the evil grows with impunity till a state of things has arisen which threatens to undermine civilisation. [Hear, hear.] The evil has grown to such dimensions in London and is, moreover, shielded by persons in high places, that only the strongest expression of the voice of the people will give us adequate legislation.'

It took four years to get this bill passed, even with the help of Benjamin Scott, the anti-vice campaigner and Chamberlain of the City of London, who approached Lord Granville to enact legislation for the protection of young girls from transportation to the continent for 'immoral purposes.' In response, the House of Lords formed a Select Committee to investigate, which confirmed there was an increase in child prostitution and white slavery. The committee's report made nine recommendations which became the basis for the *Criminal Law Amendment Bill*, including raising the age of consent to sixteen years as well as increasing penalties for sexual offences. [449]

The bill passed easily in the House of Lords in 1883, but was dropped in the House of Commons. It was reintroduced in 1884 but was again dropped during the struggle over parliamentary reform. In April 1885, the Earl of Dalhousie tempted fate by reintroducing the bill a third time. While the bill passed smoothly through the Lords in May, with some revisions, most notably lowering the age of consent to fifteen, it again faced a battle in the Commons, who were preparing to close for the Whit Week bank holiday on 22nd May and were not really interested in the bill. In addition, many

Members of Parliament were opposed to the measure, citing the curtailment of civil liberties through its increase of police powers.

Despite the effort of the Home Secretary, Sir William Harcourt, to move for a second reading of the bill, no vote was taken by the time parliament adjourned. Supporters of the bill by that time worried that it would again be put aside and decided to take action. Then, Gladstone's government resigned over the budget and a minority caretaker government was formed under Lord Salisbury while a general election was held later that year. As a result, it was decided that no time-consuming or controversial measure would be considered until then.

Even before the government crisis in June 1885, on 23rd May, W.T. Stead, the editor of the *Pall Mall Gazette* was approached by Benjamin Scott, who sought his involvement in trying to get action. His subsequent investigations were published in the *Gazette* from 6th October under the title 'The Maiden Tribute of Modern Babylon.' Not only did he base his investigations on interviews with the police, as well as those who were involved in the flesh trade, he went beyond it to purchase a girl, then wrote about it.

With the assistance of Bramwell Booth of the Salvation Army, Stead bought 13-year-old Eliza Armstrong from her parents, and prepared her for export. She was examined to prove that she was still a virgin, then she was brought to a brothel and lightly drugged to wait for Stead, her purchaser. He entered Eliza's room and, having regarded this as confirmation that he had his way, withdrew to write his story. Eliza was turned over to the care of the Salvation Army. The revelations caused an uproar. Copies of the *Pall Mall Gazette* were snapped up and while many denounced Stead's exposé, it did what it was intended to do: it prompted parliament to resume the debate over the *Criminal Law Amendment Bill* on 9.7.1885.

The Society for the Prevention of Cruelty to Children (SPCC), which celebrated its first anniversary on 13.7.1885, took advantage of the debate to make its own recommendations to the bill, including the raising of the age of consent to 18 years and more severe measures to protect children from exploitation. However, many members of parliament, already incensed by Stead's tactics, tried to obstruct any alterations to the laws. In addition to the recommendations made by the SPCC, on 31st July Liverpool MP Samuel Smith, presented to the Commons a clause to abolish the oath for child victims for sexual assault. However, despite the best efforts of its supporters, the SPCC's proposal was narrowly defeated 123 - 120.

Outraged by this defeat, Stead condemned it in the *Pall Mall Gazette*, listing the names of each member who voted against the clause. Congregationalist minister Benjamin Waugh, the leader of the SPCC, focusing on the fact that the proposal was defeated by only three votes, redoubled his efforts to lobby support. Along the way he managed to bring Henry James, the former Attorney-General, to his side and re-introduce Smith's amendment, which he did on 9th August. The Home Secretary, R.A. Cross, dropped his earlier opposition to the measure after consulting with a colleague on the provisions of Scottish law on the subject. This was influential when the measure was once again put to a vote, and the SPCC's 'oath clause' was included in the final version of the bill.

The *Criminal Law Amendment Act* was finally passed on 14.8.1885. Its provisions:

- Raised the age of consent to 16 years of age

- Made it a criminal offence to procure girls for prostitution by administering drugs, intimidation or fraud

- Punished householders who would permit under-age sex on their premises

- Made it a criminal offence to abduct a girl under 18 for purposes of carnal knowledge

- Gave magistrates the power to issue search warrants to find missing females and power to the court to remove a girl from her legal guardians if they condoned her seduction

- Provided for summary proceedings to be taken against brothels and

- Raised the age of felonious assaults to 13 and misdemeanor assault from 13 and 16

- Criminalised 'gross indecency between males' - previously the only homosexual crime was buggery

It also had sections outlining the penalties for abduction and procuring for the purpose of prostitution girls under the age of eighteen, as well as relaxing the rules on witness testimony: while children under the age of 12 were allowed to testify as proposed by the SPCC, it also gave the right of the accused to testify on his own behalf.

The effect of the law became noticeable almost immediately. While few cases of sexual offences were reported before the passage of the law, the number of reported cases skyrocketed in the months afterwards, especially child molestation cases. It may be that the actual number of cases remained the same, but the fact that more cases were reported and brought to the courts was at the very least a reflection of how the law changed perceptions about how women and children should be treated. But it had been a long time in coming.

Chapter 21 - Hidden Houses of Ill Fame

Much of social evil in Liverpool was hidden behind so-called innocent businesses, especially the more discrete establishments. Whilst those who frequented them knew where they were, and passed on details via word of mouth, they were not as completely obvious as the common prostitutes on the street. So now we walk on, round the corner to two more of Jane's houses.

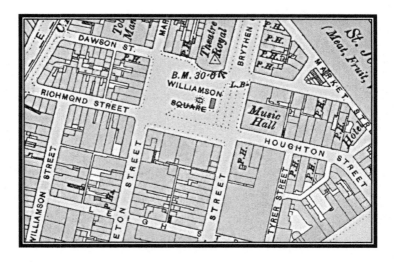

Figure 45 Upper Dawson Street, Williamson Square, the Theatre Royal

As we have noted, Houghton Street and Upper Dawson Street are parallel and No 9 Houghton Street had a back door onto it. It was a very busy thoroughfare and pedlars' markets were held in the street for many years until people complained that they blocked the way. It was full of 'amusements' and a lucrative site for two of Jane's houses. Looking at official records it is easy to see many residents based their businesses on servicing more than the cultural interests of those who attended the *Theatre Royal*.

It was built in Williamson Square at the expense of Liverpool Corporation and opened under the authority of a patent on Friday 5.6.1772 with the play of *Babemet* and an occasional *Prologue* written by the Elder Coleman.[450] However, it closed in November 1802 and a new *Theatre Royal* was built in just six months on the same site. Of semi-circular construction, it opened on 6.6.1803 and it was primarily a playhouse, though the *Italian Opera Company* did visit in 1811. The greatest performers of the time appeared there, including Paganini and Charles Dickens who took part in a series of amateur theatrical performances during the late 1840s and early 1850s, both at the *Theatre Royal* in Williamson Square and at the *Philharmonic Hall*. In February 1852, Dickens was one of the Guild of Literature and Art troupe of players, alongside Wilkie Collins, who performed works, including Dickens' own play, *Mr. Nightingale's Diary*.[451]

Figure 46 The second Theatre Royal which opened in 1803

At other times however, Dickens was in town as a researcher not raconteur. In 1860, he visited the Brownlow Hill workhouse to meet invalided soldiers from the Indian campaign and in the same year, he enrolled as a special constable with the Liverpool police force for a night, patrolling the rough and ready byways of the busy waterfront.[452]

The *Theatre Royal* offered everything from Grand Opera, Shakespeare, orchestras, pantomime, charity balls, plays and comedies. In 1871, it became the *Theatre Royal Palace of Varieties*, then the *Theatre Royal* and *Opera House*. By 1884, it was a circus and its last show was as *Sangers Hippodrome* in 1887. In 1890, it was converted into a cold store and the council demolished it in 1970.

Someone who made a considerable living for many years from his hotel's proximity to the *Theatre Royal* was John Evans, reputedly from London's Covent Garden. He opened the *Evans Hotel* on Upper Dawson Street at No 6, a few yards from the *Theatre Royal* and made full use of this attraction to offer all sorts of delights. He has more adverts in local newspapers than the *Royal Court* itself and was quite a thespian in his own right. In February 1852:

> 'Inconsequence of the unavoidable absence of the gentleman who was to have sustained the part of Lord Strongbow, our townsman Mr. John Evans, at the request of the amateurs themselves, undertook the part at half an hour's notice; and as the racy talent of that gentleman is well known amongst us, we scarcely need to add that he acquitted himself in the most creditable manner.'[453]

I was intrigued by this reference to Covent Garden and found that an *Evans Hotel* had existed there since the reign of Charles II. It was described in *Once a Week*, in 1867:[454]

> 'It is subject to peculiar and stringent regulations. Ladies are not admitted, except on giving their names and addresses, and then only enjoy the privilege of watching the proceedings from behind a screen. The whole of the performance is sustained by the male sex, and an efficient choir of men and boys sing glees, ballads, madrigals and selections from operas, the accompaniments being supplied on the piano and harmonium...

> 'We recommend Evans to the notice of steady young men who admire a high class of music, see no harm in a good supper, but avoid theatres and the ordinary run of music halls.'

However, I have failed to find a direct family connection between John Evans and the famous *Evans Hotel* of Covent Garden. Nevertheless, he obviously did very well in Liverpool, albeit it with a few hiccups along the way. One of his customers, Elizabeth Jones, was convicted of picking the pocket of William Carne taking £1 8 shillings [£112.26] whilst on his premises and she was committed for two months in March 1852.[455] Later that year John Evans himself was up in court for permitting drunkenness in his establishment, but the case was dismissed.[456]

Despite these incidents he gets positive press in February 1854 when a local newspaper says it can do no better than to direct the attention of visitors to the town during the approaching Steeple Chase [at Aintree] to the establishment of Mr. John Evans.

'His cookery is known to all his patrons as "A la Soyer" and he deals only in the best liquors.'[457]

The police at that time were quite prone to prosecute publicans for harbouring prostitutes so John Evans was not alone in being dragged to court. John Gregg of No 4 Upper Dawson Street was charged with having 11 prostitutes in his house at eleven 'clock at night on the 19.6.1845. Some of them were sitting down in the concert room, some were standing and others were at the counter. By 11.45pm there were 12 of them. Gregg's solicitor argued that if this case was proved then every public house in the area around Williamson Square would continually be in court. He added that the night in question Mr. Gregg was away from home burying his father and his wife was left in charge, but she hardly ever entered the business and therefore could not be expected to know which women were prostitutes. The judge, however, said the law was the law, but he would be lenient given the circumstances and Mr. Gregg was only required to pay £20 shillings [£80.19] and costs.[458]

And life was not a bowl of cherries for the prostitutes either. In 1844, in Upper Dawson Street at eleven o'clock on a Thursday night:

'A nymph of the pave named Maria Brown, was assaulted at the end of Upper Dawson Street by another of the frail sisterhood named Catherine Flavel, who thrust the point of an umbrella into her eye and inflicted a severe wound.'

Catherine Flavel was fined £5 [£302.09] plus costs with the threat of two month's imprisonment if she did not pay.[459]

Immorality and drink continue to go hand in hand and in 1841 Richard Murphy was charged with being a suspicious character at premises on the corner of Upper Dawson Street, which means it was either No 7 or 8. It was run by a Mr. Henry Newton, publican, and his wife who kept the establishment known as *Dick's Coffee House*.[460] On Christmas night, Mr. Newton said when he went out of the tap room in the cellar into the house, he found Richard Murphy struggling with his wife and another person in the lobby. Having learnt that Murphy had been upstairs where he had no business, he had him arrested as a suspicious person.

The servant girl, Jane Large, said she was dressing in a room upstairs when Murphy came up and asked for a light. Not being quite dressed, she handed him a candle but he pushed her door to get in the room. She managed to hold it with her foot and kept him out. Murphy told her to be quiet. She said he was an impudent fellow, upon which he laughed and pretended to be drunk. There was no drinking room upstairs but she had seen him once before when he had a glass in the back room. Jane denied he had followed her upstairs.

Mrs. Newton then gave evidence saying on that night she was with some friends and heard Jane call out. She went up and found Murphy at the girl's door. She told Murphy to get out of the house and he struck her in the belly and the head. Someone called Barnett, who had been dining with Mr. and Mrs. Newton, hearing the noise went to the bar and found Mrs. Newton upstairs. He was afraid to interfere but distinctly saw Murphy strike her. At this point her husband found her struggling with Murphy and when he went to her aid, he struck Murphy three times. When Mr. Newton had him arrested, the bridewell keeper confirmed he heard Murphy say: 'I'll ruin your house. I will say I was lured upstairs by the women.' Murphy's coat was torn to pieces in the struggle and he strongly denied the assault.

The prosecuting lawyer said Murphy had no doubt gone upstairs for the disgraceful purpose of going after the girl, but had afterwards threatened to ruin the house by giving out that he was enticed. Murphy was fined £5, [£302.09] a fine he immediately paid or he would have gone to prison for two months. Three years later, in September 1844, *Dick's Coffee House* premises are up for sale by private contract as an eligible property situated on the corner of Murray Street and Upper Dawson Street, along with a Salt Warehouse and Spirit Vaults.[461]

And Felix Patterson was just standing on that corner one day when William Craig asked him for a little tobacco and said if he did not give him some, he would stab him with a knife. He refused and Craig stabbed him in the thigh. In his defence Craig said he was intoxicated at the time and was not aware of what he was doing. He was fined £5 [£80.19] and because he could not pay was sentenced to two months in gaol.[462]

The business of drink even caused brothers to fall out as in August 1844 two came to blows, one being Jeremiah Steel who owned the *Cheshire Vaults* at No 4 Upper Dawson Street and John Steel, who punched first. John was said to be the servant of Jeremiah, but John denied it saying that Jeremiah was his servant because he had only contributed £10 [£604.17] while he, John, owned everything else. And yet another brother lived at 5 Houghton Street, one of Jane's brothels! It seems there had been a great deal of 'recriminations' between the brothers even before this assault.

One brother charged the other with borrowing money and not refunding it while a witness said that the assault came about by John trying to strike his brother Jeremiah down with a spittoon. John said he should have been the defendant in this case but he could not get out of bed to instigate an action in court as he had the lumbago. The judge dismissed the case.[463]

Not long after the brothers Steel became bankrupt. But other businesses lasted quite a long time, like at No 1 which from 1829 was occupied by John Heald, a salt merchant, with another part of it being operated as a grocery by John Hartley. But after nearly twenty years, in 1847, both were forced to sell up by order of a trustee, as they had been made bankrupt.[464]

By 1848, Thomas Porter had taken over part of No 1 with a new preservative, ice which he imported directly from the American Lakes. It was carefully packed, came in at Liverpool docks and was forwarded anywhere in the United Kingdom. You could go and view the American Ice and we even have a price list.[465] After a few years, in 1851, Edward Kelly took over the ice business but kept Thomas Porter on as an employee.

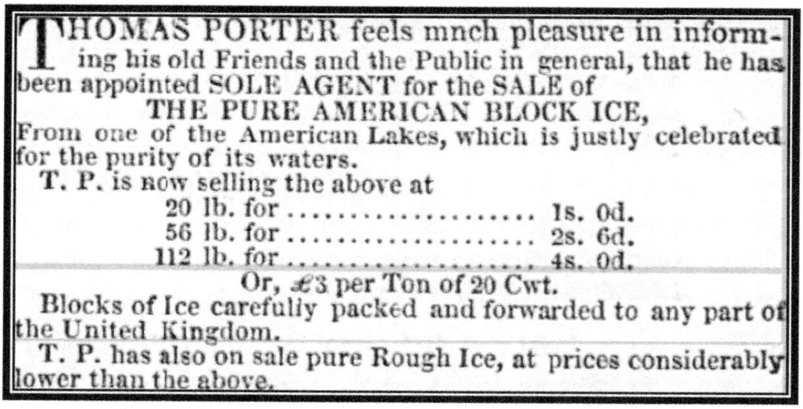

THOMAS PORTER feels much pleasure in inform-
ing his old Friends and the Public in general, that he has
been appointed SOLE AGENT for the SALE of
    THE PURE AMERICAN BLOCK ICE,
From one of the American Lakes, which is justly celebrated
for the purity of its waters.
    T. P. is now selling the above at
        20 lb. for .... 1s. 0d.
        56 lb. for .... 2s. 6d.
        112 lb. for .... 4s. 0d.
            Or, £3 per Ton of 20 Cwt.
    Blocks of Ice carefully packed and forwarded to any part of
the United Kingdom.
    T. P. has also on sale pure Rough Ice, at prices considerably
lower than the above.

Figure 47 'American Ice' Liverpool Standard Advertiser 1848

William Smith must have taken over the other part of No 1 as he carries on Heald's salt merchant's business until August 1851 when a court order appears in the newspapers ordering the sale of his premises and the one next door which is a public house run by Thomas Harrison Tate, but all are part of the same lot.[466] Curiously enough in September 1851 this same Thomas Harrison Tate, but now said to live at No 14, is found guilty of selling liquor on a Sunday morning. He was convicted by evidence given by his own witness, which was careless, and fined 40 shillings [£160.37] and costs. This was not a good autumn for him, so he sells up the following year.[467]

In 1852, Thomas Porter leaves ice work to set up his own business as a grocer round the corner not far from Williamson Square.[468] But Edward Kelly survives what must have been the battle of the preservatives, as traditionally it was salting food that kept it fit to eat, until ice came along. He runs the ice business at No 1 until at least 1864 when he turns it into a Butter Business. But there's no money in butter you say? Well, there was enough for Kelly to expand not just No 1 but to move into No 5 Upper Dawson Street as well and keep going up until the 1870s. His secret was to keep his name in the press by taking every opportunity for free advertising. Today this is common practice, but not so in 1870. This below appeared in the *Liverpool Mercury* on Friday 23.12.1853 and was part of a larger feature about Christmas Markets. It began:

'We were very much struck with the establishment of Messrs E. Kelly and Co...The warehouse was crammed with blocks of butter and similar pieces partially barricade the doorway, the whole presenting a sort of architectural pile of great magnitude; to all appearances, there is here "butter for the million...." The average sale at this establishment is no less than five tons weekly, all of which is supplied to shopkeepers. Such an enormous import to one firm is a striking proof of what Ireland is capable of producing when her resources are properly developed."

In 1853,[469] Kelly expands into a new Fish and Provision business at No 3 but November 1861 brings a headline he must have been keen to avoid: 'Summons against Kelly, the Butter Man.'[470] He was accused of smashing some crockery on Upper Dawson Street opposite one of his establishments. It came about because at that time the street was used for regular pedlars' markets and Barnard Goodman had rented a piece of ground from the Markets Committee opposite the Butter Man's shop for the purpose of selling crockery. Every Saturday he went to arrange his wares early in the morning and on this occasion found pieces of timber on his ground so he moved them away. The Butter Man shortly afterwards ordered some men to put the timber back and, in the process, broke Barnard Goodman's crockery to the value of 1 shilling and 8d [£6.68].

In his defence, Kelly said that the pedlars were the cause of great annoyance to himself and tradesmen in the locality, to which he was told that if he had any complaints, he should put them to the council or if the pedlars broke the law, to the police. The judge ordered the Butter Man to pay the damages.

But Kelly had influential friends, after all he did supply the best homes and hotels with tons of lovely butter, and he was already working behind the scenes to get rid of the pedlars. He had by this time organised a memorial [petition] signed by all but two of Upper Dawson Street occupants demanding the market committee stop using it as a market venue. Kelly was helped in some fashion by a letter sent to the council's marketing committee by Henry Carling, a street trader himself who had a standing on Upper Dawson Street on Saturdays, which was published in full by the *Liverpool Daily Post*. He and the six others who signed it were keen to disassociate themselves from the worst stand holders [471]

It said that the stall nearest Kelly the Butter Man's shop:

'Is occupied by a vendor of soiled goods, bonnets, capes, ribbons, the ground covered with his wares. The occupiers of those stands are females, who are generally drunk on a Saturday, when their conduct and language are abominable, and as a matter of course, a great annoyance to every other person having standings in Upper Dawson Street.'[472]

Figure 48 The Butter Man's shop. W.G. Herdman 1864

They suggested moving the pedlars' market to another locality, and so it happened. All sorted with the two sides satisfied, one because their businesses frontages were free of markets and the other because their ability to trade was not affected, and they got rid of the drunken women.

The 1851 census records nine occupied buildings on Upper Dawson Street and a street directory for the same year adds information on four more houses which makes thirteen. Of these, four are in the business of selling alcohol either as victuallers, hotels, lodging or beer houses, two are eating houses, two are salt merchants, a hairdresser and a butcher, which leaves three unknowns, as no trades are given.

But which houses are Jane's two brothels? Well, Nos 10 and 12 appear as eating houses, but I am sure any men wanting to use their more discrete services would know very well what else was on the menu. They were bought by Jane through her mother at the same time as No 4 Houghton Street and No 2 Tyrer Street. Part of the money was raised by a mortgage and repaid by Jane's mother as and when she made her money from the brothels. Mr. Morris, clerk to Messrs Holden who were NOT the solicitors for the purchase, paid the interest on the mortgage using the rent money of £31 [£2,485.77] a year from the houses.[473]

Thomas Hatton first appears at No 10 in a street directory at 15 Williamson Square, around the corner from Jane's brothels, in 1807 as a liquor merchant. He took over retail vaults at No 2 Houghton Street in 1821 and by 1825 he was a Wine and Spirit Dealer at 10 Upper Dawson Street. Within two years he moves to No 11. There is then a gap in the available records from 1829 until the census of 1841 when we find Thomas Gelling, a hairdresser in No 10. His daughter died here in 1842 and Jabez Laycock had moved in as well by 1845. By the 1851 census Gelling, born in the Isle of Man, age 48 is still living there with his wife.

It is hard to tell when they moved out, it being a large enough house for multiple occupancy, and they could have still been there when new people moved in around 1853, Hugh Dawson and Hugh Jones. In 1855, Nicholas Tuite was sole occupier. Thomas Mills another hairdresser was there in 1859 and by the 1861 census it was empty. The next occupier was James Midghall, yet another hairdresser in 1862, which was the year Jane was ordered to close the place down as a brothel. In 1863, it is for sale with 44 years left on the lease. The occupant at that time was Henry Robinson. A James Quinn must have bought it for he is installed as a provision dealer in 1864, having moved from No 12 as described below. He is still at both houses in 1870.

No 12 has different beginnings. Robert Glover, an earthenware dealer, has the property in 1825 but it descends into liquor between 1827-1829 when Robert Stebbing, a victualler takes it over along with John Joss who is a tobacconist. It is then occupied by John Reynolds, date unknown but he was there in 1841 as the census shows. He had had no trouble at all over his years at No 12 apart from being accused in 1853 of having defective weights and measures. He is joined in the occupancy by James Quinn in 1845, a provision dealer. It became known as the *Manchester Arms*, and he ran it with his wife, as an Eating/Lodging House. At the time of the 1851 census, he had two servants and four male lodgers all from Wales.

In 1861, he was 66 and continued the business with a housekeeper and a servant from Staffordshire, and another servant from Liverpool, along with his niece who was 26. He stayed until around 1863 when Jane had to close the brothel there due to a court case and it was sold, including all the furniture and household effects. The advert is keen to stress that it was a well-established eating house, and the rent was £35 [£2,069.52] a year. James Quinn is still there with the new occupier and eating house proprietor, Thomas Alderson, in 1867, but by 1870, James Quinn is the only occupant, according to a street directory.

If it was not for the fact that there is a full account in the newspapers of how Jane ran both Nos 10 and 12 Upper Dawson Street as brothels for many years, then you would have never known they were there.

Part Four - Judgement Day

Chapter 22 - Jane is appealing

While Chalkley was turning many people's worlds upside down following the 1860 court case, Jane is still in prison in 1861 for not paying the costs. By late November 1860 she must have been let out for a period to attend the first *Beshemel v Gallagher* trial but in the meantime her lawyers were hard at work and the appeal was heard over three days in February and March 1861.[474]

Held at Lincoln Inn's Court of Chancery in London, the court's decision was announced on 15.3.1861, based on very complex arguments about the rights of married women to separate property, and it challenged the very heart of coverture itself. Whatever you think of Jane's morals, she fought hard for her rights and those of all women in the same situation.

'With regard to personal property by common law, marriage operates as an absolute gift... As regards real estate, the husband is entitled to the receipt of the rents and profits during the continuance of the marriage.'[475]

Jane, up to becoming a widow in 1858 could not: [476]

- Manage or control any of her property
- Sell, rent it, or mortgage it without her husband's consent
- Make contracts or incur debts without his approval
- Be sued in a court of law

The bill to amend the law on married women's property Caroline Norton had been involved in was first presented to parliament in 1857 and gained widespread support, including from Mrs. Gaskell, the authoress, but it got nowhere, therefore the legal position at the time of Jane's appeal was as described above. Interestingly, her case came up at a crucial time, as another bill relating to *Married Women's Property* was introduced in April 1868, was amended, failed, reappeared in February 1869 and was eventually passed in 1870, though too late for Jane.

Therefore, any debts she incurred had to be contracted with specific reference to her separate estate. It was assumed by the law that debts involving writing bonds, bills and notes did refer to the separate estate, but spoken commands which led to Jane being in debt to tradesmen like Burton and Watson, did not. In order to recover such debts, action had to be taken against Jane's separate estate which involved a suit in Chancery, which was what the 1860 trial was, and was more expensive than the normal process under common law.

Such was the situation Jane found herself in: a judgement in Liverpool's Chancery court in 1860 against her and an appeal in London's Chancery Courts in 1861. What made it harder for her was the prevailing view that:

'By giving married women the power of holding property to their separate use... while unable to accompany the power with a fuller measure of the responsibility for contracts and obligations which property ought to carry with it, it is very questionable whether the courts of equity have not, to a serious extent, lowered the standards of honour and morality, with regard to pecuniary matters among married women. We see them resorting to shifts to avoid contracts being made good... with a frequency which... speaks very ill for the moral effect upon married women of the present condition of things by which they are allowed in Chancery the benefits without the responsibilities of property.'[477]

Victorian society obviously did not like a situation where debts cannot be collected and contracts enforced. But Jane was not alone in her situation as there were many other women all over the kingdom with drunken and brutal husbands who took earnings off hard-working wives and deserted them, so was she wrong to do the best she could for the sake of her children?

The deed of separation Thomas signed in June 1856 placed all Jane's property, especially the asserts of her business in trust for her sole use. After Jane signed over her trusteeship to Chalkley and gave him a bill of sale for her furniture, there was no money left in her separate estate. Both of them were declared insolvent debtors and Chalkley was additionally declared bankrupt following the investigation conducted by the Liverpool Tradesman's Loan Company.

To sort out Jane's complex situation, the appeal judges searched extensive bundles of case law, fifty cases at least, to find relevant precedents:

'Relating to the bonds, bills of exchange and promissory notes of married women [which] are payable out of their separate estates.'

Jane's lawyers argued she did not have one and that 'her person cannot be made liable either at law or equity.'[478]

Was all this legal manoeuvring deliberate on Jane's part to evade paying anything, in fact fraud? The 1860 trial had exonerated her of this charge but the appeal court resurrected it for rigorous review. Their final judgement was that:

'The court cannot impute to her the dishonesty of not intending to pay for goods which she purchased. The circumstances preclude the inference she expected her husband to pay: and in this particular case it is impossible that she could so intend, as she was actually supporting her husband. How then could she intend that the payment should be made otherwise than out of her separate estate?

'It is indeed stated by her answer that the agreement was that payment should be made out of the profits derived from letting the houses; but it is clear that no reliance can be placed on what this woman has stated. The statement is in the highest degree improbable and is positively denied and I cannot doubt what the verdict of a jury would be if the question was submitted to them.'

So, again she is judged not guilty of fraud – which was a big win for Jane, as the penalties were severe. The court of appeal also said that it had been perfectly legal for Jane to assign her trusteeship and all she had to Chalkley in preference to all her other creditors, and that they would not disturb that right.

'Their Lordships reversed the decision of the [Liverpool Chancery] court, holding that though the separate estate of Mrs. Gallagher was liable under the circumstances to the plaintiff's demand [Johnson's], the bills of sale subsequently executed by Mrs. Gallagher were valid, and not impeachable for fraud or on any other ground; and that consequently, Mr. Chalkley's title to the property comprised therein was preferable to that of the plaintiffs.'

Jane won the appeal, the Liverpool judgement in 1860 was overturned and she was released from prison on 15.3.1861. The final comment of the Lord Justice was:

'I am much impressed with the difficulty of the case.'[479]

Indeed, it was often cited in future cases, as a *London Standard* article of 7.5.1880 shows:

'It is a case which has a sort of legal quarry, from which arguments are dug and hewn whenever any question of separate estate comes before the courts.'

Such as this one below:

'A joint promissory note had been given by the husband and the wife: the husband being practically a pauper it was held in the Court of Common Pleas, by

Justices Grove and Lopes, that the holder of the note, in default of payment, was entitled to imprison the wife under the Debtors Act of 1869; it being proved that she had property of her own in the hands of trustees, and that, if an order were made for her imprisonment in default of payment, the debt would probably be discharged. This is an extension of the original doctrine in "Johnson v Gallagher" which would probably have astonished even Lord Justice Turner himself.'

Jane's case which had considered many other predecendents had, by 1880, become a legal precedent itself!

But she was home on 7.4.1861 when the census was taken and it shows her living at No 9 Houghton Street, one of her coffee house/brothels. There was just time for Jane to resume life and recover from her prison experience before the next scandalous court case erupted in Liverpool, this time involving Chalkley. It was held in the summer of 1861 and consumed everyone's attention until August. Jane also had to prepare for the second hearing in November 1861 of *Beshemel v Gallagher*.

However, once all this excitement died down, Jane returned to her second home in London, for what must have been very necessary rest and recuperation, leaving her staff to manage what was left of the brothels in Liverpool. The first we know for sure where she lives was July 1859 when she hosted the London Premier of the *Talking Fish* from 191 Piccadilly, in the heart of Westminster, with Charles Pollard, but she must have been firmly established there well before that time.

But back in in 1857, 191 Piccadilly is where Leah Isaacs, a cigar dealer trading as Picard and Co had her shop. She went bankrupt and all her cigar stock had to be sold. This case is interesting, as it shows once again how women, legally precluded from managing their own affairs, were easy prey to unscrupulous men, this time her own brother. [480] [481]

Leah alleged that her brother Mark Wilson had absconded with between £600 - £700 [£35,4777.52 - £41,390.44] in cash, the only capital she had and was the assumed surplus of her deceased husband's estate. Leah owed Mr. Warburg £418 [£24,716.01] for cigars and when he had called upon her to collect the money the previous week Leah told him her brother, who was her late husband's executor, was out. He had in fact run off between 2 - 6am the previous weekend with his housekeeper, taking with him a photographic machine worth £50 [£2,956.46] and all his plate and valuables. Leah was in a terrible state about it.

Mr. Warburg urged Leah to call the police and advertise for anyone who knew where her brother was to come forward. She started to cry but gave him permission to advertise, saying she was honest. However, there was no evidence that the police had been called or adverts placed, which was damning for Leah and led to allegations she had conspired with her brother to defraud their creditors. Months later the charge was 'unproven' as there was no evidence only suspicion, and the justice told Leah she was very lucky not to have been imprisoned.[482]

The next residents of 191 Piccadilly were Puttocks and Simpson who announced on 29.1.1859 they had moved from 47 Leicester Square which was the home of Sir Joshua Reynolds. By 16.4.1859, the *Talking Fish* is being advertised in the *Illustrated London News* as appearing at the address in early May. Charles Pollard must have taken the premises using Jane's money as she could not, knowing Burton and Watson were chasing her for payment for the furniture. [483]

THE TALKING AND PERFORMING FISH.—An elegantly appointed exhibition-room has been taken for the public view of this extraordinary animal, at ☐☐, Piccadilly, between St. James's Church and the Egyptian Hall, which the proprietor has the honour to announce will open on THURSDAY, May 5, 1859.—Admission, 2s. 6d.; Children, 1s. It would be in vain to attempt a written description of the wonderful performances of this lusus naturæ—they must be witnessed to be believed. The Fish possesses a sagacity bordering upon the dominions of reason, understanding thoroughly the conversation addressed to it, and by its vocal responses and amusing gyrations, gives evidence of its complete docility and comprehension. Naturalists and other scientific persons have attended its soirées in Liverpool and Manchester, and expressed their astonishment and admiration. The public Press has made it the subject of critical analysis, the result being the highest commendation. The Exhibition will be open from ten o'clock, a.m., to ten o'clock, p.m.

Figure 49 'The Talking and Performing Fish' Morning Post 26.4.1859

She must have spent a lot on the place, which was transformed into 'an elegantly appointed exhibition room.' Lying between St James's Church and the Egyptian Hall on Piccadilly and opposite the *Albany*, [484] Chapman Hall, publishers of Charles Dickens' novels, was next door at No 193 Piccadilly, so Dickens must have known about the *Talking Fish* and given his eye for the unusual and his connections with Liverpool, might have visited it.

The fish was away from its London home on tour for months at a time, where 'It will doubtless prove an attractive exhibition to cattle-show visitors....' observed *Reynolds Newspaper* sarcastically on 4.12.1859, but it always returned to its base at 191 Piccadilly, where it died, exhausted no doubt and frozen with cold. By April the premises are let to someone else.

Jane next appears in 1859 at 1 Vassall Road, Brixton, which she rented for her children so that they have somewhere to live away from her other life in Liverpool. It was an attractive area for middle class professionals and Henry Richard Vassall, third Baron Holland, began building houses for them and naming the surrounding streets after his family connections. Vassal was his wife's maiden name which he had adopted in 1800 and between 1820 - 1830 the area, known as Holland Town, was a mixture of detached and semi-detached villas and dignified terraces.

In 1860, Jane rented 1 Eltham Place, Foxley Road, Brixton, which lies at right angles to Vassall Road, using the name of William Thomas Mercer, her eldest son, who street directories that year list as being the head of the household.[485]

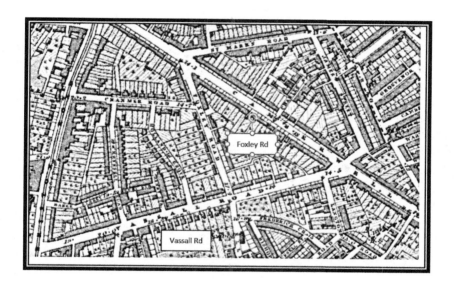

Figure 50 Vassall and FoxleyRd in Lambeth, London OS 6" map 1872

David Cox, (29.4.1783 - 7.6.185), the celebrated water-colourist, once lived in Foxley Road in 1827 where there is now a blue plaque.[486] He was an English landscape painter, one of the most important members of the Birmingham School of landscape artists and an early precursor of impressionism. In 1843, he exhibited a painting at the Royal Academy and two in 1844. He is most popularly known for his works in water colour, but he produced 300 works in oil, which is now considered 'one of the greatest, but least recognised achievements of any English painter.'[487] Jane's immediate neighbours were:

- J.T. Vincent Doyle, Esquire at No 2 whose two daughters were born there in 1861 and 1864

- Nicholas Henry Rowsell at No 3, maker of well-made rosewood and mahogany furniture who lived there until his death in 1860

- Frederick Fairlee Elderton of No 4 who was born in 1830 in Tours, France and whose father was declared bankrupt five years later. He was partner in a Bleaching and Wax Melting business. One of his daughters, Mary Amelia was born there on 19.1.1860

- Richard Price of No 5, but by 1862 he had moved to Wembley, South London

- Reuben Ripon Friend of No 9, who was born in 1805 in Durham, son of a gentleman. He was a manufacturer who gained the Freedom of the City of London in 1839

These then were Jane's middle class, well educated, respectable neighbours in Eltham Place in the early 1860s. The houses were plain three-storey terraces with basements, had cast-iron balconies which linked the first-floor windows and the ground storeys were stuccoed and channelled, containing entrances with panelled door frames and simple segmental fanlights.[488]

Very nice indeed, a far cry from a Liverpool court house and you can see why London appealed to Jane. Here she could escape from her notoriety and pass as Mrs. Jane Mercer, and she had a marriage certificate to prove it. She would have made every effort to impress the neighbours as a respectable widow, wealthy with independent means, her children well educated at expensive schools, her eldest married to a banker. It was also probably from living here close to Lambeth with their mother that Selina and Caroline met the Fox Coopers.

Interesting...

Chapter 23 - Combative Cooper

Frederick Fox Cooper Esq... who has been a critic in half the dead and living papers in London, is a Dramatic Writer.'
Literary Gazette 1835

Which was true, as between 1836-1839 Fox Cooper was for a brief time the lessee of one or more minor London theatres and produced over a dozen plays. *Hercules* was his most successful piece and by 1845 it had played on a thousand occasions.[489] However, he probably spent more of his life in the courts and debtors' prisons than in the theatre for, in 1836, he was also in the Horsemonger Lane gaol for failing to pay his bills and was not discharged for three months.[490] The petition gave 17 previous addresses for him including his current one at Garden Road, London where, as an author, he is cited along with his partner: Robson, Harrison and Co of both Wyatt and Baker Street in London, where they were known as the 'Projectors of a Plan for the Building of a New Theatre,' which was to be called '*The New King's Theatre.'*

Undeterred, Fox Cooper's next venture was *Crim Con*, described as a *Journal des Amours*, a weekly journal, thus avoiding stamp duty, in which 'heartless seducers would be held up to public indignation.' It was supposed to be published for the first time on 28.7.1838 at a price of two pence but efforts were made by many to suppress it and there was delay until 25.8.1838.

Its leading article declared that the *Crim Con Gazette* and *Journal of the Haut Ton* aimed to prevent as much as possible the progress of aristocratic vice and debauchery. Its first issue in 1836 contains gossip about the relationship between the Whig prime minister Lord Melbourne and the clever, vivacious Caroline Norton.[491][492] It was a good story to lead with as the title *Crim Con* was short for criminal conversation, the legal term for adultery. The *Gazette* also contained descriptions of disorderly houses, much personal scandal, amorous poems and a theatre column.

Another case featured was *Lord Grosvenor v the Duke of Cumberland,* who in 1770 was brought before the court of the King's Bench for 'criminal conversation.' Lord Grosvenor sued Cumberland, his wife's lover, for monetary damages and their love letters, scores of them, proved positively damning in the divorce courts in spite of being written in the lemon juice used by spies instead of ink. The couple had taken advice which appeared in the *Gentleman's Magazine.*

'If you write with any acid (juice of lemons as good as any) upon paper, then let it dry, it will be invisible, till it be held to the light. The lemon version smells better.'[493]

Cumberland not only seduced a married lady, he behaved below his station, impersonating a squire in order to visit Lady Grosvenor incognito.

'After disguising himself using the name Squire Morgan, he proceeded to act like an idiot to cover his improprieties.'

As he was the king's brother, his behaviour was doubly scandalous when the affair came to light.[494]

Figure 51 The Crim Con Gazette 25.8.1838

Then *Paul Pry* raises its head again, nearly seven years after we last heard of the publication. On 7.8.1838, Thomas Littleton Holt, the proprietor of another unstamped weekly publication entitled *Paul Pry,* was brought up by a police constable charged with committing an unprovoked assault upon Fox Cooper, who lived at 4 Wellington Street on the Strand, in London and was the proprietor and publisher of an opposition unstamped publication, also entitled the *Paul Pry.* No 4 was also next door to the *Old Bell* pub whose lease Charles Pollard claimed to hold from 1840. [495]

Two *Paul Pry*'s? Well, yes and other writers produced *Paul Pry* children's books, songs, poetry, pamphlets, etchings and cartoons. Fox Cooper edited this current version of *Paul Pry*, which sought to supply readers with instant expertise in latest fashions, and the book *Paul Pry* in the *Journal of Political Satire*.[496]

Fox Cooper had bumped into Holt at the Stamp Office that morning where he had gone to try and stop the imminent publication of an article in Holt's *Paul Pry* which depicted Fox Cooper as a pickpocket.

> 'When Holt came into the office, he saw Fox Cooper and exclaimed "Oh! This is he!" and instantly struck him in the eye and knocked him down.'

Various witnesses to this exciting event in the sober Stamp Office corroborated his account. Holt admitted he had acted in a very foolish manner, but said he had been provoked. The magistrate said Fox Cooper was within his rights to indict Holt and have him stand trial but he declined to press charges and the two left the Stamp Office together!

However, in 1839 he appears in court for a very different reason. While passing the time away in Fleet Gaol where he was once again incarcerated due to debt, Fox Cooper and his fellow debtors engaged in whatever diversions they could, including inciting a riot and assault which was reported on 13.6.1839.[497] All fourteen men charged were in Fleet Prison for debt and the new charges were for committing an assault on William Freethy and his wife Cecilia and riot in Her Majesty's prison. Two of those prisoners involved, C.C. Browning and Sarah Rigg, were not before the court and three others had not yet surrendered. Everyone else pleaded guilty including Fox Cooper so there are no statements from opposing sides or witnesses called. They were bound over on sureties of £200 [£12,083.40] each, which was a lot of money in 1839.

The Recorder told the defendants that a condition of their sentence was their good behaviour towards:[498] [499]

> 'Not only to the prosecutor and his wife, but to all liege subjects of the Queen, for the two years next ensuing; and further, that they would appear to receive judgement upon the charge of misdemeanour to which they had pled guilty, whenever the Court should call upon them. This, however, would never happen, unless some new cause of complaint should arise.'

The point was then raised that several of the witnesses for the prosecution were inmates of the prison and they stood in need of special protection.

The Recorder stated: 'Any attempt to provoke or taunt would be a breach of the peace. It was monstrous that persons, unhappily confined to prison, should be annoyed or molested by lawless associations. The defendants had heard the sentiments of the Court, and should there be new cause of complaint, they might depend upon it that they would be dealt with the greatest severity. The Court had, in the present instance, adopted the course it had, because it considered that a double restraint might answer the purpose better than codign punishment.'

Of course, the judgement might also have been a reflection of the fact that two defendants were respectably dressed, two more were genteelly attired and bowed respectfully before they departed. No doubt strings had been pulled for those with powerful fathers and relations. How or why Fox Cooper found himself in a riot and on an assault charge whilst in prison is a mystery but he did just about manage to keep his criminal record clean for the next two years.[500]

The last issue of the *Crim Con Gazette* was 11.1.1840, and, incidentally, one month later, Fox Cooper's youngest son, Alfred Edgar was born on the 1st February. They were living at Canterbury Place, St Mary's, Lambeth but the birth was not registered until 2.3.1840. No names were then given to the child but some family notes, still preserved, confirm the dates. He lived until June 1901. By Easter 1840, the family had moved to Mead's Place, Lambeth and sometime in early spring another extraordinary opportunity came up for Fox Cooper, who according to the census recorded on 7.6.1841 was living at Great Union Street, Newington.

On a pleasure boat on the river Thames, Fox Cooper met a Mr. Aglionby, a Liberal MP for Cockermouth and a director of the New Zealand Company. The MP suggested to Fox Cooper that he should start a newspaper in the developing district of Nelson at the northern end of South Island. Fox Cooper was interested and he wrote to the directors in early May outlining his reasons and qualifications for establishing a paper in the colony. He got an encouraging response so set about gaining support from journalists and friends in the form of testimonials of his abilities and experience.

These references were very good, so good you wonder whether Fox Cooper wrote them himself. One said: 'No one was more capable of successfully managing every department of a newspaper' and another mentioned that Fox Cooper had a 'Union of tact and veracity likely to render a paper interesting to the general reader.' There were other testimonies from the *Guardian*, *Courier*, and the *Public Ledger*, plus those from Lord Kenyon and Sir Charles Aldis, a distinguished surgeon.[501]

The directors agreed to his proposal and in July 1841 advanced £200 [£12,113.61]. Fox Cooper approached a friend of his called Elliott to be his partner who would provide the printing machinery and Fox Cooper would organise its transportation to New Zealand along with a timber house that they would share. A piece of land was chosen, subject to a mortgage from the New Zealand Company. In September, he asked permission to produce adverts for a trial issue to be published in London for which he was paid £100 [£6,07191] and given a loan to cover the freight charges.

But as ever with Fox Cooper and money, things get complicated. There rose a difference of opinion about whether this sum was to cover a debt from Fox Cooper to a Holborn builder, Henry Manning, in relation to the timber house. Fox Cooper said the New Zealand Company had agreed to pay the builder direct while the secretary of the company said otherwise.

During October 1841, four ships sailed from London for Nelson, New Zealand and one of these was wrecked. Another, the *Mary-Ann*, had the Fox Cooper party on it and their chattels. Either by accident or a misunderstanding, Fox Cooper had not paid Manning's outstanding debt of £68 [£4,138.56] and a writ was served on 29.9.1841 requiring costs and payment within four days. The *Mary-Ann* sailed on the fourth day, which was 2.10.1841 but not before Fox Cooper was taken off the ship against his consent, along with his family, according to the certificate of the master.

Fox Cooper was then put in Dover Castle gaol and spent his time there writing to the New Zealand company but he got nothing back except his testimonials. In these letters he maintains that the printing equipment was his own property and that the newspaper was still under his control, even though Elliott was on his way to New Zealand and would become the future sole proprietor.

After six weeks he was released on the promise that he would pay Manning's account by instalments. Fox Cooper continued to press the New Zealand Company for his passage money, freight on goods shipped, the costs of adverts and an award for the miseries he had endured. He threatened legal action but finally had to climb down and agreed to accept the company's own judgement of what they should reimburse. Even though he reckoned the amount was £177 [£10,693.81], the outcome was that in early December 1841 the company paid Fox Cooper £107 12s 6d [£6,200.29] adding they wanted no further dealings with him. Meanwhile, Elliott, his wife and his two children were still on their way to New Zealand and he took control of the newspaper when it was first published in 1842.

Fox Cooper, rolling ever onwards, put this behind him and became lessee of the *Theatre Royal* in Dover, putting to good use the enforced time he had spent there. The £100 from the New Zealand Company provided capital to open for the season and for much of 1842 he was busy managing the theatre. His eldest son Harwood then made his first appearance on stage as a youth of fifteen playing a lover, an alternative description for a harlequin. Early in the New Year, ten patent calorifere gas stoves were installed for the greater comfort of the audience, with two of them onstage for the actors. On 1st August there was a special performance of *Hamlet* and so the season went on until a fateful evening towards the end of August 1842.

The *Dover Cropping Case* caused a sensation in the national press, being reported and debated all over the country, and it was all down to Fox Cooper. As the Dover theatre business had in weeks previously been poor and Fox Cooper had got into arrears with his performers and rent for the theatre, certain members thought he did not pay them anything like a fair and honest proportion according to the receipts of the house. Consequently, on the night of a benefit he had arranged, after the audience had assembled, the cast went on strike, telling him that they would not go on until he either paid up their salaries or compromised on the matter. This proposal was rejected by Fox Cooper, the performers stood their ground and the show did not go on.

Next morning, two of the performers, who were comedians, appeared at the bar of the police court, charged with assaulting Fox Cooper. One of them was fined 10 shillings [£30.21] including costs and both of them were held for threatening Fox Cooper's life, for which they had to provide two sureties for £20 [£1,208.34] and agree to keep the peace for two months. As they had no money, they were held in the gaol for three or four hours waiting for their friends to raise it and while they were there, they suffered further indignities which resulted in a press furore. They had their hair cut off, even though it was known bail would be found in a short time.

Both comedians took out summonses against Mr. Coulthard, the Dover gaoler, for assault, claiming that the loss of their hair would be injurious to them in their business and that there was no need to cut their hair off as the surgeon of the gaol said they were clean [free of lice]. The governor however, had instructed his staff to treat the two men as misdemeanants and cut off their hair. Apparently, all prisoners were treated in the same way.

The first comedian was sworn in and said that on being placed in custody till they found bail: 'They had amused themselves with singing the song of "All is Lost."' When the gaoler came to them, he threatened if they did not leave off singing, he would place them where they could not get bail for three days. He then made them take off their coats and hats and tuck in their shirt sleeves. After this their hair was cropped short by order of the gaoler. They were placed among the debtors; but were ordered not to speak. The turnkey told them they must pick oakum, or go without their dinner. They declined both. The gaoler threatened that if they did not conform to the rules of the prison, they would be publicly whipped. The gaoler's manner was such as to intimidate and they were told by him:

'If you do not submit to the rules, you will be placed on bread and water.'

The gaoler, when called, said that he had found the two comedians bellowing and singing. He informed them that

'If they infringed the rules of the prison, they would be placed in solitary confinement for three days,' and he admitted he had ordered their hair to be cropped.

He also cited a previous case where two other men, who were in gaol for months, not the few hours the comedians were, had been cropped in Dover gaol, but he did not add that the operation was performed by a fashionable barber in the usual style while the two comedians were deprived of their hair rudely by the inexperienced hands of a common felon. [502]

One of the comedians, 'a high-spirited young fellow,' called upon the bench to censure the treatment they had suffered at Dover gaol saying that while:

'He was a poor player, he was by birth and education a gentleman... he had at no distant period occupied a situation in society equal to themselves.'

However, the decision of the court was that the governor of Dover gaol was perfectly justified in his brutal treatment of the two comedians and the charge was dismissed. This was not popular with either ordinary people or other law professionals, hence the massive publicity and debate this matter provoked across the country, mostly against this decision.[503]

The *Globe* argued:

'Different men may set a different value on their hair but we are at a loss to understand why any man under the circumstances thus described should be compelled to lose either hair, beard, nails or any part of his material substance. Because a man is committed to the custody of a jailer for an hour or so, till he can obtain surety, he ought not on that account to be subjected to any indignity.

'We can understand why it should be necessary, for the sake of the health of a number of men confined in one building, that certain regulations enforcing the cleanliness, on the innocent as well as the guilty, should be adopted. But in this case, it was not even alleged that the individuals who had the misfortune of being for an hour or two in the custody of the Dover jailer, were not in every respect clean. Why, what a tyranny, then to force those individuals to be cropped!'

The *Globe* then turned on Fox Cooper saying:

'Ought not such a person to be immediately laid hands on by the jailer, and treated like a shock dog?' Then the officials: 'With respect to the magistrates and the jailer of Dover, we say nothing; they seem well suited to each other.' [504]

The *Illustrated London News* was more subtle but still cutting:[505]

'A very notorious and ill-conditioned person of the name of Frederick Fox Cooper, whose figurings in public life have never been of a very enviable character, acquires the management of a theatre at Dover, and, failing in his payments to his actors, gets into a sort of fracas with two of them, who think proper to administer to their manager some sort of personal chastisement or assault. Whatever may be the character of Mr. Fox Cooper, or his defalcations as a manager, of course the law was strong enough to protect him against any personal violence.'

Reflecting that the assault must have been 'very trifling to earn only a fine of ten shillings,' they describe how Fox Cooper goes a little further in the adventure; and 'thinking proper to swear that he goes in fear of his life from the two persons who had used him with such considerate gentleness, they are held to bail which they haven't got.'

Well done Fox Cooper. He not only alienated his staff, his delicate reputation was in shreds, he probably had a black eye and some bruises, and both he and the theatre were out of pocket. But it shortly re-opened under the management of one of the comedians and was soon being patronised by Prince Esterhazy. However, it eventually had to close in December 1842 after a brief and unsuccessful season.[506]

Fox Cooper's next court appearance was in respect of a many-headed dog and he is now living at 17 Walcot-Place East, Lambeth and described as a dramatic author.[507] The case involved another publication which he set up between June and November 1843 called *Cerberus*. This was a beast which was also known as the *Hound of Hades*, a multi-headed dog which guarded the gates of the underworld, preventing the dead from leaving, and making sure that those who entered never left. Almost an indescribable monstrosity:

'It was a fifty-headed, relentless and strong creature which feeds on raw flesh,' and others said it had one hundred heads.[508]

Cerberus, the publication, featured four different lines of politics under four different heads which the *Theatrical Times* was quick to point out was 'three quarters true.' It cost sixpence a copy but only managed twenty-three issues before it had to close due to lack of support, though it was not before Fox Cooper had used it to expound his version of the New Zealand escapade in its 6th edition which carried an advertisement regarding emigration to New Zealand and letters written by Fox Cooper in June and July 1843:

'As the original projector of the Nelson Examiner which, in spite of every obstacle, I have firmly established... I feel every disposition to promote the success of the proposed fourth colony through the columns of *Cerberus*, the circulation of which is now 10,000 copies.'

Cerberus was obviously not making money and Fox Cooper did say in the following insolvency action that it was largely the reason why he was in debt, again. The notice of bankruptcy appeared in February 1844 and the issue as to whether an author who owed money was a business and therefore liable to being declared bankrupt, or an individual who would come into the insolvency category, was much debated. Fox Cooper was not out to change the law but to avoid becoming a bankrupt rather than an insolvent debtor because they were protected from being placed in prison for relatively small amounts and were the preferred option of gentlemen. The theory, such as it was, maintained that as no gentleman worked, he could not become bankrupt, or be arrested.[509]

His lawyer argued that the editor of a newspaper was placed in the same situation as an author or artist, who could not retrospectively be said to deal in paper or canvas, although each used the material for his business, but only the creativity of the brain gave any value to. To no one's surprise the commissioner did not accept the argument and Fox Cooper was arrested as a trader.

However, Fox Cooper is still up to his old tricks of not paying his staff a living wage and offering awful conditions. He was subject in July 1845 to police investigations of several minor London theatres and the *City of London*, which Fox Cooper was then managing, got the worst report. On the night of the inspection the gallery was crammed to suffocation with 462 people, mainly between the ages of 11 and 18. Some were from honest families but others were of doubtful character and of 'recognisable occupations.' The police uncovered the admissions of two or three people on one ticket.

Fox Cooper then tried to up his game and attract better class performers and in 1845 invited *Vandenhoff and Daughter* to appear. She was a singer and Vandenhoff was a famous actor who first appeared in the provincial theatres. In 1814, he was a member of the company at *the English Opera House (Lyceum)* where, on 4.8.1814 he was the original Count d' Herleim in *Frederick the Great*. The same year he made, as Rolla, his first appearance in Liverpool, where he was a great favourite, playing also in Manchester, Dublin and elsewhere.

On 9.12.1820, as Vandenhoff from Liverpool, he made his first appearance at Covent Garden, in London where he played *Penruddock, The Stranger, Virginius, Master Walter in the Hunchback, Richelieu, Falconbridge, Cassius, Hotspur*, and many other parts. After 1839, Vandenhoff played chiefly in the country, although he was seen occasionally at *Drury Lane* in London.

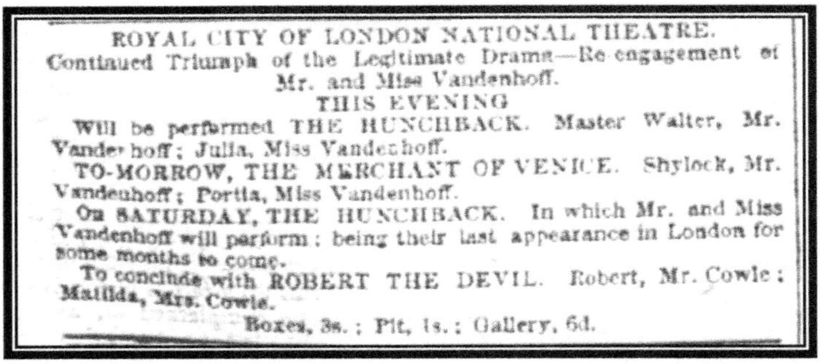

```
ROYAL CITY OF LONDON NATIONAL THEATRE.
Continued Triumph of the Legitimate Drama—Re-engagement of
              Mr. and Miss Vandenhoff.
                  THIS EVENING
   Will be performed THE HUNCHBACK. Master Walter, Mr.
Vandenhoff; Julia, Miss Vandenhoff.
   TO-MORROW, THE MERCHANT OF VENICE. Shylock, Mr.
Vandenhoff; Portia, Miss Vandenhoff.
   On SATURDAY, THE HUNCHBACK. In which Mr. and Miss
Vandenhoff will perform : being their last appearance in London for
some months to come.
   To conclude with ROBERT THE DEVIL. Robert, Mr. Cowle :
Matilda, Mrs. Cowle.
        Boxes, 3s. ; Pit, 1s.; Gallery, 6d.
```

Figure 52 The Vandenhoffs: The Sun, London 10.4.1845

Fox Cooper must have scented an opportunity to make money from them and invited the Vandenhoffs to appear at the *Royal City of London Theatre*. [510] But all did not go well. *Lloyds Weekly* takes up the tale on 20.4.1845:[511]

'Vandenhoff and his daughter have quitted this den in disgust. How he could ever have been induced to enter it, particularly under the management of Frederick Fox Cooper, is a matter of great surprise to everyone. The treasury is empty; and, when the poor actor demands his hard-earned pittance, he is met with a "knock down" argument by the management, which tends to introduce both parties to the arena of a police court.

'The theatre, as might be expected, is quite deserted: no person having the least claim to respectability would be seen within its walls. Everything that can be is brought into the play for the degradation of the drama. The judge and jury from the Garrick's Head, and all the vile penny concert singers in London, have here found a refuge: it has become the filthiest arena imaginable.

'We hardly know which to compliment most, Fox Cooper or his company; they are well worthy of each other. He must have been made reckless of public opinion to desecrate a theatre to such vile purposes. While such men are entrusted with the interest of the theatre, starvation for the actors, and total annihilation for the drama, is what all reasonable beings are reluctantly constrained to anticipate.'

It is safe to say this was not a successful production for anyone concerned and Fox Cooper's reputation drops even further as by April 1846 he is again declared bankrupt and the wrangle as to whether he is an insolvent or a bankrupt still rumbles on. But for the first time we are given some idea of the extent of his debts.[512] The amounts are considerable: between £783 [£62,785.72] and £1,625 [£130,302.41].

In June, Fox Cooper is declared insolvent once more and the notice appears, ironically, in the *Dover Telegraph*, and contains a list of all the people he has been associated with, and he has been very much busier than I suspected! Like Chalkley in the north, he has also indulged in a little speculation in the railways, which were always advertising for investors at this time due to a massive expansion in the new railway networks which devoured the countryside.

The *Hereford Journal of Railway* Intelligence had this wry comment: [513]

'Another speculator in the railway business has figured in the Insolvent Debtor's Court – a Mr. Frederick Fox Cooper, late of the Railway Atlas. He had previously tried his luck with theatres, but with no better success.'

Finally, in July 1847, Fox Cooper's bankruptcy is discharged. By now, he had been the lessee of five minor London theatres: *Marylebone, Olympic, Victoria, City of London* and *New Strand*. Does he then, age 40, with a wife and children, finally settle down? Not at all. He is back in court again in 1847, the same year as Charles Pollard is prosecuted at the Old Bailey not far away. [514]

Fox Cooper's case came about as he had re-presented a drama written by Mr. W. Collier called 'Abduction or The Farmer's Daughter' at the *Strand Theatre* where he was the lessee and it breached Collier's copyright as he had not got his permission nor had he informed Collier that he was staging it. Collier claimed he was the author of the piece which was presented at the *Queen's Theatre* several years previously and he owned the copyright, which he duly showed the court. He had found out by accident that his drama was being acted at the *Strand Theatre* under a disguised title and he wanted therefore to be paid for the six nights it had been shown, which under his rights, according to the *Dramatic Author's Act*, was 12 guineas [£1,010.34].

Fox Cooper: More than I was taking at the doors each night!

Collier's solicitor: If managers would act with common honesty and not bring out others' pieces under disguised titles, authors would not complain. If Mr. Fox Cooper had applied to Collier in the first instance, he would have let him play his piece even if he only paid him five shillings a night.

Fox Cooper: The piece he produced was a translation from French and Collier had assigned his interest in it to another party and therefore had no claim. He too was an author and had fifty or sixty pieces playing all over the country for which he never got one farthing.

After some discussion the case was settled by Fox Cooper agreeing to give Mr. Collier two guineas [£168.39] and pay all the costs in a month. [515]

Meanwhile, the war of words between rival publishers continues, blazed across the newspapers and shouted from placards in shop windows, the modern equivalent of naming and shaming. Fox Cooper, the late lessee of the *Strand Theatre*, is again suing a printer, this time J.W. Smith for libel. He claimed that for years he had contributed to the *Theatrical Journal* printed by J.W. Smith, but when Smith was discharged from that journal, he set up a rival publication and invited him to write for them, to which Fox Cooper said 'He was ready to write for any person who would pay him.'

But then they fell out and Fox Cooper:

'Having discovered a placard had been put forth reflecting on his character, he went to Smith's house and cautioned him not to repeat it, or he would take proceedings against him.'

Not taking kindly to this, Smith and his associates produced another placard stating that they would take action against any parties aiding and abetting: 'The notorious Frederick Fox Cooper of *Paul Pry* and *Crim Con Gazette* celebrity.'

A crowd collected round Smith's window where the placard was displayed and Fox Cooper said in court he had since discovered that the same bill was in several public houses where men had been employed to stick them up. Smith, after some hesitation, admitted that his two associates had written and published the libel. Fox Cooper said he only wanted an apology and the case was settled, the defendants Smith and Co being bound over to answer any additional charges Fox Cooper might take further.[516] Another feud between friends was thus settled amicably.

Later in 1848, sometime in December, Fox Cooper rents for one night the *Olympic Theatre* in London. Much effort had gone into rescuing this little theatre from disrepute and obscurity before this point and the owners had been forced to make 'temporary and pecuniary sacrifices for the sake of maintaining its rising respectability.' But as the *Era* explains:

'Its principal and most responsible manager, Mr. Davidson, however, forgetful of this fact, and contrary to the policy he has previously observed, lets the house for one night only to Mr. Fox Cooper, for a miserable five-pound note [£400.93].

'Mr. Fox Cooper, unable to produce pieces creditably, or indifferent as to who appears in them, makes a "benefit" out of scenes which we shall describe and cannot sufficiently condemn.

'On Monday night, Mr. Fox Cooper took a night there; but up to Saturday there were well founded and reasonable doubts of the house opening. Several acts appeared being judged from 'reasonable' to 'merited ridicule', and a 'farce.' A mess was made of everything else.

'The staff went on strike for their salaries forcing the stage manager, Mr. Bender, to come forward and say: "Ladies and gentlemen, I am sorry to inform you that Mr. Davidson has let the theatre this evening to a gentleman," (cries from the gallery, "Oh, oh! Fox Cooper!") for a benefit; but in consequence of that individual not having fulfilled his engagements with the company, I am compelled to say the piece of "Times Tries All" cannot be played and the performances must terminate here.'

Disappointment turned to anger, a cushion was hurled at Mr. Bender, a ginger bottle flew from someone else, the gas lights were turned off and in darkness the people were turned out. The *Era* blame the sleeping partner owner of the *Olympic Theatre*. Mr. Spicer, for they claim he merely:

'Finds the money and refuses to take any active part in the management, declining to interfere with the business of the theatre.'

They say he must accept responsibility, the moral liabilities as well as his fair share of the profits.

'It is nonsense for a man to imagine that he can remain behind the curtain of a theatre without being seen. If he is ashamed to own that he is there, there must be something discreditable in the connexion he has formed...'[517]

But nothing excuses the continuing conduct of Fox Cooper, who has once again, slipped away in the melee, to cheat and disappoint again.

Fox Cooper's association with the *Strand Theatre* from March 1847 to February 1848 also teemed with trouble and strife. He attempted to lower the prices of seats and was castigated by all concerned. Attendances plummeted by April 1847, so he resorted to presentations of animals including a mammoth horse weighing twenty-five cwt and exotic, for the time, female Ethiopians. He had to drop this too and return to English vaudeville. As one commentator said:

'The lessee has dropped the fat women, turned the horse out to grass, dispensed with the foreign caperers, refurbished the theatre and improved the company.'[518]

The venture struggled on until the following year when Fox Cooper had to give up as he owed so much money. He was hauled before the courts again in September 1849 on another matter, in a case called *Bradford v Fox Cooper* in Gravesend where he had been managing a theatre. In his defence he said he had sold all his goods, at a ruinous sacrifice but it had not been enough to pay his debts. To try and earn some money he had speculated with the *Gravesend Theatre* then the *Terrace Gardens* but the treasurer fell victim to cholera and he was left without income.

He ended up in prison in Maidstone and was brought up before the magistrates in 1850. There are more jobs and addresses than ever listed for Fox Cooper and appear to be Kent based claims. His lawyer tried to explain why Fox Cooper carried on speculating and taking risks when he already owed money:

> 'As a respected person in his profession, his only means of living was by such speculation. If after one unfortunate speculation, they were prevented from entering on another they would become ruined men.'[519]

It looks like Fox Cooper was imprisoned while he waited for this one to be heard as another newspaper said that he, along with a lot of other prisoners, would be brought before the county court in Kent at Maidstone on 9.7.1850, but Fox Cooper was used to prison by now.[520] As it turned out, he was discharged and the *Morning Chronicle* on 10.1.1852 announced the dividends to be paid to his creditors.

How easily Fox Cooper defaults and it certainly seems to run in the family. First the father, then Fox Cooper, then his brother Henry Octavius William, who, coincidentally, is in Maidstone gaol at the same time as Fox Cooper, also insolvent, so they would have been able to catch up. Henry was a clerk to a stockbroker and afterwards carried on business with John Bailey as a stock and share broker dealing in railway shares on commission. Perhaps this is where Fox Cooper got the idea to invest, another venture which did not end well. Henry Octavius spent time in prison in Norwich in 1857 too. When he died in May 1874 age 69 in Richmond, he was described as a land proprietor. As there is no trace of his will then there cannot have been any money left in his estate.[521]

This last twenty years for Fox Cooper was a roller coaster as he flipped between theatres, ran off without paying people, sued and was sued himself and somehow found time to fantasize about south sea adventures. By 1850 he is 44 and still going strong.

But how much energy have we left to read any more?

Chapter 24 - Chalkley the Fugitive

These headlines, in June 1861, were the first the world knew that Chalkley had been found, nearly a year after he had absconded.

- 'Apprehension of a Canting Knave,' *Leeds Mercury*

- 'Apprehension of Chalkley, the Liverpool Swindler at Southampton,' *Hampshire Advertiser*

- 'Apprehension of Alleged Swindler,' *Dover Express*

The main newspaper accounts were local to Southampton, then spread to Liverpool but syndication soon led to them being printed word for word in all the newspapers in the kingdom.[522]

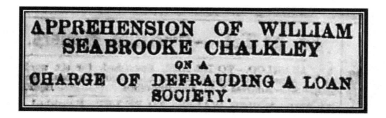

APPREHENSION OF WILLIAM
SEABROOKE CHALKLEY
ON A
CHARGE OF DEFRAUDING A LOAN
SOCIETY.

Figure 53 'Apprehension of Chalkley,' Liverpool Mercury 18.6.1861

It wasn't first class detective work that led to Chalkley's arrest, but mere coincidence or possibly divine intervention.

'It appears that among his [Chalkley's] numerous victims, was a lady named Skinner, who was a considerable shareholder in the Liverpool Trademan's Loan Society, and on whom Chalkley had also forged a bill for £400 [£23,651.68].'

This feisty lady had recently moved to Southampton and lived in Sussex Place.

'Walking down the High Street of Southampton.... with her brother-in-law, she met a man whom she immediately recognised as Chalkley, and he, it would seem, recognised her, for he tried to evade her in every possible way. He stepped into a shop but the intrepid Mrs. Skinner followed him and said she knew him. He told her she must be mistaken. She insisted he was Chalkley but he replied: "No madam, my name is William Cook."'

Then he almost immediately walked out of the shop and went up the street, pursued by Mrs. Skinner and presumably her brother-in-law. She gave Chalkley into the custody of the first policeman she met, Sergeant Blake.[523]

Reading this makes you want to shout 'At last!!!' Fancy being caught by one of his victims? But where had Chalkley, alias William Cook, been for the past year and why had he reappeared in Southampton of all places?

It became known very quickly after police questioned Chalkley and searched his papers that he had been in the town for a week, having landed on the steamer *Arago* from America.[524] This was a wooden hulled, brig-rigged, side - wheel steamer built in 1855 by Westervelt and Sons in New York.[525] Under the command of Captain Gadsden, it had sailed from New York on 25.5.1861 and was ultimately bound for Le Harve carrying mail, passengers and cargo and had arrived in Southampton on the 6th June, a day earlier than expected.[526]

This puts Chalkley in New York a week or two before 25.5.1861. But why did he take the risk and come back knowing there was a price on his head? If he thought he was safe landing in Southampton, he was, as one publication put it, 'A great fool.'[527]

On arrival, Chalkley stayed with 'a relative' in Canton Street, who the *Hampshire Advertiser* said were 'reputed to be a very pious family.' At the same time, he began to look about for a safe mooring where he might become a flourishing citizen. A house belonging to a Mr. Elliott attracted his attention, preliminaries were in course of arrangement and Chalkley, posing as the Reverend William Cook, had already paid a visit to Mr. Douglas' furnishing establishment.

'He gave himself out to be a gentleman who did a little in the preaching line: who had been apprenticed to the baking; who had gone to America and turned his attention to farming; but who inflamed with a desire to spend his days in the old country, had come home once more to resume the kneading trough. He looked at some furniture and promised to purchase when he got his house in order.'[528]

In another couple of amazing twists, it appeared that Mrs. Skinner [who used to be known as Polly Johnson in Liverpool] would be entitled to the £200 [£11, 825.24] reward for Chalkley's arrest, half of what he embezzled from her, and her brother-in-law came back from America on the same ship as Chalkley, they spent all that time together and he did not recognise him.

'The prisoner was taken before the borough magistrates on Saturday 15th June and remanded until Monday morning, then, when he was brought up, he was handed over to the authorities in Liverpool who were immediately telegraphed and a detective was sent to Southampton that night to escort him back.'

On searching the house at Canton Street in Southampton, a vast number of letters were found addressed to him as: Rev W. Cooke, Norristown Post Office, Montgomery County, Pennsylvania from the Rev W. Thompson. They gave 'our dear friend William S. Cooke' a very high character for 'piety' and 'sound doctrine,' and other good qualities and there were various sermons along with notes of others from different ministers who offered to lend him their pulpits, a list of places where he had preached, with observations on the manifestations of 'success which had blessed his ministrations' also in his luggage. One wonders whether Chalkley realised how apt the name was he had chosen. It only needed one extra letter to become 'Crook.'

But that was not all they found. There were also missives of a rather different nature, which were later published.'[529]

Liverpool, August 25th 1860.

My dear William, - I hope this letter will find you much better than when I got your dear letters, do send me word as you can, as I do feel so anxious about you.

I hope you have got the two letters I have sent you, one on the 13th and one on the 19th, safe to hand. It looks so long to me to have to wait a month before I get one from you; I wish the vessel would go and come a bit quicker than it does. O how I wish I was with you today; when it is morning, I wish it was night, and when it is night, I wish it was morning, but I must wait patiently, but I feel it hard work.

I had Mr. W......s on Thursday; he said he called to tell me he was going to live in London, that he had got so tired of the people here that he would go from them. He said he would call and give me his address, that if I wanted anything, I could write to him. My dear William, did you tell him to call upon me, as I dare not say anything to him, for fear I should be doing wrong.

Have you seen any of the papers since you went, as they have said all sorts of things about you my dear William that I know is not correct, nor all the world would not make me believe it. It has cut me to the very heart but I durst not speak. I know it is best for me to keep quiet. Oh, how I long to be with you today, dear William.

I have got large bills up in the window, 'Selling off stock at a great reduction.' I have not advertised it in the paper yet, until I get a letter from you. Polly and Sarah Ann say they are coming. I hope we shall all be with you soon dear William. Excuse the shortness of this letter, but I shall be able to say more when I hear from you. They all wish to be remembered to you, with the kindest love; and I cannot count their kisses, but double the quantity from your own dear Lilley. I remain your ever faithful and affectionate LILLEY.

P.S. – Oh how anxious I am waiting for a letter from you, dear. Dear William, may I ask if you have put one line in the paper Saturday August 25th, as I feel and believe it is you, my dear William, I am sure it is.

On the fold of the letter is written, 'Ten thousand kisses.'

So, Chalkley had yet another very secret life beneath all his pious posturing and financial subterfuge, one with Lilley, who wrote this letter exactly three months after he disappeared. He had obviously seen her and written when entire police forces and responsible citizens all over the country had been looking for him, the fugitive. Newspapers revealed the family kept a millinery or draper's shop, opposite the end of Hotham Street on London Road in Liverpool and suggested they met when Chalkley was on his extensive travels across the northern region and managing the Manchester office.

Occupants of London Road 1855-1861				
No	1855	1859	1860	1861
25	Charles Owen, shoemaker	Martin Condiff	No one	John Pepper, painter
27	Mary Condiff	Elizabeth Shaw, draper	Elizabeth Shaw, draper	Thomas Lee, shoemaker
29	John Harrison, silk dyer and scourer	John Roberts	George Warren Eating House	George Warren Eating House

I traced this shop using street directories and found that between 1859 – 1860, Lillie had No 27 London Road and her name was actually Elizabeth Shaw. Her neighbours were honest, hardworking traders: a shoemaker, plumber, a silk dyer and another ran an Eating House.

No 27 has been modernised so the photograph below, taken in 2019, shows the houses of Lilley's neighbours further up London Road and gives us some idea of what the area might have looked like.

Figure 54 London Road, Liverpool 2019

Many, with hindsight, might have suspected their relationship as when Chalkley disappeared there was talk that one of this family had gone with him. I had thought up until now they meant his wife and sixteen-year-old daughter, but on 25.5.1860 Chalkley had left them to face the music, the scandal, the horror of his 'doings' and instead devoted his letters to Lilley, known as Miss S, according to the *Liverpool Daily Post*, the only newspaper to publish even a hint of this relationship.[530] They say:

'He appears to have been on terms of peculiar intimacy with her before he ran away and she appears to have been equally fascinated with him.'

Many of her letters have survived, though none of his, but we can deduce much of what he said by her replies, written 'in a fine flowing angular hand, on tinted paper, and scented.'

From the sound of her first letter, Chalkley had departed these shores for America before 25.8.1860. I searched under his real name and the pseudonym, once I realised he had taken his mother's maiden name Cook to avoid detection, but cannot find a passenger record as his new name was too common, there were many routes from England to New York and no ID was required in 1860.

Lilley had sent other letters before this therefore she must have had some expectation he would have arrived by the 25th August and she had an address in New York. So where was he from the third week of May to August 1860? Maybe he was hiding in England, as Lilley was not worried about him until August. She refers to a 'one line' in the paper of Saturday 25.8.1860 which she feels sure was from him, so I searched and found this in the Correspondents section of the *Liverpool Mercury*, entitled: 'A Distant Reader.'

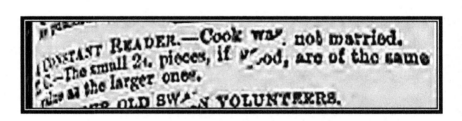

Figure 55 One liner in the Liverpool Mercury Saturday 25.8.1860

That they must have agreed to this desperate method of communication in advance says something about Chalkley. Lilley had been checking every week but by 13th September, she is panicking in Manchester as she has not heard from him, despite the three letters she sent in August and there being a post from New York to Liverpool every week.

Manchester, September 13th 1860

My dear William – I now sit down to write you a few lines, to ask you if it is not time, I should have received an answer before now. I have sent three letters, one on the 13th, one on the 19th, and 25th and it is now time, the 13th September, and I have not received one, yet it makes me feel very uneasy, wondering whether you have received my letters, and how you are, whether you are any better: do answer dear William, my letters, as soon as you can as I feel so uneasy about you. Send me word what day your vessels start and that I might know what time I may expect one.

O how I do long to see you, my dear William, the time does look so long; I don't know how the days get on, how they pass over so slowly. You say dear William, in your letter, there is a post every week; I should have had one before now. I have looked in the paper every day to see if there has one come in; you will say I am impatient, silly, but I cannot help it, I was born so; you don't know how I long to come and spoil you, and I know you would be very glad to see me.

Dear William, are there any warehouses there and can goods be bought there the same as they can here? My dear William, do send me word what sort of lodgings you have got, and what sort of people they are, whether they make you comfortable; do try to make yourself as happy as you can. As I shall come to you as soon as ever I can; I know the evenings will appear long to you, but not longer than they do to me without you.

O how I do wish I could just see you; I have many things to say to you, but I cannot until I get an answer from you. I shall be so glad to hear from you; I look out so anxiously every morning for a letter; and now I must conclude by saying that my dear mother and John, and the girls all send their kindest love to you; and I cannot tell you how many kisses, if they were with you, they say they would give you; and I cannot tell you how many from me, but I would soon show you if I was with you. I only wish I was with you tonight. You are the first and last with me.

Dear William, O how I feel I want to speak to you just now, but I do not fret, but keep your spirits up and make yourself happy until I come, as I will come, as soon as ever I can. I remain forever, your LILLEY.

Arthur Place, Rusholme, Manchester.

P.S. Does the New York vessels come near where you are?

Searching online databases, I found the exact house she mentions which is actually No:1 Arthur Place, Rusholme, about two miles south of Manchester city centre. It was a lovely area. In 1837, nearly 150 acres of land and its surroundings were laid out as an ornamental and gated park, called Victoria Park. Its mansions, designed by Manchester architect Richard Lane, made it a very fashionable address.[531]

In 1841, 1,841 people lived there but it grew rapidly in the next ten years to 3,679. By this time Rusholme had gas street lighting with fourteen gas lamps, excellent drainage and fresh supplies of water along with paved streets. In 1860, the public hall was built which was to be used for the 'moral and intellectual improvement of the people of Rusholme,' ironically in the same year that Chalkley's infamy and betrayals came to light.

No 1 Arthur Place, Rusholme was Lilley's home in 1851 as the census shows. It also told me who the other members of her family mentioned in her letters were and confirmed her father was not living with them at that time. I was then able to piece together what little information there was about the family.

From the innocence displayed in Lilley's letters, almost naivety, and the child-like eagerness of her siblings to get involved, completely unaware of the hardships in store, I assumed they were quite young and I was very surprised to find they were all, apart from Hannah, grown adults and Lilley was a mature 35 in 1860.

Lilley's father, John Shaw, had died by 1851, but does appear in the 1841 census shown as an agricultural labourer and his age is given as 45, though this could be wrong as the ages of most of the children and their mother are wrong as well, but that's par for the course with this census. However, this is undoubtably the Shaw family, as confirmed by baptism records.

John Shaw and Ann Jackson, Lilley's parents, were married in 1820 at St John the Baptist's church in Halifax, West Yorkshire. This was his parish where he worked as a clog maker and Ann could not write as she left an X as her mark on the marriage certificate. They both lived in Midgeley near Halifax which lies below Midgley Moor, a hill top village, and Elizabeth Ann (Lilley) was baptised in 1827 at Kirkburton, Yorkshire.

In 1828 John Shaw, his wife and baby daughter lived at Rowley Hill, Lepton, Kirkheaton in idyllic countryside far from the filth and stench of industrial Liverpool or Manchester. Here her sister Sarah Ann is born on 31.3.1828 but does not appear again. She probably died as John and Ann gave her name to the next daughter who turned out to be one of twins, the other being a son called John. But very quickly, the family succumb to the lure of a big city, probably in search of better paid work, and arrive in Blackley, Manchester. There are two further children Mary Ann born in 1831 at Droylsden and Grace Hannah in 1835 in Blackley, Manchester. Her father was listed as a clogger.[532]

At that time Droylsden was basically a small farming community, but with the coming of the Manchester and Ashton-under-Lyne canals and the railways in the 1840s the population increased fivefold in the 19th century. William Miller Christy developed a hat-making concern in London and his three sons continued the business. Their Droylsden branch opened in 1837 for the manufacture of shirtings at Fairfield Mills and contributed towards the building of workers' cottages nearby, a school and gas works. The canal was used to ferry coal into Droylsden from the Bradford and Snipe pits along the Ashton Canal to the five cotton mills which were established there by 1850 with another three by 1875. A total of 960 employees worked in the mill at this time.

The Lumb, Saxon and Fairfield Mills were home to the first cotton woven towel to be produced in the world on a specially adapted loom which later became known as the

Terry Towel. This was a development of the well-known Turkish towel which began in 1851 after James Christy, the son of William Miller, saw the unusually looped cloth on a visit to Turkey and brought back a sample.[533]

Chalkley's first letter to Lilley eventually arrived on 15th September. Reckoning that the voyage takes about two weeks and if Chalkley missed a post it would be at the most another week before a mail boat left New York, the latest he could have written from there was on 25th August, which is the same day he telegraphed the one liner which appeared in the Liverpool paper. If this is about right, and he had just arrived, then he must have left England between 4 - 11.8.1860. In turn, Lilley's first letter dated 13th August posted in hope that he would get it straight away was a little optimistic, but she is obviously impatient and very much in love.

Manchester, September 15th 1860.

My own dear William, I got your kind letter today, and oh, how glad I was when I heard you had got my first letter safe. I was sorry I did not wait a day longer before I sent my last, but you see I was impatient, and I am sorry I should have caused you so much pain when you received my first letter: but you see, my dear, I am here, and I can only ascribe it to the providence of God, and I do hope I shall see you soon. Often have I gone down on my knees and prayed that I might see my dear William. There is nothing I care for but you. I will come to you as soon as ever I can. You know, dear William, there is nothing I care for but you – I am always happy when with you. You say that I must and I will come at once. I will come as soon as I can get away, dear William.

I will advertise the shop and fixtures this week and I think it would be best to sell the stock with the fixtures, if I can do, but if I cannot, I will bring it with me and will send you word every week how I am getting on. They all say they will come with me: John says he can get a situation there. What do you think, dear William, and if the girls are all with us there, we can get on, as our own would be better than strangers and what little difference it would make in the expense of their coming out it would be better as it would be a saving in the end? My dear mother says that she would like to come with us.

My dear William do you not think it would be the best to come by the way of London than by here, as some ill-disposed persons had said that one of us had gone with you until they saw all three of us in the shop. They came to ask if we knew anything of you, or where you had gone to, and we told them we did not know, and we would only be glad to know; and for fear that anyone should suspect that we had gone, is there no other way than by leaving here, and would it be better to take our name or another's names. J—k—n; and John to take John J—k—n, not that we have anything to fear ourselves, but for your own dear sake.

My dear William, it is to make you secure that we will do anything that you think the best; and you do surprise me when you say you had not told Mr. W.......s to come as he just came as if you had sent him. He said he had called to put us on our guard, that if we had anything belonging to you, or you had anything belonging to us, in the way of writings. He said I don't say you have, but if you have, and I could not understand him; and I said I had nothing, and that if I wanted anything, I must apply to him; but we never have done, and I never asked him any questions, nor told him anything, for I was afraid of him. I asked him if he thought we should ever see you again, and he said he did not think we ever should; he said if there were any communications, they would come through him.

Polly said, mind what you say to that old fellow, I don't like him, he is an old pry. Polly said, when they said that one of us had gone, she wished we had, we would be taken care of by you. I wish we could get out before winter sets in. You say, dear William, that I must say when I will come. I will come as soon as I can sell off the stock and let the shop. I will send you word what day we will all of us come, as it would be better for us to get out soon as the winter is getting so near. You say, dear, you would like me to get away in a month. I will do so if I can. I would like to do so if I could, as I do not mind how soon I get to you.

Dear William, you say too, when I land, we are to be united for life with my consent. I should only be too glad to be your own. You say in your letter that I am to get a black merino frock. I will do so, but would you like me to get any other kind, as I have only the black silk one, and it is trimmed with crepe, or would you rather I did not get anything, as I will entirely leave it to you to decide. Dear William, send me word where we are to book to, New York or Philadelphia? You say you will meet us at New York, but are we to take our passage to New York or Philadelphia? As the bill states to New York only, I have enclosed one for you to look at and I and Polly have been down to Mr. Inman to make enquiries what the fare is and they say 15 guineas to New York; and whatever goods we have we send down to their office and they will see to them being packed two or three days before the vessel sails.

My dear, you say in your first letter you would like three of them to come out; Annie could be made as useful as Polly, and S.A; and if John could get a situation, then there would only be mother. But dear William, I must leave it for you to decide what way you think best. Don't you think it would be a greater blind to the public for the whole family to come out than a part of us to come as they would never imagine that the whole family would come out, not that we have had anyone trouble us any way, only Mr. W........s, and he said he was a friend of yours. My only care is to ensure your safety. I only wish we were ready to start now.

You know that two might attend to the shop and two to the millinery, and do without paying salaries. What do you think about it dear? As we could manage it amongst ourselves: that is my opinion. I must leave it to you; what do you think will be the best?

Dear William, send me word if there are vessels that go out at any other time besides those that go out on a Wednesday from here, and those that leave from New York on Saturdays; that if I wish any day would you get it any sooner than if I posted on Tuesday for the vessel that sets sail on Wednesday from here.

Now, dear, do let me entreat upon you to keep up your spirits, as I do assure you that I will come as soon as ever I have let the shop and can get away. You say, dear, that the month will appear long to you, but not longer that it will to me. I do hope that I may let in a month; now dear, I must conclude, with the hope of soon seeing you and being made your own forever; and hope we may be spared many years together for you cannot love me more than I love you. I only wish I was with you now to see off that loneliness. Polly and S.A say they are quite ready to come; and they send you lots of kisses; and as for my part, I send you all mine. Would not I give them to you if I was with you tonight; but I am, my dear, living in hopes soon to do it, now may that time come soon. Oh, how I long to be with you; and now I remain, your ever affectionate and ever faithful, LILLEY.

P.S. – Write me again by return of post and let me know how you are. I am looking out for another letter from you, dear, on Saturday; I hope I shall get it. Was so proud of this when I got it on Saturday. It is my dear mother's birthday. Now do you keep your spirits up and think that you will not be long before you have me with you. Ever yours. LILLEY

Lilley continued to try to sell the stock in their London Road shop and another letter comes from Chalkley, only five days after the first, which strengthens the argument that he must have been on a ship and out of touch until 15th September, having left England sometime in August 1860.

September 22nd 1860

My Own Dear, Dear William, - We received your very, very kind letter on the 20th, and I cannot tell you how glad I was to receive it, and to hear that you are better and keeping up your spirits; do let me entreat you to do so as I will not be long before I come, I wish I could come to you sooner. I could not tell you how delightful my dear mother and John and the girls are at the thought of coming. You say in your letter you will be proud to see us all, not more than we shall be to see you, and as for my part my dear William, I could not express my feelings but you will know them. Oh, how I wish dear William I was with you today.

I am so happy to hear you have joined yourself to the society, and that you have preached several times for them, and so thankful to hear they are so kind to you and that you are so much happier than you were, the thought of it makes me feel so much more happy. You say my own dear William how much you love us all, not more than we love you. I am sorry that I should have given you such a shock in my first letter; if I had thought of it, I would not have done it, but I am thankful that I have been spared and I hope I shall be spared to get to you under this great trial, for it has been a great trial to part with you, my dear William, the greatest trial I ever had. You say my dear William that it will not be many days before I am with you but it looks a long time to me. I wish the time was come now; I wish we were only ready to start.

I have seen Mrs. H......y today but I could not get any decisive answer from her until she has consulted her son. She has promised faithfully to give me an answer on Monday: I am trying my very best with her; I don't know what I can do with her but it shall not be for want of trying her hard; I will do my very best William to make the stock realise as near what you state as I can. I will try to dispose of the stock with the shop as I think will be the best. You ask me dear William which branch of business I like the best. I would say with all my heart the farming and so do we all; if I was sure that you would like it, but dear William we will leave it entirely up to you to decide which will be best as you are more experienced in these things than we are, and mother and John say the same; they would rather be guided by you...

You say dear, you do not know much about farming, but I think you know enough to manage one, and as for my part I will do my best to help you all I can, and if I cannot do farming I can love you, stitch a button on your shirt and darn a hole in your stocking, and Polly says that what John cannot carry to the market, she will help him, and get her pocket ready for underneath her apron to help him and Sally says if she cannot do anything else she can twist the cow's tails round and run them up the meadows and Annie says she can wash the milk cans out and scald the mugs out and John desires me to say that he thinks he would like the farming very much but he will entirely leave it to you; he does not care how soon, he thinks it would be delightful for us all to be once more together again.

You say dear William you would like us to come by [Mr.] Inman, but I think if it is agreeable to you that it would be best to come by Southampton, as it would be the safest and quietest way of coming and I would much rather come that way if agreeable to you dear. John has written to Southampton to know the particulars of the fares, what it will cost. I will send word in my next letter and as soon as I get an answer from there and from Mrs. H----y I will write immediately.

And now my dear William, just give me your opinion about Annie's piano. All she frets about is parting with it. Do you think it is possible to bring it with us or would it be best to sell it and buy her one when we get there? And now dear William make yourself as happy as you can, for soon as ever I can dispose of the shop I will. I would like to get out before November.

My dear, we got your letter all right and safe; it was directed quite right. The reason I have detained this letter is I thought I would get an answer from Mrs. H......y. I shall not let her alone until I get one and shall send you word as soon as ever I can.

And now my dear William if you think that a Millinery and Boot and Shoe shop would pay the best let us have it, as you know they cannot cheat us neither in the Boot and Shoe nor the Millinery, both of these we understand well, and as you are there and have seen the country you will know the best how to judge and as for my part I don't care which so long as I am with you and John does not mind which it is as he thinks either of the businesses, farming or the other would be better for his health.

And now dear William if you think we could manage a farm we would much rather have it. You say that you will try to make us as happy as you can and if it is in our power to make you happy nothing would give us greater pleasure than to make you happy. John says he would like to be taking the horses and cart to market to sell the butter and eggs. Polly says she will go with him, she is going to get John a pair of lace up boots and a wide-awake and she wants to know if she must bring you a pair. You say you think John would be more than happy in it, he says he would be more than happy and mother is quite delighted with it.

And now dear William we will write and let you know the time of our starting and if the letter should not reach you in time, we will go to the St Nicholas Hotel and telegraph you. How I long to be with you. I feel I cannot settle anywhere until I come to you dear William. I can do nothing now but get ready. I am beginning to pack now and I feel my spirits so much revived since I know I am coming to you. You say you want to clasp me in your arms, yes, I will show you what I will do when I come.

And now my dear William, my dear mother and John and the girls send their kindest love to you and all the kisses it is possible to give you. They say they will let you see when they come and as for my part, dear William, I have a heart overflowing with love for you. I hope shortly to be yours for ever, until death.

P.S.- My dear William, I am so happy to say we have just received your very kind letter today, the 24th September just before we were going to the post with this one. Oh! How delighted I was to get it, and to hear that you are so much better in health and happier in mind, as it leaves me the same and all the rest of the family. Now, dear William, I can be more plain now that I have received this very dear letter of yours today, that I would much rather have a farm, and mother would, and John would, and all the girls would. They are all delighted at the thought of the farm and I feel pretty sure in my mind we can manage it amongst us.

At the time we received your letter this morning we got one from Southampton. There is one vessel which sets sail on October 17, Captain Wottan. On November 14, Captain Lines and December 12, Captain Wottan; that is one card. The next card is Captain von Sauter, October 3 and October 31, Captain Wessel and there is another one November 28 and December 26.

If possible, I will get ready for the one October 31. We shall do so as we would not like it to be later and I think dear William, it would be better if you did not meet us at the vessel but let us go to the St Nicholas Hotel and telegraph you when we get in and I think it would be very much safer to come by Southampton, as I think we should come quieter than by Liverpool, for as soon as ever we have let the shop, we shall go home and start from Manchester.

Dear William, you say that we are to say that we are going to the West of England, as you are in the West; will it be safe for us to say that we are going there; would it not be better to say we are going into the country and nothing more.

Now my dear William, I shall lose no time in trying to dispose of the shop as soon as I get an answer from Mrs. H.....y, and shall write to you as soon as I get an answer as to how I am getting on.

Dear William, I will not fail to get you the little things that you want as you say that things are so much dearer than they are here and then we shall not require any clothing for some time, and if there is anything else that you require, please send me word and I will get it for you and dear John says he shall feel great pleasure in getting you anything that you require; he feels he cannot do too much for you.

Now my dear William, do not come to the vessel to meet us, as mother and John would rather you did not risk it, if you think there is any unsafety, as they would rather go to the hotel and telegraph for you; and now my dear William, I shall write you again in a few days to let you know how I am going on and now I must conclude by remaining, your own and ever affectionate   LILLEY

P.S. (No 2) – And now dear I hope to be with you in a few days. You say dear we must all pray for you. We do that daily and hourly. Dear William, if we do not come by the 2nd cabin fare at 13 guineas, we shall have all to find if we come by the one at eight guineas. Both in beds and everything else.

Figure 56 The man second left is wearing a Wide-Awake hat

Incidentally, a 'wide -awake,' which Polly says she is going to buy for her brother John, is a type of hat with a broad brim made of black or brown felt. It was inspired by the paramilitary campaign organisation, the Wide - Awakes, affiliated with the Republican Party during the 1860 election, which supported Abraham Lincoln and the Union, strongly opposing slavery. The Wide - Awakes were well-drilled and served as political police in escorting party speakers and in preserving order at party demonstrations and had over 400,000 estimated members. Their standard uniform consisted of a full robe or cape, a torch, and of course the black hat, which the Bollman Hat Company made in their factory in Adamstown, Pennsylvania in 1868.[534]

The St Nicholas' Hotel in New York, where Lilley was planning to meet Chalkley, was very fashionable in 1860. It opened on 6.1.1853, and by the end of the year had expanded to 1,000 rooms. It raised the bar for a new standard of lavishness for a luxury hotel and was the first New York City building to cost over US$1 million.[535]

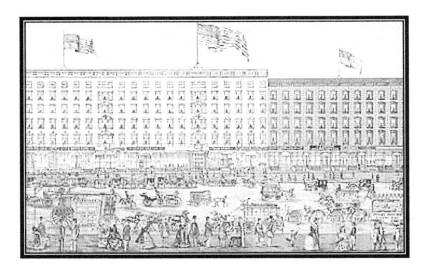

Figure 57 St Nicholas' Hotel, New York 1855: F. L. Heppenheimer

Chalkley has meanwhile made his way to Norristown in Pennsylvania and based himself at the Oak Street Station of Wesleyan Methodists with the Rev John Thompson.

> 'So zealous was he in his ministrations, and so apparently sincere was he in all his professions of piety, that there, as in England, he succeeded not only in averting suspicion as to his true character, but also in winning the esteem and the friendship of the religious body to which he had attached himself. So much so that he embodied one who was: "Allied with Heaven, [whilst] parleying oft with hell."'

But why Pennsylvania? Chalkley must have decided that one of the early centres of the American brand of methodism would be where he could reinvent himself. John Wesley (1703–1791) was an English cleric, theologian and evangelist who was a leader of a revival movement within the Church of England known as Methodism.[536] In the late 1760s, two Methodist lay preachers emigrated to America and formed societies. Philip Embury began the work in New York at the instigation of fellow Irish Methodist, Barbara Heck. Soon, Captain Webb from the British Army joined him. He formed a society in New York and travelled along the coast. The Oak Street Methodist Episcopal Church in Norristown, where the Rev John Thompson one of the elders was based, was founded in 1854 and had 198 members.[537]

Norristown, Monday morning, October 15, 1860.

Rev. W. S. Cook.—Dear brother, the Presiding Elder wishes me to fill his appointment next Sunday morning at Evansburg, and I have engaged to do it on condition you will be at home and preach for me. Will you please write and let me know whether you will be at home on Sunday so as to preach for me on Sunday morning. I will return in time to preach in the evening. Things are moving along about as usual. We had a very pleasant quarterly conference last Friday night. Yesterday morning we had a good time, brother M'Caskey preached for us, but last night the storm affected our congregation. We all join in respects. Please answer immediately.

Very truly your brother,

JOHN THOMPSON.

Figure 58 One of the letters found in Chalkley's possession in 1861

When Chalkley was not whiling away his waiting time toying with farming and cultivating his evangelical position, he had become a shareholder in the land department of the Hannibal and St Joseph's Railway Company in America and in his luggage, there was a quantity of correspondence relative to his shares, which 'would seem to be numerous.'[538]

TO BE DISPOSED OF, the GOODWILL, FIXTURES, and STOCK of an established MILLINERY BUSINESS, situate in the best part of London-road. The present parties declining business. HOUSE and SHOP TO BE LET. —Apply at 27, London-road. 27no4e3

Figure 59 'For Sale' Liverpool Mercury 27.11.1860

But for Lilley in Liverpool selling the shop was not as easy and it is as late as November 1860 when this advert appears in the *Liverpool Mercury*. It looks like Mrs. H.......y had been more difficult than Lilley had anticipated.

Lilley and her family were not ready to sail from Southampton in November or December 1860 and it is not until 19.1.1861 that Lilley is able to write and tell Chalkley they have arrived in Southampton and are going to sail for New York on 22nd. She encloses instructions to come and meet them.

The same month, Chalkley receives his preacher's licence and a glowing testimonial commending him to the Christian Fellowship.

> " LOCAL PREACHER'S LICENSE.—To all whom it may concern.—This certifies
> that William S. Cook, having been examined by us concerning his gifts,
> grace, and usefulness, we judge that he is a suitable person to be licensed
> as a local preacher in the Methodist Episcopal Church, and we accordingly
> authorise him to preach the Gospel, subject to the requirements of the discipline of
> the said church—Signed by order of the Quarterly Conference of Oak-street, M. E.
> Church in the Reading district, this 4th day of January, 1861.—F. J. THOMPSON,
> Presiding Elder."
>
> " NOTICE.—This is to Certify that the bearer William S. Cook, has been an ac-
> cepted member and Local Preacher in the Methodist Episcopal Church in Oak-
> street Station, Philadelphia Conference, January, 18th 1861, JOHN THOMPSON,
> Preacher in Charge."
>
> " TO ALL WHOM IT MAY CONCERN.— Our beloved brother, Rev. Wm. S. Cook
> Preacher in the Oak-street Station, Phil. Conference, being about to leave this
> place, I take pleasure in commending him to the Christian fellowship of those with
> whom he may unite in church relation. Brother Cook possesses gifts, grace, and
> fruits that will render him very useful wherever he may cast his lot. Praying
> that God's blessing may continue and abide with him, I remain, very truly, JOHN
> THOMPSON, Pastor of Oak-street Station."

Figure 60 The preacher's letters found in Chalkley's possession in 1861

Then, there is delay in England. According to the *Hampshire Advertiser,* on the 26.1.1861, the North German Lloyd steamer, *New York,* the only ship sailing to New York at that time which was due to leave Southampton on 23 January, only got away on 27th, having been delayed by fog in the Weser on its way back from Bremen. However, for some reason, Lilley and her family were not on it when it arrived in New York in February 1861. The Rev Thompson obviously expected them as he writes to Chalkley from Norristown on 4th February reporting on the latest news from the Wesleyan Methodists which he ends by saying:

'Let us know whether you will favour us with a visit before you go west, and give us all the news about your farming and family coming.'

Another arrangement must have then been made for May 1861, for Chalkley is in New York again waiting for them to arrive. He has asked the good Reverend Thompson in Norristown to keep an eye on the post and forward any letters for him from England. However, by some means, maybe telegraph, Lilley gets a message to him in New York which must have been urgent enough for him to take the next ship, the *Arago* on the 25th May and arrive in Southampton on 7th June.

Three times Lilley has cancelled at very short notice, the last occasion being so desperate that Chalkley leaves his good friend the Reverend Thompson in Norristown ignorant of his true whereabouts. Even in early June when he wrote to the Rev Thompson from England, Chalkley led him to believe he was still in New

York. Heaven knows what the good minister thought when the news of Chalkley's criminality and lies finally reached America and his Wesleyan flock.

Norristown, June 27, '61.

Rev. W. S. Cook.—Dear brother, your second letter came to hand this morning I am exceedingly sorry to hear that your family have not come on. I delayed writing after receiving your first letter hoping to hear of the arrival of your family, and not knowing how long you would remain in New York. You may rest assured that it was not any want of interest on my part. I saw the letter carrier at the first of this week. I told him if any letter should come for you to bring it to me. So on Wednesday one came. I paid him the one postage and told him to send the letter immediately to New York. He did so, and to my surprise, our careless Post-Master must let the letter lay in his office till last evening, and I feel sorry that your letter has been thus delayed, but you must blame our Post-Master, you may depend on me attending promptly to all your letters, and I will try and see that the Post-Master does not do the same thing again.

Our meeting goes on famously and an old man between 75 and 76 years old, powerfully converted last night, continues to pray for us. I must close in haste as it is near time for the mail to leave, and I want you to get this letter as soon as possible.

Yours in Christ,

JOHN THOMPSON.

Figure 61 Letter from Rev Thompson to Chalkley 27.6.1861

Why Chalkley came back is not known. I did my maths to see if Lilley could have been pregnant and miscarried or was perhaps too ill to travel after a birth. If she was with him in hiding, from May - August 1860 she could have given birth to a full-term child any time between February - May 1861, or had a premature child or a miscarriage.

There are no official birth records under her real name Shaw, the name of Jackson she was going to assume if they had sailed to America, a surname of Cook or Chalkley, if she had taken his name or had secretly and bigamously married him before he left for America. Nothing fits the dates. Lilley also adopted another name in 1871 so I searched that one too and again drew a blank. The only other scenario is that she miscarried or the child did not survive after the birth, in which case it was even less likely to be recorded as it was not required until 1927. None of Lilley's family died during that period and the only other reason I could come up with for her latest failure to travel, was family illness. But something very urgent must have persuaded Chalkley to come back, something which was more important than the risk to his freedom – maybe his safety?

The American Civil War was reaching its peak during the time Chalkley spent in America. In December 1860, South Carolina unanimously voted to leave the Union of States and was joined in January 1861 by Mississippi, Alabama, Georgia and Louisianna to set up the Confederate States of America. Four more states had ceded by April and civil war looked inevitable. Britain's position at this time was to stay neutral and to protect its assets in the US but by May 1861 they had recognised both parties as 'belligerent' and only a week later recognised the newer Confederacy which had a privateering fleet, which itself was a serious risk to the Union. [539]

Letters of marque had long been issued to the masters of non-government merchant ships to attack enemy shipping for their cargoes as it was a very cost-effective way for them to supplement their naval forces. These letters authorised ship's masters :

'To seize and take all ships, vessels and goods belonging to the enemy, not being within cannon-shot of the shores of a friendly state.'

Without such a letter, the ships would be seen as pirates and dealt with acordingly.

This distinction is important because another state like Britain could recognise a 'belligerent' and issue it with letters of marque, which would then put the British in a position of being set against the North or the South in this civil war, depending on whose side they wanted to support, without actually entering into warfare itself and by 6.6.1861 it looked very likely that Britain would soon be at war with the Union.

The Commonwealth of Pennsylvania, where Chalkley had set up as a Wesleyan preacher in Norristown, played a critical role in the Union, apart from providing 'Wide Awake' hats, by making available a huge supply of military manpower, equipment, and leadership to the Federal government. The state raised over 360,000 soldiers for the Federal armies, and served as a major source of artillery guns, small arms, ammunition, armour for the new revolutionary style of ironclad gunboats for the rapidly expanding United States Navy, and food supplies. The Phoenixville Iron Company by itself produced well over 1,000 cannons and the Frankford Arsenal was a major supply depot.

Pennsylvania was also the site of the bloodiest battle of the war, the Battle of Gettysburg, which became widely known as the one of the turning points of the civil war. Numerous smaller engagements and skirmishes were also fought in Pennsylvania during the 1863 Gettysburg campaign, as well as the following year when a Confederate cavalry raid culminated in the burning of much of Chambersburg and the industrial town of York was the largest city in the north to be occupied by the Confederate States Army during the war. [540]

America was no longer the promised land but riven with warfare, Pennsylvania being right in the middle of pitched battles, and more personally for Chalkley, his investments in the American railways had failed. Maybe Chalkey's decision to return was pragmatic, rather than romantic. [541]

The British ship Amelia, from Liverpool for Savannah, had arrived in New York in charge of a prize crew from the Federal vessel Union, which captured her on the 23rd off Charleston. Her cargo consists of iron crates, camp ovens, equipage, and machinery. Cargo valued at 50,000 dollars, vessel at 12,000 dollars. It was supposed that arms were concealed in the crates. The barque Virginia Ann arrived at New York; had reported that on the 10th ult, in lat 47, long 84, boarded the British ship Bramley Moore, from Mobile for Liverpool, and received from her a negro man, belonging north, who was permitted to leave Mobile. She also reported that they were boarded by the Federal steamer Massachusetts, which had the day previous taken twenty-five prizes, one the English Forfarshire, from Mobile. The Virginia Ann was chased all day and night by a privateer..

Figure 62 British ships seized: Southampton Times 13.7.1861

Chapter 25 - Chalkley Faces Judgement

Oh, what may man within him hide,
Though angel on the outward side
Measure for Measure - William Shakespeare[542]

It was Saturday 15.6.1861 when Chalkley was arrested in Southampton. No evidence could be taken that day and he was remanded in custody until Monday 17th spending his Sabbath in quiet meditation in a police cell. For Lilley, this must have been an awful time. They had only been together a week after being apart for nearly a year. Now there was nothing she could do, except wait.

In the meantime, the telegraph wires were very busy as the Liverpool police were informed their most notorious swindler was in custody. Detective Cousens set off from Liverpool by train, identified the prisoner and was in court in Southampton when Chalkley was formally handed over and he brought him back to Liverpool the same day. The solicitor for the Liverpool Trademan's Loan Company meanwhile went before the commissioner for bankruptcy and got an order to prosecute Chalkley.[543]

As part of those proceedings, it was said that Chalkley had two wives. According to the law at this time, Chalkley would have been a bigamist if he had married Lilley for his wife Jane, the mother of his seven children, still lived in Liverpool with their only surviving daughter Sarah Jane, who was just 17 in 1861. Marrying in another country was no defence, nor could he claim that he thought his wife was dead. The wanton wreckage of Chalkley's life and crimes was therefore shattering for all the women and families involved who were comprehensively shamed by his deceit and deceptions, with their trust and reputations destroyed through no fault of their own.

Mr. Raffles presided at the first hearing in the police court in Walton, Liverpool where Chalkley was described as being 'much dejected and during the inquiry scarcely looked up.' The court heard how the Liverpool Trademan's Loan Company was then in the process of being wound up in the bankruptcy court and that the case for the company was represented via the official liquidator Mr. George Morgan. The solicitor for the company then gave evidence enough for the court to remand Chalkley for seven days, after he declined to ask any of the witnesses any questions or make observations about the evidence produced.544 When one of the officers of the gaol asked Chalkley how he thought the business would terminate, he replied:

'From man I expect no mercy, but there is One to whom I can still look...'545

A week later on 25ᵗʰ June more evidence was produced, again Chalkley offered no defence and he was committed for trial on three charges of forgery and uttering forged instruments.546

On 12ᵗʰ August, at the summer assizes of the southern division of Lancaster in the Crown Court before Baron Martin, Chalkley was arraigned at St George's Hall in Liverpool, where he had appeared alongside Jane Gallagher just over a year previously. There were four indictments charging him with committing frauds on the company to a 'very large extent.'

- Embezzling sums of £10 [£591.29] and £100 [£5,912.92]

- Having on the 27 and 31.8.1859 feloniously forged and uttered two promissory notes for the payment of £200 [£11,825.84] and £850 [£50,259.82] respectively

- Having obtained by false pretences two orders of £185 5 shillings [£10,953.68] and one for £320 10 shillings [£17,886.58]

- And Chalkley pleaded guilty to a minor charge of obtaining money by false pretences but not guilty to the other indictments of forgery and embezzlement

For the defence, the court then heard the story of the two ladies Dickinson from Manchester, the office run by Goodall, Chalkley's servant. It described how Chalkley went weekly to superintend the business as many loans were granted from that district but little more was reported about F.T. Goodall so I did some research. I found that in January 1856 he was advertising loans for between 1 and 3 years at 5% from 26 Cooper Street, Manchester547 and that his accountancy partnership with a Mr. G.H. Goodall was dissolved in May the same year.548 Inspite of these financial setbacks, or maybe because of them, F.T. Goodall continued to offer loans and additionally appears in adverts selling tickets for the 'Black Ball Line of Clippers' to New Zealand, and he continues to do so for several years.549

By 20.8.1859, the Liverpool Tradesman's Loan Company has an address at Barlow's Court, 43 Market Street where George Foulkes is the Manchester agent and John

Atherton the secretary of the main office in Liverpool.[550] On 19.5.1860, just after the *Johnson v Gallagher* case began, F.T. Goodall advertises offices to be let on several floors of 19 and 21 Mount Street including four cellars, but he is still operating from 26 Cooper Street, Manchester.[551] Whilst not close to each other, these sites were certainly within walking distance.

On 28.7.1860, a month after Chalkley disappeared, Goodall is declared bankrupt and notices regarding the proceedings of the bankruptcy court were regularly reported in national newspapers until at least 1861 when it was said in Chalkley's court case that Goodall had absconded and taken with him funds from the company. Goodall's dividends were declared on the 2.7.1861.[552]

The ladies Dickinson confirmed that they had transacted all their loans with Goodall and never saw Chalkley at all and on this basis Chalkley's lawyers argued that it was Goodall who was guilty of the fraud against Ann Dickinson not him. They also put the case that there were understandable reasons why Chalkley was reckless about the loans granted, reminding the court that some four or five years previously the company had a large amount of bad debts, but:

> 'Relying on the energy and the skill and conduct of Chalkley, the directors took considerable portion of those bad debts as good and placed them in the balance sheet of the company and consequently they were enabled to pay a larger dividend. Whilst he did not defend Chalkley's actions, he thought the directors had acted very improperly and it would do well for societies if they only paid those dividends which they had fairly earned and not take bad debts to swell out dividends at the end of the year.

> 'He did not mean to say that the directors instructed Chalkley to do anything of this sort, but as they depended upon him to maintain the credit of the company, they gave him a motive to get as much business as he could – recklessly, if they liked – to show that the good debts preponderated over the bad. This being so, Chalkley might have taken the word of Goodall without making proper inquiry, honestly believing that the note was obtained from Ann Dickinson.'

If this was the case then that was the end of the charge of forgery as there was no proof that the handwriting on the promissory note was Chalkley's. In short it was all Goodall's fault and he was conveniently not there to argue.[553] The deputy chairman of the Liverpool Tradesman's Loan Company was also very keen to distance himself and said that they did not pay Goodall any salary, as he 'was the servant of Chalkley.'

After a brief consultation, the jury acquitted Chalkley of forging the order but found him guilty of uttering it knowing it to be forged. Mr. Baron Martin, in passing sentence, said Chalkley:

'Had been robbing them [the company] for years and had committed these forgeries for the purpose of covering the robberies he had committed. There was no doubt that he had defrauded his employers of many thousands of pounds. He had for a series of years been appropriating the money of the company to his own purposes and substituting these forged documents for the money.

'The consequences of such a crime were most serious, and anyone who knew anything of the administration of the law knew that a few years ago he would have been executed for this offence. Hundreds of people had been executed for this offence, and it was the duty of every person administering the law in this, probably the greatest commercial country in the world, and especially in this district where commerce was carried on to such an extent, to punish persons found guilty of this offence as severely as possible. So strongly had the legislature insisted on this, that for several years, though capital punishment was done away with, the judges were put under the absolute necessity of transporting for life everyone found guilty of forgery; no discretion being left to them.

'This restriction upon judges was also done away with, so that they could now exercise some discretion. Still that discretion was given in the belief that the judges would do their duty in endeavouring to protect the country from such frauds.'

His lordship, in spite of his lecture about more lenient sentencing practices, then sentenced Chalkley to penal servitude for 15 years and transportation.[554]

Chalkley was kept in Lancaster Castle prison until he was transported to Western Australia on the ship *York* which arrived in Freemantle on 31.12.1862, New Year's Eve. His details as taken whilst waiting, were: [555]

Prisoner No: 6541	age: 50, from Liverpool 1861	
Sentence: 15 years for Uttering a Forged Promissory Note		
accountant	male, one child	
height 5' 8 1/2"	hair grey	hazel eyes
stout build	fresh countenance	long face
birth mark back of hands	ruptured left side	mole on cheek

The official record of his crimes and the sentence below dated 10.8.1861 shows that embezzlement was given the same 15-year sentence as one for manslaughter but cutting and wounding with intent to cause grievous bodily harm resulted in a life sentence, and strangely:

- Maliciously setting fire to a stack of hay earned five years imprisonment

- Burglary with a previous conviction, three years

- Attempting to commit buggery and attempting to commit rape eighteen months for each count

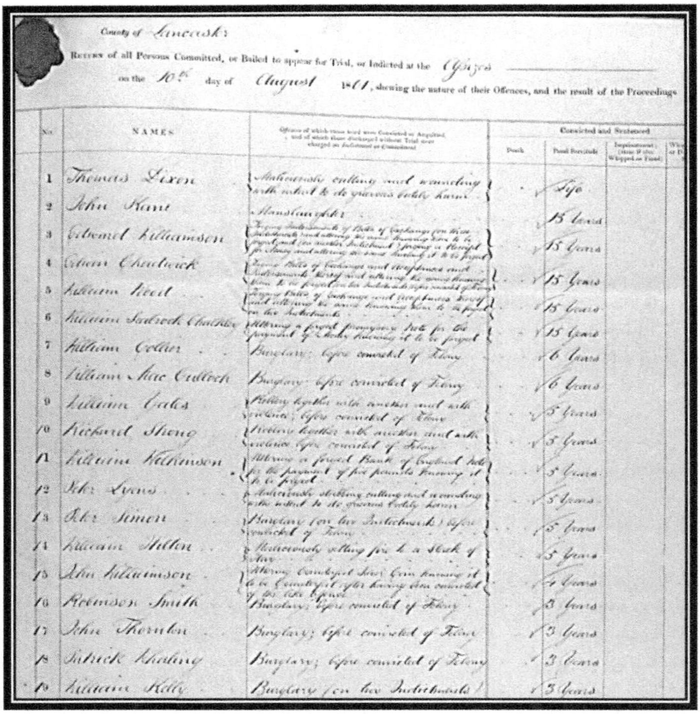

Figure 63 England & Wales, Criminal Registers, 1791-1892

It certainly gives us an idea of which crimes Victorians considered to be most serious in 1861.[556] As Chalkley was sentenced on 10th August but not transported until over a year later in September 1862, I wondered if Lilley managed to visit him during that time.

Much was printed about Chalkley after his sentence which shows how his dealings with many people caused utter misery as he persuaded them to invest their money in the Liverpool Trademan's Loan Society, honest, hardworking people who lost all they had. [557]

> 'An aged widow, residing in Toxteth Park in Liverpool, and who was possessed of about £200 [£11,825.84] which she said was all she had to support her until she was carried to the grave, was one day visited by Chalkley and after numerous inquiries respecting the nature and safety of the investment, she was induced to consent to invest the £200, a fortune to her. Chalkley, when leaving the house pronounced the benediction upon her and she, poor lady, congratulated herself she had met with such a "good, pious gentleman" into whose hands she could with confidence entrust her only means of support.'

In another case, a gentleman who had been a considerable loser by the Loan Society although he was himself a director of it, visited Chalkley whilst he was confined in Kirkdale gaol awaiting his trial. The conversation of course very naturally turned upon the loss which had been inflicted upon the visitor and at length Chalkley, assuming a very penitent air replied:

> 'Yes, I know I have wronged you. I am aware I have robbed you of every penny you possessed, and my only consolation is that I never cease to remember you in my prayers. I have made it "all right above."'

The visitor, a respected local preacher who related the story himself, could not stand this, for he felt that it was but repetition of Chalkley's old hypocrisy, and he at once turned away and left the prison in disgust.

These instances:

> 'Tell the same story, gross villainy and immorality; and yet withal a profession of the greatest piety.'

Chapter 26 - Transported to Australia

The 940-ton ship *'York'* was built at Sunderland in 1854 and was used as convict transport for Western Australia and left Portland, England on 19.9.1862 bound for the Swan River Colony, Freemantle, Western Australia, carrying the 26th of 37 shipments of male convicts. There were 108 passengers, 300 convict numbers were assigned for the voyage ranging from 6,497 to 6,796, and 299 arrived. The only death recorded was for Henry Payne, prisoner 6,701. The voyage made the fastest time to that date for a ship to travel from Portland to Freemantle, taking 84 days.

Of the 108 passengers, there were 49 pensioner guards, 24 wives, 16 sons and 15 daughters, plus another child who was born on the way. Pensioner guards were retired soldiers recruited in England to accompany convicts on their voyages to Western Australia. They were not retained as permanent staff after the voyages; however, a number were employed as assistant warders at the convict establishment. They were also used to supervise convict work parties working in the community.

An account of the voyage was written by the ship's carpenter,[558] and reading it feels like being on the voyage itself as John Gregg writes about the endless pumping out, mending leaking joints, caulking, repairing broken wooden objects from sail struts to hinges as well as painstakingly taking an air pump to pieces to mend it so the prisoners could get fresh air in the prison hold. He mentions the weather almost every day: which way the wind is blowing, the gales, the swell of the sea, the creatures they come across. They catch a shark, seven feet long and a Cape Hen, which they released back into the skies.

More telling are the accounts he gives of incidents, both tragic and amusing, which reveal the strain of 84 days at sea with guards, the military, seamen, women and children passengers mingling, and convicts constantly planning and attempting to escape.

But whatever happened, there was always Divine Service on the Poop Deck every Sunday.

John Gregg signed his articles for the voyage at Deptford, London on 16.9.1862 from where they left three days later to sail further round the south coast. I will let him speak for himself...

September 22 - 23rd. Employed making a few alterations in the cabins of the surgeon and the religious instructor. Carrying out the instructions of the surgeon with regard to a few precautions necessary to the safe custody of the convicts of whom 80 were received and shipped from Chatham.

October 3rd - 12th. Got into Portland. Took in more convicts. Fitting lids to the convicts and guards water caskets, securing their separate galleys against intruders, making boxes for their cutlery, erecting a platform for the convict's water closet on the starboard side of the forecastle.

October 13th - 19th. One of the convicts very intoxicated and confined to the punishment box. Upon taking hold of him a general disturbance broke out upon which the guards and crew stood to arms and prepared to fire... order was happily restored.

October 14th - 20th. Made a pair of scales for weighing the convicts, made another platform for the convict's water closet on the port side of the forecastle, made stools for the guards and fittings for the convicts and guard's hospital. Madeira in sight. Got a convict assistant called Watson to do routine repairs who by 22nd is officially the carpenter's mate until further orders.

October 26th – 30th. Two convicts being unruly and quarrelsome. Had to put them in leg irons. Rigged air pump for convicts which however broke down after twenty minutes. Had to take the pump all to pieces to get at the defect. Spent all day fixing air pump which required a new inside altogether. Took the irons off the two convicts who were drunk [after four days in manacles]. At 9.30am an alarm and cries of murder heard amongst the convicts, which upon investigation, turned out to be a practical joke carried rather too far.

November 1st - 22nd. The convict Watson helped to strengthen the prison doors in the main hatch. We crossed the line on 9th. Repaired a soldier's washing hut. Fixing water closets.

November 23rd. At about four bells (2am) the second officer and helmsman detect something suspicious about the port quarter life boat which seemed to be lower down than usual. The Watch being called to haul her up again, two convicts here discovered making a bold but foolhardy attempt to escape from the ship. The Watch quickly contacted the guard and the boatswain on jumping into the boat and secured one of the convicts and the other got quietly out of her and seated himself ready for leg irons, which by this time were ready for both of them. They submitted quietly to the operation of ironing, after which the uproar subsided into merely talk.

My passing opinion on the subject, the affair altogether much to be admitted to reflect little credit on the military portion of the convict guards, for although the officers of Watch called loud and often for the guard, none were forthcoming until the prisoners were actually in custody, the order for them to turn out was unanswered. Later at 5pm, the long boat was again found broken open and a convict sitting inside smoking. He made his escape before he could be secured, after which the hatch has again been fastened up, although it is feared, in vain.

The surgeon suspects the existence of a secret opening by which convicts might get out of the prison deck. At his request, I made a strict search fore and aft the deck finding nothing whatever to justify his suspicions.

November 26th – 29th. I must not miss mentioning the fact of a birth taking place this morning, the wife of a guard having been brought to bed with a son about 6.30am. This day [28th] the first death takes place. One of the convicts expired, had to rig a temporary gurney for bringing up the corpse from the hospital to the Poop, where he was sewn up and made ready for internment. [On 29th] the convict was committed to the deep this morning at 5am, the ceremony being attended by the surgeon, chaplain, captain and sergeant major and the Watch on deck of both guards and sailors.

November 30th. Some of the convicts having boasted to the surgeon that they possessed the knowledge of how 300 of them could get out of the prison and be up top in a few moments, it was deemed necessary to make a minute inspection of the prison deck. For which purpose the convicts were sent up on deck and the whole guard stood to arms, disported in various parts of the ship and the sentries doubled whilst the surgeon, captain and wardens accompanied by the boatswain and myself thoroughly overhauled every part of the prison without discovering anything to justify the boast of the surgeon's informant. The leg irons were taken off the two convicts who tried to escape [after seven days in manacles].

December 4th. I must mention that my helpmate Watson, having been employed in the hold, in some way or another, got slightly intoxicated. He has accordingly been confined in the punishment box until his recovery and, an order passed against him being admitted abaft the barricade in future, on any pretence whatever. Consequently, from this date I lose the benefit of his valuable assistance.

December 6th – 10th. The night coming in with every indication of strong breezes. At 11.30pm hands turned out to shorten sail. The wind howling loudly more to the westward the ship laboured considerably. Rehauled the doctor's water closet. Got it to work properly. The weather of last night having greatly increased at 12.30 midnight [10th] the hands turned out to shorten sail again, the wind having shifted again to the North East. The weather continued to be wet.

December 13th. Got the convict Watson to lower the water casket inside the other to make room to repair a locker. Last night a quarrel amongst the convicts. One of them threw cayenne pepper in the eyes of a fellow prisoner which of course caused the most excruciating pain. This afternoon the guard turned out and stood to arms, whilst the surgeon held an investigation which however was fruitless, owing to the contradictory evidence and the absence of light at the time of the occurrence. The prisoner was discharged accordingly, the most perfect order reigned among the prisoners during the investigation.

December 18th. Having been attacked with sickness during the night, I was placed on the Sick Report and continued in this way until Monday, four days later.

December 25th. Christmas Day. Pumping out but not much work done. The greatest jocularity among the convicts who celebrated this day of the Christian era by the execution in the military style, of abundance of local music in the shape of glees, trios, duets, probably the result of their double allowance of wine during the day. The wind hauled to the north east.

December 27th – 30th. Made another attempt at the gangway ladder which was a very harassing affair on account of the confined space and so many women and children constantly in the way. Got the ladder finished and primed by 5pm. Inspection of the prison deck, which was admirably clean and orderly.

December 30th. Religious instructors gave the children and women of the guards an amusing lecture illustrated with diagrams on the customs and religion of the aborigines of Australia. The greatest excitement prevailed amongst the convicts on account of the prospect of making land, of the proximity of which most of them seemed to be aware.

At 7.45pm information was elicited that some of the convicts intended to turn to advantage the necessity of the chain lockers which had been debarred in order to get the cables up. The surgeon of course ordered them to be re - cased which was done, the chief officer and prison wardens being present during the operation. After which the bell was sounded. This night, for greater security, all sentries were doubled and the greatest precautions and vigilance brought into play in order to guard against all possible contingencies.

December 31st. At about 10.0am we got close enough to see the shape of the land and also to recognise a lighthouse situated on a prominent headland. We then stood to the north along the coast. In a short time, the government pilot boat made its appearance, put the pilot on board who soon brought the ship to anchor in the mouth of the river near the town of Freemantle.

This concluded the voyage of the *York*, and at the end of the journal John Gregg sets out two lines in his personal accounts:

Tobacco four ounces   10 shillings [£29.56]

Wages received at Freemantle on 15.1.1863 £100 [£5,912.92]

How then, did Chalkley cope with the challenges of this voyage? He was fifty years of age, not in good health and one of only six convicts over 45. His sentence earned him a place in the most violent group of men, those who had been given 15 years or life sentences. Confined as he was with murderers, rogue military men who had been accused of mutiny, those guilty of wounding with intent and violent robberies, manslaughter and rape he must have felt very vulnerable. We can only imagine what reception his religious views would have received, if he had dared to express them.[559]

Looking further at the sentences, I saw marked differences in the prison terms awarded for the same crimes. Some men got lesser sentences than Chalkley for what, at first sight, look like much worse offences. Ten years for raping a child for example, manslaughter, attempted poisoning, striking an officer, robberies with violence. Even white-collar crimes similar to Chalkley's got lesser sentences.

For 84 days who would he have talked to, or made friends with? Chalkley would not have been allowed anywhere near the wives and children of the guards and would have had little contact with the crew. There was a religious instructor on board and a chaplain so maybe they took pity on him? Otherwise, the guards, the military and the other prisoners would have been his constant travel companions. His fellow embezzlers, all six of them, with whom he might have had something in common, were a lot younger and might not have had any interest in either him or religion. Chalkley must therefore have been very relieved to arrive in one piece, mentally and physically, and to walk on solid land.

Convict transport ships had sailed into Fremantle since 1850. The convict establishment, as the prison was first known, was built by convict labour between 1852 and 1859 using limestone quarried on the site and the first prisoners moved into the main cell block in 1855. It was renamed Fremantle Prison during Chalkley's time, in 1867. Transportation ceased the following year when the *Hougoumont* carried the last convicts to Fremantle, by which time nearly 10,000 had passed through between 1850 and 1868.[560]

Many of them suffered loneliness and social disorientation, although a survey of those who arrived in the seven convict transport ships between 1850 - 1868, which would have included Chalkley, showed these convicts lived 19 years longer than the 39 years life expectancy for a male in Britain at that time. It is also recorded that 27% of arrivals were married or widowed, Chalkley being married, allegedly, more than once.[561] The prison was a convict barracks right up to 1991 and was a place of hangings, floggings, dramatic convict escapes and prisoner riots. Inmates included imperial convicts, colonial prisoners, enemy aliens, prisoners of war and maximum-security detainees.

When the ship landed on New Year's Day 1863, it was also the first day of Chalkley's new life as a transported prisoner in Freemantle Prison, and this is what he would have seen.

Figure 64 Freemantle Prison, late 1800s

One man who made the most of his sentence, was Joseph Lucas Horrocks. [562] He was convicted of forgery in London in 1851, sentenced to 14 years transportation and arrived in Freemantle in 1852. He was different from most of the others as he was well educated and older, being 35. During Horrock's first year he worked on the construction of the convict establishment and by 1853 had earned his ticket of leave and travelled north to the convict depot at Port Gregory where he worked as a doctor. Horrocks also encouraged the settlers to grow wheat and built a mill powered by a steam engine which drew ore from the local mine. He constructed the Gwalla Church between 1861 - 1864 and carved a foundation stone which said 'My house shall be called a house of Prayer for all People.'[Isaiah]. When he died in 1865, he was buried there.[563]

We know nothing about Chalkley's life in Australia apart from the fact he had worked in the prison as a baker, returning to his simple roots, begun on the Isle of Man nearly fifty years earlier. He died on 6.7.1869 age 57 of a rupture, seven years before the end of his sentence.

And his legacy?

'Chalkley, a journeyman baker, endeavoured to increase his position. He was a local preacher, a temperance orator; he lost a great deal of money in mining speculations, obtained from those he had defrauded, and was sentenced to fifteen years penal servitude.'[564]

'The Liverpool Trademan's Loan Company, it will be remembered, was the one that collapsed through the delinquencies of Mr. Chalkley.'

Chapter 27 - Fallout

What happened to Lilley, probably the only woman outside her immediate family who trusted and believed in Chalkley? If there were more letters after he was arrested, none have come to light. She might have stayed nearby between August 1861 to September 1862, visiting him in jail while he waited to be transported but looking in the 1861 census, I found no trace of her or her siblings, anywhere.

Their mother Ann, however, was living alone in April 1861 when the census took place, at Hollin Hall, near Trawden in Lancashire. Most of the local people nearby worked in cotton mills as worsted weavers or in supporting roles, such as engine shunters, labourers, tailors, grocers and servants. She must have then rejoined the family in Southampton before Chalkley landed as one of the newspaper reports says she was at Canton Street with them when he was arrested.

Apart from the fact that Lilley's sister Grace Hannah Shaw died in 1868 age just 23 and was buried in Pendleton, Blackley, Manchester on 5.12.1868,[565] the family disappear from public view until the 1871 census which showed they had moved back to Manchester, this time to 117 Broad Street, Salford. Ann Shaw, widow, age 78, is registered as the head of the household and Elizabeth Ann (Lilley), age 47 is described as one of the daughters and a widow, which she possibly was by that time, if she had consented to a bigamous marriage. She has taken the surname of Brook, which is only two letters different to Cook, though I cannot find a marriage for her to someone of that name.

The ages and details of all her siblings are correct so this is definitely her. Curiously, her place of birth and that of Mary Ann's has now changed to Mytholmroyd which is near to Hebden Bridge and Halifax in Yorkshire. John, Lilley's brother is 41 and a cashier. Her sisters Mary (44) and Sarah Ann (41) are both working as drapers and they are all unmarried. Ann Shaw dies the same year which would have left John as head of the family supporting three sisters.

The 1881 census shows the twins, John and Sarah Ann Shaw, still unmarried, continue to live at 117a Broad Street with a housekeeper and two servants. There is no trace of Lilley or Mary Ann.

Not knowing which name(s) Lilley used from 1871 onwards makes it impossible to trace her and I have tried, under all possible permutations. She may have married again or assumed other names or maybe died early but it is clear she was not with the twins in the family home in 1881. Mary Ann may have married too but her name is also very common and hard to trace.

In 1901, brother and sister are still living together age 72 at 39 Weymouth Street, Manchester. He is a commercial clerk for the council and she a dressmaker.[566] They are no longer alive by the 1911 census.

Jane Keys, Chalkley's long suffering wife, had a difficult time after Chalkley's crimes were laid bare for all to see. Not only was she hauled in front of the authorities, expected to explain Chalkley's embezzlements and disappearance, humiliated both in private and publicly by his blatant affair with Lilley, she had to endure the endless press, the loss of her respectability and utter shame. One commentator described her as:

'A very respectable woman... of most praise-worthy character and together with her daughter, deserves great sympathy on her present unfortunate position.... Whatever Chalkley may still possess – and it is said that he had an interest in a very considerable amount of property – neither his wife nor his daughter is at present in the enjoyment of any of it, or of any pecuniary benefit from the extensive frauds.... he had heard during his enquiries of many instances which spoke volumes in favour of her character and he willingly records the fact.' [567]

By the 1861 census, Jane and her daughter Sarah Jane, who was a young-apprentice, had had to move out of their Benson Street house and were registered as visitors at 17 Thurmaston Street, Liverpool, the home of Hugh Stewart and his wife Margaret who, along with a servant, were born on the Isle of Man. I assume they were old friends of Jane's from the island. Also, in residence is a scripture reader, William F.B. Hazzell, age 26, no doubt a Wesleyan Methodist, who you would hope was able to comfort and assist Sarah Jane and her mother in those brutal times.

Before 1860, Thomas and Mary Ann, Chalkley's parents must have been extremely proud of what he had achieved and in 1859 they moved from No 7 to No 12 Sandon Street where Thomas was listed as a house agent. However, Jane Gallagher's trial alongside Chalkley and the shocking revelations about his relationship with such a notorious brothel keeper must have been awful enough, especially for his father who had devoted his working life to upholding the law, along with the accusations of extensive fraud, his sudden disappearance, the abandonment of his wife and daughter, then the later revelations about Lilley, must have been devastating. Thomas and Mary Ann were devoted Wesleyan Methodists themselves and had left the Isle of Man as pillars of a righteous society and now no newspaper in the land spared their son.

And they weren't alone in their shame, for none of the Chalkley family in Liverpool of six surviving sisters, a brother and their families, who all bore the name Chalkley, could escape the sensationalism that gripped the country for the following eighteen months. By April 1861, Chalkley's parents had fled to their daughter Mary Ann's house at 88 Brownlow Hill, Liverpool, which is not surprising as they were both in their seventies. They must have moved house again too, for there is a death record for Thomas at 7 Severn Street, Liverpool, age 76 on 7.10.1865.[568] He had, unfortunately, lived long enough to bear the full weight of his son's disgrace.

Mary, Chalkley's mother, lived another six years and died in 1871 age 80 at the same house where her daughter Mary Ann, age 52 and a widow herself by then, was living with two adult daughters.[569] They at least would have been partially shielded from any long-lasting fallout as after her marriage they were all known under her husband's name of Sayle.

One of Chalkley's nephews was not so lucky as in 1850 Thomas Richard, brother of Chalkley, and his wife Mary had a son who they named after him. It must have seemed like a good idea at the time,[570] the innocent boy's uncle being a respectable Methodist Minister and a rising figure of influence in the financial sector of Liverpool, but after Chalkley became notorious, their ten-year-old son was lumbered with his name.

When Chalkley's arrest and trial occurred in 1861, Thomas Richard had already retreated with his wife Mary and son, now 11, across the River Mersey to the Wirral and lived at 20 Chapel Street, Birkenhead, which was, strictly speaking, in Cheshire at that time. It wasn't far by today's standards, but far enough to avoid everyone who knew they were related to the infamous Chalkley. By 1871, Thomas Richard, two years after Chalkley's death, is still a joiner and builder and has moved to Clifton Crescent, Birkenhead and taken in three boarders. His son William, who has wisely dropped the 'Seabrook' middle name, is now 19 and a joiner like his father.

On the 20.12.1874, plain William married a local girl in Bebington on the Wirral,[571] called Eliza Samuels who was born in Berriew, Montgomeryshire, Wales and lived in Birkenhead but by the time of the 1881 census Thomas Richard is living alone at 3 Westbury Street, Tranmere, Birkenhead, in his early fifties as his wife Mary, age 54, died the same year.[572]

William and his wife, however, quickly had three children by the 1881 census and acquired a lodger age 76 called John Watson, a widower, who was a retired domestic missionary who had been born in Chester. By 1891, their family had increased even more, with Eliza having seven children in all. With the help of one servant, they all lived at 1 Downham Road, Tranmere, Birkenhead. Still there, is the same John Watson, who is now revealed to be a retired rope maker and, in an odd quirk of fate, a Wesleyan lay preacher, like the original Chalkley. He is held in such esteem that one of their children bears his name.

John Watson was a town missionary in the area for about twenty years and on 13.8.1860, 'around 250 people sat down to an excellent tea at the Wesleyan Chapel in Beckwith Street, Birkenhead where he was presented with a Watson's Theological Dictionary and a very handsome bible in recognition of his zealous, faithful and successful labours. The gift was acknowledged in modest terms by Mr. Watson, addresses were delivered by gentlemen present and the evening was most profitably spent.'[573]

By 1891, Thomas Richard, 64, Chalkley's brother, is an inmate of the overcrowded Birkenhead Union Workhouse, one of 282 males and 528 people altogether, where he died later that year.[574] I do not know why his only son let him end his days alone in such sordid conditions when he was still offering lodgings to a retired missionary of the same faith as his renegade uncle Chalkley. Maybe William's faith was stronger than his love for his father and he grew to regard John Watson as a worthy role model, well respected, untainted by notoriety.

The 1911 census shows William to be 60, married to Eliza for 26 years with six surviving children. They live at 17 Eldon Road, Rock Ferry, Wirral. He died in 1926 age 75 in Birkenhead.[575] When his wife Eliza died three years later, probate was awarded to Mercy Caldwell, wife of Norman Caldwell, and Margaret Chalkley, a spinster, the two youngest daughters of Eliza and William and great nieces of the original William Seabrook Chalkley. The effects were worth £332.15 shillings [£15,235.09.]

For Sarah Jane, Chalkley's sole surviving daughter, there was no respite from the Chalkley name until she married Edwin Carver, born in 1840, an accountant from Yorkshire, in 1862 in Liverpool, just after her father was shipped off to Western Australia as a transportee.[576] His father William was a shopkeeper and grocer.[577] Edwin, (22), a book keeper, and Sarah Jane (18) became man and wife in Park Place Methodist New Connexion Chapel in Liverpool. Edwin was living at Clyde Terrace, West Derby, Liverpool and Sarah Jane at 61 Squires Street, Edge Hill, Liverpool. Chalkley is clearly identified on the marriage certificate as her father but she must have been very glad to change her name.

From 1863, Edwin often appears in newspapers advertising houses to rent or for sale all over Liverpool and the Wirral as he becomes an estate and insurance agent working from 40 Church Street but then in 1866 the adverts change, as in December he advertises for a partner in a Hosiery, Glove and Shirt Business, who can invest £600 - £700 [£35,477.52 - £41,390.44]. In it, he says the business has been established for some years and is doing a profitable trade. Another advert asks for a junior to work in a Linen Shop and a third is for a youth between 14 and 15 years of age to work at Edwin's accountancy firm at 46 Church Street, Liverpool.

I doubt Sarah Jane would have had time to run a shop as she had their first son, Thomas Edwin on 7.8.1863, their only daughter Minnie on 16.5.1865 and their second son Alfred Ernest on 9.5.1867, three children in four years, all grandchildren of Chalkley. Maybe the shop was an investment.

But she must have been rather worried in 1867 when Edwin started advertising his services as an auditor of building society accounts from 48 Church Street, as the painful memories of her father's time as accountant would still have been very raw. However, he does well, so much so that by December 1867 he announces he is moving his Land, House and Insurance Agency and Accountancy Services to 66 Whitechapel, a much more prestigious address.

In 1868, Edwin branches out further into business when he is elected to the office of arbitrator for the Liverpool United Legal Friendly Burial Society in September 1869. The Imperial Loan Company then moves to No 57 Whitechapel in 1873 and Edwin becomes its secretary. He appears to be echoing Chalkley's ascent in the financial world, only the names of the companies differ, but in 1876, more worryingly for Sarah Jane, her husband is involved in a high-profile court case which consumed several editions of the *Liverpool Mercury*.

It begins with a curious news report on 7.9.1876 entitled 'A Strange Dispute about a Picture,' wherein Edwin is summoned to the police court by Lewis Lyon, a picture dealer, who wants his pictures back.[578] The case came up before Mr. Raffles at Liverpool police court five days later on 12th September and was entitled by the *Liverpool Mercury*, rather cautiously, as Edwin Carver was a respectable and influential player in Liverpool: 'Curious Transactions in the Fine Arts.' The plot is complicated but goes like this:

- A Mr. Rumer told Edwin he had been advanced £60 [£3,756.54] by a Mr. Whitehead, an auctioneer, who held two pictures of his as security

- He asked Edwin to further advance him the money to redeem the pictures so he would then be able to sell them at a profit, which they would divide between them

- Rumer then told Edwin he had several other pictures at Messrs Branch and Lees, for which he had been advanced £12 [£751.31]. He asked Edwin again to advance him the money and in return he would bring the pictures to Edwin's premises

- In due course 20 - 30 pictures were brought to Edwin and they agreed they should be sold in Manchester

- Rumer catalogued these pictures as being the works of David Cox [the celebrated water-colourist, who once lived in Foxley Road in 1827 near where Jane had a house in London] and Turner, although it was found later that they weren't painted by them at all

- Only one was sold and the others came back to Edwin's premises, who told Rumer he would let him have all the pictures back if he would return the money including expenses, all of which he had advanced to Rumer

- Rumer promised to do this but instead broke the door of Edwin's premises while he was away in Wales and took the pictures away

- Even though Rumer had paid him about £240 [£15,026.16], Edwin said he still owed him money

Rumer was committed for trial and further charged with obtaining two pictures by false pretences from Lewis Lyons, a picture dealer of 31 Chester Street, Liverpool, pictures which he claimed Mr. P.H. Rathbone had authorised him to collect. At the same time, Rumer himself summoned a man called Williams to court, because he used abusive language, calling Rumer a thief and a robber, but the case was dismissed on the grounds that the language was justified by Rumer's conduct with his fine art transactions - this before Rumer had even been found guilty.

The next hearing was at the quarterly sessions at St George's Hall in Liverpool on 23.10.1876[579] and Rumer was sentenced with considerably leniency to two months with hard labour and a suggestion to the authorities that 'he might possibly be exempted from some of the more disagreeable parts of the gaol discipline.' But Edwin did not get off without comment as the Recorder said he thought:

'Mr. Carver's transactions with the prisoner were conducted somewhat loosely for the manager of a loan company.'

And there is more... A letter to the editor of the *Liverpool Daily Post* on 12.12.1876[580] two months later showed that Rumer had complained to Her Majesty's Secretary of State for the Home Department which investigated all the facts of the case and subsequently ordered his release. The reason given was that he never signed a document saying he would deliver the 30 pictures to Edwin as security for the money he advanced. Furthermore, Rumer had instructed his solicitor to demand that Edwin produce any document that said he did, but he had not been able to. Rumer proclaimed therefore that: 'I have a free and unencumbered paid-for title to all 30 pictures.'

Four days later, a short item appeared in the *Liverpool Daily Post*[581] showing that Edwin's solicitor had produced the signed statement referred to and other associated documents which had been presented to the court. Rumer, protesting through his solicitor, said he was ready and always had been to pay back what he owed to Edwin. And still the matter did not rest.

When he was liberated from prison, Rumer instigated proceedings against Edwin and Lewis Lyon for perjury. This could not be sustained because there was still an outstanding indictment against Rumer and the magistrates refused to interfere. The Recorder in January 1877 said he had recommended the remission of Rumer's sentence because he believed Rumer was more a fool than a knave [laughter in court], but he thought he should leave the matter where it stood at the moment as:

'He had brought himself into his present position by his own excessive vanity and folly, and because he thought himself clever enough to take revenge upon people who had prosecuted him. He had no sympathy with him. If he provoked the prosecutor into pressing for punishment, he would get a severer sentence than at his last trial, because his conduct would then show that he was not only a foolish, but a wicked man. The best thing that he could do would be to leave Liverpool and go to his own country, or somewhere else.'[582]

Rumer was discharged to appear at the next sessions, if called upon. He must not have been as nothing more is reported. But this account shows how those who lived locally fared better than 'off comers' as far as the law was interpreted in Liverpool.

As this matter unravelled in the newspaper for all to see it must also have caused more than a flutter in Sarah Jane's nerves. But in March 1877, Edwin was elected an auditor of the *Rotunda Theatre* in Liverpool, in May as a member of the *Council of the Society of Accountants in England* and re-elected auditor of the *Liverpool Protective Assurance Society* in March 1881, all very respectable and worthy appointments. His three children by that time were between 10 - 14 years of age.

The 1871 and 1881 censuses show Jane Chalkley, Sarah Jane's mother, living with them at 2 Elm Villa in West Derby, Liverpool with their children, Chalkley's only grandchildren: Thomas, Minnie and Alfred.[583] Edwin, her husband, by that time was working as an accountant from 55 and 57 Price's Buildings in Liverpool. Jane, wife of Chalkley, died at 2 Hampstead Road, West Derby, Liverpool on 3.10.1881 age 65 and was buried in a private grave by her daughter.[584]

A year later in November 1882, Edwin's financial business fails and a notice in the *Liverpool Mercury* from the Chancery of the County Palatine of Lancaster, Liverpool District asks creditors of the Imperial Loan and Investment Company to put forward their claims to the liquidators. My heart sank. Sarah Jane had had to endure all her father's financial wrong doings, shame and unwanted publicity, her mother's death and now her husband's business had collapsed. What had gone wrong? Frustratingly, there is little else to be found on the matter apart from the dates of various bankruptcy hearings.

All is quiet after this, as far as the newspapers are concerned, and Sarah Jane and the children continue to live in Liverpool, though I am not sure where Edwin is or how they survived financially. Sarah Jane at least was living at 139 Salisbury Street, Everton, Liverpool in 1887 and after that it seems they left for London, where she and Edwin slip out of public notice completely.

Unfortunately, Sarah Jane died there in desperate circumstances, relatively young in Clerkenwell in 1895.[585] I only knew this because of a death notice for Sarah Jane, the wife of Edwin Carver 'late of this city' which appeared in the *Liverpool Echo* on Saturday 8.6.1895. Checking, I found her death on 19.3.1895 and a burial date of 25.3.1895 in Camden,[586] but the age on the death certificate is 56, giving a birth date of around 1839, which does not match her baptism record. It gave their address: 22 St John St Road, Holborn and showed me that Edwin was still alive and working as a walking stick mounter – which is a long way from being a financial wheeler and dealer. It also told me Sarah Jane had committed suicide by swallowing carbolic acid.

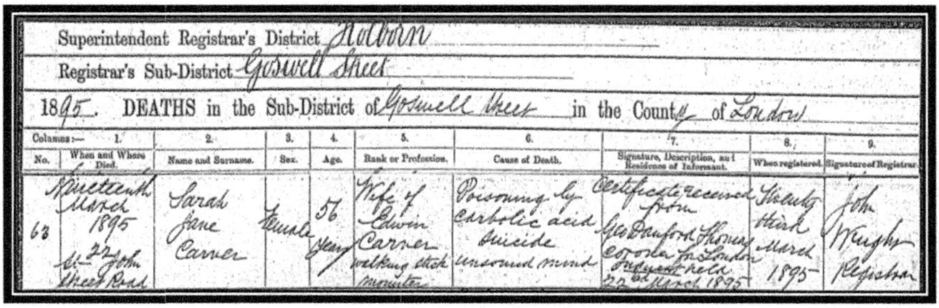

Superintendent Registrar's District Holborn

Registrar's Sub-District Goswell Street

1895. DEATHS in the Sub-District of Goswell Street in the County of London

No.	When and Where Died.	Name and Surname.	Sex.	Age.	Rank or Profession.	Cause of Death.	Signature, Description, and Residence of Informant.	When registered.	Signature of Registrar.
63	Nineteenth March 1895 St 22 John Street Road	Sarah Jane Carver	Female	56 years	Wife of Edwin Carver walking stick mounter	Poisoning by carbolic acid Suicide unsound mind	Certificate received from Geo Danford Thomas Coroner for London Inquest held 22nd March 1895	Twenty third March 1895	John Wright Registrar

Figure 65 Death certificate of Sarah Jane Carver, 1895

'Phenol (carbolic acid) is one of the oldest antiseptic agents. Apart from being used in many commercially available products in rural India, it is often used to prevent snake infestation...'[587] which I didn't think was very likely in London in 1895, though all I knew about carbolic then was its use in soap.

'Carbolic acid is a sweet-smelling clear liquid. It is added to many different products. Carbolic acid poisoning occurs when someone touches or swallows this chemical.[588] Phenol is corrosive to the eyes, the skin and respiratory tract and can cause second or third-degree burns. Drinking it rapidly leads to the paralysis of the central nervous system and a severe drop in body temperature.'

It had first been extracted from coal tar in 1841 and was later manufactured from chemicals in 1843. It was used for a wide variety of purposes, from Sir Joseph Lister using it as an antiseptic to clean wounds prior to surgery, to Carlisle officials experimenting with it in sewage treatment using it to reduce the smell of cess pits. As to why Sarah Jane took such a drastic step, the inquest report sets out her husband's version:

'His wife was addicted to habits of intemperance. On Saturday and Sunday last, she had been drinking very heavily. On Tuesday morning about 10am, his wife came close to the table, got a glass and poured something into it and then added some water and drank it. After she had taken it, she said in an excited way: "I have taken it." Edwin then found she had taken some carbolic acid. The doctor was sent for but before his arrival she died. Edwin said 'He had never heard his wife threaten to take her life, but at times she would become very excited.'

Dr Robert Faulkner of 16 Mecklenburgh Square said death was from the effect of carbolic acid poisoning, having examined the glass which showed signs of having contained carbolic acid. The jury returned a verdict of 'Suicide whilst of unsound mind.' [589]

But I have my doubts. If someone says 'I have taken it,' it usually means they are doing what they are told, for instance taking medicine, or maybe something nasty someone has given you to relieve a hangover. Regardless, the verdict stood and Edwin was now a widower age 53 and nothing more is heard of him. However, there is an entry in a national database saying he died on 13.2.1910, though there is no supporting evidence, registration of death or even a parish burial record to be found.

Maybe he took the opportunity to disappear yet again, like Chalkley his father-in-law.

Chapter 28 - Sins of the Father

Chalkley left significant wreckage behind him that's for sure, but did his wrong-doings affect the next generation of his family? 'Sins of the father' comes from biblical references primarily in the books of books *Exodus, Deuteronomy and Numbers* and refers to the iniquities of one generation passing to another. In Chalkley's case, it was his wives, parents, siblings, only child, grandchildren and namesake who had to live with his legacy.

In an attempt to find out why Sarah Jane felt so desperate and drank to excess I turned my attention to her children. Chalkley's eldest grandson was Thomas Edwin Carver and his birth was announced in the *Liverpool Mercury* as having taken place on 7.8.1863. His family lived at 30 Barnes Street, Liverpool from where his father Edwin was busy selling and letting houses, judging by the number of adverts he placed in the local newspapers.

Nothing is known about Thomas Edwin's childhood but he did emerge to the attention of the authorities in rather a dramatic fashion on 24.7.1887 when PC Charles S. Chubb found him, age twenty-four, wandering around on the streets of St Helens stark naked and took him to Prestwick Asylum, Manchester. It was over five years after the Imperial Loan and Investment Company in Liverpool run by his father went bankrupt and Thomas Edwin worked as a clerk elsewhere in the city. He was probably still living at home with his parents at 139 Salisbury Street, Everton, Liverpool from where his mother Sarah Jane was recorded as his next of kin and told them he was English and had had a good education.

The admission statement notes say:

> 'There is no history of insanity or drink in the family. The causes supposed to be influential are; pecuniary troubles and over work. His present mental condition is one of advanced paralysis. He is calm and harmless but not in habits. His bodily condition is very poor.'

The effects of paralysis were significant, attacking men in the prime of life, like Thomas Edwin. Compounding the problem was the erratic behaviour of those with general paralysis, who might get themselves into financial or legal difficulties. Delusions about their vast wealth led some to squander scarce family resources on extravagant purchases. In one case a man's wife reported he had bought 'a quantity of hats' despite their meagre income and doctors noted the frequency of thefts by general paralytics who imagined that everything belonged to them.

Thomas' case was mirrored in asylums across Britain in the late 19th century and the majority of these were men in their 30s and 40s, like Jane's husband Thomas, all exhibiting one or more of the disease's tell-tale signs: grandiose delusions, a staggering gait, disturbed reflexes, asymmetrical pupils, tremulous voice, and muscular weakness. [590] The fatal nature of general paralysis made it of particular concern to asylum superintendents, who became worried that their institutions were full of incurable cases requiring constant care. Their prognosis was bleak, most dying within months, weeks, or sometimes days of admission. But I did wonder about the diagnosis as Thomas Edwin did not die for another 28 years, all of which he spent in various asylums.

He was transferred to West Derby Union Infirmary on 26.7.1887 where he remained until he was moved to Rainhill Lunatic Asylum on 15.7.1889, two years later. There, different doctors diagnosed Thomas Edwin as having dementia, not general paralysis, and said that his first attack in their hospital lasted about a week. Their notes show he did not have epilepsy but he was suicidal and a danger to others. Further observations revealed he:

'Talks in rambling manner. Says he applies wet sheets to his body for the purpose of getting drugs out of his system. That there is no harm in a man killing himself if he feels disposed to do so. Tears his clothes. At times noisy and violent. Takes his food badly. Sleepless.

'Has an expressionless countenance. He will not speak or utter a sound and since admission has allowed himself to be fed like a baby. He will not put out his tongue or open his mouth. He is constantly waving his hands about or striking attitudes as if at one time he were declaring before an audience, or at another acting. When addressed by name he comes up, closes his eyes, forms his face upwards and makes some passes with his hands, just as if he were sign making and was forbidden to speak. "Mum" is the word apparently for him and he rigidly keeps to it; he is thoroughly self-absorbed and will give no indication by speech or by his eyes so that one might be able to surmise with probability what is actually taking place in his mind.'

Am I alone in thinking he is mimicking the gestures of a minister, like his grandfather Chalkley, delivering a sermon and pronouncing the benediction?

They recorded his physical appearance:

'Average height, fairly well-nourished body, black hair, bi-temporal diameter smaller than normal for size of head. Continence lost, eyes brown, expression one of self-absorption. Sallow complexion, ephelides well-marked [freckles]: constantly shaking his head and giving no sign of intelligence. Chest poorly developed: lungs normal. Heart normal, reflexes present. Skin harsh and pimply. Urine normal.'

Thomas was transferred to the Annexe at Rainhill Lunatic Asylum in St Helens on 22.7.1889 and remained until 1911 when the census shows he has been moved again to the Annexe of Prescott Asylum in Whiston to become one of 1,186 patients, of which 594 were men. There follows a number of annual one-line comments on Thomas every April to 1912 which all say more or less the same thing:

'Dementia with loss of memory, good health. Dull, quiet, unable to give any account of himself, has no interest in his surroundings, apathetic, and rarely speaks. Is happy and childish, contented with his lot. Never speaks unless addressed. At times he is wet and dirty. His intelligence is greatly impaired.'

There are no further notes except to say in red ink: 'Court Order.' This might have been made because Thomas' remaining parent, Edwin, died in February 1910, leaving him without immediate next of kin. However, Thomas Edwin himself died five years later on 10.8.1915 age 52, having spent the last 28 years in asylums.

Reading these notes, I immediately thought the sins of Thomas' grandfather, Chalkley, had indeed been visited upon him. And it does go some way towards explaining why Sarah Jane drank to excess and allegedly committed suicide. But she still had two other children, didn't she? Were they supporting her through this difficult time? Sadly not, as they were on the other side of the world.

Minnie was the next grandchild of Chalkley, born on 16.5.1865. When her brother Thomas Edwin was found wandering the streets in 1887, she was twenty-two years of age and a clerk at a boarding school at 113 St Domingo's Rd, Everton, Liverpool.[591] She met and married Frederick Irving, both of them age 27, in April 1892, he being a builder's clerk in Liverpool. The following year they travelled on the ship *Campania* from Liverpool to New York arriving on 27.5.1893, a voyage their grandfather Chalkley had taken over thirty years before them.[592] Within two years of them starting their new lives in the new world of America, her mother Sarah Jane committed suicide in London in 1895.

By the US census of 1900, Minnie's brother Alfred Ernest, an assistant bank cashier, has followed and is living with them at 351 Poplar Avenue, California where Frederick was a bookkeeper. However, Minnie's life took another turn for the worse as her husband died in 1904 after only eleven years of marriage. Brother and sister continued living together but they moved to 1237 R Fresno, California, Alfred Ernest is now a book keeper and rises to the position of bank teller by 1906.

Minnie marries again in 1907 to another Englishman in California, Harry H. Wilson. In the 1910 US census he is an accountant age 34, Albert, Minnie's brother is still living with them age 39 and he too by now is an accountant. In 1910, their father Edwin dies and then Minnie's second husband Harry dies young in March 1911, only lasting four years in her second marriage.

Minnie has faced in seven years the deaths of two husbands, her mother and father. In the next four years her eldest brother Thomas Edwin dies in 1915 in Rainhill Lunatic Asylum, and Albert Ernest, Minnie's youngest brother in 1916 in California. Minnie must have arranged for his death notice to be placed in the *Liverpool Daily Post* as a very brief entry appears on 29.2.1916 which says:

'A death has occurred at Fresno, USA, of Mr. Alfred Ernest Carver, formerly cashier at the Milwr Mines, Holywell, Wales and a son of the late Mr. Edwin Carver of Liverpool.'

This is quite a load she had to bear alone, but she is made of sterner stuff than her mother and survived this succession of tragedies. Somehow, she carries on but the US 1930 census shows Minnie is an inmate of the Cleveland State Hospital in Ohio, age 64 until she dies childless on 21.9.1936 age 70. Therefore, there are no surviving direct descendants of Chalkley, all of whom suffered in different ways from his legacy.

This has not been a very positive chapter therefore I want to end on a lighter note, with the landmark but curious case of the Carbolic Smoke Ball,[593] which was marketed in 1892 as a flu remedy and played on the fear of the populace as the 1889 - 1890 flu pandemic was estimated to have killed 1 million people.

It was a rubber ball with a tube attached filled with carbolic acid. The tube was inserted into the person's nose and squeezed at the bottom to release the vapour. The nose would then run, thus flushing out infections, or so the manufacturers claimed. The company published advertisements saying it would pay £100 [£8,204.93] to anyone who got sick with influenza after using its product, according to the instructions provided with it.

'£100 reward will be paid by the Carbolic Smoke Ball Company to any person who contracts the increasing epidemic influenza colds, or any disease caused by taking cold, after having used the ball three times daily for two weeks, according to the printed directions supplied with each ball. £1,000 [£82,049.30] is deposited with the Alliance Bank, Regent Street, showing our sincerity in the matter. During the last epidemic of influenza many thousand carbolic smoke balls were sold as preventives against this disease, and in no ascertained case was the disease contracted by those using the carbolic smoke ball.'

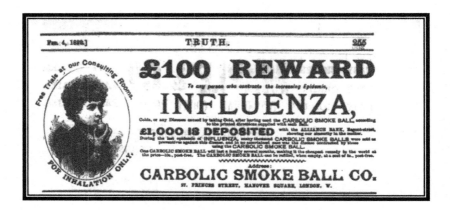

Figure 66 Carbolic Smoke Ball advert in the Truth publication 1892

'One carbolic smoke ball will last a family several months, making it the cheapest remedy in the world at the price, 10s. [£41.02] post free. The ball can be refilled at a cost of 5 shillings [£20.51] Address: Carbolic Smoke Ball Company, 27, Princes Street, Hanover Square, London.'

Mrs. Louisa Elizabeth Carlill saw the advert in a newspaper,[594] bought one of the balls and used it three times daily for nearly two months until she contracted the flu on 17.1.1892. She claimed £100 from the Carbolic Smoke Ball Company, who ignored two letters from her husband, a solicitor. On a third request for her reward, they replied with an anonymous letter which said that if it is used properly the company had complete confidence in the smoke ball's efficacy, but 'to protect themselves against all fraudulent claims', they would need her to come to their office to use the ball each day and be checked by the secretary.

Her husband brought a claim to court. The barristers representing her argued that the advertisement and her reliance on it was a contract between the company and her, so the company ought to pay. The company argued it was not a serious contract. The Carbolic Smoke Ball Company lost its argument at the Queen's Bench and appealed straight away. The court of appeal unanimously rejected the company's arguments and held that there was a fully binding contract for £100 with Mrs. Carlill. Before you dismiss this as farcical, consider the facts that:

- After it was patented, the Carbolic Smoke Ball became rather popular in many esteemed circles, including the Bishop of London, who found it 'has helped me greatly'[595]

- The action is frequently cited today as a leading case in the common law of contract, particularly where unilateral contracts are concerned as it provides an excellent study of the basic principles of contract and how they relate to every-day life. The case remains good law. It still binds the lower courts of England and Wales and is cited by judges with approval

- The Carbolic Smoke Ball Co actually increased its reward following the loss of the case

Yes, it really did. After the action, Mr. Roe, the owner, formed a new company with limited liability and started advertising again. But weren't they then inundated by thousands of claims? It was speculated that '10,000 people might now be sniffing at smoke balls hoping for their £100,' which would inflict insolvency on the company, but this did not happen at all. In a new advert on 25.2.1893, Mr. Roe cunningly turned the whole lost case to his advantage. He described the culpable advert, and then said:

'Many thousand Carbolic Smoke Balls were sold on these advertisements, but only three people claimed the reward of £100, thus proving conclusively that this invaluable remedy will prevent and cure the above-mentioned diseases. The CARBOLIC SMOKE BALL COMPANY LTD now offer £200 [£16,409.86] REWARD to the person who purchases a Carbolic Smoke Ball and afterwards contracts any of the following diseases....'

In the advertisement's small print were some restrictive conditions, with a period of three months to use the ball and claim, showing that legal advice had been adhered to. Mr. Roe then wisely left the management of the new company to other new subscribers and directors, who did not pursue such an aggressive advertising policy and by 1895 the company had fallen on harder times, as 'the new management had failed to grasp the fact that vigorous advertising was essential to success in the field of quack medicine.' It had to be wound up in 1896.

However, the proof of the pudding is in the eating. Mr. Roe himself died at the age of 57 on 3.6.1899 of tuberculosis and valvular heart disease. Mrs. Louisa Carlill, on the other hand, lived until she was 96.

Part Five - What happened next?

Chapter 29 - Prosecuted as a Procuress

'Gentlemen, - I am rejoiced to find from your paper today that the authorities are fully alive in this matter. There is another Madam Anna in the person of a woman called G-------, who I trust will ere long be in the hands of the police. But the landlords must not escape; they are equally guilty parties and pass as respectable. I had occasion lately to address myself to one of these gentlemen on the subject of suppression, who told me it was a matter of money, and met my appeal with insolence. A few indictments will bring these people to their senses.'[596]

But it took until 1862, despite folk campaigning at least since 1857 for Jane to be prosecuted. Why? Jane had influential customers, money and above all, knew too much to be brought down easily and Madam Anna has already shown us how favours were granted and then called in. Catherine Seaton, described in court as a 'lady of questionable character' who also had a brothel in Hotham Street, is another case in point. When asked if she knew a gentleman sitting in court, she tossed her head and said:

'Indeed sir, if I had to point out every gentleman here I am acquainted with, very few would escape.' [597]

This statement, while it caused considerable amusement, shows quite clearly the professional status of her clientele and the power brothel madams had to expose them.

Jane by this time was very confident of her immunity from prosecution as she was one of the most successful madams in Liverpool, with over twenty houses overall from 1839 to 1866. As such, she contributed handsomely to the economy of the town and had access to privileged information about highly placed gentlemen, but this changed significantly at the end of 1861.

It began with a letter to the editor of the *Liverpool Mercury* published on 16th December 1861 entitled: 'Refusal of the Authorities to Suppress Brothels.' Written on behalf of the inhabitants of Houghton Street, it complained that the authorities were refusing to act.

'There are three houses occupied as brothels in Houghton Street and five in a smaller street called Tyrer Street, leading from Houghton Street to Leigh Street. Two of the houses in Houghton Street and three in Tyrer Street are kept by the notorious Mrs. Gallagher, and whether or not her reputed power to expose the doings and practices of some in high office and influence in the town is the real reason of this unrebuked and glaring disregard for public morals, is a question very openly discussed.

'The inhabitants have complained so frequently and without effect, that they are now compelled to believe that for some such reason, this infamous woman dare not be too much meddled with. This belief may be wrong, but appearances and facts lead to a different conclusion.

'A memorial to the stipendiary magistrate T.S. Raffles, Esquire petitioning for their removal, was adopted about three months ago, and, after being signed by every respectable inhabitant of the street, was presented in open court, but – will it be believed? Not the slightest notice was taken of the request, no more than if it had been presented to a magistrate of the Presidency of Bengal, or, in plain words, had never been presented at all.'

Not to be discouraged, as this was just what those who were wiser in their generation had hinted would happen, the residents of Houghton Street then sent a memorial, signed again by every respectable resident of Houghton Street to the Mayor, S.R. Graves and the town council.

'After a lapse of a considerable period it was manifest that this petition was being consigned to the same oblivion as its predecessor addressed to the stipendiary magistrate.'

The residents did not give up but sent a deputation to wait upon the Mayor and their interview terminated in a request that a letter be addressed to him embodying their complaint 'of the neglect accorded to their memorial.' This was done and their hopes began to rise. In vain, as it turned out.

'An inspector of police and another official went through a farce of taking the names of witnesses and memoranda of their evidence, which must have been overwhelming, as we are one and all daily eye witnesses of the most shocking and brazen immorality that could disgrace a town, and, be it added, a town's authorities.

'An answer to the memorial to the Mayor and town council has just been received, with the intimation that the finance committee decline to direct the presentation of the brothels in Houghton Street.'

Hence their letter to the *Liverpool Mercury*, written in anger and frustration and:

'To assure your numerous readers, the public of Liverpool, that we are determined, if even by public subscription, to obtain justice at the hands of those entrusted with its administration, and to root out such dens of iniquity from our neighbourhoods.'[598]

And it came to pass, three weeks later, which is quick, as Christmas and New Year intervened, Emma Studdart of No 4 Houghton Street is accused of keeping a brothel for Jane on the 8th January 1862.[599] She was remanded for seven days then released on her own recognisances on the understanding that she was to leave the house in the meantime, and close the business. Fanny Francis, who managed No 9 Houghton Street for Jane, was also summoned and received similar treatment. The residents in the court room were told that the:

'Notorious Mrs. Gallagher was really the proprietress of both houses and whilst the keepers were poorly paid, she received the profits and lived in style in London... In order to remedy the evil, they must strike at the root and to do that they should bring Mrs. Gallagher before the court.'

They were recommended to apply for a warrant against her and then subscribe for the payment of the expenses of a detective officer to go London to execute it. This they did and the warrant was executed on the 11th January,[600] with the following comments from the Recorder, Mr. J.B. Aspinall QC, at St George's Hall at the Borough Sessions:

'The motive for taking proceedings against her has been the objection of the inhabitants of the street in which the brothel or brothels which she is charged with keeping are situated.'

He particularly pointed out that Jane was charged with keeping not one brothel but three, all in the same neighbourhood, which is strange as there were nine in that area, many others as well not far away and she had been operating with impunity for over 20 years at this point. It is as if her 1860 case produced a huge sea change in attitude towards her.

'It is a circumstance attended with danger when we find a person committing this offence upon so large a scale. The prisoner may have been assisted by persons from a distance with the means and have carried on this business with borrowed capital. There is a temptation thus afforded for procuration. It is a system fraught with much danger. There would be no limit to it if it were permitted to continue. It would be terrible in its results and undoubtedly if it was the desire of the inhabitants of the locality to put down these particular houses it was decidedly not undesirable that attention should be more particularly directed to this particular case if the facts are as they appear on the depositions.'

Long winded and very late in the day, the order for Jane's summons to the court was granted, the head of the detective department, Mr. Kehoe, communicated with Scotland Yard and as a result, London detectives were put on their watch for Jane.

Meanwhile, on 22nd January 1862 it was reported in the *Liverpool Daily Post* that:

'The war waged against the houses of ill fame still goes on...' Inspector O'Brien stated that 'the house at 5 Houghton Street was now shut up, but a quantity of wearing apparel, some furniture and about 60 dozen cases of wine remained.'

In February, while Jane was still elusive, an advert appeared in the *Cheshire Courant* for the sale of 'Magnificent Household Furniture,' which was to take place at Alyn Derwys, a public house on the river near Rossett Station and Bird Cottage on the 1st March. It comprised:

'Every necessity for a well-furnished house, in dining and bedroom suites, in rosewood and mahogany, kitchen effects, two handsome britskas [long open horse-drawn carriages with a folding top over the rear seat and a front seat facing the rear] and a beautiful London built Brougham carriage, powerful horse, harness etc.'[601]

Was this Jane's?

Eventually, on Friday the 28th. March,[602] they found her and she was arrested by Detective Officer C. Robinson of the metropolitan police. As we know, Jane had been living respectably for some time 'in a splendid house at 1 Eltham Place, Foxley Road, Brixton,' passing under the name of Jane Mercer. So why it took so long when she had said in 1860, she was living at 1 Vassall Road, which was just round the corner from Eltham Place and the London street directories listed William Thomas (Gallagher) Mercer, her eldest son, as being the householder, I don't know. Maybe they were not aware of her Mercer surname, or was Jane trying to do a deal with the police to buy her way out of this trouble like she had so many times before?[603]

The *London Evening Standard* on the 2nd April made a splash with the headline: 'Committal of a Notorious Procuress.'[604]

'Mrs. Gallagher, whose name is well known in connection with the "Chalkley frauds," and whose life as a brothel-keeper is probably without parallel, was arrested... It is stated that this woman is the owner of brothels in nearly all the chief towns in the kingdom and that she has agents in some of the principal cities on the continent.'

The *Sun, London* and the *Liverpool Albion* reported under the headline 'Apprehension of a Liverpool Notable' and were quite blunt:

'Mrs. Gallagher, the reputed owner of several notorious houses in Liverpool, kept by persons in her employment but who has hitherto escaped the clutches of the police, has at length been apprehended. Her connection with cases in which others have been prosecuted and punished, while she remained unseen and unpunished, was the cause of considerable scandal and much insidious remark.

'To clear up any misunderstanding on the subject, a warrant was obtained some time ago and transmitted to London, where she was taken into custody on Friday 28th March. She was thence transmitted to Liverpool and arrived on Saturday night about 11 o'clock. She resided in a handsome establishment at Eltham Place, and it is said, complained much of the indignity of being taken into custody. The name she went by in London was Mercer, and she will be brought before Mr. Raffles this morning to answer the charge made against her.'

It must have been very humiliating for Jane to be marched out of such a prosperous middle-class area of London where she had until then passed herself off as a wealthy, educated and respectable widow. No wonder she created a fuss.

By the 1860s, more than 10,000 miles of railway track stretched across Britain, linking cities such as Liverpool, the suburbs and remote countryside towns. When Jane was a young woman, ordinary folk thought that the train, with its erratic engine and wobbling passenger trucks, was almost a madman's toy, but it had reduced the time it took to travel distances from days to hours and in the process had broadened the horizons of every class of citizen. Jane was able to commute easily between her brothels in Manchester and Liverpool and her second home in London and close to 250 million passenger journeys just like hers were made in the 1860s as compared to the 50 million in 1838. However, this time she was being 'transmitted' under arrest.

Jane might well have been frightened, but not by the train. As a seasoned traveller, she would not have been worrying the deafening noises would hurt her ears, or that the speed would strain her eyes and bring on a total physical collapse,[605] as George Cruikshank's drawing from the late 1840s epitomises. No, Jane would have been nervous about what she might be facing in court, as all the signs were the law was going to be against her this time. Her son William Thomas travelled with her and they hatched a plan to stop the case before it started.

Figure 67 Drawing by George Cruickshank 1840

Jane arrived in Liverpool the same day they left London and was imprisoned in the main bridewell. Meanwhile, William Thomas approached the three main complainants from Houghton Street who disclosed:

> 'A young man who represented himself to be the son of Mrs. Gallagher, had been to them and offered to give £20 (£1,182.58) in payment of expenses incurred in promoting the prosecution if they would stay proceedings. Peter McDougall agreed on condition that the houses should be cleared, if the magistrates would have agreed to the withdrawal of the prosecution and the £20 were put into the poor box, provided the other promoters of the prosecution would have consented, but both Mr. Russell and Mr. Huston said "No."'

On Monday 31st March, she was brought before the magistrate.[606] Then, despite Jane's lawyer arguing that as the houses were now closed, which was all the law required, and there was no case to answer, Mr. Raffles, the magistrate, was having none of it, knowing the mood of those respectable worthies on Houghton Street. He set bail for Jane's attendance at the borough sessions in her own right for £200 (£11,825.84) and for two sureties of £100 (£5,912.92) each. It says something about Jane's friends that they stumped up the money without question.

On 10th April, Jane Gallagher, age 46, duly appeared in court again. The Recorder usually begins with a preamble about the general nature of the cases to be heard that day by the jury, but on this occasion, he spent a long time justifying why Jane was charged in a speech more suited to the summing up.[607]

'The inhabitants of a street in which a brothel is situated are entitled to insist that the offence shall no longer continue, and if the proprietor is obstinate the magistrates have no option but to institute proceedings and sometimes to bring the person before a judicial tribunal. There is one circumstance connected with this particular case which requires some little observation, because you will find that the individual is charged with keeping not only one brothel, but as many as three brothels, all in the same neighbourhood.

'Undoubtably, whatever one may think of the expediency of attempting to interfere with these houses generally, except for the purpose of regulation, it is a circumstance attended with danger when we find a person committing this offence on so large a scale.'

It is an extraordinary address, and sounds very much like he was trying to shut the stable door after the horse has bolted.

The Recorder then went on to hear many other cases before Jane was finally called on 14th April. She was variously described as 'a respectably dressed middle aged woman' by one newspaper, 'a well-known procuress of this town' by another and by the *Wrexham and Denbigh Advertiser*[608] as 'a general dealer in houses of ill fame, and as someone who had once owned a house in Rossett near Wrexham,' hence their interest.

Inspector O'Brien said Jane had been the proprietress of No 9 Houghton Street for five years and it had been a common brothel up to January 1862. He had seen her at this house frequently and Jane had told him that she not only kept this house but that it was her own property. She had given him a statement about the number of girls there, usually about six and that she had lived at No 4 first then No 5 Houghton Street and that there had been disorderly characters there too. She also described her houses in Tyrer Street and Upper Dawson Street, admitting she moved around from house to house, to keep her eye on the businesses.[609]

The neighbourhood was very disorderly and Inspector O'Brien said he had often warned Jane about complaints about her houses and told her that:

'If she did not mind, she would be indicted.'

She replied that: 'She did not think so, for she thought she could get a memorial in her favour from the inhabitants.' At which people in the court laughed.

Detective Smith said he had spoken to Jane about the brothels and she always appeared to be the mistress of the house. He had been at one looking for young merchants' clerks who had been wanted for embezzlement and said that Jane had always given him such information as he required, never attempting to screen anything. He added since the houses on Houghton Street had been closed, the street had been very quiet.

The court heard from several local residents who had complained about the nuisance caused by these houses. Mr. Peter McDougall, a picture frame maker, who lived at both 16 and 18 Houghton Street with his family, including two vulnerable teenage daughters, said he had complained to the police about the nuisance the house caused but then, damningly, had to admit he had not been above doing business with Jane. She had paid him for picture framing for No 5 and other houses. He ended rather lamely, saying when he started to work there, they were not the same as what they afterwards became.

The Recorder: They were genteel brothels then? [Laughter in court.]

McDougall: Yes, but afterwards they became noisy ones, but he had no objection to Mrs. Gallagher, more than to any of the others.

The Recorder: I should think you liked Mrs. Gallagher the best, you made picture frames for her. [Laughter in court.]

McDougall: He conceded that there were more disorderly houses in the neighbourhood than those which belonged to Jane but that his purpose in complaining was to get those suppressed as well.

Mr. William Huston, who had run the Temperance Hotel from 1859 to 1865 at No 23 Houghton Street and Mr. William Russell who also ran a Temperance Hotel for some years at No 21, gave corroborative evidence and conceded that they 'were actuated by no vindictive feelings towards the prisoner.'

Mr. Deighton appearing for Jane hadn't much to go on for all Liverpool knew about Jane's prolific businesses so he took refuge in the impotent state of the law at that time. He reminded them it was not illegal to own a brothel so all she could be prosecuted for was 'causing a nuisance.' He took exception to the wording of the indictment, which said 'continuing nuisance' whereas the evidence showed that the nuisance was a past nuisance which had abated. He quoted a recent relevant case and asked for leave to go to the court of appeal to amend the indictment, or to have the entry of the verdict altered according to the facts.

He valiantly assured the court that Jane did not appear to have done anything more than to have kept the houses in the way in which those houses were ordinarily kept. None of the witnesses had any complaint against her, the houses had been shut down, and these proceedings had been taken against Jane for the purpose of gratifying some vindictive and malignant feeling against her.

'She had also suffered from being hunted across the land and had been taken into custody at the instigation of some secret and malignant enemy, who was ashamed to come forward.'

He called upon the jury to acquit her, and sat down. He had a good point, but the Recorder did not agree, for some reason. He summed up and the jury almost immediately returned a verdict against Jane for having kept three disorderly houses up to 17.1.1862. Mr. Deighton then addressed the court saying Jane had instructed him to say:

'As regarded the houses in question she had been a very great loser. Only one of those properties was hers and it was mortgaged [No 5 Houghton Street]. The mortgagee had taken proceedings by which to avail himself of the mortgage and a Mr. Best, from Pimlico in London from whom she purchased the furniture had availed himself of the bill of sale for all her furniture [in Nos 4, 9 Houghton Street and 2 Tyrer Street].'

Figure 68 Furniture: No 5 Houghton Street, Liverpool Daily Post 3.4.1862

Indeed, the notices of sale for the furniture at No 4 Houghton Street and No 2 Tyrer Street appeared on 1st and the 3rd April in the *Liverpool Daily Post*, before Jane was in court on the 15th, showing that Jane's creditors had already begun to recoup their losses. Looking at the list of what Jane's houses contained, you will see how she ran up so many very expensive bills.

Mr. Deighton continued: 'Jane was reduced almost to a state of destitution, she had a family, whom she had brought up most respectably and apart altogether from the scenes of immorality, therefore it was highly desirable that she should not be imprisoned, but allowed to look after her children.'

Actually, in 1862 none of her children were babes in arms. Almost all were grown up, the youngest being 14 living in a boarding school in St. Albans and the eldest a mother herself, therefore Jane, age 46, was really laying it on a bit thick here.

Mr. Deighton respectfully suggested that justice in this case would be met by taking such steps with reference to Jane as would protect the inhabitants of Liverpool from any repetition of the offence of which she had been found guilty.

'If the sentence passed upon her were to go beyond that the court would be dealing with Jane with harshness. She had kept these houses for five years, since 1857, and, although the trade by which she made her living could be by no means justified, it must be recollected that she had also been permitted to carry it on for five years and that there were other persons in the town not only as bad, but worse than she was. He thought that the public would have a sufficient guarantee that Jane would not commit such practices again in Liverpool, if she were bound over in her recognisances to appear to receive judgement.'[610]

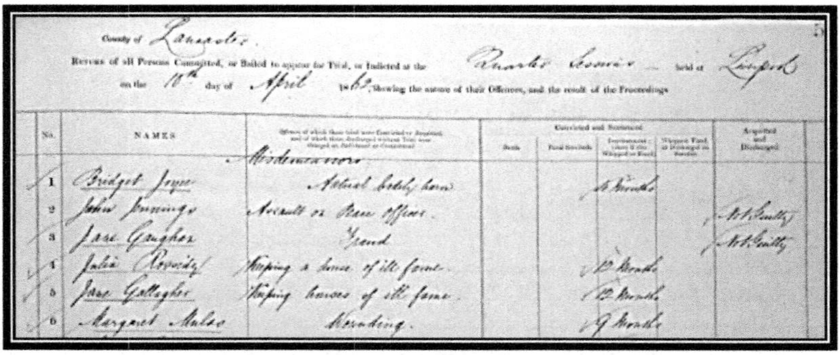

Figure 69 Committal record for Jane Gallagher of Houghton Street, 1862

The Recorder's response was that he could not enter into any bargain with the prisoner as to her future conduct.

'Yours is one of the worst cases brought under the notice of this court... there can be no question but that such houses as you have kept are a gross nuisance in any neighbourhood, and those who keep them must be taught that they are bound to close them down whenever requested to do so by lawful authority. The sentence of the court is that you be imprisoned and kept to hard labour for twelve months.'

Harsh.

I have compared the sentences passed in the same month and court for keeping a house of ill fame or a brothel. All other brothel keepers, even for those with previous records got a lighter sentence than Jane. The only exception is the 15 months awarded to Catherine Gaynor who had a particularly long list of previous convictions. Jane had none. Maybe there was after all 'some vindictive and malignant feeling' against her.

	Charge	Sentence
Jane Gallagher	Keeping three disorderly houses	12 months hard labour
Catherine Gaynor	Keeping a disorderly house with previous convictions including stabbing, prostitution and assault	15 months hard labour
Eliza Murphy	Keeping a disorderly house with previous conviction for threatening behaviour	9 months hard labour
Susan Donnelly	Keeping a disorderly house with many previous convictions including assault, fighting, stealing	9 months hard labour
Mary Flanagan	Keeping a house of ill fame	12 months

Jane was then taken away to begin her sentence and her second stay in prison, barely a year after she got out in 1861 and the residents celebrated their victory. On 11.6.1862 a report appeared in the *Liverpool Mercury* of a special gathering at William

Russell's Temperance Hotel on Houghton Street, arranged by the respectable trades people of the neighbourhood of which William Huston was the chairman. It was 'to do honour to a deserving officer.' Huston, in his victory speech, recounted how:

'They had long contended with the disorderly houses in the neighbourhood and endeavoured to remove them, and at last their efforts, aided by the kind assistance of Inspector O'Brien, had been successful... it was decided to make him a present, which was the handsome timepiece now before them.'

In response, Inspector O'Brien expressed his thanks but warned:

'The enemy is not idle, and if he was rightly informed, they had already occupied three of the outposts...'[611]

Chapter 30 - Tussles over Tyrer Street

Being imprisoned for another twelve months, this time with hard labour, must have been a bitter blow for Jane. On top of the disgrace and miserable confinement, it meant she missed the birth of her second grandson John, born on 27th April to her eldest daughter Ann Elizabeth and she could not go to the wedding of her eldest son, William Thomas Gallagher on 9th June, nearly two months later.

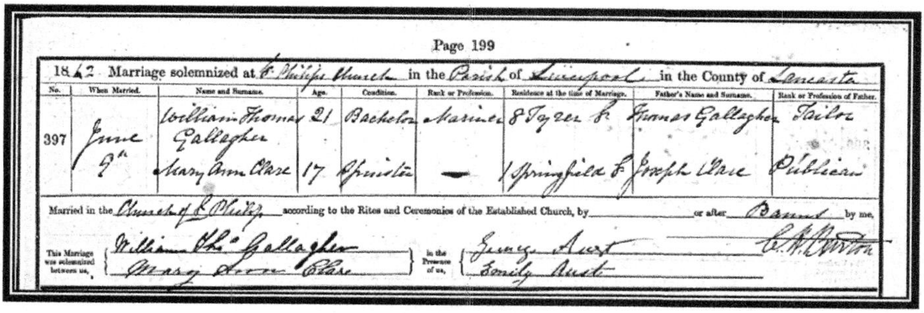
Page 199

1862. Marriage solemnized at St Philips Church in the Parish of Liverpool in the County of Lancaster

No.	When Married.	Name and Surname.	Age.	Condition.	Rank or Profession.	Residence at the time of Marriage.	Father's Name and Surname.	Rank or Profession of Father.
397	June 9th	William Thomas Gallagher	21	Bachelor	Mariner	8 Tyrer St	Thomas Gallagher	Tailor
		Mary Ann Clare	17	Spinster	—	1 Springfield St	Joseph Clare	Publican

Married in the Church of St Philip according to the Rites and Ceremonies of the Established Church, by ___ or after Banns by me, [illegible]

This Marriage was solemnized between us, William Thos Gallagher, Mary Ann Clare

in the Presence of us, George Aust, Emily Aust

Figure 70 Marriage: William Thomas and Mary Ann Clare in 1862

His young bride was Mary Ann Clare, she who had been violated by her father Joseph Clare when she was only twelve years of age whilst living with her family in a brothel at 1 Springfield Street, Liverpool,[2] one of Jane's but kept by Mary Ann's father. After serving his two years hard labour, Joseph Clare did not return home and the lodging house continued under Mary Ann's mother's management at least until 1867 but it is impossible to say if it was still a brothel.[612]

Nevertheless, Mary Ann married William Thomas Gallagher from the same house, while he lived at No 8 Tyrer Street, another of Jane's brothels. William Thomas is now a mariner and the last census he appeared in was 1851 as child living with some of his

---

2 Chapter 20

siblings in Aughton near Ormskirk. From there, Jane sent him abroad to complete his education and nothing more is heard about him until he pops up as head of the household at Vassall Road in London in 1860.

Selina's marriage to Frederick Fox Cooper, which took place 12th July in Lambeth, was another wedding her mother missed but it was probably a relief to all as it was only a few months after Jane had been publicly arrested at Eltham Place as a notorious brothel keeper and transmitted back to Liverpool under arrest.

While she is incarcerated, a court case takes place in her absence concerning the furniture ordered to be sold in the 1860 case, which was held by Best, the London auctioneer who disposed of it as per the court order. The proceeds were to be paid into the Chancery Court to meet some of her debts, but more legalities absorb countless pages as many precedents had to be taken into consideration and there is an interpleader's cause to be settled, all of which takes until 23.1.1863.

When Jane is eventually released in April 1863, her lawyers are already busy preparing her next court case and dealing with a bankruptcy notice which appears that year citing Jane Gallagher, late of May Street, Liverpool and also of Eltham Place in London.[613] It must have been hectic but very soon, in 1864 she finally gets round to applying for probate for her mother's will and moves into her next house at 41 Russell Street in Liverpool. In June that year, she would have been able to attend the wedding of her daughter Caroline to Alfred Edgar Cooper, son of Fox Cooper, in London, if she had been invited. But first Caroline has a daughter, Florence Jane, a month before in Liverpool.

I can only imagine the coming and going between London and Liverpool at that time: court cases to attend, probate to arrange, a baptism before the wedding; the discussions about whether Jane was to attend the wedding, where it would be held and who would look after the child while the ceremony was performed. It must have settled down at some point as Caroline and Alfred Edgar were to have a long and stable marriage despite the fact there were two parental wild cards, Fox Cooper and Jane, as well as complicated family relationships: Caroline and Selina were sisters but Selina was also Caroline's mother-in-law, Jane became Fox Cooper's and Alfred Edgar's mother-in-law, and Fox Cooper was father-in-law to his sister-in-law.

Finally, Jane was also brewing yet another court case which would mean all three of her daughter's names would be on the affidavit, along with their new husbands, for the women could not act independently due to coverture. Ironically Jane, as a widow, was the only *femme sole* left. You have to admire her spirit, for she does not allow herself time to recover from prison but launches a complaint in court to request the release one of her properties from the control of Chalkley, now a convicted felon.

To understand what this 1864 case is about we must move back to Liverpool and walk round another corner from Houghton Street to Tyrer Street where Jane owned or rented Nos 2, 6 and 8. Here's a 2019 photo of Tryer Street, which doesn't look very salubrious today, more like a back alley. Both Tyrer Street and Houghton Lane are currently inaccessible, as they have been gated to enhance security round the back of the scaffolded frontage onto Houghton Street and Clayton Square as the site is being redeveloped.

Figure 71 Tyrer Street Liverpool: Google maps 2019

On the map below, you can see Tyrer Street is off Houghton Street. It was where business people such as the Reverend William Tyrer lived with his daughter in 1829 along with Robert Bagott, a West Indian merchant, ship brokers and book keepers. Many master mariners lived in the street too, including Robert Martin, George Daney the captain of a steamer, Alexander Thomas the captain of the ship *Lancaster* and Robert Lawson captain of the ship *Queen Victoria*.

In later years, from 1840-1865, the area was taken over by boarding houses, billiard rooms, ale houses, the Liverpool Steam Boat company, shipwrights and bonded warehouses. It was a vibrant, lively place and very news worthy.

When, in 1858, John Basnett of No 16 Tryer Street died age 33, the *Liverpool Mercury* describes the event as 'The Drunkard's End.' The inquest heard that he was very much drunk on the Monday, was afflicted by the Horrors [delirious tremens] on the Tuesday, took two half glasses of brandy and cayenne pepper for his stomach cramps on the Wednesday and died on the Thursday after the application of mustard plasters and leeches. Inflammation of the liver was the coroner's verdict. [614]

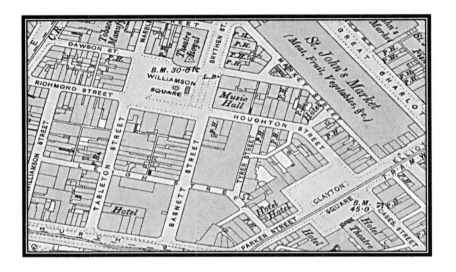

Figure 72 Tyrer St, Liverpool town centre 1890 OS map 25" 1890

Other newspapers described on 13.3.1849 how a tea dealer, Francis Edward Ward was fined 50 shillings [£151.04] for assaulting a man called Burrows, who kept a shoe shop in a brothel on Tyrer Street and on Monday 23.8.1847 how Johanna Bulger, a prostitute, died suddenly at a house of ill fame from natural causes.[615]

Tyrer Street North was renamed in around 1841 as Galton Street causing great confusion, but this did not stop Galton Street inheriting some of its distinctive characteristics. There were reports in 18.11.1851 about 'Man-Catchers,' another variation on soliciting in the streets, but this time not for sex. An emigrant, named John Beck, from Haceby in Lincolnshire, in a letter to the *Stamford Mercury*, describes the manner in which poor emigrants were victimised.

'When I arrived at Liverpool... some of the omnibus men took me to Galton Street, to a Man-Catcher's house who pretended he was an agent for Byrnes. I found he was nothing of the kind but belonged to the class of wretches called Man-Catchers. These fellows are said to give 5 shillings (£20.05) to the omnibus men for each victim they take to them. They charge the poor entrapped parties

£1 5 shillings (£100.23), more than for their passage across the sea, besides double for their board and lodging.'[616]

Another case of 'Man-Catching' ended up in court as one for slander in 1858 involving plaintiff Joseph Barnett of No 2 Galton Street and a William Anderson. It was alleged that Anderson, via 'touts' who went on board a ship just docked, poached some sailors who had promised to stay at Barnett's boarding house. They said that if the sailors stayed at Barnett's they would have their clothes seized by bailiffs as he owed a lot of money. This was untrue and Anderson was fined 40 shillings [£160.37] and costs.

Drink was the real cause of much of the violence in Liverpool streets and in 1853[617] William Fairburn:

'Who spoke with some difficulty in consequence of the injury he had received, said he had come home late, under the influence of drink and had quarrelled with his wife and hit her and the servant. A customer intervened and dragged Mr. Fairburn down the stairs and struck him three or four times. Mr. Fairburn was hauled by the police to the bridewell but Mrs. Fairburn refused to press charges so he was released.'

The customer was fined 40 shillings (£160.37) plus costs and Mr. Fairburn who struck both his wife and servant, hitting the man repeatedly, got off free, it being his right, in law, to discipline both.

On the 12.5.1857, the *Liverpool Daily Post* reports a Thomas Southeron was prosecuted for assaulting a police officer who tried to stop him stealing some pigeons. Southeron was on top of an outhouse when the officer saw him. When he came down, he 'let fly right and left' on the officer's face and head and bit him on the back of his head. The officer 'was obliged to hit him with his baton before he let go of him.' Southeron was fined 40 shillings (£160.37) and costs.

Such fun and games were daily life on Tyrer Street and it is one of her properties on this street Jane went to court over, No 8. I was lucky enough to find a reference to the case in the National Archives catalogues so I booked a visit to look at the original documents they had in storage. The complaint, as it was known, was lodged on 24.1.1865, the plaintiffs being Jane and her three daughters - and their husbands, due to coverture:

- William Brindley and Ann Elizabeth, his wife

- Frederick Fox Cooper and Selina, his wife

- Alfred Edgar Cooper and Caroline, his wife

- Jane Gallagher

The defendants were:

- Charles Turner, Richard Barlow-Potts, Brian Henshaw [lawyers for Chalkley's estate] and William Seabrook Chalkley

- William Thomas Gallagher and Alfred Hugh Gallagher, sons of Jane

The children were all legitimate beneficiaries of the estate left in Trust in Jane Oakes' will, for which, by then, Chalkley was the sole trustee. The two illegitimate daughters of Jane, Rosanna and Maria Jane Mercer, were not legally entitled to anything left in Jane Oakes' will as all the legitimate children were of age to inherit. But I was surprised to find that Jane and her daughters were on one side of this case and her two sons are on the other, along with Chalkley. What had happened?

According to the sworn affidavit in court:

'The defendants William Thomas and Alfred Hugh Gallagher left this country many years ago and have never returned to it and the plaintiffs [Jane and her daughters] have been unable to discover where they are now.'

I find this hard to believe as William Thomas offered to pay £20 to the men who were taking Jane to court over her brothels in Houghton Street in 1862 and was then away at sea as a mariner and had surely been back to Liverpool see his new wife since. And as for Alfred Hugh, we will learn about what happened to him soon, but for now I will just say he was getting regular letters from England during this period.

Moving on... This case was entitled *Brindley v Turner*, so you would never have thought that it had been instigated by Jane Gallagher but her eldest daughter's married name was Brindley and as for Turner, he represented the interests of Chalkley who could not be present as he was still in prison in Western Australia.

The records show that Jane and her daughters were 'complaining' to the Chancery Court in London because Chalkley was still legally trustee of the estate left by Jane's mother, including No 8 Tyrer Street. They wanted the Chancery Court to appoint a new trustee due to Chalkley's absence, so that the house could be sold and the monies distributed between them, which explains at last why Jane did not have any need to prove her mother's will until 1864. The affidavit goes into great detail about how matters came to this head and, knowing it was at least sworn to be true in court, I was hoping it would shed more light, with proper evidence behind it, on at least some of Jane's dealings.

It reveals that as far back as 1854, Jane Gallagher entered into an agreement to buy a leasehold house in Tyrer Street, Liverpool for £150 (£12,027.92) from William Saunders and his wife Mary Ann. Jane and her mother would have had the use of this house before that as they initially rented it.

As we already know, the house was paid for by Jane but the actual title was assigned to her eldest child. By declaration of a trust document dated 12.12.1855, Ann Elizabeth Gallagher, then fortuitously age 21 and able to sign in her own right as a single woman, said she would at any time if requested by her mother, reassign portions or the whole of both properties to any person as directed by her mother, who paid for this house with money from a building society.[618]

The 1860 court case showed us that another indenture dated 1.7.1858, which is three months before Thomas Gallagher died, is drawn up whereby Ann Elizabeth assigns this property to William Seabrook Chalkley himself, not the Liverpool Tradesman's Loan Society, before she gets married, for a sum of £150, the exact amount Jane paid for it in 1855. No money changed hands at all. Sworn legal documents show that the intention was for Chalkley to hold the deeds of the brothel at No 8 Tyrer Street and set the rents he received against what Jane owed him.

In 1860, Chalkley was declared bankrupt and sent to Western Australia to serve his sentence in 1862. In July 1864, an official assignee George Morgan was appointed to sort out his bankruptcy as even though the courts had clawed back all his assets and estate, there was not enough money left to pay everyone more than a dividend of about two shillings and sixpence [£7.39] in the pound or one eighth of what they were owed.

By the time of this court case in 1865, Chalkley had already been in penal servitude for two years and he was to die there four years later in 1869. All was not completely lost though, as when Chalkley absconded in 1860, the solicitors for the Liverpool Trademan's Loan Society took possession of his papers, amongst which they found the title deeds to the property in Tyrer Street and Ann Elizabeth Brindley's declaration of trust dated 12.12.1855 wrapped up in the same parcel.

Meanwhile, Jane and her sisters were arguing in this case that, as legally Chalkley was the sole trustee of the Tyrer Street house and a convicted felon the court should to appoint another trustee. This would enable them to work through him, sell the house and realise the profits, well the children could, the three daughters and two missing sons, not Jane as she was merely the figurehead and an ex-debtor and bankrupt to boot, but she would make sure the children would do as they were told. The important point as far as Jane was concerned was that her creditors could not claim against this estate as part of her current bankruptcy proceedings.

Jane and her family had already approached the officials dealing with Chalkley's affairs to convey the rights to the Tyrer Street house to them, but they refused to do so until they received a direction from the High Court. You cannot blame them, given the high profile of the Chalkley case, and the number of Chalkley's creditors still clamouring for a fuller pay-out for their losses.

Jane got the decision she needed on 30.1.1865 but the official document is dated much later, on 17.7.1865. She and her daughters could then appoint a new trustee and realise this asset but first they had to pay the costs of all parties.

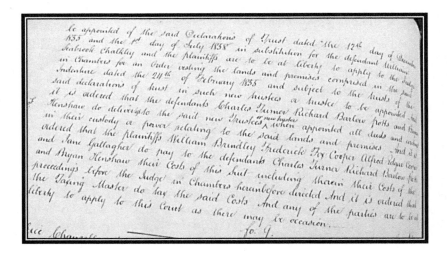

Figure 73 The Chancery Court decision on a new trustee 1865

It was a victory of sorts, but Jane had to involve for the first time, her children and their spouses, publicly in a court case. They could no longer pretend their education, respectable lifestyles, comforts, clothes, houses and probably their marriages were not funded by the ill-gotten gains of prostitution, and the *Talking Fish* of course.[619]

Who knows what impact this had on their new and comparatively respectable in - laws? And was it this money Fox Cooper was only too pleased to get his hands on when he married Selina?

Chapter 31 - Revolving Doors

Only six months later, on Tuesday 23.1.1866, Jane aged 50, unable or unwilling to keep out of trouble, is brought up on a warrant and yet again charged with keeping a disreputable house, this time at 42 Lord Nelson Street, Liverpool. Imperious as ever, she was in the same dock as a:

> 'Miserably clad, dirty-looking creature named Jane [Mary] Lovesey who afforded a striking contrast to the gay and lavishly dressed Mustrabon of the Liverpool demi-monde who stood beside her, who was also charged with keeping a house of similar repute in the same street.' [620]

I could not find any explanation for the reference to Mustrabon but:

> 'The term demi-monde became a synonym for a courtesan or a prostitute or for a woman of social standing with the power to thumb her nose at convention and throw herself into the hedonistic nightlife.'[621]

These high-class prostitutes were known as *Grandes Horizontales*, the élite, who became wealthy and famous in their own right. They enjoyed freedom and political power unavailable to other women.'[622] One such was Cora Pearl.

Born plain Emma Elizabeth Crouch in Portsmouth, England, probably around 1835, her father, Frederick Nicholas Crouch, was a famous songwriter and moved to America. He would go on to marry several times and it was said that he had 20 children. Emma became Cora when she moved to Paris after being seduced and abandoned by a man in London and was an immediate sensation, exciting patrons with her tiny waist and bountiful bosom. She was impetuous, exuberant, unembarrassed to express passion and had a string of 'protectors,' including Victor Massena, the Duke of Rivoli, who showered her with money and gifts, bought her a horse and gave her money for visits to gambling dens.

Her many influential lovers included the Prince of Orange, the heir to the throne of the Netherlands; Napoleon III's half-brother the Duke de Morny; and his cousin Napoleon Joseph Charles Paul, sometimes known as Prince Jerome Napoleon, with whom she had her longest and most lucrative relationship. However, as she reached her 40th birthday, her beauty and fortunes waned and Prince Jerome Napoleon, cut her off. Over the next decade, she slowly sold her assets out of necessity and by 1885, she had nothing left and was living in a boarding house. Cora died on 8.8.1886. One of her former lovers anonymously covered the cost of her funeral and burial in Batignolles Cemetery in Paris, though there is no grave marker. She was 51.[623]

The price those of the demi-monde paid was ostracisation from polite society and outright rejection once they grew older, which is why Jane was so careful to keep in the background of her empire and took great pains to appear to be a fashionable, well-educated and cultured woman, above all that was 'sordid.' How she must have hated to be in the dock with a common procuress - Jane Lovesey.

Nevertheless, complaints had been made by some of the respectable residents of the area about 'the annoyance arising from the manner in which the houses in Lord Nelson Street, Liverpool were conducted.'

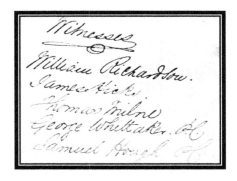

Figure 74 Complainant's names

They were from: William Richardson who lived at No 29 Lord Nelson Street and was a travelling draper with five children under 13 and a servant, and Thomas Milne who lived at No 20 and was a baker with seven boarders in his house. The others named are not listed anywhere and may have just witnessed the signatures of Richardson and Milne. [624]

Jane's other neighbours on Lord Nelson Street were a mixture of gentle folk, merchants, shop keepers, lodging house owners, estate agents, an investment and loan company, a tobacco warehouse, a temperance hotel and others selling alcohol, for the street was adjacent to Lime Street station, a hotbed of social evil and depravity as well as a focal point for all who arrived in the city by train.

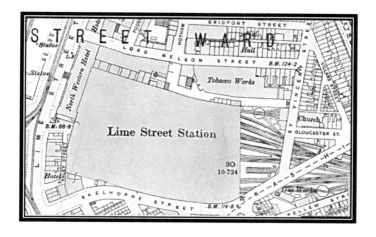

Figure 75 Lord Nelson Street, Liverpool. OS 25" map 1850

Lime Street station can be seen here bounded by Lord Nelson Street, St Vincent, Skelthorne and Pellew Streets, which were all associated with Jane's notorious brothels. It was indeed a handy location for servicing passing trade and wealthy businessmen travelling from London or other cities.

Jane's lawyer was keen to impress upon the magistrate the great differences between the two women in the dock and swiftly moved to disallow any embarrassing questions into Jane's association with the house of ill repute. He rudely interrupted the prosecution lawyer's learned discourse around the legal grounds for the case, the provisions of the act 25th Geo II, c.36, sections 5 and 6, saying he was instructed to state that Jane Gallagher, was:

> 'Willing to close her house and go away to London. She was, in fact, about to sell her furniture, having put the matter into the hands of an agent.'

This was mighty decent of her, he implied, and insisted this should put an end to the matter and satisfy all parties concerned, especially as it still wasn't illegal to run or own a brothel. The magistrate was not that easily put off and enquired if this was the house in which he had been forced to interfere with several times already, to no purpose. Inspector Hughes assured him it was not run by the woman his worship referred to and Jane's lawyer quickly added that the house had been:

'A remarkably well-conducted commercial house, [laughter in court] and though proceedings had been taken against her, there was no vindictive feeling against her.'

As Jane had been brought before the court on a warrant, the prosecuting lawyer wanted the magistrate to bind her over until the house had been closed down and for her to appear at the quarter sessions to answer any bill for indictment that might be preferred against her and here is the official record:

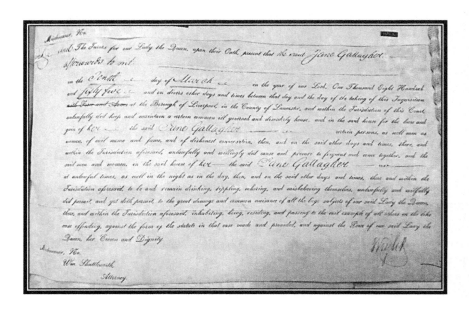

Figure 76 Jane Gallagher's Indictment

She was therefore bailed in her own right for £100 [£5,912.92] and the court demanded two sureties of £50 [£,2,956.46] each, a total of £11,825.84 at today's values, a sum anyone would struggle to muster even now. But Jane did have a habit of absconding, so maybe this was fair. Her sureties were: Joseph England Hirst of 96 Copperas Hill, Liverpool and William Phillips of 18 Bolton Street, Copperas Hill. I was curious about these two. Why would they each put up nearly £3,000 at 2017 values for Jane's bail? What was she to them?

In 1866, Hirst would have been around 38 and also owned freehold houses at 43-53 Lissant Street, West Derby, Liverpool.[625] Later, between 1878 - 1880, he acquired more property: a counting house and a smithy at 6 and 8 Rigby Street.[626] By the 1881 census age 54, he still lives at 96 Copperas Hill in Liverpool, though he was born in Kendal, Westmorland, and he worked as a Master (Scale) Beam maker employing three men and two lads.[627]

William Phillips is a very common name and he could not be found at 18 Bolton Street in the censuses and street directories for this period, so I can only assume Phillips was not a native of Liverpool but a visitor staying at Copperas Hill temporarily at the time Jane needed him to stand surety for her.

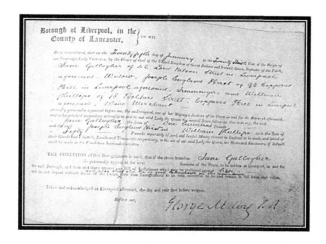

Figure 77 Jane's Bail document for the Quarter Sessions

At this point the dozy magistrate enquired if Mary (Jane) Lovesey, the miserable creature, was charged with keeping a house for her.

'Mrs. Gallagher,' the reporter wrote, 'who was attired in very fashionable costume, of exceedingly bright colours, seemed to be indignant at this question being put, and turned a most contemptuous glance upon her meaner-clad companion in the dock.' Both women were removed to the cells while bail was sorted.[628]

On the face of it, the case went as Jane planned: no shameful revelations, no influential clients were called to bear witness, she had her freedom and could still command deference and respect in court. I therefore find it very difficult to understand why Jane, and both sureties, then failed to appear in court on 19.2.1866 for the quarter sessions.

Figure 78 Jane Gallagher breaks her bail conditions

'The prisoner not answering when called upon to surrender, the court issued a bench warrant for her apprehension. This prisoner and her sureties were called three times and not answering their recognisances were forfeited.'

All £11,825.84 of it, at current values. I have searched obvious reasons for her not turning up: problems in the family, a birth, death, accident but can find nothing which explains this. It is even more mystifying when we find she actually paid all the recognisance money into court the very next day, as if nothing had happened and was then fined another £50 [£2,956.46] with the threat of 12 months imprisonment if she failed to pay.

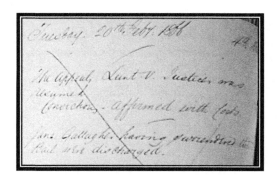

Figure 79 Jane Gallagher's bail discharged

This little adventure cost Jane nearly £15,000 at current values instead of one single fine of £2,956.46. All this money she raised in one or two days, which says something about her power, influence and financial resources. For someone who supposedly owns nothing she can certainly find the cash when she needs it. The table below gives you an idea of how this second sentence compares to those dealt with the same day.

Name	Charge	Sentence
Jane Gallagher	Keeping a house of ill-fame	Fined £50 [£2,956.46] or imprisonment for twelve months
William Howarth	Obtaining 10s 6d [£31.04] by false pretences	Three months imprisonment
John McArdle	Stealing a purse containing £5 10s [£325.21]	Seven years penal servitude
Elizabeth Shaw	Receiving the same purse	Eight years penal servitude
Thomas Hollis	Breaking into a shop and stealing meat and other goods	As a multiple offender, 14 years penal servitude
Joseph Aspinall	Breaking into a shop and stealing meat and other goods	Six months imprisonment
Catherine Caley	Stealing six pounds of cotton wool	Twelve months hard labour
Mary Lovesey	Keeping a brothel	Nine months
Ann Martin	Keeping a brothel	Eighteen months

Note: Mary (Jane) Lovesey, meanly clad or not, still got nine months for keeping a brothel at 33 Lord Nelson Street, Liverpool and there is no mention of bail for her.

Chapter 32 - The Final Curtain

'It was no unjustifiable boast that he [Fox Cooper] made in declaring that he could keep a theatre open for weeks without a treasury and that, though he could hardly be safely trusted as a manager, his company was always sought after by everybody.'
E.L. Blanchard, a well-known pantomime author and theatrical journalist

The 1851 census shows us that at the beginning of this decade, Fox Cooper's household is living at Britannia Street, City Road, near the *Grecian Theatre* in London. It comprises:

- Frederick Fox Cooper age 45, who is then described as an author, with Ann his wife

- Frederick Harwood Cooper, son, age 24, who is now a professor of elocution

- Thomas Poole age 36, a dramatic author

- Allred Edgar Cooper, son, age 11

But, also in 1851, Fox Cooper was a guest in St Giles without Cripple-gate debtors' prison on White Street, London, as one of his previous debts rolled over into this new year. How easily Fox Cooper sues and is sued. It is almost like tennis, as he is either defending a suit or volleying back. This time a Mr. Pridmore serves weakly, worn down by his money problems. He had leased *Saville House* in Leicester Square back in 1846 and in 1853, after huge losses, applied to be let out of prison for his debts but Fox Cooper and another creditor were opposing his plea.

Fox Cooper said he considered he was owed £100 [£8,018.61] for theatrical dresses and manuscripts which Pridmore had made available to his theatre. He had paid £50 [£4,009.31] for them but he and his performers were barred from the theatre on the third week and he could not access the dresses or the manuscripts. The case was adjourned and, disappointingly, nothing further is reported in the press about Pridmore's dresses.[629]

However, life for Fox Cooper as a theatre manager continues to be one long battle to balance his accounts, often chaos and more than occasionally, violent. Whilst working as the stage manager at the *Strand Theatre*, Fox Cooper was pursued by a man called Brickhill, a printer from Elephant and Castle, for non-payment of a bill he disputed for £3 [£240.56], payment for some posters and printing. Brickhill told him he was being 'Untradesmanlike,' and confronted him. Well, he did rather more than that, producing, printing and circulating throughout the neighbourhood, handbills of 'the most libellous description,' one of which, taken off a lamp post and dated 3.11.1854, read:

'Public Notice – Frederick Fox Cooper, Esq, begs to inform his inquiring friends he has removed from 24 Brook Street, West Square, Lambeth to No 9, New Street, Kennington, where all persons indebted to him are requested to remit their various amounts, and where all creditors will be paid with black guardians and a large stick.'

Fox Cooper, when asked in the ensuing court case how he knew Brickhill had printed these bills, replied:

'The fact that he has frequently threatened both myself and my wife that he would expose us. Besides, he sent persons to my house as early as seven o'clock this morning to demand the money and all morning they have been knocking at my door, to the great alarm of Mrs. Fox Cooper, who is in an extremely delicate state of health, and to our great scandal in the neighbourhood.

'I have now present a lad who is in the employment of Mr. Brickhill, whom I found knocking at my door, and he acknowledged it was his second visit to my house this morning, by direction of his master.'

Having let loose this ace, Fox Cooper demanded that the magistrate caution the lad and warn Mr. Brickhill to stop annoying him and his wife pending further summons. This the magistrate did but Fox Cooper had to drop pursuing Brickhill further.[630] Later that month however, Brickhill got his own back, charging Fox Cooper with assault.[631] So, Fox Cooper does not always get is own way! But what of his long-suffering wife, Ann? She was not a well person, with heart disease and dropsy, and had to endure much in terms of shame and disgrace because of her husband's highly strung nature and his casual approach to money and the courts. We hear very little of her.

Now, onto 1856 and a case where the *Era* itself is in court and Fox Cooper is a witness for the complainant. It devotes almost a whole page to this matter, more than four columns from top to bottom in their broadsheet and it involves: 'The Printer's Devil and the Harlequin.' Yes, even the court cases read like melodramas! This one is between Lewis Levite, a ballet dancer and a harlequin who is suing Frederick Ledger, the owner of the *Era* newspaper for £200 [£16,037.22] for a libel published in his paper on 23.3.1856.

The harlequin character came to England early in the 17th century and developed in the early 18th century to a point where it was routinely paired with the clown and was famous for slapstick comedy.[632] What happened in this case was that Mr. Levite organised a benefit at the *Garrick Theatre* in London and tasked a Mr. Till, who the *Era* described as 'a funny little printer,' with producing the advertising bills to be posted around town. They came to an agreement by which Mr. Till printed the posters and would be paid in ready money, for Mr. Till had been caught out before with people not paying him. For this Mr. Levite demanded a discount, which he got. On the day the bills were to be delivered, Mr. Till instructed his delivery boy thus:

'The gentleman whom the printing is for is a harlequin, and you know what slippery customers they can be if they like. Now, on no pretence whatever, do you let go of these bills until you get £1 19s [£156.36] good coin of the realm.'

When the lad did not come back for a long time, Mr. Till feared the worst. Mr. Levite, assisted by 'congenial spirits,' [he plied the lad with drink] had taken the printing off the boy without paying. The benefit proved to be very lucrative and when Mr. Till went around the next day for his money he was given a false address. Mr. Till appealed to the magistrate saying:

'Now, my lud, don't you think I am to be pitied – done by a harlequin, through my lad!'

The ruling was in Mr. Till's favour and the magistrate ordered Mr. Levite to pay the money and that should have ended the matter. But no. Mr. Levite took exception to way in which the *Era* had written up the proceedings and demanded an apology for the mockery they had made of him, disparaging his name and variations on it. The apology was not forthcoming, hence this case. It is gets more farcical by the minute when Fox Cooper is called about half way through on behalf of the complainant, Mr. Levite, though one wonders why given the dialogue below:

Lawyer: Do you know the plaintiff in this action? [Mr. Levite].

Fox Cooper: I know him.

Lawyer: Was he acting as a harlequin at the *Garrick Theatre?*

Fox Cooper: Not to my knowledge.

Lawyer: Have you been connected with the theatre?

Fox Cooper: I have been connected with the theatre from Easter Monday to last Saturday.

Lawyer: Did you read this pretend report of the proceedings in the Whitechapel county court?

Fox Cooper: Yes, I did.

Lawyer: Did you understand it to apply to the plaintiff?

Fox Cooper: Yes.

And so it goes on, with Fox Cooper giving little and the lawyer trying to extract blood from his stone. Fox Cooper is never this reticent, what's the matter with him? Maybe the bruising the *Era* gave him two years previously has something to do with it. Even the judge becomes exasperated and the lawyer hurriedly tries to move on saying:

Lawyer: You are a friend of the defendant, [the owner of the *Era*] are you not?

Fox Cooper: No. I have the honour to know him. [Laughter in court].

Justice: You have thrown a doubt upon the case more than it was before.

Fox Cooper was then led away.

It would have made a great sketch in the theatre for even the two opposing lawyers agreed it was a ridiculous waste of time, saying 'our unanimity is wonderful!' But it took the jury only a brief moment to award the harlequin £10 [£801.86] damages, to the astonishment of all present. Shortly after the verdict had been recorded, several gentlemen formed themselves into a committee to defray the *Era's* expenses and nearly £30 [£2,405.58] was collected in as many moments. They then all left saying they would bring the rest quite soon. Such was Victorian justice for gentlemen of power and influence.[633]

And Fox Cooper's role in all this? Who knows what game he was playing? But there is no time to ponder for within months he is a witness again in *Howe v Kennedy*, where he is the star turn. The defendants, who had both been sheriffs in London and Middlesex, were accused of neglect in executing a warrant for Mr. Howe for £21 [£1,683.91] and some odd shillings.

The plaintiff, Mr. Howe, is another printer, this time from Yorkshire and he did some work for a Mr. Sheridan Smith who was the lessee of two theatres but left Yorkshire without paying his debts. Sometime later Mr. Howe heard that Smith, now using the name Swanborough, was playing in London in another theatre and on 19.2.1856 he was to appear at the *Strand Theatre* in a benefit of his own. A warrant was taken out for his arrest and put into the hands of a Mr. Levy the sheriff's officer, who was also the proprietor of the *Garrick Theatre* in Whitechapel. Levy put it in the hands of a man called Barry, who went to the *Strand Theatre* and saw Swanborough but did not take him into custody for reasons which will be made apparent. It was for this that Howe took the case against the two sheriffs for negligence.

The annals of the stage have afforded matter for many curious anecdotes of actors and actresses, but few of late years have equalled the scene enacted in the Court of Exchequer on Tuesday last, before the Lord Chief Baron. We give it entire, as it may afford our readers a glimpse of the everyday life of members of the mimic art, and display to them the rugged and bitter life ofttimes experienced by actors, not only before, but behind the scenes :—

Figure 80 'Court of Exchequer' Morning Advertiser 10.12.1856

Mr. Swanborough was arrested in a state of great destitution and appeared in court as an insolvent debtor. He said he had purposely kept out of the way to avoid arrest on his benefit night because Fox Cooper had forewarned him. The *Morning Advertiser* takes up the tale and even reproduces the script. Fox Cooper was called and examined.

Lawyer: Those who know Mr. Fox Cooper best call him "Fox," I believe.' [Laughter in court].

Swanborough: I really do not know. I believe his name is Frederick Fox Cooper.

Fox Cooper said he was currently living at Ramsgate and he was a dramatic author. He was at the *Garrick Theatre* on 19.2.1856, had found out from Barry a warrant was out for the arrest of Swanborough and protested saying:

'Oh, you must not take him, it is his benefit tonight.'

Barry said if he did not arrest Swanborough that night he would want 10 shillings [£40.09] for himself, a bribe. Fox Cooper admitted he had acted from a mistaken feeling which he now regretted, but nevertheless he jumped into a cab and rushed off to warn Swanborough. The poor man claimed he did not owe this money but Fox Cooper went back and got the warrant and, mustering his friends, raised the 10 shillings and gave it to Barry. Now paid off, Barry left Swanborough alone with his misery in the bar, drinking.

After the failure to arrest Swanborough, Levy approached Fox Cooper asking where Swanborough's wife was and Fox Cooper told him where her mother lived. Barry heard about this and came to Fox Cooper, pleading with him not to betray him to Levy, his master.

'Mr. Fox Cooper, my bread is in your hands, and, for God's sake, don't betray me!'

Lawyer: Did you have any money from Levy for informing him of where Swanborough's wife lived?

Fox Cooper: [In a towering passion] – How dare you ask that question?

Lawyer: I ask it because I want an answer.

Fox Cooper: No, I did not. Now you have your answer! (Laughter in court)

But Fox Cooper admitted he had spoken to a Mr. Maynard about this affair and professed to tell him all he knew. 'Mr. Levy had the audacity to say he would indict him with the others for conspiracy, but that did not make him angry' - [the highly excited state of Mr. Fox Cooper while giving this portion of his evidence convulsed the court with laughter.]

He believed he had unfortunately told Levy that his officer Barry had not received anything for allowing Swanborough to escape but then said he had lent Swanborough half a crown to make up the 10 shillings paid as a bribe to Levy's agent, Barry. He was certain he saw Swanborough in the saloon where gentlemen went to drink between pieces and Levy's agent Barry was there part of the time but there were eight or nine entrances to the theatre.

Lawyer: Like a rabbit warren?

Fox Cooper: It is natural that John Doe and Richard Roe should go into a warren, isn't it? [Laughter.]

Lawyer: And these doors were guarded?

Fox Cooper: Yes, by *Cerberus*es. One was a female *Cerberus*, who received a small salary for keeping her eyes on the doors, north, east, west and south.

Lord Baron: A female *Cerberus* with four heads. [Laughter.]

Fox Cooper: Any sheriff's officer going to the *Strand* would find himself trapped in a different way from what he expected. He might have gone down below, or he might go up with a spring, heaven knows how high. [Roars of laughter.] He could not say whether Swanborough performed on the benefit night, but he supposed he did. He [Fox Cooper] could not witness any performances, more especially Swanborough's, it was so shockingly bad. [Laughter.]

Lawyer: So, you did this for Swanborough in a friendly sort of way?

Fox Cooper: Yes, just as I would do it for you, Sir, or any other gentleman. [Roars of laughter.]

Levy was called and said he had discharged Barry some months since for defalcations but not for anything arising from this current case. He admitted asking Fox Cooper for a clue to Swanborough's whereabouts who told him he would let him know if he would give him a guinea. Fox Cooper, from the body of the court, denied this, very loudly.

Summing up, the lawyer said that Mr. Howe would not have suffered anything by the non-arrest of Swanborough as he had no money at that time to pay his account. But the judge argued that was not the point. This case was about whether both sheriffs had proved conclusively that every effort had been made to arrest the man on information received. The jury found for the plaintiff, Howe and the two sheriffs lost. Fox Cooper had performed to perfection, muddying the waters and playing to the gallery, receiving the most laughs, very unlike his previous appearance in court.[634] And what is most surprising, he was not arrested for bribing a sheriff's officer.

By 1858, Alfred Edgar, Fox Cooper's youngest son, now age seventeen, was set on being a musician and only marginally involved in the theatres his father managed. Very wisely, he kept his professional life separate but family records show he did compose an overture for a pantomime Fox Cooper produced at the *Ramsgate and Sandwich Theatres* called 'Harlequin and the Magic Needle' in February 1858. It was described as a 'clever composition' introducing such delights *as Life of a Clown, Hot Codlins* and *Tippitywitchet.'*[635]

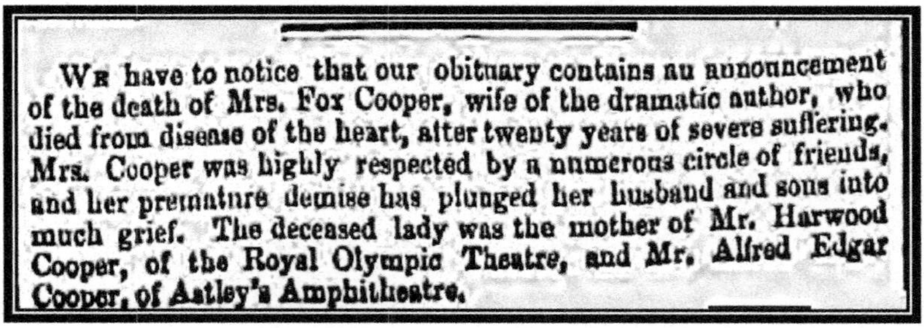

WE have to notice that our obituary contains an announcement of the death of Mrs. Fox Cooper, wife of the dramatic author, who died from disease of the heart, after twenty years of severe suffering. Mrs. Cooper was highly respected by a numerous circle of friends, and her premature demise has plunged her husband and sons into much grief. The deceased lady was the mother of Mr. Harwood Cooper, of the Royal Olympic Theatre, and Mr. Alfred Edgar Cooper, of Astley's Amphitheatre.

Figure 81 Notice of Ann Fox Cooper's death in the Era 20.5.1860

Sadly, on the 2.5.1860, Fox Cooper's wife's health failed completely and she died of dropsy at Hercules Buildings, Lambeth. An announcement appeared in the Court

Circular and Fox Cooper was present at her death. Being highly strung and a devoted husband, the blow would have been severe. Harwood, his eldest son was 34, living in Tennison Street, London with his wife Emma at the time and Alfred Edgar was 20 and lived with his father.

A year later, the 1861 census shows Fox Cooper, 55 and a dramatic author, and Alfred Edgar, 21, a musician at *Astley's Amphitheatre*, still living at 17 Hercules Buildings where the family had been since 1857. *Astley's Amphitheatre* was a performance venue in London opened by Philip Astley in 1773 and was considered to be the first modern circus ring. It was burned, rebuilt several times and went through many owners and managers. Despite no trace of the theatre remaining today, a memorial plaque was unveiled in 1951 at its site at 225 Westminster Bridge Road.[636]

At some point in the next year, father and son moved to 4 Chester Place, Lambeth which was on Kennington Road in 1862 near to Chester Street. Nos. 233 – 291 Kennington Road were formerly 2 – 31 Chester Place (Street) and built between 1788 – 1792.[637] Looking for their neighbours, I discovered that No 3 had been the home of two different Wesleyan Methodist ministers, which made me wonder about connections with Chalkley in Liverpool.

No. 235 (formerly 3 Chester Place) was between 1846 – 1847 the residence of the Rev. Jonathan Crowther, Wesleyan minister. Having been principal teacher at Woodhouse Grove School, near Bradford, Crowther was appointed in 1823 the headmaster of Kingswood School.[638] He was removed from his position there in 1826 because of his brutal use of corporal punishment. In 1837, Crowther was appointed general superintendent of the Wesleyan missions in India, returning to England in 1843 in poor health, where he was again employed in the home ministry. In 1849, he received the appointment of classical tutor in the Wesleyan Theological Institution at Didsbury, Manchester.

Between 1855 - 1856 the Rev. Frederick James Jobson, D.D., Wesleyan minister, lived at No 3 too. He was articled to an architect, but secured a reputation as a preacher by his fervour and became a minister. He served for nine years at the City Road Chapel and superintended the Methodist Magazine for twelve years.

I have not been able to find out if these Wesleyan Methodists had any connection with Chalkley apart from subscribing to the same religion. However, next door at 4 Chester Place on 12.7.1862 Fox Cooper married Selina, Jane's daughter, who was assumed in subsequent stories passed down by family, to have been his housekeeper.

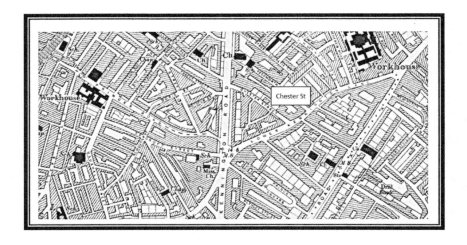

Figure 82 Chester Street on a street map of Lambeth in 1888

Around this time Fox Cooper's health got worse and it appears he developed epilepsy. After being out of debtor's prisons for nearly twelve years from the early 1850s, his name again appeared in *The Times* bankruptcy index in December 1862, only seven months after his wedding to Selina. Given that she had her own independent means Selina must have been an attractive and convenient proposition for Fox Cooper.

Many of his debts, worth £200 [£16,037.22] were due to writers who had contributed to a publication called *The Times of 1962*. This consisted of two sheets of newspaper, each about 36" by 28", printed on both sides and made to look like *The Times* as it might have been in 1962. Edited by the wits of the age, it claimed to show the revolution which a century might make in our morals, politics, laws, commerce, arts, science, literature, music and drama.

It was uncannily accurate in many respects and features a narcotic syrup which enables people to sleep at will, folk travelling to Iceland and back in day, a tunnel under the sea between Ireland and England – the wrong bit of water but the right idea – an advert for a family trip to the moon, the dangers of short sighted policy making, and various imaginative solutions to traffic problems with pedestrians having to walk only in one direction on each side of the road, a glorious one way system but for people not vehicles, and one we did not think of until COVID-19.

Regardless, it landed Fox Cooper in debt again, which must not have been one of the forecasts in this publication despite it being a highly probable event. At the hearing, Fox Cooper said his failure was due to a severe epileptic illness which prevented him from following literary pursuits, but this was pure theatre as he actually continued for another sixteen years. Nevertheless, his lawyer milked this for all its worth saying Fox Cooper 'had given so much attention to the future, that he had neglected the present.' The following week, Fox Cooper's latest bankruptcy was discharged.

While real life Fox Cooper court dramas continued to play, on the domestic front Caroline had been getting to know Alfred Edgar, for they were both of a similar age. Caroline had lived with her sister Selina and Fox Cooper since their wedding two years before and I suppose it was inevitable that she fell for her brother-in-law's son. Caroline Gallagher of Chester Place, married Alfred Edgar Fox Cooper, a musician in Lambeth on 3.6.1864 at the same church her sister had married her new husband's father in 1862. Alfred Edgar had been living at Walcot Place, Lambeth, which was probably due to propriety as Caroline had had their first daughter, Florence Jane, 26 days before in Liverpool. As Selina was still childless after two years with Fox Cooper, this must have hurt.

Fox Cooper and Selina cannot have had much money, in spite of Jane and her daughters getting permission to sell the Tyrer Street house and share the proceeds. Maybe his debts swallowed up all that Selina received, as her husband owned and controlled everything she had. They lived with her sister Caroline, Alfred Edgar and Florence Jane at the time of the 1871 census at 14 Terrace, Southwark, London along with three more of their children: Selina B, Frederick Fox and Henry G. A son also called Alfred Edgar was born after the census in April 1871 but the boy died of variola [smallpox] when he was only eleven months old. The smallpox outbreak between 1871-1872 was the last in the British Isles in terms of its scale and impact and resulted in about 42,000 deaths over two years. It was spread by refugees coming to England to escape the French-Prussian War.[639] Their last child, Helen, was born in 1876.

Alfred Edgar was always associated with the musical aspects of theatres, as a violinist, and at one time, he was leader of the orchestra at *Drury Lane Theatre*. Occasionally he arranged an overture or a 'medley of music' and there is a manuscript for piano entitled: 'Miller and his Men', being a set of five quadrilles arranged by Alfred Edgar from the beautiful melodies of popular melodrama.'[640]

Fox Cooper officially retired at a benefit especially arranged for him at the *Haymarket Theatre* on 23.12.1871 and his last play was produced at the *Adelphi* on 19.8.1876 and entitled 'A Bunch of Greens' – three men called Green all pursuing the same lady. It included some original overtures composed by Alfred Edgar.

His performances had spanned fifty years[641] and just after the final run of the play on 4.11.1876, Fox Cooper had an accident and died on 4.1.1879 on his 73rd birthday while he was living at 59 Princes Road, Lambeth. The very cold weather of that season must have aggravated his bronchitis, which was the cause of death.[642] Selina does not feature at all in his last days and family rumour had it they had separated.

Curiously, the informant, the person named on the death certificate as being with Fox Cooper when he died, was Emma Plumeridge of 64 Tyers Street, Lambeth which in 1879 was the *John Bull* pub in Vauxhall. In 1875, Edwin Webb was a beer retailer there, then by 1880 Thomas Law was the publican.[643] [644] She does not appear in any London directory or the 1881 census as living at this address but there are two possibilities for her. She was either a 50-year-old charwoman who lived at 6 Tiger Yard in Lambeth or a 23-year-old woman who married George Smith, a brewer, a few months later in Lambeth. Without more details it is impossible to say exactly who she was, but she was not family.

The funeral took place on 10.1.1879 without Selina and the bill was made out to Harriet Fox Cooper, who was Fox Cooper's step - mother, his father's second wife. Harwood, the eldest son had the bill in his possession when he too died so he might have settled it, for there was no will, no estate and no probate. Fox Cooper had probably sold the copyright of his plays and died penniless.

Various personal tributes to Fox Cooper appeared.

'He was everything by starts and nothing long, and was shifty in every sense of the word, for he changed his address at least fifty times and the safest place to look for him was in the debtors' prison... He wrote seventy-seven plays of which were many shown on the stage, yet not one of them made mark enough to be known by the compiler of the obituary section of the "Who's Who in the Theatre" where the entry merely says: "F. Fox Cooper, Actor, died 4 Jan 1879."'[645]

'In private life Mr. Cooper is the staunch friend, the kindest of parents, and one of the most companionable men of the day. He possesses a vast fund of anecdotal conversations upon every conceivable topic, and is well known to love fun for its own sake, and to be eminently the cause of it in others.' [*Theatrical Times*]

Fox Cooper's tendency for harmless pleasantry was illustrated by a story told by a wealthy resident in the East End of London who had requested the pleasure of Fox Cooper's company to dinner. His invitation was accepted and on the appointed day:

'Four cabs, heavily laden, deposited their living cargo at the door of the host, much to his astonishment.' Fox Cooper led the group and dissipated the host's surprise by remarking that: 'As his friend had signified a wish for the pleasure of his company, he had taken him at his word.' In consequence every individual connected with his establishment – which was the Strand Theatre at that time – had arrived to do honour to the proffered hospitality.'

The end of the tale is that the joke was taken as it was intended and the day was pleasantly spent![646]

His great grandson, after researching Fox Cooper's life, said he had:

'An abiding impression of Fox Cooper's quality of friendship: he thrived on it, according to an analysis of his handwriting. Between the lines, one can sense that he was often helping others, even when the cause now seems unworthy. He was a good companion, although in the material sense he had little to offer. Within the family circles little has been handed down, except that Fox Cooper had a weakness for cards, which could well explain his parlous finances. He did not "drink" but he liked champagne. Others have described him as a staunch friend, a kind parent.'[647]

There was no provision made for Selina on Fox Cooper's death and no home for her either. By the time of the 1881 census, she was living as a lodger with independent means at 378 Kennington Road, Lambeth, age forty-five. However, the Fox Cooper family records say she moved to Dublin to let rooms for theatrical folk around 1887. Whilst I cannot find any trace of her under the names she is known to have used in the past, a Mrs. Selina Cooper did apply for a passport on 11.2.1885.[648]

The only incontrovertible facts are that in the 1891 census she was a widowed lodger, one of two with independent means living at 190 Southampton Street, Camberwell, London in the household of Samuel Gillman, a farrier/smith and his wife Caroline, two children, Samuel's brother Arthur age 23, and Mary Ann Norris her co-lodger age 35.

Selina died the following year on 30.12.1892 at 220 Southampton Street, Camberwell, a little further down the road, age 56, though her death certificate says 54. She died of toxic myocarditis cardiac failure. This condition can be caused by a viral, bacterial or fungal infection, a chest infection or an auto immune disease, which occurs when your own immune system attacks your body. Common symptoms of myocarditis include:

- A stabbing pain and/or tightness in the chest which may spread across the body

- Shortness of breath when lightly exercising or walking

- Difficulty breathing when resting

- Flu-like symptoms such as a high temperature, tiredness and fatigue

- Palpitations or an abnormal heart rhythm

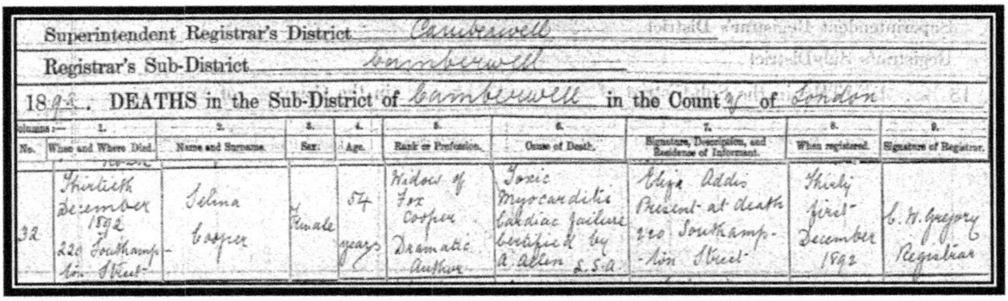

Superintendent Registrar's District Camberwell

Registrar's Sub-District Camberwell

1892. DEATHS in the Sub-District of Camberwell in the County of London

Columns:—	1.	2.	3.	4.	5.	6.	7.	8.	9.
No.	When and Where Died.	Name and Surname.	Sex.	Age.	Rank or Profession.	Cause of Death.	Signature, Description, and Residence of Informant.	When registered.	Signature of Registrar.
32	Thirtieth December 1892 220 Southampton Street	Selina Cooper	Female	54 years	Widow of Fox Cooper Dramatic Author	Toxic Myocarditis Cardiac failure Certified by A. Allen L.S.A.	Eliza Addis Present at death 220 Southampton Street	Thirty first December 1892	C. W. Gregory Registrar

Figure 83 Selina Cooper's death certificate, London 1892

An Eliza Addis was present at her death but she is not listed as living at No 220 in the 1891 census. As nothing else is known of Eliza, it is not possible to find out what connection, if any she had with Selina.

However, it is interesting to note that even though her sister Caroline was living not far away in London, she was not present, nor did she place a newspaper announcement of her sister's death.

Chapter 33 - Lust and Money

Miss B, Number 18, Old Compton Street, Soho

'This accomplished nymph has just attained her eighteenth year, and fraught with every perfection, enters a volunteer in the field of Venus. She plays on the pianoforte, sings, dances, and is the mistress of every manoeuvre in the amorous contest that can enhance the coming pleasure; is of middle stature, fine auburn hair, dark eyes and very inviting countenance, which ever seems to beam delight and love. In bed she is all the heart can wish, or eyes admire, every limb is symmetry, every action under cover truly amorous; her price two pounds.' [£172.21]

Entries like these in the 1788 London publication *Harris's Guide to Covent Garden Ladies*, aimed at the wealthier members of society like Jane Gallagher's clientele, enabled gentlemen to browse through detailed descriptions of young ladies and what they offered.[649] Later, in the 1830s and 1840s, there was a sort of tourist guide to London's lascivious women, *A Swell's Night Guide*,[650] which, whilst it was not so crude as to publish a price list, gave lavish descriptions of luxurious establishments and their key features, such as:

'Miss Allen – A perfect English beauty. She is in her nineteenth year; of symmetrical form... no-one will regret passing an hour in her company, and drinking deep at that mystic fountain of human pleasure.'

This is very different from the lewd approaches made by common street prostitutes but was equally effective in enticing the young, and not so young, but wealthy gentlemen to experience their sexual fantasies, for a price, in genteel settings where they could pretend that nothing untoward went on.

What did a visit to a prostitute cost? It depends on who you ask: Samuel Pepys' friend and diarist James Boswell in 1763 picked up a sixpenny whore in London[651] but by mid-Victorian times a shilling [£5.12] was the bargain basement and 2/6 [£12.80] the average which was a week's wage for a working girl. In the anonymous Victorian memoir, *My Secret Life* published in 1888, the writer recalls many encounters with common prostitutes in London between 1840 - 1880. For street prostitutes, he describes paying one shilling [£3.02] for a look, another shilling for a 'feel,' and about five shillings [£15.10] for intercourse. If he simply went up an alley with her, it was less.[652]

Virgins were especially prized and a highly marketable commodity, fetching anywhere between £5.00 [£330.92] and £25.00 [£1,654.62], a large amount of money, when you consider in 1880 the average wage for a skilled worker was £62.00 [£4,103.45] per year. They were very much sought after as there was less chance of catching a sexually transmitted disease. It goes without saying that enterprising madams sold their talented virgins several times over as they were well practised in the arts of innocence.

High class prostitutes received many gifts; some were ensconced in apartments, others enjoyed royal favour and while their beauty and allurements lasted, lived a very good life. It was a career path worth fighting for, if you had the wit and the wiles to survive. Common prostitutes, on the other hand, supplemented their income by robbing virtually every man they could lay their hands on, the stolen goods being swiftly exchanged in local pawnbrokers for cash. In 1843:

'A sailor, called John Murphy, charged a prostitute Margaret Gardner at the police court in Liverpool with robbing him of his clothes. It appeared that he had met the prostitute in the street and agreed to pass the night with her. He gave her eight shillings [£24.17], all the money he had. The following morning, he found all his clothes missing, which were afterwards found at two pawnbrokers, on whom the magistrate passed a severe censure and ordered the prostitute to pay a fine of fifty shillings [£151.05] and the value of the articles, or to be imprisoned for two months.'[653]

Quite where she was to get this sort of money when she was living hand to mouth is not clear so she probably went to prison where she was fed and housed for nothing. In 1847:

'Two prostitutes Margaret Wilson and Mary Davies were committed for trial on a charge of robbing Richard Robinson of £21 [£1,268.76] at a house of ill fame in Skelthorne Street, Liverpool. Richard Robinson went home with one of the prostitutes on Wednesday evening and on leaving the house the following morning, missed his money, a portion of which was found concealed in a coal vault. Both prostitutes belonged to the house.'[654]

The beauty of common prostitutes faded fast due to the rough handling they received and they were more likely to die even sooner than the six years life expectancy of a common prostitute, most usually by drink, suicide or because they were murdered.

All these women, especially the higher-class prostitutes, spent money in Liverpool on shoes, corsets, silks, gowns, hats, feathers, food, drink, carriages, trains, entertainment. As there were many thousands of them, prostitutes' earnings contributed much to the profits of businesses in the city. Just how much was presented in a lecture in the *Music Room* on 3.6.1843 by the Reverend William Bevan, Minister of Newington Chapel in Liverpool,[3] with the help of many statistical tables to show just how extensive social evil was at that time.

Remarkably, he produced calculations using police and other figures, claiming:

'In 1842 each of the 2,899 prostitutes known to the police, [mostly common prostitutes, as the better class of sex worker did not come to the notice of the police], spent between £1 5 shillings [worth £75.52] and £1 10 shillings [£90.63] a week. When these amounts are applied to the 2,899 known to the police, it comes to between: £11,384,488 and £13,662,291] a year at current values, which is more than a small contribution to Liverpool's overall economy.

However, Bevan himself admits:

'This seems to be too low a rate. It cannot cover the expenses of their lodging, their dress and their wasteful outlay in eating and drinking.'

In other words, their spending power was much greater. He then moves to a different method of calculation, again using figures drawn from police sources, to produce an average amount spent on each visit by men on prostitutes. The results are startling, especially when these are added to the amount plundered by prostitutes robbing punters. He postulates that if: one shilling and sixpence [£4.53] was spent on the 53,900 visits a year, which I assume is a police estimate, then the total amount men spent on Liverpool's common prostitutes was £2,441,670 at current values.

As well, men visiting prostitutes also spent lavishly on alcohol. In 1901, a parliamentary inquiry[655] on the evil of drink found that 75% of sailors' money was spent on drink and women. Given the numbers of sailors a night in Liverpool this was an enormous amount of money being brought into port, then spent on and by the women, the brothel keepers and all those who provided goods and services, in effect laundering immoral earnings into the profits of wealthy businessmen in the city. On top of this was all the money earned by and spent on the higher class of prostitutes and those who were unknown to the police so again, Bevan's figures are only estimates.

---

[3] Chapter Four

He goes even further now to estimate how much money was stolen from men during their visits to prostitutes, crimes classed as 'robberies in brothels.' Using police figures and only those robberies reported to the police, and many were not due to embarrassment, he calculates they accounted for: £1,986 6 shillings a week [£120,007.29] or £103,272.00 [£6,239,384.42] a year.

Money generated by social evil therefore flowed relentlessly into Liverpool's economy and shops and suppliers were eager to do business with the brothel madams knowing how much spending power they had. Respectable Liverpool traders were very willing to supply jewellery to adorn higher class prostitutes as well as other costly items, and the madams ran up debts left, right and centre. Some naive businessmen even tried to take them to court just as they would any other debtor.

One case of this kind in 1853 exposed at best the gullibility of jewellers and at worst a complete lack of morals in how they made their money. It also kept the police and magistrates busy, provided lots of clients for Liverpool lawyers and amusement to the Liverpool citizens, for whom a free day in court watching the brothel madams wipe the floor with shop keepers was better than paying for a seat at the music hall.

In *Wells and Another v Wallace*, a newspaper report described 'An Extraordinary Defence.' The defendant Isabella Wallace was accused of owing £26 5 shillings [£2,106.89] to Charles and William Wells, jewellers and silversmiths of Bold Street, Liverpool, it being the balance owed on jewellery she had bought from them.[656]

Isabella unashamedly said she was not indebted, that the goods in question were sold to her to enable her to carry on the practice of prostitution and that Wells the jewellers looked to her to be paid the price and value of the goods out of the profits and money she received by prostituting her body. As that was against the law, she argued that Wells the jewellers could not legally recover the money from her. To be sure, she also laid another charge against them, that of actually inducing her to buy the jewels on this basis in the first place.

Wells denied he knew Isabella was a prostitute, saying he had believed her to be a boarding housekeeper at No 3 Blake Street, Liverpool. When she was at his shop, she always conducted herself respectably and nothing was ever said as to her calling. Wells also admitted he had lent jewellery to a woman called Polly Storer, who he believed was a respectable woman who lived in Russell Street. At this point there was much laughter in court.

When cross examined, he admitted he might have met Isabella at her house and that he also lent jewellery to Madam Anna:

'Who was a respectable woman as far as he knew...' [Howls of laughter].

In vain, he insisted that he did not know that jewellery lent to her was also used for the purposes of prostitution. The court heard that the law said:

'No man should trade on the immorality of another and that other a woman,' and Isabella's lawyer went for the jugular asking:

'Whether the gentleman who was known to Madam Anna, Polly Storer and Isabella Wallace, was so unsuspecting and simple minded that he could be ignorant of the character of the customers he was dealing with. There could be no doubt that such ornaments were supplied for different purposes than if they were purchased by merchant's wives and daughters to attend a respectable party at an evening ball.'

Isabella, when called, freely admitted 'she was a woman of loose character.' Polly Storer confirmed her occupation and that Wells lent her jewellery too. The lawyer could not say much after that apart from:

'The jury should not find his client guilty of perjury upon the evidence of two girls such as those who had been called.'

And, amazingly, he won, but the jeweller was the laughing stock of Liverpool.

There was a similar case reported on 13'4.1855 and this time, Madam Anna herself is in the dock. Samuel Lyons, a jeweller had lent her items and visited her brothel in Hotham Street. He too said he thought the house was a respectable one, to which there was even more laughter in court. He protested he had seen respectable people in the house and that Madam Anna was a respectable woman as far as he knew. He had to agree to take £25 [£2,004.65] in settlement against an item worth £100 [£8,018.61]. A few years later his business was bankrupt.

Busy lawyers and clever barristers were quite happy to be involved in the defence of Liverpool's brothel keepers for it was well paid work, one way or another, free publicity and an excellent opportunity to display their rapier wit as they got to poke fun at respectable businessmen who could not recognise a madam even when they visited their houses.

Other ingenious methods were used to avoid repayments. In a case brought in 1854, *Mendellsohn v Edwards*, the lawyer, Mr. Godfrey, tried a different tack. He wanted to show that Mendellsohn had sold articles of dress to the prostitutes in Edwards' brothel at No 18 Trafalgar Street, where Jane too had a brothel, knowing that the dresses would be used for the purposes of prostitution. They called Forrester, a young woman to prove the practice of the profession in regard to dress.

She explained that the brothel keepers in Liverpool were in the habit of dressing the girls who board in their houses, purchasing clothes for them at exorbitant prices from people like Mendellsohn, then disposing of them to their lodgers at a large profit. But Mr. Godfrey's efforts were in vain as the judge said Edwards still had to pay the bill.[657]

In 1857, Mrs. Green, a brothel keeper turned a very neat trick, alleging that her goods were seized in execution of a warrant against Catherine Seaton, also a brothel keeper, who featured in Chapter 29 and rented a house in Hotham Street from her.[658] Catherine Seaton had some time previously, when she lived in Pellew Street, another brothel street, owned the furniture in that house and incurred a debt in the course of her business to a milliner for £164 [£13,150.52] which she did not pay off. A Mrs. Stevens took Catherine Seaton to court to recover the money.

Catherine wanted to protect the assets she had, in other words her furniture, so she came to an arrangement with Mrs. Green, who agreed to transfer it all from Pellew Street to a house in Warren Street. Between them they set up a mock sale of her furniture to Mrs. Green and Catherine attended the court case being able to truthfully say she had sold the furniture to Mrs. Green.

The judge could only decree that the furniture seized in Mrs. Green's house to pay Catherine Seaton's debts to the milliner was in fact the property of Mrs. Green, and she was entitled to have it returned. The milliner lost and Catherine was no doubt grateful to Mrs. Green and at some point, discretely got her furniture back.

You couldn't make this up! But it is striking to see how similar this case was to Jane's various efforts to hang onto her furniture. Brothel madams were also not averse to calling in favours and taking advantage of the fact that nobody dare mess with them, like Madam Anna did in 1859,[4] and Jane did successfully for years, well at least up to 1862.

It is therefore clear many businessmen, whether brothel clients or not, some of them on the council, had thinly disguised vested business interests in the spinoffs of social evil. The council itself owned the leaseholds of numerous city centre proprieties, collecting rent from many brothel keepers on a regular basis. One such brothel keeper bought the leasehold of a council property at auction in 1889 to house six ladies who regularly solicited at the American bars and music halls, then conducted clients to the property where they entertained and sold unlicensed drinks.[659]

A couple of businessmen councillors, over time, chaired the Watch Committee, which determined the priorities of the police, and collectively they set laws at a city level and had power over licencing the sale of alcohol. They also included amongst their number men who ran large Liverpool breweries. As we well know, the Victorians

---

[4] Chapter Twenty

liked to drink and they lived in a society geared towards alcohol consumption so it is no surprise to find that brewers' businesses expanded as fast as the port of Liverpool.

'Most sailors arriving in this town become intoxicated within the first 18 hours and some are deadly drunk before they are ashore one hour. The moment he lands he proceeds to draw his pay, receiving, according to the voyage, from £10 - £100 [approximately £600 - £6,0000.] Low lodging house keepers, slop clothiers, prostitutes and others are on the look - out to ease him of his cash, and the more quickly it is done the better.[660]

'There was almost no escaping the beer houses, gin palaces, refreshment rooms, restaurants, theatres, music halls, vaults, dram shops, oyster bars, private clubs and public houses that served a dizzying array of alcoholic drinks to suit people from all walks of life. Drinking went on from dawn till dusk and on into the wee small hours.'

'In Liverpool in a week more beer is drunk than in Scotland in a year,' said the *Liverpool Mail* on 23.7.1853.

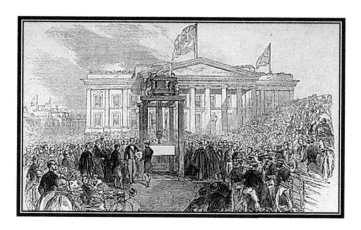

Figure 84 Prince Albert lays the foundation stone of the Sailor's Home

In the streets and alleys around the docks there were plenty of places where 'Seamen's Lodgings' were to be had, at an exorbitant charge, where the sailor would be fed and bedded, after a fashion, and many of these lodging houses were notorious.

It was therefore decided to build a Sailors' Home on Canning Street, Liverpool on the nearest dry land to the docks, to provide not only safe board and lodging but also a bank, medical facilities and a register of good character which allowed ship owners to find suitable crewmen.[661]

The foundation stone was laid by Prince Albert in 1846 but the building did not open to boarders until December 1852. Inside, the home could hold 500 men in its wooden cabins which were arranged on six floors overlooking a central hall. Each gallery had an ornamental cast-iron railing decorated in alternate layers with rope-work or mermaids. An ornamental stone over-throw with its magnificent Liver Bird was installed to prevent sailors from climbing over the gates into the home after curfew. However, in April 1860, there was a disastrous fire which caused the building to be closed for two years while the interior was rebuilt.

Ostensibly, the building provided board and lodgings to thousands of merchant seamen, but it also provided a focal point for public houses and eager prostitutes, somewhere to catch sailors before they parted with their money to others, as where better to entice seamen than the Sailors' Home right on the dockside?

How much did they spend on drink? There are figures for the estimated expenditure for working men which show that from the 2,912 drinking establishments in the town in 1864, if they took approximately £2 [£118.26] overall a day, which many felt was an underestimation, it would come to £2,125,760 [£125,694,488.19] a year paid out in drink by the lower classes.[662] Not all that was profit but it was still a great deal of money from the pockets of those who could little afford it, money which poured into the coffers of the main brewers in Liverpool.

As a result, 30 years later in 1889, Liverpool had a higher level of drunkenness than any other town in England and was the worst seaport. Putting all the commercial ports together, Liverpool had two-fifths of the population and nearly fourth-fifths of the drunken cases. In the 1870s, a Liberal MP Samuel Smith declared that:

> 'No city in the kingdom suffered so much from drunkenness and squalid vice.'
> And a visitor from France said: 'I know no place where drunkenness is so flaunted, so impudent, not only in the crooked side streets and mean courtyards where one expects to find it, but everywhere.'[663]

The *Popular Control and Licencing Reform Association's* maps of Liverpool[664] and police statistics presented to the House of Lords inquiry on Intemperance in 1877 show an overall increase in drunken arrests in the city from 11,439 in 1857 to 20,551 in 1876.[665] Other evidence at this enquiry came from William Sproston Caine, a Liberal MP and pro temperance campaigner who held radical views on prohibition. He was concerned about the social and health costs of drink and argued there was a direct link between the numbers of pubs and the death rates in certain areas of Liverpool.[666]

The minister for Liverpool prison, the Reverend James Nugent provided more data in his 1877 report on Liverpol borough gaol which showed that the majority of inmates were imprisoned for drink related crimes, some being repeat offenders having been in prison fifty, sixty or seventy times and that the prison was overcrowded with women of Irish descent who lived and worked in around the Liverpool Docks making their living through prostitution. Nugent described these women as ruthless in their pursuit of sailors who would provide them with food, shelter and drink.[667]

And what were those with power, influence and money doing about it? Sadly, too many were busy shaping municipal decisions to protect their profits, raising rhetorical arguments which proclaimed to be about the public good but were more suited to private gain, and laundering their immoral earnings in charitable donations, good works and subscriptions to public buildings as a sop to their consciences.

By 1871, there were many concerns about drink and immorality around the Sailor's Home. One Monday morning alone, eighteen women were brought before the court for soliciting there. The magistrate, after imposing fines and sending some prison, said:

'You were in that part of the town where you were least wanted - that is to say, where you may do the most mischief. What is the use of calling a place the Sailor's Home if it is to be besieged by you bad women?'[668]

A few years later in 1876, a communication from the Church of England, of all places stated that:

'On a certain night in the Spring, 102 prostitutes passed through a certain public house without touching a drink between the hours of nine and eleven pm.' This was backed up by a letter from a respectable gentleman who stated that: 'On 25th September, 148 girls passed through a public house without tasting or ordering a drink.'

Shop owners protested that the temptations to drink and lust were permitted to exist contrary to the law and demanded the Watch Committee take action.[669] But they were up against powerful brewers, like Walkers, Cains and Archibald Salvidge,[670] vice chairman of Brents Brewery in Liverpool, a conservative city councillor and a prominent freemason.

Andrew Barclay Walker followed his father, who had been brewing in Liverpool since 1836, in a partnership known as Peter Walker and Son in the late 1840s.[671] In 1879, he gained control of the business on the death of his father, turning it in 1890 into a public company, Walkers of Warrington, which was run from Duke Street in Liverpool, despite being a Warrington Company.[672]

By 1860, Liverpool had more full licenses for the sale of wine and spirits as well as beer than Manchester, and common brewers were subsumed into larger companies which meant that fewer and fewer companies controlled all the beer houses in the town. These brewers, like Walkers, were highly dependent on seamen for trade, acquired large pubs to cope with the massive influx of sailors on the docks and the centre of Liverpool where it was reported:

> 'Some of the brewers owning dockside houses have an organisation by which, when vessels are due to arrive, squads of barmen are drafted to the premises, where it is known the normal trade will for a certain period be doubled or even trebled.[673]

> 'If in the month of December 1864, the licensed public houses and beer shops in the borough of Liverpool had formed one unbroken line of buildings like some grand terrace, then the measure of that line of buildings would have been upwards of eleven and a half miles; and if the first in this line of houses were placed on the shore of Toxteth Park [in the town centre], the last in the line would be found at some point more than half way between Liverpool and Southport.'

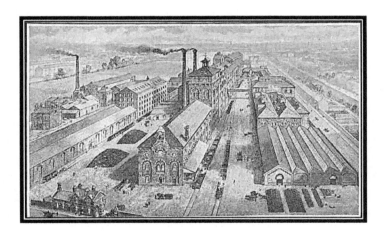

Figure 85 Walkers of Warrington by Alfred Barnard 1890

And where there's drink and sailors, there are also eager prostitutes, all hungry enough to relieve them of their pay and valuables, and folk willing to pay for their votes. In the 1879 elections in Liverpool, candidate John Hampson was charged with bribery and unduly influencing voters with evidence given of his agents giving voters free drinks in a Walker pub at the top of Brunswick Street in Liverpool.[674] Candidate

T.H Sheen was also charged with allowing his agents to bribe voters in St Anne's ward in a Walker's pub at the corner of Queen Anne Street.[675] They were both found guilty and their elections were declared null and void. [676]

Walker was a Deputy Lieutenant of Lancashire and the elected Lord Mayor of Liverpool for 1873 and 1876 and appointed High Sheriff of Lancashire for 1886 – 1887. His first action as High Sheriff was to appoint his solicitor and the future chair of the police Watch Committee, John Hughes, as undersheriff.[677] Hughes was also solicitor for Cain's Brewery.

The prestigious Walker Art Gallery was funded from the proceeds of the many Walker's Brewery licenced public houses in Liverpool, which in turn supplied all types of brothels and contributed to the huge problem of the 'demon drink' in the town. Civic philanthropy and pride were therefore in people's minds forever associated with the profits of drunkenness.[678] When the art gallery opened a very pointed cartoon was drawn by Harold Furniss, commissioned allegedly by the Liverpool Liberal councillor for St Anne's Ward, Ronald Mc Dougall.[679] It uses hard facts as well as graphics to show the misery endured by ordinary people whose money, spent on drink, funded the fine edifice:

- 52,874 people were brought before the Liverpool Justices in 1876 on drink related charges

- 8,804 drunken females were charged and 167 children overlain - died of suffocation when drunken parents inadvertently smothered them as they turned over in bed

- There were 1,183 arrests for assaults on police and 177 stabbings'[680]

- In addition, there were 472 brothels known to the police and 6,599 paupers relieved that year

- The 2,318 licensed places for drink in Liverpool produced 23,706 drunkards and the costs of 809 drink related inquests were £1,907 [£19,395.36]

- 1,206 prostitutes were known to police and 6,109 arrests were made of prostitutes in 1876 which resulted in overcrowding in prisons

Walker's efforts to buy respectability by burying his profits in charitable schemes did not end there as he, in 1886, offered £15,000 [£992,770.50] for a school of technical education and in 1887, £10,000 [£661,847.00] to fund a new Liverpool Cathedral. The newspapers were not reticent in their censure. The *Liverpool Porcupine* proclaimed:

'The city now had two godfathers - the "Slave Owner and the Drink Seller,"' saying Walker had 'scattered his gifts' across the city and that 'we shall have to drink ourselves into a cathedral, if we want one.'[681]

It was for these outcomes that he was knighted in 1877 and created Baronet Walker of Gateacre, Lancaster in 1886.[682] In 1890, Walker is referred to as a 'beer king' by Ben Tillet, a union man, who spent a week in Liverpool, saying Walker: 'presided over a beer caucus with seventy houses almost together in one street, which the men and women of the beer sodden city of Liverpool could not get rid of. The magistrates of the city were brewers or held shares in brewery concerns.'[683]

Figure 86 Peter Walker and Son, Share Certificate

Along with *Robert Cain and Sons*, Walker dominated the pubs of Liverpool in this period, adopting a new system of ownership, employing managers to run them. This worked in Liverpool but attempts to try the system elsewhere failed miserably, which led to Cains taking over Walkers after the first world war to become *Walker Cain* and power shifted to the Cain family. You can see here that *Walter Cain Ltd* owned one million five hundred thousand pounds worth of stock in Peter Walker's breweries and that Walker's was worth at that time £3.5m.[684] Conclusions that the vested interests of brewers were protected by their men in power were difficult to avoid and newspapers pointed out many instances.

The Liverpool Review on 3.1.1891 argued that it was hypocrisy for the Tory councillor John Houlding of *Brent's Brewery*, of which councillor Archibald Salvidge was the vice chairman, to vote to keep the Walker Art Gallery closed on a Sunday as a matter of principle when he opened his public houses as a matter of business.

By 1889, John Hughes' vested interests as chair of the police Watch Committee came to the fore as he was the solicitor both to Walker's and Robert Cain's breweries and Walker's previous appointee as under-sheriff of Lancaster, when he defended the policy of tolerating zones for brothels, saying it prevented the dispersal of prostitutes across the city. [685]

Religious leaders were outspoken too. Reverend Richard Acland Armstrong, Unitarian minister and temperance activist, stated in 1890 what many firmly believed, that social evil and the brewery trade worked hand in glove. He claimed that prostitutes met their customers in pubs and would hire a cab, which specialised in catering for immoral activities, to leave with their customers and after a night working the streets, prostitutes went back to the pubs and spent most of their earnings there. He came to the conclusion that:

> 'Prostitution is an essential element in building up the mighty fortunes which many of our public house proprietors enjoy. There was nothing less than the knitting together of the wholesale liquor trade, of drunkenness and of prostitution on an enormous scale in one vast compact interest which reached right to the top of the governing body of Liverpool.' [686]

He talked of a pyramid of vice, from the brewers, like Walker, outwardly respectable, pillars of Liverpool philanthropy; through to the publicans who ran the licensed premises; the landlords who accepted rent paid with immoral earnings, including the council, to the brothel madams like Jane Gallagher skimming off profits, safely at a distance, working through those who managed each house, the pimps and bullies of whatever class.

'They all,' he said, 'lived off the backs of prostitutes.'

None of this was new as even back in 1857 there were loud demands to tackle the owners of houses rented out as brothels, as this letter to the editor shows:

'In a street not a hundred miles from Norton Street, a house that formerly commanded a rent from a respectable tenant of £30 [£2,405.58] a year, and which has since changed hands as regards ownership, is now converted into a common brothel and £5 [£400.93] per month is received, just double the former rent. There is another set of persons of this description, who use bribe money and they never quit the houses as long as they have sons. Such dangerous villains ought to be found out...

'What is to prevent detectives sifting and finding out the proprietors of these filthy kennels? They must naturally know where they exist and knowing the whereabouts of each den. Why not summon the owners at once before the bench of magistrates, who have the power and the means of dealing with them?' [687]

But it was not until the law changed in 1885 that the council and the police had any power to do this. Unfortunately, at the same time, the council were made publicly and painfully aware that they too were taking money regularly from brothel keepers. A series of charges appeared in the *Liverpool Mercury* in May 1885, laid by a Liverpool magistrate, Tom Matheson, in a 'sensational' letter to the editor. Its first allegation was:

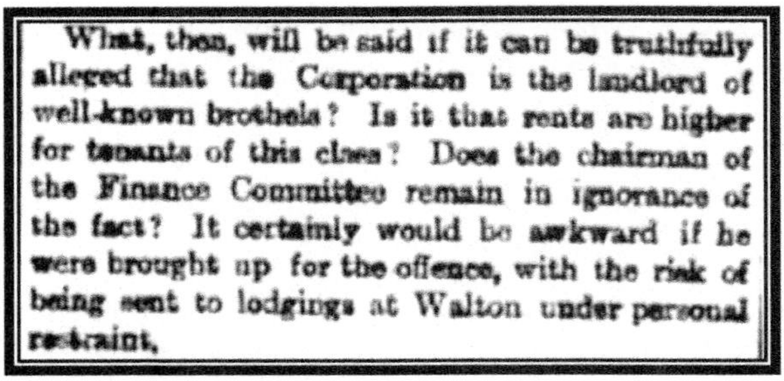

> What, then, will be said if it can be truthfully alleged that the Corporation is the landlord of well-known brothels? Is it that rents are higher for tenants of this class? Does the chairman of the Finance Committee remain in ignorance of the fact? It certainly would be awkward if he were brought up for the offence, with the risk of being sent to lodgings at Walton under personal restraint.

Figure 87 Liverpool Mercury 18.5.1885

Walton is the name of a Liverpool prison.

This charge caused an immediate backlash in the press as councillors sprang to protect the council's finances, reputation and their own business interests. Only a few supported Matheson. A response the same day was set out in a later edition of the *Liverpool Mercury* by Sir James Picton on behalf of the council promising to investigate.

But why had Matheson chosen to act now? Well, the *Criminal Law Amendment Act* of 1885[688] had just become law and said:

'Any person who kept, managed, or assisted in the management of premises used as a brothel, or was the tenant or landlord of such premises, was liable to a hefty fine or a maximum of three months' imprisonment.'

Matheson's letter to the *Liverpool Mercury*[689] raised the uncomfortable question of who was going to prosecute the council for allowing their disreputable tenants to run brothels? The Watch Committee along with the police who were controlled by them, were responsible for enacting the law but Thomas Matheson declared:

'Hitherto they have declined to do so, except under certain conditions... and the responsibility for allowing things to remain so abominably bad in Liverpool rests therefore with the Watch Committee.'

His charges were not only that the council knowingly permitted its houses to be used for immoral purposes but also that:

- The police knew the character of these houses

- Legal evidence had been given in proof by police constables and yet tenants were not prosecuted, the reason being that the Watch Committee would not sanction a prosecution unless a disturbance or other special circumstances occur

- The head constable stated the police preferred having people and such houses together in order to better control them and he would not interfere

- The council were receiving the wages of iniquity in that they did not take steps to clear obnoxious tenants out

Matheson was savaged by those with wealth and vested interests and dubbed 'Morality Tom' but he had many supporters among the respectable people of Liverpool and they would not let the matter drop.[690]

'I live in a respectable street and there is an immoral house next door to mine and situated opposite to a public school. I have complained many times to the superintendent of the police division of the district. The last time I wrote he paid me a personal visit and then told me that if I wrote any more letters, he would not notice them.'

And on 5.6.1888, the *Liverpool Association for the Suppression of Immorality* waded into the fray using their third annual meeting as a platform to memorialise [petition] the council as owners of property tenanted by immoral persons, as an opening salvo in the legal process for bringing them to court. Their memorial said:

'The alleged and uncontradicted fact that the Corporation of Liverpool, representing the rate payers, are owners of property in which there are numbers of houses known to be brothels... [we are] praying for them to free themselves and the citizens from this crying evil and shame, and instruct the Watch Committee to put in force the Criminal Law Amendment Act against immoral houses throughout Liverpool.'[691]

The council had been caught with their pants down and attempted, unconvincingly, to claim that actually, it was not their fault:

'It should be understood that the Corporation were not altogether to blame in this matter. The Corporation held a large part of the town as its freehold property and years ago leases were given. In the course of time some of those leases had expired; and so, it happened recently a number of those leases expired in certain districts of the town where those houses [brothels] abounded. When they came into possession, they [the Corporation] did not inquire too minutely into the character of their tenants. They collected the rents as if they were ordinary houses.'[692]

The *Liverpool Association for the Suppression of Immorality* wrote to the Town Clerk, Mr. Edward Samuel Smith MP, one of its supporters, raising this issue and he replied that it was not the case and that they were misinformed. Thus, the battle lines were drawn and on 5.6.1888 the *Association* were back on the attack:[693]

'The Corporation are owners of many houses in Pellew Street and Seagrave Street which are used as brothels and there are children in some of these houses... This is a grave public scandal and extremely discreditable to the Corporation... Once [a house] is let, it be conceded that the Corporation of Liverpool countenances immoral tenants of their own property and disorderly houses acquire a legality, a sanction and a security of footing that is generally supposed, in England at any rate, to be withheld.'

They point out it is little good their society setting up homes for young girls at risk, training homes and the like if:

'Liverpool ratepayers themselves allow evil to take a deeper and more secure root in the town.' A resolution was passed which said: 'They had a right to demand, as citizens, that this matter should be investigated to the bottom, that censure should be awarded wherever it was deserved and that this scandal and disgrace, in which all citizens were implicated, should be wiped out.'

On the same page of the *Liverpool Mercury*, the same day and in the adjoining column was an item called: 'The City Council in which Alderman Edward Samuel Smith resigned from the Finance Committee,' which dealt with council's rents and leases. The day after, 7th June, Mr. B. Smith for the Finance Committee, not Edward Samuel Smith the Town Clerk, was reported in the *Liverpool Mercury* confirming again the Finance Committee on behalf of the council were landlords for those properties referred to in Pellew and Seagrave Street, Liverpool but that the property came into their possession before last year [1887].

'The leases had lapsed and naturally the Finance Committee took possession and collected the rents. They put the property up for auction last year and part of it was sold. As to the character of the tenants they had no knowledge whatever.'

Really?

'Such was the state of affairs until last month [May 1888] when Mr. Thomas Hughes [previous chair of the Finance Committee] made in council the statement that he knew that the Corporation were the owners of brothels. He did not know the legal effect if it was true and consequently, he requested at the next Finance Committee that the surveyor at once to bring before the committee plans showing all the property they owned to which the character given to them by Mr. Hughes might be fairly considered applicable [that they were brothels]. This was done and the committee decided to give notice to all tenants to get vacant possession in order to sell the property.'

Therefore, the original denial by the Town Clerk was untrue. Not only that, but the current denial that the Finance Committee had only recently known was also untrue as well, as Thomas Hughes was quick to point out:

'He was amazed that Mr. Smith claimed he had only just got to know the Corporation were receiving rents from brothels.' He went on to remind Mr. Smith that:

'Only recently that Mr. Coleman, the surveyor who was the receiver of the rents had raised the question as to what his position would be in case he was taxed with the offence of receiving rents from prostitutes. In other words, he wanted a guarantee from the committee that they would hold him good against any proceedings that might be taken against him. That was how he, Mr. Hughes, got his knowledge and asked the question in committee. Mr. Smith knew some months ago at the same time as he did that this was the case.'

The discussions at Finance Committee then, predictably, moved away from this embarrassment and Mr. Coleman's concerns to financial issues and what the wealthy councillors were really bothered about: the impact of selling these properties would have on their budget and their businesses. The social reformers wanted the clearing out of tenants to include those who lived adjacent to such houses, in order to improve the integrity of the area, but, legally, they could not do this. The money men even worried that evicting brothel tenants would mean they would encamp somewhere else in the city, maybe even in their own neighbourhoods! Councillors were simply unable to get away from comments like:

'I fail to see any difference in money taken from these people, whether it is in rates or rents, it is still the wages of sin.'

Caught out and in the act, they prevaricated. The discussion was held over until 14th June,[694] weeks after Tom Matheson's letter to the editor, and Sir James Picton then put forward his motion for a full investigation to the council.

However, nothing turned out as he expected, given the previous support he had enjoyed leading up to this meeting, as the argument in the meantime had shifted into one about the police policy of keeping immoral houses in zones or designated areas. One notable speaker claimed it was not the business of the council or Sir James

Picton to require an inquiry into Tom Matheson's claims, but up to Tom Matheson himself to provide the evidence. In other words, they should do nothing!

The blood of vested interests was up, and their allies including that of Mr. Smith of the Finance Committee who had been caught out in the previous session, who said:

'If the Corporation only accepted tenants of the highest moral rectitude they would have to pay for those gentlemen. The rents of the Corporation were already going down; and soon some of these good people would be able to make their own terms. It would be a most serious thing for the Corporation if this motion was passed.'

And that is it in a nutshell. When money meets morals and community well-being, there is no contest. Sir James Picton was horrified.

'He had been long enough in the Council to be astonished at nothing; but if he were capable of astonishment, he should be vehemently astonished at the turn the discussion had taken. It had been strongly in favour of his motion, yet, after denouncing in the strongest terms the present state of things, all the speakers intimated that they would not support him.'[695]

His motion was rejected 25 votes to 4 and the matter closed, apart from a meeting of magistrates reported in the *Liverpool Echo* on 27.6.1888 which decided to set up a Select Committee of Magistrates to enquire into the state of laws affecting houses of ill fame. Some of those who voted against the motion included:

Sir James Knight JP, Ship Owner

G.H .Ball, Tobacco Broker

F.M. Robert, Wine and Spirit Merchant

Charles J. Preston, Magistrate

Patrick Houlding, Gentleman

J.R. Smith, Exotic Carpet Merchant

Sylvester Mattison, Gentleman

R Montague, Solicitor for the railway

William Radcliffe, JP with an office in Commerce Court

Sir James Poole, the Mayor

However, in 1891 another newspaper report followed detailing a Finance Committee meeting, exposing more about the council's dealings with the immoral houses they rented out to brothel keepers. A Mr. Watts said it was in respect of Pellew Street, where from 14.1.1887 to 18.6.1888 they had been drawing rent from a 'house employed for immoral purposes' that he wanted to speak.[696] 'Where's that?' asked one member of the committee. For your benefit Mr. Councillor, from the bottom right-hand corner of Lime Street station, Pellew Street runs parallel to Copperas Hill.

Mr. Watts continued, reminding the committee that a short time ago the Finance Committee said they had no property of this kind and the council appear to have cleared the tenants out over a period of two days, but:

'After selling the property to a woman of very vile character, the Finance Committee had since had the dishonesty to prosecute her for keeping the house as a house of ill fame.'

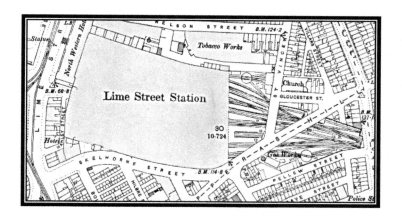

Figure 88 Pellew Street, Liverpool 1893 OS 25" map

Embarrassing, as was the explanation that:

'A woman, supposed to be respectable, signed the contract.'

It then came out there were seven of these houses and they had been occupied for 18 months during which time they had been offered for auction once or twice.

They continued to writhe and wriggle.

'If punishment is to fall, let it be on the men who bring these women into this wretched state of life. A good few of the men who support these houses are members of the Liverpool Exchange. Why not punish them?'

This was deflected by a request for a current return of how many houses of this type the council rented and a reply from the superintendent of rents for the council which said he was not aware of any such house at present being used for immoral purposes, and that was the best information they could get.

> 'They were only carrying out the policy the public asked them to carry out and had simply looked upon the property concerned from an estate point of view. If they were told that, before they sold a property, they were to inquire into the moral character of the purchaser, he protested against such a burden being imposed upon them.'

Gathering some courage, this very brave or foolish person ended saying he wanted someone else to do it and proposed setting up a subcommittee for the purpose, a tactic used still to this day to avoid doing anything. But no-one wanted to take this on and the arguments continued, alluding to the 'Purity Party' of which one of their number was a member. This led to farce, showing just what sort of puerile wit over-grown school boys produce when they are weary of boring but serious debate:

> 'If he talked about one party as the "Purity Party," then the opposite party must be called the "Impurity Party."' [Laughter.]

> 'I think two little words should be added – the 'so called "Purity Party"' [More laughter].

> '"Purity" has been withdrawn.' [Renewed laughter.]

Eventually, as it must have been time for a drink, they agreed on a new clause in future leases providing against a property being put to immoral use, and that was the end of it.

However, this clause had been in council leases since the beginning of 1800, a fact no one seemed to recall.

Chapter 34 - 'Anything, in fact, with walls and a ceiling'

Gentlemen -
There is some deep unsoundness in time
When it stares ever at the sins of women
And let's its men alone
Liverpool Mercury 1.10.1891

We have seen how even public exposure of vested interests had done little to reduce social evil in Liverpool and that the law was still pretty impotent as far as ridding Victorian society of immorality, as only a minority of those in power were willing to combine their forces to combat both it and drunkenness. Even magistrates continued to turn a blind eye to the memorials of concerned citizens until the newly empowered press started to advocate for them.

Whilst the police used the *1852 Common Lodging House Act*, which allowed them to inspect premises to disrupt their businesses, some brothel owners claimed their houses were private residences which were outside the terms of the act. Respected gentlemen in their turn, were quite willing to negotiate tenancies then hand them over to madams who developed them as brothels, in return for a share of the profits, or services in kind.

The police from the 1860s then changed their strategy to targeting prostitutes in public establishments and venues, using the *Contagious Diseases Acts* against common prostitutes, thus clearing whole streets in the 1870s but this only shifted social evil to other areas. Growing support for the repeal of the *Contagious Diseases Acts* was eclipsed in the 1880s by the vigorous efforts of Social Purity supporters who started to promote less than liberal approaches, from the reform of common prostitutes who came forward voluntarily, in favour of coercion via the law. Indeed, it is thought that this change in their priorities contributed to the creation of a 'wild and often discriminatory repressive policy towards social evil.'[697]

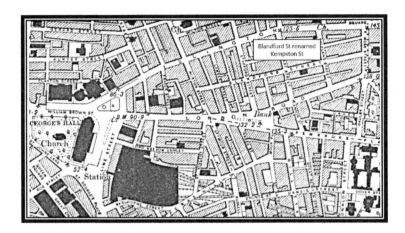

Figure 89 Blandford Street, Liverpool,1851 OS 6" map

In 1885, Liverpool council tried to localised four hundred brothels into one area where they were to be tolerated but a magistrate's report of 1889 concluded that although the police dealt firmly with street prostitution, there was still as much social evil in the designated zones, such as Blandford Street, near London Road and Lime Street station, and where Jane had No 6 in 1875. The area became so notorious it was later renamed Kempston Street. The newspapers, however, continued to pile on the pressure on behalf of their readers: [698]

> 'Much has apparently been done of late in this but as yet I am afraid a great deal of it has only been to compel the removal of brothels from one locality to another, instead of actually closing them. And in some cases, through the collusion of landlords or their agents, brothel keepers have actually only made an exchange of residence, while at the same time obeying to the very letter the notice to quit.'[699]

Meanwhile, the customer base had grown massively in the previous decade. By 1886, the numbers of seamen in Liverpool at any one time had risen to between 40,000 - 50,000 most of whom were low paid and could not afford to marry so resorted to prostitutes. Drink and social evil continued to feed each other and in the *Porcupine*[700] in September 1889, a series of articles by Harry Whiteman called 'Gay Life in Liverpool' argued it was the informal unlicensed drinking in the tolerated brothel zones that should be targeted, as this was where prostitutes spent 90% of their earnings, and not the properly licensed pubs. Whiteman also accused the temperance hotels of being a cover for brothels and went on to prove it with an enterprising investigative report showing how he had been to one and tried to hire a girl and before the deed was done, 'made his excuses' and left in the time honoured tradition of the best *News of the World* reporters in the 1970s.[701]

Next, Whiteman turned his fire onto the council's seeming inaction against social evil and the performance of their servants, the police, via the Watch Committee. He exposed an unlicensed drinking den in police headquarters in Hatton Garden in Liverpool, known to senior officers, where policemen were consuming up to £100 [£6,618.47] of beer a month, often on credit against their wages.[702] The coverage was extensive and the headlines you can well imagine.

A subsequent investigation by John Hughes, chair of the police Watch Committee, Walker's man, showed that the old store at Hatton Garden was opened to provide the police 'the necessaries of life' without having to send out for them while they were on duty. Nothing wrong with that, Hughes said. Another charge was that outsiders were allowed to use the unlicensed facility but Hughes maintained that while this was correct:

'The irregularities were by no means serious in the extent and were due to a laxity in supervision.'

Hughes recommended that the head constable set up a management committee for the place and make it a 'social club' where friends and members would be allowed to 'partake of hospitality' only to a limited extent, saying there would be no cause for complaint once this was in place.[703]

But after Harry Whiteman reported a senior police detective who had accepted a free bowl of soup and a sliced of boiled mutton in a brothel in Blandford Street,[704] the powers that be must have decided enough was enough and sued him for libel. This case turned the tables on Whiteman when a police inspector stated he was mixed up with women of ill fame, one of whom was sitting in the court room, and that Whiteman was a married man. The court sent him to prison for one month, discredited and shamed.[705] The police must have been chortling in the aisles as Harry was forced in public to 'sweep his own doorstep.'

Campaigning journalists were not daunted and Whiteman's reports marked a new era in public exposures in newspapers. Investigative articles were beginning to be an effective tool for exposing injustice and these journalists pulled no punches.

The *Liverpool Review* successfully campaigned on behalf of an Everton neighbourhood severely affected by one street's brothel tenants.[706]

'In July 1888, Howat Street had not long since been a very respectable area but of late, it has become such a social scandal that it is necessary that public attention should be directed to it.'

They printed a letter to the editor which claimed that since action taken by the *Society for the Prevention of Immorality* the street had become a hot-bed of vice and immorality as 'common brothels moved from one area had come to rest in their neighbourhood.'[707] The letter writer owned a block of property off Howat Street, all let to decent working people, who complained bitterly, he said, of the insults and annoyances their wives and children were subjected to. Prostitutes had even dragged into one of their houses a young man who was returning home with his wages, but fortunately they were foiled as he was helped by friends to escape. It appears this was a common occurrence.

He went further, saying that the police, 'as usual are quiescent and it is commonly believed they are bribed.' Another rumour heard from a scripture reader, which was believed by the neighbourhood, was that Howat Street was meant by the police to be allowed to become the haunt of these characters as there were at least twelve houses in the street known to be:

> 'Of bad character and a petition had been got up urging the police to take legal proceedings against the "black sheep" who will let their houses to any characters as long as they get their rents.'

The *Liverpool Review* conducted their own independent investigation and reported:

> 'The women located in Howat Street are of a dangerous class. With few exceptions they are filthy in their habits and appearance. They are of all ages, some of them mere girls, others old, bloated and lazy looking, but all bearing sickening evidence of debauchery. From what can be seen through the open doors, the houses are as filthy and uninviting as their occupiers. Bits of furniture; dirty, tawdry blinds; dirty, greasy floors; and scraps of food with a collection of ale bottles, seemed to be common to the kitchens of nearly all the houses.

> 'All the roads surrounding Howat Street are infested at night time by different girls, who alternately perambulate or keep house or prey on pedestrians. Young children in the neighbourhood are being contaminated and there are dozens of the little things playing about every day, and when the woman who appears to be a general servant and messenger for the "colony" is not about, they are induced to go errands for the colonists who give them halfpence for their trouble.

> 'A more serious charge made by many of the neighbours is that one or two of the police are in league with the women and pay much more attention to what they have to say than they pay to respectable residents. On investigation it appears that one specific charge can be substantiated at least and that is of a constable going into one of the most notorious houses in the middle of the night.'

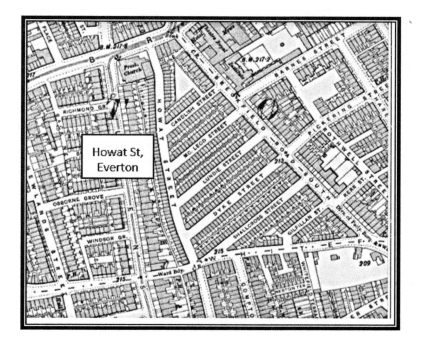

Figure 90 Howat Street, Everton, North Liverpool OS 25" 1892-1915

However, it was weeks later in August before the *Liverpool Review* were able to report that:

'Owing to the combined action of the police and landlords, twenty-four of the immoral houses had been cleared of their tenants and the street was in a much better state.'

Eventually they identified as many as thirty houses occupied by courtesans of the lowest type:

'Whose open and unabashed solicitations were the talk of the neighbourhood. Notwithstanding that some of the landlords of the houses have had the tenements cleaned down, the property is only letting anew very slowly. Several parties of the evicted tenants and others of the same class have made a determined attempt to get back again, roundly declaring that if they do, they'll "take good care nobody shifts them."

'In one case, a man who professed to be a "gentleman" and a "musician" succeeded in securing a house for two of the late tenants, but they were cleared out again in less than forty-eight hours owing to the house being secured by false pretences. It appears that three policemen are now living in Howat Street, the landlords having taken them as tenants on a reduced scale so as to keep an eye to the well-being of the thoroughfare. With the departure of the women and all appertaining to them, the neighbourhood has improved.'

But did this tactic of mass closures work? The *Liverpool Citizen* in 1888[708] showed that closing immoral houses simply makes them unknown to police, purges on drinking establishments drives the problem underground and the *Liverpool Mercury* by 1892[709] was still arguing that social evil could not be stopped unless you tackled the scourge of alcohol and the spread of drinking dens. Joint working continued to be an elusive aspiration and:

'Philanthropists make the mistake of working separately instead of unitedly,' the *Liverpool Review* were still saying five years later in 1893.

They alleged the police: 'Leave many loopholes of escape for the better class of unfortunates while they exercise scant courtesy towards the more wretched, that the approaches to social evil are piecemeal and that the evil should be rooted out "Trunk and Root," not merely shifted from place to place.

'Let all differences of creed be put aside and all join in the crusade against this giant evil. Let the government do its share, faithfully, consistently and well. Finally, so educate public opinion that vice shall be vice equally in a man as in a woman; in the bejewelled creature who rides in her brougham as well as the wretched creature in the streets who sells her womanhood for bread.'

At last, people are beginning to realise the problem was not the supply of personal services but the demands of men and the *Liverpool Mercury*, brave enough to push boundaries, published a whole series of letters from a woman called Esperanza between 1891 - 1892 which championed the rights of women and the emancipation campaign. She, the wife of a vicar, dared to suggest that men should be prosecuted for using the services of women.

'Never a man amongst all the purity crusaders has been manly enough to attack his own sex in the police courts, where thousands of women have been fined and convicted and evicted, for offences that would be impossible but for the conduct of men, the men who go scot free.'[710]

Even the head constable, Nott-Bower, was coming round by 1889 to what women like Josephine Butler said nearly thirty years previously about the *Contagious Diseases Acts of 1860*:

'It is a fatuous belief that you can oblige human beings to be moral by force, and in so doing that you may in some way promote social purity.'[711]

Or as he put it:

'Liverpool is a seaport with a population consisting of largely seamen, foreigners, and that floating class of young men, free from all restraint of home life, often with much money to spend, who cannot be made moral by act of parliament.'[712]

And a notable brothel keeper in 1893 speaking candidly to the Liverpool Review said:[713]

'I answer your question honestly when I say there is not the least improvement in Liverpool such as the raids on women were intended to produce. Why, there is not a place of public amusement in the whole of the city which is not utilised night after night by some class of women or other for assignations; even the newspapers as you know, are daily made the medium of some meeting or other; you will find a batch of them in some editions.

'Risk? Well, where the risk is great, so much is the fee the heavier. But it is not worth while discussing risk. There is not any risk under ordinary circumstances. You would be astonished if I told you the number and character of certain places. They include every kind I should think; business houses, private houses, hotels, restaurants etc – anything, in fact, with walls and a ceiling. But whatever the police may or may not do, Liverpool will not be a bit better until both women and men are made better by other means than those yet practised.'[714]

However, after decades of punitive and discriminatory solutions to age old problems, it was 1896 before even the system of zoning ended.

Part Six - Missing, presumed dead

Chapter 35 - Where is Jane?

So, how did Jane fare after her seeming loss of power and influence in this fevered, furious furore against social evil in Liverpool? I knew from Jane's mother's eventual probate, that she lived at 41 Russell Street, on Brownlow Hill in Liverpool in 1864, but not for how long. I suspect she was using it as a respectable address as there was a very well thought of servant's registry nearby supported by bishops and other gentlemen so I can only assume that Jane lay low for a while. As she did not appear in the press at all after 1866, I was beginning to think she had retired for no matter how many aliases I entered into national databases I could not find anything more meaningful than a single census return.

In 1871, she was at 13 Pembroke Gardens, Liverpool living as Jane Mercer with a couple of younger ladies she was not related to in another semi-professional neighbourhood, which indicates she had moved up in the world a little, not just in respectability but in height as Pembroke Gardens lies on one of Liverpool's hills where the air would have been somewhat cleaner.

It certainly looks like she has not given up her lodging house ways, despite heavy fines, court costs, the sale of her precious furniture and her expensive Chancery case in London, but the census does show she has emerged with an annuity, probably from the sale of No 8 Tyrer Street. From there the trail went completely cold for a long time but I knew where she wasn't as I searched for months on end, tracked hundreds of possible marriages, deaths and news reports and could not find any that matched her age and other known facts. Where was she? Not in London with Charles Pollard as that relationship was long since over and in 1872, he died in London whilst living with yet another 'wife.'

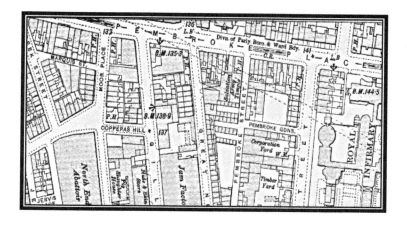

Figure 91 Pembroke Gardens, Liverpool OS 6" map 1908

Then, in 1875, Liverpool street directories show Jane at 6 Blandford Street, Liverpool which was a designated brothel zone, and 2 Hyde Street, but that does not mean Jane lived in either of these houses. It is more likely she had installed managers and moved around.

There was the hint from Fox Cooper family anecdotes that Selina, her second daughter, had gone to Dublin to run a lodging house for actors between 1887 - 1889, which made Ireland a possibility for Jane too, but there are few if any passenger records for this period and so many ports offered sailings from the west coast, including Liverpool, that I cannot check. As Selina did not return to live with Fox Cooper, I changed direction again and tracked the lives of her other married daughters who had stable families as I knew many widows in Victorian times ended up living with their children.

Ann Elizabeth and her husband William Brindley, a bank clerk, continued to live in Stafford where they had moved just after they got married from Bird Cottage in Rossett, Denbighshire, and had four sons by 1870. Jane was not with them at that time or listed in any future English censuses or street directories.

William Thomas, Jane's eldest son, after marrying Mary Ann Clare in 1862, then disappeared at sea leaving his widow in Liverpool with an adopted son. She continues to live on Springfield Street, running a grocer's shop along with her brother Joseph Clare, who becomes a scenic artist, designing stage sets in Liverpool theatres, and her adopted son Arthur Aust, who later married and had a large family in Liverpool. There is no reliable information about Mary Ann after the 1871 census.

Figure 92 The 'Doo-Da-Day Minstrels:' Glenister Matinee 1899

Caroline and Alfred Edgar Cooper stayed in London. He remained a professor of music and Caroline was busy with her many children. Alfred Edgar was also a copyist and played the violin and it is as a violinist he appeared as a member of a minstrel band in this photograph, though there is no indication as to which one of the suited gentlemen he is.

Rosanna and Maria Jane Mercer, both Jane's illegitimate daughters, I last heard of attending a Seminary for Young Ladies at 36 Chequer Street, St Albans. According to the 1861 census, Rosanna was 16, working as a junior teacher and Maria Jane was 14 and a pupil.

Michael Charles O'Brien, a printer from Talbot Street, Liverpool whose father is a stone mason, married Maria Jane in Liverpool in 1868, William Mercer, her father, signs the marriage certificate and Rosanna is a witness. On 16.10.1870 their only surviving daughter is born and named after Maria Jane's sister: Rose Edith O'Brien. Tragically, Maria Jane's husband dies on 1.6.1876 at Brick Street in Liverpool leaving his wife age 28 and his only daughter Rose Edith age eight.

In January 1870, Rosanna Mercer from Renshaw Street, Liverpool, married Thomas Crookenden, age 24, a timber merchant. They did not have any children. William Mercer, her father, died on 15.3.1881, age 83, at their next house on Herschell Street leaving Rosanna an Executor of his will. Also, by 1881, Rose Edith, age 11, appears living with her aunt Rosanna, both of whom then drop out of the official records until the 1890s, so Jane was not living with either of these daughters in the 1870s.

Thomas Gallagher, at first sight, seemed the best person to investigate for links to possible Irish in-laws, but I cannot find his birth record. His name was so common I spent ages trying to sift and sort through hundreds of Thomas Gallaghers until I eventually had to admit the futility of tracing his Irish roots without any further clues. His marriage certificate did not give either Jane's or his father's name nor was there anyone called Gallagher named as a witness, so I had to let this line of enquiry become dormant.

That left me with the most elusive child of all, Alfred Hugh Mercer, the only Gallagher child who maintained the Mercer name, and he may well have been William Mercer's son as I am still not convinced about his baptism record. I could not find him as an adult, under either the Gallagher or Mercer surname or living with any of his married sisters. The affidavit sworn by the rest of the family in the 1865 court cases about the Tyrer Street house said both brothers had gone abroad and that none of the family knew where they were, so I almost gave up on him.

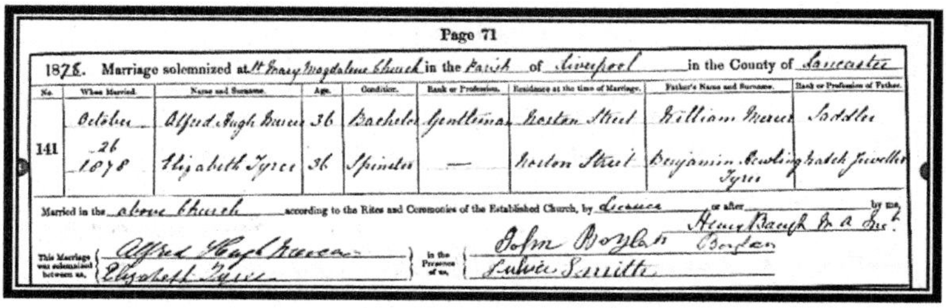
Page 71

1878. Marriage solemnized at St Mary Magdalene Church in the Parish of Liverpool in the County of Lancaster

No.	When Married	Name and Surname	Age	Condition	Rank or Profession	Residence at the time of Marriage	Father's Name and Surname	Rank or Profession of Father
141	October 26 1878	Alfred Hugh Mercer	36	Bachelor	Gentleman	Norton Street	William Mercer	Saddler
		Elizabeth Tyrer	36	Spinster	—	Norton Street	Benjamin Hewling Tyrer	Watch Jeweller

Married in the above Church according to the Rites and Ceremonies of the Established Church, by Licence or after by me, Henry Baugh M.A. Inc.

This Marriage was solemnized between us, Alfred Hugh Mercer, Elizabeth Tyrer

in the Presence of us, John Boylan, Lulia Smith

Figure 93 Marriage certificate: Alfred Hugh and Elizabeth Tyrer 1878

But then, as Mercer, he marries, age 36, in Liverpool in 1878. His occupation is given as 'gentleman' which usually implies a man with property or estates. His wife is Elizabeth Tyrer also 36, born in Liverpool, her father being Benjamin Hewling Tyrer, a London man who moved the family to Liverpool by 1841 where he worked as a watch jeweller. He died in 1869 but the word 'deceased' is not on the marriage certificate and Alfred Hugh's father is said to be William Mercer, a saddler. Bride and groom were both living at Norton Street, Liverpool.[715]

The couple do not feature in the 1881 census but the 1891 census shows them staying at 76 Boundary Lane, West Derby, Liverpool. Alfred Hugh is then 47 living off his own means and Elizabeth is 49, her age on the marriage certificate was wrong. Their neighbours are a carter, an engine fitter, a gas fitter and a cabinet maker so this neighbourhood was a significant step down from Norton Street.

Frustratingly, they then fail to appear in any other English censuses, which left me thinking maybe they died of an infectious disease. I found there were in fact four influenza epidemics between 1890 -1894. In London, the third epidemic had the highest maximum weekly mortality from influenza (506) as well as the highest maxima from bronchitis.[716] But I could find no death records for them. Why? Because I was looking in the wrong place and in the wrong time frames.

Months later, I put his name into a very obscure search engine not thinking anything interesting would result, and found this flashing up at me:

> **SUICIDE IN CUMBERLAND STREET**
>
> **A MAN SHOOTS HIMSELF THROUGH THE HEAD**
>
> **Irish Daily Independent**
> **31.8.1892**

This was Alfred Hugh Mercer, in Dublin.

Chapter 36 - Ireland?

I was shocked, flabbergasted even, then finally desperately curious. Did this mean Jane was in Ireland or just Alfred Hugh? Was it a quick visit or did she live there? A fast read of the news report showed me that she in fact lived opposite the house where he committed suicide. Had she retired? Had Selina really been in Ireland with her when she left Fox Cooper? Where had Alfred Hugh been all those years? Why did he kill himself? What about his wife Elizabeth?

Once I had calmed down a little, I devoured the Irish newspapers, archives and other sources up the end of the 19th century, collating snatches and snippets of information from all over the place, gradually piecing together the happenings of the next two decades.

Given the recent bad luck she had had in Liverpool by 1871, Jane must have had enough of the place. Maybe she thought her Gallagher surname would stand her in good stead in Ireland but, as it turned out, there were sufficient Mercers over there to hide amongst. First though, she needed to realise her assets, then coming up to sixty, Jane upped sticks and left. You have to admire her courage as it wasn't until 1852 that the last wave of the Irish potato famine was over and most migration was still from Ireland to England, not the other way round. As usual, Jane went against the tide and took the risk. But when did she go?

I went back to the 1871 census and 13 Pembroke Gardens as the last known place she actually lived. It was a respectable neighbourhood, judging by its previous occupants:

- 1860   Reverend Edward Freer, Anglican Minister[717]

- 1861   Edward William Scott, a broker

- 1870   Thomas Sparling, who also owned 65 Mulberry
  Street[718]

Then, when I searched for the address in newspapers, not Jane's name, I found a whole series of adverts in 1875 posted from 13 Pembroke Gardens in the *Liverpool Daily Post* beginning in April right through to September saying a family leaving town wanted to sell their jewellery, and it sounded to me very much like Jane. [719]

A Family leaving town wishes to sell the following Articles of Jewellery:-

- A magnificent pair of diamond earrings, three large lustrous stones in each, pure white, cost £40 – will be sold for £20

- A pair of diamond earrings, arrow shaped, patent spring fasteners, one large stone in each (first water), cost £35 in Cheapside, London – will be sold for £18

- Also, a gold graduated curb chain, hall marked 18-carat every link, nearly new, cost £16 – will be sold for £11

Apply at 13 Pembroke Gardens.

She adds a half hoop diamond ring to the pot at £14 a week later, which originally costs £26 so she was selling jewellery originally bought for £117.00 [£7,325.25] for £63 [£3,944.37]. Of course, there is nothing to say she found a buyer and a later advert showed she had reduced the price of at least one item, but when you add it all up, it is still a lot of pocket money to take to Ireland.

With 1875 as a possible date for her arrival, I searched again and found Jane Mercer cited in a court case in 1881 with, of all people, the Belfast Flour and Bread Company, who she accused of setting her house on fire, destroying all her, wait for it, furniture!

This furniture is beginning to feel like the luggage in the Terry Pratchett's *Disc World* novels, a trunk with legs, made of sapient pearwood and immensely faithful.[720] Its unceasing loyalty to its owner, often helped them out of many different situations, usually by stomping, jumping up and down on, or swallowing whatever is threatening them.[721] Likewise, Jane's blessed furniture has popped up again, having, if it was the same lot, travelled from Liverpool, via North Wales, then London and Liverpool again. Now bouncing back from her bankruptcy and public auctions when you thought you had seen the last of it, the furniture is resurrected in Belfast where it transforms into hard cash and liquidises, albeit by fire not water, at someone else's expense.

But was Jane in Belfast respectably or continuing in the business she knew so well? Was there room for another brothel madam in the city?

Ireland was one country until 1922 and between 1780 - 1840, its population increased 172%, compared to Britain's 88% and from 1841 - 1901 Belfast was the fastest growing city in the United Kingdom. By 1911, its population had surged again from 75,308 in 1841 to 386,947 with textile manufacturing, shipbuilding, engineering and rope making offering employment on huge scale.[722] Belfast's York Street Mill was claimed as the largest spinning mill and weaving factory in the world and in 1894, all Belfast mills together spun 644,000,000 miles of yarn.[723]

As weaving was predominantly a female occupation and the mechanisation of weaving replaced the home-based hand loom, huge numbers of women moved to the city to gain work, many of them young and single.[724] The 1881 census shows 73% of all people employed in the textile industry in Ireland were female and a third of these were under the age of 20. By the 1901 census Belfast had the highest proportion of women, 53.7%, of any Irish city and of which 70% were under the age of 20.[725]

For women who had moved to Belfast from the countryside away from their families and communities, life was horrible, brutal and at the very least, unpleasant. Working conditions were harsh and wages minimal with women earning on average two thirds less than men for the same the work.[726] Many turned to prostitution as a way of earning money or supplementing their income in order to feed their families, particularly if their husband was no longer supporting them either because they had died, were injured and not fit to work or had deserted them and taken up with another woman.[727] The workhouse was all too often their only option as many charitable establishments required women to give up their children. Prostitutes too found their way to the workhouse, usually when they were sick or old, and their profession became the third highest occupation represented amongst Catholic women in the workhouse between 1900 - 01.[728]

By 1835, there were at least eleven rescue homes or Magdalen asylums which tried to reform prostitutes in Dublin, run by the Sisters of Mercy. By 1914, this figure had risen to 33 and rescuing the fallen became an important part of charitable work for women of the nineteenth century.[729] Such statistics as there are only record prostitutes and establishments known to the police and in:

- 1842, there were 1,287 brothels in Dublin

- 1846 - 1855, during the famine years, there were between 330 - 419 brothels with 1,300 women working there. Other information, provided to an independent travelling researcher for the same year, compares the estimated 1,700 prostitutes in Dublin to the 236 in Belfast and well over 2,000 in Liverpool [730]

- 1870, a large number of prostitutes, 3,255, worked in Dublin according to arrest figures, far more than the 2,450 in Liverpool,[731] the 2,183 in London and 1,617 in Manchester

Arrests for prostitution in Ireland as a whole were at their height in 1870 with 3,673 prostitutes known to the police. However, not all women who worked as prostitutes were arrested even though they might be suspected of being involved in immoral activities. Instead, in 1871 police took proceedings against 17,153 women who they said were bad characters, 10,456 of whom they labelled prostitutes and they also arrested 11,864 women for crimes other than prostitution who they nevertheless believed to be prostitutes.

By 1894, the numbers had reduced and of the 74 brothels operating openly in the Monto district of Dublin there was an average of three women in each. The overall numbers of prostitutes went down to 2,970 in 1900[732] and prostitution was conducted more discretely in brothels and public houses.

The reasons why many women become prostitutes are universal but in Ireland there were additional factors such as more acute poverty, unmarried motherhood and the lure of men in uniform. Prostitutes followed the barracks while they were young and pretty, then became obliged to beg when they had lost their good looks.[733] As in Liverpool, many common prostitutes were prolific offenders, like Sarah Wilson who was inside 40 times between September 1875 and August 1877 and another woman imprisoned for five years for larceny in 1885 was recorded as a prostitute and had by the time she was 44 over 90 convictions. [734]

This meant desperate prostitutes with young children, prosecuted many times, spent their lives beween the streets, the workhouse and prisons. During October 1900, one prostitute, Mary Ann was admitted to a Belfast workhouse with her one year old daughter six times, for several days at a time. In total that month they spent 25 nights out of 31 there. Another prostitute with one child was admitted four times in the same period, but for longer periods each time.

However, admitting prostitutes was not popular with those entrusted with the management of the workhouses. In 1879, the *Freeman's Journal* printed allegations made by the Roman Catholic chaplain to Belfast Union workhouse that:

'Portions of its wards are hotbeds of immorality. Women of bad character... are freely admitted into the house.' [735] And a Belfast magistrate announced that the workhouse was: 'A den of immorality, drunkeness and vice... where women of ill-repute were mixing freely with other inmates, while young unmarried women had given birth in the workhouse.'

Jane, in Ireland in the mid-1870s, would therefore have found extreme poverty and the same legal system as in England. The:

- *Police Causes Acts* of 1847: gave police powers to arrest a woman said to be 'a common prostitute or night walker loitering or importuning passengers for the purpose of prostitution'

- *Towns' Improvements Acts* of 1854: added powers to arrest women 'otherwise offensive' such as fortune tellers, performers and beggars

- Women could also be arrested for vagrancy and there were laws against keeping bawdy houses or brothels but, they still had to be shown to cause disorder or a nuisance.

It would not have been difficult then for Jane to exploit the opportunity to open more brothels. Observing how the best money was to be made around the many barracks, she probably could not resist buying premises nearby. She had the experience to set up another empire, as well as legal knowledge and expertise in working behind the scenes where she could claim ignorance of what was going on. Managing brothels was both second nature to Jane, a lucrative business opportunity and there was pretty much nothing much to stop her. She admitted as much in a later court case:

'I have had property in Belfast but have sold it... houses all over the town, but I could not say what sort of houses they were as it was my agents who dealt with them, as the ladies who lived there were not all my tenants.'

Figure 94 Advert on 12.9.1870 in the Belfast News-Letter

When did she start? From the information I have gathered it appears that Jane spent a few years commuting between Liverpool and Ireland as she, on many occasions in the same year, features in news reports in both countries. In 1870, when Jane was still in Liverpool, this advert appeared for 46 Hill Street, Belfast, which became one of Jane's houses. She must have seen this as a good way of hiding her true profession, so she set herself up as money lender at the same time as buying houses to rent to brothel keepers.

Jane had definitely got a house of ill fame in Belfast by 1878. She had bought at auction Nos 20 - 22 Church Street which had a frontage of 55 feet with a large yard to the rear and a gateway extending into Long Lane and [736] was summoned to the police court on 27.11.1878 by James Kelly, who lived on William Street for keeping a disorderly house there. This is exactly one month after Alfred Hugh married Elizabeth Tyrer in Liverpool.

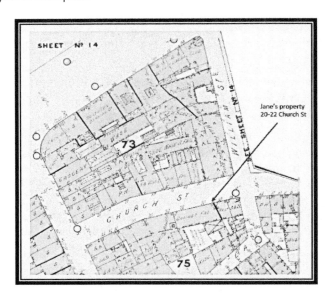

Figure 95 Goad's Insurance map of Belfast 1887

A report in the *Belfast Telegraph* reveals how Jane Mercer offered to give up the house provided the magistrates granted her sufficient time to vacate the premises and dispose of her furniture. The court adjourned the case until January 1880, over a year, but she had to lodge £200 [£13,236,94] as surety to assure them she would comply. [737]

She was living mostly in Dublin by 1880 and it looks like she travelled between the two cities until 1882 when she settled there once and for all. On the night of the fire, 11.5.1880, all her furniture and effects were stored in the stable, which had conveniently been valued recently for insurance purposes at £3,000 [£198,554.10].

On 28.3.1881, she instigated an action to recover damages for alleged negligence by the Belfast Flour and Bread Company, who she said had burnt down her stable[738] when her entire property was engulfed by a fire, resulting from the over-heating of ovens in their bakery in Church Street. She claimed £200 [£13,236.94] for the damage and the destruction of her furniture and effects.[739]

When she was cross examined in court, Jane had to admit the premises had been used as a brothel. The person she had entrusted its care to while she was in Dublin was a man called William Miller, who had been taken ill and was obliged to go to the workhouse hospital on the night of the fire. On her instructions, he had given the key to woman called Hurst who lived at 46 Hill Street, Belfast - the same address as Jane's money lending business - and she had the key when the fire occurred. She too confirmed the Church Street place had been empty for some time.[740]

The poor Belfast Flour and Bread Company could only say in their defence it was perhaps the oldest such establishment in the north of Ireland, having been set up in 1800 and there had never been any problems before to the neighbouring premises as a result of heating the ovens. Whatever our doubts about the matter, the jury found for Jane who was awarded the full £200 [£13,236.94] plus costs.

There are more glaring 'coincidences' in this case too. First the caretaker, William Miller and a Mrs. Mary Ann Miller, also known as Hurst, who was said to be a widow, had managed the brothel on 6 Blandford Street, Liverpool for Jane in 1871, and had been brought over to manage the house on 46 Hill Street, Belfast sometime before 1881.

Tracking her led me to the headline 'Shocking Immorality in Liverpool,' dated 1871[741] and confirmed that Mary Ann Miller was a lodging house keeper, age 59 and a widow. She had brought a case to recover £17 [worth £1,064.35] from a man called Isaac Parr, a licensed victualler of 237 Mill Street, for the maintenance of his illegitimate child. It appeared that three years previously he, an old man who had fathered thirteen children and a grandfather, went to Mrs. Miller's house and seduced a girl called Howard who was a servant there. She gave birth to a child, said Isaac Parr was the father and he paid her money, five shillings a week [£15.65].

Mrs. Miller had since then looked after the child as the mother was living-in as a servant somewhere else and could not have the child with her. They had already taken Isaac Parr to court once before and been awarded £10 [£626.09] for its maintenance.

Cross examined Mrs. Miller denied she kept a brothel, though Isaac Parr said she did and he also denied agreeing to pay Mrs. Miller any maintenance for the child's upkeep. When the judge asked him why he thought the house was a brothel he replied:

'I have been with a dozen women in that house. I have known that house for over ten years and this woman Mrs. Miller kept it all that time.'

The judge, summing up, said:

'I have no doubt that this house is kept as a brothel. I am exceedingly sorry that such a fine child is in charge of such a woman and kept in such a house as it is now brought up in vice and crime, whereas if it were in other hands the child might become a useful member of society and the sooner it is out of Mrs. Miller's hands the better. I will see that the attention of the authorities is directed to the matter.

'You, Parr, are an old man and a very reasonable responsibility attaches to you with respect to this child's future. You have given an account of yourself, the worst that I have ever heard from any man in this court before, and the best atonement you can make is to be a good husband in the future and to take care that this child is rescued from the peril in which it is now placed.'

He awarded the money claimed to Mrs. Miller, and undertook to see that the child was placed in a respectable family.

Less than ten years later, Mrs. Miller/ Hurst was with Jane at 46 Hill Street in Belfast. The same address came up again in an 1881 newspaper report about a woman called Kate (Catherine) Gallagher alias Jane Mercer, an alias within an alias, who in April is summoned by Constable Baile for 'Shebeening,' selling by retail a quantity of liquor in her unlicensed premises the day after the Whinney Hill races, a week previously in April 1881. It was then I knew beyond all doubt Jane was far from retired and still weaving tangled webs, albeit with Irish spiders.

Jane's case was adjourned that day because the constable had had to attend the quarter sessions. Meanwhile, five young 'sparks' of the town, some of whom had given fictitious addresses and names, one cheekily giving the 46 Hill Street as his address, were summoned for being found on Jane's premises at the time of a police raid. The four boys who turned up were all fashionably dressed and had a lawyer who made a rather 'unique' appeal on their behalf. He claimed they were from the countryside and entirely ignorant of the ways of this wicked world. It appears to have worked for they were fined 5 shillings each [£16.55] and sent on their way. The fifth boy, who had not appeared for the hearing, had his case adjourned so he could be located.

The case continued on 11th May with the constable in attendance. He said he visited Jane's house about one in the morning on 27th April and found four men, three in the parlour and two upstairs. On a bench in the kitchen there were a number of tumblers and bottles which were either half or full of porter and beer. In a press he found 24 full bottles of porter and eleven empties, a quart bottle containing spirits and an empty quart bottle and a bottle of brandy. [742]

The constable went into the kitchen first where Jane and three or four females were. He did not witness any money being passed but there was a good deal of it about. In a drawer he saw half crowns and other pieces of silver, gold and coppers. There were three females upstairs but he did not see any drink there. He did not see any of the men in the kitchen consume drink but they were sitting opposite the liquor which was on the bench. The men in the house were under the influence of liquor but he conceded they might have drunk it before they went there.

The justice had no doubt that liquor was in the house for the purposes of being sold and that in the eyes of the law a sale had actually taken place. A fine of £5 [£330.92] and costs was imposed on Jane. It is also equally clear what else was going on but as owning a brothel was not illegal until 1885 and the girls were not soliciting on the street or causing a nuisance, there was little the law could do, as Jane knew very well.

Street directories show that Jane was still listed at Nos 46 and 48 Hill Street in 1887 whilst also running another money lending business based in Dublin. This is the year Selina is reported to have been living in Ireland, managing a lodging house for actors, but as her name does not appear in the newspapers or street directories, it is impossible to be sure she was involved.

And it is from No 46 Hill Street, Belfast that Mrs. Mary Ann Miller, alias Hurst and Hutchinson by this time, was summoned by the *Belfast Vigilance Committee* for having on 11th, 17th February and 2nd March 1888 run the house as a brothel. She had lived there at least since 1880 and stated at this current hearing that she managed the place for a Mrs. Mercer who had similar houses in Dublin, London and Liverpool and that she had been brought from England by the former manager, Mrs. Hudson. Her sentence was three month's imprisonment. [743]

The *Belfast Vigilance Committee* was set up in 1885 and sprang from the *White Cross Army*, an organisation a woman called Ellice Hopkins founded in England in 1883 in attempt to improve the sexual behaviour of men. They also summoned the owners and managers of No 58 Hill Street and they too were forced to close down their very lively brothel. It sounds like it was a really popular street.

In April 1888, not content with imprisoning the manager of 46 Hill Street, the *Belfast Vigilance Committee* also summoned under the new 1885 act, the actual owner, Alfred Pelling of 31 North Street, for allowing the premises he rented to Jane Mercer to be used as a brothel. The solicitor for his defence said that since the summons had been issued, Jane had given up the keys of the house to Pelling and he therefore requested the case be adjourned for a fortnight to close the house, which was all the *Belfast Vigilance Committee* required.

A summons had been left for Jane with a Mrs. Parker at No 46, the new manager she had brought in when Mary Miller (Hutchinson, Hurst) had been sent to prison. As Jane had not been personally served, the judge ruled they had to try again and a warrant was issued for her arrest. Evidence was produced in her absence to show Jane was the person who paid the rates on this house and the taxes. The owner Alfred Pelling stood back from it all and said he did not know who was the tenant and he just received the money and did not give out receipts. The case was again adjourned until Jane could be produced in court.

The *Belfast Vigilance Committee* were incensed by her non-attendance and:

> 'Wanted to show these people; that they could not do whatever they liked and they would ask, after they had proved the case, that she be sent to jail for the full period allowed by the law, six months.'[744]

But no more reports concerning this case appear in the press. Most annoying. Maybe Jane had power and influence in Ireland too?

Chapter 37 - Social Evil in Dublin

What was the attraction of Dublin? We know Jane was fond of London as a capital city and Dublin too spent periods of time as the capital of the whole of Ireland. It has a river like Liverpool, also became a notable city in the British Empire, was a centre for administration, a transport hub and was famous for its Georgian architecture and culture.[745]

However, like all large Victorian cities, there was a distinctly less pleasant side. One shocked visitor wrote that it was a city of 'lamentable contrasts,' as close to the houses of middle-class wealthy folk were slums like the Liberties, which were dirty, full of disease and beggars, decay and depravity. In the nineteenth century there were frequent outbreaks of cholera and typhoid, which hit the poor severely, and the death rate in Dublin was much higher than in comparable British cities. The Victorians believed that toxic odours caused disease and the stench from the river Liffey was thought to be a prime cause of a cholera epidemic in 1866.

Despite this, Dublin was a hub of medical innovation during the nineteenth century. The medical schools of the city had very good reputations and there were a large number of hospitals, which meant medicine in Victorian Dublin was of a high standard. Sir William Wilde [father of Oscar] was a pioneer in eye surgery and founded St. Mark's Ophthalmic Hospital in 1844. Dublin was also the home of military Ireland, with up to half of the Irish garrison stationed there. There were parades, reviews, red coats in the streets, genteel housing for officers in Rathmines, and of course the main attraction as far as Jane was concerned, very busy brothels.[746]

Before Jane arrived in Dublin, in the 1860s and 1870s the Grafton Street area was regarded as a centre of prostitution in the city. Respectable residents complained repeatedly in the letter pages of newspapers that it had become 'impassable to virtuous women,' describing how it 'literally swarmed with women of loose character.' They appealed for help.

'Let some half-dozen men of the G Division [Dublin's intelligence police] parade Grafton Street at the hours of four to six. This was found very successful in

Sackville Street during last summer, and I have no doubt we shall soon be free of these social pests, and can again escort our wives and daughters through one of our finest streets.'

It was not until the *Contagious Diseases Acts* came into force in 1864 that greater powers were given to the police and allowed the compulsory inspection of prostitutes in certain military camps in both England and Ireland. This meant that street prostitutes were forced to undergo examination and if they were infected, they were detained in a Lock(e) hospital for up to nine months and registered as a prostitute. Like in England, these powers did not cease until 1883 when they were suspended and finally repealed in 1886.

Meanwhile, the *Industrial Schools Amendment Act* of 1880 allowed the authorities to remove children from brothels and we now know the *Criminal Law Amendment Act* of 1885 eventually gave the police power to summarily convict brothel keepers and allowed imprisonment for repeat offenders. As in Liverpool, Jane's women were not street workers, therefore she and her brothel businesses were not too affected until 1885 by which time she had firmly established herself in Dublin as a money lender, letting her disreputable houses out to others.

However, the authorities did not appear to be unduly concerned about clusters of prostitutes, even though they infested garrison towns and infected many thousands of soldiers; prostitutes even climbed over defensive walls to get to the men. They were slow to close down brothels believing that dispersing women spread the problem into new areas, something Liverpool police were very familiar with. The main Dublin police priority was responding to the inevitable violence in and around brothels, prosecuting those responsible for committing stabbings, stealing, riots, even murder, crimes which obviously concerned the public most. Social purity agencies, however, just wanted brothels closing, and worked with the police to make this happen.

'Monto' then emerged as Dublin's red-light district, its name coming from Montgomery Street, now named Foley Street. It was bounded by Talbot Street, Amiens Street, Gardiner Street and Gloucester Street [now Sean McDermott Street] and between the 1860s and the 1920s, it was reputed to be the largest red-light district in Europe. According to popular legend, the then Prince of Wales, Prince Edward (later King Edward VII), lost his virginity there.[747]

Whilst it was into this Monto area that prostitutes of Dublin were gradually confined from 1880s, they could also be found in Sackville St, [now O'Connell St.] In the late Victorian years there was nothing really new about prostitution in the city and all that tended to change over time was where prostitutes were to be found.

In 1885, the *White Cross Vigilance Association*, allied to the Church of Ireland was set up and men only were recruited on the condition that they pledged to:

'Treat all women with respect, to endeavour to put down all indecent language and jests... to maintain the laws of purity as equally binding on men and women.'

Besides attending lectures, members of the association engaged in 'patrol work,' using the new laws of 1885 to target those who owned and profited indirectly from brothels. In effect this meant keeping watch outside known 'evil houses' and, through such harassment, forcing them to close. One Dublin brothel owner offered them a bribe of £1,000 [£82,049.30] if they would stop watching his premises after they prosecuted a hotel owner for keeping a brothel in the city.

By 1891, the *White Cross Vigilance Association* had 14 branches in Dublin with 530 members. In 1893, Ellice Hopkins revitalised the association and a group of 24 members once again accosted customers leaving the city's brothels. Through their activities another 35 brothels were closed down and Mecklenburg Street was cleared of prostitutes.[748]

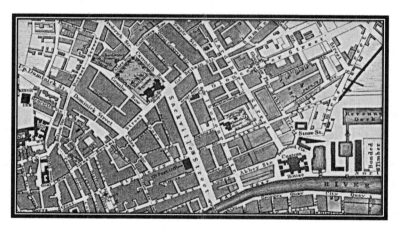

Figure 96 Map of Dublin: George Cox: London,1853

Jane moved in 1880 from Belfast to 22 Upper Gloucester Street in the middle of the Monto district and later to nearby North Cumberland Street, as its brothels flourished due to it being far enough away from upper and middle-class residential and shopping districts and more importantly, it was near to Amiens Street Station [now Connolly Station] which provided plenty of innocent young women from the countryside looking for work, and custom from Dublin's port and Aldborough

Military Barracks. In fact, Jane would have found Dublin very similar to Liverpool and Lime Street in many respects, apart from the greater presence of the military.

As a result of the Monto's notoriety, the renaming of streets was common:

- 1885 saw Lower Temple Street in Dublin became Hill Street because house prices had suffered

- In 1888 Mecklenburgh Street was renamed as Tyrone Street to please the respectable working-class residents of the area

In 1882, Jane moves to No 24 Upper Gloucester Street, which she acquired from Walter Plunkett, a commission agent, and this becomes her official money - lending office in Dublin in 1884. She was poacher turned gamekeeper and her experience of running the brothel empire would stand in her in good stead with the local madams who would always want to invest and borrow with her, given the nature of their business, for she was one of their own!

Before long Jane is in court in defence of her new role. On 15.6.1882, appears an advert showing that a cab, in good order, property of John Mc Cabe is to be auctioned by Thomas Dillon as a result of a bill of sale. Jane is the plaintiff, the one taking the action, so for a change it is not her who owes money.[749]

In 1883, John O'Brien, a grocer, brought an action against Jane in respect of an insurance policy she had sold him and his wife on 29th June. His story takes us back to Mrs. O'Brien's previous marriage to a man called Barry when a life insurance policy for £500 [£33,092.35] on the life of a Christopher Carey was put into place with the Life Insurance Association of Scotland and given to Mr. and Mrs. Barry. After Mr. Barry died Mrs. Barry, now a widow, married John O'Brien.

In order to raise some money Mrs. O'Brien then agreed to assign the policy to Jane Mercer in return for payment of £30 [£1,985.54]. Jane asked John O'Brien to sign as well, as on her marriage her husband took control of the money and anything of value his wife had - coverture rears its head once again. Both of them signed the documents drawn up by a solicitor and they agreed that £15 [£992.77] should be paid to John O'Brien and £15 [£992.77] to his wife.

The point at issue in this case is that Jane said she gave all the money to Mrs. O'Brien and got a receipt. John O'Brien took Jane to court because he said £12 [£794.22] was still owing to him. The Recorder hearing the case said that Mrs. O'Brien, who was now separated from her second husband, did not hold separate property in the insurance policy and that Jane should not have acted on the receipt without making further enquiries. He therefore held her responsible for the £12 [£794.22] claim.

It is ironic Jane lost this case on these grounds when she had got away with so many debts in England by invoking coverture. Hopefully she learned from it but really, no matter where her sympathies lay, she should have known better![750]

Jane was now living again among decent neighbours on Upper Gloucester Street, who, in 1884 had honest occupations: a house painter, a grocer, wine and spirits stores, an inspector of anatomy, a manufacturer of church furniture, a civil engineer and the secretary of the Wexford Harbour Embankment Co Draining Commission. But Nos 1, 4, 10-12, 21, 26, 27, 31-34, 36, 43 and 44 were all tenements. Nearer to Jane at No 20 was a house agent and lector [someone who reads Latin] and at Nos 23 and 28, two solicitors. But this did not mean she had given up her old ways completely, or that she had sold all her jewellery in Liverpool.

At the northern police court on 14.5.1884 Jane took a case against Mr. George Charles Garnett, age 50, alleging that:

'He, from time to time, within the last two months, obtained from her by false pretences numerous diamonds and other articles of jewellery, to the value of about £650 [£43,020.06].'

She claimed Garnett:

'Came to her house and represented himself as a man of property and said that he understood she was going to dispose of her jewellery.'

Jane produced a diamond bracelet valued at £100 [£6,618.47] and a diamond valued at £40 [£2,647.39]. Garnett said he would give her £100 [£6,618.47] for them both, an offer she accepted because she wanted cash. On the 10th March he asked to see more jewellery and she showed him some, including a keyless watch. He took this for £24 [£1,588.43] and a diamond ring for £80 [£5,294.78]. He said he wanted to show them to another person who might buy them and that he was sure he would be able to able to sell them all as they were very good. She allowed him to take them away.

On 3rd April, Garnett called again and this time took a pair of diamond earrings valued at £80, a necklace worth £80 [£5,294.78], a locket value £60 [£3,971.08], another diamond ring worth £80 [£5,294.78] and said he would see if they would suit the other party. He then asked to see the rest: a diamond brooch, two diamond rings value £70 [£4,632.93] and said he thought they would all be worth between £500 - £600 [£33,092.35 - £39,710.82]. He took some diamond studs as well and put them in his pocket saying he would come on Wednesday 23rd April with the money.

This is pretty valuable jewellery for the daughter of a carter and what follows reminded me very much of what happened between Charles Pollard and Louis-Napoleon in 1847. Garnett came on Tuesday 22nd, not with the money but an excuse, saying he would come again on the 25th, that he was a gentleman and would never break his word. Jane replied that she wanted the money, but he never came so she went on the 26th to his aunt's house where he lived on Aylesbury Road but he was not there. On the following Sunday she went again and Garnett pleaded with her 'for God's sake' not to say anything about it and that he would come to her office the next day.

Only now did Jane make enquiries and find that Garnett had no property at all and was in fact solely dependent on his aunt and that the representations he made were false and only made for the purpose of obtaining possession of her property.

Jane was 68 at this time but this does not sound like the woman who stood up to Burton and Watson in 1860, appealed the judgement and got it reversed, the Jane who won the 1865 case in London to get back control of her house at Tyrer Street and a far cry from the Jane who flouted the law of coverture blatantly to get away without paying huge debts, and enjoyed it. That Jane would never have handed over all her jewellery, the equivalent of what must have been the acquisitions of a lifetime, for a mere £100 [£6,618.47], and a bill only good for three months. What on earth was she doing?

Cross examined by Garnett's lawyer, Jane said she first met Garnett at 129 Summer Hill, Dublin, a property she had bought along with Nos 130 and 101 from Alderman Harris. She saw Garnett there, a lodging house, which was occupied by a tenant called Mrs. Smith. Answering a question, about which we can only imagine, Jane said: 'The house was proper enough when she went there.'

Jane also admitted she used to have property in Belfast but had sold it and that she never thought that the girl, who was to be the next witness, was intimate with Garnett. This was Anne Jane Booth who claimed she had first met Garnett at yet another house on Summer Hill, No 125, which was not, she said 'a proper house.' She had spent three months in Belfast in similar houses which all belonged to Jane and claimed Jane had asked Garnett and her to go and live in her house in Upper Gloucester Street.

It came out that a large basket of jewellery had been sent by Jane Mercer to their lodgings by her housekeeper, also a dress, asking Garnett to buy these things for the girl, but he would not and it appears from Ann Jane Booth's statement Garnett was not a teetotaller and she often saw him the worse for drink, even during all the transactions which took place.

Jane was recalled to the witness stand and produced the bill for £100 [£6,618.47] which was due to expire on 3rd June. Only now did she admit she had sent the basket of jewellery and she had made a mistake if she had denied it before. But she did deny she had asked Garnett to go and live at her house in Upper Gloucester Street.

Detective Officer Hayes said he arrested Garnett on the Saturday evening and found in a drawer at his aunt's house on Aylesbury Road the pawn tickets for the rest of the jewellery which he had taken to Mr. Rispin's pawn office in South Richmond Street. Garnett's lawyer asked for bail for his client as:

'It was clear these articles had been forced on him while he was in a state of intoxication by this woman, Ann Jane Booth, who had evidently considered him a good mark.'

Jane's lawyer opposed the bail saying he would be able to prove that Garnett had pawned the articles on the very day he had obtained them. The judge declined the bail and set a day the following week for the case to resume.[751]

This was long enough for matters to change completely. When the case came up again it went through in double quick time indicating some out of court deal had been struck as Jane must have realised or been advised, that she was on sticky ground. The crowded court room held its breath eager for more revelations 'as great interest was manifested in the case.' They were disappointed.

Garnett said that he had not obtained the jewellery by false pretences but had been expecting money from London which was delayed so he pawned the jewellery. He had taken the articles out of pawn, Jane got her jewellery back, Garnett was discharged and everyone went home happy, apart from those expecting more scandal.[752]

Jane was obviously learning, late but fast, that being right was not enough and sometimes discretion was better than valour. It did also make me curious about George Charles Garnett, a gentleman in need of ready money and desperate enough to take Jane's jewellery and pawn it, to say nothing of him consorting with a prostitute.

He was born in 1835, the son of Louisa, eldest daughter of the late Colonel Wade CB of the Rifle Brigade, and Hamlet Garnett. George's paternal grandfather was a vicar in Williamstown, County Meath. His uncles and aunts also married well:

- George to the daughter of Jonas Stawell of the Old Court in Cork

- William to Julia, the third daughter of John Boyse Esquire

- Ellen to the Rev John Trevor Radcliffe rector of Kilmore in Meath

- Letitia to Colonel Gerard of Bloomsbury, Meath

It was with one of these aunts George Charles Garnett was staying at Olney, Aylesbury Road in Dublin. With such a genteel background, no wonder he did not want anyone informing her. He married Anne Jane Doran in July 1858 in Dublin and apart from this there is very little to say about them. The only other newspaper reports about him appeared between 1864-67, when he was a much younger man:

- George was admitted as member of the Royal Irish Academy in 1864 when he was only 20[753]

- And he submitted his learned opinion on the art of warfare to *Saunder's Newsletter* that year saying he had for some years engaged in experiments with gunnery and the best form of projectiles, also claiming a very general knowledge of the science of war[754]

- He signs himself George Charles Garnett MRIA [Member of the Royal Irish Academy] and it is in this capacity that he arranged for the magnesium lamp and oxy-hydrogen light invented by Mr. Solomons of London to be exhibited at the Ballast Office in Dublin in May 1865[755]

- In 1867, he and his wife prosecuted Thomas Francis Cleary for assault and battery and unfortunately this case does not appear again in the newspapers.[756]

- He lived at 2 Albert Terrace in Kingstown, Dublin in 1876 and was at 4 Lansdown Road from 1879.

- He died in Rathdown in 1897 and was survived by his wife who was last noted as living back in Albert Terrace, Dublin in the 1901 census.

It does therefore appear that George Charles Garnett was an innocent sort of fellow who got himself in a mess and liked drink and prostitutes, rather than an out and out villain.

Chapter 38 - Misnomer

'Yesterday, [28.12.1887] in the Northern Division of the Police Court, Mr. Keys presiding, Jane Gallagher, described of Summer Hill and her daughter were charged on remand in the custody of Inspector Downey, of the E Division, with having, the first named prisoner made a false declaration as to the birth of an infant, and the second accused, her daughter, with having deserted the infant.'[757]

This was wholly unexpected. But which daughter were they referring to? The inspector said that between six and seven o'clock on the 19th December, the accused Jane Gallagher came to the Rathmines police station in Dublin with a female infant in her arms saying she had found the child in the porch of the Catholic Chapel, Rathmines a short time previously and that she did not know who left it there. She and the Rev Father Donegan told the police the infant was then baptised in the chapel and named Mary Byrne.

'Figure 97 South Dublin Workhouse in 1952*

That night, the infant was sent to South Dublin Union workhouse,[759] the record of her admittance saying:

Mary Byrne, female, found in the porch of an RC church by Jane Gallagher of 71 Summer Hill. Admittance No 2502.'

The police made enquiries at this address (the fifth house Jane ran or owned on Summer Hill), but failed to receive any word of her. As a result of subsequent inquiries, the inspector went to 1 Arnott Street between 5 - 6pm where he found Jane Gallagher and her said daughter Anna Maria Gallagher. But, as far as I knew, Jane never had such a daughter.

The house at 1 Arnott Street, according to an advert published in 1878, was off the South Circular Road in Dublin and had two sitting and two bedrooms, a kitchen, servant's apartment, WC, a yard and pantry. The ground rent was nominal at £3 3 shillings [£197.22] and it was at that time let for £34 [£2,128.71] a year. Available for immediate possession, the auctioneer added hopefully, 'the neighbourhood is rapidly improving.'[760]

By the time Jane and her 'daughter' lived there, the rent had gone up to £36 a year [£2,253.92] and most of the neighbours were hard working people: lodging house keepers, a dress maker at No 4, a teacher of the violin, banjo and guitar at No 7 and a nurse maid was wanted at No 2. However, further down the road at No 27 lived a couple of commission agents who pretended they were provision dealers. When the police called at their premises on King Street, they found between 700 - 800 bags on the shop's shelves filled with sawdust. They were both charged with fraud.[761]

When Jane and her daughter were charged with deserting the child, Jane's daughter being its mother, they both said they would tell the truth and explained that Anna Maria was confined on the 8th December and went to the Coombe lying-in hospital, where she gave birth to the child on 9th December, remained until Saturday 17th December then left with her baby along with Jane. If this was all true, then the baby Maria Byrne found in the chapel two days later was Jane's granddaughter.

In court, Anna Maria was described as being 'greatly affected,' and the infant was too delicate to be present. His worship said it was a most distressing case and remanded Jane Gallagher on bail until the following Monday, 2nd January, where she pleaded guilty and was remanded again. Anna Maria, who had been charged with deserting her child, was discharged from custody as there was no evidence against her.

The Minute book of South Dublin workhouse records the following:

'That on the 19th instant [they] admitted a deserted child (Mary Byrne) about 10 days old, found in the porch of Rathmines Chapel by Jane Gallagher of 71 Summer Hill, and brought to the workhouse by her and PC 23E. Baptismal certificate and declaration submitted. The police are prosecuting Mrs. Gallagher as it appears, she is the mother of the woman who gave birth to the child.'[762]

And on 14th January 1888 there is a further note:

'That the deserted child Mary Byrne admitted on 19th December last is still in the house. Jane Gallagher who deserted the child, was tried at Green Street, before the Recorder, pleaded guilty and was allowed out on her own recognisances to appear when called. Referred to the Relieving Officer to find out the mother and report to the Board.'

The role of the Relieving Officer was to visit those in need in the area to assess their health and living conditions, offering appropriate relief and medical help from the District Medical Officer where necessary. Anna Maria must have been distraught when Jane took the baby away and the authorities had a responsibility to try and help her. But a week a later, the Relieving Officer reported to the Board that he had failed to locate the two women involved and there is nothing more in the workhouse minutes or the newspapers relating to this tragedy.

Mary Byrne died on 25th January in the workhouse, six and half weeks old. I traced her baptism of the 19th December but there is nothing to show who the parents were and there is neither a death certificate or a grave record to be found.

Having now read about the Dublin South Workhouse I am not surprised the child died. As well as providing for adults, including disorderly women, the workhouse took in orphaned and abandoned children. By 1772, it had a separate establishment from the main work house and in 1730 this remit extended to include all foundling children. By 1818, the Foundling Hospital had grown rapidly, so much so that 43,254 infants had been admitted since it opened. This was probably due to their policy of 'asking no questions.'

At one of its gates, a basket was fixed to a revolving door and anyone could leave a child there, ring the porter's bell and then go before he arrived. A large proportion of the children admitted died soon after and in five years between 1791 - 1796 of the 5,126 infants admitted only one survived. A committee of the Irish House of Commons was appointed and its report was very damning.

It found sick children were stripped on being sent to the infirmary and had to wear the rags they arrived in. They were then laid five or six huddled together in cradles which were 'swarming with vermin' and covered with filthy and dirty blankets which had been cast off by others. A single bottle was used to feed the children, passed round, which had the effect of subduing the babies for a while so it must have contained either alcohol or some form of sedative, which in effect, assisted them to die.

New management were brought in by a special act of parliament but there was little improvement. In 1895, eight years after Mary Bryne died, the workhouse was visited by another commission from the *British Medical Journal* to investigate conditions. They found thirteen Sisters of Mercy acting as nurses, though they had no formal training and only worked in the day, assisted by pauper assistants, to care for more than 1,000 patients. Their report on the care of infants was very critical both of the care and cleanliness of the nursery:

> 'For healthy infants under two, there are two floors, that for the day being on the ground floor and above is a room where the mothers sleep with their infants. In the day nursery were large numbers of babies, some in wooden cradles or being nursed by their mothers. The cradles are filled with straw, covered by a sheet and blanket, some of the cots we looked into had wet sheets; in some food had been upset and not cleansed, many of the infants were untidy and ill cared for, the whole nursery showing want of control and supervision.

> 'The atmosphere, in spite of cross ventilation, was very close; there was no sense of freshness but a very powerful odour of uncleanliness. There is an officer over the nursery, but she is much handicapped in her work by the ignorant mothers, who are very difficult to manage. The lavatory and bathroom attached to this department was littered and untidy and anything but wholesome.'[763]

Nothing more appears in the newspapers after Jane was found guilty, maybe as the child died, money changed hands and the matter was quietly dropped, so I had to suspend my own judgement on the matter and concentrated on finding out if Anna Maria really was Jane's daughter.

Nothing connects them under the Gallagher, Mercer or Oakes surnames and Anna Maria does not appear in the 1901 or 1911 census either. If she was Jane's daughter she could have, in theory, been born anytime up to 1875 which would make her twelve when she gave birth in 1887 but despite the very many Anna Maria Gallaghers in England and Ireland in that date range there are no obvious candidates. As Irish census records for this period do not exist until 1901, I could not check who lived with Jane at any of her known houses in the 1880s. The 1901 and 1911 Irish censuses only show women called Anna Maria Gallagher living as daughters in established families.

But I was struck by the fact that Jane had a daughter - in - law called Mary Ann Gallagher, who had married her eldest son William Thomas Gallagher in 1862 in Liverpool. She was the Dublin born girl who had been violated by her father Joseph Clare when she was twelve, him being a brothel keeper for Jane in Springfield Street in Liverpool.[5] If you invert her name and convert it to the Roman Catholic version, it does read Anna Maria Gallagher. So where was she in 1887?

There are no records for her anywhere after the 1871 census and nothing to show if she was in Ireland at that time when she would have been 42, not too old to have a child perhaps, but was she able to conceive as she and William Thomas had no issue of their own and had a adopted a neighbour's boy?

With no other leads on Mary Ann, I decided to look elsewhere, reasoning the mother of Mary Byrne had to be someone for whom Jane would take such a big risk. Perhaps the mother was another family member: a niece, daughter or maybe even a granddaughter?

I established where all the females in Jane's immediate family were in 1887, starting with her actual daughters and granddaughters. I was able to eliminate Ann Elizabeth and Caroline as by 1887 they were age 53 and 48 and living with their large families in England. Selina who was supposed to be in Ireland in 1887, was 51, but there is nothing more about her on record. I had no idea where Rosanna (42) or Maria Jane (39) were at this time. As for the other daughter - in - law, Elizabeth Tyrer was out of the country with Alfred Hugh and they were also childless. There was only one niece for Jane, who would have been 53 in 1887 so looking into the granddaughters seemed the next logical step and there were four:

- Caroline Cooper had three daughters and in 1887 Florence Jane was 23, Selina 22 and Helen only 11

- Maria Jane O'Brien had one child, Rose Edith who was 17 in 1887

Helen can be taken off the list as she is only 11 in 1887. There are no records for Florence Jane or the younger Selina in Ireland that year and both by the 1891 census are living in London with their parents, working as theatrical actresses, neither of them marrying until after 1891.

It is too easy to assume that Rose Edith was the mother though I cannot find any reliable records for her after 1881 when she was in Liverpool age 11. Whilst there are dozens of records of girls called Rose Edith in England and Ireland, none place her in Dublin, nor can I ascertain beyond doubt when she died as searching on the O'Brien and even Crookenden surnames, as Rose Edith was at her aunt Rosanna's house in Liverpool on the night of the 1881 census, takes me no further. But what is food for thought is:

- Rose Edith's mother was called Maria (Mary) Jane

---

[5] *Chapter 20 – Preying on the Vulnerable*

- Her aunt was called Rosanna (Anna)

- Her surname was O'Brien (Bryne?)

Another possibility I considered was that Anna Maria Gallagher was actually one of Jane's prostitutes and they had both been paid to keep the father's name quiet. If so, there was no chance of tracing her and we will probably never know the truth unless more evidence comes to light, but that did not stop me being puzzled as to why Jane:

- Used her Gallagher name when for all her other dealings in Ireland after she moved from Belfast, she uses the Mercer surname

- Took a huge risk covering up this birth and giving a wrong address knowing people would know where she lived

- Left the child in a Catholic Church when she was a Protestant, then allowed the priest to baptise the child, thus lingering at the scene of the crime? This suggests the mother was a Catholic, or the unknown father, and that she felt some responsibility

Jane was not exactly the motherly type, having put all her seven children out to wet nurses as infants, then packing them off to private residential establishments until they came of age and could live independently, therefore this young mother must have been special to her in some way that I cannot account for.

As nothing else was reported, I can only assume Jane was not imprisoned for deserting the baby Mary Byrne.

Chapter 39 - Madams and Mayhem

When No 39 North Cumberland Street in Dublin became Jane's home in 1890, she bought it from Mrs. Annie Mack, who you might recall, was immortalised in James Joyce's novel *Ulysses*, where she appears in the *Nighttown* episode keeping a brothel in the heart of the red-light Monto district. She was so well known that the area was often referred to as 'Macktown' and a description of her appears in 'Tumbling in the Hay:'[764]

> 'Her face was brick-red. Seen sideways, her straight forehead and nose were outraged by the line of her chin, which was undershot and out-thrust, with an extra projection on it, like the under-jaw of an old pike ... Avarice was written by Nature's hieroglyphic on the face of Mrs. Mack. I thought of the grasping ways of her and her like ... Mrs. Mack [had] a laugh like someone guffawing in hell.'

In all, she kept eight 'flash' or superior houses on Lower Mecklenburg Street, like those Jane had in Liverpool, the street being renamed later as Lower Tyrone Street,[765] and she too had several names. Originally Anne Alexander born in Scotland in 1830, she married and became Mrs. George Leslie, having a daughter called Ada Leslie. When he died, she and her daughter moved to Dublin in 1874, about the same time as Jane arrived in Belfast. As Annie McEachern, after marrying a second husband Ronald, she first appears living at 20 Lower Mecklenburgh Street, a house transferred to her on a 41-year lease by Patrick Gilmour.

It was an 'interesting street.' At No 4, in a brothel in 1877, a 'respectable' solicitor died under suspicious circumstances and it goes without saying that his inquest was both well attended and liberally reported in the newspapers. The brothel madam, Ann Williams, was in court and said the solicitor had lived at the 'house of ill fame' for twelve years after abandoning his family, but she denied he was either the owner or the proprietor. Witnesses reported he was a 'consummate drunkard' and had been in bed for the previous nine days.

The coroner, anxious to blame someone for the death of this educated man, pressed the doctor about whether the solicitor had been neglected or starved in his last days. The doctor said it was quite the opposite, in fact:

'I never saw a body with so much fat! How his heart acted under the circumstances I am almost at a loss to know.'

The verdict was 'death from apoplexy.'[766]

In 1881, No 19, was the place where an 'Extensive Robbery of Champagne' ended up. Anne Quirk age 52 was charged with receiving stolen goods, eleven cases of champagne in all. But it was Mrs. Mack next door at No 20 who paid for them.[767]

Mecklenburgh Street had more than its share of publicity not least for its stink – it reeked of effluence and many owners were taken to court over ten years for breeching sanitary regulations in respect of their properties. It was also very well known to the police for prosecutions for 'Shebeening,' stabbings, burglaries and a mysterious suicide in 1886, by strangulation, but not via hanging. The man tied his scarf round the end of a bed post with the other end round his neck and pulled until he passed out and died. The coroner did not question whether this was possible, being more concerned that his mother was unable to give evidence because she was worse for drink.[768]

It was here that Mrs. Mack plied her trade and according to *Freemans Journal* of 18.6.1879, was charged with 'Shebeening' and fined 40 shillings [£132.37]. She keeps this address until 1885 when a Mrs. O'Brien takes over as a tenant. And guess what? This woman is Jane's youngest daughter Maria Jane O'Brien (Mercer.) I know because she too, on 22.7.1885, was charged with selling porter at 20 Lower Mecklenburgh Street without a license.[769] At last, she resurfaces, now the manager of a house of ill fame!

Knowing No 20 was an 'address of interest', I searched it more comprehensively and found a newspaper report dated 26.6.1885 which said that a Thomas Baxter Thorpe, a discharged British soldier, had been charged with having a revolver in his possession in a house in Mecklenburgh Street and was remanded. A year later Maria Jane marries for the second time to this man, them both living at the same address. Armed with these details I sent off for his attestation records, the marriage certificate and his baptism.

His parents were Charles Cooper Thorpe and Love Alder [a wonderful name, especially when you find out her maiden name was Love Eve] and they married in Lambeth, London on 10.3.1859. Thomas Baxter, their eldest, was born a month later in April and grew up in Lambeth, along with his siblings where his father Charles was a clerk and later a librarian. Charles Cooper died very young, only 39, on 21.5.1875 in Lambeth leaving his wife Love, Thomas Baxter age 16 and seven other children.

Thomas Baxter Thorpe, age 18, two years later, joined up with the 5th (Royal Irish) Lancers on 17.7.1877 and served with the regiment, mostly on garrison duties in Ireland and England, until he was discharged in Dublin on 5.7.1884 on payment of £21 [£1,389.88]. He must have liked it in Ireland as he spent the rest of his life in the city.

Maria Jane O'Brien was eleven years older than him when they married on 27.8.1886. Her second husband is described as a bachelor and a musician, though I have not been able to find out anything further about his musical abilities as compared to the antics of the Madams, he was relatively unnewsworthy. Maria Jane and Thomas, and probably Rose Edith if she was still alive, from at least 1885 were living in Mrs. Mack's old house and stayed there until 1895, by which time it had been renamed 20 Lower Tyrone Street. This possibly puts Rose Edith in Dublin and adds to the evidence she or her mother, Maria Jane, could have been the mother of the baby Maria Byrne. Unfortunately, there is no way of proving it.

Mrs. Mack, after becoming a widow for the second time in 1886, resumes this name and takes over No 39 North Cumberland Street when it first comes up for sale in 1883. She must have been a dog lover as a white Maltese Poodle goes missing from No 39 in 1885 and she offers both a reward for its return and threatens prosecution if someone is found with the little mite. [770]

The house has eight large and lofty rooms two kitchens, a pantry and a wine cellar and in 1885, using her Annie McEachern pseudonym, she acquires No 40 North Cumberland Street as well, keeping her name on the street directories even though she assigns a long lease to Ada Weatherup, her married daughter, who is then the estranged wife of William Weatherup. He is one of James Joyce's fellow rate collectors and was living on the same street as Jane at No 37 Gloucester Street between 1883 - 1884 when Jane was at No 24.

What a tangled web these brothel Madams weave! Mrs. Mack in 1886 also acquires No 85 Lower Mecklenburg Street, using the name Annie McEachern, and lives there from 1888. Ellen Cohen (alias Cannel, Charlton, or Reece), another notorious brothel keeper mentioned in Ulysses, acquires No 29 North Cumberland Street also in 1886, which is rented out for immoral purposes and produced more than normal rents - £50 [£3,309.24] a year as opposed to £15 [£992.77]. [771]

When Mrs. Mack's daughter, Ada, died aged 29 in 1887, the lease reverted to her mother who then assigns it to Lizzie Arnold, who was the wife of Leamington Arnold, a private in the 18th Royal Irish regiment. In 1893, it is his name that appears in street directories, but she was the business woman and rented it out. [772] When Lizzie died in 1915, she left a substantial portfolio of property and the trustee's sale after her

Susan Bennett

death saw eleven houses alone on Arnott Street put on the market, and business premises at Nos 46 and 46a. In what might not have been a coincidence given their shared professional interests, this is the same street Jane lived in at No 1 in 1887 when she deserted the baby Mary Byrne in the chapel porch.

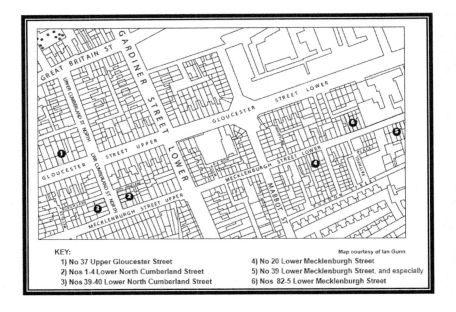

KEY:
Map courtesy of Ian Gunn
1) No 37 Upper Gloucester Street
2) Nos 1-4 Lower North Cumberland Street
3) Nos 39-40 Lower North Cumberland Street
4) No 20 Lower Mecklenburgh Street
5) No 39 Lower Mecklenburgh Street, and especially
6) Nos 82-5 Lower Mecklenburgh Street

Figure 98 Map in research by John Simpson about the Madams in 'Ulysses'

It is 1889 before Annie Mack (McEachern) starts to wind up her affairs in Dublin so she can retire to Scotland. She sells out for £1,000 [£66,184.70] to Lizzie Arnold, and gives her a long lease for Nos 85, 23 and 24 Lower Mecklenburgh Street, though Mrs. Annie Mack continues to make sure it is her name that appears in the street directories.

Jane is, as Liverpool Kate or Catherine Gallagher - on a list of madams in a book published in 1937 - along with Mrs. Mack and the likes of Maggie Arnott, another notorious brothel keeper, again mentioned in *Ulysses*. Maggie in 1881 moved into No 4 North Cumberland Street, Dublin before it was bought by Mrs. Mack in 1886. There she maintained a house of ill fame and was prosecuted for selling liquor without a license. The police found a large quantity of liquor and:

'Several showily attired girls lolling about the door smoking cigarettes, and inside five or six young men and six or seven young girls.'

Maggie Arnott's maiden name was Higgins and she used another name, Margaret Noble, when she moved to No 83 Mecklenburgh Street, which adjoined Mrs. Mack's at No 85, where she ran a brothel between 1887 to 1905. She had also adopted another name by this time: La Touché, which she claimed was her husband's mother's maiden name. Her career is notable for violence and her record shows her being summoned as follows:

- 1891 Assault and abusive and threatening language

- 1892 For having caused the death of a young girl in her house by assault, pulling her out of bed, knocking her down two flights of stairs and kicking her

- 1905 The attempted murder of her sister by striking her on the neck with an open razor

For this last offence she was committed in 1905 to Richmond Asylum as a dangerous lunatic.

Why Jane then moved such a little distance to 39 North Cumberland Street in 1890 is a mystery, especially when you consider it was not the best part of the city, being at the heart of the red-light district. The tenements were filthy, overcrowded, disease-ridden and seething with malnourished children. Perhaps she had an 'arrangement' with Mrs. Mack whereby Jane advanced her money and kept the deeds of No 39 as security?

The street had been quite grand many years before, housing the elite of the legal profession. Busy barristers and lawyers scuttled from their chambers to the courts from there every day but by 1872 it had declined and despite the optimistic hype of agents letting property in the area saying it was inhabited by 'respectable people,' the newspapers were full of the reality: 'The Garotters, Again,' 'Baby Farming' and the 'Wilful Neglect of Infants' are just some examples. [773]

There was even a famous shooting in May 1881 at No 22 North Cumberland Street which resounded nationally and was splashed in the press for weeks. Police informers were assaulted, like Mary Graham who lived on Jane's street[774] and to round the year off, there was a midnight street riot in November.

'With semi-stripped participants in hand-to-hand struggles accompanied by execrable exclamations which were distinctly audible, men and boys fought hard until the police were able to disperse them, armed with batons.'[775]

In 1882, Lord Frederick Cavendish was appointed Chief Secretary for Ireland in May but was murdered only hours after his arrival in Dublin. With Thomas Henry Burke, the Permanent Under-Secretary, he was attacked from behind by several men from an extreme Irish nationalist group, who used knives to murder them in what became known as the Phoenix Park killings. Cavendish's body was taken back to England and buried in the churchyard of St Peter's Church, Edensor, near Chatsworth, on 11 May, where 300 members of the House of Commons and 30,000 other people followed the remains to the grave.

The trial of the murderers in 1883 made it evident that the death of Cavendish was not premeditated and the assassins did not recognise him as it was Burke they wanted. Cavendish was only murdered because he happened to be with Burke in the park, which was only a short distance away from where Jane had her money lending office in Upper Gloucester Street.[776]

The investigation into these high-profile murders was led by Inspector William Thorpe of the Dublin Metropolitan Police Force, a man who had worked his way up from policeman, to sergeant, then inspector and by the end of his career was in line to become a superintendent. He was of interest not just for his career in the police, but because he was the father of John Henry Thorpe who became the Archdeacon of Macclesfield, the grandfather of another John Henry Thorpe who was MP for Rusholme in Manchester and then great grandfather of Jeremy Thorpe, disgraced ex leader of the Liberal Party, notorious for his involvement in the Christine Keeler and Profumo affair between 1960 - 1964.[777]

> 'The Profumo affair shocked the world in 1961 with details of a sexual relationship between John Profumo, the Secretary of State for War in Harold Macmillan's Conservative government, and Christine Keeler, a 19-year-old model. In March 1963, Profumo denied it in a personal statement to the House of Commons, but was forced to admit the truth a few weeks later. He had to resign and Macmillan too resigned as Prime Minister, on health grounds, in October 1963." [778]

It is true, to be fair, that the shooting and fighting died down a little by 1884 though crimes of a different sort were still being committed, like 'Knocker Wrenching.' A gentleman was charged with five others for having forced one off 30 North Cumberland Street about 6am. A neighbour heard the noise and got up in his nightdress to see a number of gentlemen running away. He hastily put his trousers on and gave chase, grabbing one and forcibly detaining him until the police arrived.[779] But for Jane, who favoured city centres, there was probably nowhere better than Dublin to catch passing trade, take advantage of teeming life and elephants. Yes, elephants.

In May 1892, Daniel Mc Donald who lived at 37 Cumberland Street, witnessed an accident which happened just as *Lord George Sanger's Circus*, with these magnificent beasts, was processing through Summer Hill. Two carts loaded with manure came along O' Connell Street and a horse, in fear of the elephants, bolted and knocked down several people. A woman died under the wheels of the cart and when lifted out, they found three children underneath her. After this loss of four lives, horses and elephants were not allowed on the streets at the same time.[780]

On 27.9.1892, James Byrne who lived at 38 North Cumberland Street attempted to commit suicide by taking sulphate of zinc. However, he was reported to the police who found him vomiting and a doctor was able to administer an emetic. Bryne was examined when he recovered and found to be suffering from a mental derangement.[781] Yes, this is the same surname as the deserted child who died in 1887 but there were lots of men called Byrne in Dublin, including a magistrate of the southern division, and many of them had children called Mary, for these were very common names.

In Jane's next court case in 1892, in which she was the victim, was bizarre. A soldier named Nicholas Shortall stole an armchair from her house on Cumberland Street and was sentenced to six weeks imprisonment.[782]

Domestic violence too was always only a fist away. Some would say, 'What's changed?' when they consider today's statistics across the whole of the UK, but the Victorians had rather different ideas about what mitigating circumstances were. In 1896, a man beat his mother to death on North Cumberland Street because she had not got his supper ready and used a knife, a strap, his boots and broke her ribs, causing internal injuries which killed her. She was between 65 - 70 years old. He was found guilty but the jury recommended mercy as his mother was known to be a habitual drunkard.[783]

Other residents had a strange sense of humour. A 'Villainous Practical Joke' was one that went wrong. George Mc Cormick 'a corner boy' was charged with having seriously injured a younger boy called Feeney who lived at 33 North Cumberland Street. Feeney said that Mc Cormick gave him a pipe and asked him to light it, but it exploded in his face. The boy's eyes were so inflamed he had to be led to the witness box. Mc Cormick was given six-month hard labour.[784]

This has been quite a whirlwind of Madams, houses, aliases, hidden ownership and tenancies in Dublin, all with connections to Jane:

- Jane and her 'daughter' in 1887, when the baby Mary Byrne was born, lived on Arnott St where Lizzie Arnold owned most of the brothel street

- Her daughter Maria Jane runs one of Mrs. Mack's houses at 20 Mecklenburgh Street, soon to become Lower Tyrone Street, for nearly ten years

- Jane acquires Mrs. Mack's most recent house at No 39 North Cumberland Street in 1890

- Mrs. Mack keeps her company at No 40 next door until 1893[785]

- Alfred Hugh commits suicide in 1892 across the road in 3 North Cumberland Street, one of Mrs. Mack's previous brothels but then owned by Jane

No wonder the newspaper reports of Alfred Hugh's death said the area was notorious, immoral and disreputable.

Chapter 40 - Eight Days, Two Deaths

Tuesday 30.8.1892:

'A man named Alfred Mercer, aged about fifty years, who was living in the house at No 3 North Cumberland Street [Dublin], committed suicide by shooting himself through the right temple. The unfortunate man occupied the front room of the second storey, where he lived for some time past together with his wife, who died four or five days ago... The deceased man did not follow any occupation.'

No 3 North Cumberland Street was built of brick or concrete, its roof of slate, iron or tiles and in 1901 it had seven rooms in all, with six windows on the front of the house. In these rooms lived 43 people crammed together, in a ratio of one room to six people, in theory. The reality was much worse for one room had ten people, another eight and yet another seven, so between those three rooms the ratio was one to eight people. The remaining eighteen occupants were split between four rooms. This was tenement life in Dublin at the end of the nineteenth century. But, at the time Alfred Hugh lived there, it appears there were fewer people.

'Immediately after the occurrence the unfortunate man was brought by Police Sergeant 6C and Constable 160C to Jervis Street hospital, where he was received by Drs Wales and Greeves, but the terrible wound which he had inflicted proved fatal and he died about twenty minutes after arrival. The remains lie at the hospital awaiting an inquest. The man has the appearance of a respectable middle-class person, with grey hair and whiskers.[786]

'Close enquiries with regard to the unfortunate man's antecedents show that he was 52 and that his father had been afflicted with lunacy. The deceased had been married some fourteen or fifteen years ago to a woman with regard to whom nothing is known. But it is known they were married in Dublin and that immediately after the marriage they emigrated to Australia. Eleven years ago, [1889] however, they returned to this city and from then till now they were supported, and amply supported, from the funds which are believed to be considerable, at the hands of his mother.'

But the 1891 census records them in Liverpool and their marriage certificate showed they were married there in 1887, not Dublin. Their emigration to Australia, however, was news and explained a lot about my failure to find Alfred Hugh before this time.

The Irish newspapers ran this story for days but even their reporters admitted they knew little about Elizabeth Mercer, Alfred Hugh's wife, apart from the fact she was:

'A well-educated woman who had no relation with the disreputable business of her mother-in-law, a portion of which was conducted in the immediate vicinity of the house in which they lived.'

However, records available today have enabled me to find out more about her father, Benjamin Hewling Tyrer. Born in London around 1802, his parents were Henry Tyrer and Charlotte Luson and he married a woman called Maria Elizabeth Watson in 1826 who was also born in London. They had eight children, some of whom were baptised on the same day. This does not mean they were necessarily twins, simply that the family waited and baptised more than one child at once. Because of the variation in the birth dates on the certificates so far, I was keen to take this opportunity to establish Elizabeth's true birth year.

As we have heard, before 1837 there was no civil registration and only churches recorded birth, marriage and death information in England.[787] Elizabeth was baptised on 17.2.1836 on the same day as her eldest brother Henry George at St Peter's Church in Liverpool where the family lived at Juvenal Place. Her father continued to work as a watch jeweller[788] and as she was born the year before the civil registration of births, I estimated it was between 1835 - 1836.

By the 1851 census, her family had moved to 52 Gerard Street in Liverpool and Elizabeth was 15, which gives us a year of birth, 1836. In the 1861 census they had moved again to 66 Finch Street [where Jane had a brothel], in the 1871 census she was at 94 Aubury Street, Liverpool working as the servant of a commercial clerk and his family.[789]

Her father died at Blandford Street, Liverpool in 1869, which in the near future was to become a designated area for tolerated brothels in Liverpool, and her mother Maria died in Liverpool in 1879, a year after Elizabeth married Alfred Hugh when they were already in Australia.

Elizabeth, on her marriage certificate claimed to be 36 in 1878 when she was in fact 42 and six years older than Alfred Hugh. On the 1891 census, Alfred Hugh is said to 47 but he was actually 48 and Elizabeth claimed to be 49 when she was 55,[790] but she would not be the first woman who felt the need to lop a few years off her age to hide the fact she was older than her husband.

Elizabeth cannot have been well when they lived in Liverpool as she herself died on 22.8.1892 at the Adelaide Hospital, which catered strictly for protestants in Dublin, having lived at 3 North Cumberland Street. Maybe they moved across the water knowing there were excellent medical facilities in the city.

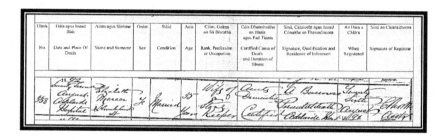

Figure 99 Death certificate of Elizabeth Mercer 22.8.1892

The death certificate shows she was age 55 and the wife of a 'store keeper,' which is new information and could only have been supplied by Alfred Hugh. The cause of death was acute dementia. In 1892, this condition was:

'Characterised by an inability to concentrate attention, memory defects and a lack of cognitive ability which was irreversible.'[791]

Someone called A. Burrows was present at her death, probably a member of staff, and the certificate was produced on 26.8.1892. [792] Elizabeth was buried at Mount Jerome cemetery in Dublin in grave number B96-380, only days before Alfred Hugh's suicide.

This cemetery has an interesting past. The newly formed General Cemetery Company of Dublin bought the lands and house of Mount Jerome in Harold's Cross, Dublin from the Earl of Meath, John Chambre, on the 23.1.1836. The first burial took place eight months later of the infant twins of a man called Matthew Pollock. 250,000 burials had taken place by 2006 and the cemetery expanded from 26 acres to 48 acres by 1874.

Figure 100 Entrance to Mount Jerome Cemetery, Dublin

Because Mount Jerome became established during the Victorian era, the monuments are 'a vivid expression of the success of the middle classes of the age.' As a result, it has one of the finest collections of Victorian memorials, tombs, vaults and crypts in Ireland. On top of one of the structures stands a howling dog and it is claimed the animal was found inconsolable on the shoreline where his master had drowned. There is also a vault which was fitted with a bell and a chain for a lady who had a phobia of being buried alive.

Many notable people are buried there including: the playwright J.M. Synge, author of *The Playboy of the Western World* and Sheridan Le Fanu, a writer who specialised in ghost stories. He is one of the founders of the genre and a huge influence on his peers, most notably Bram Stoker, author of *Dracula*. Vaults of the Guinness family and the grave of Oscar Wilde's father are also to be found at Mount Jerome.[793]

Alfred Hugh died at a different hospital, the Jervis Street charitable hospital in Dublin, which also has an intriguing history. Founded in 1718 it served the citizens of the city until 1982, over 266 years. In that time, it experienced the Act of Union, Catholic Emancipation, the Industrial Revolution, the Great Famine, the Eastern Rebellion, as well as Alfred Hugh's suicide.

The first chairman of the Board was Denis Thomas O'Brien, who held office for nearly 30 years and bequeathed much of his adjoining property to the hospital. The

Harwicke Fever hospital opened in 1803, a new Charitable Infirmary in 1804 and it then became a teaching hospital offering 75 beds, a surgery, a board room, and a matron, who in 1814 was earning £14 13s 11 and a half pence quarterly [£683.73] with board and lodging, and two nurses were appointed to assist her. The dissecting room was opened in 1813. The attending surgeons by 1821 were required every day except Sunday and:

'When patients are discharged a + shall be put in the Diet Book and in case of a Death, a mark thus ++... The Apothecary shall not absent himself from the Infirmary when the House-Keeper is away from Home and in his casual absences he shall leave directions with the Porter where he is to be found... No Patient to play at Cards, Dice or any other Game, or smoke in the Infirmary.'

A record in the Minute book of Thursday 20.7.1826 reads:

'An application having been laid before the Board from Daniel Loughlin, the Porter, soliciting a pair of shoes and stockings, as the ones handed over to him by the late porter on his dismissal were not new. Ordered, that the foregoing application be complied with.'

Another in 1830 said:

'Patients labouring under Venereal complaints be not in future admitted, being contrary to the Regulations of the Hospital.'

In 1844, the Committee of Management ordered that: 'The Matron - Housekeeper be fined £1 [£46.53] for neglecting to give a chop to a patient that was ordered by the medical gentlemen.'

Two years later, the housekeeper complained about a Mr. Farmer, a late resident pupil, saying that he had, on two evenings, noisy parties in the hospital. In 1854, the Sisters of Mercy were invited to supervise nursing by the management committee, though whether this was in response to the goings on at the hospital or not, it was successful even though the sisters were not trained nurses, as they had 'necessarily acquired an experience which renders them very efficient.'

By 1879, plans were afoot for a new hospital and in 1883 a Mr. Irving Bishop conducted a Séance in the Round Room which raised £230 [£14,400.07][794] and led to a new ward called the 'Bishop Ward.' However, not everything went to plan that night as someone forgot to tell the thought reader some of the answers to the questions planted in the audience.[795]

The new hospital opened in 1886, it had cost £55,160 16s 1d [£3,650,801.28], including purchasing the site and laying foundations, and £16,284 [£10,608,348.45] had still to be found. They held a week of fundraising events which included a Musical

Promenade, an Exhibition of Water Colours, a Full-Dress Ball, and an Undress Ball, which is not what you might think. It simply meant you did not need to dress up as for a full-dress ball in silks, fine muslins, low bodices or short sleeves, or fancy headdresses, with fans, jewellery and delicate slippers. In other words, 'Undressed' meant you could wear Morning Dress, Walking-out Dress, Carriage Dress, Promenade Dress, a Riding Habit, and Half Dress, even Afternoon Dress would do. And woe betide you if you got it wrong. The result would be a devastating social blunder as everyone was judged by their appearance. If you failed it was a sure statement about your fortune, or lack of it and your place in society.[796]

This magnificent new building had:

- Wards which were heated by hot water, 132 ft long by 30 ft wide and 20ft high which held 36 patients

- Proper windows with some double glazing, glazed corridors, conservatories, hydraulic lifts and staircases

- Fresh air vents eight feet above the floors which could be opened and closed

- Foul air exits under each ceiling leading to foul air flues which discharged above roof level

- Fireproof doors and a flat fire roof surrounded by a handsome balustrade, all in all 5,100 superficial feet which formed a splendid exercise ground for all patients, being 100ft above street level with magnificent views of the Dublin mountains and surrounding country

- An operating theatre, so arranged that every student got a full view of the operating table

The year before Alfred Hugh was admitted, a training school for nurses had been established whereby ten trainees were accepted and lived in dormitories in the hospital. Training lasted three years and applicants had to be between 22 - 55 years old, single or widowed.

Alfred Hugh's inquest was held on Wednesday 31.8.1892. Jane apparently was well known, sometimes as Madame Massey, and was said to own several houses in the city. No 3 North Cumberland Street was looked upon as:

'Of rather doubtful fame and a considerable sensation was created when the facts of the affair became known and the associations of the deceased added considerably to this feeling.'

The inquest heard how the house at 3 North Cumberland Street was let as tenements and was owned by his mother who was involved in the money lending trade.'[797]

'It is believed by the people in the neighbourhood, and indeed by the police, that he was never very strong and was afflicted with a form of paralysis and felt the loss of his wife deeply. He was observed to being in an extremely melancholy state within the past few days, and not being a man who was habitually given to the use of drink in excess, his condition was reported to have been a matter of some concern to this mother.'[798]

Jane told the inquest that her son's wife had died the previous week, that he had no occupation and she supported him. She had noticed for some years past he had been low in spirits, but not eccentric. However, the *Dublin Express*[799] reported Jane telling the Inquest that he was a money lender and a broker, when Elizabeth's death certificate said he was a store keeper and his own death certificate said he had no occupation. The newspapers were careful to state that Alfred Hugh did not follow the same trade as his mother and that:

'It appears certain that the deceased and his wife lived on friendly terms... the latter was a well-conducted woman.'

Mrs. Sly, who lived in a front room of the house, was called and said Alfred Hugh had, about an hour before his death, complained about being short of money and he had pledged a clock [with a pawnbroker]. She added that he was not drunk, but downhearted and she was preparing his dinner when he shot himself.

John Chatham, who also lived there and was regarded as a sort of caretaker, heard a noise which he 'at once conceived to have been caused by the explosion of firearms.' He rushed to the room and met Mrs. Sly who exclaimed: 'Oh Johnny, Mr. Alfred is shot!' He was lying on the bed unconscious with a revolver beside him, blood flowing from a wound to his temple and the bed was saturated with blood.'[800] Chatham went on:

'I met a young man coming down the stairs, I forgot that. He was coming down from Mrs. Sly's room. I asked him if he heard the shot and he said no. He was not in the room where the deceased was.'

Chatham said it was no more than two minutes from the shot being fired until he entered the room. He then ran as fast as he could to Store Street police station and informed the police but Constable Edward Tracy said he had been told by Mrs. Mary Chapman of the *Rotunda* that a man had shot himself at No 3.

'When he got to the house, he found the deceased lying on his back on the bed with the pistol in his right hand. He removed it from his grasp. There was a lot of blood about the bed. A cab was procured and they removed him to hospital.'[801]

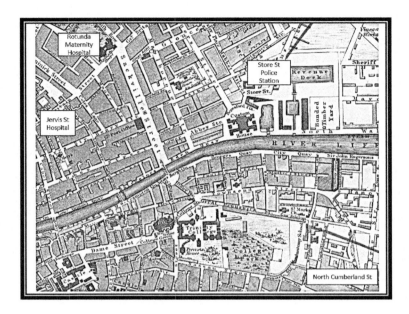

Figure 101 Map of Dublin, George Cox: London, 1853

'An old woman who said she was his mother drove up to the hospital shortly after the arrival of the police and the wounded man. She gave her name as Mercer and said she resided almost opposite in the same street.'[802]

Curiously, the young man was not called to give evidence at the inquest and it was never explained why the woman at the *Rotunda* heard about the suicide before the police if Chatham went straight to the station to report it.[803] Both places were on the other side of the river and the *Rotunda* was furthest away.[804] The doctors found there was profuse haemorrhage and a slight protrusion of the brain. There was a bullet track through the anterior portion of the brain from which they concluded the wound was self-inflicted. Alfred Hugh died at 3.20pm without regaining consciousness.

The police constable stated:

'The weapon is old-fashioned but highly finished. It is a weapon of the earlier Colt make, and has only one chamber. The handle is of a nicely-cut ivory and the weapon is fitted with a bullet which is larger in size than that used in the ordinary five-chambered Colt revolver. The size of the cartridge would suggest that the pistol is a very deadly weapon.'

It came out that Alfred Hugh had kept a diary systematically in his own handwriting since 1887 and several entries from the previous days were read out:

August 24th   Could not sleep last night, although I took eighty drops of chlorodyne. Have completed all the arrangements about the funeral. Parted from mother, but I cannot stand life any longer, now that Liz is dead.

August 29th   Feel bad. Must take some chlorodyne. If no good, must see doctor.

Chlorodyne was one of the best known patent medicines sold in the British Isles. It was invented in the 19th century by a John Collis Browne, a doctor in the British Indian Army; its original purpose was in the treatment of cholera. Browne sold his formula to the pharmacist John Thistlewood Davenport, who advertised it widely, as a treatment for not only cholera but diarrhoea, insomnia, neuralgia, migraines, etc. As its principal ingredients were a mixture of laudanum [an alcoholic solution of opium], tincture of cannabis and chloroform, it claimed to relieve pain and act as a sedative.[805]

No doubt Alfred Hugh was attracted to it for its ability to relieve, at least for a little while, his anguish, though many who committed suicide at that time used it to overdose. Other diary entries referred to his wife's illness and the unhappiness he felt at her condition. The coroner said:

'These extracts would indicate the state of the man's mind at the time, showing plainly that through grief he had lost his head and, as many had done before, had committed the fatal act.'

The jury found that death was due to laceration of the brain due to fracture of the skull, caused by the bullet wound inflicted by the deceased while labouring under temporary insanity, and they commended the promptitude displayed by the police constable in bringing the deceased to hospital.[806]

The certificate confirms Jervis Street hospital, Dublin as the place of death, that Alfred Hugh was a widower by that time, and he had no known occupation. The cause of death is harder to make out due to the handwriting but it says: 'Laceration of brain from pistol wound.' The informant was the deputy coroner of Dublin, Dr Fottrell from the hospital, the inquest was held on 31.8.1892 and the certificate produced on 1.9.1892.

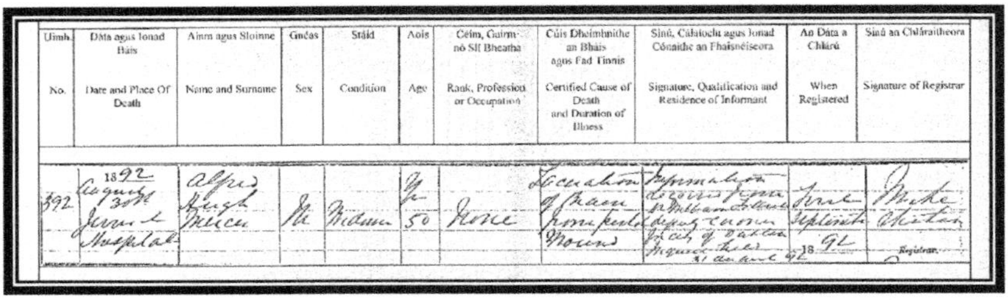

Uimh.	Dáta agus Ionad Báis	Ainm agus Sloinne	Gnéas	Stáid	Aois	Céim, Gairm nó Slí Bheatha	Cúis Dheimhnithe an Bháis agus Fad Tinnis	Sínú, Cáilíocht agus Ionad Cónaithe an Fhaisnéiseora	An Dáta a Chláraí	Sínú an Chláraitheora
No.	Date and Place Of Death	Name and Surname	Sex	Condition	Age	Rank, Profession or Occupation	Certified Cause of Death and Duration of Illness	Signature, Qualification and Residence of Informant	When Registered	Signature of Registrar
592	1892 August 30th Hospital	Alfred Hugh Mercer	M	Widows	50	None	Occupation of brain home people Mound	Hyman Leyes William Craine dated care of Bank of Ireland August the 31 Dublin	True Septent 92	Mike Whelan Registrar

Figure 102 Death Certificate 30.8.1892 Alfred Hugh Mercer

This is the second suicide in this story, the first being the daughter of Chalkley, Sarah Jane Carver, in 1895. Victorians feared suicide far more than they did murder as they regarded both acts as subversive, contrary to the ten commandments and to Victorian secular notions of self-help and the judicious exercise of willpower.

Murder might satisfy the Victorian sense of justice, since murderers could be caught and imprisoned or in turn be killed for their crimes, an eye for an eye. However, self-murder, on the other hand, might lead people toward a painful self-examination in the search for motives and it was a personal challenge to the will of God in which human justice could never really intervene.

Therefore, whilst murder caused sensation among the Victorians, suicide was more often a source of anxiety and disgrace so middle-class families often took pains to conceal it, not only because it was illegal and considered immoral but also because the insanity plea was the only way of preventing the property of a proven suicide from reverting to the Crown. They faced the awful dilemma of choosing the lesser of two evils: hereditary insanity as a future stigma, or poverty as an immediate prospect, that is, if the suicide were a breadwinner. Even clergymen were enlisted in cover-ups as, until the 1880s, proven suicides could not be buried in consecrated ground.

While Alfred Hugh and Elizabeth left nothing in their estates, Jane made sure both her son and his wife were buried at the prestigious Mount Jerome cemetery in Dublin, albeit with different grave numbers and no headstone

Chapter 41 - The Gold Rush

Up until this time I knew very little about Alfred Hugh Mercer's life after the 1851 census because he was supposedly away finishing his private education in Paris. He then missed the English censuses in 1861 and 1871 and despite being married in Liverpool in 1878 he missed the 1881 census too. But armed with the details of his death and the information Jane gave at the inquest about Australia, I renewed my searches and found that in 1862 Alfred Hugh Mercer, age 17 took an unassisted passage as an ordinary seaman bound for New South Wales, Australia departing from Liverpool on a ship called *Switzerland* which arrived in Sydney, on 12.2.1862.[807]

This would have meant that the ship set off about the end of December 1861 around the time two of Jane's brothel madams on Houghton Street were arrested for keeping houses of ill fame while Jane was supposedly living in London.[6]

Several letters sent to Alfred Hugh in Australia went unclaimed during his time, the first being in 1863. They were kept, along with all others unclaimed, and the names and addresses published in the *Queensland Government Gazette* between 1860 - 1874. This service developed because many colonists at this time moved around a lot looking for work and as a result letters were not able to be delivered as the last address was often no longer applicable. Unfortunately, the letters can no longer be claimed or accessed but there are still lists in the archives of unclaimed letters which were published monthly, usually in the month following their delivery. Therefore, for the letters unclaimed by Alfred Hugh we can assume they arrived a month before the dates given.

What was Alfred Hugh doing in Australia? His unclaimed letters give us a clue. The first dated 7.2.1863,[808] was sent to Ipswich, a place just east of Brisbane.[809] The town began in 1827 as a limestone mining settlement and grew rapidly as a major inland port. It was initially named the 'Limestone Hills' and later shortened to 'Limestone', however in 1843 it was renamed again after the town of Ipswich in England. [810]

---

[6] Chapter 29

The city became a major coal-mining area in the early 19th century, contributing to the development of railways in the region as a means of transport. The first recorded coal mines in the central Ipswich area started at Woodend in 1848, and it was perhaps the prospect of cashing in on the coal mining boom that drew Alfred Hugh to Ipswich initially.[811]

Between 1864 – 1865, an A. Mercer was issued a Crown Grant, probably for mining, at Smythesdale, Victoria which is about 85 miles west of Melbourne in South Australia. It was established during the gold rush and was known as Smythe's Creek until 1864.[812] Two more letters arrived while he was here in the next few years, both unclaimed and dated: 4.2.1865[813] and 4.2.1871.[814]

Ipswich was proclaimed a municipality in 1860 and had been a prime candidate for becoming the capital of Queensland from about 1847. However, when the Rev John Dunmore Lang had toured both Ipswich and Brisbane, despite noting the strength of Ipswich as a port town with access to the wool suppliers of the Darling Downs, Brisbane was chosen due to its mercantile and colonial interests and declared the capital of the new state of Queensland in 1859, and this is where Alfred Hugh went next.[815]

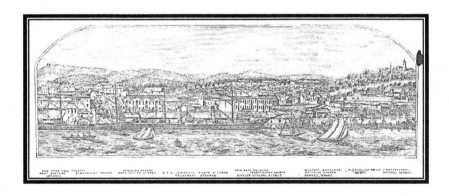

Figure 103 Part of Brisbane in 1865

Originally a penal colony, Brisbane did not permit the building of private settlements nearby for many years but as the inflow of new convicts steadily declined, the population dropped. From the early 1830s, the British government questioned its continuing suitability as a penal colony and in 1838, the area was opened up for free settlers, as distinct from convicts. From the 1840s, settlers took advantage of the abundance of timber in local forests. Once cleared, land was quickly utilised for grazing and other farming activities and the convict colony eventually closed. On 6.9.1859, the Municipality of Brisbane was proclaimed. The next month, polling for the first council was conducted and Queensland was formally established as a self-governing colony of Great Britain, separate from New South Wales, in 1859.[816]

Figure 104 Stamford's map of Queensland 1860

Gold transformed Queensland's history and landscape as it brought migrants like Alfred Hugh and established new towns. Small deposits were discovered across the Darling Downs in the 1850s before the gold rush actually began in Queensland at Canoona near Rockhampton in 1858. It was only a small deposit but explorers kept coming, then Gympie emerged as the next place to be.

Figure 105 Gympie Flood, 1873

Gympie is about 160 kilometres (100 miles) north of the state capital, Brisbane and lies on the Mary River, which flooded greatly.[817] Graziers were the original European settlers but the discovery of gold in Gympie in 1867 saved Queensland from the worst effects of the 1866 economic depression and provided an important boost for the first fifty years of the state, hence Alfred Hugh's interest. Subsequently, James Nash reported the discovery of 'payable' alluvial gold on in October 1867. [818] At the time, Queensland was suffering from a severe economic depression and Nash probably saved Queensland from bankruptcy, which is why a memorial fountain in Gympie's Park honours his discovery.[819]

The first jacaranda tree grown in Australia was planted at the City Botanic Gardens in Gympie in 1864 and Alfred Hugh, or at least letters for him, arrived in 1865. He then moved to Charters Towers in 1871, the same year as gold was first discovered there, where another letter waited dated 1.3.1871.[820] The town was founded in the 1870s[821] when gold was discovered by chance at Towers Hill on Christmas Eve 1871 by a twelve-year-old Aboriginal boy, Jupiter Mosman. He was with a small group of prospectors including Hugh Mosman, James Fraser and George Clarke when their horses bolted after a flash of lightning. While he was searching, Jupiter found not only both the horses but a nugget of gold in a creek at the base of Towers Hill.[822] The name Charters originated from the Gold Commissioner, W.S.E.M. Charters and a total of ten major gold reefs were eventually mined.

Such were the boom years, between 1872 and 1899, that Charters Towers hosted its own stock exchange. The Great Northern railway between the city and the coastal port of Townsville was completed in December 1882, when the population was approximately 30,000, making Charters Towers Queensland's largest city outside of Brisbane. The city was also affectionately known as 'The World', as it was said that anything one might desire could be had in the 'Towers', leaving no reason to travel elsewhere. What a wonderful prospect for young man like Alfred Hugh. [823]

The Charters Towers gold field produced over 200 tonnes (6.6 million troy ounces) of gold from 1871 - 1917. It was concentrated into veins and was Australia's richest major field with an average grade of 34 grams per tonne. The grade was almost double that of Victorian mines and almost 75% higher than the grades of Western Australian (Kalgoorlie) gold fields of that time. This was a fact Alfred Hugh must have appreciated for on 18.5.1872 he paid for a Gold Field Licence at Cape and the Broughton River in Queensland for Miner's Rights: No 49387.[824] He must have been a very tough to chase across unchartered lands in search of gold, and resilient in order to keep going against all the competition there must have been from other prospectors.

By 1873, he has invested as a shareholder in the Cosmopolitan Gold Mining Company at Ballarat in Victoria,[825] and applied for yet another Gold Field licence dated 6.9.1873 in Etheridge in Queensland, No 59053.[826] Originally known as Finnigan's Camp after the prospector who discovered gold nearby in 1871, the discovery of gold in 1851 meant the area could sustain high gold yields for many decades, and in the process, gold transformed the place from a small sheep station to a major settlement. Charleston Township continued to grow despite near desertion when its inhabitants, including Alfred Hugh, rushed to the Palmer River goldfield in 1874 where he got himself a licence to mine himself.

William Hann and geologist Norman Taylor found gold in a sandy bed of the river in 1872 and named the river after Arthur Hunter Palmer, the premier of Queensland at that time. Over time 20,000 people made their way to this remote gold field on the Palmer River,[827] over 18,000 of them Chinese miners for this was one of Australia's major gold rush locations.

Alfred Hugh's next application was dated 25.7.1874, when he received a Business Licence for Palmer River, Queensland, No 5233.[828] The main settlement of the gold field was Maytown replacing Palmerville after some months. It began as a camp in 1873, then grew into a town which served as the administration centre for the former Hann Local Government Area. There were several confrontations between the settlers and local Aborigines, including one at Battle Camp. This gold rush lasted three years but Alfred Hugh Mercer was long gone by 1878 as records show him age 34 arriving in London in June 1878 on the ship *Chimborazo* from Victoria, Australia.[829] Either he had made a complete fortune, or his money had run out.

Quite quickly, seeing as Alfred Hugh had been away from England for sixteen years, he married five months later to Elizabeth Tyrer on 26.10.1878, from Norton Street in Liverpool where he was probably a guest in someone's house, rather than the person who owned it. I wonder, did he come back just to find a wife, or had he been in correspondence with Elizabeth during the long years he was in Australia?

He was said to be a gentleman on his marriage certificate and 'living off his own means' in the 1891 census but does this refer to his profits, if any from the gold rush, or was he still supported by his mother's ill-gotten gains?

I cannot trace a connection between him and John Boylan, the witness at their wedding, as he did not appear in any registers near Norton Street. Scanning the lists of people registered to vote though, I found there were many counting houses on Norton Street between 1875 -1879, specifically at 21, 24, 25, 34, 40, 42 and the one owned by H. Hyman at No 44, which offered loans without surety to anyone from gentlemen to cow keepers.

There was a brothel too, disguised as a temperance house, for which the madam, Ellen Davies, was sentenced to twelve months imprisonment on 17.6.1878[830] but Norton Street also had its luxury hotels, much favoured by the Russian Ambassador and others from the same country. The Russian Princess Sonvoroff, Marchioness de Potostad and Count Kolouvrat passed through Liverpool in the first week of January that year and stayed at the *Havana Hotel*, 20 Norton Street leaving a few days later on the Cunard steamship *Scythia* for New York.[831]

It was a lively street, just off Islington and near to Lime Street Station and catered, as we have seen, for all needs, including for those who searched for milk on Shrove Tuesday in March 1877 when the demand for milk to make pancakes was the greatest. Ann Jump of No 23 Norton Street was fined 40 shillings [£125.22] and costs for adding 32 parts water to hers. The report was headlined: 'Milk and Water.'[832] But however lively it was, Liverpool must have felt very small, petty, boring and unexciting to Alfred Hugh after his glory days in Australia chasing gold.

According to Jane's statement at Alfred Hugh's inquest the couple married in Dublin, which is patently untrue, and went directly back to Australia from there. But records show the couple actually returned to Australia from Gravesend on 8.11.1878 on the ship *Kent* arriving in Melbourne, Victoria in December 1878.[833] This would have left barely enough time, thirteen days, for them to pay a quick visit to Dublin to see Jane and then get to Gravesend to catch the ship before it left. When you consider the need to be there in good time because of the unpredictable weather conditions in November and waiting for tides, it does not seem very likely they risked losing their berths with a side trip. Maybe this was wishful thinking on Jane's behalf.

After landing in Melbourne just before Christmas in 1878 where did they go? Well, staying there was one option and someone called Alfred Mercer did for a while but the last unclaimed letter for Alfred Hugh was waiting for him in Consuelo dated 4.6.1879,[834] which is currently part of the Carnarvon Gorge National Park in Queensland, with giant sandstone structures which lead to the highest plateau in the area, and the Consuelo Tableland standing at more than 1,000 feet above sea level. It was associated with coal mining for a time but maybe Alfred Hugh took Elizabeth there for their honeymoon.

But it is nowhere near Adelaide where I found an article mentioning an Alfred Hugh Mercer, in the *Express and Telegraph*, Adelaide newspaper on 7.10.1879 four months later. This Alfred Hugh had been brought before a Justice of the Peace charged as a result of information supplied by a man called George Smith:

'With using water on his premises for other than domestic purposes, namely for the washing of bottles, he not having paid the Commissioner for Waterworks in respect of the same.'

The justice asked Mr. Smith how he made out that washing bottles was not a domestic purpose, for he would be afraid to wash his own bottles in future, to which there was much laughter in court. But Smith claimed other large manufactories had to pay an extra sum for water used in washing bottles. The justice awarded a fine of five shillings but it is not clear against who. Was it Mr. Smith for bringing a frivolous charge or because he found Alfred Hugh guilty?[835]

It does not really matter now either way, as I have also found other indicators of where Alfred Hugh and Elizabeth might have lived in this next decade by searching entries in street directories, government journals and newspaper archives. None of it is conclusive and as Alfred Hugh did nothing newsworthy, there is very little else to go on as Australia is a very big place indeed to go looking for needles in haystacks. But this is what I found: Alfred Mercers who lived in and travelled to the following places:

- 1880   155B Young Street, Melbourne

- 1880   From Melbourne to Sydney on the ship *'Konoowarra'*
- 1881   3 Stafford Street, Abbotsford, Melbourne
- 1882   2 Exeter Cottages off Johnston Street, Melbourne
- 1885   From Melbourne to Sydney on the ship *'Wentworth'*
- 1886   Sydney from Victoria on the ship *'Habsburg'*

And in 1887 a man called John, alias Charles Moore, stole a sporting rifle from an Alfred Mercer at Marree which is 366 miles north of Adelaide and was committed for felony.

I would have relied upon the 1871 and 1881 censuses normally to tell me where Alfred Hugh and Elizabeth were and what occupation(s) they had but there are no census records of individuals left in the following areas after these dates:

- Victoria: 1853: Queensland: 1841; and in South Australia: 1841. This is because, after statistical analysis was completed, census forms containing information about individuals were destroyed and in 1892 all surviving Victorian household forms from earlier censuses were pulped

- And earlier, in 1882, a fire destroyed the New South Wales census records for 1846, 1851, 1856, 1861, 1871 and 1881, including the household forms from 1861, 1871 and 1881. Electoral rolls are not available for these three states for the period either[836]

What I also cannot find is a record of the voyage Alfred Hugh and Elizabeth must have taken to get back to Liverpool before the 1891 census. Jane says they were back in Dublin by 1889 so I looked there as well. But there are no census records for Ireland surviving from 1841 until 1901, as they too were destroyed either by fire or because of instructions by the government. And to make research really difficult, detailed travel records between Ireland and Liverpool are very patchy.

As a result, there are still many significant gaps in Alfred Hugh and Elizabeth's timelines both during their stay in Australia and after they are supposed to be back in Ireland in 1889, as they also appear in the 1891 census in Liverpool before they both die a year later in Dublin in 1892.

I still don't know whether they came back penniless, or because of Elizabeth's failing health. But what is sure is that the Alfred Hugh who arrived back to live in Dublin in one of his mother's houses in the red-light district of the city, allowing her to fully support both him and his wife, had lost all the fire and spirit he had shown as a pioneer in Australia.

Chapter 42 - Denouement

After the double tragedies in 1892, Jane kept calm and carried on with her business interests but then comes another strange turn of events. An act of self-harm took place in her house, only six months after Alfred Hugh died.

'Last night, [Friday 23.1.1893] a married woman called Crookenden of 39 Lower Cumberland Street, was received at Jervis Street hospital suffering from two small incised wounds in the neck which are believed to be self-inflicted. She was attended by Dr Day who does not consider the wounds dangerous.'[837]

Subsequently, Jane Crookenden, living at 39 North Cumberland Street, was charged at the beginning of February 1893 with attempting to commit suicide by cutting her own throat with a razor. Luckily, it was a mere scratch, as she was drunk at the time. When she was presented in court, she said she was sorry for her rash act and her sister paid £10 [£820.49] to guarantee her good behaviour for the next twelve months.[838]

My antennae twitched as I knew I had come across the Crookenden name before. Looking in my records reminded me Roseanna, Jane's eldest illegitimate daughter, had married Thomas Crookenden, a timber salesman, on 12.1.1870[839] in Liverpool. They initially lived with his mother, Margaret Crookenden at 49 Queens Drive in the Everton area of Liverpool. Their marriage was childless and further digging showed that Rosanna's sister-in-law had been called Jane Crookenden but she died age 13 in 1856. The 1871 census a year later shows Thomas is unemployed and again the couple are living with his mother but they have moved to 25 Venmore Street in Liverpool. This does not stop him appearing in the press though, as in 1873 he appears at a hearing to determine his right to vote under the lodger franchise where he also represents some of his fellow tenants.

Before the *Reform Act* of 1885, only lodgers who paid £10 [£661.85] or more annual rent were allowed to vote and this hearing was to adjudicate on the cases submitted by Thomas Crookenden. What follows is Thomas' evidence showing he paid 10 shillings [£41.02] a week for a sitting room and a bedroom in the house at Venmore Street where his mother was the tenant and paid £19 a year [£1,558.94] in rent.

Opposing Barrister: Does the rent include gas?

Crookenden: Yes – No, it includes a paraffin lamp. [Laughter]

Opposing Barrister: Does it include attendance?

Crookenden: Of course, you don't suppose I wait on myself, do you? [Laughter]

The attending barrister said the vote must be allowed. But Thomas, instead of quitting while he was in front, said he also represented a fellow lodger, John Lloyd Williams, who occupied the back parlour and the front bedroom of the same house for which he paid 7 shillings a week [£28.72].

Opposing Barrister: What! Two lodger claims in a house assessed at £15 [£1,230.74]! The inference was that the rent was not enough for the house.

Crookenden: You wouldn't say that if you lived there. [Laughter]

Opposing Barrister: I think in future instead of being called lodgers, you should be termed dodgers. [Laughter]

Crookenden: It might be appropriate in your case but it isn't in mine. [Renewed laughter]

Opposing Barrister: I think it is appropriate in your case. It is being suggested that deducting coals and furniture, the amount paid would be reduced below the qualifying amount.

Crookenden: Williams was only supposed to have coals three months in the year. [Laughter]

Barrister: And consider the price of coal.

Crookenden: We did not calculate three years ago that coal would be at its present price.

Barrister: You had better tell your mother to raise his rent. [Laughter]

This claim was disallowed.

Thomas Crookenden went on to advocate for a man who rented a room in his brother's house and another who lived next door to him as well and a jolly time they had of it in this hearing.

Thomas seems to have recovered from his period of unemployment in 1871 as by 1877 he lives at 35 Wentworth Street, Liverpool where he has, probably seeing the money to be made from it, set up a coal yard.[840] Continuing to do well, he is a book keeper at 66 Burleigh Rd South, Liverpool in 1878 and when in 1881 William Mercer died, Rosanna is the sole Executrix of his will and living at her father's house on Herschell Street looking after her niece Rose Edith whilst also acting as a governess to another child from Keswick who is boarding with her. Her husband is said to be away but I wonder if this is when they split up for after this there is no indication of where either Thomas or Rosanna are and Thomas himself does not die until 1913.

Armed with the details of the attempted suicide, I found a Jane Crookenden, travelling as a nurse, had arrived in Southampton from Barbados on 12.7.1891 on the ship *Medway* which came from the West Indies via: Savanilla, Colon, Jamaica, Barbados and Plymouth. There were many rich and prosperous families on board and presumably she had been hired as a nurse or governess for one of the families.[841] But how is this related, if at all, to Rosanna Crookenden and why was she in Jane Gallagher's house attempting suicide? Was this Jane again changing people's names to suit the situation, remaking her daughter as a sister so Rosanna and Jane Crookenden were the same person? Or did Maria Jane, her real sister, now married to Thomas Baxter Thorpe in Dublin, pay the fine?

One month later there is a news report about Rosanna Crookenden herself, who is in court for threatening to kill Jane Mercer of 39 North Cumberland Street and ends up in Grange-Gorman Female Prison on 16.3.1893 for one month and is then released on bail, no doubt paid by Jane.[842] She was described in the prison register as age 47, a governess, five feet two inches tall, of fresh complexion, weighing 164 lbs, born in Liverpool. This time it is definitely her.

Grange-Gorman female penitentiary, Dublin, was the only prison in the British Isles established exclusively for women and was part of a complex that held the Lunatic Asylum and a Male Prison.[843] The women who found themselves here were desperate. Many had been sentenced for theft, others for prostitution, some were convicted for fighting or abandoning a child, and there's an entire register from 1830 of women sentenced for public drunkenness. Sentences were usually short, like Rosanna's, but conditions could actually be better than the workhouse as the prison was a model penitentiary. Some women went out of their way to get arrested, using it a safety net when they could no longer survive on the streets and many were readmitted multiple times as regulars. Children were often sent to gaol with their mothers and there was a regular doctor on site for pregnant inmates.

Figure 106 Grangegorman Prison, 1836. Creative Commons

However, life there was not exactly easy. Many inmates were sentenced to hard labour, which would have included scutching [beating flax to remove the straw] or cloving which was splitting flax fibres by hand. The work was considered so onerous that it had to be approved by a doctor for the weaker women. There was a strict code of conduct and efforts were made to keep the hardened criminals away from those sentenced for the first time. For those who didn't obey the rules, punishments included being locked in solitude or in the dark with rations reduced to bread and water.[844]

This was where Rosanna spent one month, long enough to reconsider what she had done and why. We can only speculate what drove her to a drunken attempt at suicide and then threatening to murder her mother all in the first three months of 1893. Had she just found out that her sister Selina had died in 1892 along with her brother Alfred Hugh and his wife Elizabeth, and about the baby Mary Byrne, who must have been some sort of relative given the risks Jane took? And what about her other brother William Thomas? Was she told he was missing?

Her only good news must have been that her sister Maria Jane had re-married and was nearby in Dublin and, if her niece Rose Edith had survived at all, she was there too.

But moving on... Jane had seven children I know about, and maybe others died unblessed. Between them they produced for her 11 grandchildren. Ann Elizabeth and Caroline gave birth to all but one, and Maria Jane had one child who survived.

Now, alone, both husbands and a lover long since dead, I did wonder if Jane ever reflected whether using immoral means, becoming such a notorious woman in the process, in order to give her children the best possible education, ensuring they never experienced the poverty she did as a child by creating wealth enough to give them financial independence, meant they had led happy, healthy and successful lives?

She must have been proud the majority married well and into the professional classes, that some had travelled the world, and up until now, none had been to prison, ended up in the workhouse, or on the streets selling their bodies. Their choices as adults, whether they be to emigrate, or sail the vast oceans, or devote themselves to motherhood, were theirs alone but she must have grieved sorely for those who died before her, one by his own hand and been very angry at Rosanna's drunken suicide attempt and threat to murder her.

To achieve all this, yes, she had lost out on the joys of motherhood by the necessity of keeping her children away from the brothels and must have experienced some pangs over the years when she saw little of them until they popped up as newly minted adults. But she'd also had lots of fun: launching a *Talking Fish* across England, enjoying the cultivated company of influential gentlemen in Liverpool and London, possessing beautiful clothes, valuable jewellery, living in lavishly furnished houses enjoying wealth and fame, especially when she compared her life to those of her four sisters.

She alone had moved significantly up the social scale from being the daughter of a carter to a successful business woman in an era when women were wholly repressed by men, keeping her head high, conducting herself with style and finesse in court rooms across the kingdom, earning herself a reputation as a woman not to crossed. More importantly, Jane proved her resilience, surviving near ruin after the last few court cases in Liverpool with enough energy and money to start again in Ireland, accumulating more houses, money and power as well as managing a new and successful money lending business.

It goes without saying she had told a few untruths, twisted facts, changed her name a few times and committed bigamy, been in prison on three occasions at least, exploited the naiveite of tradesmen to obtain credit without disclosing her true situation, been publicly dragged up from London in disgrace as a procuress, and found guilty of deserting a child. There were probably regrets, but I expect only a few.

So, what was her legacy? Lots of good stories which have given pleasure to many and will continue to shock, amaze, enrage and above all delight for all time; a legal precedent in her name, a milestone in the long battle for the independence of married or separated women; a glorious example of what just women can do when everything is stacked against them; a unique insight into life in Victorian Britain, warts and all!

But none of us live forever. Jane is now in her late seventies, nearly the same age as her mother was when she died and I am sure must have been extremely weary of life's tribulations, endless struggles, court cases and the sheer effort to keep what she had.

There is only one more court case: *Mercer v Keys*, in 1894 and it was a very mundane swan song. She claimed she did not owe outstanding rates on her house on West Cumberland Street, Dublin after being summoned by the Collector-General for £17 [£1,394.84]. Despite her vigorous defence, the judge refused to let her off.[845]

Jane died on 10.1.1895 at 39 North Cumberland Street, Dublin, age 78. With her was her daughter Maria Jane who still lived in Mrs. Mack's house with her second husband Thomas Baxter Thorpe at 20 Lower Tyrone Street, Dublin, in the busy red-light district.[846] There is no indication Rosanna Crookenden was there when she passed.

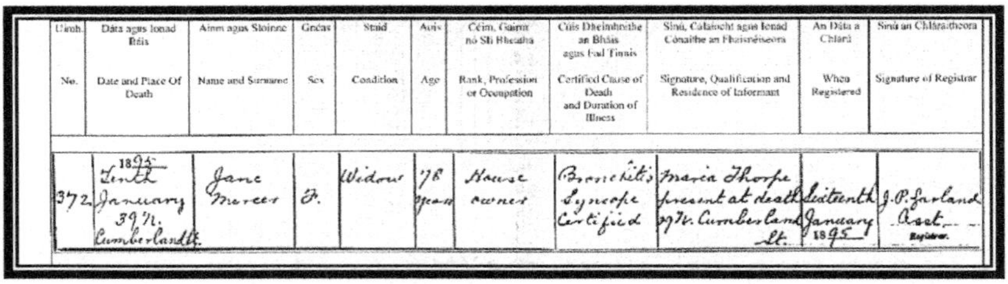

Uimh.	Dáta agus Ionad Báis	Ainm agus Sloinne	Gnéas	Staid	Aois	Céim, Gairm nó Slí Bheatha	Cúis Dheimhnithe an Bháis agus Fad Tinnis	Síniú, Cáilíocht agus Ionad Cónaithe an Fhaisnéiseora	An Dáta a Cláraí	Síniú an Chláraitheora
No.	Date and Place Of Death	Name and Surname	Sex	Condition	Age	Rank, Profession or Occupation	Certified Cause of Death and Duration of Illness	Signature, Qualification and Residence of Informant	When Registered	Signature of Registrar
372	1895 Tenth January 39 N. Cumberld St.	Jane Mercer	F.	Widow	78 years	House owner	Bronchitis Syncope Certified	Maria Thorpe present at death 39 N. Cumberland St.	Sixteenth January 1895	J. P. Farland Registrar

Figure 107 Death certificate of Jane Mercer, Dublin 1895

The cause of death was bronchitis syncope, which the French neurologist Jean-Martin Charcot first clearly described in the 1870s and labelled it laryngeal 'vertigo.' Symptoms can be blacking out, feeling light headed, falling for no reason, feeling dizzy, changes in vision. Today this condition affects 3% of men and 3.5% of women and up to 6% of people over 75. It can result from a sudden drop in blood pressure or heart rate, or an attack of bronchitis.[847]

As Jane died before 1904, an original copy of her will was in a batch which did not survive the Four Courts Fire of 1922, neither did any original wills from the 16th century until the beginning of the 1900s. Seven centuries of Ireland's historical and genealogical records, stored in a magnificent six-story Victorian archive building known as the Record Treasury, were lost in one afternoon. As well as documenting the growth of the state in Ireland across many centuries the archive's collections touched on almost every aspect of life in Ireland, including births, marriages and deaths, wills, maps, parish registers and town records from across the island. For generations, the loss of these precious historical documents has hampered research and it also means we do not know what really happened to Jane's money.[848] But we do have a summary of the probate record.

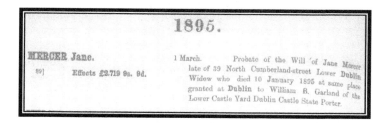

Figure 108 Probate record for Jane Mercer 1895

The High Court instructed William B. Garland to administer probate and issued the notice below which appeared in newspapers asking for claims against Jane's estate and, presumably, he eventually settled it. But as no records remain, here is yet another loose end which may never be tidied up.

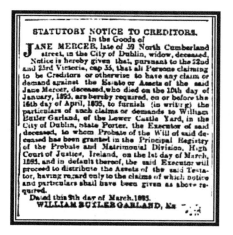

Figure 109 Statutory Note to Creditors of Jane Mercer 1895

However, we know Jane had houses on Summer Hill, Dublin including Nos 71, 101, 125, 129 and 130, as well as on North Cumberland Street and maybe other places too in Belfast. She also had an annuity which presumably would have been taken into consideration and in all, her estate is valued at £2,719 9 shillings and 9d

[£223,132.05].[849] The obvious executors, her sons, were no longer alive, or Selina so that left only two other married daughters in England and two illegitimate daughters who might have benefitted, if Jane had mentioned them in her will. [850] Who knows?

Maria Jane meanwhile made sure Jane was buried respectfully at Mount Jerome Cemetery in Dublin in grave number A64-380-9439. In the same plot are Florence Willis, age 25 who died on 1895 and Thomas Thorpe, her husband, who died two years later on 17.12.1897. He was said by then to still be an artist and died of scarring of the liver, relatively young, only 45. Maria paid the £2 [£164.10] grave fee and gave her address as 20 Lower Tyrone Street, which was just round the corner from Jane's house on Cumberland Street, Dublin.

So, who was Florence Willis who died a month after Jane,[851] at 20 Lower Tyrone Street? Maria Jane and her husband Thomas had by then moved to 39 North Cumberland Street, Jane's house. I found a couple of death records and one said Maria Jane was her mother and her actual death certificate said she was her cousin!

After all this time, Jane's life and family were still managing to surprise me.

Chapter 43 - Twists and Entanglements

Was Florence Willis' mother really Maria Jane? According to Florence's death certificate she was born around 1870, the same year as Rose Edith, Maria Jane's only official surviving child. I cannot find another marriage between Maria Jane O'Brien and a man called Willis, which might have explained two daughters born to different fathers but it is unlikely she had two children to different men in the same year when she was still married to her first husband, Michael Charles O'Brien.

Thomas Baxter Thorpe had not married before, according to his marriage certificate and would only have been eleven in 1870, so Florence Willis was not his child.

Maybe Florence Willis really was a cousin? There were three women called Florence Willis born between 1868 – 1872 in England and Wales: in Whitechapel, London, in Birmingham and Chesterfield, none of whom strayed very far from the place where they were born, and they all either died before they reached one year or lived until after 1911. There was only one born in Ireland, in Enniskillen. She was the daughter of George Willis, a hotel proprietor and Charlotte, formerly Parkinson. Born on 12.8.1870 she was baptised on 1.9.1870 and died in 1875 age only four.[852] No luck there, then.

I looked for the female children of Maria Jane's aunts who might have married a man called Willis and would have been her cousins but they were too old to have given birth to a child in 1870, being several years older than Jane herself, apart from her aunt Ellen who only had sons.

As the children of Jane's two husband's sisters could also said to be cousins by marriage, I traced as many as I could only to find that they were too old as well to have had a female child in 1870 as William Mercer was eighteen years older than Jane and as Thomas Gallagher's siblings are still unknown, there was nothing to find there either.

Next up were Maria Jane's step-nieces, and Caroline's daughter Florence Jane came up again, but as she was born in 1864 would have only been six when Florence Willis was born. As she was the eldest of the females in this generation that discounted all the younger females too.

Did Maria's first husband, Michael Charles O'Brien, have cousins who fit the profile? Well, he only had one sister who was not married by 1887 so she can be ruled out. Charles' maternal female cousins were older than his mother who was born in 1831 and only one had a child, a male who died age 12.

Finally, I turned to Thomas Baxter Thorpe's cousins next but I cannot find out if his father, Charles Cooper Thorpe, had any siblings as his parents Joseph Cooper and Sophia Thorpe were not married – she appears on the baptism certificate as a spinster and there is no other issue in this relationship. Yet another dead end.

Meanwhile, I found Maria Jane's sister, Rosanna Crookenden, died five months after Jane and four months after Florence Willis. She was 51 years old, last seen on 19.6.1895 at 28 North Great George Street in Dublin and found dead three days later on 22nd. The address is a Dancing Academy[853] run by Professor Maginni for decades, offering 'private tuition daily in fashionable dancing, waltz etc. Described as the widow of a clerk, Rosanna too died of syncope, this time of the cardiac variety. An inquest said she also had a fatty heart with both liver and kidney disease. [854]

Where Rosanna is buried I have yet to find out but it was not at Mount Jerome in Dublin with her mother, brother and his wife, brother-in-law and Florence Willis. Maybe there was no space left that wasn't already booked, or Maria Jane, the only sister in Dublin left, did not want to get involved.

That left me with three important stones left unturned in Dublin:

- Where was Rose Edith O'Brien? (Thorpe, if she took her stepfather's name)
- Who was Florence Willis?
- Who were baby Mary Byrne's parents?

Rose Edith is still elusive but she might have emigrated as there are many entries for Rose O'Brien's in the official records travelling from Ireland to the New World, but there is no way to determine if she is one of them.

If Maria Jane and Jane Gallagher accepted Florence Willis as some sort of relation, then she might also have been the mother of the baby Mary Byrne who died in 1887, as both she and Rose Edith would have been seventeen at the time, and I often wonder if Rose Edith and Florence Willis were the same person but there is no way I can prove it so I reluctantly left this mystery in order to tie up other loose ends.

Were there any connections between the different families of Thorpe we have already met? It was a very common name in both England and Ireland at that time and I spent a futile and frustrating couple of months trying to link the two branches, hoping that somehow, I might find Rose Edith and a Florence Willis in the process.

The first branch was that of Inspector William Thorpe who was in charge of the investigations into the killings of the two politicians in Phoenix Park, Dublin in 1883. He was a prolific father, having thirteen children including the one who became Archdeacon of Macclesfield, the grandfather of Jeremy Thorpe. His wife was only 17 when they married which explains why she was such an abundant mother but what renewed my interest was the fact that her maiden name was Maria (Mary) Byrne.

Knowing many parents named their first-born daughter after their mother or grandmother, prompted me to research the daughters in this family and one of them was called Florence Emily and she was born in 1873 in Dublin. This was exciting as I really thought if I could find her married or somehow living in a family called Willis, I would have found my Florence Willis. And if the families of Inspector William Thorpe and that of Thomas Baxter Thorpe were connected then that would explain why Florence Willis was living in Maria Jane's and Thomas Baxter Thorpe's house when she died and why Maria Jane buried her alongside Jane Gallagher.

Unfortunately, Florence Emily Thorpe, like several of her siblings, does not appear again in Irish records after her birth, so I have found nothing useful that connects the two Thorpe families. On the face of it, they lived on opposite sides of the fence, Inspector Thorpe's family firmly rooted in church, politics and the law and Thomas Baxter's somewhat adjacent, pursuing more hedonistic pleasures.

We now have to leave Jane with her youngest son Alfred Hugh and his wife Elizabeth close by in St Jerome cemetery, Dublin where she rests alongside the unknown Florence Willis and her son in law Thomas Baxter Thorpe, knowing her last words must have been to her youngest daughter Maria Jane, who alone held her hand while she made what must have been the most undramatic exit of her life.

Figure 110 Illustration of Jane Gallagher by George Jones, Formby 2019

R.I.P. Jane Gallagher,

alias Jane Mercer, Liverpool Kate, Madam Massey

1816 – 1895

'A woman few dared meddle with'

Mrs. Gallagher

The mystery of wives' separate trade
By me, Jane Gallagher, was made
In latter days elucubrate.[855]
I writ no writing, sealed no thing,
I dealt after a man's dealing,
Until my debt was heavy and great.
By rede of the one Lord Justice,
Albeit it was newfandgledness,
That will bind separate estate.

To tell now in what wise was meant
This law should have additament[856]
By wisdom of the Parliament,
Whereof our scriveners, as men seen,
Reck no more than an old bean,
As now it is not mine intent,
The tale were full too long.
By these ensamples yea may find
What power han wives to loose and bind;
This ends my little song.[857]

The *Pall Mall Gazette* on 11.12.1875 published this, what might have been the only commentary on Jane's achievement in respect of coverture and the law as it then applied to married but separated women.

Epilogue

Sometimes, reaching out and taking someone's hand is the beginning of a journey.
At other times, it is allowing another to take yours.[858]

And what a roller coaster it has been!

Organised research got me started with the bare bones of Jane's genealogical facts but as I hit a series of brick walls, I soon realised that I had to allow Jane to take my hand and go with her flow. Out went rational, established strategies and in rolled the scatter gun. Chaos became my lived reality as I forged along with wisps and wafts of intuition that disappeared annoyingly as I focused, the trick being to catch them while seeming to look elsewhere. Best of all were those days when synchronicity in the form of outrageously unlikely events unfolded like alchemy to reveal twists, tragic and sometimes farcical episodes in the lives of all those around Jane.

I have lost count of the number of times I have discovered information I did not know I needed until I stumbled across it whilst looking for something else. Now I have learnt to deliberately set off in illogical directions, flinging queries across the internet, talking to strangers I meet on my travels and generally spreading my net in many directions at once without wondering whether it was worth the effort or even knowing what I was looking for, because it works.

It has been exhilarating, beyond exciting as I scrambled every day, eyes and senses wide open, to see where the trail would lead me. Yes, sometimes I did need to go back to good old track and tracing as evidencing more than three ways was very necessary before believing anything that Jane said. Many, many times I was on a roll for weeks as huge swathes of landscape opened up, all waiting for me to explore – other times I was scrolling laboriously but hopefully through directories and other archived material.

Nothing came together coherently. Instead, I had spider diagrams all over the place, mind maps incomprehensible to anyone but me, whiteboards of notes and arrows, corkscrewed connectors and stick-it notes that somehow came together the more I suspended my rationality. Lockdown was a blessing in one sense, as in 2020 I was free to live a suspended life and disappear into the Victorian world of Liverpool, Ireland, the Isle of Man and London, venturing into Australia, American and the colonies online, all because of Jane Gallagher.

I have met and communicated with so many people in my explorations, learnt so much, not just about the lives of Jane, her family and associates but about the practical challenges of producing a book, at home alone when the longest work I had produced previously was a national report. When you hear this book originally had over 250 figures of tables, maps, pictures, drawings, and over 550 pages which I had to cut drastically as Word kept telling me it could not save my extra-large document, then you can see how much re-shaping and sculpturing has been necessary, but I think it was worth it.

I know I will never be finished as new information springs up all the time and I have lots of brick walls to demolish, so if anyone wants to pile in, be my guest!

sue@theinfamousmrsgallagher.co.uk

www.theinfamousmrsgallagher.co.uk

https://www.facebook.com/The-Infamous-Mrs-Gallagher-108858024410012

Acknowledgements

This book would never have emerged at all if the Museum of Liverpool had not planted the seed back in 2018 by asking me to investigate 'Brothels and Prostitution' in Liverpool. It was a great project, and just look what has come from it!

But without countless news reports about Jane's prolific exploits and those of her associates and family I would never have had enough material to justify any more than brief entries of her birth, marriages, children, and death: and what a missed opportunity that would have been!

So, many thanks to the British Newspaper Archive online where I was able to discover an enormous amount, as it gave me access to reports, court cases, addresses, incidents and more importantly, such a feel for the reality of life in England and Ireland in the nineteenth century. From these leads, I could explore with a keen focus, the main genealogy websites of Ancestry, BMD, Find My Past and Family Search along with the Government Record Offices, online Probate Services, maps from the National Library of Scotland and many other sources to check the facts and put together the stories you will read.

More particular help came from:

- Northern and Southern Ireland's archives

- National Archives in England and the Library of Australia

- The Methodist Archives in the Drew Reference Library in Madison, USA

- Members of RootsChat.com

- Lincolnshire Family History Society

- Gill Morgan and her staff at Crosby library, Liverpool

- Roger Hull at Liverpool Archives

- Geoff Oldfield who videoed many of my presentations
- All at Warren Park who gave me much needed feedback about my discoveries and were a very lively audience
- Surviving descendants of Alfred Hugh Mercer and Frederick Fox Cooper who have shared their family history and connections

However, there is no substitute for feeling and absorbing original documents held by local archives and seeking the help of their very able and interested staff, and I would like to particularly mention archives held by the Church of the Latter-Day Saints Family History Centre in Preston, Lancashire and archives held by local authorities in:

Buckinghamshire	Cheshire	City of Westminster
Denbighshire Flintshire	Halifax	Hertfordshire
Lancashire Lambeth	Liverpool	
Northamptonshire	Manchester	
Ise of Man Southampton	West Yorkshire	

My pages would have been very bare indeed without the drawings of Jane, Chalkley, Charles Pollard, William Mercer and the Talking Fish which George Jones of Formby produced. Using only bare descriptions and armed with pictures showing the fashions of Jane's day, he has produced excellent impressions of the main characters.

My special thanks go to those who have put up with me beyond all calls of friendship as I brimmed over and buzzed with excitement and could not wait to share new discoveries, even though they knew they were in for a long haul if they asked me how the book was going. They kept faith despite me locking myself away for a very long time, juggling the many strands in my head, keeping extremely odd hours, never knowing what day it was - happy because I was - even when I forgot to meet them as planned.

You know who you are: Heather, Mark, Peter, Vicky, Olivia, Eileen, Sue, Caroline, Olive and all those who I maybe only met once but were still avidly interested. Your continuing enthusiasm for my 'Brothel Woman' is what has kept me going, so:

Thank You!

Table of Figures

Figure 1 Weekly Dispatch Atlas of Liverpool 1860 12
Figure 2 Jane Gallagher, St George's Hall 1860 by George Jones 2019 15
Figure 3 Jane's city centre brothels: OS 6" map of Liverpool 1845-1864 28
Figure 4 'Women are a decidedly inferior animal.' Punch 1859 41
Figure 5 Impression of W.S. Chalkley by George Jones 2019 55
Figure 6 'For Sale' the house of Thomas Chalkley: 1839 56
Figure 7 Impression of William Mercer by George Jones 2019 69
Figure 8 Jane's marriages and children 71
Figure 9 Frederick Fox Cooper:Theatrical Times: 1847: ©V&A Museum 78
Figure 10 Fox Cooper's Obituary: London, Provincial Entr'acte: 25.1.1879 79
Figure 11 Low Hill Cemetery and Necropolis, 1825-1898 Everton, Liverpool 93
Figure 12 First section of Jane Oakes will 1851 96
Figure 13 Victorian bib or plastron: 1891 97
Figure 14 Impression of Charles Pollard by George Jones 2019 100
Figure 15 Louis - Napoleon at the time of his failed coup in 1836 103
Figure 16 King St on map of London 1868, by Edward Weller, F.R.G.S. 104
Figure 17 Young Dutch Sam – Wikipedia 106
Figure 18 Map of London 1868, by Edward Weller, F.R.G.S. 110
Figure 19 Sophia Burford's proven will dated 1851 118
Figure 20 Signatures on Sophia Burford's will 1851 119
Figure 21 Tyrer St in Liverpool City Centre. OS 25" map 1890 125
Figure 22 Advert for Rossett Hall, Chester Chronicle, 1856 125
Figure 23 A Victorian Tailor 130
Figure 24 An interior view of Lancaster Castle in 1824, J. Weetman. 139
Figure 25 Thomas' Death Certificate 20.10.1858 142
Figure 26 Lime Street, Liverpool 1890 145
Figure 27 The Hop on Lime Street, mid-1800s 148
Figure 28 Ordnance Survey 6" map of the Zoological Gardens 1851 149

Figure 29 Liverpool Zoological Gardens 150
Figure 30 ' A Lover of Decency.' Letter to the Liverpool Mercury 1869 161
Figure 31 The Marine Tiger – Congleton Mercury 5.3.1859 162
Figure 32 Punch cartoon of the Talking Fish June 1859..............................165
Figure 33 'The Talking and Performing Fish' The Field 7.5.1859 166
Figure 34 'The Elastic Baby Jumpers' Punch 1848 170
Figure 35 Illustration of the Talking Fish by George Jones, Formby 2019 174
Figure 36 Jane in court illustrated by George Jones 2019............................183
Figure 37 'Embezzlement by the Secretary of a Loan Company' 16.6.1860.........192
Figure 38 'Bankruptcy Notices' Birmingham Journal 18.1.1862....................193
Figure 39 'Bankruptcies,' the Globe 20.6.1860 194
Figure 40 Houghton, Tyrer, Upper Dawson Street. OS Liverpool 1890 201
Figure 41 Clayton Square, corner of Houghton Street, Richard Brown 1923 202
Figure 42 Corner of Williamson Sq with Houghton St. 1858 W.G. Herdman........203
Figure 43 Gambling - Liverpool Mercury 20.6.1834 205
Figure 44 Hotham St adjacent to Lime Street Station. OS map. 1846-1864 214
Figure 45 Upper Dawson Street, Williamson Square, the Theatre Royal............ 226
Figure 46 The second Theatre Royal which opened in 1803 227
Figure 47 'American Ice' Liverpool Standard Advertiser 1848 231
Figure 48 The Butter Man's shop. W.G. Herdman 1864 233
Figure 49 'The Talking and Performing Fish' Morning Post 26.4.1859 240
Figure 50 Vassall and Eltham Rd in Lambeth, London OS 6" map 1872 241
Figure 51 The Crim Con Gazette 25.8.1838................................... 244
Figure 52 The Vandenhoffs: The Sun, London 10.4.1845 252
Figure 53 'Apprehension of Chalkley,' Liverpool Mercury 18.6.1861 257
Figure 54 London Road, Liverpool 2019 261
Figure 55 One liner in the Liverpool Mercury Saturday 25.8.1860....................... 262
Figure 56 The man second left is wearing a Wide-Awake hat 271
Figure 57 St Nicholas' Hotel, New York 1855: F. L. Heppenheimer....................272
Figure 58 One of the letters found in Chalkley's possession in 1861 273
Figure 59 'For Sale' Liverpool Mercury 27.11.1860 273
Figure 60 The preacher's letters found in Chalkley's possession in 1861 274
Figure 61 Letter from Rev Thompson to Chalkley 27.6.1861...........................275
Figure 62 British ships seized: Southampton Times 13.7.1861 277
Figure 63 England & Wales, Criminal Registers, 1791-1892........................ 282
Figure 64 Freemantle Prison, late 1800s 289
Figure 65 Death certificate of Sarah Jane Carver, 1895.......................... 298
Figure 66 Carbolic Smoke Ball advert in the Truth publication 1892 304
Figure 67 Drawing by George Cruickshank 1840................................312
Figure 68 Furniture: No 5 Houghton Street, Liverpool Daily Post 3.4.1862 315
Figure 69 Committal record for Jane Gallagher of Houghton Street, 1862 316

Figure 70 Marriage: William Thomas and Mary Ann Clare in 1862 319
Figure 71 Tyrer Street Liverpool: Google maps 2019 321
Figure 72 Tyrer St, Liverpool town centre 1890 OS map 25" 1890 322
Figure 73 The Chancery Court decision on a new trustee 1865 326
Figure 74 Complainant's names 328
Figure 75 Lord Nelson Street, Liverpool. OS 25" map 1850 329
Figure 76 Jane Gallagher's Indictment 330
Figure 77 Jane's Bail document for the Quarter Sessions................................... 331
Figure 78 Jane Gallagher breaks her bail conditions 332
Figure 79 Jane Gallagher's bail discharged 332
Figure 80 'Court of Exchequer' Morning Advertiser 10.12.1856 338
Figure 81 Notice of Ann Fox Cooper's death in the Era 20.5.1860......................340
Figure 82 Chester Street on a street map of Lambeth in 1888............................342
Figure 83 Selina Cooper's death certificate, London 1892 346
Figure 84 Prince Albert lays the foundation stone of the Sailor's Home 353
Figure 85 Walkers of Warrington by Alfred Barnard 1890 356
Figure 86 Peter Walker and Son, Share Certificate 358
Figure 87 Liverpool Mercury 18.5.1885..360
Figure 88 Pellew Street, Liverpool 1893 OS 25" map...365
Figure 89 Blandford Street, Liverpool,1851 OS 6" map 368
Figure 90 Howat Street, Everton, North Liverpool OS 25" 1892-1915 371
Figure 91 Pembroke Gardens, Liverpool OS 6" map 1908 375
Figure 92 The 'Doo-Da-Day Minstrels:' Glenister Matinee 1899 376
Figure 93 Marriage certificate: Alfred Hugh and Elizabeth Tyrer 1878 377
Figure 94 Advert on 12.9.1870 in the Belfast News-Letter.................................. 383
Figure 95 Goad's Insurance map of Belfast 1887 384
Figure 96 Map of Dublin: George Cox: London,1853 391
'Figure 97 South Dublin Workhouse in 1952 397
Figure 99 Map in research by John Simpson about the Madams in 'Ulysses' 406
Figure 100 Death certificate of Elizabeth Mercer 22.8.1892 413
Figure 101 Entrance to Mount Jerome Cemetery, Dublin 414
Figure 102 Map of Dublin, George Cox: London, 1853....................................... 418
Figure 103 Death Certificate 30.8.1892 Alfred Hugh Mercer.............................420
Figure 104 Part of Brisbane in 1865..422
Figure 105 Stamford's map of Queensland 1860 423
Figure 106 Gympie Flood, 1873 424
Figure 107 Grangegorman Prison, 1836. Creative Commons.............................432
Figure 108 Death certificate of Jane Mercer, Dublin 1895 434
Figure 109 Probate record for Jane Mercer 1895 435
Figure 110 Statutory Note to Creditors of Jane Mercer 1895 435
Figure 111 Illustration of Jane Gallagher by George Jones, Formby 2019..............440

References

Prologue

1 'Scandalous Revelations in the Vice Chancellor's Court,' Liverpool Mail 15.5.1850
2 'Extraordinary Disclosures in the Chancery Court,' Liverpool Daily Post 12.5.1860
3 'Sale by auction,' Liverpool Mail 24.4.1858
4 'Extraordinary Revelations in the Vice Chancellor's Court,' Liverpool Mail 19.5.1860
5 'Johnson v Gallagher and Another,' the Law Times 30.3.1861

Part One - Early Years

Chapter 1 - Jane's Story

6 Ancestry.co.uk: Lancashire Parish Registers: 1816 Baptism of Jane Gallagher (Oakes)
7 http://www.liverpool-schools.co.uk/html/history.html
8 'The Autobiography of Mary Smith,' by Mary Smith (London: Bemrose and Sons, 1892), 1
9 'Hard Lessons,' by Purvis. (Cambridge: Polity Press, 1989), 73
10 http://www.educationengland.org.uk/history/chapter05.html#04
11 As above Purvis
12 www.liverpoolpicturebook.com
13 'Old Liverpool,' by Eric Midwinter. (David and Charles@ Newton Abbot 1971), p. 102
14 https://spartacus-educational.com/ITliverpool.htm
15 'The Sanitary Conditions of the Labouring Population,' by Edwin Chadwick (1842)
https://spartacus-educational.com/ITliverpool.htm
16 http://www.branchcollective.org/?ps_articles=paul-fyfe-on-the-opening-of-the-liverpool-and-manchester-railway-1830 by Paul Fyfe
17 https://en.wikipedia.org/wiki/Opening_of_the_Liverpool_and_Manchester_Railway
18 https://maps.nls.uk/os/6inch-england-and-wales/
19 Gores Liverpool Street Directory 1821
20 'Extraordinary Disclosures in the Chancery Court,' Liverpool Daily Post 12.5.1860
21 Ancestry.co.uk: Lancashire Parish Marriage Register: FHL 1068952
22 Liverpool Parish Register: Baptisms 1833 – 1834: p.339, Entry 2710: Source: LDS Film: 1656421
23 Liverpool Parish Register: Register: Baptisms 1836 – 1837:p. 62, Entry 492:1836 Source: LDS Film 1656422
24 Government Record Office (GRO): 1939 M Quarter: Liverpool: Vol 20 p.445
25 GRO 1841 M Quarter: Vol 20 p.393
26 Liverpool Parish Register: Register: Baptisms 1843 – 1844:p.11, Entry 87 Source: LDS Film:

93884
27 Margaret Oakes: Marriage Event Date:6 October 1828 Parish: Manchester, Lancashire, England: FHL: Film Number:1545563 Reference ID: p.660:1980
28 Ancestry.co.uk: 1851: The will of Jane Oakes
29 Ancestry.co.uk: Lancashire Parish Register Baptism: Bishop's Transcripts: 1838 Ref: Drl/2/400
30 Ancestry.co.uk Lancashire Parish Register Marriage 1828 FHL Film No: 1656197 Ref: IDit6, p.31
31 'Extraordinary Disclosures,' Liverpool Daily Post 16.5.1860
32 Find My Past: HO107, Place Number: 569, Book 3, Folio 34, p.12:1841 census
33 Ancestry.co.uk:1851 census

Chapter 2 - Building the Brothel Empire

34 'Throwing Vitriol,' Liverpool Gores Advertiser 6.5.1841 and the Reformers Gazette February 1834 and 'Extraordinary Disclosures' Liverpool Daily Post 16.5.1860
35 Reformers Gazette 1834
36 'Scandalous Revelations in the Vice Chancellor's Court,' Liverpool Mail 15.5.1850
37 'Extraordinary Disclosures,' Liverpool Daily Post 12.5.1860 p.3

Chapter 3 - Social Evil

38 'Evil Becomes Her: Prostitution's Transition from Necessary to Social Evil in 19th Century America,' Jacqueline Shelton, (2013). Electronic Theses and Dissertations. Paper 1172. https://dc.etsu.edu/etd/1172
39 'Evil Becomes Her' as above
40 'Evil Becomes Her' as above
41 'Frauds of London: The Stranger's Guide,' J Bailey, London 1809 https://www.bl.uk/romantics-and-victorians/articles/prostitution
42 'Streets of Liverpool, 'Liverpool Review 28.1.1893
43 'Prostitution in the Borough of Liverpool,' Reverend William Bevan 3.6.1843 Lecture in Liverpool published by B. Smith Castle Street, Liverpool
44 https://waywardwomen.wordpress.com/category/life-stories/liverpool/#jp-carousel-766 0
45 https://vocal.media/filthy/life-in-a-victorian-brothel
46 'Social Evil,' Liverpool Mercury 21.10.1859
47 'The Great Social Evil,' W. Logan London, 1871
48 As above
49 'Evils of the Penny Dreadful,' Liverpool Mail 3.9.1853.
50 'The Liverpool Underworld 1750 -1900,' Michael Macilwee, p.6
50 As above page 7
50 'The Slain in Liverpool by drink,' Rev John Jones 1863
50 As above
50 'Revelations of a female pickpocket,' Liverpool Mail 16.4.1842

50 As above
50 Liverpool Mercury 27.2.1849
50 Liverpool Mercury 10.1.1846
50 'The Liverpool Underworld – Crime in the City:' as above p.157
50 'The Liverpool Underworld 1750 -1900,' Michael Macilwee, p.6
50 As above page 7
50 'The Slain in Liverpool by drink,' Rev John Jones 1863
50 As above
50 'Revelations of a female pickpocket,' Liverpool Mail 16.4.1842
51 'The Liverpool Underworld 1750 -1900,' Michael Macilwee, p.6
52 As above
53 'The Slain in Liverpool by drink,' Rev John Jones 1863
54 As above
55 'Revelations of a female pickpocket,' Liverpool Mail 16.4.1842
56 As above
57 Liverpool Mercury 27.2.1849
58 Liverpool Mercury 10.1.1846
59 'The Liverpool Underworld – Crime in the City:' as above p.157

Chapter 4 – Prostitutes, Poverty and Punishment

60 https://www.legislation.gov.uk/ukpga/Geo4/5/83/section/4
61 https://api.parliament.uk/historic-hansard/acts/town-police-clauses-act-1847
62 https://en.wikipedia.org/wiki/Prostitution_in_the_United_Kingdom
63 http://www.historyandpolicy.org/policy-papers/papers/paying-the-price-again-prostitution-policy-in-historical-perspective
64 https://www.parliament.uk/about/living-heritage/evolutionofparliament/houseofcommons/reformacts/overview/reformact1832/
65 'Old Liverpool' by Eric Midwinter published by David and Charles: Newton Abbot
66 Gores General Liverpool Advertiser 3.3.1836
67 Liverpool Mail 5.3.1840
68 'Liverpool Head Constable's Annual Report,' Liverpool Mercury 1839
69 http://www.visionofbritain.org.uk/unit/10105821/cube/GENDER
70 'Mr Mansfield's charges against the police,' Liverpool Mercury 21.3.1859
71 Liverpool Mercury 1.7.1853
72 'Lecture by Dr Bevan, Minister of Newington Chapel,' 3.6.1843
73 'The effects of immorality,' Liverpool Mercury 29.10.1852
74 'Inquests' Liverpool Daily Post 12.11.1863
75 'Child killed in a brothel,' Liverpool Mercury 18.5.1864:
76 Liverpool Mail 10.6.1843
77 'Assault,' Liverpool Mercury 23.10.1849:
78 Liverpool Daily Post 18.10.1876
79 'Female Penitentiary,' Liverpool Mail 2.5.1846:
80 'Whores and the Law: A Case Study of the Sexual Double Standard and the Contagious

Diseases Acts in Mid Nineteenth Century England,' Alexandra Wallis, BA Edith Cowan University 2014

81 'Prostitution and Victorian Society: Women, class and the state' JR Walkowitz Cambridge University Press 1982

82 'Prostitution and Victorian Social Reform,' by Paul Mc Hugh 1980 (Redwood Burn Ltd Trowbridge and Escher)

83 As above

84 'The London underworld in the Victoria period: Authentic first-person accounts by beggars, thieves and prostitutes,' pp 1-108 (B Hemyng Dover Publications, Inc 1861/2005)

85 'Josephine Butler and the Prostitution Campaign: Diseases of the Body Politic,' (Jordan and Sharp) 2003

Chapter 5 - Coverture

86 'A Treatise on the Law of Husband and Wife as Respects Property, Partly Founded upon Roper's Treatise and Comprising Jacob's Notes and Additions thereto.' L.E. Bright London: 12849, p.1

87 https://www.thoughtco.com/coverture-in-english-american-law-3529483

88 'Select Committee on the Married Women's Property Bill, Q 7 and 11'

89 'Continuity and Change', as above

90 'Continuity and Change' as above

91 'Continuity and Change,' by Joanne Bailey: 17 (3), 2002, 351–372. page 353 f 2002 (Cambridge University Press DOI: 10.1017/S0268416002004253m

92 https://theconversation.com/meet-caroline-norton-fighting-for-womens-rights-before-it-was-even-cool-53668

93 https://en.wikipedia.org/wiki/Caroline_Norton

94 'The separation of mother and child by the law of "Custody of Infants," considered,' Norton, C. Sheridan. (1838)(London: Roake and Varty,) 31, Strand

95.'The Criminal Conversation of Mrs. Norton' by Diane Atkinson, published by Preface Publishing 2012

96 'Married women and the law: Coverture in England and the Common Law World,' edited by Tim Stretton and Krista Kesselring. (Published by Mc Gill at Queens University Press) 2013

97 http://www.cflp.co.uk/a-brief-history-of-divorce/

98 Lord Lyndhurst: 3 Hansard 142 (20 May 1856) p.408-10

Chapter 6 - William Seabrook Chalkley

99 'Scraps about Chalkley,' Liverpool Daily Post 29.6.1861

100 Ancestry.co.uk: England Select Births and Christenings 1538-1975 FHL No: 1736694:1787

101 Ancestry.co.uk: England Select Marriages 1738 – 1973 FHL No: 1836145 Item 212 1810

102 Archdeaconry Baptisms Kent, Canterbury 7.5.1812 Find My Past.co.uk

103 https://www.imuseum.im/newspapers/

104 https://www.myprimitivemethodists.org.uk/content/place-2/isle-of-

man/douglas_circuit_isle_of_man
105 https://www.myprimitivemethodists.org.uk/content/place-2/isle-of-man/douglas_circuit_isle_of_man
106 https://www.imuseum.im/newspapers/ Mona's Herald 12.1.1842
107 http://www.smuggling.co.uk/gazetteer_wales_14.html
108 https://www.imuseum.im/newspapers/ Manx Sun 20.3.1847
109 https://www.imuseum.im/newspapers/ Manx Liberal 14.3.1846
110 https://www.imuseum.im/newspapers/ Manx Sun 25.7.1847
111 https://www.imuseum.im/newspapers/ Isle of Man Times 1.5.1847
112 http://www.isle-of-man.com/manxnotebook/fulltext/pos1755.htm
113 https://www.imuseum.im/newspapers/ Isle of Man Times 3.6.1848
114 Ancestry.co.uk: England, Select Births and Christenings: 1538-FHL 106191, 106733 1818
115 https://www.imuseum.im/search/people/
116 http://www.toxtethparkcemetery.co.uk/Wesleyan%20Chapel,%20Upper%20Stanhope%20Street,%20Toxteth/Stanhope%20Street%20Wesleyn%20Chapel%20Burials%201827%20to%2018
69.htm
117 Lancashire Parish Records 1839 Baptisms 1814 - 1905, Page 18, Entry 371 Source: LDS Film 1595373
118 Liverpool Record Office; Liverpool, England; Reference Number:283 PET/3/24
119 Lancashire Parish Records Online: Register: 1841 Baptisms 1814 - 1905, Page 20, Entry 407 Source: LDS Film 1595373
120 Lancashire Parish Records Online: Register: 1843 Baptisms 1814 - 1905, Page 22, Entry 453 Source: LDS Film 1595373
121 Lancashire Parish Records Online: Register: 1844 Baptisms 1814 - 1905, Page 24, Entry 491 Source: LDS Film 1595373
122 Lancashire Parish Records Online: Register: 1847 Baptisms 1814 - 1905, Page 27, Entry 551 Source: LDS Film 1595373
123 Liverpool Standard and General Commercial Advertiser 22.4.1842 p.4
124 'A History of Epidemics in Britain, Vol 2 of 2,' Charles Creighton: Project Gutenberg eBook
125 'Partnership dissolved' Perry's Bankrupt Gazette Saturday 22.8.1840
126 The Dublin Morning Register - quoting the Liverpool Chronicle - 19.8.1840
127 Staffordshire Gazette and County Standard – quoting the Liverpool Standard – 22.8.1840
128 1841 England and Wales census HO107 piece 568 book number 20 folio number 27 p.19
129 'Advert for Liverpool Tradesman's Loan Society,' Chester Chronicle 7.12.1850
130 Liverpool Electoral Registers 1832-1932
131 'Bankruptcies,' Perry's Gazette 14.4.1854 p. 289
132 'Scraps about Chalkley,' Liverpool Daily Post 29.6.1861
133 http://www.thewru.com/about-us/history/
134 'Disruption among the Wesleyan Methodists,' Liverpool Mail 10.11.1849
135 As above

Chapter 7 - Married or not?

136 'Bankruptcy Court,' Liverpool Daily Post: 13.6.1862
137 'Divorced, Bigamist, Bereaved?' Probert R.(Takeaway Publishing) 2015
138 'Humour, Halters and Humiliation: Wife Sale as Theatre and Self-divorce,': Vaessen, Rachel Anne (2006), (thesis) ir.lib.sfu.ca
139 Probert as above
140 Liverpool, England, Church of England Baptisms, 1813-1917 Bishop's Transcripts Ref Drl/2/113 and Liverpool Parish Records online baptisms 1845 Entry 886, Source: LDS Film 1068892
141 Liverpool Parish Records Baptisms 1848 from the Bishop's Transcripts, p.5, Entry 1688. Source: LDS Film 1068892
142 Probert as above
143 Probert as above
144 Probert as above
145 1920s postcard in 'Divorced, Bigamist, Bereaved?' Probert, R. (2015). (Takeaway Publishing)
146 Probert as above
147 'Bigamy,' Liverpool Mercury 19.8.1851
148 'Bigamy,' Liverpool Mercury 25.3.1852
149 'Bigamy,' Liverpool Mercury 13 and 17.12.1850
150 https://moorhall.com/moor-hall/
151 Baines Directory 1824 Vol 2
152 Lancashire Church of England Parish Register 1538-1812 Baptism: 16 Dec 1798 St Mary, Lancaster. Bishops Transcripts Reference Number: Drb 2/127
153 Lancashire Church of England Parish Banns 1754:29.1.1798

Part Two - Shocks and Surprises

Chapter 8 - London Connections

154 http://collections.vam.ac.uk/item/O1285119/dramatic-authors-no-11-mr-print-unknown/
155 'Obituary,' in the London and Provincial Entr'acte 25.1.1879 p.9
156 https://www.npg.org.uk/collections/search/portrait/mw63268/The-dog-tax-Richard-Brinsley-Sheridan-William-Pitt-Charles-James-Fox-Henry-Dundas-1st-Viscount-Melville
157 https://georgianera.wordpress.com/tag/1796-dog-tax/
158 'Fashionable World,' *Morning Post* 24.1.1805 p.3
159 'A Sonnet by Henry Fox Cooper,' 28.2.1805 *Morning Post* p.4
160 'Nothing Extenuate,' by F. Renad Fox Cooper published by Barrie and Rockliff 1964 *p.16*
161 *As above*
162 King's (Queen's) Bench, Fleet, Marshalsea and Queen's Prisons: Miscellanea. Records of the King's Bench, Fleet, and Marshalsea prisons, Series PRIS 10. The National Archives, Kew, England
163 King's (Queen's) Bench, Fleet, Marshalsea and Queen's Prisons: Miscellanea. Records of

the King's Bench, Fleet, and Marshalsea prisons, Series PRIS 10. The National Archives, Kew, England

164 'Nothing Extenuate,' by F. Renad Fox Cooper published by Barrie and Rockliff 1964 p.220

165 As above F. Renad Fox Cooper

166 As above F. Renad Fox Cooper

167 'Bow Street,' *Morning Post* 3.12.1831 p.4

168 As *above*

169 'Letter to the Editor' *Morning Post* 3.12.1831 p.4

170 'Gregory v. the Duke of Brunswick', The English reports, Volume 4, 134, London: Stevens & Sons, p. 1227 and p.868 Robertson, Max, ed. (1913),

171 Boase, G. C. (1885–1900). "Gregory, Barnard" . Dictionary of National Biography. London: Smith, Elder & Co.

172 Thomas Rowlandson (1756–1827) and Augustus Charles Pugin (1762–1832) (after) John Bluck (fl. 1791–1819), Joseph Constantine Stadler (fl. 1780–1812), Thomas Sutherland (1785–1838), J. Hill, and Harraden (aquatint engravers)[1] Pyne, William Henry; Combe, William (1904) [1810] "The Stamp Office" I The Microcosm of London or London in Miniature, Volume III, London: Methuen and Company, pp.Plate 74

173 https://en.wikipedia.org/wiki/Somerset_House#cite_note-38

174 'The Satirist newspaper', later edition in the *Morning Post* 4.12.1831

175 'The Satirist Newspaper Again' Public Ledger and Daily Advertiser 7.12.1831 p.3

176 https://www.explorethepast.co.uk/2018/02/whats-in-a-name-paul-pry/

177 https://research-information.bris.ac.uk/files/210737578/Final_Copy_2019_01_23_Kilgarriff_T_PhD_Redacted.pdf

178 https://www.bmimages.com/results.asp?txtkeys1=thomas%20mclean

179 'Nothing Extenuate' by F. Renad Fox Cooper published by Barrie and Rockliff 1964

180 As above F. Renad Fox Cooper

181 King's (Queen's) Bench, Fleet, Marshalsea and Queen's Prisons: Miscellanea. Records of the King's Bench, Fleet, and Marshalsea prisons, Series PRIS 10. The National Archives, Kew, England.

182 'Nothing Extenuate,' by F. Renad Fox Cooper published by Barrie and Rockliff 1964

183 'Dicas v Thompson and Gregory,' Bucks Gazette 2.3.1833 p.2

184 'Dramatist Doubly in Debt,' in 'About the theatre' W.A. Darlington

185 'Nothing Extenuate,' by F. Renad Fox Cooper published by Barrie and Rockliff 1964

186 'Insolvent Debtors Court,' Morning Chronicle 8.7.1835 p 4

Chapter 9 - The Missing Will

187 Free BMD. England & Wales, Civil Registration Death Index, 1837-1915[database on-line]. Provo, UT, USA: Ancestry.com Operations Inc, 2006

188 'Extraordinary Disclosures,' Liverpool Daily Post 12.5.1860 page 3

189 'Scandalous Revelations in the Chancery Court,' Liverpool Mercury 14.5.1860

190 'Victorian Mourning Customs' Collier's Cyclopedia,1901.QuiltHistory.com. Quilt History. Web. 27 Sept. 2014

191 Polite Life and Etiquette. Benham, Georgene Corry. Chicago: Benham, Georgene Corry, 1891. The Funeral Source, 2001. Web. 27 Sept. 2014
192 'Most Morbid Victorian Mourning Traditions,' Breyer, Melissa. MotherNatureNetwork. MNN Holding Company, LLC, 17 Oct. 2012. Web. 27 Sept. 2014.
193 https://www.dailymail.co.uk/news/article-7188515/Sinister-portraits-families-grieving-lost-loved-ones-macabre-Victorian-trend.html
194 'Victorian Funeral Customs and Superstitions,' Friends of Oak Grove Cemetery. Web. 26 September 2014
195 'Funerary Practices in the Victorian Era' Alirangues, Loretta. Morbid Outlook. Web. 27 Sept. 2014
196 ALLOM - 1829 - old antique vintage print - art picture prints of Liverpool
197 https://www.facebook.com/photo/?fbid=10210019675396155&set=pcb.1569352299782902
198 England and Wales National Probate Calendar (Index of Wills and Administrations) 1858 - 1995 Digital folder number: 007692693 Image number: 00068
199 https://www.pbs.org/mormons/etc/genealogy.html
200 'Scandalous Revelations in the Chancery Court,' 14.5.1860 Liverpool Mercury
201 https://historicalsewing.com/1890s-plastrons-is-that-a-victorian-bib
202 'Extraordinary Disclosures,' Liverpool Daily Post page 3 12.5.1860

Chapter 10 - Charles Pollard

203 Liverpool Mercury 26.7.1853
204 https://www.campop.geog.cam.ac.uk/research/projects/transport/onlineatlas/railways.pdf
205 Ancestry.co.uk Lincolnshire Baptism records 1814: FHL no 1450474
206 Ancestry.com Baptisms 1814 St George's, Stepney: FHL 578788, 578789, 578790
207 'Marlborough Street,' Stamford Mercury 16.7.1847
208 Find My Past Surrey 1836 Marriages 1813- 37 Slip Index
209 https://en.wikipedia.org/wiki/Lord_Street,_Southport
210 https://www.britannica.com/biography/Napoleon-III-emperor-of-France
211 http://www.unofficialroyalty.com/louis-napoleon-bonaparte-emperor-napoleon-iii-of-the-french/
212 https://maps.nls.uk/geo/explore/#zoom=17&lat=51.49125&lon=-0.11184&layers=176&b=1
213 https://www.british-history.ac.uk/survey-london/vols29-30/pt1/pp180-186#fnn37
214 https://www.oldbaileyonline.org/browse.jsp?id=def1-1673-18470705&div=t18470705-1673&terms=Napoleon_Bonaparte#highlight
215 'Police Intelligence Report' 5.7.1847 London Evening Standard
216 Post Office Directory, 1848, London
217 https://www.british-history.ac.uk/old-new-london/vol4/pp165-181
218 'Bail Court Beshemel v Gallagher,' Stamford Mercury 22.11.1861
219 Wikipedia: https://en.wikipedia.org/wiki/Dutch_Sam
220 https://www.findagrave.com/memorial/18040941/samuel-evans

221 Bell's Life in London and Sporting Chronicle: 12.11.1843
222 https://abeautifulbook.wordpress.com/2018/04/09/big-hitting-hard-drinking-dutch-sam-petticoat-lane-whitechapel/
223 https://abeautifulbook.wordpress.com/2018/04/09/big-hitting-hard-drinking-dutch-sam-petticoat-lane-whitechapel/
224 As above
225 Lloyds Weekly 31.12.1843
226 https://boxrec.com/media/index.php/Famous_Fights-Past_and_Present
227 The Globe: 3.6.1844
228 John Bull article: 9.12.1843
229 Evening Standard: 16.1.1845
230 Morning Advertiser 16.1.1845
231 Era 1.11.1846
232 Era 15.11.1846
233 Ancestry.co.uk Caterham, Surrey, Bishop's Transcript of Burial Record 1847
234 Morning Advertiser 8.5.1847
235 Era 9.5.1847
236 Old Bailey trial transcripts 9.7.1847 Old Court
237 'Morning Post,' 5.7.1847
238 As above Old Bailey trail transcripts
239 'Police Intelligence,' London Morning Post 7.7.1847
240 'Marlborough Court' 3.7.1847 p.4
241 As above London Morning Post
242 Old Bailey trial transcripts 9.7.1847 Old Court
243 Devizes and Wiltshire Gazette Thursday 22.7.1847

Chapter 11 - Pretty Pickles and a Dish of Salmon

244 As above London Morning Post
245 Charles Pollard's 1847 Larceny Offence and Acquittal record Ancestry.co.uk
246 'Insolvent Debtors Court,' Stamford Mercury 10.3.1848
247 'Insolvent Debtors Court,' London Stamford Mercury, Friday 10.3.1848
248 As above
249 1851 Census London Class: HO107; Piece: 1511; Folio: 147; Page: 39; GSU roll: 87845
250 1814 baptism record London, England, Church of England Births and Baptisms, 1813-1917 Ancestry.com
251 Morning Advertiser: 15.7.1851
252 'Death of a Young Widow' Era: 25.7.1851
253 London Metropolitan Archives and Guildhall Library Manuscripts Section, Clerkenwell, London, England; Reference Number: DL/C/532; Will Number: 161
254 'Masters and Servants- Curzon v Pollard' The Era 23.5.1852
255 London Evening and the Standard: 8.10.1853
256 Bells Weekly Messenger 20.11.1853 p.7

257 London Morning Advertiser: 16.11.1853
258 London Morning Chronicle: 3.5.1854
259 'Action upon a bill of exchange,' Liverpool Mercury 25.3.1858
260' Unexplained Fracas,' Northern Times p.3

Chapter 12 – Furnishers and Furniture
261 Liverpool Mercury, 4.7.1848
262 Case number: 1865 B23. Short title: Brindley v Turner National Archives
263 'Extraordinary Disclosures' 12.5.1860 Liverpool Daily Post
264 Liverpool Archives, Council Leases 352CLECAN137
265 'To be let' Chester Chronicle May 1856
266 Revelations in the Chancery Court' Liverpool Mercury 16.5.1860 p.3
267 As *above*
268 As above
269 As above
270 'Supplying Furniture to a house of ill fame' Liverpool Mercury 19.8.1858
271 'An Extraordinary Defence' Liverpool Mercury 23.8.1853
272 McCorquodales Street Directory 1848
273 'Notice of Removal' Liverpool Mercury 21.3.1856
274 http://www.visionofbritain.org.uk/census/EW1861GEN/11
275 https://www.liverpoolecho.co.uk/news/liverpool-news/inside-old-odeon-cinema-london-15069558
276 'For Sale' Liverpool Mercury 19.8.1858
277 'For Sale' Liverpool Mail, 7.3.1857

Chapter 13 – Death, Love and Marriage
278 http://twonerdyhistorygirls.blogspot.com/2016/01/how-many-hand-sewn-stitches-in-18thc.html
279 https://www.historyextra.com/period/victorian/stitching-the-fashions-of-the-19th-century/
280 'Johnson v Gallagher' Liverpool Courier 16.5.1860
281 'Men, Women and Property in England', 1780–1870: A Social and Economic History of Family Strategies amongst the Leeds Middle Classes Robert Morris Cambridge University Press, 2005, ISBN: 521838088X; pages 379-380
282 'Johnson v Gallagher' The Law Times 30.3.1861
283 'Scandalous Revelations in the Chancery Court' Liverpool Mercury 14.5.1860 page 3
284 'Extraordinary Disclosures' Liverpool Daily Post 12.5 1860
285 'Scandalous Revelations in the Chancery Court' Liverpool Mercury 14.5.1860 page 3
286 Liverpool Archives 352 SEL/19/9
287 'Our Pauper Population' Liverpool Mercury: Liverpool Life 30.11.1857
288 http://www.workhouses.org.uk/Liverpool/
289 'Our Pauper Population' Liverpool Mercury: 'Liverpool Life': 28.12.1857

290 Liverpool Daily Post 21.11.1857
291 Clare Hartwell in the Psychiatric Bulletin 1993: 17, 113-114
292 'Annual Report of the County Lunatic Asylum at Lancaster' Liverpool Record Office M614 RAI/40/2/29, , 1863, 9.
293 Liverpool Record Office: M614/RAI/11/2
294 https://www.medicinenet.com/script/main/art.asp?articlekey=11721
295 'Liverpool Life' Hugh Shimmin 1857 published by the Liverpool Mercury
296 https://www.ncbi.nlm.nih.gov/pmc/articles/PMC2082960/
297 https://jnnp.bmj.com/content/72/3/412
298 'Epilepsy and other chronic convulsive diseases: their causes, symptoms and treatment' Gowers WR. . New York and Dover: Wm Wood, 1885, reprinted 1964
299 'Luminal bei epilepsie' Hauptmann A.. Munchiner Medizin Wochenschrift1912;59:1907–9
300 https://en.wikipedia.org/wiki/Lancaster_Castle
301 http://www.lancastercastle.com/history-heritage/people-stories/stephen-cropper/
302 'Action on a bill of exchange' Liverpool Mercury 25.3.1858
303 https://thepsychologist.bps.org.uk/volume-25/edition-10/looking-back-fascinating-and-fatal-disease
304 'General paralysis of the Insane' William Julius Mickle 1880 study
305 www.findagrave.com/memorial
306 England & Wales, Civil Registration Marriage Index FreeBMD. 1837-1915 [database on-line]. Provo, UT, USA: Ancestry.com Operations Inc, 2006. Denbighshire Marriages and Banns Vol 11b page 585

Chapter 14 - Why is it so hard to control Social Evil?

307 'The state of Lime Street – Who's to blame?' Liverpool Mercury 23.11.1858
308 Liverpool became a city in 1880
309 By Library of Congress Prints and Photographs Division Washington, D.C. 20540 USA – http://www.histografica.com/view.aspx?p=z6tjh3qx, Public Domain, https://commons.wikimedia.org/w/index.php?curid=8462990
310 http://www.visionofbritain.org.uk
311 https://williamgray101.wordpress.com/2017/10/07/liverpool-and-the-great-hunger-1847/
312 'A Friend to Morality.' Liverpool Mercury 23.11.1858
313 https://en.wikipedia.org/wiki/Social_purity_movement
314 https://api.parliament.uk/historic-hansard/acts/town-police-clauses-act-1847
315 Police Instruction Book Standing Orders No 27 20.12.1889 page 121 Liverpool Archives
316 http://www.arthurlloyd.co.uk/Liverpool/TivoliPalaceofVarietiesLiverpool.htm
317 'Liverpool Life' by Hugh Shimmin of the Porcupine Magazine Liverpool 1857
318 'Upon the Crystal Platform' the Porcupine 27.5.1865
319 https://www.flickr.com/photos/44435674@N00/5643461269
320 'Vice al Fresco' The Porcupine 4.7.1863 page 2
321 'The Liverpool Police 'Liverpool Mercury 1.6.1847 Letter to the Editor
322 Liverpool Daily Post 22.8.1871

323 1869 Annual Report for Liverpool Borough Prison Liverpool Archives

324 Liverpool Borough Prison Annual Report 1869

325 '1877 Annual Report for Liverpool Borough Prison' Liverpool Archives

326 'The Streets of Liverpool' Liverpool Review 25.2.1892 p.5

327 'The Streets of Liverpool' Liverpool Review 11.3.1893 p4/.5

328 'Catholic History of Liverpool'. Thomas Burke.Tinling and Co. Liverpool 1910

329 'Father Nugent of Liverpool' Canon Bennett, Liverpool Catholic Children's Protection Society 1949

330 'The Slain in Liverpool during 1866 by Drink' Rev J Jones

331 'The Deadly Shame of Liverpool, an Appeal to the Municipal Voters' Pamphlet 1890

332 'Condition of Liverpool, Religious and Social: including notices of the state of education, morals, pauperism and crime. Brakell, Cook Street. Liverpool 1858

333 'Disorderly Houses' Liverpool Mercury 18.11.1857

334 'Rev Skewes' Liverpool Mercury 12.12.1883

335 https://en.wikipedia.org/wiki/Washington_Irving_Bishop

336 https://www.jstor.org/stable/pdf/463136.pdf?seq=1

337 'The charges against the vicar of St Jude's' Liverpool Mercury 29.9.1883

338 Liverpool Mercury 29.9.1883

339 Liverpool Mercury 30.11.1838

340 Liverpool Mercury 5.5.1854

341 Liverpool Mercury 3.5.1856 Application for an order in bastardy against as undergraduate of Oxford

342 'The Liverpool Underworld – Crime in the City 1750 -1900' Robert Mcilwee, page 56 Oct 2011

343 'Statement of the proceedings of the Society for the Suppression of Vice' July – Nov read at their general meeting on 12.11.11804.

Chapter 15 – The Talking Fish

344 'The Talking Fish' Congleton Mercury 5.3.1859

345 'The Talking Fish' Liverpool Herald 1857

346 https://en.wikipedia.org/wiki/P._T._Barnum#cite_note-1

347 https://www.smithsonianmag.com/history/true-story-pt-barnum-greatest-humbug-them-all-180967634/

348 http://animalhistorymuseum.org/exhibitsandevents/online-gallery/gallery-8-animals-and-empire/enter-gallery-8/ii-the-animal-resource/exotic-animal-trade/

349 'The Performing and Talking Fish: Opinions of the London Press' printed by R.S. Francis, 3 Catherine Street, The Strand London 1859 – digitized by Google Books

350 'Last week of the Talking Fish' Northern Daily Times 10.2.1859 p.8

351 'The Talking and Performing Fish' The Field 7.5.1859

352 'The Talking Fish' The Morning Post 5.5.1859

353 'A Fishy Phenomenon' The Morning Herald 5.5.1859

354 'The Talking Fish' The Daily Telegraph 5.5.189

355 'A Fishy Phenomenon' The Standard 5.5.1859

356 'The Talking Fish' The Reynold's Newspaper 8.6.1859
357 London Morning Advertiser: 20.6.1859
358 'The Royal Agricultural Society's Warwick Meeting' Morning Chronicle 13.7.1859
359 'The Summer Fair' Leeds Times 16.7.1859
360 Saunder's Newsletter 11.8.1859
361 'The Talking Fish v the Bouncing Babies' Reynold's Newspaper 23.10.159 p.16
362 'The Talking Fish' The Morning Advertiser 24.10.1859
363 'First Impressions' The Aberdeen Press and Journal 29.3.1848
364 'Leeds Winter Fair' The Leeds Times 12.11.1859
365 'Swimming for Ladies' The Belfast Morning News 18.11.1859
366 'Death of the Talking Fish' Westmorland Gazette 31.12.1859
367 'The Talking Fish has died' Stamford Mercury 30.12.1859
368 'Death of the Talking Fish' Morning Post 24.12.1859
369 'The Talking Fish' Punch quoted in the Western Morning News 7.1.1860
370 'Death of a valuable member of society' Banffshire Journal and General Advertiser 10.1.1860
371 'Effingham' Reynold's Newspaper 25.12.1859
371 London Morning Advertiser: 20.6.1859
371 'Best v Hayes and Gallagher' The Law Times volume 4, March – September 1861 p.72
371 'Johnson v Gallagher' Northern Daily Times 2.12.1859 p.3
371 'Johnson v Gallagher' The Liverpool Mercury 12.2.1859
372 Advert in the Liverpool Mail 16.1.1861
373 'The Talking Fish' Newcastle Chronicle 28.6.1862 p.4
374 Letter to the Editor, London Evening Standard 18.12.1864
375 'Bankruptcy Court' Liverpool Daily Post 13th June 1862

Chapter 16 - Beshemel v Gallagher

376 'Beshemel v Gallagher - "The Talking Fish"' London Evening Standard 17.11.1860 p.7
377 'Beshemel v Gallagher' The Globe 16.11.1860
378 'The Talking Fish and its Tutor' The Era 18.11.1860 p.15
379 'Mrs. Gallagher and the Talking Fish' Liverpool Mercury 18.11.1861 p.5
380 'The Tale of the Talking Fish' The Norfolk News 24.11.1860 p.7
381 'The Talking Fish and its Tutor' The Era 18.11.1860 p.15
382 'Assault on the police' Worcester Journal 3.11.1860
383 'The Talking Fish and its Tutor' The Era 18.11.1860 p.15
384 'A memento of the Talking Fish' North London News 23.11.1861
385 'The Talking Fish' the Morning Herald in Lloyds Weekly London News 24.11.1861 p.7

Chapter 17 - Johnson v Gallagher

386 'Bankruptcy Court' Liverpool Daily Post 13.6.1862
387 'Men, women and property in England' 1780 -1870 R.J. Morris p395/6 Cambridge Press
388 'Scandalous Revelations in the Chancery Court' Liverpool Mercury 14.5.1860 p.2

389 'Johnson v Gallagher' Northern Daily Times 2.12.1859 p.3
390 'Johnson v Gallagher' The Liverpool Mercury 12.2.1859
391 'Scandalous Revelations in the Chancery Court Liverpool Mercury 16.5.1860
392 As above
393 'The Law Journal Reports for 1860-61,' vol 30
394 Liverpool Daily Post 18.5.1860
395 'Decrees under Estates in Chancery' Perry's Bankrupt Gazette 23.6.1860
396 https://doi.org/10.1080/03071022.2019.1579977
397 Liverpool Mercury 14.9.2857, p4 and 7.9.1857, p5
398 'Suggestions for Rendering Medico-Mental Science Available to the Better Administration of Justice and the More Effectual Prevention of Lunacy and Crime', Thomas Laycock, Journal of Mental Science, 14:67 (1868), 334-5.
399 Liverpool Record Office, H365.32 BOR, Reports of the Governor, Chaplain, Prison Minister and Surgeon, 18.
400 Liverpool Record Office, 347, MAG/1/3/1A, Minute Book of the Visiting Justices Sessions Gaol and the House of Correction Feb 1856 – Sept 1866

Chapter 18 – Chalkley's Downfall

401 'Embezzlement by the Secretary of a Loan Company' printed in the Lancaster Guardian 16.6.1850 p.3 citing the Liverpool Mercury
402 'The Doings of W.S. Chalkley' Published by G Vickers, London 1861
403 'Bankruptcy Notices' Birmingham Journal 18.1.1862 p.4
404 The Evening Freeman 12.6.1860
405 'Forgery and Embezzlement by a Methodist Preacher' Northern Whig 13.56.1860
406 Liverpool Daily Post 14.6.1860
407 Glasgow Herald 20.6.1860
408 Perry's Bankruptcy and Insolvency Gazette 23.6.1860 but listed 27.6.1860
409 'Bankruptcies' the Globe 20.6.1860
410 'The Committal of Chalkley' Liverpool Mercury 29.6.1861 p.3
411 'Liverpool Trademan's Loan Society' Liverpool Mercury 6.11.1860 p.3
412 As above
413 'The Doings of W.S. Chalkley' Published by G Vickers, London 1861
414 'Apprehension of Chalkley, the Liverpool Swindler at Southampton' Hampshire Advertiser 22.6.1861
415 As above

Chapter 19 - Life in the Brothel Streets

416 http://www.arthurlloyd.co.uk/Liverpool/PlayhouseTheatreLiverpool.htm#star
417 'Distinguished Personage' 4.9.1835
418 'Keeping Brothels' Liverpool Mercury: Liverpool Police Court 9.1.1862
419 Liverpool Council Lease Registers Liverpool Archives 352CLECAN137

Chapter 20- Preying on the Vulnerable

420 F.R. Lees Ph.D. in 'The Slain by Drink' John Jones 1865 p.62
421 'Child Robbing' Liverpool Mercury 17.9.1847
422 'The Road to Ruin' Liverpool Mercury 2.12.1842
423 'An awful beast' Northern Daily Times 30.4.1857
424 Liverpool Mercury 14.8.1857 and 'An unprecedented case' Liverpool Daily Post 30.5.1857
425 Liverpool Record Office: 347 QUA 2/146 Quarterly Sessions February 1867
426 'A House of Assignation' Liverpool Mercury 12.1.1863 p.6
427 'Wells and Another v Wallace' Liverpool Mercury 23.8.1853
428 'A Sporting Character' Liverpool Mercury 25.10.1850
429 Liverpool Mercury 4.7.1851
430 Liverpool Mercury 30.3.1852
431 Liverpool Mercury 18.5.1852
432 'A Disappointment' Liverpool Mail 9.9.1854
433 'Police Information,' Liverpool Mercury 6.4.1855 p.11
434 'Madam Annie' Northern Daily Times 5.9.1856 p.2
435 Liverpool Daily Post 12.12.1857
436 Liverpool Mercury 16.12.1857
437 'Where are Madam Annie's Securities?' Liverpool Daily Post 11.3.1859
438 'Bankruptcy cases' Liverpool Mercury 16.10.1859:
439 http://www.yoliverpool.com/forum/showthread.php?57892-Liverpool-Zoological-Gardens-West-Derby-Road-1832-63 and Liverpool Record Office
440 'The case of Madam la Farcie the procuress' Liverpool Mercury 14.8.1862
441 As above Quarterly Sessions registers
442 Liverpool Archives: Quarterly Sessions records
443 'Youthful Depravity' Gores Liverpool General Advertiser 23.12.1841
444 'Friend of India' Liverpool Mercury 25.12.1858 and 28.10.1858
445 Liverpool Daily Post 19.10.1867
446 Liverpool Mail 19.8.1854: Front page Saturday Supplement
447 'An Infamous Trade' Liverpool Daily Post 23.4.1867'
448 'Abduction of girls' Liverpool Mercury 5.4.1856:
449 https://en.wikipedia.org/wiki/Criminal_Law_Amendment_Act_1885

Chapter 21 – Hidden Houses of Ill Fame

450 http://www.arthurlloyd.co.uk/Liverpool/TheatreRoyalWilliamsonSquareLiverpool.htm
451 'The Theatre Royal which opened in 1803' in the Liverpool Stage by Harold Ackroyd published in 1990
452 https://www.everymanplayhouse.com/whats-more/charles-dickens-and-liverpool
453 Review in Liverpool Standard and General Advertiser 17.2.1852 p6
454 https://www.british-history.ac.uk/old-new-london/vol3/pp238-255#highlight-first
455 'Summary Convictions' Liverpool Mercury 16.3.1852 p5
456 'Informations against Publicans and Beer Sellers' Liverpool Mercury 3.8.1852 p.6

457 'The Steeple Chase' Liverpool Standard and General Advertiser 28.2.1854 p.8
458 Liverpool Mercury 4.7.1845 p.4
459 Liverpool Mail 19.10.1844 p.8
460 'Extraordinary case against a wine and spirit broker' Liverpool Standard and General Advertiser 28.12.1841
461 'For sale' Liverpool Mercury 20.9.1844 p.5
462 'A case of stabbing' Liverpool Mercury 29.5.1846 p.6
463 'Brother against brother' Liverpool Standard and General Advertiser 27.8.1844
464 Advert in the Liverpool Standard and General Advertiser 9.2.1847 p.20
465 'American Ice For Sale' Liverpool Standard and G Advertiser 13.6.1848 p 9 advert
466 A public notice in Gores Liverpool General Advertiser 14.1951 p 1
467 'Publican's and Beer Sellers cases' Liverpool Mercury 3.9.1850 p4
468 Advert in the Liverpool Standard and General Advertiser 13.7.1852 p.8
469 Gores Liverpool Directory 1853
470 'Summons against Kelly the Butter Man' Liverpool Daily Post 13.11.1861 p 7
471 Liverpool Daily Post 30.7.1861 p.7
472 'Publicans and Beer Sellers cases' Liverpool Mercury 3.9.1950 p4
473 Liverpool Mercury 14.6.1860

Part Four - Judgement Day

Chapter 22 – Jane is Appealing

474 'The Notorious Mrs. Gallagher' Liverpool Mercury 19.3.1861

475 Select Committee on Married Women's Property Bill in committee stage in the 18768 Q7, 11

476 Combs, Mary Beth (December 2005). ""A Measure of Legal Independence": The 1870 Married Women's Property Act and the Portfolio Allocations of British Wives". The Journal of Economic History. 65 (4): 1028–1057

477 Select Committee on Married Women's Property Bill in committee stage in the 1868s Q74-9

478 'Johnson v Gallagher' in English Law Reports, vol XLV, p 969 1861

479 'Men, Women and Property in England, 1780 -1870' Cambridge University Press July 2009

480 'Bankrupts' in the Morning Chronicle 27.6.1857

481 'Sales' in the Morning Post 14.1.1856

482 'Leah Isaacs – judgement' London Evening Standard 24.11.1857 p 7

483 'Notices' Illustrated London News 29.1.1859 p14

484 'The Talking and Performing Fish' Morning Post 26.4.1859 p1

485 William Mercer: London, England, City Directories, 1736-1943 Ancestry.co.uk

486 https://en.wikipedia.org/wiki/David_Cox (artist)

487 http://en.wikipedia.org/wiki/David_Cox_(artist

488 https://www.british-history.ac.uk/survey-london/vol26/pp108-122#anchorn51

Chapter 23 - Combative Cooper

489 'Nothing Extenuate' by F.Renad Fox Cooper published by Barrie and Rockliff 1964
490 'Insolvent Debtors' Leeds Intelligencer 9.7.1836 p.1
491 https://www.independent.co.uk/arts-entertainment/books/reviews/the-criminal-conversation-of-Mrs.-norton-by-diane-atkinson-7984881.html
492 https://twitter.com/DigiVictorian/status/1163192371334582272/photo/2
493 Gentleman's Magazine, xx (March 1750), 117
494 https://lifetakeslemons.wordpress.com/2011/07/26/a-criminal-conversation-grosvenor-v-cumberland/
495 'Bow Street' The Sun London 7.8.1838 p.4
496 'I Hope I Don't Intrude: Privacy and Its Dilemmas in Nineteenth-century Britain' by David Vincent Oxford \University Press in Google |Books
497 King's (Queen's) Bench, Fleet, Marshalsea and Queen's Prisons: Miscellanea. Records of the King's Bench, Fleet, and Marshalsea prisons, Series PRIS 10. The National Archives, Kew, England.
498 Ancestry.com. England & Wales, Criminal Registers, 1791-1892 Class: HO 26; Piece: 45; Page: 41
499 https://www.oldbaileyonline.org/browse.jsp?name=18390617
500 'New Court' Morning Advertiser 28.6.1839 p.4
501 'Nothing Extenuate' by F. Renad Fox Cooper published by Barrie and Rockliff 1964
502 'Hair Cropping' London Evening Standard 9.8.1842 p.2
503 'The Dover Cropping Case' Sun London 14.9.1842
504 'Justices' Justice' The Globe 9.9.1842
505 The Illustrated London News 17.9.1842
506 'Nothing Extenuate' by F.Renad Fox Cooper published by Barrie and Rockliff 1964
507 Morning Chronicle 20.12.1841 p.6
508 https://www.greekmythology.com/Myths/Creatures/Cerberus/Cerberus.html
509 'Court of Bankruptcy' The Globe 15.2.1844
510 The Sun London 10.4.1845
511 'Reviews' Lloyd's Weekly 20.4.1845 p.10
512 'Bankruptcy Court' Sun, London 24.4.1846
513 'Railway Intelligence' Hereford Journal of Railway Intelligence 22.7.1846 p 2
514 'Insolvent Debtors Court' Morning Advertiser 14.7.1846 p.4
515 'Collier v Fox Cooper' Morning Post 23.7.1847 p.7
516 'Bow Street: Libel' London Express 8.11.1848 p.4
517 'Olympic' The Era 17.12.1848 p.11
518 'Nothing Extenuate' by F.Renad Fox Cooper published by Barrie and Rockliff 1964 P.124
519 'Nothing Extenuate' by F.Renad Fox Cooper published by Barrie and Rockliff 1964 P.128
520 'Insolvent Debtors' Bells New Weekly News 30.6.1850 p.6
521 'Nothing Extenuate' by F.Renad Fox Cooper published by Barrie and Rockliff 1964 P.150

Chapter 24 - Chalkley the Fugitive

522 'Apprehension of William Seabrook Chalkley on charge of defaulting a loan society'

Liverpool Mercury 18.6.1861 p.3
523 As above
524 As above
525 'The Doings of W.S. Chalkley' published by G Vickers, London 1861
526 'North Atlantic Mail Sailings 1840-1875,' by Walter Hubbard and Richard F. Winter edited by Susan Mc Donald printed by the US Philatelic Classics Society Inc. 1988
527 https://en.wikipedia.org/wiki/SS_Arago_(1855)#cite_note-12
528 'Scraps about Chalkley' Liverpool Daily Post 29.6.1861 p.7
529 'The Doings of W.S. Chalkley' Published by G Vickers, London 1861
530 'Scraps about Chalkley' Liverpool Daily Post 29.6.1861 p.7
531 https//rusholmearchive.org/rusholme-a-century-ago
532 https://en.wikipedia.org/wiki/John_Wesley
533 https://www.tameside.gov.uk/Towns/Droylsden-Home-Page/Township-Information-Droylsden
534 https://www.hats.com/bollman-collection-1860-s-wide-awake.html
535 https://en.wikipedia.org/wiki/St._Nicholas_Hotel_(New_York_City)
536 http://files.usgwarchives.net/pa/montgomery/history/local/mchb0028.txt
537 As above
538 'The Doings of W.S. Chalkley' Published by G Vickers, London 1861
539 'Punitive Damages' Simon Daniels unpublished downloaded from http://ssudl.solnt.ac.uk/2974
540 https://en.wikipedia.org/wiki/Pennsylvania_in_the_American_Civl_War
541 Southampton Times 13.7.1861

Chapter 25 - Chalkley Faces Judgement

542 'Measure for Measure,' Act 3 Scene 2 William Shakespeare
543 'Apprehension of William Seabrooke Chalkley on a charge of defrauding a loan society' Liverpool Mercury 18.6.1861 p.3
544 'The Liverpool Trademan's Loan Company – Examination of William Seabrooke Chalkley' Liverpool Mercury 19.6.1861 p.7
545 'Scraps about Chalkley' Liverpool Daily Post 29.6.1861
546 'The Defaulting Secretary of the Tradesman's Loan Co' Liverpool Daily Post 26.6.1861 p.7
547 Advert in the Wigan Observer and District Advertiser 19.1.1856 p.1
548 'Dissolution of partnerships' Northern daily Times 12.5.1856 p.3
549 Advert in the Manchester Courier and General Advertiser 30.8.1856 p.1
550 Manchester Courier and Lancashire General Advertiser 20.8.1859 p.2
551 Advert in Manchester Courier and General Advertiser 19.5.1860 p.2
552 'Bankruptcies' Manchester Courier and Liverpool General Advertiser 30.6.1861 p.11
553 'Bankruptcies' Manchester Courier and Liverpool General Advertiser 4.6.1861 p.11
554 'The frauds upon the Liverpool Tradesman's Loan Society' Liverpool Mercury 14.8.1861 p.3

555 http://members.iinet.net.au/~perthdps/convicts/conwad31.htm
556 Ancestry.com. England & Wales, Criminal Registers, 1791-1892
557 'The Doings of W.S. Chalkley' published by G Vickers, London 1861

Chapter 26 - Transported to Australia
558 https://catalogue.nla.gov.au/Record/1502774?lookfor=author:(John%20Gregg)&offset=10&max=275
559 www.freemantleprison.com.au
560 https://fremantleprison.com.au/history-heritage/history/a-brief-history/
561 Freemantle Prison website: convict database
562 http://members.iinet.net.au/~perthdps/convicts/con-wa31.html
563 'Convict Biographies' Freemantle Prison website *as above*
564 'Defaulters' article in the Atlas 13.12.1862

Chapter 27 - Fallout
565 Lancashire FHL Film No: 559152 Ref ID:179
566 1901 census England, Wales and Scotland. RG13, piece no 3695 folio 176 p.35
567 'The Doings of W.S. Chalkley' published by G Vickers, London 1861
568 Liverpool Record Office; Liverpool, Merseyside, England; Liverpool Cemetery Registers; Reference: 352 CEM 2/2/4
569 FreeBMD. England & Wales, Civil Registration Death Index, 1837-1915 Liverpool Vol 8b p.176
570 Liverpool Record Office Civil Registration of Births Volume 20 p.490
571 England and Wales Marriages 1538 – 1988 Bebington, Cheshire, England. 1845-1883. FHS No: 1656605
572 England and Wales deaths 1837 -2007
573 'Presentation to a Town Missionary' Liverpool Daily Post 14.8.1860 p.3
574 England and Wales Deaths 1837 -2007
575 General Register Office; Birkenhead, Cheshire. United Kingdom; Volume: 8a; Page: 566
576 FreeBMD. England & Wales, Civil Registration Marriage Index, 1837-1915 [database on-line]. Provo, UT, USA: Ancestry.com Operations Inc, 2006.
577 West Yorkshire Archive Service; Wakefield, Yorkshire, England; Yorkshire Parish Records; New Reference Number: RDP43/5
578 'A Strange Dispute about Pictures' Liverpool Mercury 7.9.1876 page 8.
579 'Charge of stealing pictures – An Expert in the Fine Arts' Liverpool Mercury 24.10.1876 p.8
580 'The Case of Mr Rumer' Letter to the editor of the Liverpool Daily Post 12.12.1876 p.7
581 'Mr Alexander Rumer' Liverpool Daily Post 16.12.1876 p.5
582 'The Case of Alexander Rumer' Liverpool Daily Post 9.1.1877 p.6
583 Sub-registration district: West Derby ED, institution, or vessel:58Household schedule number:28 Piece: 3849 Folio:69 Page Number:10

584 Liverpool Record Office; Liverpool, Merseyside, England; Liverpool Cemetery Registers; Reference: 352 CEM 6/2/3
585 FreeBMD England & Wales, Civil Registration Death Index, 1837-1915
586 Deceased Online; United Kingdom; Deceased Online Burial Indexes
587 https://www.ncbi.nlm.nih.gov/pmc/articles/PMC5144530/
588 https://medlineplus.gov/ency/article/002890.htm
589 'Suicide in Clerkenwell' Islington Gazette 25.3.1895 p.2

Chapter 28 - Sins of the Father

590 https://thepsychologist.bps.org.uk/volume-25/edition-10/looking-back-fascinating-and-fatal-disease
591 1891 Census Class: RG12; Piece: 2956; Folio 96; Page 47; GSU roll: 6098066.
592 New York Passenger Lists, 1820-1957
593 https://en.wikipedia.org/wiki/Carlill_v_Carbolic_Smoke_Ball_Co
594 'Carbolic Smoke Ball' an advert in Truth publications 4.2.1892 p.255
595 'Journal of Legal Studies' 1985 345,354

Part Five - What happened next?

Chapter 29 - Prosecuted as a Procuress

596 'Yours XYZ' Liverpool Mercury 16.11.1857
597 'Green v Stevens' Liverpool Daily Mail 9.4.1857
598 Liverpool Mercury 16.12.1861
599 'Keeping Brothels' Liverpool Mercury: Liverpool Police Court 9.1.1862
600 'Police Court Report' Liverpool Mercury 9.1.1862
601 ' For Sale' in the Chester Courant 19.2.1862
602 'Apprehension of Mrs. Gallagher' Liverpool Mercury 31.3.1862
603 William Mercer: London, England, City Directories, 1736-1943 Ancestry.co.uk
604 'Committal of a Notorious Procures' the London Evening Standard 2.4.1862
605 'Mr Brigg's Hat' by Kate Colquhoun published by Little, Brown U2011
606 'Apprehension of Mrs. Gallagher' Liverpool Mercury 31.3.1862
607 'The Recorder's Remarks' Borough Sessions report in the Liverpool Mercury 11.4.1862 p.3
608 Wrexham and Denbigh Advertiser 19.4.1862
609 'The trial and sentence of Mrs. Gallagher' Liverpool Mercury 15.4.1862 page 5
610 Liverpool Daily Post Borough Sessions 1862
611 Liverpool Mercury 11.6.1862

Chapter 30 - Tussles over Tyrer Street

613 'Bankruptcies' Perry's Bankrupt Gazette 14.11.1863 p.6
614 'The Drunkard's End' Liverpool Mercury 4.1.1858
615 'Inquests' Liverpool Mercury, 27.8.1847 p 499
616 'Man Catchers' Liverpool Mercury on 18.11.1851

617 Liverpool Mercury 29.7.1853
618'Scandalous Revelations in the Chancery Court' Liverpool Mercury 14.5.1860
619 Chancery Court files, National Archives Brindley v Turner 1865/6

Chapter 31 - Revolving Doors
620 'Mrs. Gallagher before the court again' Liverpool Daily Post 24.1.1866 p.7
621 https://en.wikipedia.org/wiki/Demimonde
622 https://bookblast.com/blog/spotlight-sex-in-the-nineteenth-century-city-london-paris-and-the-demi-monde/
623 https://www.thevintagenews.com/2018/04/25/cora-pearl/
624 'Prosecutions for keeping disreputable houses' Liverpool Mercury 24.1.1866 p.5
625 Liverpool Record Office; Liverpool, England; Liverpool Electoral registers, Burgess rolls and Voters Lists; Reference: Hq324.241LIV
626 Liverpool Record Office; Liverpool, England; Liverpool Electoral registers, Burgess rolls and Voters Lists; Reference: Hq324.241LIV
627 Find My Past RG11, 3620, 69,14
628 As above

Chapter 32 - The Final Curtain
629 'Insolvent Debtors Court' Morning Post 21.12.1853 p.6
630 'Lambeth Court' Morning Chronicle 9.11.1854 p.8
631 'Lambeth Court' Morning Chronicle 16.11.1854 p.8
632 https://en.wikipedia.org/wiki/Payne_Brothers
633 'Levite v Ledger' The Era 18.5.1856 p.12
634 'Court of Exchequer' Morning Advertiser 10.12.1856 p.6
635 'Nothing Extenuate' by F.Renad Fox Cooper published by Barrie and Rockliff 1964 P.178
636 https://en.wikipedia.org/wiki/Astley%27s_Amphitheatre#cite_note-1
637 Lambeth M.B.C. Poor rate books
638 https://en.wikipedia.org/wiki/Jonathan_Crowther_(minister)#cite_note-DNB-1
639 https://www.thesocialhistorian.com/smallpox/
640 'Nothing Extenuate' by F.Renad Fox Cooper published by Barrie and Rockliff 1964 P.76
641 'Nothing Extenuate' by F.Renad Fox Cooper published by Barrie and Rockliff 1964 P. 213
642 'Nothing Extenuate' by F. Renad Fox Cooper published by Barrie and Rockliff 1964 P. 212
643 London Metropolitan Archives; London, England; London City Directories
644 https://pubwiki.co.uk/LondonPubs/Lambeth/JohnBull.shtml
645 'Dramatist Doubly in Debt' by W.A. Darlington in About the Theatre 20.1.1964
646 Illustrated Sporting and Dramatic News 22.11.1879 p.18
647 'Nothing Extenuate' by F. Renad Fox Cooper published by Barrie and Rockliff 1964 p. 222
647 1891 Census England, Wales and Scotland, Surrey: London: Camberwell: RG12 465 37 p.3
648 National Archives Index to the Register of Passport Applications 1851-1903 Ref: FO 611/14

Chapter 33 - Lust and Money

649 https://www.hackwriters.com/victorianp.htm

650 https://www.bl.uk/romantics-and-victorians/articles/prostitution

651 https://teainateacup.wordpress.com/2012/11/03/james-boswell-and-london-prostitutes/

652 https://www.quora.com/What-was-the-price-for-a-Whitechapel-prostitute-during-the-Victorian-era

653 'Robbing in a Brothel' Liverpool Mail 18.11.1843

654 'Robbery in a Brothel' Liverpool Mercury 12.3.1847

655 Parliamentary Papers LXXXIX 1901

656 'An Extraordinary Defence' Liverpool Mercury 23.8.1853

657 'Mendellsohn v Edwards' Liverpool Mercury 15.5.1854 p.3

658 'Green v Stevens' Liverpool Daily Post 9.4.1857

659 'Gay life in Liverpool. The Christian Lamb and the Gay-House Lion!' The Porcupine. 21.9.1889 pages 8-9

660 'The Slain by Drink' John Jones 1865 p.39

661 https://chesterwalls.info/gallery/sailorshome.html

662 'The Slain by Drink' John Jones 1865 p.67

663 'The Liverpool Underworld: Crime in the City,' 1750-1900 pub. 31 Oct 2011 by Dr Michael Macilwee page 10

664 'The Licensed City: Regulating Drink in Liverpool,' 1830-1920 Beckingham, David. Liverpool University Press, 2017. JSTOR, www.jstor.org/stable/j.ctt1ps31rk. Chapter 4 pages 85-124

665 'First Report from the Select Committee of the House of Lords on Intemperance:' Evidence of Major John James Grieg, Chief Constable of Liverpool HCPP. 1877

666 'First Report from the Select Committee of the House of Lords on Intemperance:' Evidence of William Sproston Caine HCPP. 1877

667 'First Report from the Select Committee of the House of Lords on Intemperance:' Evidence of Reverend James Nugent HCPP. 1877

668 'Idle and Disorderly Women' Liverpool Daily Post 4.8.1871 p.7

669 'The public houses round the sailor's home' Liverpool Mercury 7.12.1876 p.8

670 'Salvidge of Liverpool – behind the political scene 1890-1928' by S Salvidge London 1934

671 'Brewing in the North West 1840 -1914: sowing the seeds of service sector management?' Dr Alistair Mutch Professor of Information and Learning. Nottingham Trent University

672 http://breweryhistory.com/wiki/index.php?title=Walker_Cain_Ltd

673 'Advance of the Managerial System' Brewer's Journal, 5.10.1921 page 417

674 'Great George Ward' Liverpool Mercury 29.1.1879 page 3

675 'St Anne's Ward Petition' Liverpool Mercury 1.2.1879 page 7

676 http://breweryhistory.com/wiki/index.php?title=Walker_Cain_Ltd

677 'Appointments by the High Sheriff of Lancaster' Liverpool Mercury 7.4.1886 page 6

678 As above page 20

679 'The Licensed City: Regulating Drink in Liverpool, 1830-1920' Liverpool Record Office Hf708.5 doc in Beckingham, David. Liverpool University Press, 2017. Figure 5.1 page 130. JSTOR, www.jstor.org/stable/j.ctt1ps31rk.

680 Note this figure differs from that of Father Nugent's on the previous page

681 'Liverpool's Two Godfathers. The Slave Owner and the Drink Seller' the Porcupine 11.12.1886 pages 3-4 in Beckingham, David. The Licensed City: Regulating Drink in Liverpool, 1830-1920. Liverpool University Press, 2017. JSTOR, www.jstor.org/stable/j.ctt1ps31rk.

682 'London's shadows: The dark side of the Victorian city' by D.D. Gray p.149 Continuum, London 2010

683 'The Black Spot on the Mersey' Mr Ben Tillet and the 'Liverpool Drink Ring' Liverpool Daily Post 19.9.1890, page 7

684 http://breweryhistory.com/wiki/index.php?title=Walker_Cain_Ltd

685 'Immoral Houses in Liverpool, The Magistrates and the Watch Committee' Liverpool Daily Post 28.11.1889

686 'The Deadly Shame of Liverpool' pages 7-15 Rev Richard Ackland Armstrong 1890

687 'Disorderly Houses' Liverpool Mercury 18.11.1857

688 http://www.historyandpolicy.org/policy-papers/papers/paying-the-price-again-prostitution-policy-in-historical-perspective

689 'The City Council and Immoral Houses' Liverpool Mercury 31.5.1888 p. 8

690 'Read, Mark, Learn' Liverpool Mercury 21.5.1888 p3

691 5.6.1888 Liverpool Mercury Liverpool Association for the Suppression of Immorality Third Annual Meeting

692 'Liverpool Association for the Suppression of Immorality' Liverpool Mercury 5.6.1888 page 7

693 As above

694 Liverpool Mercury 14.6.1888

695 Liverpool Mercury 14.6.1885

696 'Finance Committee Meeting' Liverpool Mercury 5.5.1891p.3

Chapter 34 - Anything, in fact, with walls and a ceiling

697 'We are not beasts of the field' JR Walkowitz pages 23-4, 316-25, 365-75 Unpublished PhD thesis, Rochester University 1974

698 'The lessons of the raids' Liverpool Review 21.2.1891 p.3

699 'Disorderly Houses' Liverpool Mercury 23.11.1857

700 'Gay Life in Liverpool' the Porcupine September 1889

701 'A very serious lesson for Temperance Reformers and Teetotal Informers!' The Porcupine 12.10.1889 pages 3-5

702 'The police boozing den!' Liverpool Citizen Review Oct-Dec 1888

703 Liverpool Mercury 5.12.1888 page 5

704 'How a "D got his dinner for nothing' the Porcupine page 8 28.9.1889

705 'The Libel by Porcupine' Liverpool Courier 21.12.1889 page 7

706 'The Howat Street Scandal' Liverpool Review reports from 22.7.1888 to 1.9.1888

707 'A Hotbed of Vice in Everton' Liverpool Review p.11 on 21.7.1888
708 'Morality Tom' Liverpool Citizen 6.6.1888
709 Liverpool Mercury 3.3.1892
710 'Esperanza' in the Liverpool Mercury 3.11.1892
711 https://en.wikipedia.org/wiki/Josephine_Butler
712 'The Liverpool Underworld: Crime in the City' 1750-1900 *pub.* 31 Oct 2011 by Dr Michael Macilwee page 271
713 'The Streets of Liverpool' in the Liverpool Review 11-28.2.1893
714 'The Streets of Liverpool' in the Liverpool Review 11-28.2.1893

Part Six - Missing presumed dead

Chapter 35 - Where is Jane?

715 Liverpool Record Office: Register: Marriage 1862 - 1929, Page 71, Entry 141 Source: LDS Film 1656205 FHL 1656205.p71, no 141
716 The Project Gutenberg eBook, A History of Epidemics in Britain, Volume II (of 2), by Charles Creighton https://www.gutenberg.org/files/43671/43671-h/43671-h.htm#Page_393

Chapter 36 - Ireland?

717 1860 Gores Street Directory
718 Liverpool Record Office, Electoral Registers, Burgess Rolls and Voters Lists ref: Hq324.241LIV
719 Advert Liverpool Daily Post 29.3.1875 p.2
720 https://wiki.lspace.org/mediawiki/The_Luggage
721 https://www.discworldemporium.com/figurines-objet-d-art/330-the-luggage
722 Workshop of the empire 1820-1914' S.A. Royle in S.J. Connolly (ed.) Belfast 400: People Place and History (Liverpool, 2010)
723 'Markets and messages: Linenopolis meets the world' by E.J.Aiken and S.A. Royle in O. Purdue (ed), Belfast: The Emerging City 1850 -1914 (Dublin, 2012)
724 'Surviving the industrial city: the female poor and the workhouse in late nineteenth century Belfast' Purdue, O (2017). Urban History, 44(1), p 69-90
725 .'Census of Ireland Part II general Report with Illustrative Maps and Diagrams, Tables and Appendix,' HC 1902 [Cd 1190]
726 'A Social and Economic History of Ireland since 1800' M.E. Daly Dublin 1981 p. 105-7
727 'Diary of Rev Anthony McIntyre' Public Record Office of Northern Ireland (PRONI D/1555/2/3
728 Belfast Union Workhouse Indoor Registers January 1901 PRONI BG/7/52
729 'Abandoned women and bad characters' prostitution in nineteenth century Ireland, Women's History Review 6:4, 485-504. https://doi.org/10.1080/09612029700200157
730 'The Great Social Evil: its causes, extent, results and remedies' p.95 by William Logan: London: Hodder and Stoughton

731 State of Crime Report Liverpool Mercury 10.1.1871
732 'Judicial and Criminal Statistics for Ireland' 1872
733 'Peg Plunkett, Memoirs of A Whore' Julie Peakman (Quercus, 2015)
734 British Library
735 Freeman's Journal 14.3.1879
736 Advert in Belfast Morning News 16.12.1879 p.2 column 1
737 'The Social Evil' Belfast Telegraph 27.11.1878 p.3
738 'Exchequer Division' The Dublin Daily Express 13.1.1881 p.7
739 https://www.lennonwylie.co.uk/ccomplete1880.htm
740 'Jane Mercer v the Belfast Flour Company' 29.3.1881 p.4
741 'Shocking Immorality in Liverpool' Liverpool Mercury 23.6.1871 p.8 column 6
742 'Belfast Swells Ruralising' Belfast Telegraph 27.4.1881 and 11.5.1881 p.3 Cols 6 +7
743 'Prosecutions by the Belfast Vigilance Committee' Belfast Newsletter 15.3.1888 p.3
744 Prosecutions by the Vigilance Committee the Belfast Newsletter 17.4.1888 p.6

Chapter 37 - Social Evil in Dublin
745 https://en.wikipedia.org/wiki/Dublin
746 'Victorian Dublin Revealed' by Michael Barry Published by Andalus Press
747 https://lornapeel.com/2017/09/10/monto/
748 https://www.historyireland.com/18th-19th-century-history/women-and-the-contagious-diseases-acts-1864-1886-11/
749 'To be sold at auction' Irish Times 15.6.1882 p.8
750 'John O'Brien v Jane Mercer' in the Recorder's Court Freemans Journal 26.7.1883 p.7. col.4
751 'Strange charge of fraud' Dublin Daily Express 13.5.1884 p. 6 column 6
752 'Serious charge against a gentleman' Irish Times p.3 column 2
753 'Royal Irish Academy,' Irish Times 26.1.1864 p.3
754 'Chain armour for ships of war,' Letter to the editor in Saunder's Newsletter 29.6.1864 p.3
755 Saunder's Newsletter 9.5.1865 p.2
756 'Queen's Bench,' Dublin Daily Express 10.5.1867 p.4

Chapter 38 - Misnomer
757 'Singular charge of child desertion' Freeman's Journal 29.12.1878:
759 https://www.rte.ie/centuryireland/index.php/articles/south-dublin-union
760 'For Sale 1 Arnott Street, Dublin' Irish Times 5.10.1878 p.8
761 'A serious charge of fraud' Freemans Journal 10.6.1889 p.7
762 Dublin Board of Guardians Minute Books 22.12.1887
763 The Nursing and Administration of Irish Workhouses and Infirmaries' 1895-6 Report in the British Medical Journal

Chapter 39 – Madams and Mayhem
764 'Tumbling in the Hay,' O. St J. Gogarty: ch. 22, p 251:(1939)

765 https://www.historyireland.com/18th-19th-century-history/Mrs.-mack/
766 Freeman's Journal 29.9.1879 p.2
767 Dublin Daily Express 28.1.1881 p.7
768 Irish Times 21.4.1886 p.6
769 Dublin Daily Express 22.7.1885
770 'Lost dog,' Freemans Journal 25.5.1885
771 As above
772 Jjon/jjoyce-s-people/madams
773 'The Garotters, Again' Dublin Evening Telegraph 23.5.1872 p.2
774 Irish Times 28.7.1881 p.3
775 Weekly Irish Times 26.11.1881
776 https://en.wikipedia.org/wiki/Irish_National_Invincibles
777 https://en.wikipedia.org/wiki/Thorpe_affair
778 https://en.wikipedia.org/wiki/Profumo_affair
779 'Knocker Wrenching' Freemans Journal 21.11.1884 p.2
780 'Coroners Court' Dublin Evening Herald 9.5.1892 p.3
781 Evening Herald 27.9.1892 p.3
782 'The old armchair' Dublin Evening Herald 3.3.1892 p.3
783 Evening Herald Dublin 10.10.1896
784 Dublin Evening Herald 19.12.1892 p.5
785 As above

Chapter 40 – Eights Days, Two Deaths

786 'Suicide in Cumberland Street' the Irish Daily Independent 31.8.1892 p.6
787 https:/www.familysearch.org/wiki/en/England_Civil_Registration
788 Lancashire Parish Records online 17.2.1836 baptism of Elizabeth Tyrer Register of Baptisms 1835-1836 Page 281 Entry 2245 LDS Film 1656421 and 1656422
789 The National Archives; Kew, London, England; 1871 England Census; Class: RG10; Piece: 3822; Folio: 82; Page: 10; GSU roll: 841915
790 The National Archives of the UK (TNA); Kew, Surrey, England; Census Returns of England and Wales, 1891; Class: RG12; Piece: 2997; Folio 61; Page:9; GSU 6098107
791 'Suicide in Ireland, 1831–1921: A social and cultural history' Georgina Laragy (unpublished PhD: NUI Maynooth, 2005), pp. i–ix.
792 https://www.igp-web.com/IGPArchives/ire/dublin/photos/tombstones/1mj/mt-jerome-ndx.htm
793 https://theartofexploring.com/2014/10/17/mount-jerome-cemetery-dublin/
794 www.randombitsoffascination.com
795 'The Charitable Infirmary in Jervis Street: Chronology of a Voluntary Hospital' Eoin O'Brien, Jervis Street, Dublin 1.
796 'Mania, dementia and melancholia in the 1870s: admissions to a Cornwall asylum' by Simon A Hill and Richard Laughame in JRSM 2003 July1996 p.361-363
797 'Suicide in Cumberland Street' the Irish Daily Independent 31.8.1892 p.6
798 'Suicide in Cumberland Street' Irish Independent 31.8.1892 p.6

799 'Suicide in Cumberland Street' The Dublin Express 1.9.1892 p.6
800 Dublin Evening Telegraph 30.8.1892 p.3
801 Freeman's Journal 1.9.1892 p.3
802 Dublin Evening Telegraph 30.8.1892 p.3
803 Browne, O. Thornley Dodwell. (1947). The Rotunda hospital, 1745-1945. Baltimore: The Williams and Wilkins company
804 https://iiif.lib.harvard.edu/manifests/view/ids:10653106
805 https://en.wikipedia.org/wiki/Chlorodyne
806 'Dublin by Day' The Belfast News-Letter 1.9.1892 p.5

Chapter 41 - The Gold Rush

807 State Records Authority of New South Wales, 1862, Passenger Lists Find My Past
808 7.2.1863, Letter for Alfred Hugh, Queensland, Ipswich (Colonial), Vol IV p.93 Ref 6
809 https://en.wikipedia.org/wiki/Ipswich,_Queensland
810 https://apps.des.qld.gov.au/heritage-register/detail/?id=602567
811 https://www.ipswich.qld.gov.au/__data/assets/pdf_file/0019/9811/mining.pdf
812 En.wikipedia.org/wiki/Smythesdale
813 4.2.1865, Letter for Alfred Hugh, Queensland, Brisbane Post Office, Vol VI p.99. Ref 15
814 4.2.1871, Letter for Alfred Hugh, Queensland, Brisbane Post Office, Vol XII p.179 Ref 31
815 https://apps.des.qld.gov.au/heritage-register/detail/?id=602567
816 https://en.wikipedia.org/wiki/History_of_Brisbane
817 Queensland State Archives - https://www.flickr.com/photos/queenslandstatearchives/31256978480/, Public Domain, https://commons.wikimedia.org/w/index.php?curid=87530143
818 Qhatlas.com.au/content/gold
819 Stoodley, June. Nash, James (1834–1913) Archived 9 May 2012 at Wikiwix. Australian Dictionary of Biography, National Centre of Biography. Australian National University
820 1.3.1871, Letter for Alfred Hugh, Queensland, Charters Towers (Colonial), Vol XIV Ref 60
821 https://en.wikipedia.org/wiki/Charters_Towers
822 https://www.citigold.com/charters-towers-story/
823 https://en.wikipedia.org/wiki/Charters_Towers#cite_note-Post_Office-7
824 Queensland Licences Vol XIII p.795
825 https://en.wikipedia.org/wiki/Ballarat
826 Queensland Licences Vol XIV p. 1489
827 https://en.wikipedià.org/wiki/Palmer_River
828 Queensland Business Licences Vol XV p.1510
829 Victoria Outward Passenger Lists 1852-1915
830 Liverpool Mercury 17.6.1878 p.3
831 Liverpool Mercury 7.1.1878 p.6
832 'Milk and Water' Liverpool Daily Post 1.3.1877 p.6
833 Victoria Inward Passenger Lists 1839-1923
834 4.6.1879, Letter for Alfred Hugh, Queensland, Consuelo (Colonial), Vol XI p 697 Ref 140.
835 'Police Court' 7.10.1879 The Express and Telegraph (Adelaide) p.2

836 https://guides.slv.vic.gov.au/victorianancestors/directories

Chapter 42 - Denouement
837 'Attempted Suicide' Dublin Daily Express 28.1.1893 p.4
838 'Attempted Suicide' Dublin Evening Telegraph 7.2.1893
839 Marriage Rosanna Mercer to Thomas Crookenden 12.1.1879 Liverpool Vol 8b p.21
840 Gores Street Directory 1877
841 The National Archives of the UK; Kew, Surrey, England; Board of Trade: Commercial and Statistical Department and successors: Inwards Passenger Lists.; Class:BT26; Piece:22
842 Ireland, Prison Registers, 1790-1924 National Archives of Ireland
843 https://www.ourfamilypast.com/article/topic/6770/grangegorman-convict-depot-richmond-female-penitentiary-dublin
844 https://www.irishcentral.com/roots/genealogy/irish-womens-history-behind-bars
845 'Mercer v Keyes' Queen's Bench report Dublin Daily Express p.7 column 6
846 http://www.census.nationalarchives.ie/exhibition/dublin/poverty_health.html
847 Medlink.co./article/cough_syncope
848 https://www.irishcentral.com/news/trinity-digitally-recreates-seven-centuries-of-ireland-s-history-lost-in-1922-four-courts-fire
849 'Statutory Notice to Creditors' *published in various Dublin newspapers 1895*
850 Original data: Calendar of Wills and Administrations 1858-1920. The National Archives of Ireland. http://www.willcalendars.nationalarchives.ie/search/cwa/home.jsp: 13 January 2016.
851 Florence Willis' death: 8.2.1895 Dublin *BMD* vol 2 p.446

Chapter 43 – Twists and Entanglement
852 *Deaths* SR District/Reg Area - Enniskillen
853 Freemans Journal 20.9.1890 p.1
854 Ireland, Civil Registration Deaths Index, 1864-1958
855 https://en.wiktionary.org/wiki/elucubrate
856 https://www.merriam-webster.com/dictionary/additament

857 'Mrs. Gallagher,' in the Pall Mall Gazette 11.12.1875

Epilogue
858 https://en.wikipedia.org/wiki/Vera_Nazarian

Printed in Great Britain
by Amazon